Lives of the Popes

Also by Richard P. McBrien:

Catholicism

The HarperCollins Encyclopedia of Catholicism (general editor)

LIVES

of the

POPES

The Pontiffs
from St. Peter
to John Paul II

RICHARD P. MCBRIEN

HarperSanFrancisco

A Division of HarperCollins*Publishers*

Photograph credits begin on page 492.

HarperCollins Web Site: http://www.harpercollins.com

HarperCollins®, ⛪®, and HarperSanFrancisco™ are trademarks of HarperCollins Publishers Inc.

FIRST EDITION

Library of Congress Cataloging-in-Publication Data

McBrien, Richard P.
   Lives of the popes : the pontiffs from St. Peter to John Paul II / Richard P. McBrien. — 1st ed.
   Includes bibliographical references and indexes.
   ISBN 0–06–065303-5 (cloth)
   ISBN 0–06–065304-3 (pbk.)
   1. Popes—Biography. 2. Papacy—History. I. Title.
BX955.2.M39   1997
282'.092'2—dc21
  [B]   97–21897

97 98 99 00 01 ❖ RRD(H) 10 9 8 7 6 5 4 3 2 1

In grateful memory of

JOHN XXIII (1958–1963),
the most beloved pope in history

✌

CONTENTS

PREFACE

THIS BOOK IS IN THE NATURE OF A SPIN-OFF FROM THE ONE-volume *HarperCollins Encyclopedia of Catholicism,* published in 1995, for which I served as general editor. One of the many popular features of that encyclopedia is its twenty-page list of popes, containing not only their names and years in office (the only information contained in the usual phone directory–style lists), but also a brief thumbnail sketch of each pontificate. Many readers found it fascinating, even fun, to scan these highly compressed summaries not only because they provide a convenient overview of church history, but also because they open a window onto the great variety of men who have actually occupied the Chair of Peter over the course of almost twenty centuries, warriors and peacemakers, saints and scoundrels, politicians and pastors, reformers and nepotists alike.

This book not only greatly expands those thumbnail sketches of each pontificate, but also includes features that provide a wider historical and theological context: a time line of important papal and ecclesiastical personalities and events, on the one hand, and of correspondingly important secular personalities and events, on the other; an introductory explanation of the papacy and of the two major papal dogmas (primacy and infallibility); introductions to each of the seven historical periods in which the lives of the popes are clustered; a history of papal conclaves and a summary of the latest rules for papal elections, promulgated by Pope John Paul II in 1996; an explanation of how popes can, or have been, removed from office other than by death; a rating of the popes, from "outstanding" to "worst"; a reflection, by way of an epilogue, on the future of the papacy; a series of tables, including a chronological list of popes, calculations of the longest and shortest pontificates, a list of papal "firsts" and "lasts," a listing of key papal encyclicals, and a list of antipopes; a glossary of terms; a select bibliography of popular and scholarly resources; a sixteen-page section of photos of popes and other persons, events, and monuments related to the papacy; and an index of popes along with the usual indexes of personal names and subjects.

No reader should be under any illusion that this is a work of primary historical scholarship. If so, I hasten to issue a disclaimer to the contrary. Indeed, I cannot imagine any individual historian today writing a truly complete and comprehensive history of each of the more than 260 pontificates spread over the course of almost two thousand years. It would be the work of more than one lifetime, and probably of several. For example, the great Ludwig von Pastor's forty-volume *History of the Papacy* (in English translation) covers only the popes from the close of the Middle Ages. Horace K. Mann's eighteen-volume *Lives of the Popes* covers only the early Middle Ages. Why, then, this one-volume review of the lives and pontificates of all the popes? Has not this type of summary already been done? Yes and no. Yes, there are several recent compendia that serve very well as encyclopedic dictionaries or simply dictionaries of the popes. One thinks immediately of J. N. D. Kelly's *The Oxford Dictionary of Popes,* published in 1986. It is undoubtedly the best one-volume work of its kind in the English language. The careful reader of this book will know that I have relied on Kelly throughout, just as he relied upon Franz Xaver Seppelt's five-volume *Geschichte der Päpste* (1954–59). But this book differs from Kelly's in that it offers more than summaries of each pope's life and pontificate. It provides the reader with a theological context within which to locate and interpret these summaries. As an Anglican scholar who has been active in ecumenical dialogue with the Roman Catholic Church (he accompanied the archbishop of Canterbury, Robert Runcie, on his visit to Pope Paul VI in 1966), Canon Kelly may have been under greater constraint than a tenured Roman Catholic theologian, lest he cross the line of ecumenical propriety by raising awkward questions regarding papal claims or the implications of actions taken by individual popes, ecumenical councils, and other authoritative agencies of the Church. In any case, the aforementioned features of this book—over and above the summaries of the lives of each pope and of their pontificates—are not part of Canon Kelly's otherwise splendid and useful volume.

There are also encyclopedic dictionaries (or simply dictionaries) of the papacy in other languages. In Italian there is an excellent, richly illustrated, two-volume *Storia dei Papi,* by Francesco Gligora and Biagia Catanzaro (1989) and a more compressed, but substantive, one-volume *Dizionario Enciclopedico dei Papi,* by Battista Mondin (1995). In German there is a one-volume *Die Päpste in Lebensbildern,* by Josef Gelmi (1989), which, unlike the others, situates the popes within various historical periods (for example, the early Middle Ages, the Renaissance, from the French Revolution to the First World War) and introduces each section with a brief historical commentary. But a number of the entries in that volume are extraordinarily brief. Finally, in French there is an impressively wide-ranging, one-volume *Dictionnaire historique de la papauté,* a collective effort of more than two hundred scholars under the direction of Philippe Levillain (1994). It includes many entries on topics listed in the glossary of this book and contains a rich assortment of attractive color photos and maps. A drawback is that, unlike the other volumes mentioned above, the material on the popes had to be arranged alphabetically rather than chronologically. One loses, therefore, the sense of historical development. It becomes instead a reference work alone rather than a book that one might conceivably read from cover to cover. In addition, the entries are written by a large and very diverse group of authors. What is gained in terms of more concentrated depth and expertise may be lost in terms of coherence and consistency of style and content. But for those who read French, it is an excellent and supremely valuable reference work. Indeed, in the writing of my own book, I have relied upon all of these works, to one degree or another, and also upon the individual entries on each of the popes in the monumental *New Catholic Encyclopedia* (fourteen volumes, plus one index volume and four supplementary volumes), originally published under copyright of The Catholic University of America in 1967. This last resource, however, reflects in more than a few of the entries on the popes a pre–Vatican II, almost triumphalistic portrayal of the papacy. There is a tendency to explain away papal misdeeds and disastrous papal policies and initiatives and to avoid addressing their crucially important theological implications. But some of the entries are outstanding and the encyclopedia as a whole is a marvelous achievement.

Two other sources also deserve special mention. I have a vested interest in the first, as its general editor. That is the above-mentioned *Harper-Collins Encyclopedia of Catholicism*, which proved itself time and time again as an extraordinarily valuable reference work, not only for material concerning the papacy but also for many other related theological and historical topics. Without this resource—the product of so many excellent scholars and students with whom I was proud to work—I could not have completed this book within the time allotted to me by the publisher. The other source to which I made constant reference is the virtual classic *The Oxford Dictionary of the Christian Church*, edited by F. L. Cross and E. A. Livingstone (second edition, 1974). I also made use of the third edition, which appeared in early 1997.

However, what a nonhistorian like myself was startled to discover as he rummaged his way through these diverse secondary sources is the vast number of discrepancies, inconsistencies, and outright errors regarding dates and names and sometimes even regarding the details of significant historical events, such as papal elections. One appreciates more fully how original sin is transmitted from generation to generation. Analogously, the transmission of factual error happens in historical studies all the time. One author relies on another, who has relied, in turn, on another, and that one on another—and on and on it goes.

Given the immense historical territory covered herein, the reader can be morally certain that there are factual errors in this book as well, in spite of the efforts made to detect and expunge them. One hopes, however, that none of the errors distorts or invalidates the basic profile of an individual pope or pontificate, or especially the book's theological analyses and overarching ecclesiological perspective. The magisterial *Oxford Dictionary of the Christian Church*, for example, has gone through several printings, each time correcting errors detected in previous versions. And undoubtedly J. N. D. Kelly has discovered, or been made aware of, a number of errors in his own excellent book. Even the best of us is human and can make a mistake or two.

The originality of this book consists, first, in the material selected from the vast body of secondary literature as theologically and historically pertinent as well as potentially interesting to a nonspecialist reader; second, in the organization of the material into particular historical periods, with appropriate introductions; third, and especially, in the theological and pastoral interpretations provided throughout; and fourth, in the various features designed to expand and complement the reader's understanding of and appreciation for the institution of the papacy and its many and diverse occupants.

Is the book a reference work to be used as questions arise, or is it a book to be read as any other, from beginning to end? It is both. But it is intended, in the first instance, as a book to be read as any other, from cover to cover. Thereafter, it can serve as a reference, to be consulted as often as one has questions about the papacy or individual popes.

Perhaps the most controversial part of the book (apart from its overriding, critical view of various biblically and historically naive assumptions about the structure of the Church in general and the nature and authority of the papal office in particular) will be the ratings of the popes as "outstanding," "good" (or "above average"), "worst," and "historically important." Catholics in particular have not been accustomed to reading frank, comparative judgments about the character and performance of the various successors of St. Peter. Some of them even think it irreverent or impious to do so. Moreover, scholars and nonscholars alike will undoubtedly quarrel with the placement of individual popes in particular categories and the absence of others from one or another category. But the addition of this feature will have served its purpose well if it stimulates more lively interest in the popes and the papacy, and especially if it helps people to realize that popes do not emerge from a heavenly cookie cutter, that they frequently differ sharply one from another (in personality, leadership style, spirituality, theology, and even morality); that there is often more politics than piety involved in the selection of a new pope, and that our own personal views of the various popes are actually reflections of our views not only of the papacy, but also of the Church and of religion itself. Those, for example, who regard Boniface VIII as one of the Church's best popes rather than one of its worst, as this book claims, are evidently working out of a different ecclesiology from those who agree with the book's judgment that Pope John XXIII is the most outstanding pope in all of history. But let the arguments begin!

There remains only the always agreeable task of thanking those who have contributed in any significant way to the completion of this book. Thomas Grady, former Vice President and Executive Editor of Harper San Francisco, originally proposed the book and offered important guidance and encouragement along the way. I worked closely with John B. Shopp, former Senior Editor at Harper San Francisco during the early stages of this project and previously on the revision and updating of *Catholicism* (1994) as well as the *HarperCollins Encyclopedia of Catholicism* (1995). The final production stage was in the capable hands of Terri K. Leonard, managing editor, and Karen Levine, assistant editor. Judith Kleppe was responsible for the photo section of the book. My own assistant of twelve years, Donna J. Shearer, rendered invaluable assistance by collecting and collating pertinent research materials, assisting in the production of the lists of popes and antipopes, and especially by keeping all of my other commitments in order so that I could preserve sufficient time for this one. Beverly M. Brazauskas, a religious educator of many years' standing, prepared the index of subjects and read the manuscript to help ensure that the content and style would engage the interest of the general reader. My graduate assistant, Sally M. Vance-Trembath, a doctoral student in systematic theology at Notre Dame, ran a number of useful errands to and from the university library, seeing to it that I had all the references I required and at the time I needed them. I am also greatly indebted to Robert J. Wister, priest of the archdiocese of Newark and associate professor of Church History in the School of Theology, Seton Hall University, for reading the entire manuscript and for helping to reduce the number of errors and inconsistencies that escaped into the final version of this book. Needless to say, neither he nor anyone else except the author is responsible for the views and judgments expressed herein. Unlike the *HarperCollins Encyclopedia of Catholicism,* this has been, for the most part, a solo project—which means that, if I should be tempted to take almost all of the credit, I will also have to assume almost all of the blame for whatever deficiencies remain. I only hope the reader will enjoy using this book as much as I enjoyed writing it.

Richard P. McBrien
University of Notre Dame
March 1997

Time Line

PAPAL, ECCLESIASTICAL, AND SECULAR PERSONS AND EVENTS

PAPAL AND ECCLESIASTICAL HISTORY	SECULAR HISTORY
1–100 Christianity established in Rome (ca. early 40s) Peter comes to Rome (ca. early 60s) Peter martyred in Rome (ca. 64) Persecutions by Nero (ca. 64), Domitian (ca. 81–ca. 96), and Trajan (ca. 98–117)	**1–100** Roman emperors: Tiberius (14–37), Caligula (37–41), Claudius 41–54), Nero (54–68), Domitian (ca. 81-ca. 96)
100 Pius I (ca. 142–ca. 155): the monoepiscopate begins in Rome Victor I (189–98): the first pope to attempt to impose Roman standards elsewhere (regarding the date of Easter) Early heresies deny the humanity of Christ (Gnosticism, Docetism) Development of synods and councils	**100** Roman emperors: Trajan (ca. 98–117), Antoninus Pius (138–61), Marcus Aurelius (161–80), Septimus Severus (193–211)
200 Hippolytus (217–35): the first antipope Pontian (230–35): the first pope to abdicate Stephen I (254–57): clashed with Cyprian of Carthage over rebaptisms Persecutions by Decius (249–51) and Valerian (257–58) Period of imperial toleration (258–ca. 300)	**200** Fall of Han dynasty in China (220) Roman emperors: Decius (249–51), Gallus (251–53), Valerian (253–60), Gallienus (260–68), Diocletian (284–305) Partition of Roman Empire into East and West (285)
300 Persecution begun by Diocletian (303–13) Edict of Constantine (313) Constantine presents Melchiades (311–14) the Lateran Palace First Council of Nicaea (325)	**300** Classic period of Mesoamerican civilizations begins (300–800) Constantine the Great (306–37): sole emperor

PAPAL AND ECCLESIASTICAL HISTORY	SECULAR HISTORY
First St. Peter's Basilica constructed (ca. 330)	Beginning of Gupta dynasty in India (ca. 320)
First Council of Constantinople (381): Nicene-Constantinopolitan Creed	Seat of Roman Empire moved to Constantinople (331)
Siricius (384–99): first pope to issue decretals	Empire splits again into West and East (340)
Donatism (North African heresy)	Barbarian migrations begin (ca. 375–ca. 568)
	Theodosius the Great (392–95): last ruler of united empire

400	Innocent I (401–17): claimed supreme teaching authority; succeeded his father as pope	**400** Barbarian migrations continue
	Augustine of Hippo (354–430)	Visigoths invade Italy (401)
	Council of Ephesus (431)	Alaric captures and sacks Rome (410)
	Patrick (ca. 390–ca. 461): mission to Ireland (ca. 431)	Vandals sack Rome (455)
	Pope Leo the Great (440–61): claimed supreme and universal authority for the pope	End of Western Roman emperors (476)
		Theodoric founds Ostrogoth kingdom of Italy (493)
	Council of Chalcedon (451)	Clovis, king of the Franks, converts to Christianity (496)
	Acacian Schism (482–519)	
	Gelasius I (492–96): first pope to be called Vicar of Christ	

500	Symmachus (498–514): first pope to bestow the pallium on a bishop outside of Italy	**500** Justinian the Great (527–65)
	Benedict of Nursia (ca. 480–ca. 547) founds Monte Cassino (ca. 525)	End of Gupta dynasty in India (ca. 550)
	John II (533–35): first pope to change his birth name as pope	Rome and Naples annexed to Eastern (Byzantine) Empire (553)
	Vigilius (537–55): first pope to be excommunicated (by a synod of African bishops)	Lombards drive Byzantines from northern Italy (565)
	Byzantine emperors ratify papal elections (537–731)	
	Church of Santa (Hagia) Sophia, Constantinople, consecrated (538)	
	Second Council of Constantinople (553)	

PAPAL AND ECCLESIASTICAL HISTORY	SECULAR HISTORY
Gregory the Great (590–604): first monk to become pope; virtual civil ruler of Rome Augustine of Canterbury (d. ca. 605): mission to Britain (596)	
600 Honorius I (625–38): posthumously condemned by Constantinople III for Monothelitism Third Council of Constantinople (680–81) Monothelite controversy Byzantine emperors' required approval of papal consecrations continues	**600** Muhammad (570–632) Barbarian migrations end in western Europe (ca. 600) Arabs conquer Jerusalem (637) and destroy Carthage (697)
700 Boniface (ca. 675–754): mission to the Germans (719) Iconoclasm controversy (ca. 726–843) Stephen II (III) (752–57): forms the Papal States (given by Pepin III, 756) Consecration of Pepin III (d. 768) as king of the Franks and protector of Rome Second Council of Nicaea (787)	**700** Christianity in North Africa exterminated by Muslims (by 700) Charlemagne becomes sole ruler of Frankish kingdom (771)
800 Leo III (795–816): crowned Charlemagne as emperor (800) Cyril (826–69) and Methodius (ca. 815–85): mission to the Slavs St. Peter's Basilica plundered by Muslim pirates (846) Nicholas I (858–67): excommunicated patriarch Photius of Constantinople (863) Fourth Council of Constantinople (869–70) John VIII (872–82): first pope to be assassinated Marinus I (882–84): first bishop of another diocese elected Bishop of Rome	**800** Charlemagne crowned as first Carolingian emperor (800) Arabs sack Rome (846) and conquer Sicily (878) Emperor Basil recaptures Italy from the Arabs (880)

PAPAL AND ECCLESIASTICAL HISTORY	SECULAR HISTORY
Formosus (891–96): "Cadaver Synod" (897)	

900	Papacy sinks to moral depths; dominated by Roman families	**900**	Arabs expelled from central Italy (916)
	Monastery of Cluny founded (909)		Otto I crowned Holy Roman emperor (962)
	Hungary is Christianized (ca. 942)		Otto II crowned Holy Roman emperor (967)
	John XII (955–64): elected at age eighteen; one of the most corrupt popes in history		Otto III crowned Holy Roman emperor (996)
	Leo VIII (963–65): first layman elected pope		
	Poland is Christianized (966)		
	Benedict VII (974–83): *ad limina* visits to Rome become common		
	Russia is Christianized (ca. 988)		
	First papal canonization (993)		
	Gregory V (996–99): first German pope		
	Sylvester II (999–1003): first French pope		
1000	Clement II (1046–47): first pope also to remain bishop of his former diocese	**1000**	Muslims sack the Church of the Holy Sepulchre in Jerusalem (1009)
	East-West Schism begins (1054)		Battle of Hastings (1066)
	Nicholas II (1058–61): limited papal elections to cardinals		Henry IV excommunicated by Gregory VII (1076)
	Gregory VII (1073–85): reformer pope; claimed authority over whole Church		Henry IV imprisons Gregory VII (1084)
	Carthusians founded (1084)		Crusaders capture Jerusalem (1099)
	Roman Curia established (1089)		
	First Crusade (1096–99)		
	Cistercians founded (1098)		
1100	First Lateran Council (1123)	**1100**	Henry V crowned Holy Roman emperor (1111)
	Second Lateran Council (1139)		
	Eugenius III (1145–53): first Cistercian pope		Lothair III crowned Holy Roman emperor (1133)

Second Crusade (1146–48)

Hadrian IV (1154–59): first and only English pope

Carmelites founded (ca. 1154)

Alexander III (1159–81): decreed two-thirds majority necessary for papal election

Third Lateran Council (1179)

Lucius III (1181–85): established procedures for the Inquisition

Notre Dame Cathedral, Paris, consecrated (1182)

Third Crusade (1189–92)

Frederick Barbarossa crowned Holy Roman emperor (1155)

Thomas Becket murdered in Canterbury Cathedral (1170)

1200 Innocent III (1198–1216): claimed authority over the whole Christian world

Fourth through Seventh Crusades (1202–54)

Franciscans founded (1209)

Dominicans founded (1215)

Fourth Lateran Council (1215)

Gregory IX (1227–41): established papal Inquisition (1231)

First Council of Lyons (1245)

Augustinian Hermits founded (1256)

Second Council of Lyons (1274)

Innocent V (1276): first Dominican pope

John XXI (1276–77): first and only Portuguese pope

Nicholas III (1277–80): first pope to make the Vatican Palace his residence

Nicholas IV (1288–92): the first Franciscan pope; Catholicism established in China (1294–1368)

Celestine V (1294): first hermit to become pope; resigned after five months

Boniface VIII (1295–1303): declared that every creature is subject to the pope

1200 Crusaders capture Constantinople, establish Latin empire (1204)

England and Ireland become papal fiefs (1213)

Magna Carta (1215)

Marco Polo to China (1271–95)

Sung dynasty toppled by Kublai Khan (1279)

Crusades formally end (1291)

PAPAL AND ECCLESIASTICAL HISTORY	SECULAR HISTORY
1300 First Holy Year (1300)	**1300** Black Death in Europe (1347–49)
Avignon papacy (1309–77)	Byzantines lose last possession in Asia Minor to Turks (1390)
Council of Vienne (1311–12)	
Urban VI (1378–89): last noncardinal elected pope	
Great Western Schism (1378–1417)	
1400 Council of Constance (1414–18)	**1400** Constantine XI Palaeologus, last Byzantine emperor (1449–53)
Martin V (1417–31): his election ended the Great Western Schism	Fall of Constantinople to Turks (1453)
Council of Basel-Ferrara-Florence-Rome (1431–45)	Gutenberg Bible (1456)
Nicholas V (1447–55): first of the Renaissance popes	Lorenzo de' Medici rules Florence (1469–92)
Sixtus IV (1471–84): built the Sistine Chapel	African slave trade begins (ca. 1482)
Spanish Inquisition established (1479)	Moorish kingdom ends in Spain (1492)
Alexander VI (1492–1503): most infamous pope in history	Jews expelled from Spain (1492)
	Christopher Columbus discovers America (1492)
	Alexander VI divides New World between Spain and Portugal (1493)
1500 Julius II (1503–13): warrior pope; commissioned rebuilding of St. Peter's Basilica	**1500** Explorers: Vasco da Gama (1469–1524), Ferdinand Magellan (1480–1521), Francis Drake (1540–96)
Fifth Lateran Council (1512–17)	Michelangelo (1475–1564)
Leo X (1513–21): excommunicated Martin Luther (1521)	Copernican theory (1512)
Reformation begins (1517)	Murder of Aztec emperor Montezuma (1520)
Hadrian VI (1522–23): the only Dutch pope; last non-Italian until John Paul II (1978)	Beginning of Mogol empire in India (1526)
English Reformation begins (1534)	Thomas More executed (1535)
Society of Jesus (Jesuits) founded (1534)	Mary succeeds Edward VI (1553)
Paul III (1534–49): established the Holy Office; convened the Council of Trent	Elizabeth I succeeds Mary (1558)
	Roman catacombs discovered (1578)
	Gregorian calendar adopted (1582)
	Defeat of the Spanish Armada (1588)

PAPAL AND ECCLESIASTICAL
HISTORY

SECULAR HISTORY

Jesuit mission to India (1542–45, 1548–49)

Council of Trent (1545–63)

Jesuit mission to Japan (1549)

Index of Forbidden Books established by Paul IV (1557)

Pius V (1566–72): reformed the liturgy; excommunicated Queen Elizabeth I (1570)

Gregory XIII (1572–85): Gregorian calendar

Jesuit mission to China (1582)

Sixtus V (1585–90): reorganized Roman Curia in present form

Vatican Library opens (1588)

1600 Baroque Catholicism (ca. 1600–ca. 1750)

Jesuit missionary Matteo Ricci admitted to Peking (1601)

Paul V (1605–21): censured Galileo

Gregory XV (1621–23): decreed papal elections by secret ballot

Urban VIII (1623–44): consecrated St. Peter's Basilica (1626); Castel Gandolfo as summer residence

Galileo imprisoned (1633)

Jansenism (ca. 1640–ca. 1800)

Chinese rites controversy formally begins (1645)

Trappists founded (1664)

Gallicanism (1682–1789)

1600 Beginning of Tokugawa shogunate in Japan (1600)

First African slaves brought to North America (1619)

Peter Minuit buys island of Manhattan for $24 (1626)

Harvard College founded (1636)

Isaac Newton (1642–1727)

Ming dynasty replaced by Ch'ing (Manchu) in China (1644)

Peace of Westphalia (1648)

1700 Clement XI (1700–21): forbade use of Chinese rites

Clement XIV (1769–74): suppressed the Jesuits (1773)

Pius VI (1775–99): third longest pontificate; died a prisoner of Napoleon

John Carroll, first U.S. bishop consecrated (1790)

1700 American Declaration of Independence (1776)

U.S. Constitution (1788)

George Washington, first U.S. president (1789–97)

French Revolution (1789)

Rosetta Stone found in Egypt (1799)

PAPAL AND ECCLESIASTICAL HISTORY	SECULAR HISTORY
1800 Catholic Romanticism	**1800** Napoleon crowned king of Italy (1805), annexes Papal States (1809), defeated at Waterloo (1815)
Pius VII (1800–23): imprisoned by Napoleon; reinstated the Jesuits (1814)	
Gregory XVI (1831–46): last non-bishop elected pope	Holy Roman Empire ends (1806)
	Spanish-American wars of independence (1808–29)
Pius IX (1846–78): longest pontificate	Charles Darwin (1809–82)
Dogma of the Immaculate Conception (1854)	Karl Marx (1818–83)
	Communist Manifesto (1848)
Loss of almost all of the Papal States (1860–61)	Italy proclaimed a kingdom (1861)
"Syllabus of Errors" (1864)	American Civil War (1861–65)
First Vatican Council (1869–70)	U.S. Emancipation Proclamation (1863)
Loss of Rome and environs, last of the papal territories (1870)	Dominion of Canada established (1867)
Leo XIII (1878–1903): *Rerum novarum* (1891); second longest pontificate	Brazil abolishes slavery (1888)
	Kulturkampf in Prussia (1871)
1900 Pius X (1903–14): oath against Modernism (1910)	**1900** Sigmund Freud (1856–1939)
	Commonwealth of Australia established (1901)
Benedict XV (1914–22): halted anti-Modernist campaign	
Code of Canon Law (1917)	New Zealand attains Dominion status (1907)
Pius XI (1922–39): first pope to use radio; condemned Nazism	Chinese republic established (1911)
	First World War (1914–18)
Lateran Treaty (1929)	Russian Revolution (1917–18)
Pius XII (1939–58): first pope to use television	Irish Free State established (1922)
	Frank D. Roosevelt elected U.S. president (1932)
Dogma of the Assumption (1950)	
John XXIII (1958–63): most beloved pope in history	Adolf Hitler, German chancellor (1933)
Second Vatican Council (1962–65)	Spanish Civil War (1936–39)
Paul VI (1963–78): first pope to travel by air	Second World War (1939–45)
	United Nations charter (1945)
John Paul I (1978): first pope not to be crowned in a century or more	Cold War (1945–89)
	Republic of Ireland established (1949)
John Paul II (1978-): first Slavic pope; most traveled pope in history	Peoples' Republic of China established (1949)

PAPAL AND ECCLESIASTICAL HISTORY	SECULAR HISTORY
Revised Code of Canon Law (1983)	John F. Kennedy assassinated (1963)
Catechism of the Catholic Church (1992)	Vietnam War (1965–73)
	Communism collapses (1989)
	Apartheid ends in South Africa (1993)

INTRODUCTION

THE PAPACY IS THE OFFICE OF, AND THE JURISDICTION EXERCISED by, the Bishop of Rome, known more popularly as the pope. The papacy is also known as the Petrine ministry because the Catholic Church considers the pope to be the Vicar of Peter, that is, the one who personally succeeds to the distinctive ministry of St. Peter for the sake of the unity of the universal Church.

The title of "pope," which means "father" (It., *papa*), was in earlier centuries of church history applied to every bishop in the West, while in the East it seems to have been used of priests as well and was a special title of the patriarch of Alexandria. In 1073, however, Pope Gregory VII formally prohibited the use of the title for all except the Bishop of Rome.

In addition to the Bishop of Rome, which is his primary title, the pope has several other titles: Vicar of Jesus Christ, Successor of the Chief of the Apostles (Vicar of Peter), Supreme Pontiff of the Universal Church, Patriarch of the West, Primate of Italy, Archbishop and Metropolitan of the Roman Province, Sovereign of Vatican City State, and Servant of the Servants of God.

According to traditional Catholic belief, the papacy was established by Jesus Christ himself when he conferred its responsibilities and powers upon the Apostle Peter at Caesarea Philippi: "And so I say to you, you are Peter, and upon this rock I will build my church, and the gates of the netherworld shall not prevail against it. I will give you the keys of the kingdom of heaven. Whatever you bind on earth shall be bound in heaven; and whatever you loose on earth shall be loosed in heaven" (Matthew 16:18–19). It is because of the ancient tradition that the two principal leaders of the apostolic church, Sts. Peter and Paul, were martyred and buried in Rome that the papacy, from its beginnings, has been linked with this former imperial city.

Papal Primacy: Recognition of the papacy, or of the Petrine ministry as exercised by the Bishop of Rome, is not characteristic of the Catholic tradition alone. Other Christian traditions acknowledge the Bishop of Rome as the Patriarch of the West or as the "first [bishop] among equals" (Lat., *primus inter pares*), but only the Catholic Church accepts him as the earthly head of the worldwide Church. This is also known as the doctrine of papal primacy, which is linked, in turn, with the primacy of the

Roman see itself. St. Ignatius of Antioch (d. ca. 107) is traditionally regarded as the first major witness to the primacy of Rome. In his famous
letter to the church at Rome not long before he himself was martyred
there, he addressed "the church holding chief place in the territories of
the district of Rome—worthy of God, worthy of honor, blessing, praise,
and success; worthy too in holiness, *foremost in love* . . ." (emphasis
added). Remarkably, however, it is the only one of Ignatius's classic letters
to the seven churches of the ancient Mediterranean world that makes no
mention at all of a local bishop. This lends credence to the supposition of
historians and theologians that the monoepiscopal structure of church
governance (that is, a diocese with one bishop as its pastoral head) did
not even come to Rome until the middle of the second century, with the
pontificate of Pius I (ca. 142–ca. 155).

It would have been extraordinary, however, if Rome had *not* been sin-
gled out for a special role and position of authority in the early Church.
Not only was it the place traditionally regarded as the site of the martyr-
doms and burials of both Peter and Paul; it was also the center of the
Roman Empire. Gradually Rome did emerge as an ecclesiastical court
of last resort, the local church to which other local churches and their
bishops would appeal when disputes and conflicts could not be settled
between or among themselves. For example, in the controversies with
Gnosticism, a particularly virulent early Christian heresy that denied the
full humanity of Jesus Christ, defenders of orthodoxy appealed to the
faith of episcopal sees founded by the Apostles, and especially to the faith
of the Roman church because of its close association with Peter and Paul.
Rome subsequently intervened in the life of distant churches, took sides
in theological controversies, was consulted by other bishops on doctrinal
and moral questions, and sent delegates to distant councils.

The correlation between Peter and the Bishop of Rome, however, did
not became fully explicit until the pontificate of Leo I (also known as Leo
the Great) in the mid-fifth century (440–61). Leo insisted that Peter continued to speak to the whole Church through the Bishop of Rome. It was
Leo who decisively intervened in the great Christological controversies
and whose letter, or *Tome*, to Flavian, patriarch of Constantinople, in 449
provided the basis for the definitive formulation of faith two years later at
the Council of Chalcedon.

With the East-West Schism in 1054, the shape of the papacy changed
even more significantly. Before the split the Bishop of Rome had been
viewed primarily as patriarch of Rome, alongside the patriarchs of Constantinople, Antioch, Alexandria, and Jerusalem. After the split, however,
the Roman patriarchal office and the papal office merged. The patriarchal office was completely absorbed by the power of the papacy. In the

eyes of many Eastern Christians, Western Christianity became thereby a papal church, that is, a church that relates so predominantly to the see of Rome that the pastoral autonomy of the local churches and their bishops is all but lost. The Bishop of Rome came to regard himself, and be regarded as, the universal primate of the universal Church. It was as if he were the bishop of every local church and the local bishops were simply his vicars or delegates.

Following this long and complex history, the Second Ecumenical Council of Lyons in 1274 claimed for the Roman church "the supreme and full primacy and authority over the universal Catholic Church." That formal declaration laid the foundation, in turn, for the dogmatic definition of the First Vatican Council in 1870, that "in the disposition of God the Roman church holds the preeminence of ordinary power over all the other churches. . . ."

This is not to say, however, that the evolution of the doctrine of papal primacy has proceeded in a direct, unbroken line from the time of the New Testament to the present day. On the contrary, there is a major difference in the way the papacy was perceived and exercised by the whole Church—East and West—during the first thousand years of Christian history, and the way it has been perceived and exercised—in the West—during the second Christian millennium.

Before the beginning of the second millennium and of the pontificate of Gregory VII in particular (1073–85), popes functioned largely in the role of mediator. They did not claim for themselves the title "Vicar of Christ." They did not appoint bishops. They did not govern the universal Church through the Roman Curia. They did not impose or enforce clerical celibacy. They did not write encyclicals or authorize catechisms for the whole Church. They did not retain for themselves alone the power of canonization. They did not even convene ecumenical councils, as a rule—and certainly not the major doctrinal councils of Nicaea (325), Constantinople (381), Ephesus (431), and Chalcedon (451).

The Second Vatican Council (1962–65) brought the Church's understanding of the papacy, and of papal primacy in particular, more in line once again with that of the first millennium, in contrast with that of the second millennium. The council viewed the papacy in increasingly communal and collegial terms. In other words, the pope is no longer to be conceived of as an absolute monarch—an impression clearly left by the one-sided, because unfinished, teaching of the First Vatican Council. (Vatican I had to suspend operations because of the political turmoil in Italy.) According to the Second Vatican Council, the pope exercises supreme authority over the whole Church, but the other bishops also share in that authority. To be sure, the supreme authority vested in the college of bishops cannot be exercised without the consent of the pope. "This college, insofar as it is composed of many, expresses the variety and universality of the People of God, but insofar as it is assembled under one head, it expresses the unity of the flock of Christ" (Dogmatic Constitution on the Church, n. 22). Although the pope retains "full, supreme, and universal power over the Church," the other bishops are no longer perceived as simply his stand-ins or delegates. They also receive from Christ "the mission to teach all nations and to preach the gospel to every creature" (n. 24). They govern their own dioceses not as "vicars of the Roman Pontiff, for they exercise an authority which is proper to them . . ." (n. 27). Whatever authority the pope and the other bishops enjoy, it is always to be exercised within a communion of local churches through the faithful preaching of the gospel, the administration of the sacraments, and pastoral service.

The Catholic Church is not an absolute monarchy. Its governmental structure is communal and collegial, not monarchical. Insofar as the universal Church is a *communion* of local churches, the papal office serves the unity of the whole Church as "the perpetual and visible source and foundation of the unity of the bishops and of the multitude of the faithful" (Dogmatic Constitution on the Church, n. 23). Papal primacy, therefore, is a primacy of service—in the service of unity. Insofar as the universal Church is a communion of local *churches,* the papal office must respect the legitimate diversity of these churches and practice a collegial mode of decision making (n. 23). The bishops, therefore, truly collaborate with the pope in the work of the Holy Spirit, which is the work of unity. They do so in their collegial confession of one faith, in their common celebration of divine worship, especially the Eucharist, and in their promotion of the loving harmony of the family of God (Decree on Ecumenism, n. 2).

Papal Infallibility: The second major papal dogma defined by the First Vatican Council in the nineteenth century is that of papal infallibility. Infallibility means, literally, immunity from error. Theologically it refers to a charism, or gift, of the Holy Spirit by which the Church is protected from fundamental error when it solemnly defines a matter of faith or morals. Catholic theologians are careful to point out, however, that the charism is a negative charism, that is, it only guarantees that a particular teaching is not erroneous. The charism of infallibility does not ensure that a particular teaching is an adequate, appropriate, or opportune expression of faith or morals. Furthermore, *papal* infallibility is a dimension of the *Church's* infallibility, not vice versa. The pope's infallibility is the same infallibility "with which the divine Redeemer willed His Church to be endowed" (Dogmatic Constitution on the Church, n. 25).

Unlike the doctrine of papal primacy, there is no explicit basis for the doctrine of papal infallibility in the New Testament. It was not until the middle of the third century that special importance began to be accorded the faith of the church of Rome. Some Roman emperors included the faith of the Bishop of Rome in the official norm of orthodoxy, and the biblical image of the Church "without spot or wrinkle" (Ephesians 5:27) began to be applied to the church of Rome. Rome became *the* apostolic see. According to the *Formula of Pope Hormisdas,* written in the year 515, "the catholic religion has always been preserved immaculate" in Rome. This conviction was expressed in different ways by different sources well into the Middle Ages.

But there were also challenges to such claims, not only in the East but in the West as well. Eastern Christians regarded Rome as only one of several apostolic sees to which the protection of the faith had been entrusted. And not all of Rome's bishops effectively fulfilled this important ministry. Marcellinus (296–304) complied with imperial orders to hand over copies of Sacred Scripture and to offer incense to the gods, for which he was probably deposed. Liberius (352–66) was a weak pope who at first opposed the excommunication of St. Athanasius (d. 373), the great enemy of Arianism, but then relented under pressure. Vigilius (537–55) vacillated on the teaching of the Council of Chalcedon (451) and was even excommunicated by a synod of African bishops. Honorius I (625–38) became an unwitting adherent of Monothelitism, a heresy that held there is only one (divine) will in Christ, and after his death was formally condemned by the Third Council of Constantinople (680). Certain Western metropolitans (archbishops with some form of jurisdiction over suffragan dioceses in the same geographical area) even in the early Middle Ages sometimes contradicted papal decisions. Prophetic voices, including those of saints like Bernard of Clairvaux (d. 1153) and Catherine of Siena (d. 1380), were also raised against the style and practice of the papal ministry centuries before the Reformation. Medieval theologians and canonists admitted that individual popes had erred in matters of doctrine and even conceded that a pope could deviate from the faith.

Nevertheless, the formula "Rome has never erred" survived and over the course of time came to be understood as "Rome *cannot* err." The legal maxim "The first see is judged by no one" appeared initially in the sixth century and was later interpreted to mean that the pope's teaching authority is supreme. St. Thomas Aquinas (d. 1274) would later argue that the pope's teachings must always be followed because he represents the universal Church which "cannot err."

The formal concept of infallibility, however, was not applied to the papacy until the fourteenth century, during a controversy over poverty in the Franciscan order. Advocates of a rigorist position (that Franciscans must divest themselves of all property, regardless of practical need) employed the term "infallibility" to defend the binding authority of statements by earlier popes against the more liberal decisions of their successors. Under the impact of the Reformation, the concept gained wider currency among the Counter-Reformation theologians (St. Robert Bellarmine [d. 1621] and others). There were also appeals to infallibility in the condemnations of Jansenism and Gallicanism (two largely French dissident movements) in the seventeenth and eighteenth centuries. Under strong personal pressure from a beleaguered Pope Pius IX (1846–78), the First Vatican Council formally defined the dogma of infallibility in 1870.

The key words of the Vatican I text placed certain restrictions on the exercise of papal infallibility: "... when the Roman Pontiff speaks *ex cathedra* [Lat., "from the chair"], that is, when ... as pastor and teacher of all Christians in virtue of his highest apostolic authority he defines a doctrine of faith and morals that must be held by the Universal Church, he is empowered, through the divine assistance promised him in blessed Peter, with that infallibility with which the Divine Redeemer willed to endow his Church." Thus: (1) He must be speaking formally as earthly head of the Church (*ex cathedra*). (2) He must be speaking on a matter of faith or morals (not governance or discipline). (3) He must clearly intend to bind the whole Church. Indeed, the revised Code of Canon Law (1983) stipulates that "No doctrine is understood to be infallibly defined unless it is clearly established as such" (can. 749.3).

Infallibility, therefore, is not a personal prerogative of the pope. It would be inaccurate to say without qualification that "the pope is infallible." A pope is only infallible, according to Vatican I, when he is in the act of defining a dogma of faith or morals under the conditions specified.

Neither does the dogma of infallibility mean that the pope is somehow above the Church. Vatican I's declaration that the definitions of popes are "irreformable by themselves (*ex sese*) and not by reason of the agreement of the Church (*non autem ex consensu ecclesiae*)" was added to the definition in order to oppose Gallicanism, an attitude prevalent in France that maintained that papal definitions and other decisions did not go into effect unless and until they were subsequently ratified by the Church. On the other hand, the official presenter of the dogma of papal infallibility at Vatican I, Bishop Vincenz Gasser (d. 1879), made it clear during the debate that the consent of the Church can never be lacking to an infallible pronouncement.

Nor did Vatican I intend to say, in using the word "irreformable," that infallible teachings can never change. They are formulated in human language and are expressive of human concepts. As such they are historically conditioned (*Mysterium Ecclesiae,* Congregation for the Doctrine of the Faith, 1973).

Like the dogma of papal primacy, the dogma of papal infallibility was set in a larger context by the Second Vatican Council. The charism of infallibility, the council insisted, can be exercised by the whole college of bishops, in communion with the pope, either when assembled in an ecumenical council or when scattered throughout the world. In principle, the whole Church, not just the pope and the other bishops, is infallible (Dogmatic Constitution on the Church, n. 25).

Just as it is the whole People of God, and not only the pope and the other bishops, who constitute the Church.

Part I

FROM PETER TO THE BEGINNINGS OF A UNIVERSAL PAPACY

LTHOUGH CATHOLIC TRADITION, BEGINNING IN the late second and early third centuries, regards St. Peter as the first Bishop of Rome and, therefore, as the first pope, there is no evidence that Peter was involved in the initial establishment of the Christian community in Rome (indeed, what evidence there is would seem to point in the opposite direction) or that he served as Rome's first bishop. Not until the pontificate of St. Pius I in the middle of the second century (ca. 142–ca. 155) did the Roman church have a monoepiscopal structure of government (one bishop as pastoral leader of a diocese). Those whom Catholic tradition lists as Peter's immediate successors (Linus, Anacletus, Clement, et al.) did not function as the one bishop of Rome. (The succession lists were passed down by St. Irenaeus of Lyons [d. ca. 200] and the historian St. Hegesippus [d. ca. 180], and were attested by Eusebius of Caesarea [d. ca. 339], often called the "Father of Church History.") The Roman community seems instead to have had a corporate or collegial form of pastoral leadership. Those counted among the earliest popes, therefore, may very well have been simply the individuals who presided over the local council of elders or presbyter-bishops. Or they may have been the most prominent of the pastoral leaders of the community. In any case, the popes of the first four centuries—that is, until the watershed papacy of Leo I in the middle of the fifth century—functioned with relatively limited authority beyond Rome and its immediate environs.

For example, Pope Sylvester I (314–35) seems to have exercised no discernible influence over the first ecumenical council held at Nicaea in 325. He neither convened it nor attended it. The same can be said of Pope Damasus I (366–84) with regard to the second ecumenical council held in Constantinople in 381, and of Pope Celestine I (422–32) with regard to the third ecumenical council held at Ephesus in 431. And when the Donatist schismatics in North Africa appealed to the emperor Constantine to overturn a decision of Pope Melchiades, the emperor summoned a council of representatives from all the Western provinces to meet at Arles on August 1, 314. Melchiades died several months before the council actually met, but it is significant that the emperor, in calling the council, did not regard the pope's decision as final and that neither Melchiades nor his successor took exception to the emperor's action.

Neither is there any evidence that the bishops of Rome actually governed other local churches, legislated for them, or appointed their bishops. At most, the bishops of Rome during these first four centuries may have exercised a kind of metropolitan authority over neighboring Italian sees, which came to be known as suburbicarian sees. But there is less evidence even for this than there is for the clearly "sovereign" authority exercised by the see of Alexandria over all the churches of Egypt and Cyrenaica. Indeed, when Pope Julius I acted in support of St. Athanasius following his second expulsion from Alexandria in 339, it is significant that Julius justified his intervention not on the basis of the Petrine primacy, to which later popes would appeal, but on the basis of ecclesiastical custom and the collegiality of the episcopate. And when Celestine I (422–32) rehabilitated a presbyter excommunicated by the African bishops and who later admitted his guilt, the African bishops chastised the pope for failing to respect their autonomy and for entering into communion with persons they had excommunicated, a practice, they reminded him, that was expressly forbidden by the Council of Nicaea (325). Not until the pontificate of Leo the Great (440–61) was the claim of universal papal jurisdiction (that is, over the whole Church, East as well as West) first articulated and begun to be exercised in any really decisive manner.

Little is known about these early popes. There is reason to believe, however, that like Peter many, if not all, were married. At least four of these early popes were sons of priests: Sixtus I (ca. 116–ca. 125), Damasus I (366–84), Boniface I (418–22), and Innocent I (401–17), whose father was not only a priest but a pope, Anastasius I (399–401). If Pope Anastasius I were not married, his son would have been illegitimate and, therefore, ineligible for ordination to the priesthood, much less for election to the papacy.

The first pope who reached out to assert his authority beyond the borders of his own ecclesiastical community and its suburbicarian sees was Victor I (189–98), an African. It was Victor who ordered other churches to conform to the Roman practice of celebrating Easter on the Sunday following the fourteenth day of the Jewish month of Nisan (the day of Passover). At his urging synods were held in various parts of the ancient Christian world, from Gaul (modern-day France) to Mesopotamia (present-day Iraq), where it became gradually clear that the majority was in agreement with Pope Victor. But when Victor presumed to excommunicate those who disagreed with his ruling, he was rebuked by no less a prominent figure of the early Church than St. Irenaeus of Lyons, who pointedly reminded the pope that all of his predecessors had been indulgent toward diversity of practice and had not dared to resort to the ultimate weapon of excommunication.

When popes did begin to engage in theological disputes with the pastoral leaders of other churches, they were sometimes rebuffed as interlopers or, worse, as having erroneous views. For example, Pope Stephen I (254–57) and St. Cyprian (d. 258), bishop of Carthage, clashed over the question of the validity of baptism administered by heretics and schismatics. Cyprian followed the belief and practice of most of the churches of North Africa, Syria, and Asia Minor, namely, that those baptized by heretics and schismatics had to be rebaptized if they were to enter or be reconciled with the Catholic Church. Stephen represented the tradition of Rome, Alexandria, and Palestine, which held that baptisms by heretics and schismatics are valid and that the only condition required of those seeking to enter or be reconciled with the Catholic Church was absolution of their sins by the laying on of hands. When Stephen threatened to break communion with all the churches that practiced rebaptism, he was implored by Bishop Dionysius of Alexandria (d. 264/5), himself a supporter of the Roman position, not to take such a hard line. The situation would surely have worsened had Stephen not died in the midst of the controversy.

This incident was indicative of the papacy's newly emerging tendency to claim pastoral authority over local churches outside of Rome, but also of the readiness of other bishops to confront and challenge the Bishop of Rome when they felt he was going too far in the enforcement of pastoral practice or discipline. Stephen I seems to have been the first pope to have appealed to the classic "you are Peter . . ." text in Matthew's Gospel (16:18) as the basis of the Roman primacy. Pope Damasus I (366–84), who secured from the emperor Gratian the right of Western bishops to appeal directly to Rome, customarily designated Rome as "the Apostolic See" and rebutted Constantinople's claims to equal rank with Rome. Like Stephen before him, Damasus also applied the Matthean text to the Roman primacy. His immediate successor, Pope Siricius (384–99), ruled that no bishop should be consecrated without his knowledge (although not necessarily his approval or authorization). More forcefully than any previous pope had done, Pope Innocent I (401–17) laid claim to supreme teaching authority and he welcomed (and expected) appeals from various churches on matters of doctrinal dispute. Like Innocent, Pope Boniface I (418–22) emphatically promoted the authority of the papal office, once writing: "It has never been lawful for what has once been decided by the Apostolic See to be reconsidered." And yet his own immediate successor, Pope Celestine I (422–32), played little part in the major Christological council held at Ephesus in 431—a council concerned with the human and divine natures of Jesus Christ and with the question of whether Mary could be considered the Mother of God. Such was the gap that often existed between papal rhetoric and pastoral reality in the early history of the papacy—that is, before the pontificate of Leo the Great (440–61).

1 Peter, Apostle, St., *Galilean,*[1] *d. ca. 64.*

Jesus' chief apostle, whom Catholic tradition regards as the first pope, Peter was born in the village of Bethsaida on the Sea of Galilee. (The first succession lists, however, identified Linus, not Peter, as the first pope. Peter was not regarded as the first Bishop of Rome until the late second or early third century.) Peter's original Hebrew name was *šim'ôn,* rendered in Greek as Simon (Σίμων). It was also rendered as Simeon (Συμεών) twice in the New Testament: Acts 15:14 and 2 Peter 1:1. Jesus gave him a new name, the Aramaic word for rock, *kêpā',* later transliterated into Greek as Κηφᾶς (*Kephas*). But the name *Kephas* appears only nine times in the New Testament, once in John and eight times in the Letters of Paul. The name Peter is a Greek translation of the Aramaic word, *kêpā',* and is used more than 150 times in the Gospels and in the Acts of the Apostles. This name conveyed to Greek-speaking Christians far more about Peter's function in the Church than the noncommittal *Kephas.* The double name Simon Peter occurs about twenty times in the New Testament, mostly in John.

That Peter was married and remained so even after becoming a disciple of Jesus is clear from the account of Jesus' healing of Peter's mother-in-law (Mark 1:29–31) and from Paul's reference to the fact that Peter and the other apostles took their wives along on their apostolic journeys (1 Corinthians 9:5). The pious belief that the apostles, including Peter, "put away" their wives once they received the call from Jesus has no historical basis. Rather, it arises from the mistaken, and essentially unchristian, assumption that celibacy is more virtuous than marriage because sexual intimacy somehow compromises one's total commitment to God and the things of the spirit.

Peter's Singular Role in the New Testament: Catholic tradition has regarded Peter as the first pope because of the special commission he received from Jesus Christ and because of the unique status he enjoyed and the central role he played within the college of the twelve apostles. He was the first disciple to be called by Jesus (Matthew 4:18–19). He

---

[1]Unless otherwise indicated, the ethnic background or nationality of an individual pope should be assumed to be Italian, i.e., within the territory of the Italian peninsula.

served as spokesman for the other apostles (Mark 8:29; Matthew 18:21; Luke 12:41; John 6:67–69). According to the tradition of Paul and Luke (1 Corinthians 15:5; Luke 24:34), he was the first to whom the Lord appeared after his resurrection. (Mary Magdalene is the primary witness to the Resurrection in the tradition of Matthew, John, and the Marcan appendix, but even in Mark the angel at the tomb instructs Mary Magdalene and the other women to "go and tell his disciples and Peter" [16:7].) Peter is, in fact, the most frequently commissioned of the Twelve following the resurrection. He is also the most frequently mentioned disciple in all four Gospels and is regularly listed first among the Twelve (Mark 3:16–19; Matthew 10:1–4; Luke 6:12–16). This latter point alongside others is of particular significance because, in the ancient world, respect and authority resided in the first of a line, the first born or the first chosen. He is thus prominent in the original Jerusalem community—described by Paul as one of its "pillars" (Galatians 2:9)—and is well known to many other churches (Acts 1:15–26; 2:14–40; 3:1–26; 4:8; 5:1–11, 29; 8:18–25; 9:32–43; 10:5; 12:17; 1 Peter 2:11; 5:13). It was Peter who took the decisive step in ordering the baptism of the Gentile Cornelius without first requiring circumcision (Acts 10). Although Paul spoke of Jesus' ministry as being directed to the circumcised (Galatians 2:7), Peter's influence in gentile areas is nevertheless obvious (1 Corinthians 1:12; 1 Peter 1:1).

On the other hand, his role was not always so singular. He often shared his position of prominence with James and John, constituting with them a kind of inner elite within the Twelve. All three accompanied Jesus to the raising of Jairus's daughter (Mark 5:37), at the Transfiguration (9:2), at the Mount of Olives for a special farewell discourse (13:3), and to the Garden of Gethsemane (14:33).

Peter's activities are not reported following the Council of Jerusalem, where he exercised an important, though not necessarily "papal," role in opening the mission of the Church to the Gentiles (Acts 15:7–12). Significantly, it was James, not Peter, who presided over the council and ratified its decisions. However, there is increasing agreement among historians and biblical scholars that Peter did go to Rome and was martyred there (by crucifixion, according to the North African theologian Tertullian [d. ca. 225]). The Roman leader Clement (regarded as Peter's third successor, ca. 91–ca. 101) describes Peter's trials in Rome (*1 Clement* 5:4), and Eusebius of Caesarea (d. ca. 339) reports an ancient story about Peter's crucifixion there (*Ecclesiastical History* 2.25.5, 8). St. Irenaeus of Lyons (d. ca. 200) assumes that Peter and Paul jointly founded the church of Rome and inaugurated its succession of bishops (*Against Heresies* 3.1.2; 3.3.3). However, there is no evidence that before his death Peter actually served the church of Rome as its first bishop, even though the "fact" is regularly

taken for granted by a wide spectrum of Catholics and others (for example, in Jesuit scholar Thomas Reese's otherwise fine book *Inside the Vatican* [Cambridge, MA: Harvard University Press, 1996, p. 11]). Indeed,
there is no evidence that Rome even had a monoepiscopal form of ecclesiastical government until the middle of the second century. As was
pointed out earlier, among the letters of St. Ignatius of Antioch (d. ca.
107) to the seven churches of the ancient Christian world, Ignatius's letter
to Rome was the only one in which he makes no mention at all of its
bishop. The ancient text known as *The Shepherd*, attributed to Hermas, a
lay member of the Roman community, contains hints of disputes about
rank among church leaders (*Visions* 2.2.6; 3.9.7), who are sometimes referred to as "the elders who are in charge of the Church" (2.4.3). Significantly, the references are all in the plural. Where bishops are mentioned
(again in the plural), they are usually linked with other bishops, teachers,
and deacons (3.5.1), as if the Church were a tower under construction and
these leaders were numbered among its stones. By the late second or early
third century, however, Peter did become identified in tradition as the
first Bishop of Rome. But tradition is not a fact factory. It cannot make
something into a historical fact when it is not.

Peter is credited with writing two Letters that are part of the New Testament canon: 1 and 2 Peter. While biblical scholars generally accept his
authorship of the first, they regard his authorship of the second as unlikely. Nevertheless, as a compendium of highly flattering traditions
about Peter, the second Letter is an important witness to the stature he
enjoyed and the respect he was accorded in the early Church. He is said,
for example, to have had the gift of inspiration (2 Peter 1:20–21) and to
have received revelations about future false prophets (2:1–3), special traditions about the Parousia, or Second Coming of Christ (3:8), and the re-
generation of the world (3:11–12). A body of apocryphal literature
associated with the name of Peter emerged in the second century: the
Apocalypse of St. Peter, the *Acts of St. Peter*, and the *Gospel of St. Peter*.
Even if not authentically Petrine in authorship, these writings attest to
Peter's increasing prestige in the early Church. The account of Peter's
being crucified upside down is derived from this literature.

Peter and the Primacy: In the Catholic tradition, the biblical basis for
associating the primacy with Peter is embodied in three texts: Matthew
16:13–19; Luke 22:31–32; and John 21:15–19. The fact that Jesus' naming of
Peter as the "rock" occurs in three different contexts in these three
Gospels raises a question about the original setting of the incident itself.
Scholars are not sure if the naming occurred during Jesus' earthly ministry or after the Resurrection, with what is called a subsequent "retrojec-
tion" into the accounts of Jesus' earthly ministry. The conferral of the

power of the keys of the kingdom surely suggests an imposing measure of authority, given the symbolism of the keys, but there is no explicit indication that the authority conferred was meant to be exercised over others, much less that it be absolutely monarchical in kind (as claimed and exercised by later popes, especially in the Middle Ages and even into the late twentieth century). In Acts, in fact, Peter is shown consulting with the other apostles and even being sent by them (8:14). He and John are portrayed as acting as a team (3:1–11; 4:1–22; 8:14). And Paul confronts Peter for his inconsistency and hypocrisy in drawing back from table fellowship with gentile Christians in Antioch under pressure from some Jewish Christians who arrived later from Jerusalem. Paul "opposed him to his face because he clearly was wrong" (Galatians 2:11; see also 12–14).

Scholars, however, point to a significant trajectory of images relating to Peter and his ministry as an independent basis for the primatial claims. He is spoken of as the fisherman (Luke 5:10; John 21:1–14), an occupation that, in fact, he and his brother Andrew had practiced, as the shepherd of Christ's sheep (John 21:15–17), as the Christian martyr (John 13:36; 1 Peter 5:1), as an elder who addresses other elders (1 Peter 5:1), as a proclaimer of faith in Jesus as the Son of God (Matthew 16:16–17), as the receiver of a special revelation (Mark 9:2–8; 2 Peter 1:16–18; Acts 1:9–16; 5:1–11; 10:9–16; 12:7–9), as the guardian of the true faith against false teaching and misunderstanding (2 Peter 1:20–21; 3:15–16), and, of course, as the rock on which the Church is to be built (Matthew 16:18).

This trajectory of biblical images continued in the life of the early, postbiblical Church, and these images were enriched by others: missionary preacher, great visionary, destroyer of heretics, receiver of the new law, gatekeeper of heaven, helmsman of the ship of the Church, coteacher and comartyr with Paul. This is not to suggest, of course, that Peter was portrayed always and only in a positive fashion. He is also presented as a weak and sinful man. He is reproached by Paul (Galatians 2:11–14), misunderstands Jesus (Mark 9:5–6; John 13:6–11; 18:10–11), weakens in faith after beginning to walk on water (Matthew 14:30–31), is rebuked by Jesus (Mark 8:33; Matthew 16:23), and, in spite of prior boasts to the contrary (Mark 14:29,31; John 13:37), he denied Christ (Mark 14:66–72). But he is always repentant and was eventually rehabilitated. The Risen Lord appears to Peter and he becomes once again a source of strength to the Church (Luke 22:32).

Peter's unique importance as Jesus' first and chief disciple and as the leader of the college of the twelve apostles is clear enough. No pope in history has achieved his status, and it is no accident that none of the more than 260 individuals whom Catholic tradition regards as his successors have taken the name Peter II, including two whose own baptismal names were Peter (John XIV, elected in 983, and Sergius IV, elected in 1009). What can be said, however, about Peter's enduring significance for the papacy and for the Church itself?

Petrine Succession: History provides a long list of popes following Peter, beginning with Linus (ca. 66–ca. 78) and continuing into the twentieth century and the end of the second Christian millennium with such popes as Pius XII (1939–58), John XXIII (1958–63), Paul VI (1963–78), John Paul I (1978), and John Paul II (1978–). Catholic tradition regards all of these popes as successors of Peter. In what sense are they his successors, and in what sense are they not?

In at least two of his apostolic roles, Peter could *not* have had successors: first, as the traditional cofounder with Paul of the Apostolic See of Rome; and, second, as one of the Twelve who were personal witnesses of the Risen Lord. These are unique, nonrepeatable, and nontransmittable aspects of Peter's apostleship. On the other hand, the bishops of Rome do continue Peter's ministry of evangelizing the world and of maintaining the unity of the whole Church. They also continue to exercise within the college of bishops the same kind of pastoral authority Peter exercised within the original company of the Twelve. The word "continue" is important. The popes do not succeed Peter in the sense of *replacing* him, as a newly inaugurated president of the United States, for example, replaces his predecessor. The popes carry on Peter's ministry, but Peter as such is irreplaceable. He alone is the rock on which the Church is built.

Indeed, for St. Cyprian of Carthage (d. 258) every bishop in his own episcopal see, or diocese, is in some sense a successor of Peter. As successors of the apostles, all bishops are signs of unity and bearers of the apostolic tradition. St. Hilary of Poitiers (d. 367), too, referred to all bishops as "successors of Peter and Paul." St. Augustine of Hippo (d. 430) pointed out that in Peter the whole Church, and not only Peter, received the keys of the kingdom. Moreover, the Orthodox churches maintain that Rome is not the only see in which Peter exercised his apostolic primacy and in which an episcopal succession occurred. They cite Antioch as one of these other apostolic sees.

Nevertheless, it is a matter of Catholic doctrine that Petrine succession, like apostolic succession, is a development guided by the Holy Spirit and, in that sense, is of divine institution.

Petrine Ministry: According to Catholic tradition, the ministry that the Bishop of Rome exercises in his capacity as Vicar of Peter (see below) is a continuation of Peter's own ministry on behalf of the universal Church. As such it is called the Petrine ministry, which Jesus is believed to have conferred upon Peter at the Last Supper when he declared, "I have prayed that your own faith may not fail; and once you have turned back, you must strengthen your brothers" (Luke 22:32). The ministry of pastoral leadership exercised by Peter in the first part of Acts is the model and the norm for the Petrine ministry exercised by the pope. It involves witnessing to the faith, overseeing the way in which local churches preserve and transmit this faith, providing assistance and encouragement to fellow bishops in their own local and universal ministry of proclaiming and defending the faith, speaking in the name of the bishops and their local churches when the need arises, and articulating the faith of the Church in the name of the whole communion of local churches which together constitute the universal Church. In sum, the Petrine ministry is that of a "servant of the servants of God" (Lat., *servus servorum Dei*): a servant of his brother bishops, and a servant of the whole People of God.

Vicar of Peter: The most traditional title accorded the pope (from the end of the fourth century) is that of Vicar of Peter. The Bishop of Rome does not take the place of Peter. Unlike Peter, the pope is neither an apostle nor an eyewitness of the Risen Lord. These are qualities that cannot be transmitted to those who follow. The popes can only continue Peter's ministry by keeping alive the faith that has been handed on to them. The closest English word to "vicar" is "substitute." Like a substitute teacher in a classroom, the pope stands in for Peter, but does not replace him. Although the title Vicar of Christ is practically synonymous today with the person and office of the pope, it does not have the same historical standing in the Catholic tradition as that of Vicar of Peter. Originally, all bishops were considered to be vicars of Christ. Not until the pontificate of Eugenius III (1145–53) did the title Vicar of Christ become exclusively identified with the Bishop of Rome. Subsequently, Pope Innocent III (1198–1216) appealed to the title as the basis of his universal power, even over temporal authorities. Nevertheless, in 1964 the Second Vatican Council affirmed that "bishops govern the particular churches entrusted to them as the vicars of Christ and his ambassadors" (Dogmatic Constitution on the Church, n. 27). The pope is Vicar of Christ insofar as he is a bishop, not insofar as he is a pope. The title that captures his distinctive Petrine responsibilities is that of Vicar of Peter. Feast day (with St. Paul): June 29.

2 Linus, St., *ca. 66–ca. 78 (67–76 in the Vatican's official list).*

Because it was not until the late second or early third century that Catholic tradition came to regard Peter as the first Bishop of Rome, it was Linus, not Peter, who was considered in the earliest succession lists to be the first pope. Very little is known about Linus. St. Irenaeus of Lyons (d. ca. 200) and the historian Eusebius of Caesarea (d. ca. 339) identified him with the companion of Paul who sent greetings from Rome to Timothy in Ephesus (2 Timothy 4:21), but Scripture scholars today are generally hesitant to do so. Early sources, including Eusebius, claim that Linus held office for about twelve years, but they are not clear about the exact dates or about his exact pastoral role and authority. It should be remembered—contrary to pious Catholic belief—that the monoepiscopal structure of church governance (also known as the monarchical episcopate, in which each diocese was headed by a single bishop) still did not exist in Rome at this time. And neither was there a College of Cardinals charged with the election of a new pope. (The electoral role of the College of Cardinals did not begin until 1059.) For almost the entire first Christian millennium the pope was elected by the clergy and people of Rome, since his immediate and primary pastoral office was that of Bishop of Rome.

There is no evidence to support the legend that Linus died as a martyr and was buried on Vatican Hill close to St. Peter, nor for the tradition that he decreed, in keeping with 1 Corinthians 11:1–16, that women should keep their heads covered in church. His name occurs after those of Peter and Paul in the ancient Canon of the Mass. In Eucharistic Prayer I today his name follows those of the twelve apostles (including Paul, but not Matthias, who was elected to succeed the betrayer, Judas Iscariot), but his name and the names of other early popes and martyrs are usually given in brackets and in small type to designate the optional character of that portion of the Eucharistic Prayer. Feast day: September 23.

3 Anacletus [Cletus], St., *Greek (?), ca. 79–ca. 91 (76–88 in the Vatican's official list).*

The name of the second successor of Peter, Anacletus, is really Anencletus, a Greek adjective meaning "blameless." Since it was also a common name for a slave, it may be indicative of his social origins. Cletus, the name by which he is commemorated in Eucharistic Prayer I following that of Linus, is simply a shortened form of Anacletus. In some early sources the two names were assumed incorrectly to be those of two different popes.

Anacletus evidently exercised a position of pastoral leadership in Rome, but the monoepiscopal structure (also known as the monarchical episcopate) was still not in place there. One unconfirmed tradition is that, during his pontificate, he divided Rome into twenty-five parishes. The church historian Eusebius of Caesarea (d. ca. 339) reports that he died in the twelfth year of the Emperor Domitian's reign (81–96). The tradition that he died a martyr is also unattested. His former feast day, April 26, was dropped in the course of Pope Paul VI's reform of the liturgical calendar in 1969.

4 Clement I, St., *ca. 91–ca. 101 (88–97 in the Vatican's official list).*

Also known as Clement of Rome, he is best known for his likely authorship of the letter referred to as *1 Clement,* the most important first-
century Christian document outside the New Testament and treated by
some in the ancient Church as if it were, in fact, part of the New Testament canon. A second letter attributed to him (*2 Clement*) is not authentic. The Roman community at this time was probably divided into a
number of small house churches scattered throughout the city and its
neighboring districts, each presided over by a presbyter (and possibly
more than one). There would have been no united and coordinated leadership within the city's Christian community as a whole, but it was otherwise the case in the community's relations with the Christian
communities of other cities. One presbyter (and Clement was specifically
mentioned in *The Shepherd* of Hermas) was charged with corresponding
with these other communities and probably also with dispensing aid to
those in need. As such, Clement and others in his position would have
functioned as a kind of foreign minister of the Roman church rather
than as its monarchical bishop. But surely the presbyters, like Clement,
who fulfilled this responsibility would have stood out.

This first letter of Clement was sent ca. 96 from the church in Rome to
the church in Corinth, instructing the Corinthians to reinstate elders
(presbyters, or senior priests) who had been improperly deposed and to
exile the younger persons who had instigated the rebellion. In Clement's
view (one not grounded in the New Testament, however), the apostles
themselves had established bishops (a term he uses interchangeably with
presbyters) and deacons in all places and had stipulated that neither they
nor their successors were to be deprived of office. Significantly, Clement
offered no defense for his intervening in the pastoral affairs of the
Corinthian church (he had not been invited to do so by the Corinthians),
but neither did he appeal to any special Roman privilege. The rhetorical
character of the letter may indicate that Clement knew that he did not
possess the authority he claimed and that he had to rely instead on per-
suasion and exhortation. The hortatory subjunctive, in fact, is used with
remarkable frequency, while the imperative is used only sparingly.

The form of Clement's intervention seems to have been modeled on
the relations of the imperial capital of Rome (its Senate and emperor)
with its outlying provinces. In accordance with the practice of the imperial government, Clement sent with his letter three witnesses to observe
and to report on the restoration of peace. His recommendation of exile
for the offending parties also mirrored secular Roman practice in which
exile was an escape from trial. Indeed, the letter is marked throughout by

a laudatory attitude toward the Roman state. It praises the Roman military as a model of obedience and calls upon Christians to be similarly "obedient . . . to our rulers and governors on earth," to whom God has given the sovereignty. Underlying these words is the conviction that the empire and its rulers have been established by God as the earthly counterpart of the heavenly kingdom. As such, the Roman political system—which is at once imperial and hierarchical—is worthy of being emulated by the Church itself. The influence of the existing Roman political system on the evolving Roman ecclesiastical system, therefore, cannot be discounted. When some Catholic theologians and historians today suggest that the hierarchical structures of the Church, including the papacy, owe more to the Roman Empire than to Jesus, they do not exaggerate.

There is an unverified tradition, attested nonetheless by Tertullian (d. ca. 225) and St. Jerome (d. ca. 420), that Clement was consecrated by St. Peter himself and as his immediate successor. If that were true, Linus (ca. 66–ca. 78) and Anacletus (ca. 79–ca. 91) would have to be somehow displaced from or rearranged on the list of popes. Third- and fourth-century writers such as Origen (d. ca. 254), Eusebius of Caesarea (d. ca. 339), and Jerome equated him with the Clement whom St. Paul mentions as a coworker who "struggled at [his] side in promoting the gospel" and whose name is "in the book of life" (Philippians 4:3), which is a kind of registry of God's chosen people (Exodus 32:32–33; Psalms 69:28; 139:16).

There is no historical evidence to support the claim that Clement died a martyr or that he was banished to Crimea, where he is said to have preached the gospel while doing forced labor in the mines and was later drowned in the Black Sea with an anchor around his neck. There may be more substance, however, to the tradition that the church of San Clemente in Rome stands on the site of his house. Clement is mentioned in Eucharistic Prayer I between Cletus (Anacletus) and Sixtus I (ca. 116–ca. 125). Feast day: November 23 (in the West); November 24 or 25 (in the East).

5 Evaristus, St., *Greek, ca. 100-ca. 109 (97–105 in the Vatican's official list)*.

Evaristus is regarded by Catholic tradition as the fourth successor of Peter. The early succession lists, however, differ about the length of his pontificate and even about his exact place on the list. The historian Eusebius of Caesarea (d. ca. 339), for example, indicated that Evaristus served for eight or nine years, while the fourth-century Liberian Catalogue (which called him Aristus and placed him after Anacletus rather than Clement) calculated his term as just under fourteen years. There is little or no reliable information about him. Specifically, there is no basis for the claim that he died as a martyr and was buried on Vatican Hill near St. Peter. Two letters and two fragments of decretals associated with him are not authentic. The fact that he is on the early succession lists indicates, at the very least, that he exercised a prominent role of leadership in the Roman church, although not as its only bishop, or overseer. The monoepiscopal structure (also known as the monarchical episcopate) did not come to Rome until the middle of the second century, with the pontificate of St. Pius I (ca. 142–ca. 155). Feast day: October 26.

6 Alexander I, St., *ca. 109-ca. 116 (105–115 in the Vatican's official list).*

Alexander is regarded by Catholic tradition as the fifth successor of Peter. As in the case of his predecessors, the length of Alexander's pontificate is a matter of guesswork. The estimates of the early sources range from seven to ten years. When information about an early religious figure is sparse to nonexistent, as in this case, pious legend too often fills the vacuum. Thus, the *Liber Pontificalis,* a collection of papal biographies that began to take shape in the sixth century, attributes to Alexander the insertion of the eucharistic institution narrative from the Last Supper into the Canon of the Mass (an attempt to assign an early origin to this liturgical practice) and also credits him with inaugurating the custom of blessing houses with holy water and salt (which really stemmed from a pagan practice). The *Liber Pontificalis* also repeats a Roman tradition that Alexander was beheaded on the Via Nomentana, a road leading outside of Rome, but the tradition evidently had confused him with an actual martyr of the same name whose tomb was discovered along that road in 1855. Indeed, St. Irenaeus (d. ca. 200) identifies no martyrs among these early Roman leaders until Pope Telesphoros (ca. 125–ca. 136). Feast day: May 3.

7 Sixtus [Xystus] I, St., *ca. 116–ca. 125 (115–125 in the Vatican's official list).*

Sixtus I is regarded by Catholic tradition as the sixth successor of Peter, thus the Latin name Sixtus (meaning "sixth"), although he is more correctly known as Xystus. The dates of his pontificate are as uncertain as those of his immediate predecessors. The early sources generally agree that it lasted about ten years. Little or nothing else is known about him. The *Liber Pontificalis* (a collection of papal biographies first compiled in the mid-sixth century) indicates that he was the son of a priest and attributes to him, without historical basis, a decree that sacred vessels (e.g., chalices, ciboria) should only be touched by clergy and another decree that the people should chant the Sanctus (the "Holy, Holy, Holy" at the beginning of the Eucharistic Prayer) with the priest. There is also no foundation for the claim that he died as a martyr and was buried on Vatican Hill near St. Peter. Feast day: April 3 or 6.

8 Telesphoros, St., *Greek, ca. 125–ca. 136 (125–136 in the Vatican's official list).*

Telesphoros is the only second-century pope whose martyrdom is historically verifiable. Although the exact dates of his pontificate are uncertain, early sources are in agreement that it lasted eleven years. The *Liber Pontificalis* (a collection of papal biographies first compiled in the mid-sixth century) mistakenly attributes to him the inauguration of a seven-week fast before Easter and the use of the Gloria in the Christmas Midnight Mass. Both practices were not introduced until much later. St. Irenaeus (d. ca. 200) notes that Telesphoros always observed Easter on Sunday rather than on whatever day of the week Passover happened to fall (which was the practice of those Christians who were known as the Quartodecimans—the Latin word for "fourteenth"—because they observed Easter on the fourteenth day of the Jewish month of Nisan). Feast day: January 5 (in the West); February 22 (in the East).

9 Hyginus, St., *Greek, ca. 138–ca. 142 (136–140 in the Vatican's official list).*

Hyginus is regarded by Catholic tradition as the eighth successor of Peter. Estimates of the length of this pontificate range from as many as twelve years to as few as four (the more credible figure). According to the *Liber Pontificalis* (a collection of papal biographies first compiled in the mid-sixth century), Hyginus was a Greek from Athens with a background in philosophy. His contemporary, St. Justin Martyr (d. ca. 165), also came to Rome from the East and was, like Hyginus, a philosopher and apologist (i.e., defender of the faith). St. Irenaeus (d. ca. 200) reports that during Hyginus's pontificate the Gnostic teachers Valentinus (d. ca. 175) and Cerdo came to Rome from Egypt and Syria, respectively, indicating that Rome was becoming a major Christian center. Marcion (d. ca. 160), regarded by church historians as one of the most formidable heretics ever confronted by the Church, also came to Rome ca. 140, where he fell under Cerdo's influence. Four years later, during the next pontificate, Marcion was excommunicated by the Roman church for heresy.

Hyginus was regarded as a martyr (and was included in the Roman Martyrology), but there is no historical evidence to substantiate that belief or the pious tradition that he was buried on Vatican Hill near St. Peter. Feast day: January 11.

10 Pius I, St., *ca. 142–ca. 155 (140–155 in the Vatican's official list).*

Pius I was the first of the listed popes to have functioned as the single, or sole, Bishop of Rome. Before his pontificate, the Roman church seems to have been governed by a council or group of presbyters or presbyter-bishops. Those regarded by Catholic tradition as popes before the pontificate of Pius I may simply have been the most prominent members of those governing groups.

The early sources are confused about the dates of this pontificate. Some place Pius I after his successor Anicetus (ca. 155–ca. 166). The second-century Muratorian Canon (the oldest extant list of the books of the New Testament) identifies Pius as a brother of Hermas, a former slave and the author of a historically significant visionary work with strongly penitential themes known as *The Shepherd*. Nothing much is known of Pius's pontificate except that the Gnostics Valentinus (d. ca. 175), Cerdo, and Marcion (d. ca. 160) were actively promoting their views in the city, specifically that the Old Testament had been completely supplanted by the New Testament so that Christianity is in no sense a fulfillment of Judaism, but rather its replacement. The Gnostics also harbored a negative attitude toward the material world and the body, even denying the reality of Jesus' human body. It is thought that Pius presided over a synod of presbyters that excommunicated Marcion in July 144.

Although Pius is mentioned in a somewhat unreliable ninth-century martyrology compiled by St. Ado of Vienne (d. 875), there is no evidence that he was martyred or that he was buried on Vatican Hill near St. Peter. Feast day: July 11.

11 Anicetus, St., *Syrian, ca. 155–ca. 166 (155–166 in the Vatican's official list).*

Anicetus was Bishop of Rome at a time when the city was becoming a flourishing center of Christian activity, attracting some of the leading figures of the ancient Church, including the great anti-Gnostic Syrian scholar St. Hegesippus (d. ca. 180) and St. Justin Martyr (d. ca. 165). Although the *Liber Pontificalis* (a collection of papal biographies first compiled in the mid-sixth century) reports that Anicetus forbade clerics to wear long hair, he is perhaps best remembered for his serious but amicable discussions with one of the most revered figures in the early church, St. Polycarp (d. ca. 155/6), bishop of Smyrna (in present-day Turkey), who had been a disciple of St. John the Evangelist.

Already in his eighties, Polycarp had come to Rome to urge the pope to adopt the common liturgical practice in Asia Minor of observing the feast of Easter, regarded as the Christian Passover, on the fourteenth day of the

Jewish month of Nisan (the day of the Jewish Passover), regardless of the day of the week on which it fell. Because these Christians preferred the fourteenth day of Nisan, they were known by the Latin word for "four-teenth," namely, Quartodecimans. It is important to note that, until this time, Rome itself observed no special feast of Easter. The Roman church considered every Sunday a celebration of the Resurrection. Anicetus denied Polycarp's request that Rome conform its practice to that of the churches of Asia Minor, insisting that he felt bound by his predecessors' custom of celebrating the Resurrection every Sunday. The discussion remained friendly and Anicetus invited Polycarp to preside at the Eucharist. They departed in peace, but Rome and the East continued their separate practices. Ever since the first ecumenical council at Nicaea in 325, Roman Catholics have celebrated Easter on the Sunday following the full moon after the vernal equinox (i.e., between March 22 and April 25). However, many Eastern-rite Catholics as well as Orthodox and other non-Catholic Eastern Christians who follow the Julian rather than the Gregorian calendar celebrate Easter on a different Sunday.

It was probably Anicetus who erected a memorial shrine for St. Peter on Vatican Hill that was familiar to visitors at the turn of the century (ca. 200). Feast day: April 17.

12 Soter, St., *ca. 166–ca. 174 (166–175 in the Vatican's official list).*

The most significant development in Soter's pontificate was the introduction of Easter as an annual liturgical feast in Rome. Until this time, the Roman church had no separate feast of Easter, but instead regarded every Sunday as a celebration of the Resurrection. The date agreed upon for the new feast was the Sunday following the fourteenth day of the Jewish month of Nisan (in other words, the Sunday following the day of Passover). This contrasted with a common Christian practice in Asia Minor of celebrating Easter on the day of Passover itself, no matter what day of the week it fell on. Those who followed this practice were called Quartodecimans (from the Latin, "fourteenth," for the fourteenth day of Nisan).

The historian Eusebius of Caesarea (d. ca. 339) preserved fragments of a letter that Dionysius, bishop of Corinth, wrote to Soter in acknowledgment of the pope's letter to the Corinthian community and promising that his letter would be read regularly at gatherings of the Corinthian church. Modern historians speculate, on the basis of other letters written by Dionysius, that Soter may have expressed his disapproval of a certain moral laxity in the Corinthian community, specifically with regard to sexual conduct and a too lenient restoration of penitents to communion with the Church regardless of their sins. Dionysius's obsequious reply may have been designed to calm the waters between Rome and Corinth.

The *Liber Pontificalis* (a collection of papal biographies first compiled in the mid-sixth century) reports that Soter ordered nonordained monks not to touch altar cloths or offer incense in church—an indication that pastoral micro-management is not an exclusively modern phenomenon. Although Soter was later venerated as a martyr, there is no evidence that he died a martyr's death. Feast day: April 22.

13 Eleutherius [Eleutherus], St., *Greek, ca. 174–ca. 189 (175–189 in the Vatican's official list).*

Eleutherius is regarded by Catholic tradition as the twelfth successor of Peter, having served as a deacon (assistant) to Pope Anicetus (ca. 155–ca. 166) before being elected to the papacy himself. In 177 or 178, he received a visit from St. Irenaeus of Lyons (d. ca. 200), bearing a letter from the Christians of Lyons (in southern Gaul, or modern-day France) that set out their highly critical views on Montanism, a new religious movement that was prophesying a speedy end of the world and preaching the need to impose severe ascetical practices upon the Church. Although the historical record is not completely clear, it seems that Eleutherius failed to see the danger of Montanism and declined to pass judgment on its prophetic claims. However, Tertullian (d. ca. 225), a prominent convert to Montanism, claimed that the pope originally sent out conciliatory letters acknowledging the authenticity of the prophecies and only later rejected the movement.

The *Liber Pontificalis* (a collection of papal biographies first compiled in the mid-sixth century) dubiously attributes to Eleutherius the regulation that Christians are never to reject any food as naturally unclean. Such a regulation would have been more appropriate to fifth-century Rome, when Manichaean proscriptions of certain foods were in fashion. There was also a popular, but legendary, belief that a British king had asked this pope to send missionaries to Britain. Eleutherius is first mentioned as a martyr in the somewhat unreliable ninth-century martyrology compiled by St. Ado of Vienne (d. 875). Feast day: May 26.

14 Victor I, St., *African, 189–198.*

The first African pope, whom St. Jerome (d. ca. 420) identified as the first Latin ecclesiastical writer, Victor is best known for his firm resolution of the controversy over the celebration of Easter. With his urging, synods were held in Rome and in other Christian centers from Gaul (modern-day

France) to Mesopotamia (present-day Iraq). Although the great majority sided with the pope, the churches of Asia Minor held fast to their practice of celebrating Easter on the fourteenth day of the Jewish month of Nisan (the day of Passover), whether it fell on Sunday or not. They were called Quartodecimans, after the Latin word for "fourteenth," because of their preference for the fourteenth day of Nisan. By contrast, the Roman church, which originally had no separate feast of Easter because it regarded every Sunday as a celebration of the Resurrection, observed Easter on the Sunday following the day of Passover.

When the Quartodecimans, under the leadership of Polycrates, bishop of Ephesus, refused to bend to his will, Victor declared them out of communion (excommunicated) not only with the Roman church but with the universal Church. His harsh action evoked a storm of protest, even from those who accepted his ruling on Easter. St. Irenaeus of Lyons (d. ca. 200) pointed out to him that all previous popes down to Soter (ca. 166–ca. 174) had tolerated the Quartodeciman practice and that the issue was not one that touched the essence of the Christian faith. The fact that the churches of Asia Minor remained in communion with Rome indicates that the pope may have heeded the stern advice of Irenaeus and others and withdrawn the sentence of excommunication. But the incident itself shows the growing belief of the popes at this time that the Roman church enjoyed some kind of primatial status in the universal Church.

Victor also excommunicated Theodotus of Byzantium, the leader of an Adoptionist group that taught that Jesus was not the real Son of God, but only God's "adopted" son, and deposed Florinus from the priesthood for defending Gnostic doctrines. He is also the first pope known to have had dealings with the imperial household, supplying the emperor's mistress, herself a Christian, with a list of Christians condemned to the mines of Sardinia and thereby securing their release. Though later venerated as a martyr, there is no evidence that Victor suffered a martyr's death or that was he buried on Vatican Hill near St. Peter. Feast day: July 28.

15 Zephrynus, St., *198/9–217 (199–217 in the Vatican's official list).*

Although his pontificate lasted more than seventeen years, relatively little is known about Zephrynus except for the sharp criticisms he received, especially from St. Hippolytus (d. ca. 236), a leading and learned Roman presbyter. Hippolytus depicted the pope as a simple man without education and the puppet of his powerful deacon Callistus (who eventually succeeded Zephrynus as pope). Hippolytus and others, including the North African theologian Tertullian (d. ca. 225), were frustrated with the pope because of his apparent weakness and vacillation in the face of new challenges to the historic faith from Montanism (a religious movement that was prophesying a speedy end of the world and preaching the need to impose severe ascetical practices upon the Church), Adoptionism (a Christological theory that Jesus was an ordinary human being who became the "adopted" Son of God at his baptism), and Sabellianism (also known as Modalism and Monarchianism, a theory holding that in God there is, in effect, only one divine Person with three different modes or manifestations of divine activity). In the light of the modern emphasis on the papal office as the guardian and defender of orthodoxy, such criticisms are truly remarkable. Early popes like Zephrynus and Eleutherius were accused of actually being too easy on doctrinal dissidents rather than too censorious. Zephrynus did publish a creedal formula that emphasized the divinity of Jesus Christ as well as the Son's personal distinction from the Father, but the pope, like almost everyone else at this time, lacked the theological terminology to say this clearly.

Origen (d. ca. 254), one of the first great theologians in the history of the Church, visited Rome during this pontificate—another indication of the growing importance of "that most ancient church" (Origen's own words). There is no evidence, however, to support the tradition that Zephrynus died a martyr's death, but there is some basis for the belief that he was buried in his own cemetery near that of Callistus on the Appian Way. Feast day: August 26.

16 Callistus [Calixtus] I, St., *217–222.*

Callistus is the first pope, after Peter, whose name is commemorated as a martyr in the oldest martyrology of the Roman church, the *Depositio Martyrum* (ca. 354). Much of the information that survives about Callistus comes filtered through the highly derogatory writings of St. Hippolytus (d. ca. 236), a leading and learned Roman presbyter who also had been a persistent critic of Callistus's predecessor, Zephrynus.

In his youth Callistus had been a slave of a Christian who set him up in banking. When, to the dismay of its many Christian customers, the business failed (perhaps through some unsavory activity of his), Callistus fled. After his return, he was charged with fighting in a synagogue on the Sabbath and sentenced to hard labor in the mines of Sardinia. He was released at the same time as a number of other Christian slaves were liberated through the good offices of the emperor's Christian mistress, Marcia, and Pope Victor I (189–98). Victor had deliberately excluded Callistus from the list he had submitted to Marcia, but Callistus prevailed upon the governor to free him as well. Upon Callistus's return to Rome, the pope sent him to live in Anzio on a monthly pension, but Victor's successor, Zephrynus, recalled him and appointed him his deacon, with supervisory authority over the clergy of Rome and over the church's official cemetery on the Appian Way (now known as the catacombs of San Callisto). Because of Zephrynus's own intellectual and administrative limitations, Callistus exerted enormous influence as the pope's deacon and was elected to succeed him. Hippolytus, however, refused to accept the election and seems to have sought and received election as bishop by a schismatic group, thereby becoming the Catholic Church's first of thirty-nine antipopes (the last was Felix V [1439–49]).

Callistus's five-year pontificate was defined in large part by his constant battles with Hippolytus and his faction, who accused the pope of doctrinal deviations (Modalism, in particular, the view that in God there is only one divine Person with three modes of activity) and laxity in discipline (for example, ordaining men who had been married more than once, recognizing marriages between partners of different social classes, and readmitting heretics and schismatics to the Church without adequate prior penances). Both charges were unfair. Callistus was clearly not a Modalist, but neither did he support Hippolytus's teaching that the Word (Logos) is a distinct Person, a view the pope regarded as ditheistic (positing two Gods). And Callistus's approach to sinners was actually closer to that of Jesus than to the new rigorists in the Church. The Church, he believed, is a place where the wheat and tares grow together. As Jesus reminded his disciples, the sorting out of saints from sinners must be left to the merciful God. The Church, the pope insisted, must offer reconciliation to anyone seeking forgiveness for sins committed after baptism.

Callistus is said to have laid the foundation for Ember Days (days of fast and abstinence occurring in sets of three, four times a year), which are no longer observed in the Catholic Church.

Although his name appears in the oldest Roman martyrology, it is questionable whether he was, in fact, a martyr. As historians point out, there was no persecution during his pontificate. His tomb in the cemetery of Calepodius on the Via Aurelia (and not in the cemetery named after him on the Appian Way) was discovered in 1960 in the remains of an oratory erected by Pope Julius I (337–52) in the fourth century. The crypt is decorated with frescoes depicting his martyrdom. Feast day: October 14.

17 Urban I, St., 222–230.

Urban had a generally peaceful pontificate, because it fell within the imperial reign of Alexander Severus (222–35), in which there were no persecutions of Christians. The schism in the Roman church provoked by the bitter opposition of St. Hippolytus (d. ca. 236) to Urban's two immediate predecessors, Zephrynus (198/9–217) and Callistus (217–22), continued during Urban's pontificate, albeit in less acute form. However, there is no historical record of the relationships between Urban and Hippolytus. Contrary to pious belief, Urban did not die a martyr's death. According to the fifth-century martyrology of St. Jerome, he is buried in the cemetery of Callistus on the Appian Way. A tomb slab bearing his name in Greek letters has been discovered there. Feast day: May 25.

18 Pontian [Pontianus], St., *d. October 235, pope from July 21, 230, to September 28, 235.*

Pontian was the first pope to abdicate the papal office. (There were three, and perhaps five, others who did so after him: Silverius in 537, Celestine V in 1294, Gregory XII in 1415, and probably John XVIII in 1009. During Benedict IX's canonically confusing pontificate, he abdicated in 1045 in favor of his godfather, but was reinstated in 1047.) He did so only because he had been deported by the new, anti-Christian emperor Maximinus Thrax to labor in the mines on the island of Sardinia, known as the "island of death," from which few ever returned alive. Pontian did not want there to be a vacuum of leadership in the Roman church.

All except the last few months of his pontificate had been peaceful because the tolerant Emperor Severus was still reigning. After succeeding Severus in March of 235, however, Maximinus Thrax abandoned his predecessor's policy of toleration and initiated a violent campaign against Christian leaders. He arrested Pontian and the antipope Hippolytus (d. ca. 236), a strong critic of popes Zephrynus (198/9–217) and Callistus (217–22) and the apparent leader of a schism in the Roman church. Both were imprisoned in Rome and then exiled to Sardinia. According to the fourth-century Liberian Catalogue, Pontian abdicated on September 28, 235, the first precisely recorded date in papal history.

Neither Pontian nor Hippolytus survived the harsh treatment and conditions on Sardinia. Pontian died less than a month after his resignation. It has been suggested that Pontian and Hippolytus were reconciled while in prison or in exile. Their bodies, in any case, were brought back to Rome by Pope Fabian in 236 or 237 and were buried in the newly completed papal crypt in the catacombs of Callistus on the Appian Way. Fragments of Pontian's tomb slab were discovered there early in the twentieth century, with his name and episcopal title inscribed in Greek.

The only other matter for which Pontian's pontificate was known was the Roman church's formal approval of the condemnation of Origen (d. ca. 254), one of the first great theologians of the early Church, by Demetrius, bishop of Alexandria, in 230 or 231. It is assumed that, as the Bishop of Rome, Pontian must have presided over the Roman synod that endorsed the expulsion of Origen from Egypt, from his teaching post, and from the priesthood itself.

A fourth-century martyrology lists Pontian as the first Roman bishop-martyr (after Peter). Feast day: August 13 (with St. Hippolytus).

19 Anterus, St., *Greek, November 21, 235–January 3, 236.*

Because his pontificate was less than two months long (he died a natural death), there is nothing to be said of Anterus except that he was the first pope to be buried in the newly completed papal crypt in the cemetery of Callistus on the Appian Way. Large fragments of the inscription over his tomb have been found there. Anterus's predecessor, Pontian, was also buried in the papal crypt some months later, after his body was returned from the island of Sardinia, where he had died in exile. Feast day: January 3.

20 Fabian, St., *January 10, 236–January 20, 250.*

Fabian was one of the most respected and accomplished popes of the earliest Christian centuries. St. Cyprian of Carthage (d. 258), one of the leading bishops in the contemporary Church, described him as honorable and praised the integrity of his administration. There is a legendary story, related by the historian Eusebius of Caesarea (d. ca. 339), that when the Roman clergy were considering a successor to Pontian, a dove landed on Fabian's head. The clergy were not thinking of Fabian as a possible successor at the time, but the event seemed to them a sign of the Holy Spirit's choice, and so he was elected.

With unusual administrative skill, he reorganized the local clergy, dividing the growing Roman church into seven ecclesiastical districts with a deacon, assisted by a subdeacon and six junior assistants, in charge of each district. He also supervised numerous building projects in the cemeteries and arranged for the bodies of Pope Pontian (d. 235) and the antipope Hippolytus (d. 236) to be returned from their Sardinian exile and buried properly in Rome. Fabian must have had influence at the imperial court because the bodies of those sentenced to deportation could not be brought home or buried without the emperor's explicit and rarely given consent.

Almost all of Fabian's fourteen-year pontificate was peaceful (two emperors, Gordian III and Philip the Arab, were generally tolerant of the Church), but after Decius ascended to power (249), a new and vicious persecution was initiated. Fabian was arrested and was among the first to die, probably as a result of brutal treatment in prison. He was buried in the papal crypt in the cemetery of Callistus on the Appian Way, where the slab on his tomb, bearing his name, title, and the abbreviated word for martyr in Greek letters, was discovered in the nineteenth century. His body was later removed to the church of San Sebastiano, where a sarcophagus inscribed with his name was identified at the beginning of the twentieth century. Feast day: January 20 (with St. Sebastian).

21 Cornelius, St., *March 251–June 253.*

Cornelius's pontificate was marked by his constant and often bitter battles over the question of the validity of baptism by heretics and schismatics. The Roman practice, upheld and enforced by Cornelius, recognized the validity of such baptisms and did not require the rebaptism of those wishing to enter or be reconciled with the Catholic Church.

It had taken more than a year to elect Cornelius as successor to Fabian. The Roman clergy had postponed the election because of the violent persecution under the emperor Decius and because several members of the clergy, including a leading candidate for the papacy, were in prison. During the interregnum of fourteen months the Roman church was governed as it had been during the first century of its existence, that is, collegially, with the presbyter Novatian acting as spokesman.

The following spring the emperor left Rome to fight the Goths. During his absence, the persecution subsided and the election was held. By this time, however, the leading candidate, a presbyter by the name of Moses, had died in prison. Novatian fully expected that he would be elected, but the clergy voted instead for Cornelius, whom Cyprian (d. 258), bishop of Carthage, described as an unambitious priest who had come up through the ranks. Novatian reacted bitterly to the results of the election and had himself ordained a bishop, setting himself up as a rival (antipope) to Cornelius. What was clearly at the basis of Novatian's opposition was Cornelius's readiness to readmit to communion, albeit after suitable penance, those Christians who had lapsed during the persecution. Novatian flatly opposed reconciliation under any conditions. Indeed, this may also have been the central issue in the papal election itself.

Novatian tried to persuade the bishops of other Christian centers to accept his own title to the Roman see, and in Rome itself a faction of rigorist clergy and laity refused to recognize Cornelius's authority. However, Cornelius's election was upheld by Cyprian, who had some influence over the African clergy in Rome, and by Dionysius (d. 264/5), bishop of Alexandria. Cyprian also supported Cornelius when, in October 251, he excommunicated Novatian and his followers at a synod in Rome attended by sixty bishops and many presbyters and deacons. The synod affirmed the pope's policy (and that of a Carthaginian synod) of readmitting, after appropriate contrition and "the medicines of repentance," those Christians who had lapsed during the Decian persecution. Cornelius sent copies of the decisions of the Roman synod and of Cyprian's letter of support to Fabius, the rigorist, pro-Novatian bishop of Antioch. The pope wanted Fabius to suspend his support for Novatian and to accept the moderate course adopted by the majority of churches.

In spite of Cyprian's support of the pope, some bad blood had developed between these two leading bishops of the early Church. When Cornelius had sought backing for his election to the papacy against the challenge from Novatian, Cyprian took some time before finally giving that support. Over a year later, the pope received representatives of Fortunatus, who, like Novatian, was a schismatic bishop in opposition to Cyprian. Even though Cornelius rejected their advocacy on behalf of Fortunatus, Cyprian was upset that the pope had received these envoys in the first place and he sent Cornelius a sharp rebuke. A flurry of correspondence followed between the pope and Cyprian and also between the pope and other bishops. Cornelius made known his position on the schism and also strongly defended his moderate stance toward the lapsed.

Although it has been noted that Cornelius wrote far too harshly, even falsely, about Novatian, the letters (particularly the one to Fabius, bishop of Antioch) provide historians with detailed statistics regarding the Roman church at the time. It included forty-six priests, seven deacons, seven subdeacons, forty-two acolytes, fifty-two exorcists, readers, and porters, and more the fifteen hundred widows (who were also considered officers of the church). On the basis of these figures, it has been estimated that the membership of the Roman church in the mid-third century may have reached fifty thousand members.

When the new emperor, Gallus, resumed the persecutions in June 252, Cornelius was arrested and deported to Centumcellae (present-day Civitavecchia, the port of Rome). Before dying there the following June, Cornelius received a warm letter of support from Cyprian. His body was later taken back to Rome and buried in the cemetery of Callistus on the Appian Way. The inscription on his tomb is the first papal epitaph written in Latin (all others had been in Greek). Both his name and that of Cyprian are included in Eucharistic Prayer I (Canon of the Mass), immediately after the names of Popes Linus, Cletus (Anacletus), Clement, and Sixtus. Feast day: September 16 (with St. Cyprian).

22 Lucius I, St., *June 25, 253–March 5, 254.*

Almost immediately after his election, Lucius was banished from Rome by the emperor Gallus. His place of exile, like that of his predecessor, may have been Centumcellae (present-day Civitavecchia, the port of Rome). Upon the death of Gallus and the accession of Valerian, who seemed at first favorably disposed to Christians, Lucius managed to make his way back to Rome with other exiled Christians. After his return, he received a congratulatory letter from Cyprian (d. 258), bishop of Carthage. Another of Cyprian's letters to him suggests that Lucius maintained the moderate policy of his predecessor, Cornelius, toward those who had lapsed in time of persecution and who sought reconciliation with the Church. The Bishop of Rome evidently made no concessions to the antipope Novatian and his followers, who strongly opposed the reconciliation of lapsed Christians under any conditions.

Because he suffered for the faith in exile, Lucius can be regarded as a confessor (the technical name for one who suffers for the faith, short of death). There is no evidence, however, that he died as a martyr. Lucius is buried in the papal crypt in the cemetery of Callistus on the Appian Way, where a portion of his epitaph, written in Greek, has been found. Feast day: March 4.

23 Stephen I, St., *May 12, 254–August 2, 257.*

Stephen is best known for his theologically important dispute with St. Cyprian (d. 258), bishop of Carthage, over the question of whether those who had been baptized by heretics and schismatics had to be rebaptized upon entrance or return to the Catholic Church. Cyprian held that they had to be rebaptized; Stephen insisted that they did not. This dispute, however, had been preceded by two others.

The first clash with Cyprian occurred after a Spanish bishop, who had lapsed under persecution along with another bishop (by accepting certificates indicating that they had offered sacrifice to the gods), went to Rome and persuaded Stephen to restore him and his fellow bishop to the Church and to their bishoprics. The Spanish churches appealed the pope's decision to Cyprian, who convened a council of North African bishops. The council confirmed the deposition of the two bishops from their sees, but excused Stephen from any blame for his action because he obviously did not have all the facts.

A second clash between Stephen and Cyprian occurred over Bishop Marcian of Arles, who had adopted the rigorist views of the antipope Novatian and was refusing even deathbed reconciliation to Christians who had lapsed in time of persecution. The local bishops of Gaul (modern-day France) had written to Stephen, urging him to depose Marcian. When the pope took no action, the bishops appealed to Cyprian, who urged the pope to depose Marcian and arrange for the election of a new bishop.

The third clash was over the rebaptism of those who had been baptized already by heretics and schismatics. Cyprian, along with most of the churches of North Africa, Syria, and Asia Minor, generally held that the first baptism was invalid since baptism could only be validly administered within the Church. Stephen represented the tradition of Rome, Alexandria, and Palestine, which held that the first baptism was valid and that a second baptism would be illicit (i.e., sinful). The only action appropriate for those who came into the Catholic Church from a heretical or schismatic sect was absolution by the laying on of hands. Cyprian held a synod in Carthage in 255 which supported his position, but some North African bishops objected and sided with Rome. Cyprian thereupon convened a second synod, consisting of seventy-one bishops, the following year. The second synod came to the same conclusion as the first. Stephen, in the meantime, had written to the churches of Asia Minor warning that he could no longer remain in communion with them if they persisted in their practice of rebaptism. When Cyprian sent envoys to notify the pope of the decisions of the two North African synods, Stephen refused to receive the envoys or to offer them hospitality. On September 1, 256, a third council of some eighty-seven North African bishops again supported Cyprian. Cyprian's subsequent letter to Firmilian of Caesarea in Cappadocia is no longer extant, but Firmilian's reply is. In it, there is a violent attack on the pope and the Roman teaching on baptism by heretics and schismatics. With the danger of a major rift in the universal Church looming large, Dionysius (d. 264/5), bishop of Alexandria, himself an opponent of rebaptism, wrote to Stephen, imploring him to adopt a more conciliatory approach. One can only speculate as to how the situation might have deteriorated even further had not Stephen died in the midst of the controversy and had Cyprian himself not been martyred a year later.

These events, however, underscore the growing recognition of the Roman church as a court of appeal, certainly for the churches of Gaul and Spain, and as a church with which other churches are desirous of being in communion. Stephen, however, emerges from these controversies as "an imperious and uncompromising prelate" (J. N. D. Kelly). In spite of his office and its growing authority in the early Church, Stephen, like St. Peter before him, is confronted to his face, as it were, by other bishops and directly blamed for endangering the unity of the Church. The charge is not only profoundly serious but ironic as well, because if the papacy has had any distinctive function at all in history, it is to preserve and strengthen the unity of the Church, not divide it. When popes use the powers of their high office to support one faction against others within the Church, their claim to be bridge builders (the word "pontiff" is derived from the Latin word for bridge, *pons*) rings hollow to many.

Stephen seems to have been the first pope to have appealed to Matthew 16:18 ("... you are Peter ...") as the basis of the primacy of the Roman church and its bishop. He died a natural death and was buried in the papal crypt in the cemetery of Callistus on the Appian Way. Feast day: August 2.

24 Sixtus [Xystus] II, St., *Greek, August 30, 257–August 6, 258.*

More correctly known as Xystus, he is one of the Church's most highly venerated martyrs. He was elected just as the emperor Valerian abandoned his policy of toleration toward Christians, ordering them to participate in state-sponsored religious ceremonies and forbidding them from gathering in cemeteries. Sixtus II managed to avoid personal trouble with the authorities until Valerian issued a second, more severe edict ordering the execution of bishops, priests, and deacons and imposing assorted penalties on laypersons. On August 6, 258, while the pope was seated in his episcopal chair addressing the congregation at a liturgical service in the private (and presumably safe) cemetery of Praetextatus, imperial forces rushed in and seized and beheaded the pope and four deacons. Two other deacons were executed later the same day, and the seventh, St. Lawrence, was put to death four days after that.

Before his death, however, Sixtus II successfully devoted his energies to healing the breach between Rome and the churches of North Africa and Asia Minor created by the issue of the rebaptism of heretics and schismatics who wished to enter the Church and, in particular, by the intransigent approach taken by his predecessor, Stephen I. Although he, too, upheld the Roman policy of accepting the validity of baptisms administered by heretics and schismatics, he restored friendly relations with St. Cyprian (d. 258), bishop of Carthage, and the estranged churches of Asia Minor, probably by tolerating the coexistence of the two practices. Much credit for the reconciliation has been given to Dionysius (d. 264/5), bishop of Alexandria, who had tried in vain to persuade Stephen I to adopt a less confrontational approach. Cyprian's biographer, however, also gives credit to Sixtus II himself, describing him as "a good and peace-loving priest."

After his martyrdom, the pope's body was transferred to the papal crypt in the cemetery of Callistus on the Appian Way. The bloodstained chair on which he had been sitting when killed was placed behind the altar in the chapel of the crypt. A century later Pope Damasus (366–84) composed an epitaph describing the execution that was placed over the tomb. The name of Sixtus II was included in the Eucharistic Prayer, or Canon of the Mass, situated between those of Popes Clement and Cornelius. Feast day: August 6.

25 Dionysius, St., *July 22, 260–December 26, 268.*

Dionysius was one of the most important popes of the third century because of his organizational and charitable activities and his clarification of the Church's doctrine of the Trinity. His election to the papacy had been delayed for nearly two full years because of the emperor Valerian's severe persecution of Christians, which included the execution of many presbyters. During that period, the Roman church was governed by the remaining presbyters (all seven deacons having been martyred along with Sixtus II). Not until word was received that Valerian had died in captivity in Edessa (in modern-day Turkey) did the presbyters consider it safe to hold an election. Dionysius was faced immediately with the challenge of restoring order to a church that had been thrown into virtual chaos by the emperor Valerian's vicious persecution. Valerian's son Gallienus reversed his father's policies and returned the Roman church's confiscated properties, including its cemeteries. Dionysius assigned the care of worshiping communities and cemeteries to various presbyters and parishes and established new episcopal administrative units in the Roman metropolitan area. He also sent letters of encouragement to the church in Caesarea, which was suffering the effects of a foreign invasion, and provided funds for the ransoming of Christian captives in Cappadocia generally (in modern-day central Turkey).

Dionysius (known also as Dionysius of Rome, perhaps to distinguish him from Dionysius [d. 264/5], bishop of Alexandria) is at least an important footnote in the history of the doctrine of the Trinity. Some Christians in Alexandria had written to the pope to complain about their bishop's views on the Trinity, charging that he separated the Son from the Father by speaking of the Son as a creature and by refusing to affirm that the Son is of the same divine essence as the Father (doctrinal aberrations that were known as Sabellianism and Subordinationism). Pope Dionysius convened a synod in Rome in 260 that condemned such views and laid out the Church's traditional Christological teaching; namely, that the Son is not a creature, but that he is united with the God of all in such fashion that "the divine Trinity and the holy doctrine of the Oneness (Gk., *monarchia*) will be preserved in their integrity." The synod and the pope, therefore, struck a fine balance between the need to preserve the distinction between the three divine Persons, on the one hand, and the need to preserve their unity and equality, on the other. The pope also wrote privately to Dionysius of Alexandria to request an explanation of his position. The Alexandrian's reasoned reply, which employed the now classic formula that the Son is of the same being, or substance (*homoousios*), as the Father, satisfied the pope and the matter was settled. In 340 Pope Julius I (337–52) referred to this exchange as a precedent for Roman supervision over Alexandrian doctrine.

Contrary to one tradition, Dionysius was not a martyr. He is buried in the papal crypt in the cemetery of Callistus on the Appian Way. Feast day: December 26.

26 Felix I, St., *January 5, 269–December 30, 274.*

Felix I is one of the least known of the popes. The only matter for which he has received any attention from historians concerns a letter he received from a synod in Antioch announcing its decision to depose Bishop Paul of Samosata for his heretical teachings on the Trinity. But even this letter affords Felix only the weakest of footholds on historical durability because it was addressed originally to Felix's predecessor, Dionysius, who died before it reached Rome. In his reply to the letter, Felix seems to have accepted the synod's decision and recognized the new bishop. When the deposed Paul refused to vacate the premises, the local church leaders appealed to the emperor Aurelian (and not to the pope), who ordered the premises to be handed over to "those with whom the bishops of Italy and of Rome were in communication."

Contrary to one tradition, Felix did not die a martyr. He is buried in the papal crypt in the cemetery of Callistus on the Appian Way. Feast day: May 30.

27 Eutychian, St., *January 4, 275–December 7, 283.*

No reliable information about Eutychian or his pontificate (which occurred wholly within a period of peace) survived the devastation wrought by the emperor Diocletian's persecution of the Church beginning in 284, just after Eutychian's death. It is conjectured that the Roman church may have flourished under him because of the expansions of its official cemeteries undertaken at the time. We do know that Eutychian is the last pope to be buried in the papal crypt in the cemetery of Callistus on the Appian Way, where fragments of his epitaph, in ill-formed Greek letters, were discovered. The tradition that he died a martyr is without foundation, however. Feast day: December 7.

28 Caius [Gaius], St., *December 17, 283–April 22, 296.*

The pontificate of Caius, more accurately known as Gaius, occurred during a continued period of peace when the Roman church seems to have consolidated its position. Although he was in office for more than twelve years, there is no reliably specific information about his pontificate. By the time of his death, the papal crypt in the cemetery of Callistus must have been full because he was buried in a section nearby. Fragments of his epitaph, in Greek letters, were discovered there in the nineteenth century. The first letter of his name was clearly a gamma ("G"). Pope Urban VIII transported his body to the church of St. Caius (San Caio) in Rome in 1631. After the church's destruction in 1880, the pope's remains were placed in a private chapel of the Barberini princes. Feast day: April 22.

29 Marcellinus, St., *June 30, 296–October 25, 304.*

During the Diocletian persecution launched in 303, Marcellinus complied with imperial orders to hand over copies of Sacred Scripture and other sacred books and to offer incense to the gods. Some historians think that he was deposed or abdicated before his death. For a time, his name was actually omitted from the official list of popes.

There is little reliable information about him. The only recorded episcopal action of his pontificate was his authorizing of one of his deacons, Severus, to carry out certain structural modifications in the cemetery of Callistus on the Appian Way. On February 23, 303, the emperor Diocletian issued his first edict against the Christians, ordering the destruction of churches, the handing over of sacred books, and the offering of sacrifice to the gods by those attending courts of law. Sometime around May of that same year, Marcellinus seems to have complied with the second and the third items. Several of his clergy, including three future popes (Marcellus [306–8], Melchiades [311–14], and Sylvester [314–35]), were later accused by the Donatist heretics of having acted with him. But it is highly unlikely that any of the three did so. Indeed, when Marcellus succeeded to the papacy himself, he was merciless in his dealings with those who had lapsed during the persecution and he struck Marcellinus's name from the official list of popes. The charges against Melchiades were not made until after he had become pope and had rendered an important ruling against Donatus, the leader of the Donatists and a claimant to the see of Carthage. As for Sylvester, a contrary tradition developed that he had, in fact, suffered "most gloriously" during the Diocletian persecution. Nevertheless, the Donatists made these allegations in their controversies with St. Augustine (d. 430), who only half-heartedly denied them with reference to Marcellinus. And Pope Damasus I (366–84) completely ignored Marcellinus when composing his poetic tributes (epitaphs) to previous popes.

It is not clear when, and if, Marcellinus either voluntarily abdicated his office or was formally deposed. The *Annuario Pontificio,* an official Vatican publication, identifies the date of his termination from office with his date of death (October 25, 304). His actions, however, would have automatically disqualified him from the priesthood and, therefore, from the papacy as well, as of about May 303. If he was deposed or voluntarily abdicated, we have no date for either event.

Marcellinus was buried in the private cemetery of St. Priscilla on the Via Salaria, because the church's own cemeteries had been confiscated.

Because of various reports of his execution by the emperor after allegedly repenting of his actions, he came to be venerated as a martyr and his name was included in the ancient Roman Canon of the Mass. However, he is not mentioned in the martyrology of St. Jerome or in the Gelasian Sacramentary. Feast day: June 2 (with St. Peter, exorcist and martyr).

30 Marcellus I, St., *November/December 306–January 16, 308 (May 27 or June 26, 308–January 16, 309, in the Vatican's official list).*

Marcellus is best known for his severe attitude toward those Christians who had lapsed in time of persecution—so severe, in fact, that the new emperor, Maxentius, eventually banished him from the city as a disturber of the peace. There is some confusion, however, about his real identity and about the dates of his pontificate. Some have confused him with his predecessor, Marcellinus (Marcellus is not mentioned, for example, in Eusebius of Caesarea's history of the Church), and the *Annuario Pontificio*, an official Vatican publication, gives his dates as May/June 308–January 16, 309. (The confusion about the dates of his pontificate also affects the dating of the pontificates of his two immediate successors, Eusebius and Melchiades.) Whatever the case, he seems to have governed the Roman church during the period between Marcellinus's death in 304 until just before Eusebius (not Eusebius of Caesarea) was elected in 310.

Because of the losses suffered during the Diocletian persecution and the internal divisions it created within the church itself, the election of a successor to Marcellinus was delayed for more than three and a half years. Marcellus, a leading presbyter during Marcellinus's pontificate and the one who probably held the Roman church together during the intervening period, was elected. Perhaps the principal pastoral problem he faced as Bishop of Rome was the disposition of those Christians who had compromised their faith under Diocletian. There was no doubt in his mind how he should proceed: vigorously and mercilessly. However, the severe penances he imposed provoked a backlash in the church. There was public disorder and even bloodshed. So serious did the situation become that the emperor Maxentius banished him from the city for the sake of public peace. Marcellus died shortly thereafter. His body was later brought back to Rome and buried in the private cemetery of St. Priscilla. Feast day: January 16.

31 Eusebius, St., *Greek, April 18–October 21, 310 (April 18, 309–August 17, 309 or 310, in the Vatican's official list).*

Eusebius's exceedingly brief pontificate was completely dominated by the issue of the reconciliation of those who had compromised their faith during the Diocletian persecution (they were known as *lapsi,* "the lapsed"). Like his predecessors, Eusebius adopted a pastoral approach, offering full reconciliation to those who repented of their sin and performed an appropriate penance. And like his predecessors he was condemned by a faction, this time under the leadership of Heraclius, for not being severe enough. His opponents were against readmission under any conditions. The internal discord within the Christian community was so bitter and so disruptive that the emperor Maxentius once again intervened and deported both the pope and Heraclius to Sicily. Eusebius died soon thereafter. His body was brought back to Rome and buried in the cemetery of Callistus on the Appian Way. Feast day: August 17.

32 Melchiades [Miltiades], St., *African (?), July 2, 311–January 11, 314.*

Also known as Miltiades, Melchiades was Bishop of Rome when the emperor Constantine granted favored status to the Church via the Edict of Milan (313). Although the *Liber Pontificalis,* a collection of papal biographies that began to take shape in the sixth century, identifies him as an African, it is more likely that he was a Roman.

Even before the Edict of Milan (also known as the Edict of Constantine), the emperor Maxentius had promulgated an Edict of Toleration at Nicomedia on April 30, 311, and later ordered the return of church lands and buildings that had been confiscated during the Diocletian persecution. On October 28, 312, the emperor Constantine defeated his brother-in-law Maxentius at the Milvian Bridge and then conquered Rome itself. The following year he and his coemperor in the East, Licinius, granted religious toleration to everyone and restored all remaining confiscated property to Christians. He also presented Melchiades with the empress Fausta's palace (the Lateran) on Monte Celio, which thereafter became the papal residence.

An incident in North Africa otherwise defined Melchiades's pontificate. Caecilian was consecrated bishop of Carthage in 311. He was immediately rejected by the rigorist party, which opposed readmission of those who had compromised their faith under persecution. Caecilian had supported the more tolerant approach of the previous bishop of Carthage. The rigorists also raised an objection against Caecilian's consecrator, charging that he had handed over sacred books during the persecution. The rigorists thereupon consecrated a rival bishop, Majorinus, who was soon succeeded by Donatus. The rigorists appealed to the emperor Constantine to mediate the dispute and he, in turn, asked Melchiades to hear the case and to report to him. Melchiades added fifteen Italian bishops to the imperial commission (which was originally composed of Melchiades and three Gallic bishops nominated by Constantine) and transformed it into a synod, meeting at the Lateran Palace. On October 3, 313, the synod rendered a verdict in favor of Caecilian, and it excommunicated Donatus for having required the rebaptism of laypersons and the reordination of clergy who had compromised their faith during the Diocletian persecution. At the same time, Melchiades offered full communion to other North African bishops, allowing them to retain their episcopal sees. The Donatists were bitterly resentful of the verdict and began to spread rumors about Melchiades's own behavior during the persecution. They appealed once again to Constantine, who summoned a council of representatives from all the Western provinces to meet at Arles on August 1, 314. Melchiades died several months before the council actually met, but it is significant that the emperor, in calling the council, did not regard the pope's decision as final and that neither Melchiades nor his successor took exception to the emperor's action.

Melchiades was buried somewhere in the cemetery of Callistus on the Appian Way. Feast day: December 10.

33 Sylvester [Silvester] I, St., *January 31, 314–December 31, 335.*

Sylvester I's pontificate lasted for nearly twenty-two years, during which time Constantine was emperor. In spite of the length of his pontificate and the importance of the Constantinian period in which he served, the pope seems to have made little or no lasting impact on the Church or on the papacy itself. Indeed, it is what he did *not* do as pope that is more significant than what he did do.

Constantine, who occasionally assumed the title "bishop of external affairs," called a special council of some 130 bishops at Arles in August 314 to hear another appeal from the Donatists, who were contesting the consecration of Caecilian as bishop of Carthage. (The Donatists were rigorist opponents of readmitting to the Church those who had compromised their faith during the Diocletian persecution.) Significantly, the emperor did not convene the council in Rome, nor did he appoint the Bishop of Rome to preside over it, but assigned that responsibility instead to Marinus, the bishop of Arles, and entrusted the general conduct of the council to Chrestus, bishop of Syracuse. Sylvester sent two presbyters and two deacons to represent him. When the council ended, however, it transmitted its decisions to him in a letter that acknowledged his primacy over the West (although not over the whole Church) and asked him to circulate the decisions to the other churches.

Also during Sylvester's pontificate, the first ecumenical council, consisting of some 250 bishops, was held at Nicaea, the emperor's summer residence (in modern northwest Turkey), in July 325. This was the council that first defined the divinity of Jesus Christ, teaching that he is of the same being, or substance (*homoousios*), with God the Father (against the Arians who held that Jesus Christ was the greatest of creatures, but not equal to God). And yet, significantly, the pope played no part in the proceedings of this ecumenical council. He did not convene the council (the emperor did) or preside over it (Ossius [or Hosius], bishop of Cordoba, did). Like other bishops within the empire, Sylvester had been invited to attend the council, but he declined to do so, pleading old age. He did send two presbyters to represent him, but they were given no special status at the assembly other than in signing the acts of the council after the presiding bishop did and before the other bishops signed them.

In spite of Sylvester's lackluster pontificate, the Roman church benefited immensely from Constantine's generosity, which included the building of great churches such as the original St. Peter's Basilica on the Via Ostiensis and the Basilica Constantiniana and its baptistery (later known as San Giovanni in Laterano [St. John Lateran], which still serves as the pope's cathedral church even today). Perhaps because of the pope's unimpressive pontificate, however, a number of legends developed about him a long while after his death. A mid-fifth century "biography" attributed to him the conversion of Constantine and even of curing the emperor of leprosy. Pious reports circulated in the fifth and sixth centuries that the Council of Nicaea was really convened jointly by the pope and the emperor, not by the emperor alone, and that Ossius presided over the council because the pope had designated him to do so. There was also a growing belief in the authenticity of the "Donation of Constantine," an eighth- or ninth-century fabricated document in which the emperor allegedly conferred on Sylvester and his successors the primacy over the great patriarchates, over the city of Rome, over Italy, and over all of the provinces and states of the West. The "Donation of Constantine" was included in the *False Decretals* (ninth-century forgeries that sought to buttress episcopal independence from lay control) and Gratian's *Decretals* (an unofficial twelfth-century collection of canon law and canonical sources compiled by the monk John Gratian). By the middle of the fifteenth century, the document's authenticity was questioned by Aeneas Sylvius Piccolomini (later Pope Pius II) and others, but in the meantime this document and the other spurious sources exercised enormous influence on medieval thought. Sylvester was buried in the private cemetery of St. Priscilla on the Via Salaria, but his remains (perhaps only his head) seem to have been moved by Pope Paul I in 762 to the church of San Silvestro in Capite within the city walls. Feast day: December 31.

34 Mark [Marcus], St., *January 18–October 7, 336.*

During his exceedingly brief pontificate, Mark saw the tide turn strongly against the orthodox teaching of the Council of Nicaea (325) on the divinity of Jesus Christ. Although the emperor Constantine had been a vigorous supporter of the council's teaching against Arianism (which held that Jesus Christ was only the greatest of creatures, but not equal to God), he wavered under the influence of his Arian half sister, Constantia. A few months before Mark's election, St. Athanasius (d. 373), bishop of Alexandria, was deposed by the Council of Tyre and forced into exile to the city of Trier. Other orthodox bishops were also deposed at the same time. Arius himself would have been rehabilitated had he not died suddenly. There is no evidence, however, that Pope Mark played any role at all in these developments or in their immediate aftermath.

He is said to have established two churches in the city of Rome and to have decreed that the bishop of Ostia (a nearby Italian diocese) should be the first of the three consecrators of the Bishop of Rome. (Today the dean of the College of Cardinals holds the honorary title of bishop of Ostia.) Mark was buried in the cemetery of Balbina on the Via Ardeatina, in a basilica that was probably built under his direction. Feast day: October 7.

35 Julius I, St., *February 6, 337–April 12, 352.*

Julius I is best known for his forceful defense of the Council of Nicaea's teaching on the divinity of Jesus Christ (325) and of those Eastern bishops, including especially St. Athanasius of Alexandria (d. 373), who remained faithful to that teaching in the face of determined opposition, even to the point of deposition from office and exile. When the emperor Constantine died in 337, the orthodox bishops were allowed to return to their dioceses. The Arian bishops, however, appealed to Julius to prevent this and to recognize Athanasius's replacement in Alexandria. Julius rejected their request, having already offered support and protection to the orthodox bishops, including Marcellus of Ancyra, following his condemnation in 336 by a council held at Constantinople. After the second expulsion of Athanasius from Alexandria in 339, Julius convened a synod in Rome, in June of 341, which exonerated the orthodox bishops of doctrinal errors attributed to them by the Arians. Following the synod, Julius sent a letter to the Eastern bishops, reproaching them for not accepting his invitation to the synod, for having condemned bishops of apostolic sees without reference to the episcopate as a whole, and for ignoring, in their condemnation of Athanasius, the historic prerogatives of the Bishop of Rome concerning the see of Alexandria. It is significant that

Julius justified his intervention not on the basis of the Petrine primacy, to which later popes would appeal, but on the basis of ecclesiastical custom and the collegiality of the episcopate. ("You should have written to us all, so that justice might be determined by all.") The following summer the Arian bishops met at Antioch, with the Eastern emperor Constantius presiding, and confirmed their condemnation of Athanasius, recognized the current claimant to the Alexandrian see, and adopted a creed that ostentatiously omitted the language of Nicaea that the Son is "one in being with the Father."

Julius thereupon asked the two emperors to convene a general council of East and West at Sardica (modern Sofia, Bulgaria) in 343. (Julius himself did not attend the council.) The Easterners, however, withdrew when the Western bishops insisted on seating Athanasius and other bishops who had been deposed in the East. Under the presidency of Ossius (Hosius), the council proceeded without them, reaffirming the validity of Athanasius's claim to the see of Alexandria and ratifying the teaching of the Council of Nicaea by forbidding the use of Arian language. The council also made provisions for bishops condemned or deposed by provincial synods to appeal to Rome, "in order to honor the memory of blessed Peter."

We know little about the remainder of Julius's pontificate. He received Athanasius in 346 on his way back to Alexandria, giving him a letter for the Christian community there, and he founded several churches in Rome, including the Julian basilica (now the Church of the Holy Apostles [Santi Apostoli]) and Santa Maria in Trastevere. He was buried in the cemetery of Calepodius on the Via Aurelia. Feast day: April 12.

36 Liberius, *May 17, 352–September 24, 366.*

Liberius is the first pope not to be listed among the saints and is generally regarded to have been a weak pope. He at first opposed the condemnation of St. Athanasius of Alexandria (d. 373) by the Arians, for which he was deposed from office by the Arian emperor Constantius and sent into harsh exile in Thrace. He eventually submitted and was readmitted to his Roman see, which by that time and with the urging of the emperor had elected a second bishop, Felix II (d. 365), technically an antipope. (It is interesting to note that Damasus, Liberius's successor in the papacy, was for a time in Felix's service as a deacon—in defiance of the oath taken by the Roman clergy not to recognize anyone else as pope while Liberius was still alive.) Only after the death of Constantius in 361 did Liberius return to orthodoxy and make an effort to restore the Nicene faith to the universal Church.

Liberius was elected to the papacy at a time when pro-Arian bishops enjoyed a dominant position in the East and when the pro-Arian emperor Constantius II, now the sole emperor, was putting increasing pressure on the Western bishops to join in the condemnation of Athanasius by the Council of Tyre in 335. Athanasius had become the primary symbol of Nicene orthodoxy, that is, of support for the teaching of the Council of Nicaea (325) that Jesus Christ is "one in being with the Father" and not simply the greatest of creatures, as the Arians held.

Under pressure from the pro-Arian bishops and lacking the strength of character of his predecessor, Liberius asked Constantius II to convene a council at Aquileia to settle the dispute regarding Athanasius and the see of Alexandria. The emperor did hold a synod there and then at Arles, where he was in residence at the time. Responsive to the imperial will, both assemblies reaffirmed the condemnation of Athanasius. The papal legates also agreed to the decision. The pope was appalled by the weakness of his own envoys and demanded a general council to uphold not simply Athanasius, but the Council of Nicaea itself. But when the council met in Milan in October of 355, the emperor's will again prevailed. There was no discussion of the Nicene Creed, and the condemnation of Athanasius was reaffirmed. Three bishops who resisted were promptly exiled. Liberius continued to resist, was brought forcibly to Milan, and then, refusing to acquiesce in its actions, was deported to Beroea in Thrace. As time passed in exile, Liberius weakened. He accepted the condemnation of Athanasius as well as the ambiguous first Formula of Sirmium (351), which omitted the Nicene language "one in being with the Father," but did not explicitly reject it. He also personally submitted to the emperor. His four letters to pro-Arian bishops in 357, asking them to intercede for him with the emperor, indicated that he was prepared to do anything to return home. Taken to Sirmium in 358, he refused to sign a second formula, which was particularly Subordinationist (subordinating the Son to the Father), but he signed a more moderate formula that rejected the Nicene language but also declared that the Son is "like" the Father in being (*homoiousios*, rather than the Nicene *homoousios*).

With the Roman public clamoring for Liberius's return, the emperor thereupon allowed him to go back to Rome, but on condition that he jointly rule with the antipope Felix, who had been elected as a rival bishop during Liberius's absence. Felix, however, was regarded as a usurper and was extremely unpopular. Most of the laity and clergy preferred Liberius alone, chanting, "One God, one Christ, one bishop." In the face of a possible riot, Felix withdrew to the suburbs. Liberius, however, had already lost most of his international prestige. With two bishops in Rome, he was not invited to, nor did he, send legates to the Synod of

Rimini in 359, at which the Western bishops were bullied into accepting an Arian creed. Not until the death of the emperor in 361 did Liberius resume his role as defender of Nicene orthodoxy. He published a decree voiding the decisions of the Synod of Rimini. In 362, however, he also urged his fellow Italian bishops to reestablish communion with those bishops who had approved the Rimini decisions, on condition that they now accept the Nicene Creed. He did the same for Eastern bishops in 366. Thus did he try to restore unity to the Church—the primary ministry of the Bishop of Rome.

He built the huge Liberian Basilica, which was transformed in the fifth century into Santa Maria Maggiore (St. Mary Major). He was commemorated on September 23 in the fifth-century martyrology of St. Jerome, but his name does not appear in subsequent liturgical calendars. Later tradition remembered him as a betrayer of the faith, and his name was invoked by opponents of papal infallibility at the First Vatican Council (1870). Ironically, the antipope Felix II came for a time to be included on the official list of popes and, through some confusion with another person, was venerated as a martyr who had defended the Nicene faith with his life. Feast day: July 29.

37 Damasus I, St., *ca. 304–84, pope from October 1, 366, to December 11, 384.*

One of the most aggressive advocates of the primacy of Rome in the early Church, Damasus promoted the cult of martyrs by restoring and decorating their tombs with his own marble inscriptions (epitaphs) and authorized his secretary, St. Jerome (d. ca. 420), to compose a new Latin translation of the New Testament (later known as the Vulgate) based on the original Greek.

Born in Rome, the son of a priest, Damasus was ordained a deacon and accompanied Pope Liberius into exile in 355. He soon returned to Rome, however, and was in the service for a time of the antipope Felix II, in defiance of the oath taken by the Roman clergy not to recognize anyone else as Bishop of Rome while Liberius was still alive. This was a remarkably significant lapse in one who, later as pope, would argue vigorously on behalf of the supremacy of the papacy. It is a lapse that those who cite Damasus in support of papal primacy do not mention.

After Liberius was allowed to return from exile (having himself made some substantial compromises), Damasus became reconciled with him. When Liberius died, a bitter and violent controversy erupted over the choice of a successor. There is a curious discrepancy in two accounts of the election, however. According to the more reliable account, a faction that had been consistently loyal to Liberius met immediately in the Julian basilica of Santa Maria in Trastevere, elected the deacon Ursinus, and had him consecrated Bishop of Rome by the bishop of Tibur (Tivoli). (A second account strangely identifies this faction with supporters of Felix, not Liberius, perhaps out of concern to establish the papal credentials of the individual whom the Catholic Church officially recognizes as Liberius's legitimate successor.) Another, larger faction loyal to Felix met in the church of San Lorenzo in Lucina and elected the deacon Damasus, who hired a gang of thugs to storm the Julian basilica, routing the Ursinians in a three-day massacre. Damasus was consecrated by the bishop of Ostia in the Lateran Basilica on October 1, after his supporters had seized the church. Following his consecration, however, bloody fighting continued in the streets of Rome. In a wholly unprecedented act, Damasus asked for help from the city prefect, who sent Ursinus and two of his deacons into exile. But the violence continued, and Damasus dispatched his own forces to attack Ursinus's supporters, who had taken refuge in the Liberian Basilica (now St. Mary Major). A contemporary historian reported that some 137 died in the battle. The bishops of Italy were dismayed by the pope's use of violence. When they were gathered in a synod in honor of Damasus's birthday in 368, the pope asked them to approve what he had done and to condemn Ursinus. Their reply was curt: "*Nos ad natale convenimus, non ut inauditum damnemus*" (Lat., "We came together to celebrate a birthday, not to condemn someone without a hearing"). The conflict between Damasus and the partisans of Ursinus continued throughout his entire pontificate.

Although Damasus had badly blotted his ecclesiastical copybook, he enjoyed much favor with the court and the aristocracy, especially women of wealth. Roman gossips nicknamed him "the matrons' ear-tickler." His grand lifestyle and lavish hospitality endeared him to the upper-class pagan families.

At the same time, he was relentless in opposing heresies and other dissident movements in the Church. He was harsh in his repression of Arianism and achieved condemnations of Apollinarianism (which denied that Jesus had a human soul) and Macedonianism (which denied the divinity of the Holy Spirit) at successive Roman synods. However, his dealings with the Eastern churches were inept. Like most of his fellow Western bishops, he failed to grasp the meaning of developments in the East. Thus, when there were two rivals for the see of Antioch, Damasus threw his support behind Paulinus, described as "an unrepresentative leader of a reactionary group" (J. N. D. Kelly), instead of Meletius, on whom rested most hopes for unity in the East, including those of St. Basil the Great (d. 379), bishop of Caesarea, who described the pope as impossibly arrogant.

When Meletius died in 381, Damasus refused to enter into communion with his successor, Flavian.

Significantly, although few popes in history have made such vigorous, uncompromising claims on behalf of papal primacy, Damasus himself took no part in the ecumenical council held in Constantinople in 381, which defined the divinity of the Holy Spirit and whose third canon placed the bishop of Constantinople, "the new Rome," second only to the Bishop of Rome.

Damasus was tireless, in fact, in promoting the primacy of Rome, referring to it frequently as "the Apostolic See" and insisting that the test of a creed's orthodoxy is papal approval. While the claims of Constantinople were based on synodal decisions and political considerations ("the new Rome"), Damasus's claims for the Roman primacy were based exclusively on his being the direct successor of Peter and the rightful heir of Christ's promises given in Matthew 16:18 (". . . you are Peter . . ."). He confirmed this in the Roman synod of 381. He had also seen to it that the Roman see, with the approval of the state, was established as the court of appeal for the entire Western episcopate (but, again, not for the entire Catholic Church).

He organized the papal archives, established Latin as the principal liturgical language in Rome, and commissioned his secretary, St. Jerome, to revise existing translations of the New Testament on the basis of the original Greek. He also composed epigrams in honor of martyrs and popes and had them inscribed on marble slabs. He himself was buried in a church he had built on the Via Ardeatina, but his body was later moved to another of his churches, that of San Lorenzo in Damaso. Feast day: December 4.

38 Siricius, St., *December 384–November 26, 399 (December 15 or 22 or 29, 384, in the Vatican's official list).*

Siricius was the first pope to issue decretals, that is, legally binding directives formulated in the style of imperial edicts. The oldest surviving decretal, dated February 11, 385, was addressed to Himerius, bishop of Tarragona, in response to fifteen questions on matters of church discipline. It begins with the claim that the Apostle Peter is present in the Bishop of Rome and then proceeds to offer directives on such items as the readmission of heretics to the Church (they were not to be rebaptized), the age and qualifications of candidates for ordination, the requirement of celibacy for priests and deacons, and penitential discipline. Siricius asked that these decrees be circulated to churches in the neighboring provinces of Africa, Spain, and Gaul (modern-day France). In January 386, he sent nine canons passed by a Roman synod to various churches in Africa and elsewhere stipulating that no bishop should be consecrated without the knowledge of "the Apostolic See" or only by a single consecrator.

Siricius was elected to office unanimously, in spite of the candidacy of the antipope Ursinus. The emperor Valentinian II was delighted with the show of support for Siricius and officially confirmed his election, perhaps to ward off any residual opposition from the supporters of Ursinus. Although Siricius was as much opposed to heresies and other dissident movements as his predecessor, Damasus, he urged lenient treatment of those who repented. He rebuked and broke communion with those bishops who had been responsible for the sentencing to death of the rigorist heretic Priscillian in 386, the first person to be executed for doctrinal deviation. On the other hand, he also excommunicated Jovinian, a monk, for criticizing the value of fasting and celibacy and for denying the perpetual virginity of Mary. At the request of St. Ambrose (d. 397), bishop of Milan, he intervened successfully in a schism in Antioch and ended it by urging the council of Caesarea (in Palestine) to recognize Flavian rather than Evagrius as bishop.

Although honored as a saint in earlier centuries, his name was omitted from the first edition of the Roman Martyrology (1584) because of his personal conflicts with St. Jerome, in whose expulsion from the city of Rome he had concurred, and with St. Paulinus of Nola (d. 431), who complained of the pope's haughtiness. His name was added to the martyrology in 1748 by Pope Benedict XIV. He was buried in the basilica of San Silvestro near the private cemetery of Priscilla. Feast day: November 26.

39 Anastasius I, St., *November 27, 399–December 19, 401.*

Best known for his condemnation of the great third-century theologian Origen (d. ca. 254), with whose writings he was not even familiar, Anastasius was also the father of his own successor, Innocent I. Those who disliked his predecessor, Siricius, approved of him; namely, St. Jerome (d. ca. 420), who still had a circle of influential friends in Rome, and St. Paulinus of Nola (d. 431), both of whom thought Anastasius more sympathetic than Siricius to the practice of strict asceticism in the Church. When the African bishops, for example, asked the pope to relax the ban on Donatist clergy returning to the Church because of the shortage of priests, Anastasius wrote to the Council of Carthage (401) and urged the bishops to continue their struggle against the heresy (which held that those baptized by heretics and schismatics must be rebaptized upon entering the Catholic Church). St. Jerome even suggested that Anastasius's pontificate had been cut short because Rome did not deserve so fine a bishop.

Anastasius was buried in the cemetery of Pontian on the Via Portuensis. Feast day: December 19.

40 Innocent I, St., *December 22, 401–March 12, 417.*

One of the early Church's staunchest defenders of the prerogatives of the Apostolic See in matters of doctrine and ecclesiastical discipline, Innocent I was actually the son of Anastasius I. This is the first instance of a son succeeding his father to the papacy.

As the Western empire was buckling under the relentless onslaughts of the migrating Germanic tribes (the migrations have been conventionally referred to as the barbarian invasions), Innocent asserted papal claims with ever greater frequency and emphasis. He carried forward Pope Siricius's (384–99) novel practice of issuing decretals in the imperial style. He laid down laws for churches (all in the West, however) regarding the Canon of the Mass, or Eucharistic Prayer (insisting on the Roman custom as the norm), the sacraments of Penance (also known as Reconciliation) and Extreme Unction (now called the Anointing of the Sick), Confirmation (only bishops were to administer it), and the canon of Sacred Scripture (he excluded several apocryphal books). He also pointed out that the bishops should recognize Rome as their court of appeal, to which all "weightier causes" should be referred.

But Innocent also indirectly made claims over the East. When St. John Chrysostom (d. 407) was deposed as bishop of Constantinople and exiled in 404, the pope sent him letters of support and encouragement, refused to recognize his replacement, called for an impartial council, and organized a protest to the Eastern emperor. When the papal legates were insulted and expelled and John died in exile, Innocent broke communion with those Eastern bishops who had opposed John. (Only after Innocent's death was full communion restored.) When he was informed in 416 that St. Jerome's monasteries in Jerusalem had been destroyed by thugs and their residents assaulted, he wrote immediately to Jerome promising to apply the full authority of the Apostolic See against the offenders and he wrote to Bishop John of Jerusalem to chastise him for allowing the outrage. In general, he was intent on resisting the efforts of the see of Constantinople, with imperial encouragement, to extend its jurisdiction over the churches in Eastern Illyricum (on the Balkan peninsula).

Innocent also exercised his authority in the North African churches' efforts against Pelagianism, a heretical movement that held that one can be saved by human effort alone, without the aid of divine grace. Two African councils (at Carthage and Milevis) had reaffirmed the condemnation of Pelagius (originally issued in 411), following an effort at the Palestinian synod at Diapolis (415) to pardon him. The bishops, out of deference to the pope, asked him, in 416, to add his own condemnation to theirs. Five bishops, including St. Augustine (d. 430), also sent a Pelagian dossier to the pope, requesting that Pelagius be summoned to Rome and his errors condemned. In one of three letters written in reply (January 27, 417), the pope praised the African bishops for referring the matter to him (when, in fact, they had not). He appealed to an ancient (but hardly unequivocal or consistent) tradition that bishops everywhere should submit disputed matters of faith to Peter and his successors. Contrary to the pious belief, however, that Christ conferred supreme teaching authority on Peter and that every successor of Peter understood himself to possess this same supreme teaching authority, Innocent I was really the first pope to make this claim so clearly. The Bishop of Rome, he declared, is "the head and the summit of the episcopate."

During the middle of his pontificate, Innocent was faced with another kind of pastoral challenge: the siege of Rome by Alaric the Visigoth, with attendant famine and despair throughout the city. In 410 he led a delegation to see the emperor Honorius at Ravenna in order to arrange a truce. The negotiations failed, and Alaric stormed and sacked Rome on August 24, 410, while Innocent was away. He did not return to the city until 412. After his death five years later, he was buried in the same cemetery as his father, Anastasius I, on the Via Portuensis. Feast day: July 28.

41 Zosimus, St., *Greek, March 18, 417–December 26, 418.*

Temperamentally impulsive, politically inept, and culturally unprepared for the office, Zosimus revoked Innocent I's condemnation of Pelagius and readmitted him and his colleague Celestius to communion with the Church. But later, under pressure from the African bishops, he reversed himself.

Zosimus was a presbyter who had been recommended to Innocent I by St. John Chrysostom (d. 407), the deposed and exiled bishop of Constantinople. Unfamiliar with Western ways, Zosimus appointed a maverick bishop, Patroclus of Arles, an individual who may have had a role in manipulating the papal election, as metropolitan of Arles, with full authority to consecrate all bishops of the provinces of Vienne and the two Narbonnes and to decide all cases not subject to Roman review (making him, in effect, papal vicar of Gaul). Clergy visiting Rome from Gaul were required to bear a testimonial letter signed by Patroclus. The pope ignored the subsequent protests from bishops and clergy alike, taking his cue always from Patroclus himself.

Zosimus's handling of matters in North Africa was even worse. He reopened the question of the condemnation of Pelagius and his disciple Celestius. After reading Pelagius's profession of faith sent originally to Innocent I (but arriving after Innocent's death) and after a personal meeting with Celestius in Rome, he wrote to the African bishops to inform them that both men had cleared themselves and to reproach the bishops for having acted in haste against them. The African bishops, including St. Augustine (d. 430), were outraged. They firmly informed the pope that his predecessor's decision must stand. Zosimus backed off. After a perfunctory reminder about the Roman primacy, he assured the African bishops that the situation remained as it was under Innocent. The bishops had, in the meantime, also appealed to the emperor Honorius, who fully supported them, reaffirmed the condemnation of Pelagius and Celestius, and then banished the two as disturbers of the peace. The pope had no choice but to make a full retreat. After another council at Carthage in 418 and at the insistence of Augustine, Zosimus addressed a lengthy document (known as the *Epistola Tractoria*) to the bishops of East and West in which he condemned the Pelagians and their teachings.

But he committed yet another blunder in Africa by interfering in the case of a priest (Apiarius) who had been excommunicated by his bishop and who then appealed to the pope. The pope tried to justify his intervention by citing two canons of the ecumenical Council of Nicaea (325), which were actually canons from the local Council of Sardica (342/3), not recognized in Africa. In the last months of Zosimus's life, a number of disaffected clergy were lobbying against him at the imperial court in Ravenna. The pope was preparing to excommunicate them (and may, in fact, have done so) when he fell ill and eventually died.

Zosimus was buried in the basilica of San Lorenzo outside the walls on the road to Tivoli. The ninth-century martyrology of Ado was the first to list him as a saint, a title that in these early centuries seemed to be attached automatically to virtually every pope, without regard for evidence of the special sanctity of their lives. Feast day: December 26.

42 Boniface I, St., *December 28, 418–September 4, 422 (December 28 or 29, 418, in the Vatican's official list).*

A dedicated opponent of Pelagianism (which held that salvation can be attained by human effort alone, without the aid of grace) and a vigorous advocate of papal authority, Boniface I is the author of the axiom: "It has never been lawful for what has once been decided by the Apostolic See to be reconsidered." In its more familiar Latin form, it reads: *Roma locuta est; causa finita est* ("Rome has spoken; the cause is finished").

Almost immediately after the burial of Zosimus, the deacons of the Roman church along with a few presbyters barricaded themselves in the Lateran Basilica and elected Eulalius, Zosimus's chief deacon, who was probably also a Greek. The next day the great majority of the presbyters, with many laypersons, assembled in the Basilica of Theodora and elected the aged and frail presbyter Boniface, who was himself the son of a priest. On the day after that, both were consecrated separately. Eulalius was consecrated in the Lateran Basilica by the bishop of Ostia, who customarily ordained the Bishop of Rome, and Boniface was consecrated in the church of San Marcello in the presence of nine bishops. Boniface was installed in St. Peter's Basilica because the Lateran was under the control of the faction supporting Eulalius. The pagan prefect of the city threw his own support to Eulalius and so reported his decision to the emperor at Ravenna. Boniface was ordered to leave Rome, which he did under protest. But Boniface had many friends and supporters in Rome and at court, including the emperor's sister. When most of the Roman presbyters petitioned the emperor on behalf of Boniface, the emperor summoned both bishops to a synod at Ravenna. When no decision was reached there, a council was held at Spoleto on June 13, 419, at which bishops from Gaul and Africa were present. The emperor required both Boniface and Eulalius to leave Rome in the meantime. Boniface complied, but Eulalius refused. This caused civil disorder in Rome and infuriated the emperor, who ordered Eulalius banished from the city and declared Boniface the lawful bishop.

Boniface proceeded to undo the damage created by his predecessor, Zosimus, in establishing a papal vicariate in Arles. He restored metropolitan rights to Marseilles, Vienne, and Narbonne. With the help of the Western emperor, he also retained the prefecture of Illyricum (on the Balkan peninsula) under Roman jurisdiction in the face of continued efforts by the Eastern emperor to transfer it to the patriarchate of Constantinople. In the ongoing struggle against Pelagianism, he was firm in his defense of orthodoxy and persuaded the emperor to publish an edict requiring all bishops to subscribe to Zosimus's *Tractoria* condemning the heresy.

When Boniface died, the antipope Eulalius made no effort to claim the see. Boniface was buried in a chapel he had built in the cemetery of St. Felicity on the Via Salaria, near the tomb of the saint. Feast day: September 4.

43 Celestine I, St., *September 10, 422–July 27, 432.*

Among the events that occurred during Celestine's pontificate was the third ecumenical council of the Church, held at Ephesus in 431. Significantly, the emperor Theodosius II, not the pope, convened the council, and the pope himself did not attend. He sent three legates to represent the interests of the Roman church. The acts of the council were not submitted to the pope for his approval, but in subsequent letters he expressed his satisfaction with its accomplishments.

After his unanimous election as Bishop of Rome following his term as chief deacon (archdeacon) of the church, Celestine confiscated the churches of the large Novatianist community in Rome (those who favored the rebaptism of individuals who were originally baptized by heretics or schismatics) and began the restoration of the Julian Basilica (Santa Maria in Trastevere), which had been severely damaged in the sack of the city by the Visigoth Alaric in 410. Like his predecessor, Zosimus (417–18), he got into difficulty with the bishops of North Africa for meddling in their affairs. He ordered the second rehabilitation of the priest Apiarius, who had been excommunicated by his bishop (Pope Zosimus had rehabilitated him the first time, but the priest lapsed once again). However, at a council in Carthage (ca. 426), the priest finally admitted his guilt and the papal legate who had accompanied the priest back to Africa from Rome was forced to disavow him. This gave the African bishops an opportunity to chastise the pope for failing to respect their autonomy and for entering into communion with persons they had excommunicated, a practice, they reminded him, that was expressly forbidden by the Council of Nicaea (325). It is significant that, even after the great claims of Pope Damasus (366–84) regarding the primacy, a large body of bishops felt free to scold the pope for intruding in their affairs and for entering into communion with those with whom they had broken communion.

Celestine nonetheless continued to press the point that, as Bishop of Rome and successor of Peter, he had pastoral authority beyond the Roman church and, indeed, over the universal Church, East as well as West. He reminded the bishops of southern Gaul that they were under his supervision, objected to various practices in their region, including the wearing of distinctive episcopal garb, and warned them against the semi-Pelagian teaching of the monk John Cassian (d. 435), namely, that the first turning toward God is a matter of human effort, but thereafter God's grace is necessary for salvation. Celestine had the leaders of Pelagianism expelled from the West (Pelagianism held that it is possible to be saved by human effort alone, without the aid of grace), sent a mission to Britain to deal with Pelagianism there, and in 431 consecrated the first bishop of Ireland (Palladius).

Toward the end of his pontificate, he plunged into the debate between Nestorius of Constantinople (d. ca. 451) and St. Cyril of Alexandria (d. 444) concerning the relationship between the divinity and the humanity of Jesus Christ. Nestorius held that there were two distinct persons in

Christ and that Mary was the mother of the human person, Jesus of Nazareth, and not of the divine Person, the Son of God. Cyril held, on the contrary, that there is a fundamental personal unity in Christ, in such wise that Mary can be called the Mother of God (Gk., *Theotokos*). When both individuals submitted their views to Celestine, he received them as an appeal from the East to Rome. With Cyril's encouragement, the pope condemned Nestorius's position at a Roman synod in 430, demanding that Nestorius recant within ten days or be excommunicated. Meanwhile the Byzantine emperor Theodosius II—not Pope Celestine—decided to convene a general (ecumenical) council at Ephesus to settle the matter. The council opened on June 22 even before the papal legates or the Antiochene bishops (generally supportive of Nestorius) had arrived. Nestorius was excommunicated. When the papal legates arrived on July 10, they endorsed the decision, having been instructed by the pope to be guided by Cyril's judgment in matters coming before the council. The council also excommunicated John of Antioch (d. 441), leader of the moderate wing of the Antiochene school and the one whom the emperor had intended to have preside over the council, but Celestine refused to approve that decision, hoping that John would eventually repudiate Nestorius, accept the council's teaching, and return to communion with the Church.

Celestine was buried in the private cemetery of Priscilla on the Via Salaria. His mausoleum was decorated with paintings recalling the ecumenical council at Ephesus, which he neither convened nor attended. Feast day: April 6.

44 Sixtus [Xystus] III, St., *July 31, 432–August 19, 440.*

Also known as Xystus and himself the son of a priest, Sixtus III acted as peacemaker in the aftermath of the Council of Ephesus (431) and, aided by funds from the imperial family, directed a major rebuilding program in Rome in the aftermath of the invasion by the Visigoths under Alaric in 410.

True to his Petrine ministry of maintaining the unity of the Church by healing wounds of division and by building bridges between alienated groups (the Latin word *pontifex* means "bridge builder"), Sixtus reached out to John of Antioch (d. 441), whom the ecumenical Council of Ephesus (431) had deposed and excommunicated. Sixtus asked only that John accept the teaching of Ephesus and disavow Nestorius (who held that there are two persons in Jesus Christ, one human and one divine, and that Mary is only the mother of the human person, not the Mother of God). Sixtus knew personally what it was to be on the other side of orthodoxy in a doctrinal debate. Before his election he had been a sympathizer of Pelagius, a British monk who held that one can achieve salvation by human effort alone, without the aid of divine grace. But once Pope Zosimus (417–18) had condemned it, Sixtus, with encouragement from St. Augustine (d. 430), fully accepted the papal teaching. Sixtus's hope for reconciliation between the Antiochenes (those who regarded the humanity of Jesus to be under greater threat of theological error than his divinity) and the Alexandrians (those who regarded the divinity of Christ to be more threatened by theological error than his humanity) was realized in the spring of 433 when the Antiochenes and St. Cyril of Alexandria (d. 444), the leader of the Alexandrians, came to agreement regarding the two natures in Christ through a document known as the Formula of Union.

Although Sixtus was justifiably proud of the good relations that now existed between the Roman see and the East, there was a setback the following year (434) when Proclus, the new bishop of Constantinople, tried to detach the papal vicariate in Illyricum (on the southeastern Balkan peninsula) from Rome and to bring it under Eastern jurisdiction. Sixtus ordered his bishops there to ignore Proclus's initiative and to continue to acknowledge the bishop of Thessalonica as the papal vicar in that region. He also asked Proclus not to tolerate appeals to Constantinople from the Illyrian bishops. As a show of good faith on the pope's own part, when the bishop of Smyrna appealed to Rome against a sentence handed down by Proclus as metropolitan bishop of Asia Minor, Sixtus refused to interfere.

As part of his program to repair the damage wrought by the Visigothic invasion of 410, Sixtus rebuilt the Lateran baptistery into its present octagonal form and completely reconstructed the Liberian Basilica of Santa Maria Maggiore (St. Mary Major). The inscriptions in the baptistery highlighted the nature of baptism and the necessity of grace (against the now defeated Pelagians, who held that one could be saved by human effort alone), while the mosaics in St. Mary Major expressed the Church's triumph over Nestorianism at the Council of Ephesus. The pope also persuaded the emperor Valentinian to contribute silver and gold ornaments to the basilicas of St. Peter, St. Paul Outside the Walls, and the Lateran to replace what had been plundered by the Visigoths. He also established the first monastery in Rome, St. Sebastian's on the Appian Way.

Sixtus III was buried somewhere in the cemetery of St. Lawrence. Four centuries passed before a cult developed in his honor. The name of Sixtus III first appeared in the ninth-century martyrology of Ado. Feast day: March 28.

Part II

FROM LEO THE GREAT TO THE DAWN OF THE CAROLINGIAN EMPIRE

HIS SECOND PERIOD IN THE HISTORY OF THE papacy, from the middle of the fifth century to the end of the eighth, includes the only two popes who have been called "the Great": Leo I (440–61) and Gregory I (590–604). Leo was particularly strong in claiming supreme and universal authority for the papacy on the grounds that the pope is the heir of Peter, actively intervened to help shape the Church's definitive teaching on the humanity and divinity of Jesus Christ at the Council of Chalcedon (451), and personally persuaded Attila the Hun to withdraw from his menacing advance toward Rome in 452. With the complete breakdown of civil order in Rome a century and a half later, Gregory became its virtual temporal ruler. He was not without prior political experience, however, having served as prefect of the city of Rome for two or three years before disposing of his personal wealth and becoming a monk. Gregory was a prodigious writer; his most enduring work, *Pastoral Care*, served as a textbook for medieval bishops. At the same time, Gregory had a realistic understanding of the limits of his office. He chastised the patriarch of Constantinople for using the title "ecumenical patriarch," insisting that no bishop can claim to be a universal patriarch, including even the pope! No other popes of this period exercised as much influence as Leo I and Gregory I, either on the contemporary Church or on the subsequent development of the papacy itself.

There were several "firsts" during this period of papal history. Gelasius I (492–96), like Leo the Great a vigorous advocate of papal supremacy, was the first pope to assume the title "Vicar of Christ," although it would not become attached exclusively to the Bishop of Rome until the pontificate of Eugenius III (1145–53). It was also Gelasius who advanced the theory of the "two powers" or the "two swords" (referring to the authority of the pope in both the sacred and temporal spheres)—a theory that would be so influential in the Middle Ages. Symmachus (498–514) was the first pope to bestow the pallium (a woolen vestment worn around the neck as a symbol of pastoral authority) on a bishop outside of Italy. Boniface II (530–32) was the first pope of Germanic stock. His successor, John II (533–35), was the first pope to take a different name upon election to the papacy, but only because his own name from birth, Mercury, was that of a pagan god. Silverius (536–37) was the first and only subdeacon elected pope and the second pope to follow in the footsteps of his father (Hormisdas [514–23]) as pope. Gregory the Great (590–604) was the first pope to use the title "servant of the servants of God." Paul I (757–67) was the first to succeed his brother as pope (Stephen II [III]). John IV (640–42) was the first and only Dalmatian pope.

There were also changes in the way popes were elected. Originally determined solely by the clergy and laity of Rome (since the pope is, first and foremost, Bishop of Rome), papal elections had by this time come under the decisive influence of the emperor. Indeed, Vigilius's successor, Pelagius I (556–61), was elevated to the papacy without benefit of any formal election at all, his appointment having been secured directly by the emperor Justinian. As a rule, however, elections were not considered valid unless and until the emperor formally approved them. Benedict II (684–85) did win a minor concession from the emperor in his allowing the imperial viceroy (exarch) in Ravenna to ratify papal elections, thereby eliminating the delay in receiving approval from Constantinople for the newly elected pope to be consecrated as Bishop of Rome. The whole arrangement ended, however, after the death of Gregory III (731–41), the last pope to seek imperial approval for his consecration. Soon thereafter, Stephen II [III] (752–57), who succeeded the last of the Greek popes, Zacharias (741–52), finally established the independence of the papacy from the Byzantine Empire, placing it instead under the protection of the Frankish kingdom. It was also Stephen II (III) who formed the Papal States, assuming juridical and administrative control of territories in central Italy over which the papacy had claimed temporal sovereignty since the fourth century. Perhaps to bring some measure of internal moral integrity to the electoral process, Boniface III (607) had decreed that the penalty of excommunication would be imposed on anyone discussing a successor to a pope during the pope's lifetime and until three days after his death. Stephen III (IV) decreed in 769, following the election of the antipope Constantine, who was a layman at the time he was chosen, that henceforth only deacons and cardinal-priests (that is, those Roman presbyters who were pastors of the key parishes of Rome) should be eligible for election as pope and that the laity should no longer have any vote in such elections.

This period was also marked by instances of papal deviation from doctrinal orthodoxy, or at least disconcerting facsimiles thereof. John II, under pressure from the Eastern emperor, contradicted the teaching of a previous pope, Hormisdas (514–23), on the two natures of Jesus Christ. Honorius I (625–38) became an unwitting adherent of Monothelitism, which held that there is only one (divine) will in Jesus Christ. After his death, Honorius was formally condemned by the Third Council of Constantinople (680)—an action subsequently ratified by Pope Leo II (682–83). When the Monothelite controversy continued to divide Rome and Constantinople, Eugenius I (654–57) tried valiantly to reconcile the two sides. In doing so, however, he prematurely accepted a compromise that seemed to posit three wills in Christ. This provoked a firestorm of protest among the clergy and laity of Rome. The pope was prevented from continuing with Mass at the basilica of St. Mary Major until he had promised to reject the compromise. Such are the vagaries of papal history.

45 Leo I, "the Great," St., *September 29, 440–November 10, 461.*

Elected to the papacy while still only a deacon and while away from Rome on a diplomatic mission in Gaul (modern-day France) on behalf of the imperial court, Leo is one of only two popes in all of Church history to have been called "the Great" (the other was Gregory I [590–604]). He was a strong advocate of papal authority and of the teachings of the Council of Chalcedon (451) on the humanity and divinity of Jesus Christ. So forcefully articulated were Leo's claims for the pope's universal and supreme authority over the Church, in fact, that his own pontificate constitutes a major turning point in the history of the papacy. He was the first pope to claim to be Peter's heir, which, according to Roman law, meant that all the rights and duties associated with Peter lived on in Leo. Previous popes had spoken of their succession to Peter's chair or appealed to his martyrdom and burial in Rome as the basis of their authority. In his sermon given on the fifth anniversary of his election to the papacy, Leo insisted that "the stability which 'the Rock' [Peter] himself received from that rock which is Christ, he conveys also to his heirs. . . ." Thereafter, the popes increasingly regarded themselves as standing in the place of Peter, exercising authority not only over all of the faithful but over all of the other bishops as well.

Indeed, Leo himself exercised firm control over the bishops of Italy, including those of Milan and the northern region, enforcing uniformity of pastoral practice, correcting abuses, and resolving disputes. In replying to appeals from the bishops of Spain to help in their fight against Priscillianism, a heresy that regarded the human body as evil, he laid down precise instructions for action. Although ecclesiastical Africa was traditionally jealous of its pastoral autonomy, especially against any encroachments upon it by Rome, Leo's rulings on irregularities in African elections and other regional conflicts were eagerly sought after and embraced. When Hilary of Arles (d. 449) began acting as if his diocese in southern Gaul still possessed the special authority over other local churches in the region granted to it by Pope Zosimus (417–18) but revoked by his successor, Boniface I (418–22), Leo ordered that Hilary confine his pastoral activities to his own diocese. Specifically, he was to stop interfering in the appointment of bishops of other dioceses. Bishops were to be elected by the local clergy and leading laity, and the election was to be ratified by the people generally. Leo's electoral principle is still quoted, but unfortunately has not been in force for centuries: "He who is in charge of all should be chosen by all" (*Letter* 10). Four days after Leo's instruction to Hilary, the Western emperor, Valentinian III, ordered his military commander in Gaul to enforce Leo's orders. Leo, however, could not have been pleased that the emperor gave as one reason for the pope's authority "the importance of the city of Rome." Rome's political importance had already declined sharply, and ecclesiastical and political authorities in the East were using that decline to justify a shift in the balance of ecclesiastical power from Rome to Constantinople.

The East, therefore, was much less disposed than the West to accept Leo's papal claims. In June of 449, for example, he sent an important letter (*Letter* 28), or *Tome*, to Bishop Flavian of Constantinople, condemning the Monophysite teaching that in Christ there is only one divine nature, Christ's human nature having been absorbed by the divine. The emperor Theodosius II called a council at Ephesus in August (not to be confused with the ecumenical Council of Ephesus, held in 431). Pope Leo was represented by three delegates who had with them a copy of the *Tome*, which Leo expected to be read out and approved. But the council disregarded it, condemned Bishop Flavian, and rehabilitated the monk Eutyches, who had been censured by Flavian for his Monophysite views. Leo refused to recognize the council, referring to it as a *latrocinium*, or "robber council." Two years later another ecumenical council was convened—at the call of the emperor, not the pope!—at Chalcedon, on the eastern shore of the Bosphorus strait, which separates modern-day European and Asian Turkey. That council reversed the decisions taken at the "robber council" of Ephesus and endorsed the Christological teaching of Leo and others; namely, that in Jesus Christ there are two natures, one divine and one human, hypostatically united in one divine Person. Leo's *Tome* was respectfully received and approved as a standard of orthodoxy and as an expression of "the voice of Peter." "Peter has spoken through Leo" was one of seventeen affirmative acclamations recorded in the minutes of the council.

For the sake of historical and theological perspective, however, it should be noted that Leo had wanted the council to be held in Italy, with his own representatives presiding over it. But even so powerful and assertive a pope as Leo the Great could not get his own way on a matter of such high ecclesiastical importance. Furthermore, he also objected in vain to the council's canon 28, granting Constantinople the same "prerogatives" and ecclesiastical dignity in the East as Rome enjoyed in the West on the grounds that both were imperial cities. Leo, in fact, was so opposed to this initiative by which Constantinople was to be regarded as the second see of Christendom (supplanting Alexandria and Antioch, respectively) that he withheld his endorsement of the council's proceedings until March 21, 453, two and a half years later. (He never approved canon 28.) These points serve as additional reminders of how differently papal authority was perceived and exercised in earlier centuries in contrast to modern times and current popular assumptions.

Apart from his involvement with these important doctrinal and canonical issues and his authorship of a number of clear and theologically substantive homilies and letters, Leo is also celebrated for his courageous personal confrontation with Attila the Hun near Mantua in 452, when the warrior was laying waste to northern Italy and preparing to move south toward Rome. Heading a delegation from the Roman Senate, Leo persuaded Attila to withdraw beyond the Danube. In 455 he also met the Vandal king Gaiseric (or Genseric) outside the walls of Rome. Although Leo failed to persuade Gaiseric to withdraw, he succeeded at least in preventing the torching of the city and the massacring of its people.

Upon his death, Leo was buried in the portico, or porch, of St. Peter's. His body was moved to the interior of the basilica in 688. He was made a Doctor of the Church in 1754. Feast day: November 10 (in the West); February 18 (in the East).

46 Hilarus [Hilary], St., *November 19, 461–February 29, 468.*

The pontificate of Hilarus was generally uneventful. Having served as Leo the Great's archdeacon and one of his representatives at the "robber council" of Ephesus in 449, from which he barely escaped unharmed because of his support of Flavian, the patriarch of Constantinople, Hilarus attempted to follow in his predecessor's footsteps but without ever approximating his stature. Unlike Leo, he had almost no dealings with the Church in the East except for a decretal he may have circulated to Eastern bishops confirming the ecumenical councils of Nicaea (325), Ephesus (431), and Chalcedon (451), and Leo's *Tome*, while at the same time condemning various heresies and reasserting the Roman primacy. In Italy he opposed the spread of Arianism (a heresy that regarded Jesus Christ as the greatest of creatures, but not the Son of God) and compelled the new emperor, Anthemius, to swear that he would never permit meeting places for heretics in the city of Rome. Hilarus also frequently intervened in the ecclesiastical affairs of Spain and Gaul. Several of his letters indicate how dependent the Spanish bishops had become on Rome and how the pope seemed to have had no hesitation in exercising his authority over them. In 465 Hilarus convoked a council in Rome, at the basilica of St. Mary Major, which decreed that a dying bishop may not appoint his own successor.

Because he attributed his successful escape from Ephesus to the intervention of St. John the Evangelist (the future pope had hid himself in the burial chambers of the saint outside the walls of the city), he built three chapels adjoining the Lateran Basilica, one of which he dedicated to the Evangelist. Hilarus also bestowed gifts on Roman churches to replace the precious metals looted by the Vandals in 455 and founded a monastery at San Lorenzo fuori le Mura (St. Lawrence Outside the Walls), where he was buried. Feast day: February 28.

47 Simplicius, St., *March 3, 468–March 10, 483.*

Simplicius's pontificate saw the last of the Western emperors, Romulus Augustulus, succeeded by a German general as king of Italy and the establishment of barbarian kingdoms in the rest of the Western empire. It is ironic that his pontificate, coming so soon after Leo the Great's, was also marked by a further erosion of papal prestige and influence in the East. Faithful to Leo's firm opposition to the Council of Chalcedon's canon 28, granting Constantinople ecclesiastical status roughly equivalent to Rome's, Simplicius resisted the effort by the patriarch Acacius (d. 489) to honor the canon. He also strongly opposed the new concessions being made jointly by emperor and patriarch to Monophysitism, the heresy, condemned by the Council of Chalcedon (451), that denied that Christ had a human as well as a divine nature. Without the advantage of telephone, fax machine, or electronic mail, the pope's information constantly lagged behind the events themselves. Until 479 his letters show him struggling unsuccessfully to influence developments. After 479, however, Acacius deliberately kept the pope in the dark, and his already minimal influence declined even further. For the most part, he was a spectator rather than a major player in the continued struggle between Chalcedonian orthodoxy and Monophysite heresy in the East.

Pope Simplicius is credited, however, with a number of building projects in Rome, including the first instance of adapting a public building for use as a church, in this case the church of San Andrea in Catabarbara. He also extended the policy of delegating papal authority in Spain, where Bishop Zeno of Seville was appointed papal vicar for that country and given responsibility for the observance of papal decrees. Simplicius died after a long illness and was buried near Leo the Great in the portico, or porch, of St. Peter's. Feast day: March 10.

48 Felix III (II), St., *March 13, 483–March 1, 492.*

Felix III (so identified because, at the time of his election, the antipope Felix II [355–65] had not yet been removed from an early official list of popes) is famous for his rejection of the *Henoticon* and for his excommunication of Acacius, the patriarch of Constantinople who supported it. The ensuing Acacian Schism lasted until 519. The *Henoticon* was a statement developed jointly in 482 by the emperor Zeno and the patriarch Acacius in order to reconcile Chalcedonian orthodoxy (which taught that in Christ there are two natures, one human and one divine, united in one divine Person) and Monophysitism (which denied that Christ had a human as well as a divine nature).

The son of a priest, Felix III was himself a widower with at least two children, from one of whom Pope Gregory the Great (590–604) was descended. Immediately after his election (which was influenced by the king's praetorian prefect), Felix demanded the deposition from office of the new Monophysite bishop of Alexandria and the observance of the teaching of the Council of Chalcedon (451) on the two natures of Christ. He reproached Acacius, the patriarch of Constantinople, for supporting the new bishop of Alexandria and the *Henoticon* and summoned him to Rome to defend himself against the charges of the orthodox bishop whom the Monophysite had replaced. But the pope's legates did their job badly, failing to protest when the Monophysite bishop's name was included in the Canon, or Eucharistic Prayer, of the Mass, thereby giving the impression that Rome actually approved of him and of the *Henoticon* as well. Upon the return of the legates to Rome, the pope excommunicated them as well as Acacius at a synod held in 484 and dispatched his sentence of excommunication upon Acacius to Constantinople by special messenger. It is said that some overzealous orthodox monks pinned the notice on Acacius's vestments as he was presiding at Mass. The only immediate effect the excommunication had was on the pope himself. His name was removed from the prayers of the Mass in Constantinople. (The names to be prayed for were inscribed on two panels of wood or metal, inside a hinged folder, which were known as diptychs [Gk., "folded together"]). The longer-term effect on the Church was more serious. It precipitated the Acacian Schism, which lasted for thirty-five years (484–519) and was the first serious breach of unity between East and West. When Acacius died in 489 and a new emperor ascended to the throne two years later, there were high hopes for a settlement of the dispute, but the pope refused any gestures of reconciliation as long as the Monophysite bishop was still in Alexandria and his name and that of Acacius were still commemorated at Mass. Even after the death of the Monophysite bishop and the election of an orthodox bishop in Alexandria, however, the pope refused to make any move toward reunion until Acacius's name was removed from the Mass. And in a belligerent letter to the emperor he warned him "to learn divine things from those who are in charge of them, and not to desire to teach them." Some historians regard this as the opening shot fired in what would prove to be a long struggle between the papacy and the empire.

In his dealings with pastoral problems in the West, Felix III was no less harsh and intransigent. When asked what was to be done about the many Catholics in North Africa who had submitted under force to Arian rebaptism, he decreed in 487 that those in Holy Orders should be denied reconciliation until they were on their deathbeds and others could be reconciled only after many years of rigorous penances. Felix was buried in a family crypt in St. Paul's Basilica, close to his father, his wife, and his children. Feast day: March 1.

49 Gelasius I, St., *African, March 1, 492–November 21, 496.*

Gelasius was the first pope to be called "Vicar of Christ," although the title was not exclusively attached to popes until the pontificate of Eugenius III (1145–53). After Leo the Great (440–61), Gelasius was the outstanding pope of the fifth century. An African by birth, he is remembered for his strong stand against both the emperor and the patriarch of Constantinople in the Acacian Schism (484–519) and for his defense of papal primacy by appealing to the theory of "two powers" or "two swords" (the spiritual and the temporal)—a theory that would become so influential in the Middle Ages. It is said that if Leo the Great laid the juridical foundations of papal authority, it was Gelasius who applied those principles to Church and state alike in a series of letters that read more like legal briefs than pastoral pronouncements.

Having served as archdeacon under his predecessor, Felix III, Gelasius faced a very difficult situation upon his election to the papacy. The so-called barbarian kings, all Arian (those who held that Christ was the greatest of creatures, not the Son of God), now ruled what was left of the western empire. The Ostrogoths under Theodoric, also an Arian, were in control of most of Italy. Refugees and shortages, of clergy as well as of supplies, abounded. The Acacian Schism continued without resolution. But Gelasius befriended Theodoric, encouraging him to stay out of ecclesiastical affairs. The pope used his own private fortune to assist the poor, sent supplies from the papal estates and some that were donated by Theodoric himself to ease the famine, and temporarily lowered the standards for ordination to increase the number of clergy. But in dealing with the Acacian Schism he proved more intransigent—as difficult as that may seem—than Felix III himself. He refused even the entreaties of the orthodox patriarch of Constantinople to lift the sanctions posthumously from Acacius (d. 489), the former patriarch of Constantinople. Gelasius insisted that no reconciliation was possible until Acacius's name and those of others associated with the attempt to reconcile orthodoxy and Monophysitism were removed from the prayers of the Mass, and he continued to defend the excommunication of Acacius against the protests of the Eastern bishops who regarded it as uncanonical. The emperor Anastasius I became increasingly alienated from the pope, and the Eastern bishops blamed Gelasius for putting the whole Church at risk. Some influential groups in Rome began to murmur against the pope and applied pressure for a more reasonable approach to the schism. At the Roman synod of 494, in a gesture of good will, Gelasius revoked Felix III's excommunication of one of the legates he (Felix) had blamed for mishandling a mission to Constantinople. It was at a synod the following year that Gelasius was first referred to as the "Vicar of Christ."

In a famous letter to the emperor and in other documents, Gelasius advanced a theory that would have profound influence in the Middle Ages; namely, that two powers govern the world: the one spiritual (the "consecrated authority of bishops"), centered in the pope, and the other temporal (the "royal power"), centered in the emperor. Each power has its source in God, and each is independent in its own sphere. But the spiritual power is intrinsically superior to the temporal because it mediates salvation to the temporal. Given this view of his own authority from God, Gelasius had no sympathy for the claim of Constantinople, grounded in the teaching of the Council of Chalcedon (451), that it was equivalent in status and dignity to Rome and second only to Rome in all of Christendom. And given the persistence of the Acacian Schism throughout his relatively brief pontificate, Gelasius was consumed with the task of defending papal prerogatives against those who favored a less rigid Roman approach. General support for the papacy continued, however, in the West and in Italy in particular.

A prolific writer of letters and theological treatises, Gelasius also left eighteen Mass formularies that were preserved in the Leonine Sacramentary (sixth century). Although his public performance in office was that of an authoritarian and severe pastoral leader, contemporaries pointed out that he was, in private, a humble person, given to mortification and the service of the poor. He was buried somewhere in St. Peter's Basilica. Feast day: November 21.

50 Anastasius II, *November 24, 496–November 19, 498.*

Following a pattern that one sees repeated again and again in the history of papal elections, Anastasius II was elected to the papacy because of dissatisfaction with the policies of the two previous popes, Felix III (483–92) and Gelasius I (492–96). Both had been unyielding in their approach toward the Acacian Schism (484–519), the forerunner of the major East-West Schism that would occur in the eleventh century. Felix III had excommunicated Acacius, the patriarch of Constantinople, for supporting a Monophysite bishop in Alexandria (contrary to the Council of Chalcedon of 451, the Monophysites held that Jesus Christ had only a divine nature), and Acacius later removed the pope's name from the list of those prayed for in the Canon, or Eucharistic Prayer, of the Mass.

Himself the son of a priest, Anastasius II immediately sent two legates to Constantinople carrying a conciliatory letter for the emperor, in which the pope announced his election to the papacy and expressed his desire for the restoration of Church unity. The pope was even prepared to recognize the validity of baptisms and ordinations performed by Acacius, but insisted that Acacius's name be removed from the list of those to be prayed for at Mass. The emperor (who was also named Anastasius) suggested a compromise: he would recognize Theodoric the Ostrogoth as king of Italy if the pope would accept the *Henoticon,* a doctrinally ambiguous formula of union between orthodox Catholics and Monophysites drawn up in 482 at the instigation of the emperor Zeno. Festus (or Faustus), the senior Roman senator who was in Constantinople at the same time as the papal legates, persuaded the pope to accept it. Without consulting his own clergy, Pope Anastasius II then received and entered into communion with Photinus, the deacon of Bishop Andrew of Thessalonica, whom Pope Gelasius I had denounced as a partisan of Acacius. A number of Roman clergy felt betrayed and, in turn, broke communion with their own bishop, the pope. At the height of the crisis, the pope died suddenly (an act of divine retribution, his critics claimed), and with his death perhaps the last hope of restoring unity between East and West also died.

Anastasius II's name is not found in any of the ancient martyrologies and there is no evidence of any cult or devotion to him following his death. The medieval tradition regarding him as a traitor to the Holy See because of his efforts at East-West reconciliation is manifestly unjust. Dante, for example, placed him among the heretics in the sixth circle of hell (*Divine Comedy, Inferno* 11.6–9). He was buried in the portico, or porch, of St. Peter's Basilica. He was only the second pope of the first fifty not to be recognized as a saint. Liberius (352–66) was the first.

51 Symmachus, St., *November 22, 498–July 19, 514.*

Elected while still a deacon by a majority of the Roman clergy who were dissatisfied with the conciliatory attitude of his predecessor, Anastasius II, toward the East, Symmachus confronted a schism in Rome from the outset of his pontificate. But a smaller number of clergy who favored Anastasius's approach met on the same day in the basilica of St. Mary Major and, with the support of most of the Roman Senate and the Roman aristocracy, elected the archpriest Lawrence. Both sides appealed to Theodoric, the Ostrogothic king of Italy, even though he was himself an Arian (a heretic who believed that Jesus Christ was the greatest of creatures, but not the Son of God). Theodoric ruled in favor of the one who was ordained first and had the largest amount of support. That was Symmachus.

Soon after returning from Ravenna, where he had met with the king, the newly elected Pope Symmachus convened a synod in Rome, which banned all discussion of a successor during a pope's lifetime, but which allowed the pope himself to designate his successor if he so wished. If he died before doing so, the clergy of Rome should choose the next pope, but the laity were thereafter to be excluded from the process. Lawrence, the antipope, signed the statute and was appointed bishop of Nuceria (or Nocera) in Campania.

But the peace lasted only a short time. The aristocrats, led by the senator Festus (or Faustus), reported the pope to Theodoric for having celebrated Easter according to the old Roman calendar rather than the Alexandrian calendar. The king summoned Symmachus to his residence in Ravenna, but after the pope reached Rimini and learned that he was also being charged with unchastity and the misuse of church property, he returned immediately to Rome. The king was displeased with the pope's action, and many of his clergy declared themselves no longer in communion with him. At the urging of the pope's critics, the king appointed Peter, the bishop of Altinum, to celebrate Easter and to administer the Roman see pending the resolution of charges against the pope. The king then called a synod of Italian bishops (known as the Palmary Synod) to adjudicate the matter in 501 (some place the date at 502). The pope at first refused to appear, but later, when he attempted to do so, he and his party were violently attacked on the way. Some were killed, others wounded. The synod decided that no human court could judge the pope, that only

God could do that. The pope, therefore, was absolved of all charges, and his disaffected clergy were urged to reconcile themselves with him. (One of the by-products of this dispute were the so-called Symmachan Forgeries, a collection of documents that purported to offer precedents in support of the principle that no earthly power can sit in judgment over a pope. Although they were widely circulated in later years, the documents are without historical basis.)

Displeased with the verdict, the king immediately invited Lawrence back to Rome, where he functioned as Bishop of Rome (from the official Catholic point of view as antipope) for four years. Lawrence assumed control of the city's churches and of all papal properties, and his portrait was placed among those of previous popes. Symmachus, meanwhile, remained confined to St. Peter's Basilica (then outside the walls), surrounded by a great deal of street violence. Nevertheless, he seems to have had the support of the majority of the people as well as the archbishops of Milan and Ravenna. By the year 506, Theodoric had become alienated politically from Byzantium and its allies in Rome. With the encouragement of the Alexandrian deacon Dioscorus (a later antipope), the king confirmed the synodal verdict of 501 that exonerated Symmachus and ordered the senator Festus to return the city's churches and papal properties to Symmachus so that there would be "only one pontiff in Rome." Lawrence withdrew once again from the city, settling on a farm owned by his patron Festus.

But true peace was not restored. Many remained alienated from Symmachus. Nevertheless, he resumed his reign in full vigor. He expelled Manichaean heretics from Rome, ransomed prisoners captured in the wars in northern Italy, defended African Catholics against the persecutions of Arian rulers, restored the primatial rights of the diocese of Arles over Gaul (modern-day France) and extended them also to Spain, conferred the pallium (a woolen vestment worn around the neck as a symbol of an archbishop's authority) for the first time on a bishop outside of Italy (Caesarius of Arles), introduced the sung Gloria in the Sunday liturgy, and built and restored a number of churches in Rome, especially St. Peter's, which he used as his residence and administrative headquarters. Flushed with self-confidence because of his triumph over his pro-Byzantine opponents at home, the pope adopted a hard-line posture toward Constantinople and the Acacian Schism, intensifying the ill feeling between himself and the emperor Anastasius I. In 514, however, riots in Constantinople and Antioch and a revolt in Thrace induced the emperor to seek some sort of reconciliation with the pope. He invited Symmachus to preside over a general council at Heraclea in Thrace in order to settle the doctrinal issues behind the schism. But the pope was already dead before the invitation arrived in Rome. He was buried in the portico, or porch, of St. Peter's. Feast day: July 19.

52 Hormisdas, St., *July 20, 514–August 6, 523.*

Married before ordination, Hormisdas had a son, Silverius, who later succeeded him as pope. A peacemaker at heart, from a rich, aristocratic family, he moved immediately to restore harmony to the Church. On the home front he reestablished communion with the Roman supporters of the antipope Lawrence, and on the foreign front he brought to an end the Acacian Schism (484–519) that had divided East from West because of a difference of approach to Monophysitism (a heresy that denied that Jesus Christ had a human nature).

When the pope received an invitation from the emperor Anastasius I (an invitation originally intended for Hormisdas's predecessor, Symmachus) to preside over a general council at Heraclea in Thrace, Hormisdas consulted Theodoric, the king of Italy, and then sent legates to Constantinople on two occasions, in 515 and 517, carrying his conditions for reunion; namely, public acceptance of the anti-Monophysite teaching of the Council of Chalcedon (451) and of Pope Leo I's *Tome* on the two natures of Christ, the condemnation of Acacius, the deceased patriarch of Constantinople, and of others who were considered "soft" on Monophysitism, and the retrial by Rome of all deposed or exiled bishops, thereby establishing the jurisdictional primacy of the pope in the East. But now politically stronger than at the time he extended the invitation to the pope to preside over a general council, the emperor refused to yield.

Within a year, however, the emperor was dead. He was succeeded by Justin I, an orthodox Catholic who fully embraced the teaching of Chalcedon and made it the official faith of the empire. In response to the new emperor's invitation, the pope sent another delegation to Constantinople with the same demands. On March 28, 519, an agreement, known as the *Formula of Hormisdas,* was reluctantly signed in the imperial palace by John II, patriarch of Constantinople, and by all the bishops (about 250) and heads of monasteries who were present. More than thirteen and a half centuries later, the First Vatican Council (1869–70) would incorporate that Formula in its dogmatic constitution on papal primacy, *Pastor aeternus.*

Some historians have noted a shadow across Pope Hormisdas's achievement in the East. First, the pope could not have accomplished anything without the support of Justin I and his successor, Justinian, his nephew. Both viewed reunion with Rome as a necessary precondition for recovering Italy for the empire. Second, in restoring the exiled orthodox bishops to their sees on their own imperial authority, prior to any negotiations with Rome, they were making a point that the pope had no jurisdictional primacy in the East. Third, when patriarch John signed the Formula, he added a gloss expressing joy that the old Rome and the new Rome (Constantinople) were now one, that is, one in honor. Fourth, although the pope insisted on full compliance with the agreement, the emperor and the patriarch followed a more pragmatic approach in its enforcement. Fifth, and finally, when the pope authorized the new patriarch, Epiphanius, "to put on our person" and to remove the final traces of the schism in the East, the pope was implicitly recognizing canon 28 of the Council of Chalcedon regarding the coequal status of Constantinople with Rome.

Hormisdas was buried in the portico, or porch, of St. Peter's. Feast day: August 6.

53 John I, St., *August 13, 523–May 18, 526.*

Already elderly and sick when elected, John I was the first pope to travel to the East, albeit under pressure from the king of Italy. (It was also under John I that the practice began of numbering the years from the birth of Christ instead of the unwieldy custom of listing them according to the era of Diocletian.) Just before John's election, the emperor Justin I, headquartered in Constantinople, revived a number of laws directed against the Arians (heretics who held that Jesus Christ was the greatest of creatures, but not the Son of God). Their churches were seized; they were expelled from public office; and they were required to give up their Arian faith. The emperor's campaign against the Arians, many of whom were Goths, had infuriated Theodoric, the king of Italy, because he was both a Goth and an Arian himself. Therefore, he summoned the pope to the royal residence in Ravenna and dispatched him on a mission to Constantinople along with a delegation of bishops and Roman senators. Their charge was clear: to reverse the imperial actions against the Arians, including the demand that they renounce their Arian faith.

Although his was a humiliating mission, John I was received in Constantinople with extraordinary enthusiasm and respect in October or November 525. The emperor even prostrated himself before him, "as if he were Peter in person." A few months later, at the Easter liturgy in the Hagia Sophia church, the pope was given a throne higher than that of the patriarch's, celebrated Mass according to the Latin rite, and placed the Easter crown on the emperor's head, an honor customarily reserved to the patriarch. In subsequent discussions, the emperor acceded to the first two of Theodoric's demands, but not the third (that the Arians not be required to renounce their Arian faith). Believing that they could achieve no more than that, the pope and the rest of the delegation returned to Ravenna, only to face the king's fury. Theodoric not only bristled at the emperor's refusal to grant mutual toleration, but he also resented the pope's magnificent reception in Constantinople and his obvious satisfaction with it. Suspicious of John I's loyalty, Theodoric forced the pope to remain in Ravenna until he decided what to do with him. Already exhausted by his long journey and terrified by the prospect of severe punishment at the hands of the king, the elderly pope collapsed and died (some said because of maltreatment and starvation). His body was taken back to Rome, where it was venerated as that of a martyr's and as possessing miraculous powers. John I was buried in the nave of St. Peter's. His epitaph honors him as "a victim for Christ." Feast day: May 18.

54 Felix IV (III), St., *July 12, 526–September 22, 530.*

Because there was an antipope who took the name Felix II in 355 and whose name was included for a time on the official list of popes, Felix IV is really the third Pope Felix in the official line of successors of St. Peter. His pontificate is best known for its support of Caesarius, bishop of Arles, against the semi-Pelagians, a heretical group who held that, although grace is necessary for salvation, the first move toward salvation is an act of human freedom without grace. Only thereafter does grace enter into one's progress toward salvation. The pope's teaching, drawn mainly from St. Augustine (d. 430), was adopted by the Second Council of Orange in July, 529.

Felix IV is also remembered for the manner in which he left the papacy. As death approached, he gathered his clerical and political supporters around his sickbed and gave them an order to elect his archdeacon Boniface as his successor. (It is said that he did so because he feared that fierce factional fighting would erupt among the clergy after his death.) He gave Boniface his pallium (a woolen vestment worn around the neck as a symbol of pastoral authority) on condition that it be returned to him if he should recover. The pope had his order published in Rome and a copy sent to the royal court in Ravenna. The majority of the Senate, however, rejected the pope's action and published an edict forbidding discussion of a papal successor during a pope's lifetime and the acceptance of a nomination as successor.

It was Felix IV who, with the support of the queen-regent of Italy, converted two pagan temples into a church dedicated to Sts. Cosmas

and Damian. A mosaic portrait of the pope in the apse is the first contemporary papal likeness to have survived, although in a highly altered
state. He was buried in the portico, or porch, of St. Peter's. Feast day:
September 22.

55 **Boniface II,** *September 22, 530–October 17, 532.*

Though born in Rome, Boniface II was the first pope of Germanic stock.
Archdeacon under his predecessor, John I, he was summoned along with
a number of clergy and senators to the pope's sickbed and given the
pope's pallium (a woolen vestment worn around the neck as a symbol of
pastoral authority) along with an order nominating him as the next
pope. This action precipitated a reaction in the Roman Senate, which forbade any discussion of a successor during a sitting pope's lifetime or the
acceptance of a nomination as successor. Most of the Roman clergy
agreed with the Senate's action. When they met in the Lateran Basilica to
elect a new pope, they elected the deacon Dioscorus of Alexandria, who
had been a close confidant of and collaborator with two previous popes,
Symmachus (498–514) and Hormisdas (514–23). The defeated minority
withdrew to an adjacent hall and elected Boniface. Both were consecrated
on the same day, September 22, 530. Dioscorus, however, died twenty-two
days later and his supporters, bereft of their leader, acknowledged Boniface as pope. Although Dioscorus is not officially recognized as a legitimate pope, there is little or no doubt that, according to the church law of
the day, he, not Boniface, was the rightly elected pope. Unfortunately,
Boniface was vindictive in victory. He forced the sixty priests who opposed his election to sign a declaration admitting their guilt, promising
never to do anything like that again, and condemning the memory of
Dioscorus.

Like his predecessor, Felix IV, Boniface II wanted to assure the election
of a pro-Gothic successor. At a Roman synod in 531, he formally proposed Vigilius as the next pope and obliged the clergy to subscribe to his
order with an oath. But his action provoked strong opposition, and he
had to retract his nomination of Vigilius and to burn the document
mandating the nomination at a subsequent synod and in the presence of
the Senate.

In 531 Boniface confirmed the acts of the Second Council of Orange
(529) which taught, against the semi-Pelagians, that grace is always necessary for salvation, even from the very first moment when human freedom can be exercised. He also practiced great charity during a famine in
Rome. Although he is buried in St. Peter's, there is no evidence of any cult
devoted to him.

56 John II, *January 2, 533–May 8, 535.*

Because his name from birth was that of a pagan god, Mercury, John II was the first pope to take a different name upon his election to the papacy. He was also famous for contradicting, under pressure from the Eastern emperor, the teaching of a previous pope (Hormisdas) on a matter of doctrine.

The events leading up to his election, two and a half months after the death of his predecessor, Boniface II, are a reminder of the all too human nature of the papacy. It was, according to historians, "a period of intrigue and corruption, with aspirants to the papal throne and their partisans resorting to canvassing and bribery; even church plate and funds collected for poor relief were squandered to obtain votes" (J. N. D. Kelly, p. 57). Afterward the king of Italy confirmed a decree of the Senate outlawing under pain of severe penalties various improper practices in papal elections and ordered that the decree be inscribed on marble and posted in St. Peter's for all to see.

An elderly priest, John II was a compromise choice, on good terms with both the Ostrogothic king of Italy, Athalaric, and the Eastern emperor, Justinian I. Following a synod, the new pope formally accepted a dogmatic decree the emperor had published in March 523. The decree acknowledged the teaching of the first four ecumenical councils, but it also included the so-called Theopaschite formula ("One of the Trinity suffered in the flesh"), which Pope Hormisdas had rejected as both unnecessary and open to misunderstanding. The emperor favored it because, while it was orthodox, the formula appealed to the Monophysites under his jurisdiction (the Monophysites were heretics who held that Jesus Christ had only a divine nature) because of its anti-Nestorian tone (the Nestorians were heretics who held that in Jesus Christ there were two persons, one divine and one human, rather than one divine Person). When the Acoemetae ("sleepless") monks of Constantinople, known for their fidelity to the teaching of the Council of Chalcedon (451), protested the pope's acceptance of the formula, the pope tried to persuade them to withdraw their opposition. But they refused, and the pope excommunicated them as Nestorians because they seemed to have gone even so far as to deny the title *Theotokos* (Mother of God) to Mary. The pope wrote to the emperor to inform him that his decree was orthodox. The emperor, in turn, incorporated the pope's letter and his own (in which he acknowledged the Apostolic See as "the head of all the Churches") in his famous Code of Justinian. The whole episode, however, is remembered mainly as an example of one pope's contradicting another in a matter of doctrine.

John II died on May 8, 535, and was buried in the portico, or porch, of St. Peter's.

57 Agapitus I, St., *May 13, 535–April 22, 536.*

The son of a priest who had been killed by supporters of the antipope Lawrence in 502, Agapitus I was strongly opposed to the practice of a pope's designating his successor and, therefore, began his pontificate by having Pope Boniface II's (530–32) condemnation of the antipope Dioscorus of Alexandria publicly burned (see Boniface II, number 55, above).

As pope, Agapitus also took a forceful stance against former Arians (heretics who held that Jesus Christ was not the Son of God, but only the greatest of creatures) in North Africa and in the East. He forbade them from exercising their clerical office, in spite of an appeal from the emperor Justinian. At the same time, the pope was forced to pawn sacred vessels in order to pay for his trip to Constantinople, under explicit threats from the last Ostrogothic king of Italy, Theodahad. The king had learned of the emperor's plans to invade Italy in order to reincorporate it into the empire after almost sixty years as a Germanic kingdom. Although given a triumphal welcome in Constantinople, the pope's mission failed. The emperor explained that his plans for the invasion could not be called off.

While in Constantinople, however, Agapitus I did persuade the emperor to remove Anthimus, the patriarch of Constantinople, on the grounds that he was a Monophysite (a heretic who held that in Jesus Christ there is only a divine nature, and not a human nature as well). The pope consecrated the new patriarch, Mennas. He also acceded to the emperor's request that he confirm the orthodoxy of the Theopaschite formula, which Pope Hormisdas (514–23) had disapproved of but which Pope John II (533–35) had accepted. The pope died in Constantinople on April 22, 536, and his body was brought back to Rome in a leaden casket and buried in the portico, or porch, of St. Peter's. Feast day: September 20 (in the West); April 17 (in the East).

58 Silverius, St., *d. December 2, 537, pope from June 1 or 8, 536, to November 11, 537.*

The son of Pope Hormisdas (514–23), Silverius was the first (and only) subdeacon to be elected pope and one of only three (or perhaps five popes) to resign their office: Pontian in 235, Celestine V in 1294, Gregory XII in 1415, and probably John XVIII in 1009. (During Benedict IX's canonically confusing pontificate, he abdicated in favor of his godfather in 1045, but was reinstated in 1047.) Silverius's election, however, occurred under threat of violence against the Roman clergy by the last Ostrogothic king of Italy, Theodahad, who wanted a pro-Gothic pope at a time when the Eastern emperor was about to invade his kingdom.

The Monophysite empress Theodora, upset with the previous pope's deposing of the Monophysite patriarch Anthimus of Constantinople, urged Pope Silverius to step down in favor of the Roman deacon Vigilius, the papal nuncio to Constantinople, with whom she had made a pact to restore Anthimus to Constantinople. When Silverius refused, he was summoned to the headquarters of the emperor's general, Belisarius, and accused of plotting with the Goths, who were then laying siege to the city. The pope was stripped of his pallium (the woolen vestment worn around the neck as a symbol of his pastoral authority), degraded to the status of a monk, and deposed on March 11, 537. (By implication, even the Vatican's official list of popes in the *Annuario Pontificio* acknowledges the validity of his deposition by the emperor, because it begins his successor's pontificate in the same month, even though Silverius did not formally abdicate until the following November.) He was deported to Patara, a seaport town in Lycia, whose local bishop directly interceded on his behalf with the emperor Justinian himself. The emperor ordered the pope back to Rome to face trial. If found innocent, he would be restored to the papal throne.

By this time, however, Vigilius had already been elected the new pope. When Silverius reached Rome, Vigilius arranged to have him taken to Palmaria, an island in the Gulf of Gaeta, where he resigned from the papacy under threat on November 11. Silverius died less than a month later, on December 2, probably from physical abuse and starvation designed to avoid a potentially embarrassing trial. He was buried on the island and his grave became an attraction for those seeking cures and miracles. From the eleventh century he has been venerated as a martyr, but not until the fourteenth century was he venerated in Rome itself. Feast day: June 20.

59 Vigilius, *March 29, 537–June 7, 555 (the Vatican's official list also recognizes Vigilius as pope from March 29, 537, even though his predecessor, Silverius, had not yet formally abdicated until November 11 of that same year).*

Vigilius was clearly one of the most corrupt popes in the history of the Church. As papal nuncio to Constantinople, he entered into a secret pact with the Monophysite empress Theodora to restore the Monophysite patriarch Anthimus to the see of Constantinople and to disavow the Council of Chalcedon (451). (The Council of Chalcedon had condemned Monophysitism as a heresy because it denied that Jesus Christ had a human as well as a divine nature.) In return for his cooperation, she showered him with gifts and assured his election to the papacy upon the death of Agapitus I (535–36). (Vigilius had already been nominated by Pope Boniface II [530–32] as his successor, but the nomination was nullified as uncanonical.) By the time Vigilius returned to Rome, Silverius had already been elected as Agapitus's successor. Under orders from the empress, the imperial general in Rome, Belisarius, saw to it that Agapitus was deposed and exiled and Vigilius "elected" to succeed him. Vigilius then blocked the fair trial that the emperor Justinian ordered for Agapitus and had the pope kidnapped and taken to the island of Palmaria in the Gulf of Gaeta, where he was forced to abdicate and was probably starved to death to avoid the potentially embarrassing trial. The Roman clergy seem to have retroactively validated Vigilius's "election" upon the resignation of Silverius in November 537.

Vigilius played a duplicitous game with the East. Privately, he assured Anthimus and other Monophysites that he agreed with them, but he also wrote to assure the emperor Justinian that he fully endorsed the teaching of Chalcedon and that he supported the emperor's deposition of Anthimus and other Monophysites. When Justinian published an edict condemning the "Three Chapters," that is, the writings of three theologians (the most famous of whom was Theodore of Mopsuestia) whose work the Council of Chalcedon had not questioned, he demanded that the pope sign it along with the other patriarchs. When Vigilius resisted, the emperor had him arrested while he was saying Mass on November 22, 545, and had him taken to Sicily. After a long stay there, the pope was brought to Constantinople in January 547. While there, he and Mennas, the patriarch of Constantinople, excommunicated one another. But by June Vigilius relented. He resumed communion with Mennas and promised the emperor and empress that he would condemn the "Three Chapters." When he did so, however, his *Iudicatum* ("decision" or "judgment") was interpreted throughout the West as a betrayal of Chalcedon.

A synod of African bishops at Carthage excommunicated the pope in 550. Even the pope's nephew, the deacon Rusticus, publicly repudiated the *Iudicatum* on Christmas day, 549, and was subsequently excommunicated by his uncle in early 550. The crisis became so severe that the pope and the emperor agreed that a council would be necessary to resolve it. Vigilius was allowed to withdraw his edict condemning the "Three Chapters," but soon thereafter the emperor issued a fresh edict of condemnation. The pope excommunicated the emperor's theological adviser and took refuge with his clergy in the basilica of Sts. Peter and Paul. After being physically assaulted by the imperial police while at the altar and then treated like a prisoner, the pope fled across the Bosphorus in December 551 and took refuge, ironically, in the basilica of St. Euphemia in Chalcedon, where the council had been held.

After further threats and conflicts between the pope and the imperial forces, there was, in June 552, a reconciliation initiated by the emperor Justinian himself. The pope returned to Constantinople and plans for the council went forward once again. Although the pope wanted the council held in Sicily or Italy (or at least preceded by a synod there), the emperor decided that it would be held in Constantinople on May 5, 553, in the great hall attached to Hagia Sophia church. The pope refused to attend because of the tiny representation of Western bishops. On May 14 he issued his First Constitution, signed by sixteen other bishops, which condemned the teachings, but not the person, of only one of the three theologians (Theodore of Mopsuestia) included in the "Three Chapters." The emperor rejected it and then humiliated the pope by revealing the secret correspondence he and the pope had over the whole issue. He also had the pope's name removed from the list of those to be prayed for at Mass, while making it clear that he was only breaking communion with Vigilius personally, but not with the Holy See itself.

The emperor had the council condemn the "Three Chapters" and then he threw the pope's deacon into jail, deposed and exiled uncooperative Latin bishops, and placed the pope himself under house arrest. After six months, the ill and isolated pope gave in and, on December 8, 553, wrote to the new patriarch, revoking his earlier defense of the "Three Chapters" and admitting they needed to be condemned. But the emperor was still not satisfied. On February 23, 554, Vigilius issued his Second Constitution, which completely endorsed the action of the council in condemning the "Three Chapters." (Opponents of papal infallibility at the First Vatican Council in 1869–70 cited the case of Pope Vigilius in their arguments against the proposed dogma, even though infallibility was not at issue in this whole sorry episode.) Vigilius was freed and allowed to return to Rome, if he wished. Although his presence was demanded there, the pope remained in Constantinople for another year, where he obtained from Justinian, in return for his cooperative behavior, the so-called Pragmatic Sanction (August 13, 554), assuring the Church important rights and privileges in Italy.

When Vigilius finally left for Rome in the spring, he suffered another of many attacks of gallstones and died in Syracuse, Sicily. When his body was brought back to Rome, it was not buried in St. Peter's because of his unpopularity. He was buried instead in San Marcello on the Via Salaria.

60 Pelagius I, *April 16, 556–March 4, 561.*

Because of the circumstances surrounding his election to the papacy, Pelagius I's pontificate was marred from the outset. Upon the death of Pope Vigilius, the deacon Pelagius, the papal nuncio in Constantinople, returned to Rome as the emperor Justinian's personal choice to be the new pope. The Roman clergy were very unhappy about having to accept Pelagius without even an election. Not surprisingly, he encountered a very hostile reception when he reached Rome. Many religious and nobles broke communion with Pelagius, and his consecration had to be delayed for several months because no bishop would agree to officiate. Later, only two bishops consecrated him in the presence of a presbyter representing the bishop of Ostia, who was normally a papal consecrator.

There were rumors circulating that he was involved somehow in the death of Pope Vigilius, and he was being widely criticized in the West for his flip-flopping on the "Three Chapters" (see Pope Vigilius, number 59, above), having first opposed the condemnation of the three anti-Monophysite theologians (Theodore of Mopsuestia, Theodoret of Cyrrhus, and Ibas of Edessa) and then, under pressure from the emperor (who wanted to placate the Monophysites in the empire), agreeing to their condemnation. After his ordination and consecration, Pelagius took the unprecedented action of solemnly affirming his loyalty to the first four general councils of the Church (Nicaea, Ephesus, especially Chalcedon, and Constantinople) and of swearing on the cross and the book of the Gospels that he had done no harm to Vigilius.

As pope, Pelagius acted with determination to restore law and order to Rome and to Italy generally after the wars. He was especially devoted to the alleviation of poverty and famine and to the ransoming of war prisoners. He reformed papal finances and reorganized papal properties in Italy, Gaul, Dalmatia, and North Africa, diverting their income to the poor. He also took a firm stand against simony (the buying and selling of spiritual benefits and church offices) and against clerical corruption. But his efforts on these and other fronts were of little avail in winning acceptance of his papal authority outside of the city of Rome itself. Resentment and hostility toward him were deeply rooted and widely dispersed. Because of the stand he had taken on the "Three Chapters," the bishops of the great dioceses of Milan and Aquileia, for example, refused communion with him. For the same reason, he continued to be distrusted and despised in Gaul (modern-day France). Already elderly when consecrated as pope, Pelagius died after five years in office and was buried in St. Peter's.

61 John III, *July 17, 561–July 13, 574.*

Little is known about the thirteen-year pontificate of John III. Known as a pro-Easterner, he was elected with the support of the emperor Justinian and of Narses, the imperial exarch (viceroy) in Italy. He was the second pope to change his birth name (Catelinus) upon election to the papacy. (The first was John II [533–35], whose birth name was Mercury.) Seven years into John III's reign, the Lombards invaded large sections of Italy. This crisis helped to ease the schism that had existed between Rome and the great churches of the West during the pontificate of Pelagius I. Relations with North Africa had already improved after the death of Justinian in 565. The new bishop of Milan, his city now in the hands of the Lombards, decided that it was politically prudent to renew communion with Rome in 573, but the diocese of Aquileia continued to hold back.

As the Lombards moved south, John III rushed to Naples to persuade the unpopular imperial viceroy, Narses, to return to Rome and take charge of the crisis. But the Roman people were displeased, and Narses's unpopularity began to contaminate the pope as well. To avoid being drawn further into the conflict between the Romans and Narses, John withdrew from the city, taking up residence and headquarters in the church of Sts. Tiburtius and Valerian, two miles outside of Rome on the Via Appia, until Narses died. But soon thereafter the pope himself died and was buried in St. Peter's.

62 Benedict I, *June 2, 575–July 30, 579.*

Very little is known about the pontificate of Benedict I. Because of the breakdown in the lines of communication between Rome and Constantinople, he had to wait eleven months before receiving imperial confirmation of his election to the papacy. During his reign, the Lombards continued their push southward, finally laying siege to Rome itself in the summer of 579. Appeals to the emperor for help were of little avail. The troops he sent were too few in number. As the siege intensified and famine spread, Benedict died. He was buried in the sacristy of St. Peter's.

63 Pelagius II, *August 579–February 7, 590 (the Vatican's official list gives the beginning of his pontificate as November 26, the date of his imperial confirmation, but theologically he became pope as soon as he was ordained Bishop of Rome, in August).*

Elected when the Lombard siege of Rome was at its height, Pelagius II, the second pope of Germanic extraction, was ordained as Bishop of

Rome immediately (probably in August), without waiting for the emperor's formal approval. The new pope immediately sent his deacon (the future Gregory the Great) to Constantinople as his representative (apocrisarius) to explain the departure from precedent and to beg for military aid. But the emperor did not have the necessary forces to dispatch. Appeals to the Franks also failed. In 585, however, the imperial exarch (viceroy) in Ravenna arranged a truce with the Lombards, which lasted for four years. The pope tried to take advantage of this pause in hostilities to mend ecclesiastical fences with the churches of northern Italy, but these efforts generally failed as well, except in the case of Aquileia, with which communion was restored.

During Pelagius II's pontificate, the Visigoths were converted to Christianity in Spain, and yet another controversy with Constantinople erupted over the patriarch's use of the title "ecumenical patriarch," a custom dating back to the previous century. When Patriarch John IV assumed the title at a synod in 588, the pope refused to endorse the acts of the synod because of his conviction that the title infringed upon papal supremacy. Pelagius ordered Gregory, his nuncio, to break communion with John until the latter repudiated the title.

In Rome itself the pope was an active builder. He reconstructed the church of San Lorenzo fuori le Mura (St. Lawrence Outside the Walls), where his portrait appears in a contemporary mosaic on the triumphal arch. When a plague broke out in the aftermath of flooding caused by the overflow of the Tiber River, Pelagius II was among its first victims. He was buried in the portico, or porch, of St. Peter's.

64 Gregory I, "the Great," St., *ca. 540–604, pope from September 3, 590, to March 12, 604.*

Only the second pope in all of church history to be called "the Great" (Leo I [440–61] was the first), Gregory I was the first pope to have been a monk and was one of the papacy's most influential writers. His *Pastoral Care,* which defined the episcopal ministry as one of shepherding souls, became the textbook for medieval bishops. Although only a junior deacon at the time of Pelagius II's death, he was unanimously elected to the papacy. But Gregory immediately wrote to the emperor asking him to withhold his consent from the election, which he had neither sought nor wanted. In the meantime, Gregory engaged in intense pastoral work among the plague-stricken inhabitants of Rome. After the imperial mandate arrived, however, he accepted consecration as Bishop of Rome under protest.

His early letters disclose his unhappiness over having been forced to leave the contemplative life to assume the heavy responsibilities of the papacy. Indeed, those responsibilities were far heavier than usual because of the general breakdown of civil order at the time. Gregory found himself drawn as deeply into temporal and political affairs as into spiritual and ecclesiastical concerns. (He had been prefect of the city before selling all his possessions, giving the proceeds to the poor, and converting his home into a monastery.) He immediately organized the distribution of food to the starving, and, in order to expand the reservoir of resources, he reorganized the papal territories in Italy, Sicily, Dalmatia, Gaul, and North Africa. He admonished each rector of the papal estates "to care for the poor" and "to promote not so much the worldly interests of the Church but the relief of the needy in their distress." He insisted that he was not dispensing his own property but property that belonged by right to the poor, given originally by St. Peter, who continued to care for his flock through Gregory.

When the imperial exarch (viceroy) in Ravenna proved incapable of doing anything about the Lombard threat, the pope took the lead and fashioned a truce with the duke of Spoleto. When the exarch broke the truce and the Lombards moved against Rome, Gregory saved the city by bribing the Lombard king and promising yearly tributes. As a result of all these efforts, Gregory became virtually the civil as well as the spiritual ruler of Rome. He negotiated treaties, paid the troops, and appointed generals and governors. At the same time, he carefully attended to the need for reform in the government of the Church as well. He imposed a detailed code, for example, for the election and conduct of bishops in Italy and enforced clerical celibacy. He also secured better relationships with the churches of Spain and Gaul (modern-day France). When he discovered that the Anglo-Saxon invaders had not been evangelized by the native clergy of Britain, he dispatched Augustine (later of Canterbury), with forty other monks, to England in 596 and later conferred the pallium (the woolen vestment worn around the neck as a symbol of pastoral authority) on Augustine as archbishop of the English.

His relations with the East were complicated by the presence of the emperor, to whom he as pope was subject. Gregory frequently had to defer to the emperor even in matters of ecclesiastical governance. But the pope continued to insist on papal primacy and on the Roman see's role as a court of appeals even for the East. The conflict with the patriarch's use of the title "ecumenical patriarch" continued throughout Gregory's pontificate. Gregory insisted that there is no universal patriarch in the Church (including the pope!) and that his own primatial claim required humility. Indeed, he referred to himself constantly as the "servant of the servants of God."

Given his own monastic background, Gregory was a vigorous promoter of monasticism and of the liturgy, particularly of liturgical music. Indeed, his name was so closely identified with plainsong that it came to be known as Gregorian chant. Many of the prayers recited in the Eucharist are said to be attributable to Gregory, for example, the Christmas Preface and the Prefaces of Easter and the Ascension. He is also credited with the placement of the "Our Father" in the Mass. His support of monasticism and of monks, however, created divisions within the ranks of the Roman clergy that were to last for many years and would affect several subsequent papal elections, with the electors divided between pro-Gregorian and anti-Gregorian forces, that is, between pro-monastic clergy and pro-diocesan clergy.

His writings were more practical than theoretical and more derivative than original. But he was such an effective synthesizer, especially of the work of St. Augustine of Hippo (d. 430), that he came eventually to be included with Ambrose, Augustine, and Jerome as a Doctor of the Church. Even in his own lifetime his *Pastoral Care* was translated into Greek and Anglo-Saxon. In it he set out a vision of pastoral care adapted to the needs of the people and rooted in personal example and preaching, with a fine balance between the contemplative and active aspects of all ministry. In four books he treated the type of person and motives necessary for pastoral ministry, the virtues required in a pastor, the manner of preaching to many different types of people, and the need for pastors to examine their own consciences. The *Dialogues* describe the miracles and deeds of Italian saints, especially St. Benedict of Nursia (d. ca. 547). One of his goals was to encourage people to bear the trials of earthly life as a preparation for the eternal life to come. His *Forty Homilies on the Gospels* are examples of his popular preaching, blending storytelling with doctrine and biblical texts, and the *Homilies on Ezekiel* are examples of more learned discourse addressed to clerics and monks. His *Moralia*, a mystical and allegorical exposition of the book of Job, was an influential spiritual text centuries later. St. Thomas Aquinas (d. 1274), for example, cites him 374 times in the second part of the *Summa Theologiae*. Gregory's own spirituality was marked by a vivid sense of the imminent end of the world, intensified perhaps by the ill health that hindered him throughout his pontificate. He was so racked with gout that, by the time of his death, he could no longer walk. Unfortunately, Rome, under yet another siege, was once again in the grip of famine. In their desperation, the Romans turned against the pope who had done so much for them. He died on March 12, 604, and was buried in St. Peter's with the epitaph "consul of God." Feast day: September 3.

65 Sabinian, *September 13, 604–February 22, 606.*

Sabinian was one of the most unpopular popes in history. In fact, his funeral procession had to make a detour outside the city walls to avoid the hostile demonstrations. How did this pope come to such an end? Having fallen out of favor with Gregory the Great for his unsatisfactory perfor- mance as nuncio to Constantinople (he was considered too conciliatory toward the emperor and the patriarch), Sabinian was elected to the pa- pacy as a reaction to Gregory, who had himself become unpopular with the Roman populace by the time of his death. (Contrary to historically uninformed assumptions still current today, papal electors very often choose a new pope decidedly different in style and even in policy from the previous pope, even when that pope was someone as distinguished as Gregory the Great!)

Sabinian reversed Gregory's policy of favoring monks and promoted diocesan, or secular, clergy instead. But he reversed another Gregorian policy as well. With the renewal of hostilities with the Lombards and the return of famine, Sabinian maintained tight control over food supplies and, unlike Gregory, sold them to the people rather than giving them away freely. Accused of profiteering, he was as despised in death as in life. Thus, the diverted funeral procession. He was buried in a secret location in the Lateran.

66 Boniface III, *February 19–November 12, 607.*

It was Boniface III who, following a Roman synod, forbade under penalty of excommunication all discussion of a successor to a pope or to any other bishop during the pope's or a bishop's lifetime and until three days after his death. His action may have been prompted by the rivalries (be- tween pro- and anti-Gregorian factions) that preceded his own election. Indeed, a full year passed before the vacancy created by Sabinian's death was even filled. A second interesting point about Boniface III's brief pon- tificate was the declaration of the new emperor Phocas (actually a repeat of a declaration by the emperor Justinian) that the see of St. Peter was the head of all the churches, thereby putting to a temporary end the patri- arch of Constantinople's use of the title "ecumenical patriarch." While papal nuncio to Constantinople under Pope Gregory the Great, Boniface III had forged a particularly friendly relationship with the new emperor. The imperial declaration regarding the Roman see was a logical outcome of that relationship. He died on November 12, 607, and was buried in St. Peter's.

67 Boniface IV, St., *August 25, 608–May 8, 615.*

A disciple and imitator of Pope Gregory the Great (590–604), Boniface IV converted his house in Rome into a monastery upon his election to the papacy and, like Gregory, favored monks and promoted monasticism.

The ten-month vacancy in the papal office was caused by a delay in receiving imperial approval from Constantinople for his consecration as Bishop of Rome. The new pope held a synod (at which the first bishop of London was present) in 610 to regulate monastic life and discipline. The pope enjoyed good relations with the emperor, Phocas, and his successor, Heraclius (the former allowed him to turn the Roman Pantheon into a church dedicated to the Blessed Virgin Mary and all the martyrs), but his pontificate was constantly disturbed by famine, plagues, and natural disasters. Like Gregory, he was especially devoted to the poor. He was buried in St. Peter's; his cult apparently did not begin until the Middle Ages, during the pontificate of Boniface VIII (1295–1303). Feast day: May 25.

68 Deusdedit [Adeodatus I], St., *October 19, 615–November 8, 618.*

Deusdedit (later Adeodatus I) was the first priest to be elected pope since John II in 533. All the intervening popes were deacons when elected (except for Silverius in 536, who was the first subdeacon elected to the papacy). Already elderly when elected, Deusdedit was the choice of the clerical faction opposed to the pro-monastic policies of Gregory the Great and Boniface IV. As a diocesan priest himself, he promoted diocesan clergy over religious to offices. He ordained fourteen priests—the first to be ordained since the death of Gregory the Great in 604. Almost nothing is known about his pontificate except that Rome was hit with an earthquake and another plague. His epitaph describes Deusdedit as simple, devout, wise, and shrewd. On his deathbed he gave the first recorded bequest by a pope to his clergy, the equivalent of a year's salary to each. He was buried in St. Peter's. Feast day: November 8.

69 Boniface V, *December 23, 619–October 25, 625.*

Like his predecessor, Deusdedit, Boniface V was elected by the clerical faction opposed to the pro-monastic policies of Gregory the Great and Boniface IV. And like Deusdedit, he had to wait almost a year for imperial confirmation of his election and approval of his consecration as Bishop of Rome. He promoted policies favorable to the diocesan clergy, decreeing, for example, that only priests could transfer the relics of martyrs, and he took a special interest in the English church, conferring the pallium (a woolen vestment worn around the neck of an archbishop as a symbol of pastoral authority) on Justus when he became archbishop of Canterbury in 624. He wrote directly to King Edwin of Northumbria, urging him to study the Catholic faith, and to Queen Ethelburga, already a Christian, to encourage her to procure the conversion of Edwin and his subjects.

(Edwin was baptized sometime after Boniface V's death.) The pope also established the principle of asylum in churches.

Boniface V was known for his compassion and generosity, having distributed his entire personal fortune to the poor. And like his predecessor he left generous bequests to his clergy. Buried in St. Peter's, he is described in his epitaph as "generous, wise, pure, sincere, and just." One only wonders why he was not eventually recognized as a saint, since the title had been conferred on many less deserving popes in the past.

70 Honorius I, *October 27, 625–October 12, 638.*

Honorius is one of the few popes in history to have been condemned by an ecumenical council (the Third Council of Constantinople in 680–81) for doctrinal deviation. One source indicates that Honorius, elected on October 27, 625, only two days after the death of Boniface V, did not await imperial approval of his consecration, that he was ordained Bishop of Rome on November 3. If that were the case, the beginning of his pontificate would be November 3 rather than October 27. But the *Annuario Pontificio,* which contains the official Vatican list of popes, indicates the beginning of his pontificate as October 27. The *Annuario* obviously accepts the judgment of other sources that Honorius had indeed received imperial confirmation of his election from the exarch Isaac, who was in Rome at the time, and immediate consecration as Bishop of Rome. The matter is not a small point. Theologically, a person does not become pope until he is Bishop of Rome. Canonically, there have been periods in the Church's history when election, not consecration, was sufficient for validity. The present canon law of the Church (can. 332.1) conforms with its theology, namely, that a person who is elected pope without being a bishop is not pope until he is ordained a bishop. One must keep in mind that the overwhelming majority of the popes of the first millennium were either priests (presbyters) or deacons (in one case, a subdeacon) when elected. The first person elected pope who was already a bishop was Marinus I (882–84), who was bishop of Caere (now Cerveteri) at the time. During almost all of the first Christian millennium, bishops were prohibited by canon 15 of the Council of Nicaea (325) from moving from one diocese to another.

In 634 Honorius I received a letter from Sergius I, the patriarch of Constantinople, proposing that the second Person of the Trinity, the Word of God, was the subject of every "operation," human and divine, in the God-man, Jesus Christ. Sergius pointed out that the formula "two distinct natures but one operation" had been found useful in the East to win over the Monophysites (heretics who held that in Christ there was no human nature, only a divine nature). Sophronius, the new bishop of Jerusalem, and others branded the formula as Monophysitism in disguise. Nevertheless, Honorius not only accepted the formula, but took it a step further. Since the Word of God acted through both natures (human and divine), he had only one will. In a second letter the pope rejected the formula "two wills," although he strongly defended the teaching of the Council of Chalcedon (451) that in Christ there are two natures, one human and one divine. Honorius and Sergius's position came to be known as the heresy of Monothelitism and was condemned by the Third Council of Constantinople (681), which read aloud and condemned his two letters to Sergius for having "confirmed his [Sergius's] wicked dogmas."

Because Honorius's formula of the "one will" was incorporated in Emperor Heraclius's decree on the subject, called the *Ecthesis* (638), which came to be regarded as the classic expression of Monothelitism, the council censured Pope Honorius (along with others) by name: "But since, from the first, the contriver of evil did not rest, finding an accomplice in the serpent and through him bringing upon human nature the poisoned dart of death, so too now he has found instruments suited to his own purpose— namely . . . Honorius, who was pope of elder Rome . . . —and has not been idle in raising through them obstacles of error against the full body of the church, sowing with novel speech among the orthodox people the heresy of a single will and a single principle of action in the two natures of the one member of the holy Trinity. . . ." The condemnation, or anathema, was explicitly ratified by Pope Leo II in 683 when he approved the acts of the council in a letter to the emperor Constantine IV. Honorius was thereby joined with Pope Vigilius (537–55), who had been excommunicated by a synod of African bishops in 550 and put under a doctrinal cloud by the Second Council of Constantinople in 553 for his vacillation on a similar matter of Christological doctrine (see Vigilius, number 59, above).

The record of both popes (Honorius and Vigilius) was cited by opponents of papal infallibility at the First Vatican Council (1869–70). Honorius's condemnation was specifically discussed in the negotiations in the fifteenth century regarding the possible reunion between Catholic and Orthodox churches, and again in the seventeenth and eighteenth centuries during the controversies over Gallicanism (a French-based movement to assert greater local autonomy for the church in France over against Rome). The arguments subsequently employed in defense of the pope were that he was guilty only of imprudent expression, not heresy, and that he was not teaching in a solemn or definitive manner for the universal Church.

Otherwise, Honorius was a reasonably successful pope. He ended a local schism in Italy. Like Gregory the Great (590–604), he turned the papal residence into a monastery, actively supported the young church in Britain, conferring the pallium (the woolen vestment worn around the neck of an archbishop as a symbol of pastoral authority) on the archbishops of Canterbury and York and sending congratulations to King Edwin of Northumbria on the occasion of his baptism, reformed the education of the clergy, and assumed temporal responsibilities the civil authorities could no longer manage. He restored the Roman aqueducts, maintained the corn supply, and acted as paymaster for the imperial troops. He was such an efficient administrator of the papal estates that he never lacked for funds for the building, maintenance, and improvement of the churches of Rome, including the complete restoration of St. Peter's, where he was eventually buried with the epitaph "leader of the common people."

71 Severinus, *May 28–August 2, 640.*

Already elderly at the time of his election, Severinus had to wait almost twenty months before receiving imperial approval for his consecration because he refused to accept the emperor's *Ecthesis* (638), the classic expression of Monothelitism (a heresy that held that in Christ there is only one will, not two). In the meantime, the pope-elect was subject to brutal treatment. The imperial troops surrounded the papal residence at the Lateran Palace for three days, demanding to be paid. The papal treasury was subsequently plundered and the contents divided between the soldiers and civic officials. Severinus died two months after his consecration, before having to take a definitive stand on the *Ecthesis*.

Elected by the anti-Gregorian, pro-diocesan clergy faction, Severinus raised the pay of his diocesan clergy and granted them a full year's salary upon his death. He was buried in St. Peter's.

72 John IV, *Dalmatian, December 24, 640–October 12, 642.*

Although he was the son of the legal adviser to the imperial exarch at Ravenna, John IV refused to endorse the imperial line on Monothelitism (the heresy that held that in Christ there is only one divine will, and not a human will as well). In January 641 he held a synod in Rome to condemn Monothelitism as heretical. When the new patriarch of Constantinople, Pyrrhus I, appealed to Pope Honorius's endorsement of Emperor Heraclius's *Ecthesis* (the classic expression of Monothelitism, which the emperor himself later repudiated before his death), John IV wrote to the new emperor, Constantine III, to express his disgust at the patriarch's attempt to link his predecessor with heretical views and to demand that copies of the *Ecthesis* be taken down from their public postings in Constantinople.

Concerned about the plight of his homeland, he sent an abbot to Dalmatia (modern-day Croatia) with substantial sums of money to ransom captives taken into slavery by the Avar and Slav invaders and later endowed a chapel next to the Lateran baptistery for the relics of Dalmatian martyrs that the abbot brought back to Rome.

There is one interesting development connected with his election to the papacy. While he was awaiting official confirmation from the emperor (in this instance, a period of five months), the Roman church sent an official letter to certain Irish bishops and abbots censuring their custom of observing Easter on the day of the Jewish Passover rather than on the following Sunday and also warning them against Pelagianism (a heresy that held that one can be saved by human effort alone, without the aid of grace). What is striking about this document is that the pope-elect was the second signatory, not the first, and that the first signatory, the archpriest Hilarus, and the chief secretary (also named John) described themselves as "vicegerents of the Apostolic See." For a long period of church history, election to the papacy was sufficient for validity. If that were the case in this time period, John IV would have already been pope and would have functioned as such. But apparently it was not: since the pope is Bishop of Rome, John could not be pope unless and until he was ordained a bishop. That is once again the present canonical requirement: election *and* ordination as a bishop, if the one elected is not already a bishop (can. 332.1).

John IV died on October 12, 642, and was buried in St. Peter's.

73 Theodore I, *Greek, November 24, 642–May 14, 649.*

Theodore I was an implacable foe of Monothelitism (the heresy that held that in Christ there is only one divine will, not two: divine and human). A Greek, born in Jerusalem and the son of a bishop, Theodore probably came to Rome as a refugee from the Arab invasions of the Holy City. The choice of an Easterner with close ties to opponents of Monothelitism indicated the electors' desire to resist the imperial pressure in support of this heresy. One of the new pope's first acts was to write to the boy-emperor Constans II to ask why the *Ecthesis* (the imperial decree in support of Monothelitism) was still in force despite its repudiation by Pope John IV and even by its author, the emperor Heraclius, before his death on February 11, 641. The pope also wrote to Paul II, the new patriarch of Constantinople, demanding that he repudiate the *Ecthesis* and have it removed from public places in the city. When the exiled patriarch Pyrrhus I renounced the *Ecthesis* after being defeated in a public debate with Maximus the Confessor in Carthage, he went to Rome, made a public profession of faith in St. Peter's, and was received by the pope with great honors and was recognized anew as the rightful bishop of Constantinople. The pope excommunicated and deposed the sitting patriarch, Paul II, who came out in support of the *Ecthesis*. But when Pyrrhus I failed to regain his patriarchal throne, he went to Ravenna, renounced his recantation, and made his peace with the imperial court. Pope Theodore thereupon convoked a synod and excommunicated Pyrrhus. It is said that he signed the decree on St. Peter's tomb in consecrated eucharistic wine.

By 648 the young emperor Constans II had come to the realization that the *Ecthesis* had failed to reconcile the Monophysites (heretics who held that in Christ there is only one divine nature, and not a human nature as well) in the East and was so unpopular in the West that it threatened political stability. Therefore, he promulgated a decree known as the *Typos* ("Rule"), which abrogated the *Ecthesis,* prohibited all further discussion of the number of wills in Christ, and ordered that official church teaching should be limited to what had been defined by the first five ecumenical councils (thereby excluding the Third Council of Constantinople, which had condemned Monothelitism as heretical). When the papal nuncio in Constantinople refused to sign it, he was arrested and exiled. The Latin chapel in the Placidia Palace, official residence of the papal nuncios, was closed down and its altar demolished. Pope Theodore died on May 14, 649, before issuing an official response to the *Typos,* which surely would have been strongly negative. He was buried in St. Peter's.

74 **Martin I, St.,** *d. September 16, 655, pope from July 5, 649, to August 10, 654 (the Vatican's official list gives as the end of his pontificate September 16, 655, the day of his death in exile, rather than August 10, 654, the day a successor, Eugenius I, was elected).*

Martin I was the last pope to be recognized as a martyr. He was also the first pope in decades to be consecrated without waiting for imperial approval, an act that infuriated the emperor, Constans II, who refused to recognize him as a legitimate pope. A strong and resolute opponent of Monothelitism (the heresy that held that in Christ there is only one divine will, not two: human and divine), Martin I paid a heavy personal price for his defense of Catholic orthodoxy.

Three months after his election, the new pope held a synod, attended by 105 Western bishops and a number of exiled Greek clergy, which affirmed the doctrine of the two wills in Christ and condemned both Monothelitism and the emperor's *Typos* (the decree banning further discussion of the number of wills in Christ). Martin then excommunicated Bishop Paul of Thessalonica for refusing to subscribe to the synod's decisions and appointed an orthodox apostolic vicar for Palestine, the intellectual center of Monothelitism. He also sent a copy of the synodal decisions to the emperor, inviting him to repudiate the heresy, while diplomatically laying the blame for the heresy on certain patriarchs rather than on the emperor himself. The emperor, in turn, sent Olympius as exarch to Italy with orders to arrest the pope and bring him to Constantinople (others say it was to assassinate the pope). But Olympius soon discovered that such a move was impossible because of the widespread support for the pope (a pious version is that Olympius was struck blind and converted). He subsequently joined the pope against the emperor.

In the summer of 653 a new exarch, Theodore Calliopas, seized the pope, bedridden from gout, in the Lateran Basilica, where he had taken sanctuary. The exarch handed the clergy an imperial decree declaring that Martin was not the legal pope and was therefore deposed. The exarch smuggled the ailing pope out of Rome and forced him onto a ship to Constantinople on June 17, 653. The ship arrived in September 653 and, after three months of solitary confinement, the pope was tried for treason, allegedly for having supported Olympius in his attempts to gain the throne. During the trial, Martin was treated not as a pope but as a rebellious deacon and former papal nuncio. He was publicly stripped of his episcopal robes, his tunic was ripped asunder from top to bottom, and he was put in chains. He was found guilty, condemned to death, and publicly flogged. However, the dying patriarch of Constantinople, Paul II, pleaded for Martin's life and the sentence was commuted to exile. After three more months in prison under terrible conditions, the pope was taken by ship to Chersonesus in the Crimea, where he died on September 16, 655, from the effects of starvation and harsh conditions and treatment. He was buried there in a church dedicated to the Blessed Virgin Mary.

Martin's situation in exile was exacerbated by the lack of support he received from the church in Rome. Not only did it not come to his aid, but it even elected a successor while he was still alive. Was his successor, Eugenius I, a legitimate pope? Can the Church have two popes at the same time? These are the kinds of questions that challenge much mistaken popular belief about the papacy, even today.

The ending date of his pontificate given above, therefore, is in some doubt. Some (even J. N. D. Kelly) place it on the day he was deported to Constantinople and therefore no longer in a position to lead the Roman church. Others place it on the day a successor was elected. Others place it on the day of his death in exile. His successor, Eugenius I, accepted election while Martin I was still alive, but only after the Roman clergy had waited more than a year, all the while resisting pressure from the emperor

Constans II to replace Martin. Eugenius and the other Roman clergy probably concluded that Martin would never return to Rome and that if they waited any longer, the emperor would impose a Monothelite pope on the Church. It may have been a matter of choosing the lesser of two evils. However, a month or so before Eugenius was elected, Martin sent a letter to a friend in Constantinople in which he mentioned three ecclesiastical officials who were acting as his deputies in governing the Roman church. And just before his death on September 16, 655, he sent another letter to his friend, mentioning that he prayed especially "for the one who is now ruling over the Church." Was this a tacit acquiescence or approval of Eugenius's election? We do not know. Accordingly, even though the official *Annuario Pontificio* begins Eugenius's pontificate in 654, he cannot be considered incontestably to have been pope until after Martin's death a year later. (Ideally, Martin should have resigned in order to remove all ambiguity about Eugenius's election during his imprisonment in exile.) One wonders, in the meantime, why the *Annuario Pontificio* lists the end of Martin's pontificate as September 16, 655, and the beginning of Eugenius I's as August 10, 654. Does the Vatican wish to affirm that the Catholic Church at one time had two legitimately elected and consecrated popes serving concurrently? That would be an extraordinary assertion indeed. But that is exactly what the Vatican's official list of popes implies.

Although the Third Council of Constantinople (680–81) could not rehabilitate Martin I some twenty-five years later because it was under the control of Constans II's son Constantine IV, it was not long after that council that the Roman church came to venerate Martin I as a martyr, and he is actually mentioned by name in the Mass in the Bobbio Missal (an eighth-century collection of liturgical texts). Feast day: April 13 (formerly November 12).

75 Eugenius [Eugene] I, St., *August 10, 654–June 2, 657.*

Eugenius I is best known for the dubious circumstances under which he was elected to the papacy. His predecessor, Martin I, was still alive in exile. Eugenius was elected and consecrated on August 10, 654, but Martin I did not die until September 16 of the following year. There is no evidence that Martin resigned the papacy, although he did know that someone had been elected to succeed him and, in a letter to a friend in Constantinople, acknowledged that he was praying for the one placed over the Roman church. The Vatican's official list of popes, given in the *Annuario Pontificio,* places the end of Martin I's pontificate on September 16, 655, and the beginning of Eugenius I's on August 10, 654. According to the *Annuario,* therefore, there were two legitimate popes occupying the Chair of Peter simultaneously! It seems theologically appropriate to characterize Martin I's lengthy exile as tantamount to a resignation (much like an individual who is declared legally dead after a certain amount of time has elapsed) and Eugenius I's election, therefore, as pastorally prudent and canonically valid, even though Martin was still alive in distant exile.

Indeed, it seemed clear to the Roman clergy that Martin I was never going to return from exile and that if they waited any longer (they had already stalled for a year, in spite of pressure from the emperor to elect a successor), the emperor might impose a Monothelite pope (that is, someone who agreed with the heretical view that in Christ there is only one divine will, not two: human and divine). A mild, elderly priest (presbyter) at the time of his election, the new pope immediately sent envoys to Constantinople to restore friendly relations between Rome and the emperor. The emperor insisted that they recognize Peter, the new patriarch of Constantinople, who proposed to them a compromise formula stating that, while each of Christ's two natures had its own will, the divine Person possessed only one will. Even though this seemed to suggest that Christ actually had three wills (one for each nature and one for the divine Person), the papal representatives accepted the formula and entered into communion with the new patriarch. The patriarch handed them his profession of faith to be taken back to pope. When it was read out in the basilica of St. Mary Major, however, the clergy and laity were so outraged that they prevented the pope from continuing with Mass until he promised to reject the formula. Eugenius I relented, and a schism was begun once again between Rome and Constantinople. The emperor threatened to do to Eugenius what he had already done to Martin I, but at the time he was distracted with warfare on another front. Before any action could be taken against the pope, Eugenius I was dead (June 2, 657). He was buried in St. Peter's, but his name was not included in the martyrologies until inserted into the Roman Martyrology by the church historian Caesare Baronius (d. 1607). Feast day: June 2.

76 Vitalian, St., *July 30, 657–January 27, 672.*

Unlike some of his immediate predecessors, Pope Vitalian adopted a conciliatory attitude toward imperial and ecclesiastical Constantinople on the question of Monothelitism (the heresy that posited only one will, not two, in Jesus Christ). In return, the emperor Constans II sent the pope elaborate gifts and officially confirmed various privileges for the Roman church, while the patriarch Peter included the pope's name among those to be prayed for at Mass, the first pope to be so included since Honorius

I (625–38). When the emperor paid an official visit to Rome in 663, the pope and the Roman clergy greeted him with pomp and circumstance, ignoring the brutal treatment he had inflicted on Pope Martin I (649–54) and the publication of the *Typos* (a decree that banned further discussion of the wills of Jesus Christ and that was formally condemned as blasphemous by the Lateran synod of 649). However, the emperor did not do everything to the pope's liking. For example, against the pope's objections he transformed Ravenna into an independent see that had the right of electing its own bishop, subject only to imperial confirmation.

When the emperor was assassinated in 668, Pope Vitalian gave his strong support to the emperor's son Constantine IV against the army's preferred choice of a successor. In gratitude, the new emperor did not enforce his father's decree (the *Typos*), leaving the pope free to teach the orthodox doctrine that in Christ there are two wills (divine and human), not one (divine). The emperor even refused to accept the official documents of the new patriarch, John IV, because he deemed them unorthodox. When the next patriarch, Theodore, tried in retaliation to erase the pope's name from the list of those to be prayed for at Mass, Constantine IV resisted the move.

Pope Vitalian had a deep concern for the church in Britain and supported the efforts of the king of Northumbria, following the Synod of Whitby (664), to establish in England the Roman, as opposed to the Celtic, date for Easter (that is, the Sunday after the Jewish Passover, rather than the day of Passover itself) and other Roman practices as well. The pope consecrated Theodore of Tarsus, a Greek monk living in Rome, as the new archbishop of Canterbury in 668, but took care that the new archbishop did not impose Greek ideas or customs in his see. In Rome Vitalian supported the music school at the Lateran in order to train singers for the more elaborate Byzantine-style rites. The chanters were called "Vitaliani." Vitalian died on January 27, 672, and was buried in St. Peter's. Feast day: January 27.

77 Adeodatus II, *April 11, 672–June 17, 676.*

Very little is known about the pontificate of Adeodatus II. An elderly monk when elected, he rejected the synodical letters and profession of faith sent to him by Constantine I, the new patriarch of Constantinople, who like several of his predecessors was a Monothelite (a heretic who held that in Jesus Christ there is only one divine will, and not a human will as well). The pope did have a reputation for kindness and generosity to the poor, to pilgrims, and to his clergy. He was buried in St. Peter's.

78 Donus, *November 2, 676–April 11, 678.*

Like many other early pontificates, including that of his immediate predecessor, Donus's pontificate was generally wrapped in obscurity. Already elderly when elected in August (he had to wait about three months
for imperial approval of his consecration), he did reach an understanding with the archbishop of Ravenna whereby the latter abandoned his
see's claim to be completely independent of Rome in terms of governance and the appointment of bishops, a privilege granted by the emperor in 666 (see Vitalian, number 76, above). Donus also discovered that
the Syrian monks occupying a well-known Roman monastery were actually Nestorians (heretics who held that in Jesus Christ there were two persons, one divine and one human, rather than one divine Person). He
replaced the monks with orthodox monks and dispersed the Nestorians
to a number of other monasteries. It is said that Donus was an active
builder and restorer of churches and that he laid down a marble pavement in the atrium of St. Peter's. He died on April 11, 678, and was buried
four days later in St. Peter's.

79 Agatho, St., *June 27, 678–January 10, 681.*

Agatho's pontificate was marked by the end of imperial support for
Monothelitism (the heresy that held that in Jesus Christ there is only
one divine will rather than two wills, one divine and one human) and by
the restoration of friendly relations between Rome and Constantinople.
It was soon after his election (date unknown) and consecration that
Agatho received a letter from the emperor Constantine IV (a letter originally addressed to Agatho's predecessor, Donus) proposing a conference
at which the whole issue of the wills of Christ could be discussed and by
which unity between Rome and Constantinople might be restored. The
emperor had come to realize that support for Monothelitism was no
longer a viable strategy for reconciling the Monophysites (heretics who
held that in Jesus Christ there is only one divine nature rather than two,
human and divine) in the East.

Agatho welcomed the emperor's idea and invitation but decided to
hold some preparatory synods in the West (the largest and most important was held in Rome in 680; others were held in Milan, England, and
Gaul) in order to formulate a united position on Monothelitism to take
to the council. The papal delegation to Constantinople included two future popes (John V and Constantine) and brought with it two lengthy
documents: a letter from the pope to the emperor condemning
Monothelitism and stressing Rome's role in preserving the true faith and

the decree of the Roman synod, signed by 150 bishops, condemning Monothelitism.

The emperor decided to upgrade the conference to a general council (the Third Council of Constantinople), to meet in the imperial palace (November 7, 680–September 16, 681) and to be presided over by the emperor himself. Beforehand he replaced the Monothelite patriarch of Constantinople with an orthodox patriarch and instructed him to order all the bishops under his jurisdiction to attend the council. At the council's thirteenth session it condemned (anathematized) the Monothelite leaders, including Pope Honorius I (625–38) for his approval of the Monothelite formula, "two distinct natures but one operation," but only after overcoming the objections of the understandably reluctant papal delegates. (The emperor withheld his approval of the election of Agatho's successor until the delegates dropped their objections.) The condemnation read: "But since, from the first, the contriver of evil did not rest, finding an accomplice in the serpent and through him bringing upon human nature the poisoned dart of death, so too now he has found instruments suited to his own purpose—namely . . . Honorius, who was pope of elder Rome . . . —and has not been idle in raising through them obstacles of error against the full body of the church, sowing with novel speech among the orthodox people the heresy of a single will and a single principle of action in the two natures of the one member of the holy Trinity. . . ." The condemnation, or anathema, was explicitly ratified by Pope Leo II in 683 when he approved the acts of the council in a letter to emperor Constantine IV. Pope Agatho had died eight months before the council ended, but his contribution was acknowledged in the council's congratulatory address to the emperor, which acknowledged that Peter had spoken through Agatho.

Agatho finalized the terms of the agreement with the archbishop of Ravenna (initiated by his predecessor Donus) whereby future archbishops of Ravenna would be consecrated by the pope and receive the pallium (the woolen vestment worn around the neck as a sign of pastoral authority) from him. Given an acute shortage of funds in the Roman church, Agatho succeeded in having the emperor abolish the tax assessed on the occasion of papal elections. In return for that concession, however, the emperor restored the earlier, time-consuming practice of seeking imperial approval for papal consecrations from Constantinople rather than from the exarch in Ravenna. Agatho also supported the bishop of York's appeal to Rome against the archbishop of Canterbury's unexpected division of York into three separate dioceses and also promoted the spread of the Roman liturgy in Britain. Widely regarded as a kindly, cheerful person, he died during an epidemic on January 10, 681 (one source says he was 107 years old), and was buried in St. Peter's. He came to be venerated in the East and the West alike. Feast day: January 10.

80 Leo II, St., *August 17, 682–July 3, 683.*

A Sicilian, Leo II was the pope who formally approved the acts of the Third Council of Constantinople (680–81), which condemned Monothelitism (a heresy that held that in Jesus Christ there is only one divine will rather than a human and a divine will) and which also included an explicit condemnation of a previous pope, Honorius I (625–38), for doctrinal deviation. Honorius had given his approval in 638 to an imperial document known as the *Ecthesis,* which supported Monothelitism. In the Latin text of his letter of May 7, 683, to the emperor Constantine IV, Leo II spoke of Honorius as having "attempted to undermine the pure faith by his profane betrayal." In the Greek text, however, the words were softened to: "by his betrayal he permitted the pure teaching to be tainted." In letters to the Spanish and perhaps other Western bishops, Leo II only accused Honorius of being negligent in extinguishing the flame of heresy.

Elected in January 681, the new pope had to wait eighteen months before receiving imperial approval for his consecration. The letters from the guardians of the Holy See (those responsible for its governance during a vacancy) to Constantinople announcing Pope Agatho's death and Leo II's election reached there on March 10 while the council was in progress. However, the emperor deliberately delayed his ratification of the election until the council had formally condemned Pope Honorius I and other leading advocates of Monothelitism and until Rome's approval of the council's condemnations had been assured. The Roman legates at the council were extremely reluctant to agree to the condemnation of a previous pope and it required lengthy negotiations, even after the adjournment of the council in September, to gain their acquiescence. The emperor's withholding approval of Leo II's consecration proved a powerful incentive. It was not until the following July (682) that the envoys returned to Rome with the acts of the council and the imperial mandate for Leo II's consecration. By exception, the *Liber Pontificalis* (a collection of early papal biographies) noted the names of Leo II's consecrators: Andrea, bishop of Ostia; Giovanni, bishop of Porto; and Piacentino, bishop of Velletri. These were three of Rome's neighboring (or suburbicarian) dioceses.

The emperor Constantine IV showed his approval of the newly elected pope's cooperation by inviting him to send a resident papal nuncio to the imperial court in Constantinople and by lowering the taxes on the papal patrimonies in Sicily and Calabria as well as the corn requisition for the army. The emperor also revoked the decree of his predecessor Constans II (666) granting the archdiocese of Ravenna independence from Rome in the naming of its archbishops. Thereafter, they would be consecrated by the pope and granted the pallium (the woolen vestment worn around the neck as a sign of pastoral authority) by him as well. Leo II, in turn, had the acts of the council translated into Latin and circulated to all ecclesiastical and political leaders in the West, with his mandate that they be accepted. Given the new understanding with the see of Ravenna, the pope exempted it from fees traditionally levied at the time of its archbishop's consecration and also dispensed him from the obligation of personally attending the annual Roman synod.

A well-trained singer in the papal choir school prior to his election to the papacy, Leo II was deeply concerned with the promotion of church music. He was also celebrated for his devotion to the poor and his efforts to improve their condition. He died on July 3, 683, and was buried in St. Peter's. In 1607 Paul V had the remains moved to a place under the altar in the basilica's Chapel of the Madonna della Colonna, where three other popes are buried: Leo III, Leo IV, and Leo XII. Feast day: July 3.

81 Benedict II, St., *June 26, 684–May 8, 685.*

Serving less than a year as pope, Benedict II was known primarily for his humility, gentleness, and love for the poor. He had to wait nearly a year from the time of his election by the Roman clergy in early July 683 until the emperor sent formal approval of his consecration. The emperor also granted the new pope's request that the imperial exarch in Ravenna be allowed, as before, to grant such approvals for papal consecrations, thereby reducing the time between a papal election and consecration.

Benedict II confirmed his predecessor's support of the Third Council of Constantinople (680–81) and sent a delegate to Spain with copies of the acts of the council and Leo II's letters. But the strongly independent Visigothic church of Spain did not approve the acts of the council without subjecting them first to an exhaustively analytical examination at the Fourteenth Council of Toledo (684). When the archbishop of Toledo learned that the pope had been verbally critical of some passages in a profession of faith that he had sent to Benedict II following the council, he sent the pope a blistering protest. The pope was also unsuccessful in persuading Macarius I, the deposed Monothelite patriarch of Antioch now residing in a Roman monastery, to abandon his heretical views. He did carry out restorations of various Roman churches, including St. Peter's, where he was buried after his death on May 8, 685. Feast day: May 7.

82 John V, *Syrian, July 23, 685–August 2, 686.*

Because his short pontificate was marked by illness, John V established practically no record at all. Like Leo II (682–83), he was consecrated by the bishops of Ostia, Porto, and Velletri, three of Rome's neighboring (or suburbicarian) dioceses. John V suspended a bishop in Sardinia for having consecrated another bishop in his province without permission from Rome, and he was also generous in his will to his clergy, the charitable monasteries of Rome, and the lay sacristans of churches.

His life before becoming pope was more interesting. A Syrian from Antioch (probably a refugee from the Arab invasions), as a deacon he was one of three representatives sent by Pope Agatho to the Third Council of Constantinople (680–81); he took a leading role in its discussions and personally brought back to Rome copies of the acts of the council and the emperor's letter approving Leo II's election. He was archdeacon when he was unanimously elected to the papacy. He was buried in St. Peter's.

83 Conon, *Thracian, October 21, 686–September 21, 687.*

A compromise candidate elected in old age, Conon had a short, but unfortunate, pontificate. He nominated a deacon of the church of Syracuse as rector of the papal patrimony in Sicily, a lucrative post traditionally reserved for a member of the Roman clergy, and allowed him the use of ceremonial saddlecloths that were also reserved for members of the Roman clergy. Moreover, his appointee proved to be an extortionist. The papal tenants revolted and the rector was arrested and deported by the governor of Sicily.

Conon had been a compromise choice between the archpriest Peter, favored by the clergy, and the priest Theodore, favored by the local militia, which prevented the clergy from entering the Lateran Basilica for the election. When negotiations between the two sides failed, the clergy put forward the elderly, uncommitted Conon who, because his father had been an army general, was also acceptable to the militia. J. N. D Kelly describes this pope as "[u]nworldly and of saintly appearance, . . . simple-minded and continuously ill." His election and performance in office left the Roman church deeply divided. Conon was buried in St. Peter's.

84 Sergius I, St., *Syrian, December 15, 687–September 8, 701.*

A strong pope, Sergius I asserted the authority of the Bishop of Rome in the West and resisted the efforts of the emperor Justinian II in the East to make the pope bow to his will. Thus, he consecrated Damian as the new archbishop of Ravenna in Rome (the first such papal consecration since 666, when Ravenna was declared autonomous), baptized Caedwalla, the young king of the West Saxons, granted the pallium (the woolen vestment worn around the neck as a symbol of pastoral authority) to Beorhtweald, the new archbishop of Canterbury, ordered that Wilfrid be restored to the see of York, authorized Willibrord's mission to Frisia and consecrated him later as archbishop of the Frisians, and received the see of Aquileia back into communion with Rome, ending a schism begun in 553. And when the emperor demanded that the pope approve the acts of a council he called in 692, ostensibly to complete the work of the Second and Third Councils of Constantinople (553 and 680–81, respectively), Sergius I refused.

The council (known as the Trullan Council because it met in the domed room ["trullus"] of the imperial palace) had not included any Western bishops, ignored Western canon law, banned certain practices observed in the West (such as clerical celibacy and the Saturday fast in Lent), and expressly renewed the twenty-eighth canon of the Council of Chalcedon (451), granting Constantinople equivalent status to Rome. When the emperor learned of the pope's response, he sent the commander of the imperial bodyguard to force the pope to sign or to arrest him and bring him to Constantinople. But the imperial troops in Ravenna and elsewhere rallied to the pope's support, forced their way into Rome, and hunted down the imperial commander. Only the pope's pleas saved the man's life. The humiliated emperor was overthrown and exiled in 695.

Sergius I's election was marked by great division in Rome. Upon the death of his predecessor, Conon, one faction of the Roman clergy elected the archdeacon Paschal (who promised a bribe to the imperial exarch in Ravenna in return for his support) and the other elected the archpriest Theodore. Because of the stalemate, leading public officials, army officers, and the majority of the Roman clergy met in the Palatine Palace and unanimously chose Sergius. Sergius was installed in the Lateran only after its gates were stormed, because it had been occupied by the rival factions and their candidates. Theodore thereupon withdrew his claim to the papal throne and endorsed the election of Sergius, but Paschal held out until the exarch came to Rome with the intention of overturning the election of Sergius. Upon his arrival, however, the exarch saw the popular support for Sergius, threw his own support to him as well, and issued the necessary imperial mandate for his consecration (but only after obliging Sergius to hand over the one hundred pounds of gold that Paschal had originally promised him).

Sergius I restored many Roman churches, including the basilicas of St. Peter's and of St. Paul's. He also removed the remains of Pope Leo the

Great (440–61) from their inconspicuous resting place to an ornate tomb in a prominent place in St. Peter's. An accomplished singer himself, he introduced the singing of the Agnus Dei ("Lamb of God") at Mass and processions on the four principal feasts of the Blessed Virgin Mary. He was buried in St. Peter's and there is some indication that a cult developed soon after his death. Feast day: September 8.

85 John VI, *Greek, October 30, 701–January 11, 705.*

Very little of enduring importance or interest seems to have occurred during John VI's pontificate. Elected and consecrated on the same day, he did spend large sums of money ransoming prisoners taken during battles in defense of papal territories under attack from the duke of Benevento. He was also instrumental in saving the life of the imperial exarch Theophylact when he was threatened by mutinous members of the Italian militia. In 703 Wilfrid of York came once again to Rome after having been driven from his diocese a third time. The pope held a four-month-long synod in 704 that supported Wilfrid. In the only letter remaining from John VI's pontificate, the pope asked the kings of Northumbria and Mercia to direct the archbishop of Canterbury to reach a settlement of the matter at a synod. Failing that, all parties should come to Rome to work toward a solution in a fuller council. He died on January 11, 705, and was buried in St. Peter's.

86 John VII, *Greek, March 1, 705–October 18, 707.*

John VII was the first pope who was the son of an imperial official, an individual responsible for the maintenance of the imperial palace on the Palatine. Elected and consecrated on the same day, the new pope enjoyed good relations with the Lombards, whose king returned valuable estates in the Cottian Alps that had been taken from the papacy in previous military actions. In 706, however, the ruthless emperor Justinian II, who had been overthrown in 695, returned to power and sent two bishops to Rome with copies of the canons of the Trullan Council (692). Pope Sergius I had firmly refused to sign these documents. John VII was less forthright. He simply returned the documents unsigned without expressing assent or dissent. In other matters, he showed a readiness to defer to Byzantine policy, for example, in the matter of church decorations. A patron of the arts and a builder, he constructed a new papal residence at the foot of the Palatine and restored a number of churches, adorning them with mosaics and frescoes, some of which included representations of himself. One such mosaic is extant in the crypt of St. Peter's. John VII died on October 18, 707, and was buried in a Chapel of the Blessed Virgin Mary, which he had added to St. Peter's Basilica.

87 Sisinnius, *Syrian, January 15–February 4, 708.*

Although greatly respected for his high moral character and pastoral sensitivity, the aged Sisinnius was so crippled with gout at the time of his election and consecration on January 15, 708, that he could not even use his hands to feed himself. His only recorded ecclesiastical act was the consecration of the bishop of Corsica. He also ordered the walls of Rome to be reinforced, but he died before the job could be undertaken—only twenty days after his election. He was buried in St. Peter's.

88 Constantine, *Syrian, March 25, 708–April 9, 715.*

The key event in Constantine's pontificate was his yearlong trip to Constantinople at the request of the emperor Justinian II and in the hope of normalizing relations between Rome and Constantinople. The pope was received enthusiastically everywhere along the journey, and upon his arrival in Constantinople was greeted by the emperor himself, who kissed the pope's feet and received absolution and Holy Communion from him as well. Successful negotiations were held between papal and imperial sides at Nicomedia. The deacon Gregory (the future Pope Gregory II, Constantine's immediate successor) was convincing in his explanation of the pope's objections to a number of the canons approved by the Trullan Council of 692 (because of their anti-Western content and tone), and the pope himself seems to have given at least verbal approval to other canons. The emperor was so pleased with the results that he published a decree confirming the privileges of the Roman church.

Pope Constantine returned to Rome on October 24, 711, after a long journey marked by illness. Less than two weeks later the emperor was murdered by mutinous troops and was succeeded by Philippicus Bardanes, a fanatical Monothelite (a heretic who held that in Jesus Christ there is only one divine will, rather than a divine and a human will). The new emperor sent the pope his own Monothelite profession of faith and demanded that the pope accept it. Pope Constantine refused. The emperor's name was dropped from the list of those to be prayed for at Mass and his image was removed from churches. When the imperial exarch, headquartered in Ravenna, tried to enforce the emperor's demand, the Roman citizenry rebelled and there were bloody battles in the streets. The pope and his clergy pleaded for calm. Happily, the emperor was overthrown and his successor promptly assured the pope of his own orthodoxy and his acceptance of the teaching of the Third Council of Constantinople on the two wills of Christ (680–81). Pope Constantine died on April 9, 715, and was buried in St. Peter's.

89 Gregory II, St., *ca. 669–731, pope from May 19, 715, to February 11, 731.*

The first Roman to be elected pope after seven consecutive popes of Greek, Syrian, or Thracian background, Gregory II was perhaps the outstanding pope of the eighth century. He persuaded the Lombard king to return valuable papal properties, led the resistance of the Italian people to the new, heavy taxes imposed by the emperor Leo III, and saved the city of Rome from a siege mounted by the Lombard king and the imperial exarch. He also firmly resisted the emperor's efforts to ban the use and veneration of sacred images (known as iconoclasm) out of concern, the emperor insisted, that such practices were an obstacle to the conversion of Jews and Muslims. The pope formally rebuked the emperor at a Roman synod in 727.

Nevertheless, the new policy of iconoclasm was officially promulgated in an edict signed by the patriarch of Constantinople in 730. Gregory II stoutly refused to support it, even branding iconoclasm as a heresy, and warned the emperor that he was exceeding his temporal authority. The Italian populace resented the emperor's ultimatum to the pope, and there were uprisings in the north. Indeed, the emperor had contemplated assassinating the pope, but thought better of it because of the pope's strong support among the people.

Gregory II was also celebrated for his support of the mission to Germany in the person of Boniface (d. 754), a name given to Wynfrith by the pope himself. Boniface had come to Rome from England in 718 and left the following year, under direct commission from Gregory II, to evangelize the people of Frisia. In his instructions to the missionaries, the pope counseled leniency in dealing with marriage among the newly converted Germans, authorizing separation in certain cases and other exceptions to marriage laws. Given Boniface's success, the pope consecrated him a bishop in 722 and gave him a letter of recommendation to Charles Martel, ruler of the Franks (d. 741), who would provide protection for Boniface's missionary work. Because of the close working relationship between Boniface and Gregory II, Roman liturgical practice was adopted everywhere in the emerging German church.

At home, the pope repaired the walls of the city ravaged by war, initiated repairs made necessary by the flooding of the Tiber River, extensively restored many churches, and promoted monasticism, especially the Benedictines, by rebuilding and repopulating deserted and decaying monasteries, including the famous Monte Cassino, reduced to ruins by the Lombards. He was also liturgically active, introducing a Mass for the Thursdays of Lent. Evidence of his cult first appeared in the ninth-century martyrology of Ado. Gregory II died on February 11, 731, and was buried in St. Peter's. Feast day: February 11.

90 Gregory III, St., *Syrian, March 18, 731–November 28, 741 (the Vatican's official list gives only the month of November as the end of his pontificate).*

Gregory III, a Syrian by birth, was seized by cheering crowds at the funeral of Gregory II, brought to the Lateran, and elected pope by popular acclaim. He was consecrated five weeks later after obtaining official approval from the imperial exarch in Ravenna. He was the last pope to seek such approval. His pontificate was marked by growing tensions over iconoclasm (the emperor's policy of forbidding the display and use of sacred images). The new pope urged the emperor Leo III to back away from the policy, but when he received no reply, he called a synod which condemned iconoclasm and declared excommunicated anyone who destroyed sacred images. That would have included the emperor himself and the patriarch of Constantinople. However, the papal envoys who were carrying these decrees to the East were intercepted by imperial officials in Sicily and imprisoned. After one envoy successfully got through with the documents, the emperor decided to use force against the pope. He first dispatched an armed fleet to Italy, which was lost in a shipwreck, seized papal properties in Calabria and Sicily, and declared the ecclesiastical provinces of Illyricum and Sicily to be under the jurisdiction of the patriarch of Constantinople rather than the pope. And yet Gregory III remained loyal to the empire, viewing it as the only legitimate political authority. Indeed, the pope's support of the empire was crucial to the recapture of Ravenna from the Lombards in 733. Both the emperor and the exarch showed their gratitude, respectively, by making a truce with the pope and by donating six onyx columns that were placed in front of the tomb of St. Peter in the basilica.

Gregory III, however, realized that Rome was now vulnerable to attack by the Lombards. He rebuilt the walls of the city and restored those of Civitavecchia. He also entered into defensive alliances with the dukes of Spoleto and Benevento. The king of the Lombards was infuriated. After capturing Spoleto, he marched on Rome itself. Given the empire's weakened state, Gregory III called upon the Franks for help in the person of their ruler, Charles Martel (d. 741). But Charles refused, given his earlier alliance with the Lombard king in his fight against Arab invaders of Provence. The pope then entered into a politically disastrous alliance with the despised duke of Spoleto, thereby widening the gap between Rome and the Lombard king.

In church matters, the pope gave his full support, as his predecessor had, to the missionary efforts of Boniface (d. 754) in Germany, promoting him to archbishop in 732, with the authority to establish dioceses. The pope also strengthened relations with the English church, bestowing the pallium (the woolen vestment worn around the neck as a sign of pastoral authority) on Egbert of York and Tatwine of Canterbury and appointing the latter papal vicar for all of England. At the same time, he devoted his energies to the beautification of Rome and its churches, making a special point of erecting numerous colorful images in defiance of iconoclasm. He promoted monasticism, made necessary improvements in cemeteries, and constructed an oratory in St. Peter's, dedicated to Christ the Savior and the Blessed Virgin Mary, for the reception of relics of the saints. Gregory III died November 28, 741, and was buried in St. Peter's in the oratory he had built. The first evidence of his cult, like that of his predecessor, appears in the ninth-century martyrology of Ado. Feast day: November 28.

91 Zacharias [Zachary], St., *Greek, December 10, 741–March 22, 752.*

Zacharias was the last of the Greek popes and also the last pope to send official notification of his election to the imperial court and patriarch in Constantinople. Through personal diplomacy, he reestablished peaceful relations with the Lombards in northern Italy, although eight years later a new Lombard king revived the old expansionist policies, capturing Ravenna in 751 and then turning his attention toward Rome itself. Relations with Constantinople were also improved. Both the pope and the emperor played down their differences on the iconoclast controversy (the East opposed the use and veneration of sacred images; the West approved the practice). Indeed, the emperor bestowed two large estates in southern Italy upon the Holy See, perhaps because he had appreciated Zacharias's refusal to recognize a temporary usurper of the imperial throne and the pope's earlier efforts to persuade the Lombards to desist from their planned attack upon the imperial exarchy in Ravenna.

Like his two predecessors, Gregory II and Gregory III, Zacharias gave his full support to the missionary efforts of Boniface in Germany and through Boniface forged even closer relations between Rome and the Frankish church and kingdom. When Pepin III, son of the deceased Charles Martel (d. 741), sought a ruling from the pope on the status of his royal title, the pope decreed that it was better for the title to belong to the one who exercised effective authority than to one who had none. Subsequently, the last king of the Merovingian line was deposed (with papal approval) and Pepin, of the Carolingian line, was elected at Soissons in November 751. Boniface anointed him king. The pope's support for the transfer of power from the Merovingian to the Carolingian lines would have extraordinary significance later on in relations between the pope and the emperor.

Zacharias built no new churches, but continued Pope John VII's decorative work in Santa Maria Antiqua, where a contemporary fresco of him can still be seen. He also moved the papal residence back to the Lateran (John VII had moved it earlier to the Palatine). A learned and cultured man, Zacharias translated Pope Gregory the Great's *Dialogues* into Greek, making it possible for the work to be read widely in the East. Zacharias died on March 22, 752, and was buried in St. Peter's. Feast day: March 15 (in the West); September 5 (in the East).

92 Stephen II (III), *March 26, 752–April 26, 757.*

Stephen II (III) established the independence of the papacy from the Byzantine Empire and placed it under the protection of the Frankish kingdom, thereby shifting the sphere of influence over the papacy from the East to Western Europe. Stephen II (III) also formed the Papal States.

The confusion over whether he was the second or third Stephen in the papal line stems from the fact that an elderly Roman priest, who would have been Stephen II, was elected pope on March 22 or 23, 752, and was duly installed in the Lateran, but had a stroke three days later and died before being consecrated. In those years (as again today) consecration as a bishop, as well as the acceptance of one's valid election, was the essential canonical requirement, because the pope is the Bishop of Rome. The *Annuario Pontificio* (the official Vatican directory) included the original Stephen II in its official list of popes until 1960, but suppressed his name in 1961, giving all subsequent popes called Stephen a dual numbering. This Stephen was a Roman priest who was unanimously elected pope in St. Mary Major Basilica immediately after the death of the elderly priest of the same name who had just been elected to succeed Zacharias.

Soon after the consecration of Stephen II (III), Rome faced a new threat from the Lombard king Aistulf, fresh from his conquest of Ravenna. The king obviously now regarded the duchy of Rome as his fief and imposed an annual tax on all of its inhabitants. He also rebuffed every effort to achieve a fair and peaceful settlement of disputes over expropriated imperial territories, in spite of pleas from the pope. When the pope's appeal to the emperor Constantine V for military assistance went unanswered, Stephen II (III) turned to Pepin III, king of the Franks, just as Pope Gregory III had turned to Charles Martel for help in 739. Mindful of the invaluable support he had received from Stephen's predecessor, Zacharias, Pepin agreed to the pope's request for a meeting. He sent Bishop Chrodegang of Metz and his own brother-in-law, Autcar, as escorts. The pope's trip, beginning on October 14, 753, took him across the Alps (he was the first pope to make that journey) and he was received by Pepin on January 6, 754, at Ponthion. The next day the pope and some of his clergy who had accompanied him came before the king in penitential garb and threw themselves down at his feet, begging him in the name of St. Peter to save the Roman people from the Lombards. Not only did Pepin agree to help, but he also gave a written promise (known as the "Donation of Pepin" or the "donation of Quierzy [Quiercy]," where the matter was finally settled) to guarantee as the pope's rightful possessions the duchy of Rome, Ravenna, and other cities held by the Lombards and perhaps also extensive territories in northern and central Italy. Although Stephen had spent the winter seriously ill at the abbey of St.-Denis near Paris, he was able on July 28, 754, solemnly to anoint Pepin, his wife, and sons (thereby confirming the legitimacy of the Carolingian dynasty) and to bestow on Pepin and his sons the title "patrician of the Romans."

Pepin tried peaceful means at first with the Lombards, but when they failed, he attacked and defeated them quickly in August 754, forcing them to hand over expropriated territories to the pope. Stephen received a tumultuous welcome upon his return to Rome. Once the Franks had recrossed the Alps, however, the Lombard king Aistulf broke the peace and laid siege against Rome and its neighboring territories. In response to Stephen's repeated pleas in the name of St. Peter, Pepin once again invaded Italy, crushed the Lombard king, and forced upon him even harsher terms of peace in June 756. When the Byzantine emperor protested the transfer of former imperial possessions to the pope, Pepin replied that he had taken up arms solely out of love for St. Peter and for the forgiveness of his sins and, therefore, could not hand over his conquests to anyone but the pope. Fulrad, the abbot of St.-Denis, deposited the keys of the various cities and the decree of donation upon St. Peter's tomb. Thus were the Papal States created and thus began the pope's role as temporal sovereign—a mixed blessing indeed.

When Aistulf died without heir, the pope successfully maneuvered to have a Tuscan placed on the Lombard throne, in return for which the pope received additional cities, including Bologna. The pope also persuaded the dukes of Spoleto and Benevento to switch their loyalty from the Lombards to Pepin and the Holy See. Through the pope's influence Pepin arranged that the Roman liturgy would replace the Gallican liturgy throughout his kingdom. Stephen II (III) died on April 26, 757, and was buried in St. Peter's.

93 Paul I, St., *May 29, 757–June 28, 767.*

Paul I is the only instance of a pope's succeeding his older brother to the papacy. He had been ordained a deacon by Pope Zacharias (741–52) and served his brother Stephen II (III) as a close adviser and negotiator.

Although he was elected unanimously in late April, Paul I's consecration had to be delayed for a month because a minority faction that opposed the Frankish alliance preferred the archdeacon Theophylact. His pontificate was marked by persistent efforts to consolidate the papacy's control over the newly granted Papal States, which were threatened by a new Lombard king, Desiderius, who repudiated the peace treaty that had been carefully forged between Pepin, king of the Franks, and the Lombard king Aistulf. Pepin chose not to intervene again militarily, lest he drive the Lombards into an unholy alliance with the Byzantine emperor in an effort to regain lands taken from both of them. Instead, he pursued a diplomatic course, forging a compromise between Desiderius and Pope Paul I in which the pope would have to scale back his grandiose vision of the Papal States.

In the meantime, the iconoclast controversy (regarding the use and veneration of sacred images) began heating up once again. The emperor Constantine V held a council at Hiereia (754) which denounced images and their veneration. Paul I welcomed refugees from the East fleeing from persecution for their devotion to sacred images. Fortunately for the pope, Pepin rebuffed the emperor's efforts to win his support for the iconoclastic policy. At a synod held at Gentilly in 767, at which Franks and Greeks debated iconoclasm and Trinitarian doctrine, the papal view prevailed. Paul I died shortly thereafter, on June 28, 767, in St. Paul's Basilica, having sought relief there from Rome's excessive heat. He was buried in St. Peter's.

Regarding his own personal and pastoral life, opinion is divided. Some underscore his compassion and his devotion to the poor and to prisoners, but others note his harsh style of administration in which he relied on tyrannical subordinates to carry out his policies. In the process, he alienated the lay aristocracy of Rome and laid the foundation not only for a brief schism following his death, but also for the end of lay involvement in papal elections. His pontificate was also noted, however, for the transfer of many bodies (or relics from them) from the catacombs to churches and chapels in Rome. There is no evidence of his cult before the fifteenth century. Feast day: June 28.

94 Stephen III (IV), *August 7, 768–January 24, 772.*

(For an explanation of the dual numbering, see Stephen II (III), number 92, above.) The unhappy pontificate of Stephen III (IV), a Sicilian raised in Rome, began under a cloud and ended in disaster. Because of the severe administrative style of Stephen's predecessor, Paul I, the lay aristocracy of Rome had become so alienated that they even contemplated the pope's murder. They decided against that course of action, however, and placed their hopes in electing a successor sympathetic to their interests. As it turned out, one of their number violated the oath not to circumvent normal canonical procedures and had his brother Constantine, a layperson, acclaimed pope by a mob of soldiers. He was installed in the Lateran, ordained a subdeacon and deacon, and then consecrated as pope by three bishops in St. Peter's Basilica on July 5, 767. Constantine wrote to Pepin III informing him of his "election," but received no reply. In the meantime, complex political intrigues in Rome shifted the alliances that had prepared the way for Constantine's selection as pope. His brother and chief supporter was killed in street fighting with Lombard troops, and Constantine fled to the Lateran oratory, where he was soon arrested. Taking advantage of the chaotic situation, the Lombards briefly installed a pope of their own, Philip, a chaplain at a local monastery, but he was almost immediately rejected and expelled from the Lateran. The powerful chief notary of the Holy See, Christopher, saw to it that Stephen was canonically elected to replace Constantine the following year, on August 1, 768. He was consecrated as Bishop of Rome on August 7.

The antipope Constantine was dragged from his hiding place, paraded through the city, and at a synod stripped of the insignia of office, deposed, and imprisoned in a monastery. While at the monastery, he was attacked by a gang and his eyes were gouged out. At a subsequent synod (769) the acts of Constantine's election and of his brief administration were burned (one should keep in mind, however, that Pope Stephen III (IV) had originally signed those acts, along with all the Roman clergy), his ordinations were declared invalid (which the synod could not really do since Constantine had been validly, although illicitly, ordained a bishop), and Constantine himself was sentenced to lifelong penance in a monastery. The synod also decreed that henceforth only deacons and cardinal-priests (that is, those Roman presbyters who were pastors of the key parishes of Rome) should be eligible for election as pope and that the laity should no longer have any vote in such elections.

Upon his own election, Stephen III (IV) sent an envoy to inform the Frankish king, Pepin III, of his accession to the papal throne and to invite some of the Frankish bishops to attend the synod that would dispose of the canonical problems created by Constantine's "election." Thirteen Frankish bishops attended. Dominated from the start by Christopher, the one who had engineered his election, Stephen's pontificate was marked by vacillation, intrigue, and stupendous blunders. When the pope finally tried to break free of Christopher's influence, he entered into a disastrous alliance with Desiderius, king of the Lombards, who arranged the murders of both Christopher and his son Sergius. The pope wrote to the new Frankish king, Charles (Charlemagne), and lied about the circumstances of their deaths, insisting that they had been plotting against his life and that Desiderius had saved him. Desiderius, however, broke all of his promises to the pope and, for all practical purposes, reduced him to a state of complete subservience. In 771 Charles, now sole ruler of the Franks, repudiated his marriage to the daughter of Desiderius and thus became the Lombard king's mortal foe. Stephen's position deteriorated even further, and his pontificate ended in total failure. Stephen III (IV) died on January 24, 772, and was buried in St. Peter's.

95 Hadrian [Adrian] I, *February 9, 772–December 25, 795.*

During Hadrian I's lengthy pontificate (the fourth longest in history, after Pius IX [1846–78], Leo XIII [1878–1903], and Pius VI [1775–99]), Charlemagne, king of the Franks, conquered the Lombards (774), deposing the antipapal king Desiderius, and confirmed the transfer to the Holy See of territories that together constituted the Papal States (because of which Hadrian I is sometimes called the second founder of the Papal States, after Pope Stephen II [III]). Ordained a deacon by Stephen III (IV), Hadrian was unanimously elected on February 1 and was consecrated as Bishop of Rome on February 9.

It required three separate visits of Charlemagne to Rome (in 774, 781, and 787) before the boundaries of the Papal States were finally fixed. They were to remain in that essential form until their final dissolution in 1870. The Second Council of Nicaea was also held during his pontificate (787). The pope, of course, gave the council his full support for its teaching against iconoclasm (the Eastern prohibition against the use and veneration of sacred images). Charlemagne, on the other hand, was unhappy with the council (perhaps because he had not been invited) and had a detailed refutation of its decisions prepared by theologians on the basis of a faulty translation of its acts (they thought, for example, that the council had approved the "adoration" of images, which clearly it did not). In 794 Charlemagne held a great synod in Frankfurt, which condemned the adoration of images and also Adoptionism (which held that there was a dual sonship in Christ, one natural and the other adopted), a heresy that was especially strong in Spain.

In Rome, the pope took advantage of the peaceful conditions made possible by Charlemagne and built and restored many churches, strengthened the walls of the city and the embankments of the Tiber River (after devastating floods in December 791), and completely reconstructed four great aqueducts. He was also devoted to the care of the poor and to the promotion of monasticism and of church-operated farms that generated income for charitable projects. Charlemagne is said to have grieved at the pope's death on Christmas, 795, "as if he had lost a brother or a child," and had a magnificent marble slab inscribed with memorial verses that can be seen in the portico, or porch, of St. Peter's. Hadrian I was buried in the crypt of the basilica.

Part III

FROM THE CAROLINGIAN EMPIRE TO THE BEGINNING OF THE MONARCHICAL PAPACY

LTHOUGH THERE HAVE BEEN MANY LOW PERIODS in the history of the papacy, the period between the beginning of the Carolingian Empire (800) and the end of the pontificate of Damasus II (1048) was undoubtedly its lowest, some happy exceptions to the rule notwithstanding. The period was marred by papal corruption (including simony, i.e., the buying and selling of church offices, nepotism, lavish lifestyles, concubinage, brutality, even murder) and the domination of the papacy by German kings and by powerful Roman aristocratic families. During this period at least five popes, and possibly a sixth, were assassinated. One pope, Sergius III (904–11), was himself a murderer, having ordered the murders of his predecessor, Leo V, and the antipope Christopher. Two popes were imprisoned and mutilated or starved to death (Stephen VIII [IX] [939–42], and John XIV [983–84], respectively), and the body of one pope (Formosus [891–96]) was even exhumed from its resting place, on orders of one of his successors, and put on public trial in the so-called Cadaver Synod.

The events following the election of the first pope of this period, Leo III (795–816), gave warning of the chaos that was to come in the next two and a half centuries. Although elected unanimously, Leo had many enemies among the Roman nobility, led by Paschalis, a relative of his predecessor, Hadrian I, and others. While riding in procession to Mass one day, a gang attacked the pope and tried unsuccessfully to gouge out his eyes and cut off his tongue. After a formal ceremony of deposition, the pope was placed under house arrest in a monastery. With the help of friends he escaped to Charlemagne's royal court at Paderborn, but his opponents soon followed, bearing with them charges of perjury and adultery, which the Franks thought to be well founded. It was not until December of the following year, however, that, with the overt assistance of Charlemagne himself, the pope ceremonially purged himself of the charges. But a moral cloud would hang over the remainder of his pontificate.

Why did the worldwide Church not suffer greater harm than it did during this two-hundred-year period of papal degradation and decline (although not all the popes of this time were "bad popes")? Why were the churches outside of Italy not so seriously affected by this deplorable state of affairs? How to explain the fact, for example, that the Anglo-Saxon Church experienced a period of vigorous revival and reform? While it is true that the power of the church of Rome over other local churches had been steadily expanding in the preceding years, the exercise of that power was only occasional and intermittent. Even under such strong popes as Leo the Great (440–61), Gregory the Great (590–604), and Nicholas I (858–67), there was no such thing as a central government of the Church. Unlike today, there were no systems of communications to make it possible. The Church was less like a centralized monarchy or empire than a loose federation of local churches, which were themselves synodal federations of monarchical sees. Once the monarchical papacy was clearly established in the pontificate of Gregory VII (1073–85), however, corruption could more easily spread out from the center of a now excessively centralized institution.

There were also many "firsts" during this period. Fortunately, some of the "firsts," such as the trial of the exhumed Formosus, have never been repeated. Thus, Leo III (795–816) was the first—and only—pope to offer obeisance to a Western emperor. Stephen IV (V) (816–17) was the first pope to anoint an emperor. John VIII (872–82) has the dubious distinction of being the first pope to be assassinated, having been poisoned and then clubbed to death. Marinus I (882–84) was the first bishop of another diocese to be elected Bishop of Rome, in violation of canon 15 of the Council of Nicaea (325). Therefore, he was also the first *bishop* to be elected Bishop of Rome! The practice of electing bishops of other dioceses as Bishop of Rome soon became common, however, and it remains so to this day. Boniface VI (896) was the first and only pope to be elected after having twice been defrocked for immoral conduct, once as a subdeacon and later as a priest. John XI (931–35/6) was the first and only illegitimate son of a pope who himself became pope. John XV (985–96) was the first pope formally to canonize a saint, Ulric of Augsburg, in 993. Gregory V (996–99) was the first German-born pope. (Boniface II [530–32] had been the first pope of Germanic stock.) Sylvester II (999–1003) was the first French pope. Leo VIII (963–65) was the first layman elected pope, although the canonical legitimacy of his election has been questioned because of the manner in which his predecessor was deposed. The antipope Constantine, also a layman, had been elected and consecrated in 767, but both acts were later declared null and void by a Lateran synod. A series of three laymen were elected to the papacy in the eleventh century: Benedict VIII (1012–24), Benedict's younger brother, John XIX (1024–32), and Benedict IX, who was also the only pope in history to have held the papal office at three different times (1032–44, 1045, and 1047–48). John XII (955–64) was the first and only teenager elected to the papacy (he was eighteen). However, he did not have a long pontificate, dying of a stroke suffered less than nine years later, allegedly while in bed with a married woman. Clement II (1046–47) was the first pope to remain bishop of his previous diocese (Bamberg, Germany) while serving as Bishop of Rome. His immediate successors, Damasus II (1048), Leo IX (1049–54), and Victor II (1055–57) did the same, retaining the dioceses of Brixen, Toul, and Eichstätt, respectively. Stephen IX (X) (1057–58) remained as abbot of Monte Cassino during his pontificate, and Nicholas II (1058–61) remained as bishop of Florence during his.

The laity participated in papal elections for most of the first Christian millennium—sometimes directly along with the Roman clergy and sometimes representatively through the Roman nobility. Through much of the period covered in this section, the emperors were also directly involved in papal elections, either through subsequent approval or through direct nomination of candidates. Nicholas II (1058–61) was the first pope to attempt to restrict such elections to cardinal-bishops, with the subsequent assent of the clergy and laity. In any case, many of the popes elected during this period served extraordinarily short terms. Thus, there were twenty popes elected in the ninth century and twenty-three in the tenth century, in comparison with only six popes elected in the nineteenth century and eight popes in the twentieth century (and that includes the thirty-three-day pontificate of John Paul I in 1978).

This period also witnessed serious breaks between the churches of East and West, leading eventually to the East-West Schism that continues to this very day. As this period came to a close in the middle of the eleventh century, the need for reform had grown increasingly apparent. The five popes just before the crucially important Gregory VII (1073–85), whose pontificate marked the beginning of yet another major period in papal history, were all reformers with varying degrees of success. But there is no more vivid emblem of this period than the so-called Cadaver Synod, at which the deceased Pope Formosus was exhumed from his grave, placed on public trial, sacramentally degraded, and then mutilated—all under the direction of one of his successors, Stephen VI (VII). Stephen, however, would pay for his sin. He himself was deposed, stripped of his papal insignia, imprisoned, and then strangled to death. Such were the antics of more than a few of the successors of the Apostle Peter in the ninth, tenth, and eleventh centuries.

96 Leo III, St., *December 27, 795–June 12, 816 (the Vatican's official list begins his pontificate on the day of his election, December 26, rather than the day of his consecration as Bishop of Rome, December 27).*

Leo III is best known for his crowning of Charlemagne, king of the Franks, as the first Carolingian emperor (and the forerunner of the Holy

Roman Empire) in St. Peter's on Christmas day, 800. He is also the first and only pope to offer obeisance to a Western emperor.

As mentioned above, his election to the papacy on December 26, 795, although unanimous, was not without real opposition, particularly from members of the aristocracy who were relatives of Leo's predecessor, Hadrian I. (He was consecrated the next day.) On April 25, 799, he was violently attacked while in procession to Mass and an unsuccessful attempt was made to cut out his tongue and blind him. He was then formally deposed and sent off to a monastery, from which he later escaped with the help of friends. He made his way to Charlemagne's court at Paderborn and was received with all due pomp.

The Frankish king refused to recognize the pope's deposition from office. Soon thereafter, however, representatives of the anti-Leonine faction arrived bearing charges of perjury and adultery against the pope. Although many Franks regarded the charges as credible, they were inhibited from making a judgment about them because of the commonly accepted principle that no power could judge the Apostolic See. Charles had the pope escorted back to Rome, but the problems in the city persisted. A year later Charles himself arrived in Rome and was greeted in a manner appropriate for a visiting emperor. On December 1, 800, the king held a council in St. Peter's and explained that its purpose was to examine the charges against the pope. But the assembly said it did not wish to do so because it could not sit in judgment of the pope. On December 23 Leo declared himself ready to be purged of these "false charges" and thereupon took an oath of purgation, swearing to his innocence. His opponents were condemned to death, but the pope had their sentences commuted to exile. Two days later, as Christmas Mass was beginning, Charles rose from his prayers in front of St. Peter's tomb and the pope placed an imperial crown on his head. The congregation hailed him as "Emperor of the Romans" and Leo knelt in homage before him.

The coronation was of great benefit to both sides. Charlemagne now enjoyed at least equal status to his imperial counterpart in Constantinople and a clearer legal position with regard to Rome and the Papal States. For Leo III the coronation established a secular power in Rome to maintain order, ended the papacy's dependence on the Byzantine emperors, and added prestige to the papal office itself since it was the pope who bestowed the crown upon the emperor. The coronation, however, also sowed the seeds of eventual conflict between the two powers—a conflict that would perdure through much of the Middle Ages.

Although now rehabilitated and enjoying the full support of the new emperor, Leo III found himself overshadowed by Charlemagne, who, in turn, did as he pleased not only in the temporal realm but even in ecclesiastical matters. He interfered in the business of the Roman church and in the management of the Papal States, and he induced Leo in 798 to elevate Salzburg to an archdiocese with metropolitan status and to convene a synod in Rome to condemn Spanish Adoptionism (a heresy that held that Jesus Christ is both the natural and the adopted son of God). It is significant, therefore, that Leo III resisted Charlemagne's effort to add the phrase "and from the Son" (Lat., *Filioque*) to the Nicene Creed. (It was already in use in the Frankish Church.) Leo had no problem with the doctrine implied in the phrase, but he opposed any alteration of the historic creed. He did not want to alienate the Greeks, who strongly opposed the change on doctrinal grounds. When Charles died (January 28, 814), Leo began to act more independently, but unfortunately not more wisely. When another conspiracy against him came to light, he personally tried the conspirators on charges of treason and condemned scores of them to death (815).

Otherwise, Leo III was an efficient administrator of the Papal States and of the Church's vast welfare system. He also continued his predecessor's program of building, restoring, and embellishing the churches of Rome. In foreign matters, he maintained a close interest in the affairs of the English Church, helping to restore the king of Northumbria to his throne, settling a dispute between the archbishops of Canterbury and York, and withdrawing the pallium (the woolen vestment worn around the neck as a sign of pastoral authority) from the bishop of Lichfield. In spite of his severe, divisive, and morally dubious pontificate, he was included in a catalogue of saints in 1673, because of the presumed "miracle" of the restoration of his eyes and tongue in the attack upon him in 799. He died on June 12, 816, and was buried in St. Peter's. Feast day: June 12.

97 Stephen IV (V), *June 22, 816–January 24, 817.*

(For an explanation of the dual numbering, see Stephen II (III), number 92, in Part II.) Stephen IV (V) was the first pope to anoint an emperor (Louis the Pious), suggesting thereby that papal approval was necessary for the exercise of full imperial authority—a remarkable reversal of the centuries-old practice by which the Byzantine emperor's approval was necessary for the validity of a papal election. Conciliatory by nature, Stephen had been a widely popular choice for pope. He was probably elected (on June 22, 816) to heal the divisions created by his predecessor, Leo III. (He was consecrated as Bishop of Rome the same day.)

Stephen immediately sought a meeting with Charlemagne's successor, Louis the Pious. It took place at Rheims in October 816. After an elaborate welcome by the emperor, Stephen anointed and crowned Louis and his consort, Irmengard, in the cathedral, using an alleged "crown of

Constantine" he had brought with him from Rome. Extensive private discussions between the pope and the new emperor followed, presumably to reaffirm the terms of the pact between the Frankish crown and the papacy, including the autonomy of the Papal States and the freedom of papal elections. For the sake of peace at home, the pope won a concession from Louis the Pious to grant pardons for the aristocratic conspirators whom Charlemagne had exiled to Gaul in 800 because of their part in the rebellion against Pope Leo III. Stephen returned to Rome with the pardons and with many gifts. But he died three months afterwards, on January 24, 817, and was buried in St. Peter's.

98 Paschal I, St., *January 25, 817–February 11, 824.*

During Paschal I's pontificate the practice of crowning the emperor in Rome became established. However, this pope was so detested by the Roman people because of his harsh manner of governance that his body could not be buried in St. Peter's as almost every other pope had been. Abbot of St. Stephen's monastery when elected to the papacy on January 24, 817, Paschal was consecrated as Bishop of Rome the very next day, apparently out of concern that the emperor might interfere. But the new pope immediately announced his election to the emperor Louis the Pious, stressing that the office had been thrust upon him and that he had not sought it.

Soon thereafter the emperor confirmed the agreements he had reached with Paschal's predecessor, Stephen IV (V), at Rheims, confirming papal authority over the Papal States and pledging noninterference in papal elections and other internal ecclesiastical affairs unless explicitly invited to do so. (The official document is known as the *Pactum Ludovicianum.*) The harmonious relationship with the emperor continued throughout Paschal's pontificate. There were frequent official contacts between Rome and the imperial court. When the pope chose Archbishop Ebbo of Rheims to evangelize the Danes, Louis sent him to Rome in 822. The pope commissioned him and designated him as papal legate for the northern regions. When Louis's son Lothair, having already been crowned as coemperor in 817, with the pope's approval, came to Italy in 823, Paschal invited him to Rome and solemnly anointed him on Easter Sunday. The pope also presented him with a sword as a symbol of his temporal authority (a theologically dubious gesture for a pope, whose primatial authority is spiritual, not temporal).

Lothair, however, proved more independent than his father. Exercising his royal rights, he held a court and rendered a judgment whereby the abbey of Farfa, just north of Rome, would be exempt from taxation by the Holy See. The pope's supporters in Rome were angered, but his aristocratic opponents were not. They turned to the young emperor for support against the clerical party. After Lothair left Rome, however, members of the papal household blinded and beheaded two leaders of the pro-Frankish group in the Lateran because of their loyalty to the emperor. Paschal denied any personal involvement, but the emperor sent an investigating team to Rome. Following the example of his predecessor, Leo III, Paschal took an oath of purgation before a synod of thirty-four bishops, adding that the murdered men had been lawfully executed as traitors. The event convinced the Frankish court to exercise closer supervision over Rome, but Paschal died before any change occurred.

During his pontificate, iconoclasm (the movement against the use and veneration of sacred images) flared up again in the East. Paschal appealed to the Byzantine emperor Leo V, but without success. In the meantime, he devoted himself to the building and restoration of churches in Rome. Three of the new churches contain mosaics with lifelike portraits of Paschal, including Santa Prassede on the Equiline, where he had to be buried because, as noted above, the people would not allow his body to be buried in St. Peter's following his death on February 11, 824. Paschal's name was included in the catalogue of saints in the late sixteenth century, but his feast (May 14) was suppressed in 1963.

99 Eugenius [Eugene] II, *May 11(?), 824–August 27 (?), 827 (May 824–August 827 in the Vatican's official list).*

During Eugenius II's pontificate, the papacy came under more direct control of the emperor. The change was prompted by factionalism in Rome between the pro-Frankish nobility and the Roman clergy and by the emperor's concern about the chain of events in the previous pontificate, of Paschal I, leading to the murder and exile of leading pro-Frankish officials. Eugenius's election followed several months of disturbances in Rome, with the clergy and aristocracy making rival nominations. The clergy and ordinary laity favored the presbyter Sisinnius, while the nobility favored Eugenius, archpriest of Santa Sabina on the Aventine. After prolonged discussions, the monk Wala, of the Benedictine abbey of Corbi, who was also a trusted adviser of the two coemperors, Louis the Pious and his son Lothair, engineered Eugenius's election, probably in early May 824. He was consecrated as Bishop of Rome on May 11 or thereabouts.

Eugenius not only informed the imperial court of his election but acknowledged its sovereignty in the Papal States and swore an oath of allegiance to Louis. After a meeting between the new pope and the coemperor Lothair in Rome, a "Roman Constitution" was published (November 1,

824), strengthening Frankish control over Rome and the papacy. Among the terms was the restoration of the ancient practice, suspended since Pope Stephen III (IV)'s synod of 769, of the people of Rome as well as the clergy participating in papal elections. However, before being consecrated, the pope-elect was required to take an oath of loyalty to the emperor before the imperial legate. All citizens of the Papal States were also to take an oath of allegiance to the emperor. At a Lateran synod called by Eugenius II in November 826, the terms of the constitution were ratified.

However, the synod also showed its independence from the Frankish court in matters ecclesiastical. It applied to the Frankish Church a collection of disciplinary canons dealing with simony (the buying and selling of church offices), the qualifications and duties of bishops, clerical education, monastic life, Sunday observance, marriage, and other matters. And when Louis sent an envoy to urge the pope to accept a compromise in the iconoclastic controversy with the East, the pope insisted that the matter had been settled by the Second Council of Nicaea (787). On November 1, 825, Louis convened a commission of Frankish theologians in Paris, with the pope's knowledge and approval, in order to examine the whole issue. Their report rejected Nicaea II and censured the pope for protecting error and superstition. But the pope would not yield, and Louis did not push the point. In the meantime, the pope remained in correspondence with Theodore of Studios (d. 826), the leader of the pro-image faction in the East. Among other activities of Eugenius II's pontificate was his blessing of Ansgar and his companions' mission to the Danes in the fall of 826. He died in late August 827 and was buried in St. Peter's.

100 Valentine, *August–September 827.*

Upon the death of Eugenius II, Valentine was unanimously elected by the clergy, nobility, and people of Rome, in accordance with the terms of the new constitution promulgated by the emperor in 824. Valentine was properly consecrated, probably the next day, but he died a month to forty days later. There is no record of any official activities during his brief pontificate. He was probably buried in St. Peter's.

101 Gregory IV, *March 29, 828–January 25, 844 (827–January 844 in the Vatican's official list).*

Although Gregory IV's pontificate lasted some sixteen years, it was generally undistinguished. He came from an aristocratic Roman family and was elected with the support of the lay nobility, whose voting rights in papal elections had been restored by the Frankish emperor Lothair's "Roman Constitution," promulgated during the pontificate of Eugenius

II (824). It seems that he tried to escape his election by taking refuge in the basilica of Santi Cosma e Damiano, but the crowd followed him there, joyously acclaimed him as pope, and conducted him to the Lateran Palace. In accordance with the terms of the constitution, however, Gregory's consecration was delayed until he received formal approval from an imperial legate and had himself sworn allegiance to the emperor. He was consecrated as Bishop of Rome on March 29, 828.

When a dynastic dispute arose between the emperor Louis the Pious and his sons Lothair, Pepin, and Louis the German, Gregory IV supported Lothair. The Frankish bishops were angered by the display of partisanship, reminded the pope of his oath of loyalty to Louis, and threatened to excommunicate him. The pope held his ground, asserting that the authority of St. Peter's successor was greater than imperial authority. As the armies of the sons were gathered against the army of their father near Colmar in the summer of 833, the brothers persuaded the pope to go to Louis's camp to negotiate. When he returned with what he thought to be a reasonable settlement, the pope found that Lothair had deceived him. On the night the pope returned, most of Louis's supporters deserted him and the emperor was forced to surrender unconditionally and was subsequently deposed. Gregory IV returned to Rome dejected. Louis was later restored to power, but after his death a bloody conflict developed among the sons. The pope once again tried to mediate a settlement, but without success.

Little else is known about Gregory IV's pontificate. He did build a fortress at Ostia, which he named Gregoriopolis, to defend against the Saracens, who had established themselves in Sicily. In 831 or 832 he also received Ansgar, who had been sent on a mission among the Danes, and bestowed on him the pallium (the woolen vestment worn around the neck of an archbishop as a sign of his pastoral authority) and named him papal legate for Scandinavia and the Slav missions. Around the same time he received Amalarius of Metz (d. ca. 850), a famous liturgical scholar, and assigned an archdeacon to teach Amaralius Roman liturgical practices. The pope spent vast sums of money building and decorating churches. He commissioned a portrait of himself in mosaic which can be seen in the apse of St. Mark's, the church where he had been cardinal-priest at the time of his election to the papacy. He died on January 25, 844, and was buried in St. Peter's.

102 Sergius II, *January 844–January 27, 847.*

The pontificate of Sergius II was one of the more corrupt in the history of the papacy. The cardinal-priest of the church of Santi Martino e Silvestro ai Monti, he was elderly and gout-ridden when elected in late January 844 by his fellow Roman aristocrats in his titular church. The Roman people had earlier elected John, a deacon, and had him enthroned in the Lateran Palace, from which he was quickly expelled. Given the unsettled situation, Sergius's consecration as Bishop of Rome took place without awaiting formal approval from the Frankish court, as required in the Roman Constitution of 824. The emperor Lothair reacted angrily to this breach of protocol. He sent his son Louis, the new viceroy of Italy, to Rome with an army. Along the way it plundered the papal territories as an act of retribution. When he reached Rome, Louis ordered a synod, held in St. Peter's, to investigate the circumstances of Sergius's election and consecration. Twenty Italian bishops attended. Although Sergius II's election was ratified, he and the Roman citizenry had to swear allegiance to Lothair and accept the principle that a pope-elect could not be consecrated without imperial approval and in the presence of the emperor's representative. Sergius then crowned and anointed young Louis as king of the Lombards.

Sergius (or, perhaps more accurately, his brother Benedict) proved to be an ambitious builder, including among his accomplishments the enlargement of the Lateran basilica. But he (and Benedict) engaged in dubious methods of fund-raising to accomplish these construction projects, including simony. Bishoprics and other church offices were sold to the highest bidder. In August 846, in spite of advance warning, Saracen pirates successfully and thoroughly plundered St. Peter's and St. Paul's (both outside the Aurelian walls of the city)—acts that many contemporaries viewed as divine retribution for papal corruption. Sergius II died less than six months later, on January 27, 847, and was buried in St. Peter's.

103 Leo IV, St., *April 10, 847–July 17, 855 (the Vatican's official list begins his pontificate in January, the month of his election, but he was not consecrated as Bishop of Rome until April 10).*

Leo IV did much to repair the city of Rome after the Saracen attacks of 846, including the erection of a forty-foot wall surrounding St. Peter's and much of Vatican Hill, creating what came to be called the "Leonine City." He was unanimously elected pope on the day his predecessor, Sergius II, died (January 27, 847), and was consecrated as Bishop of Rome six weeks later, on April 10. He did not await the imperial consent required by the Roman Constitution of 824, on the grounds that the recent Saracen attacks on the city ruled out delay.

Besides giving his attention to the walls of Rome, Leo organized an alliance among several Greek cities in Italy and in 849 launched a successful sea attack against the Saracens just outside of Ostia, as they were preparing to attack Rome once again. In 854 he rebuilt Centumcellae (now Civitavecchia), naming it Leopolis. The pope's prestige grew with each new initiative and success. However, his relations with the Frankish emperor were strained. Outwardly he remained deferential, but he acted independently of the imperial court most of the time. Thus, although he agreed to crown and anoint the emperor Lothair's son Louis II in Rome on Easter 850, he also had three imperial agents executed for murdering a papal legate.

Leo's authoritarian style was also reflected in his denunciation of powerful Frankish prelates like Hincmar, archbishop of Rheims, and John, archbishop of Ravenna, for their excessive use of episcopal authority, his excommunication of Anastasius, cardinal-priest of San Marcello (and a later antipope), and his refusal of Lothair's request that he appoint Hincmar apostolic vicar and grant the pallium (the woolen vestment worn around the neck as a sign of pastoral authority) to the bishop of Autun. He also annulled the Synod of Soissons (853), which had invalidated the ordinations of the temporarily deposed bishop of Rheims, and he demanded that another council be held, presided over by papal representatives. He adopted a high-handed approach to the patriarch of Constantinople, chastising the patriarch for having deposed the bishop of Syracuse (in Sicily) without first consulting the pope, and summoning both parties to Rome.

Leo IV was generally a strict disciplinarian on internal church matters such as penitential practices. He also promoted church music and is said to have added the asperges (the sprinkling of holy water) to the Mass. Like many of his predecessors, Leo IV rebuilt or restored several churches in Rome, and his portrait in fresco can still be seen in the lower basilica of San Clemente. He died on July 17, 855, and was buried in St. Peter's. His feast day, now suppressed, was July 17.

104 Benedict III, *September 29, 855–April 17, 858.*

Little is known of Benedict III's brief pontificate. When Leo IV died, the first choice of the Roman clergy and laity was Hadrian, cardinal-priest of San Marco. When Hadrian refused election, Benedict, the pious and learned cardinal-priest of San Callisto, was chosen. But he, too, resisted and took refuge in his titular church of San Callisto. The crowds followed him and conducted him directly to the Lateran Palace, where he was installed on July 20, 855. However, some influential pro-imperialist individuals preferred Anastasius (known as Anastasius Bibliothecarius), the cardinal-priest whom Leo IV had excommunicated because he had sought refuge with the emperor, residing mainly in the diocese of

Aquileia, and refused to return to Rome when the pope ordered him back. Since Benedict could not be consecrated without imperial approval, the pro-imperial party took advantage of the situation, brought Anastasius to Rome, and installed him in the Lateran Palace, after having dragged Benedict from the throne and imprisoned him. But after three days of anarchy it became clear that Benedict had wide popular support, while Anastasius was reviled. The pro-imperialist group relented and allowed Benedict's consecration to go forward on September 29, 855. Anastasius was stripped of his papal insignia and ejected from the Lateran. He was reduced to lay status and confined to a monastery. However, he would reemerge in the next three pontificates as an important counselor to popes and be named librarian of the Roman church (hence, his name: Anastasius Bibliothecarius, Anastasius the Librarian).

Very little else survives of Benedict III's pontificate. He intervened in various ecclesiastical disputes, but with no clear pattern of accomplishment. He remained firm in asserting Rome's primatial jurisdiction over Constantinople and, like his predecessor, Leo IV, refused to ratify the patriarch's deposition of the bishop of Syracuse (in Sicily) until both parties came to Rome and he (the pope) had an opportunity to examine the case. The pope also restored several churches in Rome, including St. Paul's.

One interesting side note to Benedict's pontificate concerns the legendary Pope Joan. In one medieval version of the legend Leo IV was succeeded not by Benedict III but by a John Anglicus, who is said to have reigned for two years, seven months, and four days and who was in fact a woman. As the story goes, she was a native of Mainz. After a brilliant career as a student in Athens, she came to Rome, where she astonished people with her learned lectures and edifying life. Upon the death of Leo IV, she was unanimously elected pope. Her secret, however, was disclosed when she gave birth to a child while riding in procession from St. Peter's to the Lateran. In another version of the legend she succeeded Pope Victor III in 1087, but there is simply no contemporary evidence for either version.

Benedict III died on April 17, 858, and was buried in St. Peter's.

105 Nicholas I, St., *ca. 820–67, pope from April 24, 858, to November 13, 867.*

Like Leo the Great (440–61), Gelasius I (492–96), and Gregory the Great (590–604) before him, Nicholas I conceived of the pope as God's representative on earth with authority over the whole Church, East and West, including all of its bishops, and with the right to watch over and influence the state and to receive protection from it. Upon the death of Benedict III, a number of the Roman clergy turned once again to Hadrian, the cardinal-priest of San Marco, who had refused election three years earlier. And once again he removed his name from consideration. Nicholas, counselor and friend to the previous pope, was elected in the presence and with the approval of the emperor Louis II, who had rushed to Rome as soon as he had heard of Benedict III's death. Nicholas I was consecrated as Bishop of Rome on April 24, 858.

Nicholas's exalted view of the papacy shaped his whole pontificate. He excommunicated and deposed the archbishop of Ravenna and reinstated him only after he promised to subject himself to Rome in the future. The pope also clashed with Archbishop Hincmar of Rheims, the most powerful metropolitan in the empire, over the archbishop's deposing of certain of his clergy and the bishop of Soissons. In overruling Hincmar's actions, Nicholas I appealed to forged documents, known as the *False Decretals* (attributed to Isidore of Seville), which asserted the superior authority of popes over synods and metropolitans. When King Lothair of Lorraine's wife appealed to the pope after being abandoned by her husband for another woman, and after a synod at Aachen and another at Metz ratified the divorce and approved Lothair's second marriage, the pope deposed and excommunicated the two archbishops (of Cologne and Trier) when they delivered the synodal decrees to him in Rome. The emperor Louis II sent troops to Rome, and Nicholas took refuge in St. Peter's. But eventually the emperor backed off, and Lothair returned to his wife, at least temporarily.

Nicholas I was equally assertive in his relations with the East. He revived the long dormant jurisdictional claims of Rome over Illyricum, and when the patriarch of Constantinople, Ignatius, was forced to abdicate in favor of Photius, the pope refused to recognize Photius and deposed and excommunicated him at a synod held in the Lateran in 863. When the Byzantine emperor Michael III protested, the pope rebuked him, pointing out that he acted in accordance with the rights of the Apostolic See. Relations with the East worsened when the pope dispatched missionary bishops to Bulgaria in response to an appeal from its king, Boris I. The papal delegation's advice on moral and canonical matters was anti-Byzantine in tone, and Photius was indignant over it. Since Bulgaria had been evangelized originally by Byzantine missionaries, he felt that it fell under his own spiritual jurisdiction. After denouncing the Latin interference to the other patriarchs of the East, Photius convened a synod in Constantinople (867) which excommunicated and deposed Nicholas. The pope had died (on November 13, 867) before word of the synod's action reached Rome, but the mutual excommunications clearly laid the foundation for the East-West Schism of 1054—a schism that perdures to this very day. Although Nicholas I's successor, Hadrian II, recommended that his name be included in the prayers of the Mass, Nicholas I's name was not listed among the saints until 1630. He was buried in St. Peter's. Feast day: November 13.

106 Hadrian [Adrian] II, 792–867, pope from December 14, 867, to December 14, 872.

Married before ordination, Hadrian II, cardinal-priest of San Marco, was so widely respected that he twice declined election to the papacy (in 855 and 858) before finally accepting election in 867, and then only because the supporters and opponents of Nicholas I's hard-line style could not agree on a successor. Although we do not know the date of his election, he was consecrated as Bishop of Rome in St. Peter's on December 14, 867, by bishops Donato of Ostia, Formosus of Porto (who would himself be elected pope in 891, only to have his corpse exhumed and placed on trial in 897), Pietro of Cave, and Leone of Silva Candida.

Hadrian II's pontificate was marred from the start, when the duke of Spoleto attacked and plundered Rome. Then his own daughter was raped and murdered along with her mother, the pope's wife, by a brother of the former antipope Anastasius, whom Hadrian II had appointed papal archivist. Hadrian fired and excommunicated Anastasius, but less than a year later gave him another position in the chancery. The elderly pope also showed weakness in other areas. He restored King Lothair of Lorraine to communion, even though the pope had no firm evidence that the king had complied with Nicholas I's order to take back his divorced wife. He also lifted the excommunication from Lothair's mistress. Moreover, he failed in his attempts to influence the line of succession in Lorraine after Lothair's death and to bring civil and ecclesiastical disputes in the Carolingian realms before the papal court. For the latter he received a stinging rebuke from Archbishop Hincmar of Rheims. Unlike Nicholas I, however, Hadrian II immediately backed down.

When he learned of the excommunication and deposition of his predecessor by the patriarch Photius, Hadrian convened a synod in 869 which condemned Photius and his associates. At the same time, he sent two (and perhaps three) personal representatives to the Fourth Council of Constantinople (869–70), although they were not allowed to preside as the pope requested. The council upheld the Roman synod's condemnation of Photius, but also listed the patriarchates in the order of precedence followed in the East: Rome, Constantinople, Alexandria, Antioch, and Jerusalem. Rome had always opposed the placement of Constantinople ahead of Alexandria, but it relented in this case, thereby restoring peace temporarily between East and West. However, three days after the council's adjournment the emperor Basil ruled that Bulgaria came under the jurisdiction of Constantinople, not Rome. A Byzantine metropolitan was consecrated for it and the Latin clergy were ordered to leave. Hadrian did retain Roman control over Moravia by approving the use of the Old Slavonic liturgy and by consecrating Methodius as archbishop of Sirmium and papal legate to the Slavs. Hadrian II's last recorded act was the recrowning of Louis II in St. Peter's on Pentecost (May 18), 872. The pope died on December 14, 872, and was buried in St. Peter's.

107 John VIII, *December 14, 872–December 16, 882.*

John VIII was the first pope (but not the last) to be assassinated. A close collaborator of Pope Nicholas I (858–67) and for twenty years archdeacon, he was unanimously elected pope and consecrated as Bishop of Rome on the same day that his predecessor, Hadrian II, died. These were violent and chaotic times, and John VIII's pontificate was faced with one major problem after another. Although elderly when elected, he had great energy and drive. Indeed, he was determined to reign in the manner of Gregory the Great (590–604) and his mentor, Nicholas I. He personally took charge of the defensive efforts against the attacks of the Saracens from the south, working diligently to forge a military alliance among the states of southern Italy. He built a defensive wall around St. Paul's Basilica and personally commanded a papal fleet. But the alliance soon fell apart when some of the states made their own separate "peace" with the invaders. The pope himself was reduced to bribing them as well.

Upon the death of the emperor Louis II in 875, the pope jumped headlong into imperial politics and rallied the clergy and senate of Rome to the support of Louis's uncle, Charles the Bald, crowning him emperor on Christmas. In gratitude Charles extended the boundaries of the Papal States and renounced the imperial right to have envoys in Rome and any direct influence in papal elections. But John's political sense proved disastrous. Charles the Bald was of no real help to the papacy and died soon after Carloman, the son of Louis the German (whom the pope had rejected in favor of Charles), marched into Italy to assert his claims on the throne. After a series of bizarre and complicated events (Carloman became ill and withdrew; the dukes of Spoleto and Tuscia occupied Rome and imprisoned the pope; the pope was set free and traveled to Provence, where he inserted himself once again in matters of temporal succession), John VIII turned eastward for help against the Saracens. Photius by now had been reinstated as patriarch of Constantinople and there was still much bad blood between him and Rome. But the pope was willing to compromise to secure military aid. With Photius presiding, a council was held in the Hagia Sophia in Constantinople in November 879, at which the Second Council of Nicaea (787) was recognized, even though it had condemned iconoclasm (the Eastern view that the use and veneration of sacred images is idolatrous). The council also annulled the synods that had anathematized Photius and forbade any additions to the creed of Constantinople (381). John VIII ratified the council's decisions so long as they did not contradict any of the instructions he had given his legates, and he recognized Photius as patriarch.

Although he was largely a political pope, John VIII promoted the sanctity and indissolubility of marriage and the freedom of episcopal elections. He supported Methodius, the apostle of Moravia, in his conflict with the German and Hungarian clergy and approved the use of Old Slavonic in the liturgy in 880 (after having at first forbade it). He was the first pope to be assassinated, having been poisoned by some of his associates, perhaps even by his own relatives, and then clubbed to death on December 16, 882. None of the sources indicates a reason for his murder. He was buried in St. Peter's.

108 Marinus I, *December 16, 882–May 15, 884.*

Marinus I was the first bishop of another diocese (Caere, now Cerveteri) to be elected Bishop of Rome, in violation of canon 15 of the First Council of Nicaea (325). The son of a priest, he entered the service of the Roman church at the age of twelve, was ordained a deacon by Nicholas I (858–67), and served as one of three papal legates to the Fourth Council of Constantinople (869–70). He later served as archdeacon and treasurer of the Roman church and then bishop of Caere in Etruria. Sometimes mistakenly listed as Martin II, he was elected and consecrated as Bishop of Rome on December 16, 882, without consulting the emperor, Charles III. However, when Charles III visited Italy, he gave his recognition to the new pope and had constructive discussions with him. Marinus tried his best to maintain good relations with Photius, the patriarch of Constantinople. Although John VIII had excommunicated Photius in 869 (later recognizing him in 879), Marinus retained a friend of the patriarch's as papal librarian (an important position in those days). The pope also maintained excellent relations with King Alfred the Great of England and, at the king's request, exempted the English quarter in Rome from taxes. Marinus I died on May 15, 884, and was buried in the portico, or porch, of St. Peter's between the Porta Argentea and the Porta Romana. (As with many of the popes of this period who were buried in the portico, his body was later transferred to the crypt.)

109 Hadrian [Adrian] III, St., *May 17, 884–September 885.*

Almost nothing is known of Hadrian III's brief pontificate, but he may have been one of the few popes in history to have been assassinated. His election to the papacy, two days after the death of Marinus I, is shrouded in obscurity. He was consecrated the same day, May 17, 884. He seems to have been a supporter of the policies of Pope John VIII (872–82) rather than of his immediate predecessor, Marinus I, thus underscoring the point that popes are not usually succeeded by carbon copies of themselves. One of his few recorded acts was the blinding of a high official of the Lateran Palace, an enemy of Pope John VIII whom Pope Marinus had permitted to return from exile. There is also a report that Hadrian III had a noblewoman whipped naked through the streets of Rome. These acts suggest that the bloody vendettas that erupted after Pope John VIII's assassination in 882 were continuing.

Hadrian III maintained his predecessor's conciliatory approach to the East, sending notification of his election to the patriarch of Constantinople, Photius, whom John VIII had excommunicated in 869 (although he subsequently recognized him in 879). At the request of the emperor Charles III, the pope set out from Rome in the summer of 885 to attend the imperial Diet of Worms (in Germany). Lacking a legitimate male heir, the emperor expected the pope to approve his illegitimate son's right of succession to the throne. In return for his cooperation, the pope apparently hoped that the emperor would lend his support to the pope's bitter fight with his enemies in Rome. However, the pope seems to have met with foul play during his journey near Modena (in Italy). His body was buried in the abbey of Nonantola. In spite of his ordering of the blinding of a palace official and the crude punishment of the noblewoman, Hadrian III was regarded as a saint in Rome, and his name was officially added to the list of saints in 1891. He is also said to have authored a four-volume history of Charlemagne. Feast day: July 8 (or 9).

110 Stephen V (VI), *September 885–September 14, 891.*

(For an explanation of the dual numbering, see Stephen II [III], number 92, in Part II.) Stephen V (VI) is largely responsible for pushing the Slavs away from Rome and eventually into the arms of Orthodoxy when, after the death of St. Methodius (885), one of the apostles to the Slavs, he forbade the Old Slavonic liturgy. A priest of the church of Santi Quattro Coronati, Stephen was unanimously elected sometime toward the end of September 885 and was consecrated as Bishop of Rome by Bishop Formosus of Porto (who become pope himself in 891) in a ceremony witnessed by Bishop Giovanni of Pavia in his capacity as imperial legate. Nevertheless, because he had been elected without the emperor's consultation, Stephen was threatened with deposition. However, the new pope managed to dissuade the imperial chancellor from taking such action when he pointed out that he had been the unanimous choice of all the electors (Roman clergy and leading laity) and that the resident imperial ambassador had even assisted him in taking possession of the papal palace (the Lateran).

Stephen faced problems on two fronts: continued factional conflict in Rome and increasing Saracen raids. The emperor Charles III could be of no assistance to the pope because he had troubles of his own in France; in 887 he himself was deposed. The Carolingian Empire had ended. When no one stepped in to fill the power vacuum, the pope turned in desperation to Guido III, the duke of Spoleto, who had seized the throne of Italy. The pope crowned him emperor in St. Peter's in 891. The duke thereupon asserted his own supremacy over the Papal States.

Stephen V (VI) maintained friendly relations with Constantinople, with the hope that the Byzantine emperor could provide military aid against the Saracens. When Methodius died on April 6, 885, the pope selected Methodius's disciple Godarz as his successor. However, at the prodding of the German clergy, the pope summoned Godarz to Rome, informed him that he could not use the Old Slavonic liturgy, and appointed one of Methodius's suffragan bishops as administrator of the metropolitan see. When it became clear to Methodius's disciples that Moravia was to be organized according to the wishes of the German hierarchy, they escaped to Bulgaria, where they reverted to the Byzantine rite in the Slavonic language. Eventually this Slavonic-speaking church would spread into other countries, including especially Russia. Stephen V (VI) died September 14, 891, and was buried in the portico, or porch, of St. Peter's.

111 Formosus, *ca. 815–96, pope from October 6, 891, to April 4, 896.*

Formosus is most famous (or infamous) for what happened to him after his death. His body was exhumed, propped up on a throne in full pontifical vestments, and subjected to a mock trial (the so-called Cadaver Synod) in which the dead pope was found guilty of perjury, of coveting the papacy, and of having violated the canons forbidding the transfer of a bishop from one diocese to another (he had been bishop of Porto before being elected Bishop of Rome). Formosus's official papal acts and ordinations were declared null and void, and three fingers of his right hand (by which he swore oaths and gave blessings) were cut off. He was reburied in a common grave and then exhumed a second time and thrown into the Tiber River. A hermit retrieved the body and gave it a third burial. Pope Theodore II (897) exhumed the body a third time and gave it a fourth and final burial with honors in St. Peter's.

Already about seventy-six years of age when elected pope, Formosus had enjoyed an extraordinarily colorful career. He was consecrated bishop of Porto in 864 and was later sent as a missionary to Bulgaria in 866–67, where he performed so brilliantly that King Boris I urged both Popes Nicholas I and Hadrian II to appoint Formosus as metropolitan of the country. But the two popes refused because of the canonical prohibition against moving a bishop from one diocese to another. Formosus also served as a papal ambassador in France and Germany and played a leading role in the Roman synod that excommunicated the patriarch of Constantinople, Photius, in 869. Unfortunately, he ran afoul of Pope John VIII, who was fearful of a political rivalry, and in 876 was excommunicated and deposed on charges of treason, for deserting his diocese, and for coveting the papacy. After Formosus admitted his guilt and promised not to return from exile or seek to regain his diocese, he was readmitted to lay communion. But John VIII's successor, Marinus I, recalled Formosus from exile, canonically rehabilitated him, and restored him as bishop of Porto. As bishop of Porto, Formosus consecrated Pope Stephen V (VI) in 885 and was unanimously elected to succeed Stephen on September 19, 891. The fact that Formosus was already the bishop of another diocese was, for some unexplained reason, not held against him—until after his death. Formosus was consecrated as Bishop of Rome on October 6.

As pope, he strengthened and promoted Christianity in England and northern Germany. He also maintained friendly relations with Constantinople, although he failed in his attempts to mediate a dispute between the followers of the former patriarch, Ignatius, and the new patriarch, Stephen I, whom the Ignatians opposed because he had been ordained by Photius. Unfortunately, his pontificate was placed under great political pressure because of the aggressive behavior of the duke of Spoleto (whom Formosus's predecessor, Pope Stephen V (VI), had crowned as emperor). Formosus sought help from Arnulf, king of the Franks, who eventually invaded Italy. The duke of Spoleto died in the meantime and Arnulf was crowned emperor in St. Peter's in mid-February 896. But Arnulf was struck with paralysis and had to abandon any further military actions against the house of Spoleto.

Although Formosus was a man of exceptional intelligence, ability, and even sanctity, he made some bitter political enemies, including one of his own successors, Stephen VI (VII). Indeed, it was Stephen VI (VII) who, under pressure from the coemperor Lambert and his mother (who resented Formosus for having crowned Arnulf emperor), ordered Formosus's body exhumed nine months after his death, at age eighty, and put on trial, over which Stephen himself presided. A deacon acted as defense attorney. Obviously, the defense was insufficient. The deceased pope was found guilty and his body was mutilated before being thrown into the Tiber River. The "Cadaver Synod" divided the Italian church in two and was a major factor in several subsequent papal elections in which pro-Formosans and anti-Formosans were pitted against one another. It is perhaps little wonder that there has never been a Pope Formosus II, although Cardinal Pietro Barbo had to be dissuaded from taking the name in 1464. He took the name Paul II instead.

112 Boniface VI, *April 896.*

Boniface VI was the only man elected to the papacy after having been defrocked twice (by Pope John VIII, no less) for immorality, once from the subdiaconate and the other time from the ordained priesthood, or presbyterate. His was probably the second shortest pontificate in history, after Urban VII (twelve days in 1590). (It is possible that it was the shortest or the third shortest pontificate, but we do not know the exact day of his consecration as Bishop of Rome or the exact day of his death.) He died after only about fifteen days in office, the victim of a severe case of gout. The son of a bishop, Boniface was elected almost immediately after the death of Formosus, probably on April 4 or 11, under pressure from rioting mobs. He was consecrated as Bishop of Rome on the Sunday following his election. The Roman people's action may have reflected their hostility toward the absent German emperor, Arnulf, and his resident governor. A Roman synod convened by Pope John IX in 898 deplored Boniface VI's election, since he had been twice defrocked for unworthy conduct and had never been canonically reinstated. The synod ordered that this should never happen again. Boniface VI was buried in the portico, or porch, of St. Peter's.

113 Stephen VI (VII), *May 896–August 897.*

(For an explanation of the dual numbering, see Stephen II (III), number 92, in Part II.) The name of Stephen VI (VII) belongs among the infamous popes for having ordered the exhumation of Pope Formosus's body and then for presiding over a mock trial (the so-called Cadaver Synod) of the deceased pope in January 897, nine months after the aged pope's death. For his disgraceful action, Stephen himself was later deposed, stripped of his papal insignia, imprisoned, and strangled to death.

The trial of Formosus (see Formosus, number 111, above) was surely inspired by fanatical hatred, but perhaps also by canonical calculation.

Formosus, after all, had appointed Stephen as bishop of Anagni. If Formosus's papal acts and ordinations were declared invalid (which the Cadaver Synod did do), then Stephen's appointment and ordination as bishop of Anagni were invalid. In that case, his own election as Bishop of Rome could not be challenged canonically on the grounds that he was already the bishop of another diocese. The First Council of Nicaea (325) had ruled that no bishop could be transferred from one diocese to another. Indeed, that was one of the very charges brought against Formosus himself, namely, that he had been bishop of Porto when elected pope.

Following the mock trial Stephen VI (VII) required clergy ordained by Formosus to submit letters renouncing their ordinations as invalid. A few months later, however, an outraged populace, including many of Formosus's supporters, rebelled. Stephen was deposed, imprisoned, and strangled to death. He was buried in St. Peter's.

114 Romanus, *date of death unknown, pope from August to November 897.*

Little or nothing is known of the pontificate of Romanus. After the deposition, imprisonment, and murder of Stephen VI (VII), Romanus was elected and consecrated as Bishop of Rome on a date uncertain, sometime in August 897. He had earlier been created a cardinal by Stephen VI (VII) in the title of the church of San Pietro in Vincoli (St. Peter in Chains). Nevertheless, we do know that Romanus was a member of the pro-Formosan faction, which shows again how often popes are succeeded by men different from themselves in outlook and loyalties. He seems to have become a monk after his brief period on the papal throne. If so, he was probably deposed by the same pro-Formosan faction that elected him in the hope of replacing him with a more vigorous and effective defender of their hero's memory. In any case, the precise date of his death is unknown. Nor do we know where he was buried.

115 Theodore II, *November/December 897 (December 897 in the Vatican's official list).*

Although he was in office only twenty days (the exact dates are unknown), Theodore II held a synod invalidating the so-called Cadaver Synod of 897, which had placed the corpse of Pope Formosus on trial (see Formosus, number 111, above). Theodore II rehabilitated Formosus, recognized the validity of his ordinations and papal acts, and ordered to be burned all the letters solicited by Pope Stephen VI (VII) from the clergy— letters in which they were forced to renounce the validity of their ordinations by Formosus. Theodore then ordered the body of Formosus to be exhumed from the private grave in which it had been placed after being flung into the Tiber River, reclothed in pontifical vestments, and reburied with honors in its original grave in St. Peter's. The circumstances of Theodore II's own death are unknown, but one historian believes that the pope's courageous acts cost him his life. Given the highly charged atmosphere at the time, such speculation is probably not without foundation. He was buried in St. Peter's.

116 John IX, *January 898–January 900.*

John IX also convened a Roman synod annulling the so-called Cadaver Synod of 897, which had placed the deceased Pope Formosus on trial (see Formosus, number 111, above). The circumstances of John's election to the papacy mirrored the chaotic situation in Rome at the time. The enemies of the late Pope Formosus seized the initiative and elected Sergius, bishop of Caere (now Cerveteri), as pope. After Sergius had taken possession of the papal residence at the Lateran, the pro-Formosan party appealed to Lambert, king of Italy, whom Formosus had crowned as emperor in 892. With Lambert's help, Sergius was expelled from the palace and John, a Benedictine abbot, was elected pope and consecrated as Bishop of Rome in early January 898.

John moved quickly to complete his predecessor's efforts in rehabilitating Pope Formosus. He called a synod in Rome, attended by a number of bishops from northern Italy, which burned the acts of the Cadaver Synod, pardoned some of the participants (who pleaded that they had acted under compulsion), and deposed others, including Sergius, the bishop who was first elected to succeed Theodore II. Formosus's ordinations were recognized as valid, and so, too, was his crowning of Lambert as emperor (but not his crowning of Lambert's rival, Arnulf, king of the East Franks). The synod reaffirmed the canonical prohibition against the transfer of bishops from one diocese to another, but stipulated that the case of Formosus was an exception to the rule. The synod also prohibited trials of deceased persons and decreed that, while the pope should be elected by bishops and clergy at the request of the senate and people of Rome, his consecration should take place in the presence of imperial representatives. This was a revival of the terms of the Roman Constitution of 824, decreed by the emperor Lothair I. Shortly after this synod, the pope held a second, larger synod in Ravenna, which confirmed not only the acts of the Roman synod but also the ancient privileges of the Holy See and its territorial possessions. However, the death of the young emperor in a hunting accident and the irregularity of the imperial succession prevented the matter pertaining to papal elections from being enforced. Total chaos would follow John's pontificate.

On other fronts, John IX did his best to maintain good relations with Constantinople, sent representatives to deal with problems in the Moravian Church (but was rebuked by the bishops of Bavaria for interfering), and restored the bishop of Langres (France) to his diocese after he had been deposed by Pope Stephen VI (VII). John IX also confirmed the privileges of the abbey of Monte Cassino. He died in January 900 and was buried in St. Peter's. However, no monument honors his memory.

117 Benedict IV, *February 900–July 903.*

Very little is known of Benedict IV's pontificate except that Rome continued to be torn apart by partisan conflict between the supporters and enemies of the late Pope Formosus (891–96). Because of the political and social chaos, few reliable records remain from this period—which explains why the circumstances and date of Benedict IV's election and consecration as Bishop of Rome are uncertain. We do know that he held a synod at the Lateran (the papal palace) on August 31, 900, which confirmed Arginus as bishop of Langres (France) and ratified Pope Formosus's granting of the pallium (the woolen vestment worn around the neck as a sign of pastoral authority) to him. (Arginus had been deposed by Pope Stephen VI [VII], but later restored by Pope John IX.) The pope also formally excommunicated those who had murdered the archbishop of Rheims and urged the French bishops to promulgate the decree throughout the country. Significantly (in view of the canonical prohibition against a bishop's transferring from one diocese to another), he approved the election of Stephen, formerly bishop of Sorrento, as archbishop of Naples. He also supported Malcenus (also Maclacenus), a bishop in Cappadocia (modern-day Turkey), who had been driven from his diocese by the Saracens. The pope furnished the bishop with letters commending him to the care and protection of all Christians.

With the accidental death of the young Lambert of Spoleto, who left no male heir, Italy was thrown into political chaos. Berengar of Friuli, king of Italy since 888, might have filled the void, but he was defeated by the Magyars in 899 and his supremacy in Italy was subsequently challenged by the young king Louis "the Blind" of Provence, grandson of the emperor Louis II. The pope crowned Louis emperor in February 901, but soon thereafter Berengar regained his political and military strength and defeated Louis in August 902, driving him permanently out of Italy. Without an imperial protector, Rome once again fell into political and social anarchy.

Remembered as a pope who was generous to the poor and those in distress, Benedict IV is believed by some to have been murdered by agents of Berengar, probably in July 903. He was buried in St. Peter's.

118 Leo V, *d. early 904 or October 905, pope from July/August to September, 903.*

After less than two months in office, Leo V was overthrown by an antipope, Christopher, imprisoned, and murdered. At the time of his election, Leo was a priest in a town about twenty-two miles southwest of Rome. Historians do not know how a man who was not a member of the Roman clergy could have been elected pope in this period. Possibly he was a compromise candidate, chosen because of his good reputation. But perhaps because he was an outsider, he was overthrown in a palace revolution by Christopher, cardinal-priest of San Damaso, who declared himself pope and had Leo thrown into prison. But Christopher was, in turn, overthrown by Sergius (later Pope Sergius III) and sent to prison with Leo. After enduring several weeks of misery, both were murdered. (Another version has it that Christopher ordered Leo murdered, and then he was murdered himself on order of Sergius.) An eleventh-century legend confuses Leo V with Tugdual (also Tutwal and Tual), a Breton saint who was thought to have been miraculously elected pope while on a pilgrimage to Rome. Tugdual, however, actually lived in the sixth century, not the tenth. (Levillain's *Dictionnaire historique de la papauté* insists that Leo V died "*sans doute*" [Fr., "without doubt"] in October 905. J. N. D. Kelly places his death in early 904.) Leo V may have been buried in St. Peter's or in the Lateran.

119 Sergius III, *January 29, 904–April 14, 911.*

Although the conventional wisdom makes Alexander VI (1492–1503) the historic symbol of papal corruption, few other popes in history can vie with the murderous Sergius III, who was responsible for the deaths of his predecessor and his predecessor's rival, the antipope Christopher. Subsequently, he held a synod that reaffirmed the infamous Cadaver Synod of 897, which had placed the corpse of Pope Formosus on trial. Once again all of Formosus's ordinations were declared invalid, and the Church was thrown once more into a state of total confusion. Sergius III is also said to have fathered an illegitimate son who became a future pope (John XI).

Sergius himself had been consecrated bishop of Caere (now Cerveteri) by Pope Formosus and took part in the Cadaver Synod. When the synod invalidated Formosus's ordinations, Sergius regarded himself as reduced to the diaconate and had himself reordained by Pope Stephen VI (VII). Even then, Sergius was ambitious for the papacy and did not want the fact that he was once the bishop of another diocese to be held against him, because of the canonical prohibition against a bishop's being transferred from one diocese to another. (The origin of the prohibition was canon 15 of the Council of Nicaea, in 325.) Gripped by hatred of Formosus, Sergius was originally elected pope to succeed Theodore II in 897 and was even installed in the Lateran Palace, but was quickly ejected in favor of the pro-Formosan John IX, who had the support of the emperor Lambert of Spoleto. Sergius was deposed and driven into exile, but found himself with a second chance when, seven years later, the antipope Christopher overthrew Leo V. Sergius marched on Rome with an armed force, threw Christopher into prison, was acclaimed pope, and was consecrated on January 29, 904. Soon afterward, he had both Leo and Christopher strangled to death in prison.

Sergius dated his own reign from December 897, when he was first "elected," and he regarded all subsequent popes as intruders. He forced his clergy under threat of violence to attend a synod that nullified John IX's two synods (898), one in Rome, the other in Ravenna, and reaffirmed the acts of the Cadaver Synod of 897, including that synod's invalidation of Pope Formosus's papal acts and ordinations. Since Formosus had created many bishops and they, in turn, had ordained many priests, there was complete confusion in the Church. Sergius ordered, again under threat, that all those ordinations be repeated. There was some scattered opposition outside of Rome (the Frankish priest Auxilius wrote very effective defenses of Formosus's ordinations, and Bishop Stephen of Naples also weighed in on the side of the deceased pope), but public opposition was impossible in the city itself. Sergius had the support of the noble families, particularly that of Theophylact, a powerful official who commanded the local militia. Sergius was so close to his family, in fact, that he was reputed to have had a son (the future Pope John XI) by the fifteen-year-old daughter of Theophylact's wife, Theodora. So corrupted were Sergius and his immediate successors by the Theophylact family, that the subsequent decades have been called the "pornocracy" of the papacy.

Acting according to form, Sergius also threw the Eastern Church into confusion when, in opposition to Eastern canon law, he approved the Byzantine emperor Leo VI's fourth marriage, in quest of a male heir. The patriarch of Constantinople who had opposed the marriage was deposed and exiled.

Sergius III completed the restoration of the Lateran Basilica, which had been badly damaged during an earthquake while the Cadaver Synod was being held. The supporters of Pope Formosus saw the earthquake as a sign of divine displeasure with the synod. Many Catholics might wonder today why that divine displeasure did not land directly on the head of Sergius in the form of falling stones and wooden beams. He died on April 15, 911, and was buried in the Lateran Basilica. His tomb has not been preserved.

120 Anastasius III, *ca. June 911–ca. August 913 (April 911–June 913 in the Vatican's official list; Levillain's* Dictionnaire historique de la papauté *begins his pontificate in September 911 and ends it in October 913).*

The pontificate of Anastasius III was completely dominated by the Theophylact family, specifically by its powerful head of household (consul, senator, financial director of the Holy See) and his ambitious wife, Theodora. No records survive of Anastasius's election and consecration as Bishop of Rome, and little of his pontificate. There is only one extant document, a bull granting the pallium (the woolen vestment worn around the neck as a sign of pastoral authority) to the bishop of Vercelli. He did receive a lengthy letter from Nicholas, the reinstated patriarch of Constantinople, that deplored Pope Sergius III's approval of the emperor Leo VI's fourth marriage in 906 and the behavior of the papal legates. There is no record of the pope's reply, but it probably was unsatisfactory because Nicholas removed the pope's name from the list of those to be prayed for at Mass and once again relations between Rome and Constantinople had soured. After a pontificate of just over two years, Anastasius III died and was buried in St. Peter's.

121 Lando [Landus], *ca. August 913–ca. March 914 (July 913–February 914 in the Vatican's official list; Levillain's* Dictionnaire historique de la papauté *begins his pontificate in November 913 and ends it in March 914).*

Historians do not agree on the date of Lando's election and consecration as Bishop of Rome. It is likely that his candidacy had been approved by the powerful Theophylact family in Rome. His brief pontificate of about six months was undistinguished. Indeed, nothing is recorded of his reign except a donation, given in memory of his father, to the cathedral church in his home territory of Sabina. He was buried in St. Peter's.

122 John X, *March/April 914–May 928 (March 914–May 928 in the Vatican's official list; Levillain's* Dictionnaire historique de la papauté *says that his pontificate began in early April and places his death in 929).*

Because he tried to distance himself from the powerful noble families of Rome, John X was deposed, imprisoned, and suffocated to death after a pontificate of some fourteen years. He had been archbishop of Ravenna for nine years when, at the instigation of the Roman nobility and especially of the Theophylact family, he was elected to the papacy. The irony was not lost on those who were loyal to the memory of Pope Formosus (891–96), a pope whose body was exhumed from its grave and placed on public trial, among other things for having moved from one diocese (Porto) to another (Rome) in accepting election to the papacy. However,

with the growing prominence of the Roman see, the long-standing canonical objections to electing bishops of other dioceses to the papacy was
beginning to weaken.

Perhaps the Roman nobility's real motive for summoning John X from
Ravenna to Rome was his reputation for leadership, at a time when their
grand estates were threatened by the continued Saracen raids on central
Italy. John X immediately organized a coalition of Italian princes and persuaded the Byzantine emperor, Constantine VII, to provide naval assistance. After a three-month siege in which the pope himself took part, the
alliance decisively defeated the Saracens in August 915. The next month he
crowned Berengar I as emperor in St. Peter's, eliciting from him the traditional oath to guarantee the rights and possessions of the Holy See.

On the ecclesiastical front, John X approved the strict monastic rule of
the newly founded abbey of Cluny (910), promoted the conversion of the
Normans, settled disputes over episcopal succession to the dioceses of
Narbonne and Louvain, respectively, and worked (unsuccessfully) to
bring Croatia and Dalmatia back to communion with Rome and to suppress the liturgical use of the Slavonic language. Toward the end of 923 he
restored unity with the Eastern Church, a unity that had been broken
once again in 912 because Popes Sergius III (904–11) and Anastasius III
(911–13) had approved the emperor's fourth marriage, in violation of
Eastern canon law. In Rome itself John X completely reconstructed and
decorated the Lateran. But he also took some bizarre actions, such as
confirming the election of Count Heribert's five-year-old son, Hugh,
as archbishop of Rheims, in return for which he secured the release of
King Charles the Simple, whom Heribert had imprisoned.

What led to the pope's downfall, however, were his deliberate efforts
to mark a course independently of Rome's powerful noble families. Two
years after the emperor Berengar's murder in 924, John X made a pact
with the new king of Italy, Hugh of Provence. This alarmed Marozia, the
powerful daughter of Theophylact, who had died about six years earlier.
She and her husband, Guido, the marquis of Tuscany, organized a revolt
against John X and his brother Peter, whom the pope had come increasingly to rely upon. Peter was killed in the Lateran before John X's eyes,
and a half year later the pope himself was deposed and imprisoned at
Castel Sant'Angelo. He died after several months (probably in early 929),
almost certainly by suffocation on orders of Marozia. He was buried in
the Lateran Basilica.

123 Leo VI, *May–December 928.*

The brief pontificate of Leo VI, an elderly man (a priest in the title of
Santa Susanna) when elected in order to keep the papal throne warm for

a son of the powerful Theophylact family, has left no significant historical trace. It is canonically significant, however, that he was elected and consecrated as Bishop of Rome while his predecessor, John X, was still alive and in prison. Had John's deposition from office been canonically valid? If not, Leo VI's election was invalid and he does not belong on the official list of popes. The only surviving letter from Leo's pontificate was written to the bishops of Dalmatia and Croatia, asking them to be obedient to their archbishop to whom the pope had granted the pallium (the woolen vestment worn around the neck as a sign of pastoral authority) and to be content with their territorial boundaries. Leo VI died before his predecessor, John X, was murdered in prison. Leo VI was buried in St. Peter's.

124 Stephen VII (VIII), *December 928–February 931.*

(For an explanation of the dual numbering, see Stephen II (III), number 92, in Part II.) Stephen VII (VIII) was elected to succeed Leo VI while Leo's predecessor, John X, was still alive and in prison. The same canonical question that can be raised about the validity of Leo VI's election to the papacy can be raised about Stephen's. Had John's deposition from office been canonically valid? If not, Stephen's election was invalid and he, like Leo VI, does not belong on the official list of popes. Like Leo VI, Stephen VII (VIII) was a stopgap appointment, manipulated by the powerful Theophylact family, and particularly by Marozia, who wanted to ensure that her son John would someday be pope. Because of the absence of written records from this turbulent and chaotic period of papal history, Stephen's only recorded actions concern the confirmation or extension of privileges granted to certain monasteries and religious houses in Italy and France. He was buried in the crypt of St. Peter's.

125 John XI, *March 931–December 935 or January 936 (March 931–December 935 in the Vatican's official list).*

Elected and consecrated as Bishop of Rome while still in his early twenties, Pope John XI was the illegitimate son of Pope Sergius III (904–11) and Marozia, the head of the powerful Theophylact family. This is the only recorded instance of an illegitimate son of a previous pope succeeding to the papacy himself.

Among John XI's first official acts was to confirm that the new reformist abbey of Cluny (founded in 909) was under the protection of the Holy See and that its abbots were to be freely elected. When the Byzantine emperor Romanus I asked the pope early in 932 to approve the appointment of his sixteen-year-old son Theophylact as patriarch of Constantinople, the pope did so and the following year sent two bishops as his representatives to consecrate and enthrone the young man—an action that shocked many in the Eastern Church. That same summer John XI officiated at the wedding of the widowed Marozia and Hugh of Provence, king of Italy. The wedding and the pope's participation in it were highly controversial because Hugh was Marozia's brother-in-law. The marriage was contrary to the canon law of the day. It was also unpopular with the Roman people because of their suspicions of foreign rule. A revolt was incited by Alberic II, Marozia's son by her first marriage, whom Hugh had insulted at the wedding banquet. In December an armed mob stormed Castel Sant'Angelo, where the couple was residing. Hugh escaped, but Alberic imprisoned his mother and his half brother, the pope, and proclaimed himself prince of Rome, senator of all the Romans, count, and patrician. Nothing more was heard of Marozia, but John XI was later released from prison and placed under house arrest in the Lateran, where Alberic treated him as his personal slave. A later historian of the century described the pope as "powerless, lacking all distinction, administering only sacraments." He was buried in the basilica of St. John Lateran.

126 Leo VII, *January 3, 936–July 13, 939.*

Elected through the direct influence of Alberic II, the absolute ruler of Rome at this time, Leo VII was consecrated as Bishop of Rome on January 3, 936, and restricted thereafter to purely ecclesiastical functions during his pontificate. Probably of Benedictine background himself, Leo VII promoted the revival of monasticism. He invited the reformist abbot Odo of Cluny to Rome for a visit and entrusted him with the task of reforming the religious houses of Rome and its environs. At the same time, the pope renewed the privileges of the restored abbey at Subiaco, fifty miles east of Rome, and also of Cluny in Burgundy. A serious moral blot on his record occurred in 937 or thereabouts when he encouraged his newly appointed archbishop of Mainz to expel Jews who refused to be baptized. He died on July 13, 939, of unknown causes and was buried in St. Peter's.

127 Stephen VIII (IX), *July 14, 939–October 942.*

(For an explanation of the dual numbering, see Stephen II (III), number 92, in Part II.) Like his predecessor, Leo VII, Stephen VIII (IX) was elected (on the same day Leo VII died) through the direct influence of Alberic II, the absolute ruler of Rome at this time. He was consecrated as Bishop of Rome the next day, July 14. And like Leo VII, he was restricted by Alberic to purely ecclesiastical matters. He supported the new reformist monastery in Cluny and the reform of monasteries in Rome and central Italy (but so, too, did Alberic because of his deep personal interest in monasticism). Stephen did support Louis IV as king of France and ordered the people and nobles of France and Burgundy to do so under pain of excommunication. Later that year (942) he restored the archbishop of Rheims to his diocese after having been displaced for several years. This pope's conciliatory gesture also helped to soften the opposition to Louis. In the last months of his life, Stephen VIII (IX) fell out of favor with Alberic, perhaps because he became involved in a conspiracy against him. The pope was imprisoned, mutilated, and died of his wounds sometime in late October 942. He was buried in St. Peter's.

128 Marinus II, *October 30, 942–May 946.*

Like his two immediate predecessors, Marinus II was the creature of Alberic II, the absolute ruler of Rome, and was allowed to do little during his pontificate. Elected and consecrated as Bishop of Rome a few days after the death of Stephen VIII (IX), Marinus II left little or no historical trace. Among his recorded acts were his defense of the privileges and properties of the abbey of Monte Cassino against the avaricious bishop of Capua and his appointing its abbot as head of the monastery attached to the Roman basilica of St. Paul's Outside the Walls. He also confirmed the appointment of Frederick, archbishop of Mainz, as papal vicar and envoy to Germany with the authority to convene synods and to deal with abuses among the clergy and monks—the same office conferred two centuries earlier on St. Boniface (d. 754), apostle to Germany. Marinus II is sometimes mistakenly listed as Martin III (just as the first Pope Marinus [882–84] was mistakenly listed as Martin II). He died sometime during the month of May 946 and was buried in St. Peter's.

129 Agapitus II, *May 10, 946–December 955.*

Agapitus II was forced by Alberic II, the dying absolute ruler of Rome, to swear an oath, in direct violation of the decree of Pope Symmachus in 499, that the next pope would be Alberic's son Octavian. Like his three immediate predecessors, Agapitus II had been elected through Alberic's direct influence. He was consecrated as Bishop of Rome on May 10, 946.

Agapitus II confirmed the special status of the reformist abbey of Cluny in Burgundy and arranged for German monks from the abbey at Gorze to come to Rome to restore discipline at the abbey attached to the basilica of St. Paul's Outside the Walls. With King Otto I of Germany and King Louis IV of France, the papal delegate presided over a synod at Ingelheim, which resolved the dispute over episcopal succession in the diocese of Rheims and ordered Louis's rival in France to submit to Louis under pain of excommunication. The pope ratified these decisions at a Roman synod in 949. He also gave broad support to Otto, granting him jurisdiction over monasteries, permitting his brother Bruno, archbishop of Cologne, to wear the pallium (the woolen vestment worn around the neck as a sign of pastoral authority), and indirectly extending Otto's jurisdiction over Denmark through powers granted to the metropolitan of Hamburg. When Otto asked the pope to transform the monastery he had founded at Magdeburg into a metropolitan see, with supervisory authority over the mission to the Slavs and with the right to establish bishoprics and archbishoprics and to define ecclesiastical boundaries, the pope agreed, much to the consternation of the archbishop of Mainz.

As Alberic lay dying, he summoned the clergy and the nobility to St. Peter's, where he compelled them, in the presence of the pope, to take an uncanonical oath that his illegitimate son Octavian would be elected to succeed Agapitus II. The pope died a year later and was buried in the apse of the basilica of St. John Lateran.

130 John XII, *December 16, 955–May 14, 964.*

Elected (at age eighteen) because of the oath exacted illegally from the clergy and nobility by his dying father, Alberic II, absolute ruler of Rome, John XII was the third pope in history to change his name (Octavian) upon election (the first to do so was John II in 533, whose name from birth was Mercury, and the second was John III in 561, whose name was Catelinus). He established the Holy Roman Empire, crowning Otto I in 962, and allowed the emperor to reassert imperial influence over papal elections. The pope's private life was marked by gross immorality (some accused him of converting the Lateran Palace into a brothel), and he was deposed by a Roman synod in December 963 at the emperor's urging, but he resumed the papacy two months later after deposing his successor, Leo VIII. John XII died at age twenty-eight—of a stroke suffered allegedly while in the bed of a married woman.

In spite of this deplorable record, he did manage somehow to engage in normal ecclesiastical activities from time to time. The Spanish Church, under pressure from Muslim attacks, sought his counsel. He presented the pallium (the woolen vestment worn around the neck as a sign of pastoral authority) to the visiting archbishops of York and Canterbury in 957 and 960, respectively, and shared his father's interest in monastic reform, even going on pilgrimage to the abbey of Subiaco, fifty miles east of Rome. On the other hand, he engaged in a disastrous attempt to enlarge the Papal States by military force against Capua and Benevento, while the northern regions of the papal territories were being plundered by the king of Italy. The pope dispatched two envoys to the king of Germany, Otto I, to ask for his help and to offer the imperial crown in return. Otto accepted the invitation and the terms. He restored papal sovereignty in the north of Italy and entered Rome on January 31, 962. On February 2 the pope anointed and crowned him emperor, along with his queen, Adelaide, in St. Peter's. This act established the Holy Roman Empire, which was to last until 1806.

A Roman synod called upon the pope to mend his personal ways and decided certain issues affecting the Church in Germany. On February 13 Otto published the "Ottonian Privilege" (*Privilegium Ottanianum*), which solemnly confirmed the donations of Pepin and Charlemagne, but which added substantial new territories to the Papal States comprising between two-thirds and three-quarters of Italy. The decree bound the emperor to defend the Church's rights and possessions and restored the rules for papal elections, subjecting them once again to imperial approval. The popes were to swear their allegiance to the emperor and recognize him as the overlord of the Papal States, as stipulated by the constitution of Lothair I in 824.

John XII was resentful of the arrangement. As soon as the emperor left Rome to fight battles elsewhere, the pope began intriguing against him with the emperor's hated enemy Berengar II, king of Italy. In November 963, the emperor returned to Rome, and John XII fled with the papal treasury to Tivoli. Otto presided over a synod in St. Peter's at which, after hearing charges from the clergy of the pope's unworthy behavior, he accused the pope of perfidy and treason. The synod wrote to the pope three times asking him to appear before the synod. He refused and threatened excommunication. In his absence, he was deposed on December 4, 963. At the request of the synod, Otto proposed the name of Leo, a layman, as a worthy successor, and Leo was elected on December 4, 963, and consecrated as Bishop of Rome two days later, after receiving all the requisite Holy Orders in sequence. There is a serious canonical question, of course, whether the synod had the right to judge the pope and to depose him—which, in turn, raises a question about the validity of Leo VIII's election and consecration.

Leo's own behavior in office disturbed the Roman people, who rallied to John's support after the emperor left the city once more. Leo VIII fled, and John XII exacted severe reprisals against the imperial partisans. At a synod on February 26, 964, the previous imperial synod was nullified, Leo VIII was deposed and his ordinations were declared invalid. But soon thereafter Otto marched back into Rome and John retreated from the city once again. In early May he suffered a stroke (it is said, while in bed with a married woman) and died a week later, still in his middle twenties. He was buried in the Lateran Basilica.

131 Leo VIII, *December 6, 963–March 1, 965.*

Leo VIII's pontificate overlapped with two others: John XII's (between December 4, 963, and John's death on May 14, 964) and Benedict V's (between May 22 and June 23, 964). The legitimacy of Leo's own election in 963 has been a matter of canonical debate because of the questionable nature of John XII's deposition by a Roman synod presided over by the German emperor on December 4, 863. Significantly, the official list of popes in the Vatican's *Annuario Pontificio* accepts the overlapping without resolving the canonical question.

Leo VIII had been a skilled Lateran official of good reputation. Still a layman when elected by acclaim on December 4, 963, following the deposition of John XII and with the emperor Otto I's approval, he had to be rushed through the various minor and major Orders before being consecrated as Bishop of Rome two days later by the bishops of Ostia, Porto, and Albano. Leo's election, however, proved unpopular with the Roman people. They were encouraged in their dissatisfaction by the deposed John XII from his refuge in Tivoli. As soon as the emperor and his troops left Rome in mid-January, widespread disturbances erupted in the city and Leo VIII was forced to seek asylum in the imperial court, thereby allowing John XII to regain the papal throne. A synod convened by John in St. Peter's on February 26 deposed Leo as a usurper and declared his ordination and consecration invalid, as well as the Holy Orders of those whom Leo had himself ordained.

When John XII died after suffering a stroke, allegedly while in bed with a married woman, the Romans ignored Leo VIII and urged the emperor to elect the cardinal-deacon Benedict. The emperor refused because he had personally arranged Leo's election after John XII had been deposed. But the Romans ignored the emperor's wishes and proceeded to elect and enthrone Benedict as Benedict V on May 22. The emperor reentered the city on June 23 and reinstated Leo VIII as pope. A few days later Leo convened yet another synod which deposed and ecclesiastically degraded Benedict V, who was later deported to Hamburg in 865. Nothing else is known of Leo VIII's brief and canonically dubious pontificate. He was buried in St. Peter's.

132 Benedict V, *d. July 4, 966, pope from May 22 to June 23, 964.*

Benedict V's one-month-long pontificate was canonically dubious because another claimant to the papacy, Leo VIII, was still alive. When the licentious John XII died on May 14, 964, the Roman people and many of the clergy ignored the wishes of the emperor Otto I to reinstate Leo VIII (whom John XII had deposed as a usurper). Instead, on May 22 they acclaimed Benedict, a learned, reformist cardinal-deacon, as pope, had him consecrated as Bishop of Rome, and enthroned him in the Lateran Palace.

The emperor laid siege to the city of Rome, threatening to starve the people into submission. The people soon yielded and handed over Benedict to the emperor on June 23. A synod was immediately held in the Lateran, presided over jointly by Leo VIII and the emperor Otto I. Benedict was condemned as a usurper (which he was only if Leo VIII's own dubious election and consecration in December 963 had been canonically valid), was stripped of his pontifical vestments and insignia, and had his pastoral staff, or crozier, broken over his head by Leo himself as Benedict lay prostrate.

The emperor allowed Benedict to retain the rank of deacon but deported him to Hamburg, where the local bishop treated him with courtesy and dignity. When Leo VIII died on March 1, 965, some called for Benedict V's restoration to the papal throne, but there was no general interest in him. Nevertheless, Benedict was still widely admired and respected for the holiness of his life (in sharp contrast to the libertine John XII). Just over twenty years after his death in Hamburg (July 4, 966), Benedict's body, which had initially been buried in Hamburg's cathedral, was returned to Rome by the emperor Otto III. His place of burial in Rome, however, is unknown.

133 John XIII, *October 1, 965–September 6, 972.*

John XIII's pontificate was largely in the service of the ecclesiastical and political agenda of the German emperor Otto I, who had directly influenced John's election. Once again the ancient canonical prohibition against the transfer of bishops from one diocese to another was ignored. John had been bishop of Narnia in Umbria when elected and consecrated as Bishop of Rome.

His pontificate began on a negative note. The Roman people resented his dependence on a foreign sovereign and hated him for his authoritarian style of governance. In the midst of a popular revolt less than three months after his election, John was assaulted, imprisoned, and exiled to the Campagna. He escaped and made contact with the emperor. The Romans eventually repented of their actions and, on November 14 of the following year, welcomed John XIII back to the city. The emperor himself returned to Rome at Christmas, severely punished the leaders of the revolt, and remained in Italy until the summer of 972, all the while bestowing protection on the pope.

A synod in Ravenna in 967, presided over by the pope and the emperor, passed legislation against clerical marriages and restored large territories to the Papal States. John XIII, in his turn, complied with the emperor's desire, against the opposition of the German hierarchy, to have Magdeburg raised to an archdiocese, and the following year the pope consecrated Adalbert as its first and most important archbishop. At Christmas, 967, John crowned Otto's twelve-year-old son Otto II as co-emperor. Less than five years later, with the hope that relations between East and West could be improved, John XIII officiated at the marriage of Otto II and a Greek princess, a niece of the Byzantine emperor John I, and crowned her as empress. But tensions deepened, especially when the pope elevated Capua and Benevento to metropolitan archdioceses, even though they fell within provinces under Byzantine control. In order to limit Rome's influence in the Byzantine provinces of Apulia and Calabria, the patriarch of Constantinople retaliated by making the bishop of Otranto an archbishop with five suffragan bishops under him.

After his death on September 6, 972, John XIII was buried in the basilica of St. Paul's Outside the Walls.

134 Benedict VI, *January 19, 973–July 974 (January 19, 973–June 974 in the Vatican's official list).*

When his protector, the emperor Otto I, died, Benedict VI was seized, imprisoned, and strangled to death by order of the antipope Boniface, a tool of the newly powerful Crescentii family in Rome. The circumstances of Benedict's election (in September or October 973) remain obscure. He seems to have had the support of both the pro-imperial party and the reformers, who opposed another political pope. He did not have the support of the Roman aristocracy. Benedict's consecration as Bishop of Rome was delayed until January 19, 973, because, under the restored rules, formal imperial approval was required, and the emperor was back in Germany at the time.

Benedict VI's early decisions were consistent with the emperor's interests as well as the reformers'. He confirmed the premier status of Trier, the oldest diocese in Germany, promoted the reform of monasteries, and forbade bishops from charging fees for ordinations and consecrations. But when Otto died on May 7, the pope lost his pillar of support. The new emperor, Otto II, preoccupied with his own troubles in Germany, could provide no help when a nationalist faction, led by the head of the Crescentii family, mounted a revolt against Benedict VI. In June 974 the pope was seized and imprisoned in Castel Sant'Angelo.

A cardinal-deacon named Franco, who was the candidate originally favored by the Crescentii family to succeed John XIII, was quickly elected and consecrated as pope, taking the name Boniface VII. The imperial representative hurried to Rome the next month to demand Benedict's release, but Boniface, the antipope, had Benedict strangled to death by a priest named Stephen, in order to strengthen his own claim on the papacy. The imperial representative led a force that stormed the castle, but Boniface escaped, taking a portion of the papal treasury with him. Another pope was elected (Benedict VII) and Boniface was excommunicated. However, Boniface returned to Rome six years later, upon the death of emperor Otto II, to reclaim the papacy from the unpopular Benedict VII (who was subsequently imprisoned, deposed, and murdered).

Remarkably, the antipope Boniface VII remained in office for some eleven months without significant imperial or popular protest. He died suddenly on July 20, 985, giving rise to suspicions that he had been murdered. His body was stripped of its vestments, dragged naked through the streets, and left at the foot of Marcus Aurelius's statue (then in front of the papal Lateran Palace), where it was trampled upon and stabbed repeatedly with spears. He was referred to now as "Malefatius" ("evildoer") rather than "Bonifatius" ("doer of good"). Until 1904 Boniface VII was classified as a legitimate pope, and the next pope to assume the name Boniface took the number VIII. Some have argued that Boniface VII was a legitimate pope from the date of John XIV's death in August 984. The legitimate pope, Benedict VI, had died by strangulation in June 974 and was buried in St. Peter's.

135 Benedict VII, *October 974–July 10, 983.*

During the pontificate of Benedict VII official visits by bishops and laity (known as *ad limina* visits, that is, "to the thresholds," or tombs, of the Apostles Peter and Paul) became more frequent, as did the practice of referring disputed issues to the pope. After Benedict VI was murdered by the antipope Boniface VII, Benedict VII, then bishop of Sutri, near Viterbo, was elected pope with the support of the emperor Otto II and the pro-imperial party and aristocratic families of Rome. He was consecrated as Bishop of Rome sometime in October 974. The new pope immediately convened a synod at which the antipope Boniface VII was excommunicated. However, Boniface mounted a revolt against Benedict VII in the summer of 980, forcing the pope to leave the city. The pope appealed to the emperor, but it took until the following March to be restored.

Benedict VII was primarily a spiritual rather than a political pope. He promoted monasticism and monastic reform in France, Germany, and Italy, and at a synod in St. Peter's in March 981 he prohibited simony (the buying and selling of church offices and spiritual benefits). But in other ecclesiastical matters, he was little more than a tool of the emperor. For example, he suppressed and divided the diocese of Merseburg in Germany so that its bishop, a favorite of the emperor, could be promoted to the more prestigious diocese of Magdeburg. Some have judged this act of suppression a setback in efforts to convert central Europe. Benedict also advanced the emperor's anti-Byzantine agenda by agreeing to elevate Salerno to an archdiocese and to establish Trani as a Latin diocese independent of the Byzantine-controlled diocese of Bari.

After his death on July 10, 983, Benedict VII was buried in Santa Croce in Gerusalemme, one of the seven ancient basilicas of Rome, perhaps because of the report that he had once gone to Jerusalem as a pilgrim (before being elected pope) and brought back a fragment, or relic, of the True Cross.

136 John XIV, *December 983–August 20, 984.*

John XIV was not the first pope to change his name upon election to the papacy (John II had done so in 533, John III in 561, and John XII in 955), but he is the first one to have done so because his baptismal name was Peter. He did not wish to take the papal name of the Blessed Apostle himself. (The only other pope to forgo the name of Peter was Sergius IV in 1009.) Upon the death of Benedict VII on July 10, 983, the emperor Otto II offered the papacy to Maiolos, the well-regarded abbot of Cluny in Burgundy, who declined it. Without consulting the clergy and people of Rome, the emperor then selected Peter Canepanova, his former archchancellor for Italy and now bishop of Pavia. Evidently, the negotiations with Peter took some time because it was not until December that he accepted the appointment. Indeed, there seems to have been no election at all. Consequently, the new pope came into office with no allies in the city and the emperor as his sole constituent.

No sooner had John XIV been installed when Otto II was stricken with malaria and died in the pope's arms. The empress, Theophano, immediately left Rome for Germany to defend the claim of her three-year-old son Otto III. John XIV was now completely defenseless against his enemies. The antipope Boniface VII returned from exile in Constantinople in April 984. John was arrested, beaten, deposed from office, and imprisoned at Castel Sant'Angelo. He died four months later of starvation. Some reports indicate that he was poisoned. The only surviving document from his pontificate is a decree bestowing the pallium (the woolen vestment worn around the neck as a sign of pastoral authority) on the archbishop of Benevento, an act with political overtones because of the emperor's interests in southern Italy. John XIV was buried in St. Peter's.

137 John XV, *August 985–March 996.*

John XV was the first pope formally to canonize a saint: Ulric, bishop of Augsburg, in 993. Cardinal-priest of the church of San Vitale when elected with the support of the powerful Crescentii family, John XV, it should be noted, was regarded as the successor of the antipope Boniface VII, who died on July 20, 985, rather than of Pope John XIV, who died of starvation or poisoning on August 20, 984, after having been deposed and imprisoned by Boniface. Indeed, Boniface VII has only been considered as an antipope since 1904. Before that, he was included on the ancient lists of popes, even though usually described as an intruder. Moreover, the next pope to take the name Boniface took the number VIII, not VII. Thus can the Holy Spirit cross the canonical wires!

Immediately after his election, John XV allied himself with the Roman nobility and alienated his clergy in the process. His greed also fueled their contempt for him. Nevertheless, the new pope attended to (mostly) political business. He mediated a dispute between the king of England and the duke of Normandy in 991. The following year he accepted Poland from Duke Mieszko as a papal fief, with responsibility for protecting Poland from Germany and Bohemia. Even his historic canonization of Ulric of Augsburg in 993 advanced the imperial interests. On another front, and at the prodding of the German hierarchy, he intervened in 992 in the dispute over the deposition of Arnulf (also Arnoul) as archbishop of Rheims, instigated by the king of France and approved by the synod of St.-Basle, Verzy, in 991. The new archbishop chosen by the king was Gerbert of Aurillac (the future Pope Sylvester II). The French bishops had acted independently of Rome and insisted that they were within their canonical rights to do so. They rebuffed the pope's efforts to call them "on the carpet" for their actions. A synod held at Mouzon in the Ardennes subsequently condemned and suspended Gerbert (995), but it should be noted that only German bishops were in attendance. (After the king's death, Arnulf was restored to Rheims.)

The head of the powerful Crescentii family had died in 988 and was succeeded by his tyrannical brother, who seized power in the Papal States and ruled them in a dictatorial manner. After the empress Theophano died in June 991, the pope's position deteriorated precipitously. In March of 995, facing the contempt of his own clergy for his avariciousness and nepotism and suffering under the harsh thumb of the Crescentii family, John XV was forced to seek asylum in Sutri, from which he sent envoys to the young emperor Otto III to seek help against his enemies. When word began to circulate of John's contact with the emperor and of the emperor's decision to come to Rome, the Roman nobility invited the pope back to the city and reinstalled him in the Lateran Palace with all appropriate honors. Otto III set out from Regensburg in February 996, but the pope died of fever before the emperor reached Rome. John XV was buried in St. Peter's.

138 Gregory V, *Saxon, 972–99, pope from May 3, 996, to February 18, 999.*

Gregory V was the first German pope. He was only twenty-four years old when chosen by his father's cousin, the emperor Otto III, whom he served as chaplain. The pope-designate, Bruno by name and the great-grandson of the emperor Otto I, was accompanied to Rome by two German bishops and was formally elected and consecrated on May 3, 996, taking the name Gregory V out of respect for Pope Gregory the Great (590–604). He is the first pope, therefore, to take a new name upon election as pope other than for the reason that his birth name was pagan (Mercury, Catelinus, or Octavian) or that of the Blessed Apostle Peter.

On the feast of the Ascension, a little more than two weeks later, Gregory V crowned Otto as emperor and patrician in St. Peter's and named him protector of the Church. In an effort to restore harmonious relations between the papacy and the Roman centers of power in the aristocracy and in the Curia, he began to mark out an independent course from the emperor. The emperor, in turn, refused to renew Otto I's pact with the Holy See or to restore certain territories to the Papal States as Gregory demanded. Gregory V also declared the emperor's friend Gerbert (the future Pope Sylvester II) an intruder in the archdiocese of Rheims (see John XV, number 137, above) and Arnulf (also Arnoul) as its rightful bishop.

After the emperor left Rome in June 996 for the cooler climate of Germany, the local resentment toward the foreign pope boiled over and the pope was driven out of Rome by a group headed by the leader of the powerful Crescentii family—a man whom the newly elected pope had urged the emperor to pardon rather than send into exile as punishment for his treatment of Pope John XV. Gregory V sought refuge in Spoleto, from which he made two armed attempts to recover Rome. Both attempts failed. He moved to Lombardy in January 997 and early the next month held a synod at Pavia, which excommunicated the head of the Crescentii family and restored the ancient rule of Pope Symmachus (499) that no agreements regarding papal succession could be made while the incumbent pope was still alive.

Later that month the now excommunicated head of the Crescentii family in effect declared the papal office vacant and, with the connivance of the Byzantine envoy, had John Philagathos, archbishop of Piacenza, elected and consecrated as John XVI. The new antipope was soon excommunicated by the Western bishops and Gregory V returned to Rome in the company of the emperor, where he presided over a synod that deposed the antipope John XVI, already blinded and severely mutilated, and imprisoned him in a monastery. (Later he was formally tried, deposed, defrocked, and stripped of his pontifical robes.) Crescentius, the head of the Crescentii family, was beheaded at Castel Sant'Angelo.

For the remainder of his pontificate, Gregory maintained an uneasy relationship with the emperor. Although he suspended the French bishops who had participated in the deposition of Arnulf (Arnoul) from Rheims and restored Arnulf to his archdiocese, he had to accept the emperor's appointment of Gerbert as archbishop of Ravenna and in 998 to send him the pallium (the woolen vestment worn around the neck as a sign of pastoral authority). On the other hand, against the emperor's wishes he began the process of restoring the see of Merseburg, which had been suppressed and divided at the emperor's behest in 981.

Gregory V died of malaria in February 999, not yet thirty years of age. If he had entertained any hopes of being on the papal throne at the turn of the millennium the following year, those hopes were upset by Divine Providence. He was buried in St. Peter's.

139 Sylvester [Silvester] II, *French, ca. 945–1003, pope from April 2, 999, to May 12, 1003.*

Sylvester II was the first French pope. His choice of the name Sylvester represented a conscious decision to associate himself with Pope Sylvester I (314–35), who had long been considered a model of papal cooperation with the emperor. Before his selection as pope by his friend and advisee, the emperor Otto III, he was Gerbert of Aurillac, archbishop of Ravenna and previously the archbishop of Rheims, although his claim to that see was disputed by Popes John XV and Gregory V (see John XV, number 137, and Gregory V, number 138, above).

Well-educated in literature, music, mathematics, philosophy, logic, and astronomy, Sylvester made an about-turn after his election to the papacy. A strong supporter of the rights of the French bishops and an equally strong critic of the papacy in the midst of the dispute over the archdiocese of Rheims (991–95), he became a tenacious advocate of papal rights. He reinstated his former rival Arnulf (also Arnoul) as archbishop of Rheims, on the grounds that his original deposition had not been authorized by the pope, and acted in an authoritarian manner toward various bishops who incurred his displeasure. On the other hand, he was a dedicated reformer, denouncing simony (the buying and selling of spiritual goods and church offices), nepotism, and violations of clerical celibacy. He also insisted on the free election of abbots by monks.

So determined was the emperor to maintain a cooperative relationship with the papacy that he added eight counties of the Pentapolis to the

Papal States, which he had previously refused to give to Pope Gregory V. Together they organized the churches of Poland (the pope named its first archbishop in 1000) and Hungary, and in 1001 the pope sent a royal crown to King Stephen I of Hungary in recognition of his right to the throne. But in February 1001, the Romans revolted once again against foreign domination. The emperor and pope were forced to leave the city. Otto died the following year before he could reestablish his authority in Rome. The new head of the Crescentii family, John II Crescentius, allowed the pope to return, but on condition that he limit himself to spiritual functions. The pope died less than a year later, on May 12, 1003, and was buried in the Lateran Basilica.

140 **John XVII,** *May 16–November 6, 1003 (June–December 1003 in the Vatican's official list; but J. N. D. Kelly and Levillain's* Dictionnaire historique de la papauté *give the May–November dates).*

John XVII's short pontificate left little or no trace in the history of the papacy. He took the number XVII because there was an antipope named John XVI, between John XV and himself. John XVII was probably a relative of the dominant Crescentii family in Rome and his election was undoubtedly engineered by the family's leader, John II Crescentius. Born John Sicco, he was married before ordination and was the father of three sons. The pope's only notable recorded papal act was his authorizing of Polish missionaries to work among the Slavs. It is not known how he died or how old he was when he died. He was probably buried in the Lateran Basilica.

141 **John XVIII,** *December 25, 1003–June/July 1009 (January 1004–July 1009 in the Vatican's official list; J. N. D. Kelly and Levillain's* Dictionnaire historique de la papauté *disagree only on the end of this pontificate: Kelly gives June/July, Levillain gives late June).*

Little is known of John XVIII's pontificate, but he may have abdicated shortly before his death and become a monk at the basilica of St. Paul's Outside the Walls, where he is buried. He was cardinal-priest of St. Peter's when elected to the papacy through the decisive influence of the head of the powerful Crescentii family, who ruled Rome from 1003 to 1012. In 1004 he did restore the diocese of Merseburg, which Pope Benedict VII had suppressed and divided in 981 at the request of the emperor Otto II, and also approved in 1007 the establishment of the diocese of Bamberg in Bavaria. In late 1007 he summoned the bishops of Sens and Orleans to Rome under pain of excommunication to confront them about their threats to the papal privileges granted to the abbey of Fleury, also known as Saint-Benoît-sur-Loire. There is evidence that relations between Rome and Constantinople improved during this pontificate, perhaps because of the pro-Byzantine sympathies of the Crescentii family head. In any case, the pope's name was restored to the list of those to be prayed for at Mass in Constantinople. John XVIII followed the precedent set by John XV in 993 and solemnly canonized five Polish martyrs in 1004. He also sent the pallium (the woolen vestment worn around the neck as a sign of pastoral authority) to the archbishops of Trier and Canterbury. If John XVIII did abdicate before his death in late June or early July 1009, it is probable that he was forced to do so. As noted above, he was buried in the basilica of St. Paul's Outside the Walls.

142 Sergius IV, *July 31, 1009–May 12, 1012.*

Sergius IV was the second pope to have changed his name upon election to the papacy because his baptismal name was Peter. He did not want to take the name of the Blessed Apostle Peter (the first pope to have made the same change of name, for the same reason, was John XIV in 983). Like that of his immediate predecessors, his elevation to the papacy was the product of the powerful Crescentii family of Rome. He was bishop of Albano when elected, which is another indication that the ancient and long-standing prohibition against bishops' transferring from one diocese to another was no longer honored. Very little is known of this pontificate.

Sergius IV did send representatives to the consecration of the Bamberg cathedral and ratified the privileges bestowed on it by Pope John XVIII. He also confirmed the properties of the newly restored diocese of Merseburg. In May 1012 there was a violent revolt in Rome. Both the pope and the head of the Crescentii family, John II Crescentius, disappeared within a week of one another, and a new pope was elected under the influence of the rival Tusculan family. These circumstances have given rise to the not improbable belief that both Pope Sergius IV and John II Crescentius were murdered. The pope was buried in the basilica of St. John Lateran.

143 Benedict VIII, *ca. 980–1024, pope from May 18, 1012, to April 9, 1024 (J. N. D. Kelly begins the pontificate on May 17, and Levillain's* Dictionnaire historique de la papauté *identifies the date of consecration as May 21).*

The first in a series of three laymen elected consecutively to the papacy, Benedict VIII (born Theophylact) established himself from the outset as a political and even military pope. Elected on May 17, 1012, he was given minor and major sacramental Orders and consecrated as Bishop of Rome on May 18 (or possibly on May 21).

A product of the newly ascendant Tusculan family, he used armed force to crush the rival Crescentii family (which had elected another pope, named Gregory) while his brother Romanus (later Pope John XIX) assumed the reins of civil government in Rome. Benedict VIII restored good relations with the German emperor, inviting Henry II to Rome and crowning him in St. Peter's in February 1014. At a synod following the coronation, the pope consecrated the emperor's half brother Arnold as archbishop of Ravenna. Then the parties moved to Ravenna itself for another synod, which established minimum ages for Holy Orders and passed laws against simony (the buying and selling of spiritual goods) and other abuses.

The pope spent most of the next six years in military campaigns designed to solidify the political power of Rome throughout central Italy. He personally led a naval alliance against Saracen invaders in northern Italy and liberated Sardinia in 1016. He also supported anti-Byzantine revolts in southern Italy in order to protect the material interests and claims of the papacy in the region. When the Byzantine forces crushed the revolt and moved northward, the pope left for Germany to seek the emperor's help. So impressed were the Germans with the pope's appearance in their country that the emperor verbally restored the Ottonian Privilege (962), which had solemnly confirmed the donations of Pepin and Charlemagne, but which also added substantial new territories to the Papal States comprising between two-thirds and three-quarters of Italy. The emperor also promised military aid, but his armies were unable to do more than fight the Byzantines to a draw. Their advance to the north was at least halted.

Later, at a synod in Pavia (1022), the emperor and the pope together pushed through legislation prohibiting clerical marriage, including those at the rank of subdeacon (an order that was suppressed after the Second Vatican Council [1962–65]), and reducing to serfdom the children of clerical unions. The emperor was principally behind the reforms and immediately incorporated them into the imperial code. The pope, on the other hand, was more concerned with the loss of church properties to the children of clerical unions. Indeed, Benedict VIII was ever jealous of the canonical power and rights of the Holy See. Thus, when the archbishop of Mainz banned all appeals to Rome on disciplinary matters (insisting that such appeals should only be directed to the appropriate metropolitan archbishops), the pope severely reprimanded him. Some have referred to this pope as more powerful than all of his immediate predecessors, but he wielded a power—political and military especially—that is far removed from the original meaning and purpose of the Petrine ministry. He died on April 9, 1024, and was buried in St. Peter's.

144 John XIX, *April 19, 1024–October 20, 1032 (May 1024–1032 in the Vatican's official list; J. N. D. Kelly and Levillain's* Dictionnaire historique de la papauté *agree with our dates rather than those in the* Annuario Pontificio).

John XIX was the first and only pope to succeed his older brother to the papacy. Like his older brother, he was still a layman (born Romanus) when "elected" (a word that needs to be in quotation marks because he actually bought the election through bribery). John's bribery and his canonically illicit passage from lay status to the papacy in a single day shocked and infuriated many of the Romans, although certainly not the newly powerful Tusculan family that was responsible for his selection.

Early in 1027 John XIX crowned Conrad II emperor in St. Peter's, but Conrad did not renew the traditional imperial privileges granted to the Holy See, nor did he promise to be its protector, as previous emperors had done. Indeed, the emperor treated the pope with little respect and ordered him around at will. Thus, he compelled the pope to do a favor for a loyal friend, the German patriarch of Aquileia, by decreeing that another patriarchate, Grado, was subject to Aquileia and that Aquileia was the metropolitan see of all the dioceses of Italy. And when the bishop of Constance complained to the emperor that the pope had granted the abbot of Reichenau the right to wear pontifical vestments at Mass, the emperor ordered the abbot to hand over to the bishop the papal decree and the insignia and had them burned publicly.

On other ecclesiastical fronts, the pope gave his full support to the reformist abbey of Cluny in Burgundy, reaffirming its privileges and defending it against criticism from the bishop of Mâcon, but relations with East soured once again and the pope's name was dropped from the list of those to be prayed for at Mass in Constantinople. Perhaps because of the unseemly manner in which he ascended to the papacy, a moral cloud hung over John XIX's head throughout his pontificate. There were charges, for example, that he demanded money in return for appointments to the hierarchy. He died on October 20, 1032, and was buried in St. Peter's.

145 Benedict IX, *d. ca. November/December 1055, pope from October 21, 1032, to September 1044; March 10 to May 1, 1045; November 8, 1047, to July 16, 1048 (the Vatican's official list of popes gives the three sets of dates* *as 1032–1044; April 10–May 1, 1045; and November 8, 1047–July 17, 1048; J. N. D. Kelly and Levillain's* Dictionnaire historique de la papauté *agree with our dates rather than those in the* Annuario Pontificio).

Benedict IX (born Theophylact) was the third consecutive layman to assume the papal office and the only pope in history to have held the office for three separate periods of time (although that accounting depends on how one assesses the legality of his two depositions from office and his abdication). In any case, his was one of the most canonically confusing pontificates in all of papal history.

Upon the death of John XIX, Alberic III, the new head of the ruling Tusculan family in Rome and John XIX's brother, arranged through bribery to have his own son Theophylact, the nephew of the previous two popes, elected and enthroned as Benedict IX. Generally speaking, the new pope put the interests of himself and his family ahead of the spiritual concerns of the Church. Nevertheless, he did manage to have a relatively active pontificate. He placed the abbey of Monte Cassino under direct papal protection in 1038, and at a Roman synod in April 1044 he restored Grado's patriarchal status, which John XIX had removed in deference to the emperor Conrad II. In September of that same year, however, there was another revolt in Rome, mostly in reaction to the pope's immoral life and the dominance of the Tusculan family over Church and state alike. Benedict IX fled the city.

The following January (1045) even though Benedict had never been formally deposed, a branch of the rival Crescentii family installed John, bishop of Sabina, as pope. He took the name Sylvester III. Benedict promptly excommunicated him and on March 10 managed to expel him from Rome and reclaim the papal throne. Two months later, however, for reasons that are not clear (perhaps it was the money he would earn from the sale of his office), he abdicated in favor of his godfather, John Gratian, who took the name Gregory VI. In the fall of 1046 the emperor Henry III came to Italy with a desire to be formally crowned by the pope. He summoned all three claimants—Benedict IX (who had withdrawn to his family estate outside of Rome), Sylvester III, and Gregory VI—to a synod at Sutri, near Rome, on December 20, where Sylvester and Gregory were deposed. Benedict was formally deposed four days later at a Roman synod on Christmas Eve. The emperor then named Suidger of Bamberg as pope, who took the name Clement II. Clement died suddenly eight months later, and the people, perhaps encouraged by bribes, demanded that Benedict IX be restored to office.

Benedict IX was reinstated on November 8, 1047, and remained in office until July 16, 1048, when he was forced from the papal throne by order of the emperor. Poppo of Brixen was installed as Damasus II. Benedict retreated to his Tusculan homeland, continuing to regard himself as the lawful pope against the intruder Damasus and, later, against Damasus's successor, Leo IX. A Lateran synod in April 1049 summoned Benedict to face the charge of simony (the buying and selling of spiritual goods and church offices), and when he refused to appear, excommunicated him. Benedict IX lived at least another seven and a half years, died sometime between mid-September 1055 and early January 1056, and was buried in the abbey church of Grottaferrata in the Alban hills.

146 Sylvester [Silvester] III, *d. 1063, pope (or antipope?) from January 20 to March 10, 1045 (January 20–February 10, 1045 in the Vatican's official list; J. N. D. Kelly gives our dates and Levillain's* Dictionnaire historique de la papauté *gives January 13 or 20 for the beginning and March 1046 as the end).*

The legitimacy of Sylvester III's pontificate is open to question. If his election was not valid, he belongs on the list of antipopes. After Benedict IX was expelled from Rome, Sylvester was elected as the candidate of the Crescentii family, which had dominated Roman politics until displaced by the newly powerful Tusculan family. As soon as Benedict IX heard of Sylvester's election, he excommunicated him. Two months later Benedict returned to Rome and had Sylvester removed from the papal throne. Sylvester thereupon resumed his duties as bishop of Sabina, a post he had never relinquished. Eighteen months later, on December 20, 1046, Henry III, king of Germany, had Sylvester III condemned at the synod of Sutri, confined to a monastery, and stripped of his Holy Orders. The sentence must have been suspended, however, because Sylvester continued to function in Sabina until 1062, when a successor was named. He is probably buried in Sabina.

147 Gregory VI, *d. late 1047, pope from May 5, 1045, to December 20, 1046.*

Given the circumstances of his election, upon the abdication of Benedict IX, Gregory VI was accused of simony (the buying and selling of spiritual goods and church offices) by the emperor and synod of Sutri and deposed. Born John Gratian, he was archpriest of San Giovanni a Porta Latina (St. John at the Latin Gate) when his godson Benedict IX abdicated in his favor on May 1, 1045—and for a great sum of money. Although Benedict's designation of his own successor was explicitly prohibited by church law, it is said (on what basis, we do not know) that the proper electoral process was observed. Many church reformers greeted his election with enthusiasm (they were not aware as yet of the financial arrangements). Henry III came down from Germany with the hope of being crowned emperor by the pope, but there were at least three possibilities from which to choose: Benedict IX, Sylvester III, and Gregory VI. At a synod in Sutri (about twenty-five miles north of Rome) on December 20, 1046, the king and the synod pronounced Gregory guilty of simony and deposed him from office. Gregory VI was taken back to Germany, accompanied by his chaplain and friend, the future Pope Gregory VII, and placed under the supervision of the bishop of Cologne. He died toward the end of that same year. His burial place is unknown.

148 Clement II, *Saxon, December 25, 1046–October 9, 1047.*

Clement II (Suidger) was the first pope to remain bishop of another diocese (Bamberg) while serving as Bishop of Rome. He was also the first of four German popes imposed upon the Church by King Henry III of Germany in order not only to rescue the papacy from the power of feuding Roman families but also to ensure German control over it. In fact, Clement II crowned Henry and his wife as emperor and empress on the same day (Christmas) he himself was enthroned as pope.

At the time of Clement's selection by Henry, there were three possible claimants to the papal throne: Benedict IX, who had abdicated in favor of his godfather, Gregory VI, and Sylvester III, who was elected after Benedict was expelled from Rome in January 1045. At two successive synods (at Sutri and Rome), the three were formally deposed and the emperor nominated Suidger, bishop of Bamberg. Suidger's choice of the name Clement (traditionally regarded as the third successor of the Apostle Peter) underscored his intention to return to early Christianity for his pastoral inspiration. As for Henry, he acclaimed himself patrician, with the power to approve the election of a pope. Within a few days (January 5) the new pope presided over a synod which condemned simony (the buying and selling of spiritual goods and church offices) and declared a forty-day penance for anyone knowingly ordained by a simoniacal bishop. Then the pope accompanied Henry to the south of Italy, where he confirmed the appointment of the archbishop of Paestum and placed Benevento under condemnation for refusing to open its gates to the emperor. Later on he affirmed his support for the reformist abbey of Cluny in Burgundy and confirmed the privileges of his other diocese, Bamberg. Because he suddenly fell ill and died in an abbey near Pesaro in early October, rumors circulated that he had been poisoned by Benedict IX. An exhaustive examination of his remains in 1942 disclosed that Clement II had probably died of lead poisoning. He was buried in the Bamberg cathedral.

149 Damasus II, *Bavarian, July 17–August 9, 1048.*

The pontificate of Damasus II, the second of the four German popes imposed by King Henry III, was brief and uneventful. Like his predecessor, he retained his diocese of Brixen after election and consecration as Bishop of Rome and was only the second pope in history to do so. Upon the sudden death of Clement II in October 1047, the emperor, in his capacity as patrician (with the authority to appoint the pope), nominated Poppo, bishop of Brixen, on Christmas day. In the meantime, however, the deposed Benedict IX returned to Rome to reclaim the papal throne with the support of the powerful count of Tuscany, who prevented Poppo from reaching Rome. When Poppo returned to Germany and informed the emperor, Henry III threatened the count that, unless he obeyed his orders, he would come to Rome himself and place a new pope on the throne. The count relented and had Benedict IX expelled from Rome on July 16, 1048. The next day Poppo was consecrated and enthroned. Like his predecessor, he took the name of an ancient pope, Damasus, to show his regard for early Christianity. Twenty-three days later, however, he died at Palestrina, where he had retreated to escape the Roman heat. Although some charged that he was poisoned, malaria is the probable cause of his death. He was buried in the basilica of San Lorenzo fuori le Mura (St. Lawrence's Outside the Walls).

150 Leo IX, St., *Alsatian, 1002–54, pope from February 12, 1049, to April 19, 1054.*

The third and best of the German popes imposed on the Church by the emperor Henry III, Leo IX (Bruno of Egisheim), like his two immediate predecessors, retained his diocese of Toul (until 1051) while serving as Bishop of Rome. It is said, however, that he accepted the emperor's nomination only on condition that it would subsequently be approved by the clergy and people of Rome. When he reached Rome, dressed in the simple garb of a pilgrim, he was greeted with acclaim and crowned on February 12, taking the name Leo to recall the ancient, still uncorrupted Church.

Two months later he convened a synod in Rome which denounced simony (the buying and selling of spiritual goods, including church offices) and violations of clerical chastity. Several simoniacal bishops were deposed and the penance imposed by his predecessor Clement II on priests knowingly ordained by such bishops was reaffirmed. He gathered a "kitchen cabinet" of distinguished persons from Lorraine to help in the reorganization of the Curia. These included Hildebrand (later Pope Gregory VII) and Humbert of Moyenmoutier (later cardinal-bishop of Silva Candida). He also sought counsel from the abbot of the reformist abbey of Cluny in Burgundy and Peter Damian (d. 1072). Called the "Apostolic Pilgrim," Leo promoted his reforms by traveling extensively throughout Europe—in Italy, Germany, France, and even Hungary—holding a dozen synods in Rome, Bari, Mainz, Pavia, Rheims, and Rome. At Rheims, for example, he insisted that bishops and abbots must be elected by clergy and laity.

Unfortunately, Leo IX's last years in office were marked by failure In 1053 he led a disastrous military expedition against the Normans in southern Italy in defense of the Papal States, and he himself was captured and held for nine months. He was released only after making humiliating concessions. Meanwhile, the anti-Latin patriarch of Constantinople, Michael Cerularius (d. 1058), angered by the pope's interference in southern Italian areas claimed by Byzantium and by his naming of Humbert archbishop of Sicily, closed down the Latin churches in Constantinople in 1053 and vehemently attacked various Latin practices, including the use of unleavened bread in the Eucharist. In January 1054, while still a prisoner, Leo IX sent a delegation to Constantinople led by Humbert. The mission was a spectacular failure because of the intransigence of both sides. On July 16, 1054, in the presence of the whole congregation at the Hagia Sophia, Humbert placed on the altar a bull excommunicating the patriarch and his supporters. Cerularius countered with his own condemnations on July 24. The East-West Schism, which has lasted to this very day, is conventionally dated from this tragic series of events in the summer of 1054. Although Leo IX had died a few months earlier, the breach is laid at the doorstep of his pontificate since the envoys were acting in his name. His last days were marred by illness and deep regret, but soon thereafter he came to be regarded as a saint. He is buried in St. Peter's. Feast day: April 19.

151 Victor II, *Swabian, ca. 1018–57, pope from April 13, 1055, to July 28, 1057 (April 16 in the Vatican's official list, but J. N. D. Kelly and Levillain's Dictionnaire historique de la papauté both agree on the April 13 starting point for this pontificate).*

The fourth and last of the German popes nominated by the German king Henry III, Pope Victor II (Gebhard), like his three predecessors, continued as bishop of his diocese (Eichstätt) after being elected to the papacy. Following the death of Leo IX in April 1054, there were extensive discussions about papal succession in Mainz between the Roman delegation headed by the deacon Hildebrand (later Gregory VII) and the emperor and his representatives. It was not until November that Henry III nominated Gebhard as pope. But Gebhard resisted for about four months until he received assurances that certain properties and treasure taken from the Holy See would be returned and that he could retain the diocese of Eichstätt. He was not enthroned until almost a year after Leo's death. Canonically and theologically, he should have been considered the pope and the Bishop of Rome as soon as he accepted election, since he was already a bishop. Enthronement is purely ceremonial and adds nothing essential. However, if Victor II withheld his assent until the day of his enthronement, April 13, 1055, that would be the day on which his pontificate officially began.

The new pope and the emperor convened a synod in Florence in June, which condemned simony (the buying and selling and spiritual goods, including church offices), clerical marriage, violations of clerical chastity, and the alienation of church property (selling church property for private gain). Several bishops were deposed from their sees. Similar decisions were taken at synods in southern France (Lyons and Toulouse) presided over by local bishops as representatives of the pope and by Hildebrand as his special delegate. As an expression of confidence in Victor II, the emperor appointed him duke of Spoleto and count of Fermo, making the pope in effect an imperial officer. After a brief illness in October 1056, Henry III died, having personally entrusted the care of the empire and of his five-year-old son to the pope, who was in Germany at the time seeking military assistance against the Normans in southern Italy. Victor II adroitly ensured the succession of the boy (Henry IV), crowning him at Aachen, with his mother, Agnes, as regent, and later negotiated a reconciliation between the imperial house and two of its most powerful adversaries (Lorraine and Flanders).

The pope returned to Italy in mid-February 1057 and held a synod at the Lateran in April. In order to please one of his new allies, Godfrey of Lorraine, the pope appointed Godfrey's brother Frederick as abbot of Monte Cassino and made him cardinal-priest of San Crisogono. But six days after holding a local synod at Arezzo on July 23, the pope died of fever. His German staff wanted to take his body back to Eichstätt, but the people of Ravenna seized the body and it was buried in Santa Maria Rotonda (the mausoleum of Theodoric the Great [d. 526]), just outside the walls of the city. With the deaths of Pope Victor II and the emperor Henry III, the ten-year period of imperial-papal reform had come to an abrupt end.

152 **Stephen IX (X)**, *French, ca. 1000–1058, pope from August 2, 1057, to March 29, 1058 (the Vatican's official list marks the beginning of his pontif-*

icate on August 3, the day of his enthronement, rather than August 2, the
day of his election and consecration).

(For an explanation of the dual numbering, see Stephen II (III), number 92, in Part II.) Another in a long series of very brief eleventh-century pontificates, Stephen IX (X)'s promoted the reformist agenda, but without the direct collaboration of the German imperial court that had dominated the four preceding pontificates. Born Frederick (of Lorraine), Stephen was abbot of Monte Cassino when elected and consecrated on the same day, August 2, 1057. He took the name Stephen because August 2 was St. Stephen I's feast day. No effort was made to contact the imperial court in Germany before proceeding to the election. The Romans were undoubtedly taking advantage of the fact that the new emperor, Henry IV, was a very young child. Another possible reason for not consulting the imperial court and for proceeding quickly to the election was the fear that the aristocratic families of Rome might try to reassert their influence over papal elections. Four months later a delegation to the imperial court led by Hildebrand (the future Pope Gregory VII) seems to have received retroactive approval for Stephen's election.

Stephen IX (X) remained abbot of Monte Cassino, where he tried to restore the rule of poverty. He promoted the reformist activities of Peter Damian (d. 1072) by naming him cardinal-bishop of Ostia, and the reformers Humbert of Silva Candida and Hildebrand were among the pope's closest advisers. The pope died in Florence on March 29, 1058, while trying to arrange an alliance against the Normans in southern Italy and was buried in San Reparata. Before leaving Rome for Florence, Stephen had solemnly bound the clergy and laity, in the event of his death, not to elect a successor until Hildebrand returned from his mission to the imperial court in Germany.

153 Nicholas II, *French, ca. 1010–61, pope from December 6, 1058, to July 27, 1061 (the Vatican's official list begins this pontificate on January 24, 1059, the day of enthronement, rather than the day of his acceptance of election).*

During Nicholas II's pontificate the election of a pope was restricted to cardinal-bishops, with the Roman clergy and people giving their subsequent assent. Bishop of Florence when elected Bishop of Rome on December 6, 1058, in Siena, Nicholas continued to serve in both capacities after his election to the papacy. He may have also been the first pope crowned with the *camelaucum,* the original form of the papal tiara.

Upon Stephen IX (X)'s death on March 29, 1058, the reformist cardinals honored the late pope's solemn mandate that they should wait until the leading reformer Hildebrand (the future Pope Gregory VII) returned from his mission to the imperial court in Germany before proceeding to the election of a successor. An anti-reformist faction within the Roman aristocracy, however, seized upon the delay and on April 5 elected John, bishop of Velletri, who took the name Benedict X. He had to be irregularly consecrated because Peter Damian, the bishop of Ostia, would not participate. The reformist cardinals refused to recognize Benedict, left Rome, and elected Gerard, bishop of Florence, in Siena in December. The new pope, who took the name Nicholas II, convened a synod at Sutri, twenty-five miles north of Rome, in early January 1059 and in the presence of the imperial chancellor condemned the antipope Benedict X. Nicholas II then went to Rome in the company of the duke of Lorraine's troops, where he was received enthusiastically (Benedict had already fled the city). The new pope was installed at the Lateran on January 24, 1059.

Like his predecessor, Stephen IX (X), Nicholas II was greatly influenced by the leading reformers of the day: Humbert of Silva Candida (d. 1061), Hildebrand (d. 1085), and Peter Damian (d. 1072). At a Lateran synod on April 13, which declared Benedict X's election uncanonical, the pope promulgated a historic decree mandating that, in order to avoid the risk of simony (the buying and selling of church offices), papal elections should be conducted by the cardinal-bishops, with the subsequent assent of the Roman clergy and laity. (There was great opposition to this change, and it had to be amended after Nicholas's death.) The synod also allowed for the election of a non-Roman cleric and for holding the election outside of Rome. This practice was already in place, of course, in the election of Nicholas II himself. He was a Frenchman and his election was held in Siena, not Rome. And he was certainly not the first non-Roman cleric to become pope. The synod left open the possibility of imperial involvement in the elections, but the imperial right was not unconditional and could be forfeited through abuse. In addition, the synod legislated against clerical marriage and concubinage, required that the clergy of the cathedral church share a common life, and issued the first formal prohibition of lay investiture, that is, the receiving of church offices from laypersons. Other synods were held in 1060 and 1061, dealing once again with simony and simoniacal ordinations. Archbishop Guido of Milan attended the 1060 synod and, by accepting his ring from the pope, tacitly acknowledged that his previous investiture by the emperor had been simoniacal (that is, given for a price).

Politically Nicholas II reversed the policy of his immediate predecessors toward the Normans in southern Italy. Instead of fighting them, he entered into an alliance with them and thereby secured a political and economic foothold for the papacy in most of the south. However, the new alliance (as well as the stringent disciplinary measures) generated re-sentiment in the imperial court and within the German hierarchy, led by the archbishop of Cologne. A cardinal-delegate of the pope sent in 1061 to explain the pope's policies to the imperial court was not received. Moreover, a synod of German bishops declared Nicholas II's acts null and void and broke off communion with him. Before there were any repercussions in the Holy See, the pope died in Florence, his second diocese, on July 27, 1061. Like Pope Stephen IX (X), who also died in Florence, he was buried in San Reparata.

154 Alexander II, *September 30, 1061–April 21, 1073 (the Vatican's official list gives October 1 as the starting point of this pontificate; it is the day of enthronement rather than election).*

A reformer pope like his immediate predecessors, Alexander II (born Anselm) supported the liberation of Christian lands from the Muslims as well as the victorious Duke William of Normandy against Harold of England in the battle of Hastings in 1066. He was bishop of Lucca when elected Bishop of Rome on September 30, 1061, with the support of the reformist leader Hildebrand (the future Pope Gregory VII) and backed by Norman troops in the face of disturbances in Rome.

However, the cardinal-electors had not consulted with the German imperial court, in keeping with the decree of the Lateran synod of 1059 on papal elections, The court, in turn, nominated a rival pope, Honorius II (Cadalus, the wealthy, anti-reformist bishop of Parma), at an assembly in Basel and with the support of the members of the Roman aristocracy. The antipope Honorius II defeated Alexander's armed forces in April 1062 and installed himself in Rome. But the powerful duke of Lorraine arrived the next month with superior forces and persuaded both claimants to the papal throne to withdraw to their original dioceses (Lucca and Parma) until the German court settled the conflict. After hearings in Augsburg in October and in Rome in December, a judgment was rendered in favor of Alexander II. The following May (1063) Honorius anathematized Alexander and attacked Rome, taking possession of Castel Sant'Angelo for several months. Meanwhile, Alexander II pressed forward with his reformist agenda. At a Lateran synod that same year he renewed the decree of his predecessor, Nicholas II, against simony (the buying and selling of church offices), forbade attendance at Mass celebrated by married priests, prohibited lay investiture without the permission of the diocese, and commended the common life to cathedral clergy. There was also a flurry of synodal activity, with the participation of papal legates, in Lombardy, France, Spain, England, Germany, Bohemia, Croatia-Dalmatia, and Scandinavia.

The pope also sent banners and granted indulgences to Norman soldiers and French knights fighting the Muslims in Sicily and Spain, respectively. Indeed, the reconquest of lands previously taken by the Muslims was an important prelude to the Crusades. But in 1063 the pope also intervened in southern France and Spain to defend Jews who had suffered in these military campaigns. He renewed the prohibition of Pope Gregory the Great (590–604) against the mistreatment of Jews.

As the schism between the followers of Alexander II and of Honorius II dragged on, Peter Damian persuaded the archbishop of Cologne to convene a synod of German and Italian bishops in Mantua in May 1064, to which both claimants to the papal throne would be invited. Honorius refused to attend because he was denied the right to preside. Alexander did attend, presided, and took an oath of purgation, swearing that he had never been guilty of simony. As a consequence, Alexander II was acknowledged as pope and Honorius II was formally condemned, after which he returned to his diocese of Parma, never abandoning his claims to the papacy.

In 1068 the king of Aragon placed his country under the feudal protection of the pope and in 1071 replaced the Mozarabic liturgy with the Roman liturgy. In 1070 Alexander II came down hard against German bishops whom he suspected of practicing simony and forced the resignation of the bishop of Constance. Even King Henry IV retreated from his intention to divorce his wife, given the pope's firm opposition to breaches of the marriage bond. But a serious rift developed between the pope and the emperor when in 1071 Henry IV tried to impose his nominee as the new archbishop of Milan, while the pope supported another candidate in the reformist tradition. Because of the emperor's stubborn support of his own candidate, the pope excommunicated five of his counselors for simony. Also in 1071 the pope sent a representative to the Byzantine emperor, the first such contact since the mutual excommunications of pope and patriarch in 1054. Nothing came of this contact before Alexander II's death in April 1073. But the stage was now set for the truly pivotal pontificate of Gregory VII, which would mark the effective beginning of the monarchical papacy that many Catholics and others assume to be a product of the will of Jesus Christ rather than of the vicissitudes of human history. Alexander II was buried in the Lateran Basilica.

Part IV

FROM THE GREGORIAN REFORM TO THE PROTESTANT REFORMATION

NE OF THE GREATEST THEOLOGIANS OF THE twentieth century, Cardinal Yves Congar, O.P. (d. 1995), argued that "the great turning point in ecclesiology [the theology of the Church] is the eleventh century. That turning point is, of course, embodied in the person of Gregory VII." Congar acknowledged that Gregory VII faced overwhelming internal and external problems when he was elected in 1073: simony (the buying and selling of spiritual goods and church offices), nepotism, violations of clerical celibacy, and the interference of lay princes in the appointment and installation of bishops and abbots ("lay investiture"). Gregory VII had his canon lawyers comb the archives for every trace or shred of support for the kind of exercise of papal power that he deemed necessary to meet these challenges. Some of the materials they uncovered were authentic; others were spurious—forgeries.

Cardinal Congar pointed out that by seeking to rely on legal precedents for the exercise of what should be only spiritual authority, Gregory VII "ended up by making the Church itself into a legal institution." Thus, when the Church opposed the temporal power, "it was led to adopt very much the same attitudes as the temporal power itself, to conceive of itself as a society, as a power, when in reality it is a communion, with ministers, servants." What led to the Church's becoming a legal institution, Congar argued, was "the affirmation of papal power as the basis of everything" (*Fifty Years of Catholic Theology: Conversations with Yves Congar,* ed. Bernard Lauret [Philadelphia: Fortress Press, 1988], pp. 40, 42). Gregory VII, in other words, launched the second-millennial papacy as a legalistic, monarchical office—a concept foreign to the first-millennial Church and to the whole of the East, past and present alike. It was also Gregory VII who decreed in 1073 that the title of "pope" should thereafter be restricted to the Bishop of Rome. Previously, the title applied to every bishop in the West, while in the East it seems to have been used of priests as well and was a special title of the patriarch of Alexandria. It is still used by the Coptic patriarch of Alexandria.

Some Catholics regard this period from Gregory VII to the Protestant Reformation as the apex of the papacy, whose glory, grandeur, and power have only recently been restored by Pope John Paul II (1978–). Others, however, regard the developments of this period as an aberration, albeit of many centuries' duration. Whatever one's point of view, the period undoubtedly yielded men of unusual talent and ability, beginning with Gregory VII himself. Some of the most important popes in all of history reigned during these four and a half centuries—and some of the very worst. Innocent III (1198–1216), one of the most powerful popes of all time, claimed authority not only over the whole Church, as Gregory VII had, but over the whole world as well. Boniface VIII (1295–1303), like Innocent III, also claimed papal supremacy over the temporal as well as the spiritual realms. At least three other popes from this period are well known for different reasons. Celestine V (1294) is always cited by the media and their "expert" sources on the Catholic Church as the only pope to have ever resigned from office. That is factually untrue. There were at least two, and probably four, other popes before him who resigned from the papacy for one reason or another: Pontian (230–35), who was arrested and deported in the year 235 by the anti-Christian emperor Maximinus Thrax; Silverius (536–37), who was forced to resign by his successor, Vigilius (537–55); John XVIII (1003–9), who probably resigned and entered a monastery; and Benedict IX, who, during his canonically confusing pontificate, abdicated in 1045 in favor of his godfather, but was reinstated in 1047. Following Celestine V, Gregory XII resigned in 1415 to help resolve the Great Western Schism (1378–1417). Another well-known pope from this period is the infamous and spectacularly corrupt Alexander VI (1492–1503), who is at the top of nearly everyone's list of so-called bad popes. Less well known but no less important is Leo X (1513–21), who helped launch the Protestant Reformation with his "sale" of indulgences and church offices and his excommunication of Martin Luther in 1521. Leo X was, in turn, preceded by a string of some of the worst popes in all of history, including his immediate predecessor, Julius II (1503–13), who spent almost as much time on the field of military battle as he did tending to his pastoral responsibilities.

Among the less celebrated and, in some cases, notorious popes of this period are the following. Urban II (1088–99) established the Roman Curia and launched the First Crusade (1096–99) in an ill-conceived and utterly counterproductive attempt (repeated at least three more times by subsequent popes) to recapture the holy places in Palestine from the Muslims. Eugenius III (1145–53), a Cistercian, retained the habit and lifestyle of a monk throughout his entire pontificate (Urban V, a Benedictine, did the same, 1362–70). The election of Alexander III (1159–81) provoked a twenty-year schism, covering almost his entire twenty-two-year pontificate. Lucius III (1181–85), because of the hostility of the Roman people toward him, had to spend most of his pontificate living outside the city (the same was necessary for Urban IV, 1261–64, Clement IV, 1265–68, and Martin IV, 1281–85); Lucius III also laid the foundation for the infamous Inquisition in defining procedures by which alleged heretics could be suppressed and punished. Celestine III (1191–98), although already eighty-five years of age when elected, managed to serve for almost seven years. Innocent III, mentioned above, also called the Fourth Lateran Council (1215), which mandated annual confession for all Catholics and the wearing of a distinctive garb by Jews and Muslims—the latter a disturbing forerunner of the requirement in twentieth-century Nazi Germany that Jews wear the Star of David to make them easily identifiable. Gregory X (1272–76) was elected in the famous conclave in Viterbo in which the civil authorities locked the cardinals inside the papal palace and then, because of their long delay in electing a new pope, removed the roof and threatened them with starvation. John XXI (1276–77) issued the papal bull that the bishop of Paris relied upon to condemn nineteen propositions of St. Thomas Aquinas. During the pontificate of Nicholas IV (1288–92), Catholicism was established for the first time in China. Clement V (1305–14) was the first of a seventy-year line of French popes who made their official residence in Avignon rather than Rome. Clement VI (1342–52) laid the groundwork for the doctrine of indulgences, the abuse of which would become one of the immediate causes of the Protestant Reformation almost two hundred years later (according to Catholic teaching, indulgences are spiritual merits won for us by Christ and the saints, to be drawn upon by the faithful through their prayers and good works). Innocent VI (1352–62) was denounced by St. Bridget of Sweden as a persecutor of Christ's flock. Gregory XI (1371–78), at the urging of St. Catherine of Siena, returned the papacy from Avignon to Rome in 1377. Urban VI (1378–89) was so unstable and abusive that an antipope was elected to replace him, thereby launching the Great Western Schism of 1378–1417, during which there were at least two and sometimes three claimants to the papacy at the same time. During the pontificate of Nicholas V (1447–55), Constantinople, the center of Eastern Christianity for almost the entire history of the Church, fell to the Turks in 1453. Sixtus IV (1471–84) outdid all others in the field of nepotism, having named six of his nephews cardinals (he also transformed Rome from a medieval to a Renaissance city, built the Sistine Chapel, and established the Vatican archives). Julius II (1503–13), was the patron of two of history's greatest artists, Michelangelo and Raphael, and the one who commissioned plans for the new St. Peter's Basilica, to be funded by the sale of indulgences. And Leo X (1513–21) continued both his predecessor's construction project and his methods of raising the necessary funds—and excommunicated Martin Luther as well.

There were also many "firsts" during this period. Victor III (1087) was the first pope to be beatified without subsequently being canonized a saint. Eugenius III (1145–53) was the first Cistercian pope. Hadrian (Adrian) IV (1154–59) was the first and only English pope. Callistus III (1455–58) was the first of two Spanish popes (the second was the infamous Alexander VI, 1492–1503). Alexander III (1159–81) was the first of many lawyers to be elected pope. In 1276, for the first time, there were four canonically recognized popes in the same year: Gregory X (1272–76), Innocent V (1276), Hadrian V (1276), and John XXI (1276–77), although by present canonical standards and the standards of good theology, Hadrian V was not a pope, that is, the Bishop of Rome, because he was not a bishop when elected and died before being consecrated. Innocent V (1276) was the first Dominican pope. Because he continued to wear his white Dominican cassock while pope, subsequent popes adopted it as their ordinary papal dress, although the custom seems not to have been finally established until the pontificate of another Dominican, Pius V (1566–72). John XXI (1276–77) was the first and only Portuguese pope and also the only medical doctor to occupy the Chair of Peter. Nicholas III (1277–80) was the first pope to make the Vatican Palace his official residence. Nicholas IV (1288–92) was the first Franciscan pope. Boniface VIII (1295–1303) was the first pope to proclaim a Holy Year (in 1300). Nicholas V (1447–55) was the first of the Renaissance popes, acting as a patron of literature, the arts, and architecture, as well as the founder of the Vatican Library. And, once again, Celestine V (1294) was *not* the first and only pope to have resigned from the papacy. There were at least two, and possibly four, before him (Pontian in 235, Silverius in 537, John XVIII in 1009, and Benedict IX in 1045), and one since (Gregory XII in 1415).

At least three popes of this period were assigned their destinies by Dante Alighieri (d. 1321) in his *Divine Comedy:* Hadrian V (1276) was placed in Purgatory for the sin of avarice; John XXI (1276–77), in Paradise; and Nicholas III (1277–80), in Hell for nepotism and avarice.

Nearly half of the Catholic Church's twenty-one ecumenical councils were held during this period as well: Lateran I (1123), which ended the controversy over lay investiture (the practice of lay rulers' determining appointments of bishops and abbots); Lateran II (1139), which nullified all the papal acts and ordinations of the antipope Anacletus II; Lateran III (1179), which decreed that henceforth a two-thirds majority of cardinals was necessary for the election of a pope; Lateran IV (1215), which decreed that Catholics must make an annual confession of sins; Lyons I (1245), which excommunicated and deposed the emperor; Lyons II (1274), which forged a short-lived union between Rome and the Greek Church; Vienne (1311–12), which condemned the Knights Templar and supported the stricter Franciscan observance of poverty; Constance (1414–17), which ended the Great Western Schism by deposing two claimants to the papacy and compelling the third to abdicate, before conducting a conclave in which Martin V (1417–31) was elected; Basel-Ferrara-Florence-Rome (1431–45), which was held in four different cities and which unsuccessfully tried to reunite the Latin and Greek Churches of West and East; and Lateran V (1512–17), which invalidated the council of Pisa-Milan (1511–12), which had, in turn, declared Julius II suspended. Lateran V also reaffirmed the Pragmatic Sanction of Bourges (1438), which had asserted the independence of the French Church from papal control.

In summary, this was a period in papal history when the papacy became essentially a Western office and the Roman Catholic Church essentially a papal church. Neither development was a theologically or pastorally happy one. Indeed, the bad popes of this period (and there were many in the fifteenth and early sixteenth centuries) did far more harm to the Church than the bad popes of the ninth, tenth, and eleventh centuries had done, because the newly centralized form of ecclesiastical government made it possible for the corruption to spread rapidly through many other parts of the Church. In the ninth, tenth, and eleventh centuries—before papal centralization really took root—the corruption had relatively limited effects beyond Rome and Italy. At this period's end the Western Church was torn apart by a Reformation, the effects of which are still with us almost five centuries later.

155 Gregory VII, St., *ca. 1020–85, pope from June 30, 1073, to May 25, 1085 (the Vatican's official list gives as the beginning of his pontificate April 22, 1073, the day on which he was elected by popular acclaim; a deacon at the time of his election, he was not consecrated as Bishop of Rome until June 30).*

The pontificate of Gregory VII, one of the most important and influential popes in the entire history of the Church, marks a real watershed in the history of the papacy, from the first to the second Christian millennium. In the first Christian millennium the papacy functioned to a great extent as a mediator of disputes, ecclesiastical and political alike. The Bishop of Rome was only one of several Western patriarchs (although today there are honorary patriarchs in Lisbon, Venice, and the East and West Indies, and a Latin-rite patriarch in Jerusalem, the pope implicitly claims to be the Church's universal patriarch, in contradiction to Pope Gregory the Great's [590–604] insistence that the Church has no universal patriarch). To be sure, individual popes of the first millennium such as Leo the Great (440–61) readily donned the mantle of the Apostle Peter and claimed a primacy of pastoral jurisdiction—but for the most part over the West alone, and even then only over key regions of the West. At the same time, there were constant tugs-of-war between Rome and Constantinople (involving both the Byzantine emperor and the patriarch), but the East never fully accepted papal primacy in the sense in which it has come to be understood since Gregory VII. Gregory was the first pope effectively to claim universal jurisdiction over the whole Church—laity, religious, and clergy, princes and paupers alike—and he did so on the basis of canonical and legal precedents to which no other pope before him had appealed. He is also the pope who restricted the use of the title "pope" to the Bishop of Rome. Before that, the title was used of all bishops in the West.

Born Hildebrand, he served under several popes before being himself elected to the papacy: Gregory VI (1045–46), as chaplain; Leo IX (1049–54), as treasurer of the Roman Church (or administrator of the Patrimony of St. Peter); and Nicholas II (1058–61) and Alexander II (1061–73), as archdeacon, chancellor, and principal counselor. Upon the death of Alexander II, he was elected pope by acclamation (contrary to the detailed procedures established by Nicholas II in 1059) and took the name Gregory, after both his patron, Gregory VI, and Gregory the Great (590–604). He delayed his consecration until after the feast of Sts. Peter and Paul on June 29 out of respect for the two apostles. He did not inform or seek the approval of the German king, Henry IV.

Gregory made reform the centerpiece of his pontificate. But in order to accomplish his reforms, he inflated traditional papal claims over spiritual and temporal spheres alike. In March 1075 he issued his *Dictatus papae* ("Pronouncements of the Pope"), containing twenty-seven propositions about the powers of the pope, including such claims as: "That he alone can use imperial insignia"; "That only the pope's feet are to be kissed by all princes"; "That it is licit for him to depose emperors"; "That it is licit for him to transfer bishops, under pressure of need, from see to see"; "That no synod ought to be called 'general' without his command"; and "That he ought to be judged by no one." (The document is generally considered to have been a collection of chapter titles from an unfinished compilation of canon law.) The norm of Catholic fidelity was unquestioning obedience to the Bishop of Rome, who exercised a universal rule over the whole of Christendom, including kings and emperors.

At the Lenten synods of 1074 and 1075 Gregory VII reaffirmed his predecessors' decrees against clerical marriage and simony (the buying and selling of spiritual goods, including church offices), and, in the teeth of strong opposition, enforced them through the agency of papal legates in France, Germany, and England. Even the powerful archbishop of Rheims was successfully deposed. From this point on, papal legates (today known as nuncios, and apostolic delegates) became an important administrative arm of the papacy. The Lateran synod of 1078 threatened bishops with suspension if they allowed their clergy to marry and remain in office. The pope also demanded that newly elected bishops take an oath of obedience and that all bishops visit the Holy See. Given the composition and content of the Lateran synods under Gregory, it was almost natural that they should have evolved into general, or ecumenical, councils (of which there were eventually five in the medieval period).

Gregory's prohibition of lay investiture, that is, the interference of lay princes and other temporal rulers in the appointment and installation of bishops and abbots, provoked even stronger opposition, this time from the king of Germany himself, Henry IV. After defeating the Saxons in 1075, Henry nominated his own men as archbishop of Milan and as bishops (and abbots) in Germany and other parts of Italy, including Spoleto and Fermo. When the pope rebuked the king, Henry IV convened a synod of twenty-six German bishops at Worms (January 24, 1076), which deposed the pope, referring to him as the "monk Hildebrand." Henry himself called upon Gregory to resign. At Piacenza the Lombard bishops followed suit. Then, at the Lenten synod of 1076, Gregory excommunicated Henry, suspended him from the exercise of his royal powers, and released the king's subjects from all allegiance to him. Bishops who supported Henry were either excommunicated or suspended. As a political ploy, Henry IV asked forgiveness and sought absolution, wearing penitential garb and kneeling in the snow at Canossa, near Reggio, in northern Italy in January 1077. Gregory forgave and absolved the king. But three years later he again excommunicated and deposed Henry over a persistent dispute Henry was having with Rudolf of Swabia, whom the German princes had elected as a rival king. After a violent civil war in Germany and after the pope's failure to bring the two sides together, Gregory VII recognized Rudolf's claim to the throne. Henry thereupon called a council of imperial bishops at Brixen on June 25, 1080. The council deposed Gregory (his second deposition!) and elected Guibert, archbishop of Ravenna, as Clement III to replace Gregory. (Guibert had been suspended by Gregory for not attending the synod of 1075 and then was excommunicated for taking part in the meeting of Lombard bishops at Piacenza, which supported the synod of Worms's first deposition of the pope.)

Henry was still open to compromise because he wanted to be crowned as emperor, but Gregory was inflexible, so much so that he lost many of his supporters, including thirteen cardinals. After Henry seized Rome in March 1084 following a two-year siege, the Roman clergy and laity elected Guibert (Clement III) pope and he was enthroned in the Lateran Basilica on March 24, 1084. A week later, on March 31, while Gregory VII was still at Castel Sant'Angelo, the antipope Clement III crowned Henry emperor in St. Peter's. But both Henry and Clement left Rome when Robert Guiscard, duke of Apulia, marched on Rome with Norman troops and rescued Gregory. (Clement returned to Ravenna, where he remained as archbishop while carrying on a fierce pamphlet war against Gregory and the Gregorian reformers. He would later return to Rome to exercise his role as presumptive pope once again during the pontificates of Victor III, 1087, and Urban II, 1088–99.) The violent behavior of Robert's troops infuriated the Roman people and they turned on the pope who had invited them in. Gregory VII left Rome, going first to Monte Cassino and then to Salerno, where he died on May 25, 1085. He was buried in Salerno's cathedral.

Many letters survive from Gregory VII's pontificate. They show his deep interest even in the distant churches of Denmark, Spain, Poland, Hungary, Russia, France, and England. He emphasized always the virtue of justice, insisting that the Catholic king's duty was to be a lover of justice. He insisted that archbishops should come to Rome to receive the pallium (the woolen vestment worn around the neck as a sign of pastoral authority). Under him, the Roman liturgy, already in use in Aragon, replaced the Mozarabic rites in regions of Spain controlled by the king of Castile. He also fixed the Ember Days (a series of penitential days of fasting and partial abstinence observed four times a year) in the Latin Church. He had hoped to liberate the Holy Sepulchre in Jerusalem from the Turks and to restore union with the Eastern Church, but the many controversies closer to home dashed those plans.

Although one of the great reformer popes in history, his single-mindedness, approaching fanaticism at times, undermined much of his reformist agenda. Subsequent papal conclaves were often marked by division between Gregorian and anti-Gregorian cardinal-electors. Nevertheless, he is the pope who, more than any other, shaped the development of the papacy in the West throughout the second Christian millennium—for good or for ill. He was beatified in 1584 and canonized by Pope Paul V in 1606. Feast day: May 25.

156 **Victor III, Bl.,** *ca. 1027–87, pope from May 9 to September 16, 1087 (the Vatican's official list begins his pontificate on May 24, 1086, the date of his first election—an election he did not formally accept—and almost a year before his consecration as Bishop of Rome on May 9, 1087).*

Victor III was the first pope to be beatified without being subsequently canonized a saint.

When the great reformer pope Gregory VII died in exile in Salerno, the reform party was in a state of confusion and disarray. Some of its leading cardinals had shifted their support to the antipope Clement III, elected in 1084, while Gregory was still in Rome at Castel Sant'Angelo. It took almost a year—and with much pressure from the Norman prince Jordan of Capua—until the cardinals elected Desiderius (born Daufer or Daufari), abbot of Monte Cassino since 1058 and perhaps the most influential abbot in the Church at this time. A year after being elected abbot, he was named by Pope Nicholas II as cardinal-priest of Santa Cecilia and papal vicar of the monasteries of southern Italy. (He also gave refuge to Gregory VII when he fled Rome in 1084 and was present at Gregory's death in Salerno.) The electors concluded that Desiderius might bring about a reconciliation with the emperor Henry IV. So, on May 24, 1086, they elected him pope in the diaconal church of Santa Lucia in Rome. Desiderius resisted the election, insisting that the cardinals should select Cardinal Oddone di Châtillon (who would be elected the next time, as Urban II). The abbot then fled Rome for Terracina. After a long period of indecision, Desiderius's resistance finally ended. The Norman leader Jordan of Capua had intervened and urged Desiderius to convene a synod in Capua, not as pope but as papal vicar for the monasteries of southern Italy. The synod persuaded him to accept his election as pope, despite the intense, residual opposition of a minority led by the archbishop of Lyons. Abbot Desiderius was canonically elected at Capua on Palm Sunday, March 21, 1087, taking the name Victor III, in honor of Pope Victor II, who had been Henry's father's nominee to the papacy and had served as guardian to Henry IV when he was a very young boy. (Before his death Gregory VII had recommended three possible successors. Desiderius was not one of them.)

Four days after his canonical election the pope-elect was forced to flee Rome because of riots in the city. Discouraged by the civil disturbances and the bitter factional disputes between the Gregorians and the anti-Gregorians that his election had exacerbated, Victor III put aside his papal insignia and returned to his monastery at Monte Cassino, where he resumed his duties as abbot. On May 9, 1087, however, he was safely conducted to Rome and consecrated as Bishop of Rome in St. Peter's, while the antipope Clement III, having been dislodged by Norman troops, took refuge in the Pantheon.

The rest of the city, however, was still under the control of the antipope's supporters. Discouraged, Victor III returned once again to Monte Cassino. He came back to Rome by sea in early June in response to pleas from the countess Matilda of Tuscany. On July 1 those loyal to him were able to retake the entire city. Then, just a couple of weeks later, with rumors circulating about the emperor Henry IV's impending arrival in Italy, the pope returned yet again to Monte Cassino, where he remained as abbot until three days before his death on September 16, 1087. In late August he did hold a local council at Benevento which reaffirmed Gregory VII's prohibition of lay investiture (the appointment and installation of bishops and abbots by lay rulers), invalidated simoniacal ordinations (those conducted by bishops who had obtained their offices through bribery), and excommunicated the antipope Clement III and the leader of the extreme Gregorians, the archbishop of Lyons, who had opposed his taking the papal throne. During the council, however, Victor III's health deteriorated. He returned immediately to Monte Cassino where he died and was buried. Victor III was beatified by Pope Leo XIII in 1887, but he has never been canonized a saint. Feast day: September 16.

157 Urban II, Bl., *French, ca. 1042–99, pope from March 12, 1088, to July 29, 1099.*

During the pontificate of Urban II, the Roman Curia was established and the First Crusade (to liberate Jerusalem from the Muslims) was launched (1096–99). He was also the first of eight consecutive popes who had the number "II" after their papal names.

Baptized Oddone (di Châtillon), he was former prior of the reformist abbey of Cluny in Burgundy and current cardinal-bishop of Ostia when Victor III died at Monte Cassino on September 16, 1087. Rome was once again under the control of forces loyal to the antipope Clement III and his supporters. Accordingly, the election of a successor to Victor III had to be conducted in the Duomo di San Pietro (St. Peter's Cathedral) in Terracina, south of Rome near Gaeta. There were about forty cardinals, bishops, and abbots present, as well as representatives of the German court. The cardinal-bishop of Porto represented the Roman clergy. The abbot of Monte Cassino represented the cardinal-deacons. The cardinal of San Clemente represented those who were impeded from coming from Rome. The prefect of Rome represented the Roman people. After observing three days of prayer, the cardinals elected Cardinal Oddone unanimously on March 12, 1088, and he was consecrated the same day, in the same place, by the cardinal-bishops of Porto, Tuscolo, and Albano. He took the name Urban upon his election as pope, for what reason we do not know; Urban I (222–30) left little historical trace in papal history other than, like Urban II, he had to contend with an antipope (Hippolytus) during his reign.

Urban II attempted from the outset to mark a more moderate course on church reform. Although he reaffirmed Gregory VII's legislation against clerical marriage, simony (the buying and selling of church offices), and lay investiture (the appointment and installation of bishops and abbots by lay rulers) at a council in Melfi (1089), he adopted a more benign approach to bishops who had been invested by their sovereigns but canonically elected and to the validity of Masses celebrated by priests who had been properly ordained but who had given themselves over to schism. While his conciliatory efforts won him some points in Germany and elsewhere, they did not mollify the emperor, Henry IV, who forced the pope in 1090 to surrender Rome (the pope had entered the city the previous year) to the antipope Clement III and to seek asylum with his Norman allies in southern Italy.

After the defection of Henry's son Conrad to the pope's side, however, Urban II managed to return to Rome in late 1093 and, through bribery, to recover the Lateran Palace in 1094 and Castel Sant'Angelo in 1098. By 1095, even though the imperially supported schism supporting the antipope Clement III continued, Urban II's position was now secure enough for him to convene a number of synods. In March 1095 the synod of Piacenza nullified the ordinations of the antipope and his followers, condemned the eucharistic teaching of Berengarius of Tours (who had denied the Real Presence of Christ), and encouraged Christians to rally to the military support of the Eastern Church beleaguered by the Muslims. A synod at Clermont in November 1095 forbade bishops and clergy to become vassals of lay rulers or of any layperson, decreed that the so-called Truce of God (the suspension of all military hostilities on a given day of the week) should be observed, and issued a summons to the First Crusade (1096–99) to liberate Jerusalem from the Muslims. A synod at Bari in 1098 sought a reconciliation with the Greek bishops of southern Italy. Anselm of Canterbury (d. 1109) was present at the synod in order to try to persuade the Greeks to accept as an addition to the creed the so-called *Filioque* (Lat., "and of the Son") clause, which posited a double procession of the Holy Spirit from both the Father and the Son, rather than from the Father through the Son (*per Filium*). But the pope's overall attempts at reconciliation with the East did not succeed.

His European "foreign policy" may have been somewhat more successful, winning some support for his reforms in France and reorganizing the Church in Spain, including the establishment of the archbishop of Toledo as primate of the country. But because of the pope's distractions with the schism at home, the sovereigns of England, France, Spain, and Sicily (not to mention Germany itself) were able to ignore at will the papacy's reformist regulations. Urban II died on July 29, 1099, in the Palazzo dei Pierleone, next to the church of San Nicolò in Carcere. Two weeks before his death the Crusaders had reconquered Jerusalem, but the news of the victory did not reach the pope in time. He was buried in St. Peter's. A person of monastic piety and humility, he was beatified by Pope Leo XIII in 1881. Feast day: July 29.

158 Paschal II, *August 14, 1099–January 21, 1118.*

Under pressure from the emperor Henry V, Paschal II reversed many of the reforms initiated by Pope Gregory VII (1073–85). Consequently, the papacy suffered a decline in prestige during Paschal's pontificate.

Born Raniero (Rainerius), he served as abbot of St. Paul's Outside the Walls (it was the abbey of St. Lawrence, according to one source) and as cardinal-priest of the church of San Clemente. Sixteen days after Urban II's death, Raniero was elected pope on August 13, 1099, and took the name Paschal. Why he did so is unknown. The first Pope Paschal was so detested by the people of Rome that, after his death, his body could not be buried in St. Peter's. Paschal II was consecrated as Bishop of Rome the next day. Because he was not yet a bishop when elected, he could not theologically be Bishop of Rome (and, therefore, pope) until his consecration, in spite of canonical norms to the contrary.

Paschal II's personality (timid and weak, but also stubborn and inflexible) did not aptly suit him to face the problems inherited from his predecessor: the lay investiture controversy (the appointment and installation of bishops and abbots by lay rulers) in Germany, France, and England; a hostile emperor (Henry IV); and a determined and durable antipope (Clement III). Indeed, there would be four antipopes during Paschal II's pontificate: in addition to Clement III, there were Theodoric, who was cardinal-bishop of Albano; Albert (or Adalbert), who was cardinal-bishop of Silva Candida; and Sylvester IV, who was archpriest of the church of San Angelo. With the help of financial backing from the Normans, Paschal II had the antipope Clement III removed from Rome. But the investiture problem got worse, not better. Although Henry IV had no interest in supporting any of the three antipopes after the death of Clement III in September 1100, he did want to continue to invest bishops and abbots with ring and crozier. But Paschal II renewed the prohibition of lay investiture at a synod in Rome in 1102. After Henry V successfully overthrew his father, it soon became obvious that he, too, wanted to continue the practice of lay investiture. The pope saw to it, however, that lay investiture was condemned and prohibited by synods in Guastalla (1106), Troyes (1107), which deposed bishops who had been invested by laymen, Benevento (1108), and the Lateran (1110).

In spite of all this, Henry V still wanted to be crowned emperor in Rome. A short-lived compromise was worked out at Sutri on February 9,

1111. Henry would renounce investiture and allow the free election of bishops and abbots, and, in return, the German churches would surrender all properties and rights and privileges that had been bestowed by the empire, except for strictly ecclesiastical revenues, such as tithes. When the agreement, or concordat, was read out at the coronation ceremony in St. Peter's three days later (February 12), there were cries of protest and the service had to be brought to an abrupt end. Henry withdrew his acceptance of the agreement and had the pope and the cardinals arrested (including Cardinal Giovanni, who would succeed Paschal II as Gelasius II). After two months of harsh imprisonment, the pope agreed to the emperor's terms (known as the Privilege of Ponte Mammolo) on April 12. The king would retain the right to invest bishops and abbots with ring and crozier after their canonical election, with royal consent to the election to be given before consecration. Paschal also had to swear that he would never excommunicate Henry. The next day he crowned Henry V as emperor in St. Peter's.

Paschal II's abject surrender to the emperor's demands evoked a storm of protest and recrimination against the pope by the reformers. Paschal was so distraught that he considered resigning the papacy. He agreed to a nullification of the Privilege of Ponte Mammolo at a Lateran synod in 1112 and personally condemned and withdrew the privilege in 1116, while renewing the ban on lay investiture. Meanwhile, the lay investiture matter was being peacefully negotiated elsewhere, with the pope's involvement. In England, the king renounced the right of investiture but retained the right to receive homage from bishops before their consecration, and in France the king also renounced investiture in favor of an oath of allegiance.

Paschal II's relations with the East were unhappy. He gave his blessing to a military expedition against the Eastern empire in 1105, thinking it to be a crusade against the Muslims. The Greek Church reacted with acute hostility. In 1112 the Eastern emperor attempted reunion with the pope, but the effort collapsed under the weight of the pope's insistence that the East recognize the primacy of Rome as a precondition.

The last years of Paschal II's lengthy pontificate were even less happy. In 1116 rioting in the city forced him to flee to Benevento. He did so again the following year when Henry V arrived in Rome for a few months' stay. From Benevento he excommunicated Archbishop Maurice of Braga (who later became the antipope Gregory VIII) for solemnly crowning Henry as well as his wife, Matilda, at Easter. A few days after returning to the city in early 1118, the pope died at Castel Sant'Angelo on January 21 and was buried almost secretly in the Lateran Basilica because St. Peter's was under the control of the emperor's forces.

159 **Gelasius II,** *March 10, 1118–January 28, 1119 (January 24, 1118–January 28, 1119, in the Vatican's official list; January 24 is the date of election; consecration as Bishop of Rome did not occur until March 10).*

An elderly man when elected, Gelasius II was attacked and imprisoned immediately after his election by the head of a patrician family in Rome who detested his predecessor, Paschal II. The pope eventually fled to France and died at the monastery in Cluny.

Baptized Giovanni (John) and educated at Monte Cassino, where he became a monk, he was cardinal-deacon in the title of Santa Maria in Cosmedin and chancellor of the Holy Roman Church for some three decades under both Urban II and Paschal II, who also named him archdeacon and librarian. Upon his election on January 24, 1118, not at the Lateran but secretly in the monastery of Santa Maria in Pallara on the Palatine Hill because of the dangerous political and military situation in Rome, he was violently assaulted and imprisoned by Cencius Frangipani, head of a patrician family that detested Paschal II, to whom the new pope had been intensely loyal. At the urging of the other aristocratic families and the Roman people, Gelasius II was released, but he and the cardinals had to flee Rome almost at once because the emperor Henry V was on his way to the city. In his native Gaeta, Gelasius II was ordained a priest (he was still only a deacon at the time of his election in January) and consecrated as Bishop of Rome on March 10.

Henry V demanded that the pope return to Rome so that they could work out together their differences over the investiture controversy (the appointment and installation of bishops and abbots by lay rulers). When the pope refused to return, the emperor had the archbishop of Braga proclaimed as pope; he took the name Gregory VIII. Gelasius excommunicated both the emperor and the antipope a month later at Capua (April 9) and sent letters denouncing the antipope to all the major Christian centers. When Henry left Rome because of the approach of Robert of Capua's army, Gelasius II returned only to find the city under the control of the antipope Gregory VIII and other hostile forces. He could not formally be installed in the Lateran Palace or St. Peter's, and on July 21 was once again attacked by the agents of Frangipani during the celebration of Mass at Santa Prassede. Although the pope managed to escape, he decided to flee to France, along with several of his cardinals. Gelasius II held a synod at Vienne in southern France in early January 1119, but after falling ill he retired to the abbey of Cluny, where, a few weeks later (January 28, possibly 29), he died and was buried near the main altar of the abbey church.

160 Callistus [Calixtus] II, *French, 1050–1124, pope from February 2, 1119, to December 13, 1124.*

Callistus II was the pope who agreed to the Concordat of Worms in 1122, which finally settled the investiture controversy. The Church would retain all spiritual rights in the appointment and installation of bishops and abbots, while the emperor's role would be largely limited to Germany. The concordat was formally ratified at the First Lateran Council in 1123.

On February 2, 1119, at Cluny, the handful of cardinals who had accompanied Gelasius II to France (see Gelasius II, number 159, above) unanimously elected Guido, the reform-minded archbishop of Vienne, as pope; he was crowned a week later in the cathedral of Vienne. (Because Guido was already a bishop, his acceptance of election was sufficient for his becoming Bishop of Rome.) The majority of cardinals, still in Rome, along with the clergy and laity ratified the election on March 1.

Upon the failure of an initial attempt at reconciliation with the emperor Henry V over the issue of lay investiture (the appointment and installation of bishops and abbots by lay rulers), the new pope reaffirmed the ban on lay investiture and the excommunication of Henry at a council in Rheims (October 29–30, 1119), attended by some four hundred prelates and the king of France, Louis VI. The pope thereupon marked a triumphal path through Lombardy and Tuscany and was received enthusiastically in Rome on June 3, 1120. The antipope Gregory VIII had already fled to Sutri, from which he was handed over to Callistus II, publicly humiliated, and then confined to a monastery. The antipope's ordinations were subsequently declared invalid at the First Lateran Council in 1123.

In the meantime, the German princes urged Henry V to recognize the new pope and to enter into negotiations with him over the lay investiture matter without harming the interests of the empire. After three weeks of hard bargaining, the historic Concordat of Worms was approved on September 23, 1122. Under the agreement the emperor renounced his putative right to invest bishops and abbots with ring and crozier (symbols of spiritual authority), and the free elections and consecrations of bishops and abbots were guaranteed. In return, the pope conceded to Henry the assurance that the elections of bishops and abbots in Germany would be held in his presence and that Henry would invest those elected with the symbol of temporal authority (the scepter). In disputed elections, the emperor would make the selection. Outside of Germany, the emperor's presence would not be required at elections, and the investiture of the symbols of temporal authority would follow within six months of consecration. The long struggle between Church and state over lay investiture was finally over. In March 1123 the pope convened a general, or ecumenical, council at the Lateran, which solemnly ratified the Concordat of Worms. The council also reaffirmed a number of previous laws on simony (the buying and selling of church offices), clerical marriage, the forging of ecclesiastical documents, and other matters. Callistus II died on December 13, 1124, in the Lateran and was buried there next to the tomb of Paschal II (1099–1118).

161 Honorius II, *December 21, 1124–February 13, 1130.*

The most memorable aspect of this pontificate is the way in which Honorius II came into office. Upon the death of Callistus II, a majority of the cardinals, allied with the Pierleoni family of Rome, at first supported Cardinal Saxo of the church of San Stephano. Then they quickly abandoned him in favor of the elderly cardinal-priest Teobaldo, who was elected on December 15, 1124, as Celestine II. Lamberto, cardinal-bishop of Ostia, was elected the same day by cardinals favorable to the Frangipani family. While Celestine II's installation was in progress on December 21, the Frangipani family, with the secret support of Aimeric, the chancellor of the Holy Roman Church, broke into the ceremony and at swordpoint had their nominee, Lamberto, acclaimed as pope. Celestine, who suffered severe wounds in the attack, thereupon resigned. (Because Celestine II had not been formally consecrated or enthroned, he is not included in the official list of popes but is classified as an antipope.) The city prefect and the Pierleoni family were bought off with substantial bribes, and Lamberto was then formally "reelected" by the assembled cardinals and enthroned as Honorius II. (Why he took the name Honorius is puzzling, because the first Pope Honorius was formally condemned after his death by the Third Council of Constantinople in 680 for unwittingly supporting Monothelitism, a heresy that held that Jesus Christ had only one divine will rather than a divine and a human will.)

It is worth noting that the divisions revealed in the papal election were not confined to the Roman families. The cardinals themselves were divided between the older Gregorians, who still thought in terms of the struggle between the Church and the empire, and a younger group of reformers, less fixated on the issues that Gregory VII (1073–85) had contended with and more concerned with the moral and spiritual reform of the Church itself.

Because of the peace with the emperor secured through the Concordat of Worms (1122) and the death of Henry V in 1125, Honorius II was able to move his reformist agenda forward. He promoted the moral and spiritual renewal of the Church, showing special favor toward the newer religious orders that combined the contemplative with the active life, such as the Premonstratensians (Norbertines), whose establishment he approved in 1126, and the Knights Templar, protectors of Holy Land pilgrims, whose rule he approved in 1128. He also supported Count Lothair III as the new German king, who, in turn, asked the pope to confirm his election. He coaxed the king of France, Louis VI, to settle his differences with the French hierarchy and secured the admission of papal legates to England. He was less successful controlling the Normans in southern Italy.

When the pope fell ill in January 1130, his powerful chancellor Aimeric had him taken to the monastery of San Gregorio on the Caelian Hill, protected by the Frangipani family. And after the pope died several weeks later, during the night of February 13/14, Aimeric had him temporarily buried in the monastery so that an election could be held immediately. Once his successor, Innocent II, had been elected, Honorius II's body was taken to the Lateran for final burial.

162 Innocent II, *February 23, 1130–September 24, 1143 (the Vatican's official list gives the date of the beginning of his pontificate as February 14, the day of his election; however, he was not yet the Bishop of Rome until February 23).*

Innocent II called the Second Lateran Council in 1139, which annulled all of the acts of the antipope Anacletus and reaffirmed the reform legislation of the past.

Born Gregorio Papareschi, he was cardinal-deacon of the church of San Angelo when elected to the papacy on the night of his predecessor's death in a clandestine meeting of a minority of (younger) cardinals in the fortified convent of San Andrea. Actually, the election consisted of five members of the electoral committee of cardinals that had originally been formed to prevent schism. Although the overall majority of cardinals were older, the younger cardinals had a majority on the committee because of the system whereby the cardinal-bishops, cardinal-priests, and cardinal-deacons voted separately. The rest of the younger cardinals immediately acclaimed him pope. He took the name Innocent II. (The first Innocent [401–17] had made the strongest claim to date of the supreme teaching authority of the Apostolic See.) When word of the election had reached about twenty-four other, older cardinals, mostly old-line Gregorians (that is, loyal to the memory and administrative style of Pope Gregory VII [1073–85]), they refused to accept the result and met themselves later that same morning in the church of San Marco, where they elected Cardinal

Pietro Pierleoni, who took the name Anacletus II. Both elections were canonically irregular.

Because Innocent II and his supporters could not use either St. Peter's or the Lateran for his consecration as Bishop of Rome, since they were both in the hands of the Pierleoni family, they conducted the newly elected pope on February 23 to the Roman chancellor Aimeric's titular church of Santa Maria Nuova in Campo Vincino, where he was consecrated by the cardinal-bishop of Ostia. The antipope Anacletus II was also consecrated on the same day—in St. Peter's Basilica. If a modern-day Catholic were miraculously transported back in time to February 23, 1130, which of the two consecrated cardinals would that Catholic recognize to be the true pope: the one consecrated in Santa Maria Nuova or the one consecrated in St. Peter's? The *Annuario Pontificio* recognizes the former as the legitimate pope and the latter as an antipope. But it would not have been so apparent to an eyewitness of these events.

The result was an eight-year schism. Anacletus's position was at first more secure than Innocent's, perhaps because he had better political connections in Rome and the support of the Norman king, Roger II. Innocent II fled to France, where he gradually won recognition as pope from everywhere except Scotland, Aquitaine, and southern Italy, perhaps because most active members of the Church preferred the spiritual emphasis in his reform agenda. His most effective supporters were Bernard of Clairvaux (d. 1153), who won over King Louis VI of France and King Henry I of England, and Archbishop Norbert of Magdeburg, founder of the Norbertines (Premonstratensians), who swung the German bishops and the king, Lothair III, to Innocent's side.

Innocent met Lothair III at Liège and won his support in his fight against Anacletus II (whom the Catholic Church today regards as an antipope). In return, Innocent II promised Lothair the imperial crown, but not the restoration of investiture rights lost in the Concordat of Worms (1122). Innocent subsequently condemned Anacletus at a synod in Rheims. Lothair marched on Rome in the spring of 1133, but the supporters of Anacletus II held firm to St. Peter's and the old Leonine city (a walled area around St. Peter's created by Pope Leo IV in 852). Therefore, Lothair III had to be crowned in the Lateran Basilica, on June 3. After Lothair returned to Germany, Innocent II's position in Rome became untenable, forcing him to retreat to Pisa, where he held another synod excommunicating Anacletus and his Norman supporter, Roger II. The strife between Innocent II and Anacletus II, however, never ended until Anacletus's death on January 25, 1138. (The antipope Victor IV was elected to succeed Anacletus, but he quickly resigned and his supporters transferred their loyalty to Innocent.)

In April 1139 Innocent II convened the Second Lateran Council, which annulled all the official acts (including ordinations) of Anacletus and his allies and reaffirmed the reform legislation of previous decades. In July of that same year, however, Innocent was captured during a military expedition against Roger II and was forced to acknowledge Roger's title as king of Sicily. In turn, Roger accepted Innocent II's claim to the papal throne. In 1141 he and the king of France, Louis VII, became adversaries over an appointment to the diocese of Bourges. The pope imposed an interdict over any region that gave shelter to the king. Two years later he had more trouble on his own ground. After a period of violence and rioting, the Roman citizens established a commune with an independent senate. Innocent II died on September 24, 1143, and was buried in the Lateran Basilica. His remains were transferred to the church of Santa Maria Trastevere after the Lateran Basilica was destroyed by fire in 1308.

163 Celestine II, *October 3, 1143–March 8, 1144 (the Vatican's official list marks the beginning of his pontificate on September 26, the day of his election; but he was not a bishop at the time and did not become Bishop of Rome until he was consecrated as such on October 3).*

Because Cardinal Teobaldo Boccapecci is regarded officially, though unfairly, as an antipope, having taken the name Celestine II when elected to succeed Callistus II in 1124 (see Honorius II, number 161, above), this Pope Celestine took the number II rather than III when elected to succeed Innocent in 1143. (The first Pope Celestine [422–32] had claimed oversight as the successor of the Apostle Peter over the whole Church, East and West.) Born Guido, he was cardinal-priest of the church of San Marco when unanimously elected pope two days after Innocent II's death.

Celestine II's first two official acts were reversals of positions taken by his predecessor, Innocent II. First, he lifted the interdict on all places sheltering King Louis VII of France (who had originally opposed Innocent II on the appointment of the duly elected archbishop of Bourges). Second, he refused to ratify the treaty that Innocent had been forced to accept while a prisoner of King Roger II of Sicily. The treaty called for the pope to recognize Roger's sovereignty over southern Italy as well as Sicily. But Celestine eventually had to soften his approach to Roger because of military pressure on the borders of the Papal States. Already elderly when elected, Celestine II served less than six months as pope. He died on March 8, 1144, and was buried in the Lateran.

164 Lucius II, *March 12, 1144–February 15, 1145.*

The pontificate of Lucius II was marked by serious political strife in Rome, where a new senate, independent of the papacy and critical of the clergy, was established under the leadership of the brother of the late antipope Anacletus II. (The first Pope Lucius [253–54] was banished from Rome by the emperor Gallus, but was restored by the emperor Valerian. Little is known about Lucius thereafter.) Born Gherardo Caccianemici, he was cardinal-priest of the church of Santa Croce in Gerusalemme and chancellor and librarian of the Roman Church when elected pope on March 12, 1144. The details of his election are unknown. He was immediately consecrated as Bishop of Rome.

Although he restored the metropolitan jurisdiction of the archdiocese of Tours over Brittany, confirmed the primacy of the archdiocese of Toledo over Spain and Portugal, and accepted Portugal as a papal fief, his pontificate was preoccupied with events closer to home, in the city of Rome, where an independent senate was now functioning under the leadership of Giordano Pierleoni, the brother of the late antipope Anacletus II, and where many of the citizens were demanding that the clergy confine themselves to spiritual functions. The pope turned for help first to Roger II of Sicily and then to the new German king, Conrad III. Both efforts failed. The pope decided, in the end, to lead his own military force against the insurgents. He was injured by heavy stones during an attack upon the Capitol, where the senate met, and died shortly thereafter in the monastery of San Gregorio on February 15, 1145. He was buried in the Lateran.

165 Eugenius [Eugene] III, Bl., *February 18, 1145–July 8, 1153 (the Vatican's official list gives the date of his election, February 15, as the beginning his pontificate, but since he was not yet a bishop, he could not be Bishop of Rome until consecrated on February 18).*

A Cistercian, Eugenius III retained the habit and lifestyle of a monk while serving as pope and proclaimed the Second Crusade in 1145. He is also regarded as the last of the reform popes of this particular historical period.

Born Bernardo Paganelli (or Pignatelli), he was abbot of the Cistercian house of SS. Vincenzo and Anastasio outside of Rome when elected to the papacy on the very day (February 15, 1145) that his predecessor, Lucius II, died from wounds sustained while leading a military expedition against the Roman senate. The election was held secretly in the church of San Caesareo (Pope John Paul II's titular church as a cardinal). The pope-elect was conducted immediately to the Lateran, where he was installed.

Since Eugenius III refused to recognize the popular commune now governing Rome, he had to be consecrated three days later at Farfa, twenty-five miles north of the city, and to take up residence in Viterbo. The commune, however, soon accepted him as pope as well as his sovereignty, and he celebrated Christmas in Rome that year. But the agreement collapsed and he was back in Viterbo in January 1146; from there the following year he went to France.

On December 1, 1145, Eugenius III had proclaimed the Second Crusade after having learned of the Turks' capture of the Crusader outpost of Edessa, and he commissioned his fellow Cistercian, Bernard of Clairvaux (d. 1153), to preach on its behalf. The Second Crusade, although impressive in scope, was a great failure. At Bernard's urging, Eugenius III promoted clerical and monastic reform at such important synods as Paris (1147), Trier (1147–48), and Rheims (1148). In his invitation to the last of the three synods, the pope claimed that Christ had bestowed on the papacy, through St. Peter, supreme authority over temporal as well as spiritual matters. He also intervened in the affairs of the English Church, supporting Theobald, archbishop of Canterbury, against King Stephen, and deposing William Fitzherbert as archbishop of York. He established four metropolitan archdioceses in Ireland.

Eugenius III returned to Italy in June 1148 and at Cremona the next month excommunicated Arnold of Brescia, who had allied himself with the antipapal commune movement in Rome, become the leader of the senate, and denounced the pope as a "man of blood." The pope, after a brief return to Rome in December 1149, reached an understanding with the Roman citizens with the help of the new German king, Frederick I Barbarossa, which enabled Eugenius III to return once again in 1152. On March 23, 1153, the pope concluded a treaty with the king at Constance in which the pope promised the imperial crown to the king and the king, in his turn, promised not to make peace with the Roman commune or the Normans without the pope's consent. Each side also agreed to make no territorial concessions to the Eastern empire.

Eugenius III died of a violent fever at Tivoli on July 8, 1153, long before Frederick could come to Rome to be crowned. The pope's body was transported back to Rome and buried in St. Peter's next to Gregory VII (1073–85). Because of the austere simplicity of his life, Eugenius III was beatified by Pope Pius IX in 1872. Feast day: July 8.

166 Anastasius IV, *July 12, 1153–December 3, 1154.*

Peaceful relations were established between the papacy and the Roman commune during the brief pontificate of Anastasius IV. Born Corrado della Suburra, he was cardinal-bishop of Santa Sabina and papal vicar for Rome during the absences from the city of Innocent II and Eugenius III. A very old man, he was unanimously elected pope on July 12, 1153, four days after his predecessor, Eugenius III, died, and was immediately installed in the Lateran. He seems to have enjoyed the confidence of the Roman senate, because he was not only enthroned in the Lateran, but he was allowed to remain in Rome afterwards without any resistance. He was also respected by the Roman people, having assisted them during a period of famine. Unlike his predecessor, he agreed to bestow the pallium (the woolen vestment worn around the neck of an archbishop as a symbol of pastoral authority) on the new archbishop of Magdeburg, and he reinstated the deposed archbishop of York, William Fitzherbert, and sent him the pallium. Anastasius IV died on December 3, 1154, and was buried in the Lateran.

167 Hadrian [Adrian] IV, *English, December 4, 1154–September 1, 1159.*

Hadrian IV was the first and only English pope. Born Nicholas Breakspear, he had left England as a young man to study in France, where he entered an Augustinian monastery and eventually became abbot. When the community complained that Nicholas was too strict, Pope Eugenius III removed him and brought him to Italy as cardinal-bishop of Albano. He also served as a highly successful papal legate to Scandinavia, reorganizing the churches of Sweden and Norway, and after his return was unanimously elected pope upon the death of Anastasius IV. He was crowned in St. Peter's Basilica the next day. During his pontificate the title "Vicar of Christ" became commonly applied to the pope.

Hadrian resumed the papacy's domestic battle with the Roman commune, placing the city under interdict until it expelled its leader, Arnold of Brescia. With the cooperation of the German king Frederick, the pope had Arnold arrested and executed in 1155. The commune subsequently negotiated separately with Frederick, offering him the imperial crown in return for his recognition of them. He declined. The pope's personal relations with the king, however, were not positive. They had an unpleasant meeting at Sutri on June 8, 1155, during which Frederick only reluctantly paid the pope the proper courtesies. When Hadrian finally crowned Frederick in St. Peter's on June 18, he altered the service to emphasize the emperor's subordination to the pope. Frederick returned to Germany after putting down a brief revolt of the Roman people, who were angry at him for refusing their own offer of the crown.

The pope thereupon entered into a very unpopular treaty with William I of Sicily, which recognized him as king with authority over most of southern Italy and with special rights over the Church in Sicily.

In return, William recognized the pope's feudal sovereignty and agreed to pay him an annual tribute. To Frederick, this Treaty of Benevento (1156) seemed a betrayal of the Treaty of Constance, which he had reached with Pope Eugenius III in 1153. Tensions between the pope and the emperor worsened even more at the Diet of Besançon (1157) to which the pope had sent envoys. The envoys carried a papal letter referring to the empire as a *beneficium* of the papacy. The Germans drew the inference that the pope regarded the empire as his fief and the emperor as his vassal. The papal envoys were asked to leave. The next year Hadrian sent the emperor a letter explaining that he meant no offense in his use of the term "*beneficium*." After a very brief period of peace between the two parties, tension rose once more when Frederick, at the Diet of Roncaglia (1158), made claims over northern Italy and Corsica that were in conflict with papal prerogatives there. Hadrian, in turn, refused to approve the emperor's nominee as archbishop of Ravenna. As tensions continued to mount, the pope withdrew to Anagni for security purposes. He threatened to excommunicate Frederick unless he annulled the decrees of Roncaglia within forty days. The pope died on September 1, 1159, before the deadline was reached. He was buried in the crypt of St. Peter's Basilica. His tomb was opened for inspection in 1607 and his body was found to be undecayed, clothed in black vestments.

168 Alexander III, *ca. 1105–81, pope from September 20, 1159, to August 30, 1181 (the Vatican's official list takes the date of his election, September 7, as the beginning of his pontificate, but since he was not yet a bishop, he could not become Bishop of Rome until consecrated as such on September 20).*

Alexander III was the first of many lawyers to become pope. Unfortunately, his election provoked a twenty-year schism between those loyal to him and those loyal to the three antipopes supported by the German emperor, Frederick Barbarossa. He is also the pope who imposed a penance on the English king, Henry II, for the murder of St. Thomas Becket (1172) and who called the Third Lateran Council in 1179, which decreed that a two-thirds majority of cardinals is necessary for papal election.

Born Orlando (or Rolando) Bandinelli, he served as chancellor and papal legate under his predecessor, Hadrian IV, and was a cardinal-priest at the time of his own election to the papacy. A handful of pro-imperial cardinals (probably seven in number) had voted for Cardinal Ottaviano of Monticelli, but the great majority (probably twenty-two) supported Cardinal Bandinelli. Since there had been an agreement that the election should be unanimous, a violent dispute erupted. Cardinal Ottaviano's armed supporters broke into the meeting and tore the red papal mantle from Orlando's shoulders, and the new pope had to seek refuge in the

Vatican fortress next to St. Peter's. Ottaviano's supporters conducted him in a triumphal procession to the Lateran. Alexander III was consecrated as Bishop of Rome three weeks later, on September 20, at Ninfa, southeast of Velletri, by the bishop of Ostia. Ottaviano was consecrated as Victor IV at the imperial abbey of Farfa, northeast of Rome, on October 4.

Thereupon, the emperor convened a synod of about fifty German and Italian bishops at Pavia in February 1160, which endorsed Victor IV and excommunicated Alexander III. The pope had already excommunicated Victor, and on March 24 he condemned the emperor Frederick. In October the bishops and heads of monastic orders of most Western countries, meeting at Toulouse in the presence of King Henry II of England and King Louis VII of France (who had already announced themselves for Alexander at the council of Beauvais in July), heard arguments on behalf of both claimants to the papal throne, declared their support for Alexander III, and condemned Victor IV. Because of imperial opposition in Italy, the pope moved to France in April 1162, locating eventually in Sens (along with his Curia) from 1163 to 1665. He returned to Rome at the people's invitation in November 1165, but could not prevent the recoronation of Frederick and the coronation of his wife as empress in 1167 by the antipope Paschal III (whose election, following the death of the antipope Victor IV in 1164, had been conducted by two schismatic cardinals, two German bishops, and the prefect of Rome). A third antipope, Callistus III, was elected in 1168 and served until 1178, when he submitted to Alexander III.

Alexander III eventually moved to Benevento. While there, the pope's political position gradually improved. After the Lombard League of northern Italian cities defeated Frederick at Legnano in 1176 with the pope's support (and for which the League named the new city of Alessandria after him), the emperor was ready to negotiate. At Venice he and the pope agreed that the excommunication would be lifted from Frederick in return for his acknowledgment of Alexander as pope. Not only did Alexander impose sanctions on King Henry II of England for the murder of Thomas Becket, but he also confirmed the king of Portugal in his position and placed the king of Scotland and his realm under interdict for interfering in church appointments.

From March 5 to March 19, 1179, Alexander III presided over the Third Lateran Council, which brought the schism to a definitive end. It also decreed that a two-thirds majority of voting cardinals is necessary for election to the papacy; it encouraged universities and cathedral schools; and it provided for the punishment of heretics (in particular the Cathari, or Albigensians, in southern France). Soon after the council, however, the popular commune forced the pope to leave Rome, and in September 1179 a fourth antipope, Innocent III, was installed and quickly disposed of. Alexander spent the last two years in various parts of the Papal States and died on August 30, 1181, at Città Castellana, about thirty-five miles north of Rome. His body was taken back to Rome for burial in the Lateran, but the citizens desecrated it beforehand.

169 Lucius III, *September 1, 1181–November 25, 1185 (the Vatican's official list gives his death as August 25, 1185, but the November 25 date appears in J. N. D. Kelly, Levillain's* Dictionnaire historique de la papauté, *and* The New Catholic Encyclopedia).

In concert with the emperor, Lucius III established procedures for the repression and punishment of heretics. Born Ubaldo Allucingoli, he was a Cistercian monk early in his life and then cardinal-bishop of Ostia and Velletri when elected pope. Because of the hostility of the Roman people, however, the new pope's coronation was held in Velletri on September 6, 1181.

Apart from the period between November 1181 and March 1182, Lucius III spent his pontificate outside of Rome, mostly in Velletri and Anagni. Early in his pontificate, there were attempts to mediate the disputes between the emperor Frederick and the papacy. After some unsuccessful negotiations, Frederick and Lucius III met at Verona in October and November 1184, where they reached no agreement on three secular issues: the pope's request for military assistance against the rebellious Romans; a dispute over papal lands inherited by the Countess Matilda of Tuscany; and another dispute over the emperor's request that the pope crown his son Henry (Henry VI) and the son's engagement to the daughter of Roger II of Sicily and niece of the reigning king of Sicily (the Curia feared an alliance between the empire and Sicily would be dangerous to the Holy See).

On some ecclesiastical matters there was agreement: a program for dealing with heretics (they were to be excommunicated by the Church and then handed over to the state for punishment) and preparations for a new crusade in the Holy Land. On other ecclesiastical matters there was no agreement, particularly with regard to the validity of schismatic ordinations in Germany and Italy. Lucius died on November 25, 1185, before relations with the emperor broke down completely. He is buried in the Duomo (cathedral) in Verona.

170 Urban III, *November 25, 1185–October 20, 1187.*

So dedicated an opponent of the German emperor was Urban III that he remained archbishop of Milan during his pontificate so that the customary year's revenues from the archdiocese would not pass to the emperor after his resignation from the see.

Born Umberto Crivelli, he was unanimously elected to the papacy in Verona on the very day of Lucius III's death. He was crowned on December 1, 1185. The cardinal-electors were looking for a candidate less beholden to the emperor than Lucius III had been, but they got an even more independent-minded pope than they had expected. Urban III swore not to consecrate the anti-imperial candidate (of two elected) for the archdiocese of Trier and he sent representatives to the marriage (opposed by the Curia for political reasons) between the emperor's son and Constance of Sicily. But the pope also refused to crown the emperor's son Henry VI as coemperor, suspended the patriarch of Aquileia for crowning the son as king of Italy, opposed the practice of granting the revenues of a vacant diocese or abbey to the crown, and also opposed the right of spoils, that is, the appropriation by the crown of the movable property of a deceased prelate. The final break occurred, however, when, contrary to his oath, the pope rejected the emperor's candidate for Trier and consecrated his rival as archbishop.

The emperor Frederick immediately ordered his son to invade and occupy the Papal States and to isolate the pope and the Curia in Verona, where they were under virtual house arrest. Urban III then supported an ill-fated revolt against the emperor in Cremona and a rebellion of the German bishops under the lead of the archbishop of Cologne. But at the Diet of Gelmhausen in 1186, the emperor isolated the archbishop of Cologne and retained the support of the German bishops. At that point, the pope capitulated, dropping his support for the anti-imperial candidate for the archdiocese of Trier and approving the emperor's plan for a new election. However, the pope soon reverted to type and was actually planning to excommunicate Frederick, that is, until the pro-imperial civil authorities of Verona learned of it and asked the pope and his party to leave the city. After setting out on horseback for Ferrara, Urban III fell ill on the road and died upon reaching the city on October 20, 1187. He was buried in the Duomo (cathedral) of Ferrara.

171 Gregory VIII, *ca. 1100–1187, pope from October 25 to December 17, 1187 (the Vatican's official list begins his pontificate on the day of his election, October 21, but since he was not yet a bishop, he could not become Bishop of Rome until consecrated as such on October 25).*

Already about eighty-seven years of age when elected pope in Ferrara the day after Urban III's death in that city, Gregory VIII served just under two months. Born Alberto de Morra (or Mora), he served for nine years as chancellor of the Holy Roman Church and was, since 1158, cardinal-deacon in the title of San Lorenzo in Lucina. In the election held after Urban III's death, the cardinals at first unanimously chose Enrico di Castel Marsiaco, monk of Chiaravalle and bishop of Albano, but he refused election and recommended Cardinal Alberto de Morra. Morra took the name Gregory VIII and was consecrated as Bishop of Rome on October 25, 1187. In both preferences, the cardinals were expressing their unhappiness with Urban III's virulently anti-imperial policy, just as they had previously elected Urban because they thought *his* predecessor, Lucius III, had been too accommodating toward the emperor. (Thus swings the pendulum of papal elections, contrary to today's popular assumption that popes are usually succeeded by carbon copies of themselves.) Gregory VIII immediately moved to restore harmony to papal-imperial relations. He sent Frederick and his son Henry conciliatory letters and rebuked the anti-imperial candidate for the archdiocese of Trier for his severity toward his rival's supporters. The emperor lifted the virtual house arrest under which Urban III and the Curia had been placed and ordered that Gregory VIII could travel wherever he wished and with a military escort.

Gregory, like his famous namesake Gregory VII (1073–85), was concerned with the reform of the clergy. He forbade them from taking up arms and from wearing extravagant clothing. But he was principally concerned with preparations for another crusade, prompted by the news of a Muslim victory at Hattin in Galilee and then the shocking report of the capture of Jerusalem itself (October 2, 1187). He sent legates to Germany, France, Denmark, and even Poland to preach the crusade. Gregory VIII viewed the Muslim conquests as a sign of God's displeasure with the sins of Christians and ordered that all Crusaders should wear penitential dress. In mid-November he left Ferrara and moved south toward Rome. He paused at Lucca, where the antipope Victor IV had died and was buried. He ordered his tomb (in a monastery outside the city walls) opened and his remains thrown out of the church—hardly a pious and penitential act by any standards. When he reached Pisa on December 10, he fell ill and died a week later, on December 17, 1187. He was buried in the Duomo (cathedral) of Pisa, but his tomb was destroyed in a fire in 1595.

172 Clement III, *December 19, 1187–March 1191.*

The pontificate of Clement III was dominated by preparations for the Third Crusade (1189–92). Born Paolo Scolari, he was the cardinals' second choice when they voted in Pisa two days after the death of Gregory VIII in that city. (Their first choice, Cardinal Teobaldo of Ostia, declined.) Clement III had been cardinal-bishop of Praeneste (now Palestrina) at the time of his election. He was crowned the next day.

The new pope arranged to return the papacy to Rome after a six-year exile. Following discussions with the leaders of the Roman commune, he was received triumphantly back in the city in mid-February 1188 and took up residence at the Lateran. The senators acknowledged his sovereignty and restored papal revenues and the right to mint coins. In return, Clement III had to make substantial annual and special-occasion payments to the commune and leave the administration of the city largely to them. Peace was also restored with the empire. The rival candidates for the archdiocese of Trier withdrew their names and a new election was prepared. The Papal States, occupied by the emperor's son Henry since 1186 as a reprisal against Urban III, were returned to the Holy See, although the empire reserved some proprietary rights. The pope also agreed to confer the imperial crown on Henry VI (but the pope would die before Henry reached Rome).

Clement III made these concessions because of the financial difficulties the papacy labored under at this time and also because he wanted to devote his time and energies to the preparation of the Third Crusade, which would have to be coordinated by the emperor Frederick. Like his predecessor, Gregory VIII, he urged the Crusaders to adopt a penitential dress and diet (since he regarded the Muslim victories in the Holy Land as a sign of God's punishment for the sins of Christians) and he sent legates throughout Europe not only to preach the crusade but also to promote harmony among Christian nations. As a result, the papacy enhanced its role as an instrument of unity. The exact date of the pope's death in mid- or late March 1191 is unknown. He was buried in the Lateran, but no trace of his tomb remains.

173 Celestine III, *ca. 1106–98, pope from April 14, 1191, to January 8, 1198.*

Already eighty-five years of age when unanimously elected, Celestine III had a surprisingly long, if undistinguished, reign of nearly seven years. Born Giacinto Bobo, he was cardinal-deacon of Santa Maria in Cosmedin at the time of his election in late March, having been at that rank for forty-seven years. He had to be ordained a priest and a bishop on April 13 and 14 (Easter), respectively, and he took the name of his old friend and patron, Celestine II (1143–44).

Celestine III's pontificate was dominated by his relations with the new young king of Germany, Henry VI, who was waiting outside the city limits to receive the imperial crown, promised by Gregory VIII. With some reluctance the aged pope crowned Henry on April 15. Upon the emperor's return to Germany (after a failed campaign to the south of Rome), he began arbitrarily making appointments of bishops to various dioceses, rejected the newly elected and papally confirmed bishop of Liège and had him murdered, and imprisoned the English king, Richard the Lion-hearted, although Richard was under papal protection as a returning Crusader. But the pope took no direct action against the emperor, not even for these last two outrages. He also employed delaying tactics against Henry's efforts to get him to approve his controversial plans for a permanent union between Sicily and the empire as a hereditary monarchy. Henry VI died in Sicily on September 28, 1197.

By now the pope was already in his nineties, and at Christmas, 1197, he indicated his wish to resign provided the cardinals elected his close collaborator, Cardinal Giovanni of Santa Prisca. They rejected his proposal and he died a few weeks later, on January 8, 1198. He was buried in the Lateran.

174 Innocent III, *ca. 1160/1–1216, pope from February 22, 1198, to July 16, 1216 (according to the Vatican's official list, canonically he was pope once he accepted election on January 8; theologically he was not pope until consecrated as Bishop of Rome on February 22).*

Innocent III was one of the most important and powerful popes in the entire history of the Church, and his pontificate is considered the summit of the medieval papacy. Indeed, as pope he claimed authority not only over the whole Church but over the whole world as well. "Princes have power in earth, priests over the soul," he wrote. "As much as the soul is worthier than the body, so much worthier is the priesthood than the monarchy." He thought of himself, in fact, as Melchizedek, the biblical priest-king. Although he was not the first pope to use the title Vicar of Christ, he was among the most emphatic in its use. He thought of himself as pope placed somewhere between God and humankind—less than God but greater than humans.

Born Lotario di Segni, he was made a cardinal-deacon of SS. Sergio and Bacco in 1190 at age twenty-nine by his uncle, Pope Clement III, and in 1198, on the day of Celestine III's death, he was unanimously elected pope (probably on the second ballot) at age thirty-seven. He was ordained a priest on February 21 and consecrated and crowned as Bishop of Rome the next day by the bishops of Ostia, Albano, and Porto. He immediately established his authority in the city of Rome, replacing officials of the empire and the Roman commune with men loyal to himself. He reasserted papal control over the Papal States and added other territories to them.

When two rival candidates elected to succeed Henry VI as king of Germany applied to the pope for the imperial crown, he indicated that he had the right to intervene because he alone could bestow the crown and because he had to choose the man best suited to the needs and interests of the Church. Moreover, he argued, the transfer of the empire from the Greeks to the Germans took place through the pope. He chose Otto of Brunswick when Otto promised to recognize the enlarged Papal States and to renounce the right of spoils (the right of rulers to appropriate all the movable property of deceased prelates) in Germany. But when Otto IV later invaded southern Italy and Sicily, Innocent III excommunicated and deposed him and shifted his support for the crown to Frederick of Sicily, who made the same promises to the pope that Otto had.

Innocent intervened elsewhere as well. He excommunicated King John of England for refusing to recognize Stephen Langton as archbishop of Canterbury. When the king made his submission and handed over his Anglo-Irish domains as a papal fief, Innocent III declared the Magna Carta void because it had been extorted from the king by the barons without papal consent. He failed in his attempts to bring the king of France, Philip II, under his thumb (the king did take back his divorced wife, but probably for political, not spiritual, reasons), but the pope acquired as papal fiefs kingdoms such as Aragón, Portugal, Sicily, and Poland and sent the royal crown to the new monarch of Bulgaria. He also made his authority felt in Scandinavia, Spain, the Balkans, Cyprus, and Armenia and supported the Cistercian evangelization of Prussia.

Although Innocent III was a masterful political pope, he also had a clear ecclesiastical agenda: the Fourth Crusade (1202–4), church reform, and the combating of heresy. When the crusade failed (Constantinople fell in 1204), he appealed in 1213 for another one and fixed the date at the Fourth Lateran Council (1215) for 1217. The clergy were to contribute one-twentieth of their income for its support while the pope and cardinals were to contribute a tenth. Regarding church reform, he insisted on simplicity of life for members of the Curia and honest business practices. (His pontificate was one of the few not to experience financial difficulties.) He limited appeals to Rome and encouraged provincial and national councils, but encouraged bishops to refer more serious matters to him and to visit Rome every four years. (Local bishops were not happy with his view of them as subordinates, mere emanations of the pope's plenitude of power given directly by Christ.) He worked to elevate the moral conduct of priests and to enforce the observance of the rule in religious houses. Sympathetic to increasing calls for the practice of evangelical poverty in the Church, he authorized the first Franciscans to preach on the road. He fought hard against heresy, especially Albigensianism in southern France, and commissioned Dominic Guzmán (d. 1221), better known today as St. Dominic, the founder of the Dominicans, to dispute publicly with the heretics. The effort failed, and, after the murder of the papal legate in 1208, Innocent III ordered a full-scale crusade against the heretics, resulting in much bloodshed and destruction.

More than twelve hundred prelates and many representatives of lay princes attended the Fourth Lateran Council in 1215. Its seventy decrees included a definition of the Eucharist in terms of transubstantiation (the sacramental changing of the bread and wine at Mass into the Body and Blood of Christ), the condemnation of heresies (and an appeal for help from the secular powers in suppressing heresies), a ban on the founding of new religious orders, the requirements that all Catholics should make an annual confession and that Jews and Muslims should wear distinctive dress (a forerunner of the requirement in twentieth-century Nazi Germany that all Jews should wear the yellow Star of David on their outer clothing), and the mandate that all Christian rulers observe a four-year truce in preparation for the launching of the next crusade in 1217.

In the summer following the council, while on a trip north to settle personally the differences between the two seaports of Pisa and Genoa, he died suddenly of a fever on July 16, 1216, in Perugia. He was buried in Perugia's cathedral of San Lorenzo. In 1891 Pope Leo XIII (1878–1903), himself a former bishop of Perugia, had Innocent III's remains transferred to the basilica of St. John Lateran in Rome.

175 Honorius III, *July 24, 1216–March 18, 1227.*

Old and frail when elected pope, Honorius III continued the reform program of Innocent III and approved the rules of the Dominican, Franciscan, and Carmelite orders. Born Cencio Savelli, he was cardinal-priest of SS. John and Paul when elected pope in Perugia two days after Innocent III died there. The cardinals had delegated the choice to two of their number, and they unanimously elected Cardinal Savelli on July 18, 1216. He was consecrated as Bishop of Rome in Perugia on July 24.

Honorius III's pontificate was principally concerned with the new crusade proclaimed by Innocent III and the Fourth Lateran Council (1215). But the Fifth Crusade (1217–21) ended, like the previous one, in failure. Honorius III had crowned Frederick II, king of Germany, as emperor in 1220 in order to facilitate his participation in the next crusade, but Frederick instead left Rome to settle problems in Sicily. The emperor only agreed to embark on the crusade in 1225 because of the pope's threat to excommunicate him if he failed to set out by the summer of 1227. In the meantime, Frederick tried to control church appointments in Sicily

and to recover territories given over to the Papal States during the pontificate of Innocent III. And when the emperor also tried to reorganize
northern Italy, the Lombard League of cities successfully blocked him—
at which point the emperor manipulated the pope into assuming the un-
enviable role of mediator between the emperor and the League.

Honorius III promoted the missions in the Baltic states, launched a
crusade against the Moors in Spain, and intensified the campaign against
the Albigensian heretics in southern France under the direction of the
king of France, Louis VIII. With the pope's approval, Louis and the emperor Frederick published ordinances that imposed severe penalties on
heretics and that were the forerunner of the Inquisition. On December
22, 1216, Honorius III formally approved the Dominican order; on December 29, 1223, he approved the rule of the Franciscan order, and on
January 30, 1226, the rule of the Carmelites. He authorized a collection of
his decretals (the *Compilatio quinta*), considered to be the first official
book of canon law. He died on March 18, 1227, and was buried in the
basilica of Santa Maria Maggiore (St. Mary Major).

176 Gregory IX, ca. *1170–1241, pope from March 19, 1227, to August 22, 1241.*

Gregory IX was the pope who established the papal Inquisition under the
direction of the Dominicans. He was also a strong supporter of the Franciscans. Born Ugolino (or Ugo) da Segni, he was the nephew of Innocent
III; he was cardinal-bishop of Ostia and Velletri when elected pope the
day after the death of his predecessor, Honorius III. The cardinals had
delegated three of their number to select the new pope. Ugolino was their
second choice (after the cardinal-bishop of Porto, Conrad d'Urach, who
refused election). He was crowned two days later, on March 21.

Gregory IX proved to be a strong supporter of the Franciscans (he had
been their protector before his election) and the Dominicans, canonizing
his personal friend Francis of Assisi (d. 1226) in 1228, Anthony of Padua
(d. 1231) in 1232, and Dominic (d. 1221) in 1234 and promoting the growth
of the Poor Clares. In 1234 he also published a collection of papal decretals
(*Liber extra*), compiled at his request by Raymond of Peñafort (d. 1275),
that would remain as the fundamental source of canon law until the early
twentieth century, when a new Code of Canon Law was promulgated
(1917). In 1231 he made heretics liable to the death penalty at the hands of
the civil authorities and instituted the papal Inquisition under the direction of the Dominicans who would act with his direct "apostolic authority." (From October 1235 to May 1236 the pope himself was in Viterbo
issuing verdicts against heretics in open meetings in order to impress the
general population.) He reopened the University of Paris also in 1231 (it
had been closed for two years) and modified the ban on the philosophical

writings of Aristotle. In 1233 he founded a new university in Toulouse with the same basic constitution as that of the University of Paris.

Unfortunately, most of his pontificate was marked by the ongoing and deep-seated tensions between Gregory IX and the emperor Frederick II. The emperor, who had delayed embarking on the crusade during the previous pontificate of Honorius III, had been warned to depart for the Holy Land by the summer of 1227 or be excommunicated. Although the emperor set sail in August, he fell ill (or at least said he had) and returned to port. Gregory did not accept the excuse and excommunicated him on September 29. The following June, having "recovered" from his illness, the emperor set sail again and, despite obstacles put in his way by the pope (he had proclaimed an interdict over his lands and over any lands where he might reside, even for a time), reconquered Jerusalem. Because Gregory IX was infuriated that someone who was excommunicated should lead the crusade, he left the condemnation of the emperor in force. The pope then tried to set up a rival king in Germany, released the emperor's subjects in Sicily from their allegiance to him, and gathered an army to oppose the imperial forces in the Papal States and to invade Sicily. As soon as Frederick returned in June 1230, he crushed the papal forces while respecting the borders of the Papal States. After another brief flurry of recriminatory pronouncements, the pope and the emperor achieved a peace at Ceprano in July 1230 whereby the emperor made concessions in Sicily and promised not to violate the papal territories and the pope, in his turn, lifted the excommunication. The uneasy truce held, more or less, for several years.

The emperor offered the pope help from time to time when he encountered renewed problems with the Roman citizens and had to flee the city (1234), and the pope reciprocated by attempting to mediate between the emperor and the Lombard League of cities. However, relations with the emperor once more deteriorated in 1236 when the emperor asked the pope to excommunicate his enemies in the Lombard League. Gregory IX instead reminded the emperor of his transgressions against the Church in Sicily and of his subjection to the successor of the Apostle Peter. By 1238, after Frederick had conquered the Lombard army, it became evident that he intended to take over all of Italy, including Rome. In 1239 the pope once again excommunicated the emperor for his invasion of Sardinia, a subject of the Holy See. Frederick then called for a general council to judge the pope, and the pope, in turn, called the emperor a blasphemer and the forerunner of the Antichrist. In a circular letter addressed to all the princes, Frederick charged that in Gregory IX "wickedness was seated on the throne of the Lord." Gregory, in turn, circulated his own letter referring to the emperor as the "monster of calumny." Frederick would not be outdone. Gregory, he wrote, was a "Pharisee seated on the chair of pestilence, anointed with the oil of wickedness"—thereby bringing "pope bashing" to a new level of eloquence. Then the war of words turned into a real war. Frederick invaded the Papal States and surrounded Rome.

Gregory IX summoned a general council to meet in Rome on Easter, 1241. But the emperor intercepted all the bishop-delegates traveling to Rome from outside of Italy, having closed off all the land routes and having taken control of the sea lanes. Imperial ships captured the ships carrying the French bishops and cardinals and imprisoned all those on board. In the suffocating August heat, with the emperor's forces still surrounding the city, the pope died on August 22, 1241, and was buried in St. Peter's. The emperor withdrew to Sicily to await future developments.

177 Celestine IV, *October 25–November 10, 1241.*

An aged and sick man, Celestine IV was elected as a compromise candidate by eight other cardinals who were forcibly confined for sixty days. The new pope died about two weeks (or sixteen days) later. His was the third, and possibly even the second, shortest pontificate in history. Urban VII was in office for twelve days in 1590 and Boniface VI for possibly fifteen days in 896. The exact length of Boniface VI's and Celestine IV's pontificates is impossible to determine.

Born Goffredo Castiglioni, he was cardinal-bishop of Sabina when elected pope. After Gregory IX's death, the cardinals were reduced to twelve in number, and two of those were held prisoner by the emperor Frederick II. The remaining ten were divided between those who supported the late pope's hostile attitude toward the emperor and those who deplored it. To compel them to reach a decision, a Roman senator, Matteo Rosso Orsini, who was effectively the absolute ruler of Rome, confined them to a wretchedly dilapidated palace known as the Settinozio, or Settesoli. Goffredo, the candidate of the emperor's ally, Cardinal Giovanni Colonna, had the majority of the votes over the anti-imperial candidate, but not the necessary two-thirds required by the Third Lateran Council (1179). When they decided to elect a noncardinal, senator Orsini blocked that idea with threats of violence. As the days dragged on, some of the cardinals became ill and one died. On October 25, after two months of virtual house arrest, the cardinals elected the man who had led on the very first ballot, Goffredo, who took the name Celestine IV. Two days later, the new pope fell ill and died on November 10, probably before being crowned and performing any official papal acts. He was buried in St. Peter's.

If Celestine IV had not already been a bishop when elected pope, would he have been a legitimate pope if he was not consecrated as Bishop of Rome? The canon law of this period marked the beginning of a pontificate as the date of election, whether the individual was already a bishop or not. Through most of the history of the Church, including today, valid consecration as a bishop is necessary along with valid election because the pope is, first and foremost, the Bishop of Rome. He cannot be the Bishop of Rome if he is not a bishop!

178 Innocent IV, *ca. 1200–54, pope from June 28, 1243, to December 7, 1254 (the Vatican's official list marks the beginning of his pontificate on the day of his election, June 25, but he was not yet a bishop until June 28).*

Innocent IV was the first pope to approve the use of torture in the Inquisition to extract confessions of heresy. Born Sinibaldo Fieschi, he was a cardinal-priest in the title of San Lorenzo in Lucina, vice-chancellor of the Holy See, and a distinguished canon lawyer when elected pope at Anagni after a vacancy of eighteen months. He was consecrated as Bishop of Rome and crowned as pope three days later, on June 28. The delay in the election of more than eighteen months was caused by the emperor Frederick II, who held two cardinals prisoner and who was still smarting under the excommunication imposed on him by Gregory IX in 1239. The emperor wanted to be sure that the new pope would be sympathetic to him.

Although he possessed many of the same leadership qualities that Gregory IX had, Innocent IV did not have Gregory's temperament—or virtue. He followed the principle, "the end justifies the means." He raised nepotism to a high art, placing relatives in key positions in order to create a network of loyal supporters, and erased the distinction between church revenues and personal revenues. He believed, like his previous namesake, Innocent III (1198–1216), that as the Vicar of Christ the pope is supreme over all, but he recognized that it was a *de iure* (Lat., "by right"), not a *de facto* ("in fact") supremacy.

While the emperor was scheming to have his excommunication lifted in return for various concessions to the Holy See, the distrustful pope fled secretly in the summer of 1244 to Lyons, France, by way of Genoa (his home city). In Lyons he was under the protection of King Louis IX of France. Between June 26 and July 17, 1245, he held the First Council of Lyons, which included representatives from the whole Christian world except those regions under imperial control, with an agenda that included ongoing matters of church reform, the liberation of the holy places in Palestine, and continued difficulties with the emperor, who was found guilty *in absentia* of perjury, sacrilege, and heresy and then deposed. The emperor challenged the right of the pope to depose him, but the pope argued that Christ had given Peter and his successors absolute temporal as well as spiritual authority. The excommunication against him was renewed in April 1248, and the emperor died at the end of 1250.

Innocent IV returned triumphantly to Rome in the following year and immediately tangled with the emperor's son, Conrad IV, in the hope of regaining Sicily as a papal fief. After Conrad died (1254), the pope annexed Sicily to the Papal States and moved his residence to Naples, where he died less than two months later, on December 7, 1254, just as a rebellion was being raised against papal rule in Sicily. His original tomb was in the basilica of Santa Restituta in Naples, which was incorporated into the cathedral in the thirteenth century.

179 Alexander IV, *December 12, 1254–May 25, 1261.*

Alexander IV's pontificate was characterized by constant conflict with political powers, in which the papacy generally came out second best. Born Rinaldo dei Conti di Segni, a nephew of Gregory IX (1227–41), he was cardinal-bishop of Ostia when elected pope in Naples on December 12, 1254, five days after the death of Innocent IV. Actually the cardinals had wanted to return to Rome for the election, but the mayor of Naples bolted the city gates to keep them there. The new pope was crowned on December 20.

From the outset of his pontificate, Alexander IV was faced with the new Sicilian revolt, and he excommunicated its leader, Manfred, the illegitimate son of the late emperor Frederick II. A military effort to recapture Sicily for the papacy failed and most of the Papal States came under Manfred's control. Alexander IV also mishandled most of the other political problems that pressed in on him, including the royal succession in Germany following the death of Conrad IV in 1254 (he could not quite decide upon whom to support). He could not even reside in Rome for most of his pontificate, given the power struggles there. He spent most of his time in Viterbo.

Alexander IV canonized Clare of Assisi (d. 1253), foundress of the Poor Clares, in 1255 and founded the Augustinian Hermits in 1256 (by amalgamating several Italian communities of hermits under the Rule of St. Augustine). He died in Viterbo on May 24, 1261, around the time that his archenemy Manfred was being elected a senator in Rome. The pope was buried in Viterbo's cathedral of San Lorenzo.

180 Urban IV, *French, ca. 1200–1264, pope from August 29, 1261–October 2, 1264.*

The pontificate of Urban IV left no lasting image in papal history, having failed to resolve (or even improve) a number of continuing political problems inherited from previous popes. On a minor note, he was the pope who extended the feast of Corpus Christi to the whole Church and who commissioned St. Thomas Aquinas (d. 1274) to prepare an office (Liturgy of the Hours) for it.

Born Jacques Pantaléon, the son of a shoemaker, he was patriarch of Jerusalem and was visiting the Curia on business when he was elected in Viterbo on August 29, 1261, to succeed Alexander IV, who had died in that city. Because Alexander IV had created no cardinals during his six-and-a-half-year pontificate, the number of cardinals was down to eight at the time of the election. The new pope took the name Urban IV, perhaps in honor of Urban II (1088–99), who was also French. He was crowned on September 4. Almost immediately he named fourteen new cardinals, six of them highly qualified Frenchmen.

Urban's first move was to replace the hostile Manfred as head of the kingdom of Sicily and to eliminate the power of the Hohenstaufen dynasty from Italy. Within a few months he recovered most of the Papal States (lost by his predecessor) in the south and began rebuilding papal prestige in the north. In June 1263, Urban IV offered the kingdom of Sicily and southern Italy to the French king's brother Charles in return for a large sum of money and an annual tribute and guarantees of freedom for the Church in those territories and of military assistance when needed. When Manfred heard of the arrangement, he resumed military operations in Tuscany, Campagna, and the Papal States. The pope had to take refuge in Orvieto, where he was compelled to modify the treaty with Charles and to accept Manfred's election as a Roman senator. When Orvieto itself was threatened militarily, the pope retreated to Perugia, where he died on October 2, 1264. He was buried in Perugia's cathedral of San Lorenzo.

181 Clement IV, *French, February 5, 1265–November 29, 1268.*

During his pontificate, Clement IV decreed that appointments to all benefices in the West were papal appointments, thereby preparing the way for the present, relatively recent system in which the pope makes all episcopal appointments.

Born Guy Foulques, son of a successful French judge, he was a widower with two daughters and was cardinal-bishop of Sabina at the time of his election as pope in Perugia, the city where his predecessor, Urban IV, had died. There was a four-month gap between Urban's death and the election of Clement, however. The cardinals had been sharply divided. They finally turned to Cardinal Foulques, who was not even present at the conclave. He was elected on February 5, 1265, and took the name Clement IV. He was crowned, also in Perugia, on February 15. At the time he was on his way home from a diplomatic mission to England, where he had given the Holy See's support to King Henry III against the barons. He arrived in Perugia disguised as a monk because of the hostile political atmosphere in northern Italy. As pope he would reside first in Perugia and then in Viterbo, but never in Rome, because of hostile conditions there.

On the political front, he completed his predecessor's expulsion of the Hohenstaufen dynasty from Italy and the installation of Charles of Anjou as king of Sicily and Naples in place of the papal enemy Manfred, the illegitimate son of the deceased emperor Frederick II. (Charles was crowned in St. Peter's in 1266 by five cardinals appointed by the pope.) The pope then borrowed large sums of money to finance a military campaign against Manfred. A strong French army defeated and killed Manfred at Benevento in 1266. But two years later, with much of the population upset with Charles's regime, the last of the Hohenstaufens, Conradin, duke of Swabia and king of Jerusalem, marched on Italy. The pope excommunicated him and his supporters and deposed him from his Jerusalem throne. Conradin was at first received triumphantly by the Romans in July 1268, but he was defeated the next month by Charles at Tagliacozzo, captured, and, after a trial, beheaded. The pope did nothing to stop or protest this action, although he did on several other occasions chastise Charles for his greed and cruelty toward his new subjects. Technically, Charles had the authority to impose capital punishment because Clement IV had appointed him imperial vicar in Tuscany just a few months earlier. Ironically, now that the pope had gotten rid of the Hohenstaufen dynasty, he found himself and the papacy under the threat of a new aggressive force in Italy, the Angevin house in the person of Charles of Anjou.

As in previous pontificates of this period, gestures toward the East came to nothing, mainly because Rome demanded complete submission from the Greek Church. In his bull *Licet ecclesiarum* (August 27, 1265) Clement IV reserved to the Holy See the right to make appointments to benefices that became vacant while the incumbent was visiting the Curia. The preamble of the bull asserted the principle that the appointment to all benefices was a papal prerogative. Although it might be said that the pope was trying to curtail the influence of local nobles and rulers in ecclesiastical appointments, this was one more instance, in the centuries following the watershed pontificate of Gregory VII (1073–85), of the growing centralization of power in the papal office.

Clement IV died in Viterbo on November 29, 1268, and was buried in the Dominican convent of Santa Maria in Gradi outside the walls of the city. His remains were transferred in 1885 to the basilica of San Francesco in Viterbo.

182 Gregory X, Bl., *1210–76, pope from March 27, 1272, to January 10, 1276 (the Vatican's official list begins his pontificate on September 1, 1271, the day of his election, but he was not consecrated as Bishop of Rome until March 27, 1272).*

Gregory X is famous for the manner in which he was elected to the papacy—in the extraordinary conclave in Viterbo in which the civil authorities locked the cardinals in the papal palace and then, on the advice of Bonaventure (d. 1274), the minister general of the Franciscans (and later canonized as a saint), removed its roof and threatened them with starvation if they did not quickly proceed to the election of a successor to Clement IV. (It had taken them nearly three full years already!) The cardinals thereupon delegated the choice of a successor to a committee of six cardinals. The cardinal-electors had been divided along political lines: those who wanted to break the papacy's alliance with Charles of Anjou and those who wanted to maintain the pro-French orientation of Urban IV and Clement IV. Gregory X's pontificate was also significant for the decree, formulated at the Second Council of Lyons (1274), that papal elections should be held within ten days after the death of a pope, in the city where the pope died, and with the cardinal-electors having no contact with the outside world.

Born Teobaldo (or Tebaldo) Visconti, Gregory was not yet a priest or a cardinal when elected to the papacy on September 1, 1271. He was archdeacon of Liège and was away at the time in Acre (Akko, in modern-day Israel) on a crusade in the Holy Land with the future King Edward I of England. He had earlier served for years with Cardinal James of Palestrina, was one of the organizers of the First Council of Lyons in 1245, accompanied Cardinal Ottobono on a diplomatic mission to England in 1265, and was close to the royal families in France and England. Teobaldo reached Viterbo on February 10, 1272, more than five months after his election, and then went to Rome, where neither of his two immediate predecessors had set foot as pope. He was ordained a priest on March 19 and consecrated as Bishop of Rome in St. Peter's on March 27, 1272.

Because of his background as a Crusader, Gregory X made the liberation of the holy places the central theme of his brief pontificate. On April 13, 1272, he began sending out invitations to another general, or ecumenical, council with a threefold agenda: a new crusade, reunion with the Greek Church, and the reform of the clergy. To win support for the crusade, Gregory X sent envoys to Constantinople in October 1272 and upon their return invited the Byzantine emperor Michael VIII Palaeologus to send delegates to the council. He also moved to unite the European powers for the crusade. Having persuaded Alfonso of Castille to withdraw his claim to the German throne, Gregory approved the election of Rudolf, count of Hapsburg, as king of Germany and crowned him king of the Romans at Aachen on October 1, 1273. At the Second Council of Lyons (which the pope held in Lyons to avoid pressure from Charles of Anjou, king of Sicily and in control of much of central and northern Italy), Rudolf renounced all rights to papal territories and recognized the permanent separation of Sicily from the empire (a point that the Curia had favored for years). Rudolf confirmed these promises at a meeting with Gregory X at Lausanne in October 1275, on the pope's way home from the council.

The council opened on May 7, 1274, and the Greek delegates arrived on June 24. They assented to the primacy of the Holy See and to the Roman creed, including the controversial *Filioque* (Lat., "and of the Son"), to which the Greek Church had consistently objected because it diminished the monarchical status of God the Father within the Trinity (a point not all readers will immediately appreciate, through no fault of their own!). At the council's fourth session (July 6) the pope formally ratified the (short-lived) union of the Latin and Greek Churches. In addition to establishing a system for financing the crusade (which was never launched), the council decreed in the constitution *Ubi periculum* (July 7, 1274) that, once there is a vacancy in the Holy See, the cardinals must assemble within ten days after the pope's death in the city or town where he died and proceed to the election of a successor without any further contact with the outside world. The longer the electoral process takes, the more austere the living conditions for the cardinals were to become. (The pope and the council were obviously influenced by the circumstances of Gregory's own election.) Other conciliar decrees prohibited lengthy absences from benefices or other ecclesiastical posts and placed tight restrictions on religious orders, with the exception of the Franciscans and the Dominicans.

After crossing the Alps, the pope visited various northern Italian cities to settle local disputes, but he came down with a severe fever and died at Arezzo on January 10, 1276. He was buried in the Duomo (cathedral) of Arezzo. A cult soon developed there, in Piacenza, and in other places he had visited. It was approved by Clement XI in 1713. Gregory X's name was later added to the Roman Martyrology during the pontificate of Benedict XIV (1740–58). Feast day: January 9.

183 Innocent V, Bl., *French, ca. 1224–76, pope from January 21 to June 22, 1276.*

Innocent V was the first Dominican pope, and the still current papal custom of wearing a white cassock may have begun with him when he decided to continue wearing his white Dominican habit as pope. (Others suggest that the custom was not finally established until the pontificate of another Dominican, Pius V [1566–72].) Innocent V was the second of four individuals listed as popes in the year 1276. Born Pierre de Tarentaise, he was a renowned and well-published theologian and cardinal-bishop of Ostia when unanimously elected to the papacy on January 21, 1276, in Arezzo, where Gregory X had died. The new pope went as soon as possible to Rome, arriving on February 22. He was immediately enthroned in the Lateran and then crowned on February 25.

Innocent V had been a friend of St. Bonaventure and preached at his funeral in 1274. He was also an active participant in the Second Council of Lyons (1274); before that he had twice been Dominican provincial of France and archbishop of Lyons. His election signaled a change of course in papal policy (which many papal elections have done). The Curia wanted to move away from Gregory X's cultivation of the Germans in order to counterbalance the domination of Italy by Charles of Anjou, king of Sicily. Accordingly, on March 2 Innocent V confirmed Charles as a Roman senator and as imperial vicar in Tuscany and asked Rudolf, the king of Germany, to postpone his trip to Rome, originally planned for his coronation as emperor by Gregory X. He also tried to resurrect Gregory's plans for a new crusade and his efforts to unify the European powers so they could more effectively conduct the crusade itself.

His handling of relations with the East was generally inept. He almost apologized to the Byzantine emperor Michael VIII Palaeologus for Charles's plans for recapturing Constantinople on the grounds that it had been forcibly taken away from the Latins, and he demanded that the Greek clergy should take personal oaths accepting the *Filioque* (Lat., "and of the Son") in the creed and the primacy of the pope. Innocent VI died on June 22, only five months after his election and before his envoys reached Constantinople. He was buried in St. John Lateran Basilica, and was beatified by Pope Leo XIII in 1898. Feast day: June 22.

184 Hadrian [Adrian] V, *ca. 1205–76, pope from July 11 to August 18, 1276.*

Hadrian V's "pontificate" (see below) was noted for its brevity (five weeks) and for the fact that he died before he could be ordained a priest (he was a deacon at the time of election) and consecrated and crowned as pope. Canonically, he may have been a legitimate pope—the Vatican's official directory, the *Annuario Pontificio*, so regards him—because during this period acceptance of valid election was sufficient. But theologically he could not have been pope, because the pope is, first and foremost, the Bishop of Rome and, since Hadrian was not yet a bishop, he could not have become the Bishop of Rome until consecrated as such. The 1983 Code of Canon Law once again makes consecration as a bishop as essential as valid election (can. 332.1). Hadrian V was the third of four canonically recognized popes in the year 1276.

Born Ottobono Fieschi, he was a nephew of Innocent IV (1243–54) and cardinal-deacon of the church of San Adriano (the name he would take as pope) at the time of his election. He had also served as a very successful papal legate to England and returned to Rome to become one of the most respected and influential members of the College of Cardinals. On the day after his election, he assembled the cardinals in the Lateran and suspended the rules for a papal election laid down by Gregory X (1272–76), promising to develop new ones. A few days later he left Rome to escape the oppressive summer heat and went to Viterbo, north of Rome, where he became seriously ill and died on August 18. His tomb in the basilica of San Francisco in Viterbo is considered one of the masterpieces of Arnolfo di Cambio, a contemporary Florentine sculptor. Hadrian V is memorialized in Dante's *Divine Comedy* as a temporary inhabitant of Purgatory for the sin of avarice (*Purgatory*, 19.88–145).

185 John XXI, *Portuguese, ca. 1210/15–77, pope from September 8, 1276, to May 20, 1277.*

John XXI was the first and only Portuguese pope, the first and only medical doctor to be pope (his father was also a doctor), and the fourth canonically recognized individual to occupy the Chair of Peter in the year 1276. He is numbered as John XXI, although no pope took the name John XX. There may have been confusion at the time created by the fact that as many as ten popes had taken the name John in the tenth and eleventh centuries.

Born Pedro Julião (better known as Peter of Spain, or Petrus Hispanus), he was cardinal-bishop of Tusculum when elected pope in Viterbo ten days after Hadrian V's death in that town. He was crowned on September 15. The new pope had taught medicine at the new University of Siena and served as the personal physician of Pope Gregory X (1272–76). In addition, he was an accomplished scholar and author, having written a widely used and influential textbook in logic, a treatise on the soul, and even a study of ophthalmology entitled *The Eye* (*De oculis*). But it was on the basis of John XXI's bull *Relatio nimis implacida* (January 18, 1277) that Stephen Tempier, bishop of Paris, condemned 219 philosophical and theological propositions, including nineteen of St. Thomas Aquinas (d. 1274).

Because John XXI was a scholar with no interest in administration, he left the details of policy making to Cardinal Giovanni Gaetano, of the noble Orsini family and the future Pope Nicholas III (1277–80). In a reversal of the anti-imperial approach of Innocent V (January 21–June 22, 1276), John XXI refrained from confirming Charles of Anjou, king of Sicily, as a Roman senator and imperial vicar in Tuscany and sought to reconcile Charles with King Rudolf I of Germany in order to prepare the way for Rudolf's coronation as emperor. He also sought to bring together the European rulers to provide a united effort in another crusade to liberate the holy places in Palestine, and made (unsuccessful) efforts to heal the breach with the Greek Church.

John XXI's death was bizarre. Immediately after his election as pope, he built a small study for himself at the rear of the papal palace in Viterbo. Because it was hastily constructed, the ceiling fell in on him and he died on May 20, 1277, a few days after suffering the injuries. Although he was criticized by some of his contemporaries for alleged moral instability and a dislike of religious orders, the great poet Dante placed the pope among the saints of heaven in the *Divine Comedy* (*Paradise*, 12.134). He was buried in the Duomo (cathedral) of Viterbo.

186 Nicholas III, *1210/20–80, pope from December 26, 1277, to August 22, 1280 (the Vatican's official list gives the beginning of his pontificate as the day of his election, November 25, but he was not yet a bishop when elected; he became Bishop of Rome on December 26).*

Nicholas III was the first pope to make the Vatican Palace his residence. He also had the unfortunate distinction of having been placed in Hell in the *Divine Comedy* by the Italian poet Dante for nepotism and avarice (*Inferno*, 19.61ff.).

Born Giovanni Gaetano of the noble Orsini family, he had been archpriest of St. Peter's and a cardinal-deacon in the title of San Nicolò in Carcere for more than thirty years when elected pope in the papal palace in Viterbo on November 25, 1277, after a deadlock of six months. Three cardinals supported him and three others opposed him because of his animosity toward Charles of Anjou, king of Sicily. When the deadlock was broken, he was elected and took the name Nicholas III, the name of his titular church in Rome. More likely he took the name in honor of Nicholas I (858–67). He returned immediately to Rome the day after his election and on the day after Christmas, 1277, was consecrated as Bishop of Rome and crowned.

Nicholas's pontificate was fashioned in reaction to Innocent V's (1276) and in support of Gregory X's (1272–76); namely, to restore the political independence of the Holy See in Italy. Therefore, he persuaded Charles of Anjou to resign as imperial vicar of Tuscany and not to seek reappointment as a Roman senator when his term expired, and he decreed that in the future no prince may become a member of the senate without the pope's permission (the pope had himself elected to the senate for life). Meanwhile, he negotiated with King Rudolf I a formal renunciation of imperial claims on papal territories in Romagna, which had the effect of enlarging the Papal States and establishing boundaries that would remain more or less in place until the dissolution of the Papal States (except for Rome) in 1860. The pope also arranged a marriage between Rudolf's daughter and Charles's grandson to ensure peace between the houses of Hapsburg and Anjou (and papal supremacy in Italy).

Like John XXI, Nicholas III tried unsuccessfully to restore unity between the Latin and Greek Churches, on Rome's terms. He made some excellent appointments to the College of Cardinals and promoted Franciscans (whose protector he had been) and Dominicans to diplomatic and episcopal posts. By his bull *Exiit qui seminat* (August 14, 1279), he settled at least temporarily the dispute within the Franciscan order (between the Spirituals and the Conventuals) over the interpretation of the vow of poverty. Adopting St. Bonaventure's (d. 1274) approach, Nicholas III distinguished between the total lack of possessions, which he deemed meritorious, and the "moderate use" of things necessary for life and the fulfillment of one's vocation and ministry. He also carried out a major restoration of St. Peter's (where he had formerly served as archpriest) and made the Vatican Palace his residence. He enlarged and remodeled it and purchased plots for its gardens. He died on August 22, 1280, of a stroke at his new summer residence in Soriano, near Viterbo. In accordance with his instructions, his body was taken back to Rome and buried in the Orsini chapel of St. Nicholas, whose construction he had directed, in St. Peter's.

187 Martin IV, *French, ca. 1210/20–85, pope from March 23, 1281, to March 28, 1285 (the Vatican's official list begins this pontificate on the day of his election, February 22, but since he was not yet a bishop, he could not become Bishop of Rome until he was consecrated on March 23).*

Martin IV, who was actually the second Pope Martin (Popes Marinus I and II were incorrectly given as Martin II and III in the official lists of the thirteenth century), voided the union with the Greek Church forged at the Second Council of Lyons (1274) when he excommunicated the Byzantine emperor Michael VIII Palaeologus in 1281.

Born Simon de Brie, he was cardinal-priest of Santa Cecilia when elected pope in Viterbo after six months of animosity and intrigue between forces sympathetic to Charles of Anjou, king of Sicily, and those hostile to him. The deadlock was broken only after a new mayor favorable to Charles imprisoned two cardinals of the Orsini family (the deceased pope, Nicholas III, was an Orsini) and prevented another from participating in the election. Simon was elected through powerful pressure exerted by Charles. The Romans, however, refused the new pope entrance into the city, so he had to be crowned in Orvieto, where he spent most of his pontificate. He was consecrated as Bishop of Rome and crowned and enthroned in Orvieto on March 23. He took the name Martin in honor of the patron saint of France, Martin of Tours (d. 397).

Once again, this election undercuts the conventional assumption that popes are generally succeeded by duplicates of themselves. Martin IV's election represented a complete rejection of his predecessor's policies, and his pontificate did, in fact, reverse them. Thus, when the Romans elected the new pope senator for life (a position Nicholas III had secured for himself while forcing Charles to relinquish his membership in the senate), Martin IV transferred the office to Charles and effectively handed over control of the Papal States to him as well.

Unlike his predecessors, Martin IV supported Charles's efforts to recover Constantinople for the West by military means, and in 1281 he excommunicated the Byzantine emperor Michael VIII Palaeologus as a schismatic, even though the emperor had done all in his power to accommodate himself to the demands of the Holy See. Thus was the formula of union for the Latin and Greek Churches forged at the Second Council of Lyons in 1274 effectively annulled. The "crusade" to liberate Constantinople, however, was derailed by a revolt in Sicily against French control—a rebellion signaled by the tolling of bells for Vespers on March 30, 1282 (the so-called Sicilian Vespers). The victorious rebels offered the island to the pope as a vassal state, but Martin IV rejected the offer and urged the rebels to submit to Charles. He later excommunicated and deposed King Peter III the Great of Aragón when he accepted the Sicilian crown.

Martin IV also had problems within the Church. A friend and protector of the Franciscans, he relaxed their rules on poverty and granted them expanded spiritual rights of preaching and hearing confessions and, in the process, upset the diocesan clergy and provoked debates within the universities. (His initiative was later modified by Pope Boniface VIII in 1300.) His excessively pro-French policies alienated many Catholics, especially in Germany. Martin IV died in Perugia on March 28, 1285, just a few weeks after his friend and patron Charles I of Sicily. He was buried in the cathedral of San Lorenzo in Perugia.

188 Honorius IV, *1210–87, pope from May 20, 1285, to April 3, 1287 (the Vatican's official list begins this pontificate on the day of his election, April 2,* *but since he was not yet a bishop, he could not become Bishop of Rome until he was consecrated on May 20).*

The pontificate of Honorius IV, the grandnephew of Honorius III (1216–27), was without particular shape or distinction. Born Giacomo Savelli, he was the elderly and arthritic cardinal-deacon of Santa Maria in Cosmedin when unanimously elected pope in Perugia four days after the death of Martin IV. His election was received with enthusiasm in Rome, and he was consecrated as Bishop of Rome and crowned in Rome itself on May 20 and later elected senator for life. He resided in Rome throughout his pontificate, first in the Vatican and then in a new, sumptuous palace he had built on the Aventine Hill.

Since most of the cardinals were French, the new pope was responsive to their wishes to retrieve Sicily for the Angevins (the house of Anjou). But the means were highly complex and ultimately unsuccessful. A crusade launched against the Spanish rule of Sicily by the French king, Philip III, led to Philip's death and the death of the reigning king of Sicily, Peter III. When Peter's son James had himself crowned king of Sicily, Honorius IV excommunicated him. But then Charles of Anjou's heir, Charles II of Salerno, renounced his title to Sicily in favor of James in order to obtain his own release from imprisonment. The pope refused to approve the agreement, but Sicily was lost.

The pope resumed contacts with the German king Rudolf I and set the date of his coronation as emperor for February 2, 1287. But Rudolf could not make the journey to Rome in time and the date had to be postponed. Then it was postponed a second time when the papal legate to the Diet of Würzburg (March 16–18) was rebuffed in his efforts to secure financial contributions on the occasion of the planned coronation. The coronation never took place.

Honorius IV was a strong supporter of the Dominicans and the Franciscans, confirming and extending their privileges and appointing a number of them to bishoprics. He also promoted the study of oriental languages in Paris in the hope of reuniting the Churches of East and West. He died in Rome on April 3, 1287, and was buried in St. Peter's, but his remains were later transferred by Paul III (1534–49) to the Chiesa dell' Aracoeli, to be placed next to those of his mother.

189 Nicholas IV, *1227–92, pope from February 22, 1288, to April 4, 1292.*

Nicholas IV was the first Franciscan pope. During his pontificate, Catholicism was established for the first time in China. Born Girolamo Masci, he was a Franciscan friar (the successor of St. Bonaventure [d. 1274] as general of the order) and the pastorally attentive cardinal-bishop of Palestrina when he was unanimously elected (the first time) in the new papal palace on the Aventine Hill on February 15, 1288. He was a compromise candidate after a conclave of some eleven months, in which six cardinals had died of intense summer heat and others fell ill before the proceedings were suspended for a time. However, when Girolamo declined election out of Franciscan humility, the cardinals elected him again on February 22. This time he accepted. He took the name Nicholas IV in honor of Nicholas III, who had made him a cardinal. He was crowned on the same day.

Like his predecessor, the new pope was elected senator for life, but, unlike his predecessor, was unable to reside without interruption in Rome during his pontificate because of intermittent civil disorders that were stirred in part by his own blatant favoritism toward the Colonna family, for which he was roundly mocked. He created one member of the Colonna family a cardinal, arranged for another to be elected sole senator, and appointed others to administrative posts in the Papal States.

Nicholas IV had no more success in manipulating political developments in Sicily than his predecessor had. He proposed alliances, annulled a treaty, and crowned a pretender to the throne of Sicily—all without positive effect. So, too, nothing came of his efforts to mount another crusade to liberate the holy places in Palestine from the Muslims. He is known in history, however, as a missionary pope for having sent his fellow Franciscan friar Giovanni di Monte Corvino to the court of the Great Kubla Khan, an initiative that led to the first establishment of the Catholic Church in China (Giovanni was later appointed archbishop of Peking by Pope Clement V in 1307). Nicholas IV also sent missionaries, mostly Franciscans, to the Balkans, Persia, Ethiopia, and the Near East. In 1289, facing increasing unrest in the Papal States, he issued a bull *(Caelestis altitudo)* assigning one-half of the Holy See's revenues, as well as some of the administration, to the College of Cardinals and made the appointments of rectors and other officials in the Papal States contingent upon the college's approval.

Nicholas IV welcomed famous artists to Rome and drew upon their talents to remodel and embellish the basilicas of St. John Lateran and St. Mary Major (Santa Maria Maggiore). He also had a palace constructed near the latter and made his principal Roman residence there. He died on April 4, 1292, and was buried in Santa Maria Maggiore.

190 Celestine V, St., *1209/10 (or 1215?)–96, pope from August 29 to December 13, 1294 (the Vatican's official list begins his pontificate on July 5, the* *day of his election; but he was not yet a bishop until his consecration as Bishop of Rome on August 29).*

Celestine V is best known for being constantly, and erroneously, identified as the only pope ever to have resigned from the papacy. There were two other popes before him (and possibly a third and fourth) who resigned from the papacy for one reason or another, the first being Pontian, who was arrested and deported in the year 235 by the anti-Christian emperor Maximinus Thrax, and the second being Silverius, who was forced to abdicate in 537. A third pope, John XVIII (1003–9), may have also resigned under pressure. A fourth, Benedict IX, did abdicate in favor of his godfather in 1045 but was reinstated in 1047. A fifth pope, Gregory XII, resigned in 1415 in order to help bring to an end the Great Western Schism (1378–1417).

Born Pietro del Murrone (also Morrone) in the Abruzzi region of Italy, the eleventh child of peasant parents, he was a simple hermit under the Rule of St. Benedict at the time of his election as pope, at about the age of eighty-five, in Perugia after a vacancy of twenty-seven months. The twelve cardinal-electors, split by family loyalties between the Orsinis and the Colonnas, could not muster the necessary two-thirds vote required for election following the death of Nicholas IV on April 4, 1292. Twice several of them left Rome to escape the stifling heat, while the cardinals of the powerful Colonna family stayed behind and attempted to carry out an election on their own. In October 1293, the conclave reassembled in Perugia and pressure mounted on the cardinals to elect someone—pressure from Charles II, king of Sicily and Naples, and from disorders in Rome and the Orvieto region. On July 5, 1294, the dean of the College of Cardinals cited a prophecy by the renowned hermit Pietro del Murrone to the effect that the cardinals would suffer divine retribution if they did not elect a pope soon. The cardinal-dean also announced that he was going to vote for Pietro. By stages Pietro's margin reached two-thirds and then unanimity. He was hailed as the "angel pope" based on a thirteenth-century dream of a pope who would usher in the age of the Holy Spirit.

Sitting upon a donkey, Pietro was escorted by Charles II and his son to L'Aquila (a town in Charles's domain), where he was consecrated as Bishop of Rome in his own church of Santa Maria di Collemaggio on August 29. He took the name Celestine V. Charles saw to it that the new pope took up residence in Naples, at the Castel Nuovo, rather than in Rome, as the Curia demanded. From Naples Celestine did whatever Charles ordered him to do, placing his men in key positions in the Curia and the Papal States, creating twelve cardinals whom Charles proposed, including seven Frenchmen, and naming Charles's son, Louis of Toulouse, as archbishop of Lyons. He also reintroduced the conclave rules established by Gregory X (1272–76) making the king the guardian of the next papal election. Uneducated (he could not speak Latin) and generally befuddled (he sometimes named two people to the same benefice), he proved an inept administrator. As Advent approached, he proposed that three cardinals should assume responsibility for the government of the Church while he fasted and prayed. When the plan was rejected, he consulted Cardinal Benedetto Caetani (who would succeed him as Boniface VIII), a noted canon lawyer, about the possibility of resigning. Caetani encouraged him to do so and prepared all the documents and procedures. On December 13, in full consistory, Celestine V read out the formula of abdication Caetani had prepared for him. He stripped off his papal insignia and, in a final appeal, urged the cardinals to proceed immediately to the election of his successor. The resignation provoked a war of treatises for and against its validity.

When Caetani himself was elected, he saw to it that Pietro did not return to his hermitage on Mount Murrone, as he wished. The new pope feared that Pietro could be made a rallying point for a schism. So he placed the former pope under guard (from which he escaped for a few months) and eventually confined him to the tower of Castel Fumone, east of Ferentino, where he seems not to have been mistreated. He died of an infection caused by an abscess on May 19, 1296. His body was at first buried in Ferentino but was transferred in 1317 to Santa Maria di Collemaggio, in L'Aquila, where he had been crowned pope. Under later pressure from King Philip IV of France, a dedicated foe of Boniface VIII, Pope Clement V canonized Pietro on May 5, 1313, as a confessor (that is, one who had suffered for the faith, short of death) rather than as a martyr, as Philip had wished. Feast day: May 19 (not observed universally).

191 Boniface VIII, *ca. 1235–1303, pope from January 23, 1295, to October 11, 1303 (the Vatican's official list begins his pontificate on December 24, 1294, the day of his election, but since he was not yet a bishop, he could not become Bishop of Rome until consecrated on January 23, 1295).*

Few popes in history have made greater claims for the spiritual *and* temporal powers of the papacy than Boniface VIII, who declared that every creature is subject to the pope. As such, he was the last of the medieval popes and one of the three most powerful medieval popes, along with Gregory VII (1073–85) and Innocent III (1198–1216).

Born Benedetto Caetani, he was cardinal-priest of San Martino and possessor of many lucrative benefices at the time of his election as pope on Christmas Eve in Naples, eleven days after the resignation of Celestine V.

A renowned canon lawyer, he arranged for the abdication of his predecessor, for which he was bitterly criticized by the Spiritual Franciscans
(those who called for the literal and uncompromising observance of the
rule of poverty). Upon election, Boniface annulled most of the privileges
granted by Celestine V, dismissed various curial officials imposed by
Charles II of Sicily, and moved the papal court from Naples to Rome,
where he was consecrated as Bishop of Rome and crowned on January
23, 1295. He took the name Boniface VIII (there had been an antipope by
the name of Boniface VII in 974 and again in 984–85, but no officially recognized pope with that number). By all accounts, he was a man of exceedingly irascible temperament, given to outbursts of impatience and
rage, and a person bent on the acquisition of wealth and power for himself and his family.

Boniface made a lasting contribution to the field of canon law with
the publication in 1298 of the *Liber sextus,* which continued the five books
of Pope Gregory IX's *Liber extra* (1234) and which forms the third volume
of the *Corpus Iuris Canonici,* the forerunner of the Code of Canon Law of
1917. He also reorganized the Curia and Vatican archives and catalogued
the papal library. To reduce friction between the mendicant orders (Franciscans and Dominicans) and the diocesan clergy he severely limited the
mendicant orders' right to preach and hear confessions. In 1303 he
founded a university in Rome known as the Sapienza. On the other hand,
he commissioned or permitted so many statues of himself that he was accused of encouraging idolatry.

Most of Boniface VIII's pontificate, however, was taken up with political matters. He tried and failed to restore Charles II of Naples to the
throne of Sicily (seized earlier by rebels and transferred to the house of
Aragón). His efforts to mediate a dispute between Venice and Naples, to
defend Scotland's independence from England, and to secure the Hungarian crown for Charles II's grandson all came to naught. His attempts
to end hostilities between France and England opened a more serious
conflict between himself and Philip IV (Philip the Fair) of France. Both
countries were financing the war by taxing their clergy, a practice forbidden by canon law without the consent of the pope (Fourth Lateran
Council, 1215). In an effort to stop the practice, Boniface VIII issued one
of the most famous of papal bulls, *Clericis laicos,* on February 25, 1296,
which began with the assertion that "the laity have always been hostile to
the clergy." Philip IV retaliated by prohibiting the export of gold, nego-
tiable currency, and other valuables and by expelling foreign merchants,
knowing that the pope depended upon revenue from France. The pope
thereupon backed down and in 1297 empowered the king to impose the
tax on clergy in case of need and without consulting the Holy See. The

peace (through papal capitulation) was sealed by Boniface's canonization of Philip's grandfather, Louis IX (d. 1270).

Meanwhile, the pope was having problems on his home front. The Colonna family, which had supported Boniface's election, had become his strongest critics. They resented his high-handed, autocratic style of governance and were opposed to his Sicilian policy. They also now questioned the validity of Celestine V's resignation and Boniface's subsequent election to succeed him. When a relative of the Colonnas highjacked a convoy bearing papal treasure in 1297, Boniface ordered the two Colonna cardinals to hand over to him three strategic family castles. When they refused and later declared Boniface had usurped the papacy through Celestine V's illegal abdication, Boniface VIII deposed and excommunicated the two, who then took refuge in the court of Philip IV of France. Boniface proclaimed 1300 a year of Jubilee (the first Holy Year) and granted plenary indulgences (the remission of all temporal punishment in Purgatory) to the tens of thousands of pilgrims to Rome and the shrines of the apostles. He began dressing occasionally in imperial regalia, declaring himself as much an emperor as a pope.

But in the fall of 1301 the conflict with Philip was reignited. The king had imprisoned the bishop of Parmiers and demanded his degradation (reduction to the lay state). Boniface VIII viewed the king's action as an intrusion upon his spiritual authority. Without examining the case any further, the pope condemned the king's action, withdrew certain privileges from the French Church, and summoned its leadership to Rome for a synod in November 1302. Thirty-nine French bishops attended in spite of the king's order not to attend. Following the synod, Boniface VIII published his second famous bull, *Unam sanctam,* on November 18, 1302. Among the claims contained in it are: (1) that "outside this [Catholic] Church there is neither salvation nor remission of sins"; (2) that "of this one and only Church there is one body and one head—not two heads, like a monster—namely Christ, and Christ's vicar is Peter, and Peter's successor . . ."; (3) that "in this Church and in her power are two swords, the spiritual and the temporal. . . . Both are in the power of the Church, the spiritual and the material. But the latter is to be used for the Church, the former by her; the former by the priest, the latter by kings and captains but at the will and by the permission of the priest. The one sword, then, should be under the other, and temporal authority subject to spiritual"; (4) that "if . . . the earthly power err, it shall be judged by the spiritual power. . . . But if the supreme power err, it can only be judged by God, not by man"; and (5) that "it is altogether necessary to salvation for every human creature to be subject to the Roman Pontiff."

Philip responded with a vitriolic personal attack on the pope, drawing upon materials provided by the Colonna family. The charges touched upon illegitimacy, sexual misconduct, blasphemy, simony, usurping the papal office, and heresy. Philip called for a general council to depose Boniface VIII. After preparing a bull of excommunication against the king, the pope moved from Rome to the papal palace at Anagni, where he intended to promulgate the bull. The palace, however, was stormed by a band of mercenaries under the head of the Colonna family. When the pope refused to resign, he was arrested while dressed in his full pontifical robes. His captors planned to take him to France to be judged by a council, but the citizens of Anagni (the city of his birth) and the surrounding countryside rescued him after three days and drove off his captors. After a period of rest from his ordeal, Boniface VIII returned to Rome under the protection of the Orsini family on September 25, 1303, but he died a broken man less than three weeks later, on October 12, and was buried in the crypt of St. Peter's Basilica. In 1605, his tomb was opened for inspection and his body was found intact.

By the standards of some Catholics given to equate a healthy and vibrant Catholicism with strong and militant popes, the pontificate of Boniface VIII had to be one of the Church's major success stories. But the standards are wrong. Other popes were more inept and more corrupt, but none made claims for the papacy that were further removed from the spirit of the Apostle Peter, not to mention the Lord himself.

192 Benedict XI, Bl., *1240–1304, pope from October 22, 1303, to July 7, 1304.*

Benedict XI's pontificate was marked by his weak acquiescence to the demands of the king of France. Born Niccolò Boccasini, of an ordinary working-class family, he was the cardinal-bishop of Ostia and a Dominican (he had been Master of the Order) when unanimously elected pope in Rome on October 22, 1303. He chose the name Benedict, after his predecessor's baptismal name, as a show of support and solidarity with the powerful but tragic Boniface VIII. The new pope had been one of two cardinals who had faithfully stood with Boniface during the assault upon him at Anagni. (There had been an antipope who had taken the name Benedict X in 1058. It is interesting here, as in some other cases cited earlier, that those whom the Catholic Church now clearly characterizes as antipopes were not always so regarded in earlier centuries. Why else would Cardinal Boccasino have taken the name Benedict XI rather than Benedict X?) He was crowned on October 27, 1303, in Rome.

Benedict XI has been described by historians as a scholarly, but weak, man who felt at ease only with his fellow Dominicans. Indeed, he appointed only three cardinals during his pontificate, and all three were Dominicans. He also revoked his predecessor's bull restricting the rights of mendicants (the Dominicans and Franciscans) to preach and to hear confessions. A man of peace, he immediately lifted Boniface VIII's excommunication from the heads of the two Colonna cardinals, but without restoring their properties or their cardinalatial rank. Although the pope's gesture did not completely satisfy the Colonna partisans, it did exasperate the Bonifacians. The factional conflict that erupted afterward forced Benedict XI to leave Rome for Perugia in April 1304.

Meanwhile, the king of France, Philip IV (Philip the Fair), was still demanding a general council to denounce the memory of his despised adversary Boniface VIII. On March 25, 1304, Benedict XI published a bull absolving Philip and his family of all ecclesiastical censures and penalties. But the king's insistence on the council continued. The pope thereupon revoked all other penalties imposed on France and the French court by Boniface VIII, and he even offered assurances of pardon to those (except the leader of the gang) who had committed the outrage against Boniface VIII at Anagni, just before Boniface's death. Moreover, Boniface's famous bull, *Clericis laicos* (1296), prohibiting temporal rulers from taxing their clergy without the pope's consent, was almost completely withdrawn, and Philip was granted tithes for two years. The king was temporarily appeased and the call for a general council subsided. On July 7, 1304, the pope died of acute dysentery in Perugia. He was buried, in accordance with his wishes, in the church of San Domenico in Perugia, where there were later reports of miraculous cures at his tomb. He was beatified by Pope Clement XII in 1736. Feast day: July 7.

193 Clement V, *French, ca. 1264–1314, pope from June 5, 1305, to April 20, 1314.*

With Clement V's pontificate began the seventy-year "Babylonian captivity" of the papacy in Avignon, France. Born Bertrand de Got, he was archbishop of Bordeaux when elected pope in Perugia on June 5, 1305, after an eleven-month deadlock between pro–Boniface VIII cardinals opposed to King Philip IV of France and the pro-French, anti-Boniface cardinals allied with the Colonna family. Bertrand was eventually chosen only because the Bonifacians allowed themselves eventually to be split. He took the name Clement V out of respect for the previous Pope Clement (IV, 1265–68), who was also French. He intended at first to be crowned at Vienne, where he hoped to mediate a peace between the English and French kings, thereby preparing the way for another crusade to liberate the holy places in Palestine from the Muslims. But King Philip IV had other ideas, and Clement V was crowned instead in the king's presence at Lyons on November 15, some five months after his election. (Since he was already a bishop when elected, his pontificate did not begin with his coronation, but with his election.) Like many other popes, Clement V entered office in less than vigorous health. Afflicted with cancer, he would have to withdraw from public view for months at a time.

A month after his coronation, the new pope created ten cardinals, one of whom was English and nine of whom were French—and four of the Frenchmen were his nephews! The Italians were now in a minority within the College of Cardinals. After wandering around Provence and Gascony, notably in Poitiers (1307–8) for the first several years of his pontificate, Clement V finally settled with the Curia at the Dominican priory in Avignon, because the town belonged not to the French king but to his vassals, the Angevin kings of Naples, and offered easy access to the sea. He also lived in Venaissin, which was papal territory. Meanwhile, the king renewed the pressure for a general council to condemn his old nemesis Boniface VIII. After stalling for a long period of time, the pope finally relented and agreed to open the case on February 2, 1309. Because of political distractions, the king suspended the proceedings in April 1311. But he exacted a staggeringly high price from the pope. The Colonna cardinals who had been excommunicated by Boniface VIII were completely rehabilitated and the Colonna family was fully compensated for its losses. All of Boniface's official acts against French interests were annulled, the leader of the armed assault on Boniface at Anagni was absolved, and a papal bull, *Rex gloriae* (April 27, 1311), was issued praising Philip for his zeal in attacking the dead pope. Finally, Celestine V, the elderly pope whom Boniface VIII had maneuvered out of office, was canonized a saint on May 5, 1313.

But there was more. Because Philip coveted the wealth of the Knights Templar, a religious order devoted to the liberation of the holy places in Palestine from Muslim control, he had them arrested upon their return from the Holy Land in October 1307 and extracted confessions under torture. These confessions were turned over to Clement V with the demand, fortified by threats, that he condemn the order. After an initial hesitation, the pope called a general, or ecumenical, council at Vienne (October 1311–May 1312) at which the Knights Templar were dissolved by unilateral papal action. The pope also ruled that all of the property of the Knights Templar should be transferred to the Knights of St. John of Jerusalem (the Hospitallers, known today as the Knights of Malta). In effect, however, King Philip IV held their considerable property until his own death in 1314.

In accordance with other decrees of the Council of Vienne, Clement V fashioned a compromise settlement on the dispute between the Conventual and Spiritual Franciscans and, for the sake of promoting missionary work in the Far East, established chairs of oriental languages in Paris, Oxford, Bologna, and Salamanca. He also founded universities in Or-léans and Perugia and published the decrees of the Council of Vienne along with a collection of his decretals and those of his two predecessors in a single work known as the *Clementines* (or Constitutions of Clemen-tine), which formed a part of the *Corpus Iuris Canonici,* the forerunner of the Code of Canon Law of 1917. Centralization of church government also increased during this pontificate. New types of benefices (income-producing ecclesiastical offices) were reserved to papal nomination, and the papacy and the Curia alike profited.

There were other, less significant official acts during this pontificate. In 1306, for example, Clement suspended Robert of Wilchelsea as arch-bishop of Canterbury, whom the English king, Edward I, accused of trea-son for his support of Boniface VIII, and then, two years later, reinstated him at the request of Edward II. Also in 1306 he excommunicated Robert I the Bruce of Scotland for the murder of an old enemy, Red Comyn, and deposed two Scottish bishops for supporting the rebels. The next year he settled a long-standing controversy over the Hungarian throne. After the German emperor Henry VII died in 1313, the pope published a famous bull, *Pastoralis cura,* which went beyond even Boniface VIII's exaggerated claims for papal authority. The pope, Clement V declared, is superior to the emperor and, in times of vacancy, has the right to name imperial vic-ars. He thereupon nominated Robert of Naples as imperial vicar of Italy.

Clement V died of stomach cancer on April 20, 1314, in Roquemaure, near Carpentras, while traveling to his birthplace, Villandraut. By the time of his death, the papal treasury had been depleted from excessive personal use. He was buried in a parish church at Uzeste, about three miles from his place of birth. A monument erected in his memory was destroyed by the Calvinists two centuries later.

194 John XXII, *French, ca. 1244–1334, pope from August 7, 1316, to Decem-ber 4, 1334.*

John XXII, the second of the Avignon popes, was one of the relatively few popes to be accused of heresy, in this case because of his stated belief that the saints do not see God (the Beatific Vision) until after the final judgment.

Born Jacques Duèse (of Cahors), he was cardinal-bishop of Porto at the time of his election to the papacy on August 7, 1316, in Lyons, more than two years after the death of his predecessor, Clement V. Evidently, the cardinals had some difficulty deciding upon a candidate, given the conflicting political currents. They met first in the episcopal palace at Carpentras, in accordance with canon law requiring that a papal election be held in the place where the previous pope had died. But the conclave had to be moved to Lyons in March 1316 because of local disturbances. (An armed band had broken in on the cardinals shouting, "Death to the Italians! We want a pope! Death to the Italians!") The seventy-two-year-old Cardinal Duèse was obviously a compromise choice, but one supported by Philip, count of Poitiers (and the future King Philip V), and King Robert of Naples. He was crowned in Lyons on September 5 by Cardinal Napoleone Orsini. His electors obviously considered him a transitional pope, given his age. His pontificate lasted more than eighteen years!

Although small of stature and in weak health, this elderly pope plunged into his new duties with uncommon energy and enthusiasm. He restored efficiency to the Curia and financial stability to the Church, both having suffered badly under Clement V. He extended the powers of the papacy over appointments to benefices (income-producing ecclesiastical offices), prohibited anyone from holding more than two benefices at a time, and removed the election of bishops from the cathedral chapters (bodies of diocesan priests, known as canons, responsible for the spiritual and temporal welfare of diocesan cathedrals). He also divided the territories of large dioceses and redrew the boundaries of others. To improve the flow of revenue into the Holy See (which was Rome, not Avignon, however), he created a new system whereby each country would pay the first year's revenue of a benefice to the pope. These payments were called annates. In 1319 John XXII reserved all minor benefices to himself for a period of three years and imposed other papal taxes. He also compiled a new tax book that established a scale of fees for church documents. All of his appointments to the College of Cardinals were French, except for one Spaniard and four Romans. His worst fault was his shameless nepotism, bestowing money, gifts, and church offices on relatives and friends.

In 1318 he intervened in the ongoing dispute between the Conventual and Spiritual Franciscans, coming down on the side of the former. He banned the Spirituals' simplified habit and ordered them to obey their superiors and accept as legitimate the storing up of provisions. Twenty-five recalcitrants were handed over to the Inquisition, and four were actually burned at the stake in 1318. But the pope ran completely afoul of the Franciscan order when its general chapter, meeting in Perugia in 1322, defied a decision of the Inquisition and declared it to be orthodox teaching that Christ and the apostles owned nothing as their own property. John XXII denounced the Perugia declaration as heresy (1323), thereby infuriating members of the order who, in turn, denounced the pope as a heretic. The majority of Franciscans eventually submitted to the pope in the summer of 1325, but a minority bolted, including the minister general of the order, Michael of Cesena, and the famous Franciscan philosopher William of Occam (d. 1347). John XXII excommunicated them in April 1329 and then issued a bull later that same year declaring that the right to hold property predated the fall of Adam and Eve and that the New Testament depicts Christ and the apostles as owning personal possessions. Occam answered the bull, item by item, in the first of many writings directed against the pope.

The dissident Franciscans became allies of the pope's enemy Louis IV, who had defeated his rival for the German throne, a man whom John XXII had supported. Because of Louis IV's aggressively antipapal actions in Italy, the pope excommunicated him in 1324. Whereupon Louis called for a general council to denounce the pope for heresy because of his attitude toward the Spiritual Franciscans' understanding of evangelical poverty. Louis was supported not only by the dissident Franciscans but also by Marsilius of Padua (d. 1342), whose *Defensor pacis* (1324), which promoted the notions of a lay state and the superiority of a general council over the pope, had been condemned by John XXII in 1327. Accompanied by Marsilius, Louis entered Rome in January 1328 and had himself crowned emperor by the aged senator Sciarra Colonna, the so-called captain of the Roman people. Three months later Louis published a decree declaring "Jacques de Cahors" (the pope) deposed on grounds of heresy, and a straw effigy of him in pontifical robes was solemnly burned. Louis then had a Spiritual Franciscan, Pietro Rainalducci, elected pope by representatives of the Roman clergy. The antipope took the name Nicholas V and installed himself! After Louis left Rome in early 1329, however, the antipope lost his support, went into hiding, and eventually made his way to Avignon, where he submitted to John XXII and was pardoned and placed in comfortable captivity.

Among the other acts of this remarkably active pontificate were the establishment of dioceses in Armenia, India, and Iran, the beginning of a papal library in Avignon, the founding of a university in Cahors, and the condemnation of twenty-eight sentences of Meister Eckhart (d. 1327), the famous German mystic. But between All Saints Day (November 1, 1331) and the feast of the Annunciation (March 25, 1332), the pope delivered four sermons that were to haunt him for the remaining years of his pontificate. He had said that the saints would not see God face-to-face until after the final judgment—in opposition to the traditional doctrine that the saints enjoy the Beatific Vision immediately after death. Before the final judgment, he suggested, the saints could only contemplate the humanity, not the divinity, of Christ. He also proposed that the demons and the damned were not yet in Hell. These views were condemned at the

University of Paris in the fall of 1333, and the pope's enemies, including William of Occam, took full advantage of the controversy. Louis IV plotted with Cardinal Napoleone Orsini toward the pope's condemnation and deposition at a general council, but the pope fell ill. On his deathbed and in the presence of his cardinals, he modified his position. Before the final judgment, he said, the saints see God face-to-face as clearly as their condition allows, and he insisted that he never held the contrary view except as a personal opinion he was prepared to reject if it were contrary to the faith of the Church. One wonders how such an insignificant issue could have created such turmoil. But it did.

John XXII died on December 4, 1334, at age eighty-nine and was buried in the cathedral of Notre-Dame-des-Doms in Avignon.

195 Benedict XII, *French, 1285–1342, pope from January 8, 1335, to April 25, 1342 (the Vatican's official list begins his pontificate with his election on December 20, 1334, but he was not yet a bishop; he could not become Bishop of Rome until consecrated a bishop on January 8, 1335).*

The third of the Avignon popes, Benedict XII settled a disputed theological question about whether the saints see God face-to-face before the final judgment.

Born Jacques Fournier, of economically poor parents, he was a Cistercian, cardinal-priest of the church of Santa Prisca, and the former counselor of his predecessor, John XXII, when elected pope on December 20, 1334, in Avignon. (There were twenty-four cardinals present for the conclave—mostly French.) It is said that the leading candidate, Cardinal John de Cominges, was defeated because he refused to promise not to move the papacy back to Rome. In any case, Cardinal Fournier was elected on the seventh day of the conclave and took the name Benedict XII. He was consecrated as Bishop of Rome and crowned by Cardinal Napoleone Orsini on January 8, 1335, in the Dominican church in Avignon. One wonders if any of the Avignon popes saw the irony of their consecration as Bishop of Rome, a diocese many hundreds of miles away that they would never even visit.

Almost immediately after his consecration and coronation, Benedict XII was pressured by envoys from Rome to return the papacy there. The new pope may have thought of doing just that because he did initiate a restoration and reroofing of St. Peter's that same year and in 1341 spent large sums on both St. Peter's and the Lateran. But the majority of cardinals and the French king himself were against the move, and the continued political unrest in Rome and the Papal States gave much practical strength to their argument. Indeed, it soon became clear that Benedict XII agreed with that position. He had the papal archives moved from Assisi to Avignon and began construction of a permanent papal palace (the Palais Vieux) to serve both as a residence for himself and the Curia and also as a military fortress. He also added to the French contingent of the College of Cardinals, naming five Frenchmen and only one Italian.

Benedict XII had come into office with a reputation as a learned theologian and an indefatigable inquisitor, skilled at extracting confessions from alleged heretics, some of whom were burned at the stake. The previous pope, John XXII, on two occasions congratulated him for his efforts in eradicating heresy from his diocese. Unlike his tiny and feeble predecessor, Benedict XII was tall, heavyset, and forceful in speech. Soon after his coronation, he dismissed large numbers of clerics from the papal court at Avignon and sent them back to their benefices (income-producing ecclesiastical offices). He was convinced that clergy should remain in residence at their pastoral posts and that wandering monks should return to their monasteries. He also prohibited the transfer of money when spiritual services were rendered, limited the fees that could be charged for documents, and banned the drawing of revenue from vacant benefices (except in the case of cardinals and patriarchs). Indeed, he laid down such strict criteria for filling benefices that many remained vacant for long periods of time. In addition, he regulated the temporal authority of the Cistercians, Franciscans, and Benedictines, mandated regular chapters (formal house meetings) and visitations of monasteries, established houses of study, and reformed the training program for novices. (Unfortunately, most of these measures proved largely ineffective because of the relative brevity of his pontificate and the failure of his successor to follow through on the enforcement of these initiatives.) He also strictly defined the rights and duties of the Sacred Penitentiary, which issued indulgences and dispensations, and the first recorded decisions of the tribunal known as the Rota occurred during his pontificate.

In 1336 Benedict XII settled a controversy that had stirred the last years of his predecessor's pontificate; namely, whether the saints see God face-to-face immediately after death or not until after the final judgment. John XXII had speculated that the saints did not see God until after the final judgment. Benedict XII ruled in *Benedictus Deus* (1336) that souls have an intuitive, face-to-face vision of the divine essence, which theologians call the Beatific Vision, and that this vision of God occurs immediately after death in the case of those who die in the state of grace.

Benedict XII encountered a number of problems on the political front. He could not prevent the outbreak of the Hundred Years' War (1337–1453) between England and France or terminate hostilities after it began, so his hopes were dashed for the launching of another crusade to liberate the holy places in Palestine from Muslim control. His open favoritism toward French policy, of course, created much resentment in England. He also failed to defend the integrity of papal territories in Italy, losing control over Romagna, the March of Ancona, and even Bologna. Relations with the emperor Louis IV of Germany were full of mutual hostility. The first Diet of Frankfurt (1338) decreed that imperial authority is derived directly from God, not from the pope. The second Diet in 1338 declared that imperial rank and power rightfully belong to Louis IV and that the confirmation or consent of the pope is not required.

Benedict XII died on April 25, 1342, and was buried in the cathedral of Notre-Dame-des-Doms in Avignon.

196 Clement VI, *French, 1290/91–1352, pope from May 7, 1342, to December 6, 1352.*

The fourth—and most partisanly French—of the Avignon popes, Clement VI laid the groundwork for the doctrine of indulgences that would figure so largely in the Protestant Reformation some two centuries later.

Born Pierre Roger, he was a Benedictine, archbishop of Rouen, chancellor of France, and cardinal-priest of the church of Santi Nereo e Achilleo when he was elected pope by some seventeen cardinals meeting in Avignon on May 7, 1342. He chose the name Clement to make the point that power should be exercised with clemency and was crowned on Pentecost Sunday, May 19, by Cardinal Napoleone Orsini in the Dominican church in Avignon. Although the king of France, Philip VI, had sent his son to the conclave to influence the election in Cardinal Roger's favor, the gesture proved unnecessary. He was elected unanimously because, as in so many cases throughout the history of papal conclaves, the cardinals had grown tired of the previous pope's style and longed for a change. Thus, they chose to replace the austere and rigid Benedict XII with the more easygoing, worldly Clement VI.

About six months after his election, Clement received a delegation from Rome, conferring upon him the rank of Roman senator and begging him to return to the city. The delegation also petitioned for a reduction in the interval between Jubilee years (their motive was more economic than spiritual, since Jubilee years attracted many pilgrims to Rome). The new pope did grant that request, and the 1350 Jubilee year yielded great economic benefits for an impoverished Rome. More important than the Jubilee year itself was the bull, *Unigenitus*, that announced it. The pope defined therein the treasury of merits, a vast reserve of merit built up by Christ and the saints that can be applied to individuals, upon the recitation of certain prayers and the performance of certain spiritual works, to offset the burden of sin. The means by which these merits are applied came eventually to be called indulgences. Disputes over the sale of indulgences were a major factor in provoking the Protestant Reformation some two centuries later.

The new pope rejected the Roman delegation's appeal for his return to the city. Indeed, he actually purchased the city of Avignon and the county of Venaissin from Queen Joanna I of Naples in 1348, enlarged the papal palace, and appointed mostly Frenchmen to the College of Cardinals. His intrusion into political affairs was marked by consistent failure. He at first supported Cola di Rienzo as civil ruler of Rome, but then abandoned and excommunicated him when Cola asserted the independence of the Roman people from the pope and the emperor alike. Clement VI, like his predecessor, was unable to stop the Hundred Years' War between England and France and, in any case, could hardly pretend to be an honest broker. The papal army failed to regain Romagna for the papacy, and the pope was forced to cede control over Bologna to his adversary, the archbishop of Milan. His efforts toward union with the Greek Church also failed. On the other hand, the accidental death of the emperor Louis IV of Germany in 1347 improved papal fortunes in that country. The pope had previously supported Charles, king of Bohemia, to replace Louis, and now that Louis was dead, the pope had a friendly occupant of the German throne for the first time in many years.

Unfortunately, Clement VI's pontificate was modeled less on the example of the Apostle Peter, whose successor he claimed to be, than on that of a worldly prince. His court was bathed in luxuries and punctuated by sumptuous banquets and grand festivities. Charges were raised about his own sexual life. He shamelessly conferred church offices and gifts on relatives, friends, and fellow countrymen. The purchase of the city of Avignon and the county of Venaissin, the construction of a new papal palace (Palais Neuf), generous loans to France, and military expenditures in Italy and in the fight against the Turks eventually depleted the papal treasury that had been so painstakingly replenished by John XXII (1316–34) and Benedict XII (1335–42). New taxes had to be imposed, and appointments to an increasing number of dioceses and revenue-producing benefices were reserved to the pope. These initiatives provoked a strongly negative reaction in Germany and England especially. In 1351 King Edward III of England issued the First Statute of Provisors, reserving to the king the right of presentation in all papal appointments to benefices.

In 1348–49 when the Black Death hit Avignon itself, the pope defended the Jews against the charge that they were responsible for it. He also reached out to assist the poor and the afflicted during the crisis. Clement VI died on December 6, 1352, after a short illness. He was buried at first in the cathedral, but his body was moved in April to the Benedictine abbey of La Chaise-Dieu, where he had once studied and where he desired to be buried. His tomb was subsequently desecrated and his remains burned by the Huguenots in 1562.

197 **Innocent VI,** *French, 1282–1362, pope from December 18, 1352, to September 12, 1362.*

The pontificate of Innocent VI, the fifth of the Avignon popes, was marked by much activity, both ecclesiastical and political, but with little lasting effect. Born Étienne Aubert, he was cardinal-bishop of Ostia when elected pope in Avignon on December 18, 1352. As usual, the cardinals wanted not a carbon copy of the old pope but rather a wholly new style and approach. The new pope, already seventy-two years of age, was crowned in the Avignon cathedral by Cardinal Gaillard de la Mothe, the senior cardinal-deacon, on December 30.

In spite of his age and unstable health (the cardinal-electors regarded him as a transitional pope), he immediately revived the reformist spirit of Benedict XII (1335–42). He invalidated an agreement reached by the twenty-five cardinals in the conclave (including himself) that revenues would be thereafter divided between the pope and the College of Cardinals and that papal appointments of new cardinals would be subject to approval by the college. Innocent VI also reduced the size of the papal household and simplified the lifestyle of the papal court, which had been financially and morally exhausted during the previous pontificate. Once again, clergy were required to reside in their benefices (income-producing ecclesiastical offices), candidates for office had to establish their credentials for the position, and no one could hold more than one benefice at a time. The pope also gave his support to the reformist agenda of the Master of the Dominican order and was particularly severe with the Spiritual Franciscans (those who insisted that a Franciscan should own absolutely nothing), turning some of them over to the Inquisition to be imprisoned or even burned at the stake. So extreme were some of his measures that Bridget of Sweden (d. 1373), who was in Rome at the time and had welcomed Innocent VI's election, denounced him as a persecutor of Christ's flock.

Because he expected to return the papacy to Rome sometime during his pontificate, Innocent VI devoted much of his time and attention to the pacification of the Papal States and their return to allegiance to the pope. (The failed effort would bankrupt the papal treasury.) Innocent VI's chief instruments in this regard were the Spanish Cardinal Gil de Albornoz, the papal legate in Italy, and Cola di Rienzo, whose excommunication (by Clement VI) the pope lifted after a trial in Avignon. Cola died soon thereafter in a riot, and Charles IV of Bohemia was elected king of the Romans, later to be crowned emperor, with the pope's approval, by the cardinal-bishop of Ostia (1355). The following year Charles published his so-called Golden Bull, in which he decreed that elected German kings need not be approved by the pope. Significantly, Innocent VI did not object.

Most of the pope's other political activities proved similarly fruitless. He failed to prevent the resumption of the war between England and France in 1355 (although he effected a temporary peace in 1360), to persuade the emperor Charles IV to release King John II of France from capture, to mount a new crusade to liberate the holy places in Palestine from Muslim control, to mediate peace between Castille and Aragón, and to reunite the Latin and the Greek Churches (actually the Greeks lost interest when it became obvious that the pope could not mount an army to fight the Turks). To add to his political burdens, Innocent VI faced new dangers in Avignon itself, now increasingly subject to plundering by marauding bands of mercenary troops idled by temporary truces of war. At one point in late December 1360, communications between Avignon and the outside world were cut off and Innocent had to bribe the marauders lest they wreak further destruction. Innocent VI died two years later, on September 12, 1362, and was buried in Holy Trinity chapel, in the charterhouse of Villeneuve-lès-Avignon, which he had built.

198 Urban V, Bl., *French, ca. 1310–70, pope from November 6, 1362, to December 19, 1370 (the Vatican's official list marks the beginning of his pontificate on the day of his election, September 28, but he was not yet a bishop and could not become Bishop of Rome until consecrated on November 6).*

The sixth—and probably the best—of the Avignon popes, Urban V restored the papacy to Rome for three years, returning to Avignon just before his death.

Born Guillaume de Grimoard, he was a Benedictine monk, a canon lawyer, abbot of Saint-Victor in Marseilles, and papal legate in Italy—but not a cardinal—when elected pope in Avignon on September 28, 1362. During the conclave he was actually on a diplomatic mission in Naples. The cardinals at first elected the brother of Pope Clement VI (1342–52), but he declined. When they could not agree on one of their own number, they turned to the deeply spiritual Abbot Grimoard and elected him unanimously. Upon his return to France, the pope-elect was enthroned on October 31 in Avignon and then consecrated as Bishop of Rome on November 6 by Cardinal Aldeimo Alberto, bishop of Ostia. His enthronement and coronation were done without the usual pomp.

Retaining his black Benedictine habit and rule of life, Urban V continued his predecessor's reformist agenda. He reduced even further the luxury of the papal court and combated the holding of more than one benefice (incoming-producing ecclesiastical office) at a time, while cutting the rate of tithes in half. In 1363, however, he reserved to the pope the appointments to all patriarchal and episcopal sees and to major monasteries. He also exhausted the papal treasury once again by his generous support of impoverished students, of colleges, and of artists and architects. He founded new universities in Orange (southern France), Kraków, and Vienna.

Two of the main goals of his pontificate were reunion with the East and the liberation of the holy places in Palestine from Turkish control. Neither was fulfilled. He failed to mount the necessary forces for the crusade, even entering into a humiliating peace agreement with his enemy in Milan, Bernabò Visconti, in the hope of enlisting his participation. At the same time, he sincerely hoped to return the papacy once and for all to Rome. He had good reasons to do so, apart from its historic connection with the Apostle Peter. He could better organize (1) an alliance against the marauding bands of mercenaries who were wreaking havoc everywhere, (2) a crusade, and (3) efforts toward reunion with the East. Moreover, the emperor Charles IV was urging the pope to leave Avignon for Rome and offered to be his escort. Although the pope's skilled legate, the Spanish cardinal Gil de Albornoz, had managed to restore the allegiance of the Papal States, Rome itself was in chaos and the Vatican was uninhabitable.

Nevertheless, on April 30, 1367, against the strong objections of the French cardinals and the Curia, Urban V left Avignon, landing at Corneto (now Tarquinia) on June 3. After a brief stay in Viterbo, he entered Rome with an impressive military escort on October 16. Since the Lateran Palace was in disarray, he took up residence in the Vatican, which had been sufficiently restored before his arrival. He remained there for three years, but moving in the summer to Viterbo and Montefiascone to escape the intense Roman heat. While in Rome, the pope directed the repairs and refurbishing of churches and other buildings and completely rebuilt the basilica of St. John Lateran, which had burned down in 1360. In September 1368, he created seven new cardinals: six French and only one Roman. The next month the emperor Charles IV arrived in the city for discussions with the pope, who crowned his queen as empress. The following June (1369) the Byzantine emperor John V Palaeologus visited Rome to enlist Western assistance against the Turkish threat to Constantinople. In order to obtain this help, the emperor switched his allegiance from Eastern Orthodoxy to Latin Catholicism and submitted himself to the pope on the steps of St. Peter's. No Byzantines were present at the ceremony, and no reunion occurred. The Eastern bishops urged the pope to call an ecumenical council, but he declined. He preferred to organize a

Latin Church within the Greek empire and to send missionaries to the East.

By the end of his pontificate, Urban V seriously contemplated moving back to Avignon. The French cardinals were constantly pressuring him to do so. The situation in Italy was unsettled. In the spring of 1370 the Romans joined forces with rebels in Perugia (now under papal interdict), and the pope's adversary in Milan, Bernabò Visconti, was massing his troops in Tuscany. The pope fled Rome for the walled city of Viterbo and then Montefiascone. Meanwhile, the Hundred Years' War between England and France had flared up once again. In spite of the pleas of the Romans and the warning of the saintly Bridget of Sweden (d. 1373) that he would suffer an early death if he returned to Avignon, Urban V left Montefiascone on August 26, 1370, and set sail from Corneto (Tarquinia) on September 5, arriving in Marseilles on September 16 and then in Avignon on September 27. Less than two months later, he fell gravely ill and died on December 19. He was buried in the Avignon cathedral (Notre-Dame-des-Doms) at first, but his brother, Cardinal Angelico, transferred his remains on June 5, 1372, to the abbey of Saint-Victor in Marseilles, where the pope served as abbot at the time of his election to the papacy. His tomb became the center of a cult. Urban V was beatified by Pope Pius IX in 1870. Feast day: December 19.

199 Gregory XI, *French, 1329/30–78, pope from January 4, 1371, to March 27, 1378 (the Vatican's official list begins his pontificate on the day of his election, December 30, 1370, but he was not yet a bishop and could not become Bishop of Rome until consecrated on January 4, 1371).*

The last of the Avignon popes and the last French pope, Gregory XI returned the papacy to Rome under pressure from St. Catherine of Siena (d. 1380).

Born Pierre Roger de Beaufort, he was appointed to the College of Cardinals (as cardinal-deacon of the church of Santa Maria Nuova) by his uncle, Pope Clement VI (1342–52), at the age of eighteen or nineteen. (At the time, there were only nineteen cardinals still living: three Italians, one English, and the rest French.) Although he repeatedly tried to refuse, Cardinal Pierre Roger was unanimously elected to the papacy in Avignon on December 30, 1370, at the age of forty-two, after a two-day conclave comprised of seventeen cardinals. Since he was still only a deacon, he was ordained a priest and consecrated a bishop on January 4 by Cardinal Guido di Bologna, bishop of Porto. The next day he was enthroned and crowned. Unlike his predecessor, Urban V, who refused the usual pomp and circumstance following his coronation, the new pope, Gregory XI, acceded to the traditional triumphal procession through the streets of Avignon, while the duke of Angiò, brother of the king of France, Charles V, held the bridle of the pope's horse.

Gregory XI's pontifical agenda was straightforward enough: to return the papacy to Rome (so that he could more effectively exercise authority over the Papal States), to mount another crusade to liberate the holy places in Palestine from Muslim control, to bring about reunion with the Eastern Church, and to replenish the depleted papal treasury. Gregory formed a league of cities against the papal nemesis, the Visconti of Milan, in 1371 and placed an interdict on the family in early 1373. (An interdict is an ecclesiastical penalty that prohibits persons from participating in public worship and from the reception of the sacraments). By spring of 1375 the pope was ready to set out for Italy to strike the final blow against the Visconti, but he had to back off when the alliance began to dissolve and the money ran out. Then the kings of England and France asked the pope to mediate their conflict. That meant that Gregory XI's departure for Italy was delayed yet again. The delay proved costly. Because Florence, ordinarily a papal ally, had been angered by the Holy See's sending agents to reassert papal power in central Italy and its withholding of food supplies during a shortage in 1374–75, it led a revolt in the Papal States. The pope imposed an interdict on Florence, its allies, and the rebellious cities, which had a negative impact even on their banking and commercial life. He also sent an army of mercenaries under the command of Cardinal Robert of Geneva (later the antipope Clement VII), which reconquered the Papal States.

Meanwhile, Catherine of Siena spent the summer of 1376 in Avignon and finally persuaded Gregory XI to return the papacy to Rome. In spite of the pleas of his relatives, the French cardinals, and the Curia, the pope left the city for good on September 13. He set sail from Marseilles on October 2, but did not reach Corneto (now Tarquinia) until December 6 because of stormy seas. It was only on January 17, 1377, that Gregory XI entered Rome and took up residence in the Vatican.

Although he was preoccupied with the business of ruling over the Papal States and with protecting the papacy's economic and political interests in Italy generally, the pope also devoted himself to the reform of religious orders and was particularly active, unfortunately, in the repression of heresy in Provence, Germany, Spain, and especially France. On May 22, 1377, he addressed five papal bulls to King Edward III of England, the archbishop of Canterbury, the bishop of London, and Oxford University, condemning nineteen propositions from the earlier writings of the Oxford theologian and reformer John Wycliffe (d. 1384). Wycliffe had rejected a number of traditional Catholic teachings on the Eucharist (transubstantiation), Purgatory, and indulgences. The pope failed in his efforts to mount a new crusade and had been politically embarrassed when the emperor Charles IV had his fifteen-year-old son, Wenceslas, elected and crowned king of the Romans in the early summer of 1376, without prior consultation with the pope.

After Gregory XI's return to Rome, however, the situation in Italy went from bad to worse. Peace negotiations with Florence broke down because the pope's demands were too severe (for which Catherine of Siena sharply rebuked him), and hostility toward the pope in Rome intensified because of Cardinal Robert of Geneva's particularly brutal attack on Cesena the previous February. Gregory XI retreated to Anagni, where he died on March 27, 1378, before more realistic peace terms with Florence could be worked out and on the eve of the Great Western Schism (1378–1417). He was buried in the church of Santa Maria Nuova, his former titular church as a cardinal, known today as the church of Santa Francesca Romana (in the Roman Forum).

200 Urban VI, *ca. 1318–89, pope from April 8, 1378, to October 15, 1389.*

Urban VI was one of the most unstable popes in history and the last non-cardinal to be elected pope; his intransigence and unreasonableness provoked the French cardinals into electing an antipope, thus beginning the Great Western Schism of 1378–1417.

Born Bartolomeo Prignano, he was archbishop of Bari when elected pope on April 8, 1378, in the first papal conclave to be held in Rome since 1303. And a tumultuous conclave it was. The Roman people gathered outside the Vatican Palace demanding a Roman, or at least an Italian, pope. At one point, some of the crowd actually gained entrance into the palace to lobby the cardinal-electors directly. The heads of the city's regions also visited the palace to warn the sixteen cardinals (six cardinals were still in Avignon) against ignoring the will of the people. The next morning rioting broke out anew, and all but one of the cardinals voted for Archbishop Prignano. Before they could contact him to gain his consent, a mob broke in. The terrified cardinals placated them by pretending that they had elected an elderly Roman cardinal. The next day, however, twelve cardinals returned to the palace and confirmed the election of Bartolomeo Prignano. The last noncardinal elected to the papacy, he had been regarded as a conscientious and efficient administrator, having served for twenty years as a leading figure in the Curia in Avignon and then as regent of the papal chancery after Gregory IX returned to Rome. The other, more obstinate and irascible side of his personality had not yet been disclosed. He was enthroned as Urban VI on Easter Sunday, April 18.

That summer the new pope alienated the very cardinals who had elected him by making abusive remarks and by threatening to appoint enough Italian cardinals to tip the balance of the college in favor of the Italians. As he began to manifest a darker side of his personality, including uncontrollable tirades, the French cardinals withdrew to Anagni to consider their options. After a failed attempt to reach an accommodation with the new pope (for example, a system of coadjutors or a council of regency), they published on August 2 a declaration that the April election was invalid because it was conducted not freely but under threat of mob violence. The French cardinals invited Urban VI to abdicate. Five days later (August 9) they sent out a notice to the Christian world that the pope had been deposed as incompetent and as an intruder. They moved then from Anagni to Fondi, where, under the protection of Count Onorato Caetani, they elected the French king's cousin, Cardinal Robert of Geneva, as pope on September 20. His coronation as Clement VII on October 31 began the Great Western Schism (1378–1417), which would not be settled until another ecumenical council, the Council of Constance (1414–18), disposed of three simultaneous claimants to the papal throne and elected Martin V (1417–31). However, the council never settled the controversy over Urban's and Clement's claims to the papacy.

Europe's loyalties were divided between the two competing claimants. France, Burgundy, Savoy, Naples, and Scotland accepted Clement VII, while England, Germany, most of Italy, Scandinavia, Portugal, and the central European countries (Hungary, Poland) declared for Urban VI. Spain remained temporarily neutral. Catherine of Siena (d. 1380) strongly supported Urban. When Urban's original Curia defected to Clement, he organized a new one, naming twenty-nine new cardinals of various nationalities on September 17, 1378. The two rivals fought each other on two fronts: the spiritual and the temporal. First, they excommunicated one another, and then they sent armed mercenary forces against each other. Urban's forces won the decisive battle near Marino in April 1379, captured Castel Sant'Angelo, and secured control of the city of Rome. Clement retreated south to Naples and then to Avignon in June, where he established a papal court full of pomp and luxury. The two men had no direct contact after that. Clement died of apoplexy on September 16, 1394.

Since Urban VI never had a doubt about the legitimacy of his own claim to the papacy, he responded with indifference to appeals from various academic and political sources to find a solution to the crisis. He was mainly preoccupied with securing the kingdom of Naples for one of his nephews. He excommunicated and deposed Queen Joanna in 1380 for having recognized and supported the antipope Clement and replaced her

with his cousin, Charles of Durazzo, whom he crowned in Rome in 1381 but with whom he later quarreled. Charles plotted with certain cardinals to replace Urban because of his apparent mental instability. When he heard of the conspiracy, the pope preached a crusade against Charles, revoked his royal title, and placed Naples under interdict (an ecclesiastical penalty depriving the kingdom of spiritual and sacramental benefits). He also personally led a force against Charles, but was besieged at Nocera. He escaped and fled to Genoa with the six cardinals who plotted against him. Once there he threw them into prison and had them brutally tortured. Five of the cardinals were executed. After Charles died in Hungary in February 1386, Urban VI moved to Lucca in December 1386 and then to Pisa in October 1387, where he recruited mercenaries for a campaign against Naples, now in the hands of supporters of the antipope, Clement VII. But Urban lacked the necessary funds (the papal treasury was empty), and the campaign never got under way. In October 1388, he returned to Rome, where he quickly alienated the people.

With the Papal States in a condition of anarchy, Urban VI died the next year, on October 15, 1389, probably of poisoning. He was buried in St. Peter's. (The antipope Clement VII was still alive in Avignon, but there was no interest in recognizing him in order to end the schism.) Given the erratic and even brutal character of his pontificate, it is at least mildly amusing that standard biographies bother to point out that it was Urban VI who decreed that a Holy Year be celebrated every thirty-three years (in honor of the length of Jesus' life) and who placed the feast of the Visitation of the Blessed Virgin Mary on the liturgical calendar for the universal Church.

201 Boniface IX, *ca. 1350–1404, pope from November 9, 1389, to October 1, 1404 (the Vatican's official list marks the beginning of his pontificate on the day of his election, November 2, but since he was not yet a bishop, he could not become Bishop of Rome until consecrated on November 9).*

The second of the popes in the Roman line during the Great Western Schism (1378–1417), Boniface IX ruled like a benevolent despot in a pontificate marred by nepotism and simony (the buying and selling of ecclesiastical offices and spiritual benefits, such as indulgences). Born Pietro Tomacelli, he was cardinal-priest of the church of Santa Anastasia when he was elected pope by fourteen Roman cardinals on November 2, 1389. He was consecrated as Bishop of Rome and crowned on November 9.

As in many other instances, Boniface IX was completely different from his predecessor, Urban VI, in style and temperament. He had a pleasant personality and was a skilled and practical leader. The new pope was immediately excommunicated by the Avignon pope (the antipope Clement VII), and he, in turn, excommunicated his rival in France. Boniface IX also rejected as sinful Clement's request for a general council to resolve the schism as well as the demands of the French and the Germans that he abdicate. Soon after his election, he received back into communion with Rome several cardinals who had gone over to Clement primarily because of their disillusionment with the unstable Urban VI.

Boniface IX won his first major struggle with Clement VII on the battlefield, regaining the allegiance of the kingdom of Naples. The pope also regained control over northern Italian territories lost during the previous pontificate. At first the pope's relations with the Romans were very amicable, so relieved were they to have been liberated from the erratic and dyspeptic rule of Urban VI. But the atmosphere soon changed and Boniface IX had to move to Perugia and then to Assisi. But when the Romans began to worry that the pope might once again remove the seat of the papacy from Rome, they relented and welcomed him back to the city. In the summer of 1398, however, he discovered a plot against himself and used that as an excuse to abolish Rome's republican government and to set himself up as its absolute ruler, with certain senators as his designated administrators. He rebuilt the ruined Castel Sant'Angelo and refortified the Capitol.

Boniface IX did nothing, on the other hand, to deal with the schism in the Church. He cultivated his ties with Germany and England while ignoring all appeals for a resolution of the division. But he did offer to make the antipope Clement VII a legate for France and Spain and to allow him and his cardinals to retain their cardinalatial rank—in return for Clement's abdication. Clement VII died in 1394 without agreeing to Boniface's terms. The king of France, Charles VI, urged the twenty-one Avignon cardinals not to elect a successor to Clement VII, but they went ahead and elected Cardinal Pedro de Luna before opening the king's letter. The new Avignon pope, Benedict XIII, deeply convinced of the legitimacy of his own claim to the papacy, nevertheless tried to open the channels of communication with Rome, but Boniface again refused. And for good political reason: even the French king himself withdrew recognition from the Avignon claimant to the papacy from 1398 to 1403 because Benedict refused to honor the oath all the Avignon cardinals had taken at the conclave to abdicate if and when the majority judged it proper to do so.

Although an able, even outstanding, administrator, Boniface IX was infamous for his blatant nepotism and financial skullduggery. Because of the papacy's desperate need for money, he openly sold church offices to the highest bidders. He also increased church taxes exorbitantly, sold indulgences (spiritual means of drawing upon and applying the merits of Christ and the saints to offset the burden of sin) during the Holy Years of 1390 and 1400, and authorized income-producing Jubilees in cities far beyond the city of Rome (for a price, of course).

On September 22, 1404, he received a representative from the antipope Benedict XIII seeking a meeting to discuss a settlement of the schism, with the possibility of mutual abdication on the agenda. Boniface, however, was already too ill for such a meeting, but he would not have agreed to it in any case. A second meeting on September 29 was marked by violent exchanges. Boniface IX died two days later, on October 1, and was buried in the crypt of St. Peter's Basilica. The Romans held the antipope's representatives responsible for the sudden deterioration of the pope's health and threw them into jail. They were released only after a substantial ransom of 5,000 gold florins (over $200,000) was paid.

202 Innocent VII, *ca. 1336–1406, pope from October 17, 1404, to November 6, 1406.*

The third of the popes in the Roman line during the Great Western Schism (1378–1417), Innocent VII rebuffed all efforts to resolve the crisis. Born Cosimo (or Cosma) Gentile de' Migliorati, he was for ten years the papal tax collector in England, then cardinal-priest of Santa Croce in Gerusalemme and archbishop of Bologna when elected pope by eight cardinals in Rome on October 17, 1404, in spite of the pleas of the Avignon pope, Benedict XIII, who was in Rome at the time, to postpone the election and also in spite of the opposition of many Romans to his election. He was crowned on November 11.

Although the new pope and the other cardinals had taken an oath at the conclave to do everything in their power, if elected, to end the schism, Innocent VII refused Benedict's request for a face-to-face meeting. Toward the end of the year, however, Innocent yielded to pressure from Rupert, the newly elected king of Germany, to summon a council to meet the following November. Because of civil unrest in Rome, the council was twice postponed and then called off entirely. Innocent VII appealed to Ladislas, king of Naples, to put down a revolt, but the pope had to swear that he would not enter into any agreement with the Avignon pope that did not recognize Ladislas's title to Naples. Several months later the Romans revolted again. This time the pope's corrupt nephew had eleven leading citizens murdered, provoking a mob to storm the Vatican. Innocent VII and his cardinals were fortunate to escape unharmed to Viterbo. But after several months of Ladislas's rule in Rome, the people were ready to welcome Innocent back in early March 1406. The pope had to impose the penalty of excommunication on Ladislas to get him to vacate Castel Sant'Angelo, but after Ladislas and his troops left, the pope named him defender and standard-bearer of the Church! Innocent VII died two months later and was buried in St. Peter's.

203 Gregory XII, *ca. 1325–1417, pope from December 19, 1406, to July 4, 1415 (the Vatican's official list begins his pontificate on the day of his election, November 30, but he was not yet a bishop and could not become Bishop of Rome until consecrated on December 19).*

The fourth and last of the popes in the Roman line during the Great Western Schism (1378–1417), Gregory XII exacerbated the crisis by breaking a preelection pledge not to name new cardinals, thereby provoking the election at the council of Pisa (1409) of a third claimant to the papal throne. Gregory XII was the last pope to resign from the papacy.

Born Angelo Correr, he was cardinal-priest of San Marco and papal secretary when elected pope, at age eighty-one, by fourteen cardinals on November 30, 1406. He was crowned on December 19. Along with the other cardinals, the new pope had sworn during the conclave that, if elected, (1) he would abdicate—on condition that the Avignon pope, Benedict XIII, would also abdicate; that (2) he would, in any case, not create any new cardinals, except to maintain numerical parity with the Avignon cardinals; and that (3) he would within three months enter into negotiations with his Avignon rival about scheduling a meeting between the two of them.

At first it seemed that the octogenarian pope, Gregory XII, would fulfill his pledges. A meeting with Benedict XIII was set for the city of Savona, to be held by the following November 1 at the latest. But then pressure began to be applied to the elderly pope by the kings of Naples, Hungary, and Bohemia, as well as by his nephews who enjoyed the benefits of kinship with a reigning pope. The negotiations dragged on for months, and it became increasingly evident to Gregory XII that Benedict XIII had no intention of abdicating the Avignon throne. But when the cardinals who had supported Gregory XII grew impatient, he became suspicious of their loyalty and broke his preelection pledge not to appoint any new cardinals. On May 4, 1408, he created four, two of whom were his nephews. All but three of his cardinals abandoned him and fled to Pisa. They entered an alliance with four of Benedict's cardinals at Livorno and together, in early July, dispatched a summons for a general council to be held in Pisa in March 1409. Both claimants to the papacy were invited to attend the council, but both refused, each summoning councils of their own.

The Council of Pisa met in the Duomo (or cathedral) on March 25, 1409, and charges of bad faith and even of collusion were immediately levied against both claimants. On June 5, at the fifteenth session, both Gregory XII and Benedict XIII were formally deposed as schismatics, intractable heretics, and perjurers. The Holy See was declared vacant, and on June 26 the cardinals assembled at Pisa elected a new pope, Alexander V.

Meanwhile, Gregory XII opened his own council at Cividale, near Aquileia, on June 6, 1409. Very few attended, but before he brought it to a close on September 6, Gregory excommunicated both Benedict XIII and Alexander V. Because the archbishop of Aquileia was hostile to him, Gregory fled in disguise to Gaeta with the protection of King Ladislas of Naples (Gregory also retained the support of the rulers of Hungary, Bavaria, and Germany). When Alexander V died suddenly on May 3, 1410, the Council of Pisa elected Cardinal Baldassare Cossa to succeed him. He took the now famous name John XXIII and eventually negotiated a cynical treaty with Ladislas of Naples, who banished Gregory XII from Naples on October 31, 1411. Gregory took refuge with Carlo Malatesta, lord of Rimini.

After the Council of Constance (1414–18) deposed John XXIII on May 29, 1415, it sought to open negotiations with Gregory XII with a view to his abdication. He agreed to consider it on condition that he would be allowed formally to convoke the council, since he did not recognize the authority of John XXIII to have done so originally. The request was agreed to and, on July 4, 1415, Gregory's cardinal, John Dominici, read aloud Gregory's bull convoking the council and resigning from the papal office. The two colleges of cardinals (Rome and Avignon) were united, Gregory's papal acts were ratified, and he was appointed cardinal-bishop of Porto and legate of the March of Ancona for life. He was also declared ineligible for election as pope, but would rank next in precedence to the new pope. (The Avignon pope, Benedict XIII, still refused to abdicate, but the council declared him a heretic and deprived him of all rights to the papacy.) Three weeks before the election of Martin V, which ended the Great Western Schism, Gregory XII, already beyond the age of ninety, died at Recanati, not far from Ancona, on October 18, 1417. He was buried in the cathedral of Recanati. In 1623, during a renovation of the cathedral, Gregory XII's tomb was opened. His perfectly preserved body was reclothed in pontifical vestments.

204 Martin V, *1368–1431, pope from November 21, 1417, to February 20, 1431 (the Vatican's official list begins his pontificate on November 11, the day of his election, but he was not consecrated as Bishop of Rome until November 21).*

With Martin V's election to the papacy, the Great Western Schism (1378–1417) finally came to an end.

Born Oddo Colonna, he was cardinal-deacon of San Giorgio in Ve-
labro when unanimously elected pope on November 11, 1417 (the feast of
St. Martin), after an unusual three-day conclave at which twenty-two cardinals and thirty representatives of the five nations present at the council
participated and voted (the first—and last—papal conclave since 1058 to
include lay electors). He was immediately ordained a priest, consecrated
as Bishop of Rome, and crowned on November 21 in the cathedral
church of Constance. A triumphal procession through the streets of the
city followed the coronation. As a sign of their submission to the new
pope, the German king, Sigismund, and Frederick of Brandenburg held
the bridle of the pope's horse.

The new pope had originally been loyal to Gregory XII but broke with
him in the summer of 1408 and was active in the preparations for the
Council of Pisa (1409), which elected the antipope John XXIII. Martin V
(then Cardinal Colonna) remained loyal to John XXIII over Gregory XII
until John suddenly fled Pisa in disguise when the Council of Constance
(1414–18) asked for his resignation as well as that of the two other
claimants to the papal throne.

Martin V's election effectively ended the schism, even though first
Benedict XIII (the Avignon antipope) and then his successor, Clement
VIII, held out until their followings dwindled to insignificance. But Gregory XII's abdication and then John XXIII's acceptance, under duress, of
his own deposition by the council were the decisive events that cleared
the way for the almost universal acknowledgment of Martin V as the only
legitimate pope. (Clement VIII renounced his claim to the papacy and,
along with the few cardinals still supporting him, submitted to Martin V
in 1429.)

Although Martin V was publicly committed to carrying out the reforms of the Council of Constance, he was also interested in strengthening the canonical and financial status of the papacy. He brought loyalists
from Rome and Avignon alike into the Curia, but he failed to remove
abuses and he maintained papal rights over benefices. On March 20, 1418,
he promulgated seven reforms, among which were the relinquishment of
papal claims to revenues from vacant sees. He formally adjourned the
Council of Constance on April 22, 1418, and on May 10, in an unpub-
lished constitution, prohibited the appealing of acts of a pope to a general council.

Concerned about the chaos that had developed in the Papal States
during the course of the schism (1378–1417), Martin V resisted pressures
to make his papal residence in Germany or in Avignon and on May 16,
1418, left Constance for Rome (with intermediate stops in Mantua and
Florence, the latter for more than a year). He arrived in Rome on Sep-

tember 28, 1420. He quickly negotiated an agreement with Queen Joanna II of Naples, and her troops were withdrawn from the city. In 1424 papal troops (a theologically and pastorally dissonant concept, to be sure) defeated Braccione di Montone, the dominant ruler of central Italy, in the battle of L'Aquila, and in 1429 they crushed by force of arms a revolt by Bologna. Now free to reorganize the Papal States with the support of his troops, Martin V recovered the lost papal treasury, thereby enriching not only the Holy See but also his Colonna relatives.

His diplomatic initiatives in Europe restored some of the papacy's prestige, but he failed in his attempts to make progress toward reunion with the Greek Church and the Byzantine emperor in Constantinople or in mounting a crusade against the followers of the reformer John Hus (d. 1415) in Bohemia. On the other hand, he displayed unusual sensitivity toward Jews. He denounced anti-Jewish preaching and forbade the compulsory baptism of Jewish children under the age of twelve.

In Rome he organized a vast program of reconstruction of ruined churches and public buildings. His appointments to the College of Cardinals were of high quality, but he kept all of its members in their place. Although he was not sympathetic to the Council of Constance's decree (*Frequens*, 1417) that councils be held at regular intervals, he did summon one to meet in Pavia in 1423. Because of an outbreak of plague, his legates transferred the council to Siena (the pope himself did not attend). But when antipapal sentiments were expressed there, as they had been previously at Constance, Martin V used the poor attendance as an excuse to dissolve the council in March 1424. At the same time, he announced that the next council would be held in Basel in 1431. Martin V died of apoplexy on February 20, 1431, before the council began. He was buried in the basilica of St. John Lateran.

205 Eugenius [Eugene] IV, *ca. 1383–1447, pope from March 11, 1431, to February 23, 1447 (the Vatican's official list begins his pontificate on March 3, but since he was not yet a bishop, he could not become Bishop of Rome until consecrated on March 11).*

Having failed to dissolve the Council of Basel in 1431, Eugenius IV convened the Council of Florence in 1439 in a commendable but vain attempt to reestablish communion between the Latin and Greek Churches.

Born Gabriele Condulmaro (also Condulmer), he was the nephew of pope Gregory XII (1406–15), who had appointed him cardinal-priest of San Clemente in 1408. At the time of his unanimous election to the papacy on March 3, 1431, in the basilica of Santa Maria sopra Minerva, Cardinal Condulmaro was governor (by appointment of Pope Martin V) of

the March of Ancona and of Bologna. As in so many other papal conclaves, the other thirteen cardinal-electors (of a total of twenty-two in the
college itself) were looking for a change, not a continuation, of the policies and style of the deceased pope, whom they regarded as too authoritarian. They wanted a pope who would be committed to the reform
agenda of the impending Council of Basel and who would work collabo-
ratively with the College of Cardinals in the reform of the Church and in
the administration of the Papal States. Upon his election as Eugenius IV,
he published a bull confirming the electoral pact, but he would completely ignore it during his sixteen-year pontificate. He was consecrated
as Bishop of Rome and crowned in St. Peter's Basilica on the following
Sunday, March 11, and then conducted in a solemn procession to the
pope's cathedral church, St. John Lateran Basilica.

The new pope first moved against his predecessor's family (the Colonnas), forcing them to return the vast territories Martin V had given to his
nephews, but his main preoccupation at the start of his pontificate was
the reform council of Basel, which Martin had called. The council
opened on July 23, 1431, and Eugenius IV dissolved it on December 18,
using the sparse attendance as an excuse. He assured the delegates that he
would call a new council in eighteen months' time and that he would
himself preside over it. But the pope's action was regarded as precipitous
and was widely resented. The council refused to disperse. On February 15,
1432, the Council of Basel appealed to the teaching of the Council of
Constance (1414–18) that a general, or ecumenical, council is superior in
authority to the pope and on December 18 issued an ultimatum to Eugenius IV. Only six of the twenty-one cardinals sided with the pope. It required the efforts of the German king Sigismund to avert a schism. The
following year (December 15, 1433) the pope had to withdraw his bull dissolving the council and to acknowledge its legitimacy.

Meanwhile, the pope faced terrible problems at home. The Papal
States were occupied by hostile lay powers and a revolt, instigated by the
Colonna family, erupted in Rome in May 1434. Like other popes before
him, Eugenius IV had to flee the city in disguise. He went to Florence,
where he would reside until 1443 (and where he would come under the
influence of its extraordinary artistic culture). On June 9, 1435, the Council of Basel decreed the end of annual papal taxes (known as annates) and
called for a limitation on the powers of the papacy and the Curia. The
following June (one notes how long it took to react to events in those
days), the pope denounced the council's actions in a letter circulated to
various Christian rulers. But the final rupture between Eugenius IV and
the Council of Basel came on an issue to which both were committed,
namely, the reunion of the Latin and Greek Churches. The great majority

of the council delegates favored Basel itself, or Avignon, or Savoy for the negotiations, while the Greeks favored Constantinople. The pope preferred an Italian city. He won over the Greeks to his point of view and the council was transferred to Ferrara on September 18, 1437, opening on January 8, 1438.

The pope had sent a fleet to transport the emperor, the patriarch, and a retinue of seven hundred. Since they did not arrive until early March, the council was solemnly inaugurated on April 9. The following January, however, the council had to move once again, this time to Florence. (A number of conciliar delegates defiantly remained in Basel, however.) The given reason for the move was the outbreak of plague, but the more plausible reason was financial. The pope had accepted full responsibility for the entire Byzantine delegation and now found himself behind on his payments. An act of union between the Latin and Greek Churches (entitled *Laetentur coeli,* July 6, 1439) was forced on the Byzantine emperor John VIII Palaeologus because of the imminence of a Turkish invasion. The terms of the union included recognition of papal primacy, the existence of Purgatory (a post-death state of purification of the effects of sins that have already been forgiven), the legitimacy of the use of unleavened bread in the Eucharist, and the legitimacy of the use of the *Filioque* (Lat., "and of the Son") in the creed. The *Filioque* had been added to the creed by Pope Benedict VIII in 1024 at the request of the German emperor Henry II and was vehemently opposed by the East because it undercut the unique status of God the Father.

Subsequently, the pope signed agreements with the Armenians (1429), the Copts in Egypt (1443), certain dissident Nestorian groups in Mesopotamia (1444), and the Chaldeans and Maronites of Cyprus (1445). (Nestorians held that in Jesus Christ there are two persons, one divine and the other human, rather than only one divine Person, as taught by the Council of Ephesus in 431.)

Those conciliar delegates who remained in Basel after the transfer of the council to Ferrara and then to Florence first suspended and then deposed Eugenius IV on January 24, 1438, and June 25, 1439, respectively. The pope replied on September 4, 1439, challenging the ecumenicity of the earlier phases of the Council of Constance and condemning the Council of Basel. On November 5, 1439, those remaining in Basel elected a layman, Amadeus VIII, the duke of Savoy, as an antipope (Felix V). The election was conducted by only one cardinal and thirty-two other electors nominated by a commission and was not generally recognized except in those territories the duke had ruled and in some smaller states. For a time, Felix V employed a future pope as his secretary and ablest adviser, Enea (also Aeneas) Silvio Piccolomini (later Pius II, 1458–64), who subsequently made his peace with Eugenius IV (1442). Piccolomini even helped to arrange a concordat between the pope and the new German king, Frederick III, and won the support of the German electors and eventually the whole of Germany for Eugenius's authority as pope. Given the antipope's own difficult relations with the rump council of Basel, his personal scruples, and threats to his family, Felix V abdicated on April 7, 1449, and was appointed by Eugenius IV's successor, Nicholas V, as cardinal-bishop of Santa Sabina and as papal vicar and legate in Savoy and adjacent dioceses. Felix V was the last of the antipopes.

In the spring of 1443, when Eugenius IV recognized the claims of Alfonso V of Aragón to the throne of the kingdom of Naples, Alfonso ordered his bishops to withdraw their support from the antipope Felix V and made possible the pope's return to Rome from Florence in September, after an absence of some nine years. The following year a crusade he had financed against the Turks ended in defeat at Varna, Bulgaria. And, although concessions had been made on both sides in the agreements between Eugenius IV and Germany on matters pertaining to the administration of temporal property and appointments to vacant benefices, Eugenius issued a deathbed bull in which he declared that he did not intend by these agreements to diminish the authority or privileges of the Holy See. It is said that, as he lay dying, he expressed regret that he had ever left the monastery he had lived in during his youth. He was at first buried in the crypt of St. Peter's next to the tomb of Eugenius III, but his body was eventually moved to the church of San Salvatore in Lauro in Rome.

206 Nicholas V, *1397–1455, pope from March 6, 1447, to March 24, 1455.*

Nicholas V was the first of the Renaissance popes, a patron of literature, the arts, and architecture. Born Tommaso Parentucelli, he was archbishop of Bologna (although the city refused him entry), a cardinal-priest of Santa Susanna, and a papal legate in Germany when he was elected pope on March 6, 1447, in the Dominican convent of the basilica of Santa Maria sopra Minerva, as a compromise choice. Eighteen cardinals were present. On the first ballot there were eight votes for Cardinal Domenico Pantagale (known as "Capranica"), and ten for cardinal Prospero Colonna. But eventually the balloting swung to Cardinal Parentucelli, whose election was announced by none other than Cardinal Colonna. This led another cardinal, Antonio Martino di Chaves, from Portugal, to exclaim: "God has elected the pope, not the cardinals." The new pope took the name Nicholas V as a sign of respect and affection for his old saintly patron, Bishop (later Cardinal) Niccolò Albergati of

Bologna, whom he served for twenty years. He was crowned on March 19, also by Cardinal Colonna, with the tiara of St. Sylvester.

Nicholas V had almost immediate success in areas where his less patient and less politically skilled predecessor, Eugenius IV, had failed. He restored order in the city of Rome, rid the Papal States of mercenary troops, and won (or bought) back the allegiance of various cities. He ratified the agreement Eugenius had reached with the German Church and court, and in the Concordat of Vienna (1448) King Frederick III recognized papal rights to annual taxes (annates) and over church appointments in Germany. Nicholas V persuaded the antipope Felix V to abdicate (April 7, 1449), in return for which he named Felix a cardinal-bishop and a papal vicar and legate, with a substantial income. He also persuaded the rump council of Basel (now transferred to Lausanne) to dissolve itself (April 24, 1449) after accepting Felix's abdication and then "electing" him as pope and admitted several of the antipope's cardinalatial appointees to the College of Cardinals. In thanksgiving for these achievements on behalf of church unity, Nicholas V proclaimed 1450 a Year of Jubilee and thousands of pilgrims flocked to Rome, increasing its prestige as the center of Christendom and also adding to the city's and the papacy's financial coffers. The Jubilee year, however, was marred by the outbreak of plague (during which the pope left the city) and by a traffic disaster on the Ponte Sant'Angelo in which at least 172 persons were trampled to death. In the same year, he underscored his commitment to reform by canonizing the Franciscan reformer Bernardino of Siena (d. 1444) and by sending Cardinals Nicholas of Cusa and Capistrano to northern and southern Germany, respectively, and Cardinal d'Estouteville to France to promote reform in those countries.

Having served as a tutor in his youth for wealthy Florentine families while a student at the University of Bologna, he was at home with scholars and artists. He amassed a great personal library of books and manuscripts (807 in Latin and 353 in Greek), which, upon his death, became the basis of the Vatican Library. He arranged for the translation into Latin of numerous Greek authors, both classical and patristic, and sponsored the rebuilding of numerous churches, palaces, bridges, and roads in Rome, as well as the renovation of the Leonine City (a walled section of Rome, including St. Peter's and much of Vatican Hill, created by Leo IV after the Muslim attacks of 846). For the decoration of these buildings, he employed various outstanding artists from many nations, including the celebrated Fra Angelico. He sought in all these enterprises to establish the Church as a cultural leader.

On March 19, 1452, Nicholas V crowned the German king Frederick III as emperor in St. Peter's, the last imperial coronation to take place in

Rome. In early January 1453, a republican plot on the pope's life was uncovered. Its leader, Stefano Porcaro, was executed along with his co-conspirators. In June of that same year the news of the sack of Constantinople by the Turks (on May 29) sent shock waves through the whole of Europe. Nicholas tried to mount a crusade in September, but to no avail. On April 9, 1454, after the pope himself failed in his efforts to convene a peace conference of Italian states in Rome, the Peace of Lodi was agreed to by Venice and Milan, and then Florence. Nicholas V and the king of Naples and Sicily subsequently agreed as well, thereby forming the Italian League.

Weakened by gout, Nicholas V died on March 24, 1455. In the early Church he would probably have been proclaimed a saint, given his morally upright life in the midst of much contemporary corruption and brutality. He was buried in St. Peter's, near the tomb of his predecessor, Eugenius IV.

207 Callistus [Calixtus] III, *Spanish, 1378–1458, pope from April 8, 1455, to August 6, 1458.*

The first Spanish pope, Callistus III created two of his nephews cardinals, one of whom would become the second—and last—Spanish pope, the infamous Alexander VI (1492–1503). He was also a former supporter of an antipope, Benedict XIII (1394–1417), during the Great Western Schism (1378–1417), but eventually persuaded Benedict's successor, Clement VIII (1423–29), to submit to Pope Martin V in 1429, for which service the pope promoted him to bishop of Valencia the same year. Born Alfonso de Borja (Borgia, in Italian), he was cardinal-priest of the church of Santi Quattro Coronati as well as bishop of Valencia when elected pope on April 8, 1455, as a compromise candidate between the competing Colonna and Orsini factions—and a presumably safe one, given his health (he was weakened by gout) and age (seventy-seven). He was crowned in St. Peter's Basilica on April 20 by Cardinal Gaspare Colonna.

Callistus III immediately threw himself into his new responsibilities, organizing a crusade to liberate Constantinople from the Turks (captured in May 1453). He dispatched preachers, offered indulgences, imposed taxes, and sold gold and silver works of art and valuable book bindings to finance the cost of building a fleet. Although there were some initial successes (the defeat of the Turks outside of Belgrade, for which the pope ordered the feast of the Transfiguration universally observed on August 6; the defeat of the Turkish fleet off the island of Lesbos; and the liberation of several Christian islands in the Aegean), Christian rulers in the West, preoccupied with domestic concerns, were generally indifferent to the cause. Meanwhile, the pope's heavy-handed methods of raising money began to stir resentment and opposition in France (the University of Paris called for a general council) and Germany (where church leaders began demanding the same freedoms from papal interference as France enjoyed). Callistus III also incurred the wrath of Alfonso, king of Aragón and Naples, when he diverted a Crusader fleet to Genoa to advance papal territorial interests.

Like many seemingly pious individuals, Callistus III was a stubborn man who tolerated no opposition from anyone, including his cardinals. His blatant nepotism angered and embittered many. He enlisted Spanish commanders to lead the troops in the fortresses of the Papal States and appointed one nephew as governor of Castel Sant'Angelo and prefect of Rome and conspired to seat another on the throne of Naples. He filled the Curia with Spanish appointees from Valencia and Catalonia and appointed two other nephews, still in their early twenties, as cardinals, including Rodrigo Borgia (later Alexander VI), whom he named as vice-chancellor of the Curia.

He reopened the case of Joan of Arc, burned at the stake as a witch and heretic in Rouen on May 30, 1431; her sentence was annulled and she was declared innocent (June 16, 1456). In the same year, however, he shamed his pontificate by reviving harsh anti-Jewish legislation, left moribund by his predecessors, banning all social communication between Christians and Jews. Callistus III died on August 6, 1458 (the feast of the Transfiguration that he had ordered to be celebrated universally). Upon his death, the Italians vented their wrath upon the Catalans, who fled in terror. Callistus III was buried originally in the chapel of San Andrea in St. Peter's, but his body was transferred in 1610 to the church of Santa Maria di Monserrato, the Spanish church in Rome.

208 Pius II, *1405–64, pope from August 19, 1458, to August 15, 1464.*

The third of the Renaissance popes and a renowned humanist in his own right, Pius II encouraged the arts and literature and promoted the lavish pageantry associated with the papacy of this period. He also canonized St. Catherine of Siena (his home region) in 1461.

Born Enea (Aeneas) Silvio Piccolomini (or de' Piccolomini), he had been a firm opponent of Pope Eugenius IV (1431–47), secretary and principal adviser to the antipope Felix V (1439–49), a strong conciliarist at the Council of Basel (1431–49) and the author of a series of dialogues (*Libellus dialogorum de concilii auctoritate*, 1440) defending the authority of a general, or ecumenical, council. In 1445, with encouragement from King Frederick III of Germany, whose imperial poet (poet laureate) and secretary he had become, Piccolomini severed his connection with the antipope Felix V and reconciled himself with Eugenius IV. In the same year, he changed his immoral way of life (he had fathered several illegitimate children), and the next year was ordained a priest. He worked hard thereafter to win support for Pope Eugenius IV in Germany, in reward for which Pope Nicholas V appointed him bishop of Trieste in 1447 and of Siena in 1450. Callistus III made him a cardinal in the title of Santa Sabina e lo volle a Roma in 1456, in gratitude for his efforts in reconciling the king of Aragón and Naples with the pope. Cardinal Piccolomini was elected pope on August 19, 1458, at the chronological age of fifty-three, but he was already prematurely old. He chose the name Pius in honor of the Roman poet Virgil's "pius Aeneas." He was crowned on September 3.

He immediately issued a bull (October 1458) calling for a three-year crusade against the Turkish advance into Europe and summoned a congress of Christian rulers to meet in Mantua the following June. But his proposals for raising troops and money met strong opposition, and the congress was a failure. Pius II was convinced that this diminution of papal influence had occurred because of the newly inflated prestige of councils. So he abandoned his own long-standing support for the conciliar movement and published a bull, *Execrabilis,* on January 18, 1460, in which he forbade submitting papal acts to any future general, or ecumenical, council on appeal. He reinforced his change of mind in a second bull, *In minoribus agentes* (April 26, 1463), in which occur the famous words, "*Aeneam reiicite, Pium suscipite*" ("Reject Aeneas, submit to Pius").

The pope's continuing difficulties with France were rooted in his support for the Spaniard Ferdinand I over the Frenchman René I as king of Naples. After Louis XI came to the French throne, Pius II did not waver in his support for Ferdinand. As a result, Louis XI reintroduced the traditional liberties of the French Church (over against Rome). The pope also ran into difficulty in Germany, where antipapal sentiment had come to a head when Pius II excommunicated Duke Sigismund of Tirol for opposing the reform program Cardinal Nicholas of Cusa was trying to introduce in Brixen. The pope also deposed the archbishop of Mainz when he appealed to a general council in a dispute over efforts to replace Frederick III as king of the Romans. He clashed with the king of Bohemia, who challenged Pius II's leadership of the crusade and his traditional position as mediator of disputes in Christendom.

In October 1463, he again called for a crusade, with the stipulation that he himself would lead it. As before, the Christian rulers withheld their support. Although by now seriously ill, the pope took the cross in St. Peter's in June 1463 and headed for Ancona, which he had previously designated as the rendezvous point. When he arrived, he found only a handful of Crusaders. As the Venetian galleys came into view, Pius died, on August 15, 1464, at age fifty-nine. His heart was buried at Ancona and his body was taken to Rome. He was buried in the chapel of San Andrea in St. Peter's, but his body was transferred in 1614 to the church of Sant'Andrea della Valle, also in Rome.

209 Paul II, *1417–71, pope from August 30, 1464, to July 26, 1471.*

One of history's least popular popes, Paul II reneged on his promise to the cardinals who elected him to promote the reform of the Church, angered humanists for his treatment of scholars, and was absorbed in luxury, sport, and entertainment.

Born Pietro Barbo, he was the nephew of Pope Eugenius IV (1431–47), who saw to his rapid rise in the Church—from archdeacon of Bologna to bishop of Cervia and then of Vicenza, protonotary of the Roman church, and then, at age twenty-three, cardinal-deacon. His uncle's successor, Nicholas V (1447–55), named him cardinal-priest of San Marco. Upon Pius II's death in August 1464, the cardinal-electors (as so often has been the case) were looking for a different kind of pope, someone less self-indulgent and more committed to reform. The cardinals swore themselves to an eighteen-point electoral pact, defining the next pope's agenda and calling for a general, or ecumenical, council within three years' time. (Other points included fixing the number of cardinals at twenty-four, reforming the Curia, and resuming the war against the Turks.) Cardinal Barbo was unexpectedly elected on August 30 on the first ballot and immediately declared that the pact provided only guidelines for his pontificate, not mandates. When he forced the cardinals to modify them, he also lost their trust. He was crowned on September 16. (Although he took the name Paul, he actually toyed with taking the name Formosus, after the famous pope whose body was dug up from the grave, placed on trial, and found guilty in the so-called Cadaver Synod of January 897.)

Paul II was among the worst of the Renaissance popes: a vain, intellectually shallow, ostentatious playboy. He was a promoter of carnivals, to whose expense he forced Jews to contribute. When he decreed on April 19, 1470, that, beginning with 1475, there would be a Holy Year every twenty-five years, his motive was hardly religious or spiritual. He loved festivities. In 1466 he moved his principal residence to the newly built and magnificent Palazzo San Marco (now the Palazzo di Venezia). Meanwhile, he lost the respect of humanists and scholars for abolishing in 1466 the college of abbreviators, or papal draftsmen, which was composed mainly of literary figures. Then he earned their hatred when he imprisoned and tortured the historian Bartolomeo Platina for protesting that decision. He also suppressed the Roman Academy in 1468 because he suspected it of cultivating pagan rituals and ideas and banned the study of pagan poets by Roman children. On the other hand, he surrounded himself with scholars, collected works of art, restored monuments, and installed the first printing press in Rome.

Like his predecessors, Paul II tried to mount a crusade against the Turks, but his efforts bore little fruit. The Christian ruler most qualified to lead such a crusade, the king of Bohemia, was suspected in Rome of being a Hussite (John Hus was a Czech theologian-reformer who, among other things, demanded that the faithful be allowed to receive Holy Communion under both species, bread and wine). Paul II excommunicated the king in December 1466 and even called for a crusade against him. The major Christian rulers of Europe—the kings of Germany and France—urged the pope to call a general council at Constance, but that was the last thing the pope wanted. Paul II died suddenly of a stroke at age fifty-four on July 26, 1471, while still negotiating a marriage between Ivan III of Russia and the Catholic daughter of the Byzantine emperor. Bartolomeo Platina, the Vatican librarian during the next pontificate, took his revenge on Paul II (who had imprisoned and tortured him) by painting his portrait in the blackest colors and by writing a highly unfavorable biography. Paul II was buried in St. Peter's.

210 Sixtus IV, *1414–84, pope from August 25, 1471, to August 12, 1484 (the Vatican's official list begins his pontificate on the day of his election, August 9, but since he was not yet a bishop, he could not become Bishop of Rome until consecrated on August 25).*

Sixtus IV transformed the city of Rome from a medieval to a Renaissance city, built the Sistine Chapel, founded the Sistine choir, established the Vatican archives, but also blatantly practiced nepotism (making six nephews cardinals), established the Spanish Inquisition, annulled the decrees of the reformist Council of Constance (1414–18), was personally involved in a conspiracy that included murder, and helped prepare the way for the Protestant Reformation.

Born Francesco della Rovere in poverty (one of the relatively few popes not to have come from an aristocratic or economically prosperous family), he was educated by Franciscans and joined the order early in his life. A celebrated preacher and respected theologian, he became minister general of the Franciscans in 1464 and was appointed cardinal of San Pietro in Vincoli in 1467. In the confusion following Paul II's sudden death at age fifty-four, Cardinal della Rovere quickly emerged as the favorite, with the support of the duke of Milan and with his own nephew making many promises to the cardinal-electors before the vote on August 9, 1471. He was consecrated as Bishop of Rome and crowned by Cardinal Borgia (the future Alexander VI), who functioned as archdeacon, on August 25 in St. Peter's Square, the first time such a ceremony was held there.

Soon after his election, Sixtus IV named two of his young nephews cardinals (one of whom would become Pope Julius II) and advanced and enriched a number of other relatives. (He would later name four other nephews to the College of Cardinals.) Like many of his predecessors, he was eager for a crusade against the Turks, but he, too, was faced with the general indifference of Christian rulers in Europe. After a weak effort in 1472, he proclaimed another crusade in 1481, when Otranto, on the Italian mainland, fell. It was recovered the following year with the help of Venetian and Hungarian forces and probably because of the sudden death of the sultan.

As a Franciscan, Sixtus IV was happy to increase the privileges of his order and to canonize in 1482 the great Franciscan theologian Bonaventure (d. 1274). But he was preoccupied during much of his pontificate with the well-being of the Papal States. In 1478 he was drawn by one of his nephews into the Pazzi conspiracy, in which Giuliano de' Medici was killed and his brother Lorenzo was wounded. (That same year he annulled the decrees of the reformist Council of Constance [1414–18] and established the Spanish Inquisition, later sought to check its abuses, and then confirmed the infamous Tomás de Torquemada as grand inquisitor.) This murderous act drew the pope into a useless and scandalous war with Florence (1478–80), and then he incited Venice to attack Ferrara—only to change sides and impose spiritual penalties on Venice. The princes and cities of Italy forced the pope to accept the Peace of Bagnolo in 1484, leaving him with no additional territories and much trouble in Rome and Latium.

Sixtus IV's vain military expeditions and his unseemly generosity toward his family had depleted the papal treasury and forced him to engage in the sale of indulgences and other dubious forms of revenue raising (including the doubling of curial offices). In March 1482, a former ally of the pope's, the Croatian archbishop Andrea Zamometič, had tried to reconvene the Council of Basel (1431–49) in order to pass judgment on Sixtus IV. The following year the pope renewed the ban on appeals to general councils over a pope.

Very few of the thirty-four cardinals he created (including six nephews) were qualified, and he reigned as a Renaissance prince—an odd posture indeed for a lifelong Franciscan. As a Renaissance prince, however, he did improve the roads, buildings, and bridges of the city, built churches (including the Sistine Chapel), and restored Holy Spirit hospital. He attracted painters, sculptors, and musicians to Rome and, as mentioned above, founded the Sistine choir, established the Vatican archives, and reorganized and enlarged the Vatican Library and opened it to scholars, as a result of which he is generally regarded as the Library's second founder (Nicholas V [1447–55] was its initial founder). Sixtus IV died on August 12, 1484, following the imposition of the distasteful Peace of Bagnolo and was buried in St. Peter's, where his bronze tomb is considered a masterpiece.

211 Innocent VIII, *1432–92, pope from August 29, 1484, to July 25, 1492.*

With the pontificate of Innocent VIII, the papacy sunk to the depths of worldliness—a fitting prelude to the most notorious pontificate in history, that of Alexander VI. Born Giovanni Battista Cibò, he was the bishop of Molfetta and a cardinal-priest of Santa Cecilia (and the father of three illegitimate children prior to ordination and while a member of the Neapolitan court) when elected pope in a conclave filled with intrigue and bribery. Cardinal Giuliano della Rovere, the nephew of the deceased Sixtus IV, knew that he could not be elected at this time (he would be elected pope nineteen years later, as Julius II), so he threw his support behind someone he felt he could dominate, namely, Cardinal Cibò. He was crowned on September 12 by Cardinal Piccolomini. Less than three months later (December 5), he issued a bull, *Summis desiderantes*, in which he ordered the Inquisition in Germany to punish alleged witches with the greatest severity.

Innocent VIII's papal court was indistinguishable from that of any contemporary prince, and his cardinals (appointed mostly by Sixtus IV) lived in the grand style. Because of the enormous financial debts left by his predecessor, the new pope created new and unnecessary offices in the Curia and elsewhere in order to sell them to the highest bidders (which is the essence of simony). Persuaded by Giuliano della Rovere, Innocent VIII foolishly sided with rebel barons against King Ferdinand I of Naples, who refused to pay the papal taxes. The alliance with the barons had disastrous consequences for Rome and the Papal States, and the pope was forced to make a distasteful peace with Ferdinand in 1486. (In the same year he recognized Henry VII as king of England.) Then he entered into an alliance with Lorenzo de' Medici, whose daughter was married to one of the pope's sons, Franceschetto. (The pope appointed their thirteen-year-old son a cardinal!) In 1489 Ferdinand broke the peace and Innocent

VIII excommunicated and deposed him. There was a reconciliation in January 1492, but the papacy lost L'Aquila and most of its remaining political prestige.

As in the case of almost every pope before him, Innocent VIII's efforts to mount a crusade against the Turks went nowhere. In 1489, however, he entered into an agreement with the Turkish sultan in which the pope detained his fugitive brother and rival in Rome in return for forty thousand ducats (almost $1.7 million) a year and the gift of the holy lance (presented to the pope in 1492) believed to have pierced the side of Christ on the cross. As Innocent VIII's pontificate neared its end, there was jubilation in Rome over the news that the Moors had been expelled from Granada (January 2, 1492). In gratitude, the pope awarded the Spanish king Ferdinand V (and his wife, Isabella of Castile) and his successors the title "Catholic Kings." Upon the pope's death on July 25 (with Christopher Columbus less than three months from landfall in America), the Papal States were in a condition of anarchy. It is said that, as he lay dying, he begged the cardinals to elect a successor better than himself. They surely did not! Innocent VIII was buried in St. Peter's.

212 Alexander VI, *Spanish, 1431–1503, pope from August 26, 1492, to August 18, 1503 (the Vatican's official list begins his pontificate on the day of his election, August 11, but since he was not yet a bishop, he could not become Bishop of Rome until consecrated on August 26).*

Alexander VI was the most notorious pope in all of history. His pontificate was marked by nepotism, greed, and unbridled sensuality.

Born Rodrigo de Borja y Borja (Borgia in Italian) near Valencia, he was the nephew of Pope Callistus III (1455–58), who named him a cardinal-deacon at age twenty-five and the next year vice-chancellor of the Holy See, a position that made it possible for him to amass such wealth that he was accounted the second richest cardinal. He also lived an openly promiscuous life, fathering several children before and after his election to the papacy. Rodrigo had hoped to succeed Sixtus IV to the papacy in 1484, but had to wait for the next conclave in 1492 to realize his ambition, although not without the help of generous bribes and promises of lucrative appointments and benefices. Therefore, his election in the Sistine Chapel on August 11, 1492, was simoniacal (i.e., purchased). (It is said that only five of the twenty-two cardinals, excluding Borgia, could not be bought: Carafe, Piccolomini, della Rovere, lo Zeno, and del Portugal.) Alexander VI was crowned in St. Peter's on August 26. (He had taken the name Alexander VI rather than Alexander V, even though Alexander V was, in accordance with present thinking, an antipope elected by the Council of Pisa in 1409. Evidently, Alexander V's claim to legitimacy was stronger than now.)

Although the new pope seemed to make a strong beginning, restoring order in Rome and promising reform of the Curia and a crusade against the Turks, it soon became evident that the consuming passions of his pontificate would be gold, women, and the interests of his family. He named his son Cesare, at age eighteen, a cardinal, along with the brother of the current papal mistress. He also arranged several marriages for his daughter Lucrezia and often left her in charge of the papacy, as virtual regent, when he was away from Rome.

After the death of Ferdinand I, king of Naples, in early 1494, Alexander VI crowned Ferdinand's son Alfonso II as his successor, an act that provoked King Charles VIII of France to invade Italy, voicing threats to call a council to depose the pope. Because Alexander VI could not defend Rome against the invaders, he had to come to terms with Charles. Later, in league with other Italian rulers, he forced the French king out of Italy. Later still, however, the pope did an about-face and reestablished friendly relations with France, even approving the partition of Naples between France and Spain in 1501. But the pope's main political preoccupation during his pontificate was with the transformation of the Papal States and central Italy into a family enterprise and with the containment of the great Roman families. The means employed included assassinations, seizures of properties, and the creation of cardinals for a high price.

The political act for which Alexander VI is best remembered occurred in 1493 when he drew a line of demarcation between Spanish and Portuguese zones of exploration in the New World (although it had to be modified the following year because it was designed to favor Spain unduly). The ecclesiastical act for which he is also remembered was his excommunication, torture, and execution in 1498 of the famous Florentine preacher and reformer Girolamo Savonarola, who had been denouncing papal corruption and calling for a council to reform the Church and depose Alexander VI. On an artistic note, the pope restored Castel Sant'Angelo, had the Borgia apartments in the Vatican decorated by Pinturicchio, the celebrated Umbrian painter, and persuaded Michelangelo to draw up plans for the rebuilding of St. Peter's.

In June 1497, when his favorite son, Juan, was murdered and suspicion centered on Cesare, Alexander VI was so shattered that he resolved to dedicate himself thereafter to church reform. But his resolution could not withstand the continued temptations of the flesh and the demands of his family. And so nothing came of it. In August 1503 he and his son Cesare were at dinner hosted by a cardinal. Both ingested a poison evidently meant for their host. The pope died but his son survived. Pious accounts say that Alexander VI died of fever in an epidemic. He was buried first in the chapel of San Andrea in St. Peter's, and then in 1610 his remains, along with those of his uncle, Pope Callistus III (1455–58), were transferred to the Spanish church of Santa Maria di Monserrato in Rome.

213 Pius III, *ca. 1439–1503, pope from October 1 to October 18, 1503 (the Vatican's official list marks the beginning of his pontificate on the day of his election, September 22, but apparently, although he had been appointed archbishop of Siena, he had not yet been ordained a priest or a bishop; his consecration as Bishop of Rome did not occur until October 1).*

A compromise, or stopgap, candidate in poor health, Pius III died only seventeen days after his consecration and coronation as pope. Taking the day of his episcopal consecration as the beginning of his pontificate, his was possibly the fourth shortest pontificate in history, and even the second or third shortest because of the difficulty in determining the exact dates for Boniface VI (896) and Celestine IV (1241).

Born Francesco Todeschini-Piccolomini, he was a nephew of Pope Pius II (1458–64), who appointed him archbishop of his home city of Siena at age twenty-one and a few weeks later made him cardinal-deacon of San Eustachio. He also allowed him to use the surname Piccolomini (Pius II's family name). He was placed in charge of Rome and the Papal States when his uncle Pius II embarked on a crusade in 1464 and was for many years cardinal-protector of England and Germany and then papal legate to Germany. During the pontificate of Alexander VI, however, he kept his distance from the papal court. In the conclave that elected Alexander VI, Cardinal Piccolomini (Todeschini) refused to be bribed and five years later was the only member of the College of Cardinals to protest Alexander VI's transfer of substantial papal territories to his son Juan. Although he had been considered for the papacy in previous conclaves, he owed his election this time to the need to break a deadlock. (The conclave was moved from the Vatican to the basilica of Santa Maria sopra Minerva because of threats of force from Cesare Borgia, the son of Alexander VI.) Piccolomini took the name Pius III after his uncle.

At the time of his election, Pius III was in poor health (afflicted with gout) and prematurely old, both of which made him an attractive candidate to provide the Church with a bit of breathing space following Alexander VI's pontificate. But the new pope's reign proved to be even shorter than the cardinals themselves had expected or hoped. He was ordained a priest (he was only a deacon at the time of election) and consecrated a bishop on October 1 and crowned on October 8. He was so weak, however, that the ceremonies had to be abbreviated. He died seventeen days later and was buried in the chapel of San Andrea in St. Peter's. Pius III's remains were transferred in 1614 to the church of Sant'Andrea della Valle in Rome.

214 Julius II, *1443–1513, pope from November 1, 1503, to February 21, 1513 (the Vatican's official list begins his pontificate on October 31, but he was actually elected the next day, November 1).*

A patron of artists like Michelangelo, Raphael, and Bramante, Julius II commissioned plans for the new St. Peter's Basilica, to be funded by the sale of indulgences—the kindling for the Protestant Reformation soon to follow.

Born Giuliano della Rovere of impoverished but noble parents, he was, like so many other popes, a nephew of a previous pope, Sixtus IV (1471–84), and, like these others, he benefitted greatly from favors granted by his uncle the pope. He was named bishop of Carpentras at age eighteen and later the same year cardinal-priest of San Pietro in Vincoli. He was quickly given other dioceses (including Avignon), abbeys, and benefices (income-producing ecclesiastical offices), including appointment as cardinal-bishop of Santa Sabina. As a cardinal he fathered three daughters.

He had lobbied (with the aid of bribes) for the election of Innocent VIII in 1484 when he realized he could not be elected himself and then exercised great influence over the new pope. Giuliano was an enemy, however, of Alexander VI and fled to France to escape possible assassination in 1494, but he failed in his attempts to win the king's support for a general council that would depose Alexander VI for simony. Indeed, Charles VIII signed a treaty with the pope in 1495. Upon Alexander VI's death in 1503 Giuliano returned to Rome, but was not elected pope at the conclave. However, the one chosen, Pius III, died almost immediately after his coronation and Giuliano finally succeeded in his ambition at the next conclave. He was elected unanimously in a single day, November 1, 1503, with the help of substantial bribes and promises of ecclesiastical preferments, especially to Cesare Borgia. He was crowned on November 18 and took possession of the pope's cathedral, the basilica of St. John Lateran, on November 26, after a triumphal procession through the streets of Rome.

Apart from his interest in art and architecture, Julius II was a thoroughly political, even military, pope, far removed from the example of the Apostle Peter and the mandate of Jesus Christ. He restored and enlarged the Papal States, forced the still dangerous Cesare Borgia out of Italy, won back most of Romagna, and in 1506, in full armor and in the lead, captured Perugia and Bologna from their tyrannical rulers. In 1508, having joined the League of Cambria (France, Germany, and Spain), he defeated Venice so completely that it had to surrender Rimini and Faenza as well as all taxation rights. Fearing French domination in northern Italy and concerned about the need for Venetian assistance against the Turks, Julius II then made peace with Venice and, to win the support of Spain, recognized Ferdinand II of Aragón as king of Naples, disregarding France's claims on it.

With himself at the head of his army, Julius II seized Mirandola in January 1511, but barely escaped capture during the fall of Bologna to the French. With the support of nine anti-Julian cardinals, King Louis XII of France convened a council at Pisa on October 1, 1511, with the intention of deposing the pope. The council even had the support of the emperor Maximilian I. After the pope stripped the rebellious cardinals of their rank, the council moved to Milan, where it declared the suspension of the pope. (It later moved to Lyons, where it came to an end after losing the sponsorship of the French.) The year before, Julius II had formed the Holy League with Venice and Spain for the defense of the papacy, which Henry VIII of England joined later in the year. Although the League's armies were initially defeated at Ravenna, with the help of Swiss troops the tide turned and the French were driven from Italy. The Papal States were increased by the addition of Parma, Piacenza, and Reggio Emilia, and Julius regarded himself as their re-founder.

Julius II was primarily a politician and a warrior, for which he was scathingly attacked by the humanist Erasmus (d. 1536) in his *Praise of Folly* (1509). Julius paid little attention to ecclesiastical, much less spiritual, concerns. He did issue a fateful dispensation to Henry VIII of England, enabling him to marry his brother's widow, Catherine of Aragón, published a bull (January 14, 1505) declaring papal elections (like his own?) nullified if engineered through simony, and established the first dioceses in South America. He also convened an ecumenical council, Lateran V, in May 1512. The five-year council concerned itself mainly with condemnations of the council held at Pisa in 1511–12 and the Pragmatic Sanction of Bourges (a 1438 decree that curtailed papal rights in France). The pope was especially gratified by the emperor Maximilian's submission to him at the council's third session. The council, however, was poorly attended from the very beginning. Of the eighty to ninety bishops in attendance, most were Italian.

Julius II is perhaps best remembered for his patronage of great artists like Michelangelo, Raphael, and Bramante. Among the works inspired and funded by Julius were Michelangelo's statue of Moses in the church of San Pietro in Vincoli (St. Peter in Chains) and the paintings in the Sistine Chapel and Raphael's frescoes in the Vatican. The pope commissioned

Bramante to prepare plans for the new St. Peter's Basilica and he assisted at the laying of the cornerstone on April 18, 1506. In a historically momentous decision, Julius II arranged to finance the construction by the sale of indulgences, thereby lighting the match that ignited the Protestant Reformation. The sale of indulgences was the occasion of Martin Luther's historic Ninety-five Theses. When Julius II died of fever on February 21, 1513, he was mourned by some as the liberator of Italy from foreign domination and was subsequently hailed by others as a forerunner of its eventual unification. He was buried in the church of San Pietro in Vincoli, of which he had been cardinal-priest.

215 Leo X, *1475–1521, pope from March 17, 1513, to December 1, 1521 (the Vatican's official list begins his pontificate on March 9, the day of his election, but since he was not yet a bishop, he could not become Bishop of Rome until consecrated on March 17).*

The Protestant Reformation began during the pontificate of Leo X, in large part because of his decision to sell church offices and indulgences in order to pay off debts incurred through personal extravagance, military campaigns, and the construction of St. Peter's Basilica.

Born Giovanni de' Medici, son of Lorenzo the Magnificent, he was tonsured (i.e., admitted to the clerical state) at age seven, named a cardinal-deacon of Santa Maria in Dominica at age thirteen, and was the effective ruler of Florence at the time of his election to the papacy on March 9, 1513, at age thirty-seven. The College of Cardinals was not at full strength at the time because nine anti-Julian cardinals (i.e., those opposed to Pope Julius II) who participated in the council held at Pisa and Milan (1511–12) were excluded. Once again (as has been so often the case in papal elections), the twenty-five cardinal-electors wanted a pope far different from the deceased soldier pope Julius II. Cardinal de' Medici won the support of the younger cardinals and then of the older cardinals, who thought his state of health would ensure a brief pontificate. Leo X was ordained a priest on March 15 (he was a deacon at the time of election), consecrated as Bishop of Rome on March 17, and crowned as pope on March 19.

A Renaissance prince who loved books, music, art, hunting, and the theater, Leo X made Rome once against the cultural center of the Western world. Politically, he was concerned with preserving Italy, and especially his beloved Florence, from foreign domination. To do so, he entered into an unpopular treaty with France in 1515 (after a series of French military victories in Italy, including Milan). Leo X surrendered Parma and Piacenza in return for Florence's independence, under Medici control. He also arranged a concordat with France that would last until the French Revolution in 1789. The concordat conceded to the French crown the right of nomination to all higher church offices (bishops, abbots, and priors), reserving only lesser benefices to the pope. But the concordat also finally removed the Pragmatic Sanction of Bourges (a 1438 decree that curtailed papal rights in France). In 1516 he waged a politically and financially disastrous war in an effort to impose his nephew Lorenzo as duke of Urbino. The next year, discovering a plot by some cardinals to poison him, Leo X executed their leader, Cardinal Alfonso Petrucci, imprisoned four others, and packed the College of Cardinals with thirty-one new members.

When elected pope, Leo X had sworn to continue the Fifth Lateran Council, convened by his predecessor, Julius II, in 1512. He opened the sixth session on April 27, 1513, and at the eighth and ninth sessions (December 19, 1513, and March 5, 1514) received the French king's repudiation of the schismatic council of Pisa-Milan (1511–12) and the submission of the French bishops. Lateran V also ratified Leo X's concordat with Francis I of France and the abolition of the Pragmatic Sanction of Bourges. Although the council also addressed a number of reform measures (e.g., condemnations of pluralism, or the holding of more than one church office at the same time, and of absenteeism), there were no effective means of enforcement. When Leo X closed the council on March 16, 1517, there was no apparent sense of urgency about the gathering clouds of revolution on the horizon.

Leo's personal extravagance and his patronage of the arts forced him to pawn his palace furniture and silver and gold plates, but his official debts pushed him into even more serious measures. To finance his military expeditions, the projected crusade against the Turks, and the construction of the new St. Peter's, he had to borrow money on a mammoth scale and to sell church offices, including cardinals' hats. For the construction of the new basilica he renewed the sale of indulgences authorized by Julius II, and then he arranged a highly lucrative (but simoniacal) deal with Albrecht, the archbishop of Brandenburg and Mainz, for the indulgence to be preached in his dioceses. (When the wealthy archdiocese of Mainz fell vacant, Albrecht had applied for it but could not raise the necessary funds for the installation tax and for the papal dispensation to hold a plurality of dioceses. On condition that Albrecht would allow preachers of the indulgence to go into his dioceses, the money was advanced to the pope by the banking house of Jacob Fugger. One-half of the money raised by the preaching would go to the Fuggers, the other half to the pope.) When the Dominican John Tetzel (d. 1519) began preaching the indulgence in January 1517, the Augustinian monk Martin Luther (d. 1546) posted his famous Ninety-five Theses of protest on the church door in Wittenberg.

When a summary of Luther's views reached Rome in early 1518, the pope ordered the general of Luther's order to silence him, but the effort was unsuccessful. After a series of debates between Luther and the theologian John Eck (d. 1543) at Leipzig in 1519, Leo X published his famous bull, *Exsurge Domine* (June 15, 1520), condemning Luther on forty-one counts. When, on December 10, 1520, Luther publicly burned the papal bull, Leo X excommunicated him in the bull *Decet Romanum pontificem* on January 3, 1521. Ironically, on October 11 of that same year, the pope conferred the title "Defender of the Faith" on England's King Henry VIII for his defense of the seven sacraments against Luther.

Unfortunately, Leo X and the Curia did not comprehend the significance of these reform movements or of the Church's urgent need to root out corruption and abuses. Indeed, he was probably too distracted with military and political affairs (he continued, for example, as ruler of Florence throughout his pontificate). When Leo X died suddenly of malaria on December 1, 1521, Italy was in political turmoil, northern Europe was about to erupt in an explosion of religious conflict, and the papal treasury was empty and the papacy in great debt. Leo X was buried first in St. Peter's, but his remains were transferred in 1536 to the basilica of Santa Maria sopra Minerva, where a great monument to him was erected.

Part V

FROM THE COUNTER-REFORMATION TO THE BEGINNING OF THE MODERN PAPACY

ERHAPS THE FOUR MOST SIGNIFICANT EVENTS affecting the Catholic Church in the second Christian millennium are the East-West Schism of 1054, the sixteenth-century Protestant Reformation, the Catholic Counter-Reformation mounted by the Council of Trent between 1545 and 1563, and the Second Vatican Council of 1962–65. While it is true that the Church is "at once holy and always in need of purification" and must constantly follow "the path of penance and renewal" (Vatican II, Dogmatic Constitution on the Church, n. 8), the Protestant Reformation should not have been necessary. It was the product of a series of tragic and unforgivable mistakes and corrupt actions on the part of the Church's leadership, the papacy in particular. The fourteenth and fifteenth centuries were among the worst in the Western Church. The monarchical papacy, rooted especially in the pontificate of Gregory VII (1073–85), that had developed in the twelfth and thirteenth centuries became a bloated bureaucracy wallowing in lust for money and power. The Avignon papacy (1305–78) and then the Great Western Schism (1378–1417) so diminished the papacy's standing in the Church and in the secular world that the councils of Constance (1414–18) and Basel (1431–49) sought to replace the pope as earthly head of the Church by a general, or ecumenical, council.

During these same years, the clergy became increasingly corrupt, church offices were for sale, and the principal motive of many officeholders was wealth, not ministerial service. Ecclesiastical careerists accumulated as many benefices (income-producing offices) as possible (a practice known as pluralism), knowing that they could never serve them all personally (a situation known as absenteeism). Poorly paid substitutes in these benefices were usually uneducated and pastorally incompetent. The need for reform was almost universally recognized. Indeed, in many of the papal conclaves during these pre-Reformation centuries, the cardinal-electors compelled candidates for the papacy to commit themselves under oath to carry out certain reforms of the Church if elected. Unfortunately, many of the newly elected popes ignored their solemn promises. Moreover, the self-interest of the popes, the bishops, and the secular rulers mitigated against an authentic commitment to reform, because so many of them profited personally from the abuses. The growing popular dissatisfaction and anticlericalism created a powder keg that would be sparked by Martin Luther and the other Reformers early in the sixteenth century. The papacy, as we saw in Part IV, was woefully unprepared for the challenge. On the contrary, it was the largest part of the problem.

Luther posted his famous Ninety-five Theses on a church door in Wittenberg in 1517. It was not until 1545, after most of the damage had been done to the unity of the Church, that the papacy began to mount a serious response to the incessant calls for renewal and reform. However, most of the activities of the papacy during these years were reactive rather than proactive. The Protestant Reformation had placed the Catholic Church on the defensive, and it would remain there until the middle of the twentieth century, fiercely combating the Enlightenment, the French Revolution, Italian nationalism, modern intellectual movements, and especially theological and biblical scholarship. No pope of this period better typified that negative defensiveness than the last, Gregory XVI (1831–46), the first and only Camaldolese monk to serve in the papacy. Gregory XVI was a reactionary pope in the literal sense of the world. He feared and despised almost every modern development. He banned railways in papal territories, opposed Italian nationalism, ruled the Papal States with an iron hand, even crushing an uprising with the use of Austrian troops, and condemned freedom of conscience, freedom of the press, and the separation of Church and state. The only glaring exception to his reactionary agenda was his denunciation of slavery and the slave trade.

Paul III (1534–49) convened the Council of Trent in 1545 and thereby launched what is known as the Catholic Counter-Reformation. That this Counter-Reformation bore the seeds of its own excesses became quickly evident during the pontificate of Paul IV (1555–59), who strengthened the Inquisition, established the Index of Forbidden Books, and confined Jews to a special quarter in Rome and required them to wear a distinctive headgear. (Leo XII [1823–29] also confined Jews to ghettos.) Paul IV's successor, Pius IV (1559–65), reconvened the Council of Trent after a ten-year suspension and committed his pontificate to reform. His successor, Pius V (1566–72), the only canonized saint among the thirty-six popes of the period covered in Part V, enforced the decrees of the Council of Trent, published the *Roman Catechism*, and reformed the Roman Missal and the Divine Office (Liturgy of the Hours). Unfortunately, he also excommunicated Queen Elizabeth of England, thereby placing the Catholics of that country in a life-threatening situation. Gregory XIII (1572–85) was also a firm supporter of the Tridentine reforms. He reconstructed and endowed the old Roman College, which was renamed in his honor as the Gregorian University, and also reformed the Julian calendar by dropping ten days and adding a leap year. The name of the reformed calendar also honors his memory. It is known as the Gregorian calendar.

It was Sixtus V (1585–90) who set the maximum number of cardinals at seventy—a figure not exceeded until the pontificate of John XXIII (1958–63)—and who reorganized the Roman Curia in a form that would remain essentially unchanged until the Second Vatican Council (1962–65). He also transformed Rome from a Renaissance to a great Baroque city. Paul V (1605–21) will always be remembered as the pope who censured the astronomer Galileo—a censure removed almost four centuries later in the pontificate of John Paul II (1978–). Gregory XV (1621–23) decreed that papal elections should thereafter be conducted by secret ballot—a practice still in effect today. Urban VIII (1623–44) consecrated the new St. Peter's Basilica in 1626 (the manner of funding its construction in the early sixteenth century was one of the immediate causes of the Protestant Reformation), and he adopted Castel Gandolfo as the papal summer residence—it is still in use today for that purpose. Alexander VII (1655–67) permitted Jesuit missionaries in China to use Chinese rites in the Mass and the sacraments and also commissioned Bernini to enclose St. Peter's Piazza with two semicircular colonnades. Clement XI (1700–1721) reversed Alexander VII's approval of the use of Chinese rites—a disastrous decision that completely undercut the Catholic missionary effort in China. (The prohibition was eventually lifted by Pius XII in 1939.) The memory of Clement XIV (1769–74), a Franciscan, is dishonored by his suppression of the Jesuits in 1773. The Society of Jesus (the Jesuits' formal title) was reinstated by Pius VII (1800–1823) in 1814. Pius VI (1775–99) denounced the French Revolution and died a prisoner of Napoleon Bonaparte.

There were not many "firsts" during these three centuries of papal history. Hadrian VI (1522–23) was the first and only Dutch pope, and the last non-Italian until the pontificate of John Paul II in 1978. Hadrian (Adrian) was also one of only two popes since the sixteenth century to retain his baptismal name as pope. The other was Marcellus II in 1555. The last pope to retain his former diocese while serving as Bishop of Rome was Benedict XIII (1724–30). He remained as archbishop of Benevento. (The practice was known as pluralism and was always strongly condemned by reformers.) The first pope to issue an encyclical (or circular letter to all the world's Catholic bishops) was Benedict XIV in 1740. This period also witnessed the shortest pontificate in history, that of Urban VII who was elected on September 15, 1590, and died on September 27, before he could be crowned.

216 Hadrian [Adrian] VI, *Dutch, 1459–1523, pope from January 9, 1522, to September 14, 1523.*

The first pope of the Catholic Counter-Reformation, Hadrian [Adrian] VI was the only Dutchman to serve as pope and the last non-Italian until John Paul II (1978–). He is also one of only two popes in the second Christian millennium to retain his baptismal name as pope (Marcellus II did the same in 1555).

Born Adrian Florensz Dedal in Utrecht, he was, like Jesus, the son of a carpenter. He was cardinal-archbishop of Utrecht when unanimously elected to the papacy on January 9, 1522, with the support of the emperor Charles V. He had previously been professor, rector, and chancellor at the University of Louvain; regent of Aragón; bishop of Tortosa; inquisitor for Aragón, Navarre, Castile, and León; and viceroy of Spain for the emperor Charles. When elected pope in a deeply divided conclave (England's lord chancellor, Thomas Woolsey, was a leading candidate), Cardinal Dedal was away in Spain. He came to Rome by sea to underscore his independence from both France and the empire. Accordingly, he was not crowned until August 31.

From the outset of his pontificate, Hadrian VI saw his task as one of containing the Reformation by attending to the reform of the Church's central administration and of uniting the Christian West against the Turks (with whom most of the popes of this period were obsessed). Both were to end in failure. First, he was badly received by the Roman people, who regarded him as a northern "barbarian." They also resented his belt-tightening economies (made necessary by the extravagance of his predecessor, Leo X) and his disinterest in Renaissance art and culture. Because the cardinals were also unhappy, having expected some generous "payoffs" for their election of him, they refused to cooperate with his attempts at reforming the Curia.

Hadrian VI's legate at the Diet of Nuremberg (December 1522) was instructed to acknowledge that blame for the disorder in the Church lay primarily with the Curia itself—an admission that historians have described as the first step in the Catholic Counter-Reformation. The pope, however, was firm in his opposition to the doctrinal positions taken by Martin Luther and his followers—opinions that he had previously condemned as an inquisitor in Spain. Hadrian VI ordered the enforcement of the ban on Luther's teachings decreed in the Edict of Worms (May 8, 1521). But the pope (like many others) did not really appreciate the seriousness of Luther's revolt.

Hadrian VI's hopes for a crusade against the Turks foundered diplomatically, in spite of the fall of Rhodes to the Turks in December 1522 and the impending threat to Hungary. The pope had alienated Charles V by remaining neutral in Charles's fight against Francis I of France. Then he alienated Francis by arresting Cardinal Soderini, an ally of the French king. Francis stopped the flow of money from France to Rome and prepared to invade Lombardy. This forced the pope into a defensive alliance with the empire, England, Austria, Milan, and other Italian cities. A little over a month later, worn out by these developments and weakened by the searing Roman heat, Hadrian fell seriously ill and died in September 14, 1523. He was buried first in the chapel of San Andrea in St. Peter's between the tombs of Pius II and Pius III. That the ill will of the Roman people toward him continued even after his death is revealed in the Latin graffito written on his tomb: "*Hic jacet impius inter Pios*" (Lat., "Here lies an impious [pope] between [two] Piuses"). His remains were transferred ten years later to the German national church of Santa Maria dell'Anima in Rome.

217 Clement VII, *1478–1534, pope from November 19, 1523, to September 25, 1534.*

During Clement VII's pontificate, the Protestant Reformation continued to spread across northern Europe and into England, when Clement refused to grant Henry VIII a divorce from Catherine of Aragón. Born Giulio de' Medici, the illegitimate son of Giuliano de' Medici, he was cardinal-archbishop of Florence (appointed by his cousin, Leo X, who dispensed him from the canonical prohibition against ordaining those of illegitimate birth) and vice-chancellor of the Holy See when unanimously elected (actually, proclaimed) pope on November 19, 1523, after a conclave of six weeks' duration (October 8–November 19). He had been a strong candidate at the previous conclave in 1523, but lost to Hadrian VI. Clement VII was crowned on November 26.

  Politically, the new pope was mainly concerned with preserving his family's hold on Florence and the papacy's on the Papal States. He flip-flopped in his loyalties: first by supporting Francis I of France and thereby infuriating the emperor Charles V; then, after the French defeat at Pavia and the capture of Francis I, by seeking the emperor's protection; and then by joining a military league (with France, Milan, Florence, and Venice) against the emperor. As a result, the emperor invaded Italy and sacked Rome on May 6, 1527. The pope escaped to Castel Sant'-Angelo but was forced to surrender and was imprisoned for over six months. He was released only after agreeing to the French occupation of major cities in the Papal States, promising neutrality, and paying a huge indemnity. Clement VII, however, left the now devastated city of Rome to reside first in Orvieto and then in Viterbo. He came to recognize that his interests lay with the emperor, both for combating the Lutheran heresy in Germany and for mounting a united crusade against the Turks, who were advancing on Vienna. The reconciliation of pope and emperor was sealed by Charles V's coronation at Bologna on February 24, 1530, the last imperial coronation by a pope, and by the restoration of Medici rule in Florence. But the relationship rested on a thin reed. The pope hedged his bets by traveling personally to Marseilles to marry his own grandniece to the French king's second son.

During the period of open enmity between the pope and the emperor, the Diet of Speyer (June 1526) rejected the Edict of Worms (1521), which had banned Martin Luther's writings. In doing so, Speyer gave the Reformers valuable breathing space. Clement VII fumbled another opportunity to confront the new Lutheran challenge when he refused to heed the emperor's call for a general council to deal with the crisis. He also mishandled Henry VIII's divorce from Catherine of Aragón, first appearing to be sympathetic to the English king's request for a dispensation, then delaying for time, and then, under pressure from Catherine's nephew, Charles V, transferring the case to Rome, subsequently pronouncing a deferred sentence of excommunication on Henry on July 11, 1533 (later imposed by his successor, Paul III, in 1538), and voiding his divorce and remarriage. The English Church went into schism.

Clement VII also failed to check the spread of the Reformation in the Scandinavian countries and in Switzerland and showed no sympathy for the reform movements already at work within the Church, for example, the Oratory of Divine Love (whose members included the future Pope Paul IV) and the activities of those who would found major religious orders such as the Jesuits, Capuchins, and Ursulines. (Clement's successor, Paul III, would approve these groups and inaugurate the reformist Council of Trent in 1545.)

True to the Medici tradition, Clement VII was a patron of great artists like Michelangelo, Raphael, and Cellini and of political theorists like Niccolò Macchiavelli. He commissioned Michelangelo to paint the *Last Judgment* in the Sistine Chapel and to fashion monuments to the memory of his family in the Sagrestia Nuova of San Lorenzo in Florence. Clement VII died on September 25, 1534, and was buried in the basilica of Santa Maria sopra Minerva.

218 Paul III, *1468–1549, pope from October 13, 1534, to November 10, 1549 (if he was not yet ordained a bishop at the time of his election, his pontificate would begin on November 3, assuming he was consecrated a bishop as well* *as crowned on that day; on the other hand, he was already cardinal-bishop of Ostia when elected; see below for the reason for the confusion—he had been bishop of several dioceses before he was even ordained a priest).*

A leading pope of the Counter-Reformation, Paul III convened the Council of Trent in 1545.

Born Alessandro Farnese, he was sixty-seven years of age, dean of the College of Cardinals, and cardinal-bishop of Ostia when unanimously elected pope on October 13, 1534, after a two-day conclave. (He had been a serious candidate in the conclaves of 1521 and 1523, but was opposed by the Colonna and Medici families.) He wanted to take the name Honorius IV, but the cardinals objected and he chose instead the name Paul III after the man who was pope when Alessandro was born. Paul III's election was greeted with delirious joy and excitement because he was the first Roman to be elected pope in 103 years. He was crowned on November 3. He had been treasurer of the Holy See and cardinal-deacon under appointment of Alexander VI (1439), bishop of Corneto and Montefiascone, and then bishop of Parma in 1509, all before his ordination to the priesthood in 1519! He had held off ordination in order to continue his promiscuous lifestyle, fathering four illegitimate children by a noble Roman mistress. His nickname was "Cardinal Petticoat" because his sister Giulia had been Alexander VI's mistress. After his ordination he allied himself with the reformers in the Curia.

Paul III was a Renaissance pope in the fullest sense of the word. He loved to hunt, patronized artists and writers, appointed prominent theologians to professorships in the Roman university, contributed valuable manuscripts to the Vatican Library, commissioned Michelangelo to complete the *Last Judgment* in the Sistine Chapel (after Paul censured Michelangelo for the nudity of his figures, the artist depicted the pope among the damned with a donkey's ear and a serpent around his body), and initiated the construction of the Palazzo Farnese as a tribute to his family. He also staged masked balls, held splendid banquets, and revived the carnival. His nepotism was also in the Renaissance tradition. Two months after his election he named two of his grandsons cardinals, at ages fourteen and sixteen, respectively, and then gave them important church offices. On the other hand, he also made some excellent appointments to the College of Cardinals, including Gian (Giovanni) Pietro Carafa (later Paul IV), Reginald Pole (archbishop of Canterbury and papal legate in England), St. John Fisher (a leading defender of the Catholic faith in England), Giovanni Morone (a leading reformist bishop), Marcello Cervini (later Marcellus II), and Gasparo Contarini (a leading lay reformer).

Paul III is listed among the popes of Catholic reform because of his tentative efforts toward the renewal of the Church, culminating in the Council of Trent in 1545. That council only met after several false starts. Paul III originally announced the council for Mantua in 1537 and then for Vicenza in 1538, but both had to be postponed because of objections from the emperor, Charles V, and King Francis I of France. He formed a commission of cardinals in 1536 to examine the state of the Church. Its scathing report became the basis for the Council of Trent. On December 17, 1538, the pope excommunicated Henry VIII (Clement VII's earlier sentence having been suspended) and placed England under interdict (an ecclesiastical penalty that prohibited the administration of the sacraments). The European powers, however, refused to accede to the pope's wishes that they impose sanctions of their own against England. England drifted further away from Rome. At the same time, however, the pope promoted the reform of religious orders and the development of new ones, including the Society of Jesus (or Jesuits), which he formally approved on September 27, 1540. Alas, he also established the Congregation of the Roman Inquisition (also known as the Holy Office and today as the Congregation for the Doctrine of the Faith) on July 21, 1542, granting it wide-ranging and punitive powers of censorship.

Only after the Peace of Crépy on September 18, 1544, ending the war between France and the empire, was the pope able to hold the general council he had always wanted. (The persistent state of war between the two powers made it impossible for the pope to mount a crusade against the Turks, who were threatening the coasts of Italy and Christian outposts in the East.) The council opened on December 13, 1545, in Trent, a northern Italian city recommended by the emperor. The pope was represented by various legates. The council did not meet the expectations of the Reformers, who had hoped for a more representative body (to include some of the Reformers themselves), or of the emperor, who urged that it confine its agenda to matters of discipline and reform so as not to upset the Lutherans.

The opening Mass of the Holy Spirit in Trent's cathedral was attended by four cardinals, four archbishops, twenty-one bishops, five generals of religious orders, and fifty theologians and canon lawyers. The first seven sessions were concerned with the relationship between Scripture and tradition, original sin, justification, and the seven sacraments. When renewed tension developed between the pope and the emperor, the pope used an outbreak of typhus as an excuse for moving the council to Bologna, a city within the papal sphere of influence, on March 11, 1547. However, the emperor objected and forbade the German and Spanish bishops to attend (he was also king of Spain). Paul III, therefore, had no option but to suspend the eighth session on February 1, 1548 (the suspension was not formally published until September of the following year).

His last years were marred by family difficulties. In 1545 he had given control of Parma and Piacenza (then duchies within the Papal States) to his undeserving son Pierluigi, an enemy of the emperor. Four years later Pierluigi was murdered and the emperor Charles V claimed the two duchies for his own son-in-law, Ottavio, who was also the pope's grandson. The pope on his deathbed forgave Ottavio and ordered Parma to be given to him. Paul III died of violent fever on November 10, 1549, at age eighty-one and was buried in St. Peter's. His tomb by Michelangelo's student Giacomo della Porta is considered one of the basilica's finest.

219 Julius III, *1487–1555, pope from February 8, 1550, to March 23, 1555.*

During Julius III's pontificate, the Council of Trent was reconvened for a year (1551–52). Born Giovanni Maria de' Ciocchi del Monte, he was elected pope on February 8, 1550, in a conclave that lasted ten weeks. The English cardinal Reginald Pole missed election by a single vote (he reached twenty-five votes, but needed twenty-six for the required two-thirds for victory). Ciocchi del Monte was elected only after a compromise was forged between the French and Farnese (those created by the Farnese pope, Paul III) cardinals, against the strong opposition of the emperor Charles V (who resented the cardinal's role in attempting to move the Council of Trent to Bologna in 1547). Before election, Cardinal Ciocchi del Monte had been an assistant (chamberlain) to Julius II, which is why he chose his name. He had also been bishop of Pavia, governor of Rome (twice), successor to his uncle as archbishop of Siponto, cardinal-priest in the title of Santi Vitalis, Gervase, and Protase, and then cardinal-bishop of Palestrina and a copresident of the Council of Trent (with Cardinals Cervini and Pole). He was crowned on February 22. He took possession of the Lateran Basilica, the pope's cathedral church, on June 24.

In spite of his strong canonical background, Julius III proved to be a typical Renaissance pope, given to hunting, banqueting, the theater, advancing the interests of his family, and an assortment of other sensual pleasures. He created a scandal because of his infatuation with a fifteen-year-old boy whom he picked up in the streets of Parma, had his brother adopt, and then made a cardinal and head of the Secretariat of State. (The boy ended up in prison for criminal activity.) Because of a preelection oath he had sworn with other cardinals at the conclave, he reconvened the Council of Trent on May 1, 1551, with the gratitude and support of the emperor Charles V. King Henry II of France, however, forbade

French participation. There were several sessions (eleven through sixteen), some of which were attended by German Protestants. But the council had to be suspended once again because of the German-French war precipitated by the pope's effort to expel the pro-French Ottavio Farnese (Paul III's grandson) from Parma. When the combined papal and imperial forces were defeated by the French, the German princes revolted against Charles V and the council lost its main political support.

The pope retired to his new, luxurious villa (Villa Giulia, at the Porto del Popolo), where he spent most of his time on idle pursuits, interrupted by occasional ventures into church business. For example, he confirmed the constitution of the new Society of Jesus (Jesuits) on July 21, 1550, and at the urging of St. Ignatius of Loyola established the German College in Rome to train German diocesan priests to restore Catholicism to their country. When the Catholic Queen Mary succeeded Edward VI to the English throne on July 6, 1553, Julius III appointed Cardinal Reginald Pole, a relative of the queen, as legate in England. On November 30 Pole solemnly absolved England from the papal interdict placed upon it by Julius III's predecessor, Paul III.

The pope also appointed Marcello Cervini (the future Marcellus II) as Vatican librarian, Michelangelo as chief architect for the new St. Peter's, and the composer Palestrina as choirmaster of the Cappella Giulia (Julian Chapel) in St. Peter's. He died of gout (from which he had suffered for years) on March 23, 1555, and was buried in the crypt of St. Peter's.

220 Marcellus II, *1501–55, pope from April 10 to May 1, 1555 (the Vatican's official list begins his pontificate on the day of his election, April 9, but since he was not yet a bishop, he could not become Bishop of Rome until consecrated the following day).*

One of only two popes in modern times to retain his baptismal name as pope (the other was Hadrian VI in 1522), Marcellus II died of a stroke before he could implement his ambitious reform program. Born Marcello Cervini, he served as administrator of three Italian dioceses, cardinal-priest of Santa Croce in Gerusalemme, papal legate to the imperial court, one of three copresidents of the Council of Trent, and head of the Vatican Library. As head of a reform commission first established by Paul III, he was so critical of the nepotism and lifestyle of his predecessor, Julius III, that he had to retire to his diocese of Gubbio. Few papal elections held out such high promise for reform. Unanimously elected on April 9, 1555, and consecrated a bishop and crowned the next day (even though opposed by the emperor), he drastically reduced the expenses for his coronation and decreased the size of the Curia. To prevent nepotism from infecting his pontificate as it had so many others before him, he forbade his relatives from coming to Rome. He gathered all the reform documents prepared under Julius III with the intention of promulgating them in a single papal bull. After only twenty-one days as Bishop of Rome, Marcellus died of a stroke on May 1 and was buried simply in the crypt of St. Peter's Basilica. He is memorialized in Palestrina's *Missa Papae Marcelli*.

221 Paul IV, *1476–1559, pope from May 23, 1555, to August 18, 1559.*

At first hailed as a reformer, Paul IV soon showed himself to be a pope in the old medieval style: authoritarian, triumphalistic, censorious, and intolerant. He created the Index of Forbidden Books.

Born Gian (Giovanni) Pietro Carafa, he had been a model bishop of Chiete (or Theate), where he founded a religious order known as the Theatines, dedicated to a life of strict poverty and to church reform. He was also a papal legate to England, archbishop of Brindisi, and nuncio to Flanders and Spain. Although known as a reformer, he was hostile to all efforts at reconciliation with the Lutherans, and as head of the reactivated Inquisition he exercised his authority with unusually brutal severity. He was appointed a cardinal in 1536, archbishop of Naples in 1549, and dean of the College of Cardinals in 1553. The conclave of some forty cardinals was divided between pro-French and pro-imperial factions. Neither could elect their own candidate, so the conclave turned finally to their seventy-nine-year-old dean, Cardinal Carafa, and unanimously elected him pope on May 23, 1555, over the opposition of the emperor Charles V. He took the name Paul IV to honor the memory of the pope (Paul III) who named him a cardinal. Three days later he was crowned in St. Peter's Square with great solemnity and splendor. He took possession of his cathedral church, the Lateran Basilica, on October 28.

Paul IV's ventures into politics were generally marked by failure. His involvement in a war against Spain ended in defeat. On political-ecclesiastical matters he fared no better. He denounced the Peace of Augsburg (1555), which recognized the coexistence of Catholics and Protestants in Germany, and upon the death of Queen Mary I of England in 1558 he insisted on the restitution of all church properties and demanded that Queen Elizabeth I submit all of her claims to him. The fortunes of Protestantism in England were immeasurably aided by the pope's behavior.

He was strongly opposed to the reconvening of the Council of Trent, because he felt he could wage war against the Protestants more effectively on his own. He tried to set up a kind of para-council consisting of a commission of some sixty prelates, but it never fulfilled its purpose. He then turned his attention to the Roman Inquisition, increasing its authority and regularly attending its sessions. So extreme was his sense of ortho-doxy that he had an innocent man like Cardinal Giovanni Morone im-prisoned for heresy in Castel Sant'Angelo. In 1557 he instituted the Index of Forbidden Books, severely restricting the reading and writing of books. Because he suspected Jews of aiding the Protestants, he restricted them to ghettos in Rome and the Papal States and compelled them to wear distinctive headgear.

On the positive side, Paul IV was generally careful in his choice of car-dinals (although he made his unworthy nephew Carlo a cardinal and pro-moted other relatives to lucrative benefices), and he insisted that bishops reside in their dioceses and monks in their monasteries (even ordering the arrest of those who were found in Rome outside of their monaster-ies). Because of his harshness and nepotism, however, he and his family were despised in Rome. Upon his death on August 18, 1559, rioting crowds destroyed the headquarters of the hated Inquisition and released its pris-oners. The pope's statue on the Capitol was toppled and disfigured. Paul IV was buried in the basilica of Santa Maria sopra Minerva.

222 Pius IV, 1499–1565, December 25, 1559, to December 9, 1565.

Pius IV provided a strikingly positive contrast to his predecessor, Paul IV. A reformist pope, he reconvened the Council of Trent after a suspension of ten years.

Born Gian (Giovanni) Angelo de' Medici (no relation to the famous Florentine family), he had held a number of diplomatic and political po-sitions under Paul III (1534–49), including governor of Parma in the Papal States, and, while still a layman, he was appointed archbishop of Ragusa (Sicily) and, four years later (1549), created a cardinal-priest in the title of Santa Pudenziana (and later in the title of Santa Prisca) by Paul III. He held a curial position under Julius III (1550–55), whose elec-tion he had supported, but was in general disfavor with Paul IV, his own predecessor, because he disagreed with the pope's anti-Spanish attitude. At the conclave following Paul IV's death, the French and Spanish fac-tions in the College of Cardinals were deadlocked after almost four months. Then a third group, led by Cardinal Carlo Carafa (Paul IV's nephew), rallied behind Cardinal de' Medici and he was elected pope by acclamation on Christmas Eve. The vote was canonically confirmed on Christmas morning, December 25, 1559. The newly elected pope took the name Pius, he said, because he wanted to be "pious" in both name and deed. Once again, it should be noted, a papal conclave elected a man very different from the deceased pope. In contrast to the severe and autocratic Paul IV, Pius IV was warm and friendly. He was crowned on January 6,

1560. (Significantly, he had been born on Easter, elected pope on Christmas, and crowned on Epiphany.)

Pius IV immediately rehabilitated Cardinal Giovanni Morone, who had been imprisoned by Paul IV under suspicion of heresy, revoked the arrest warrants for vagrant monks, reined in the Inquisition, and began revision of the complicated Index of Forbidden Books. He also reestablished friendly relations with the Hapsburgs, Philip II of Spain and the emperor Ferdinand I, and filled the vacant nunciatures in Vienna, Venice, and Florence. However, he also placed on trial two of Paul IV's despised nephews, Cardinal Carlo Carafa and Giovanni, duke of Palino. They were found guilty of instigating the war against Spain, of murder, and of other crimes and were executed. It is one of the enigmas of Pius IV's otherwise positive reign that he should have treated Cardinal Carafa so harshly after he had worked so effectively for his election to the papacy.

Although Pius IV indulged in a favorite Renaissance practice of nepotism, one of his choices proved remarkably fortunate. Within a week of his coronation, he appointed his young lay nephew Carlo Borromeo (d. 1584) as cardinal-archbishop of Milan, where he proved himself an able and committed reformer. Borromeo opened seminaries for the education of future priests, challenged his clergy to live more moral lives, established a Confraternity of Christian Doctrine for children, and, often with his own money, cared for the poor and the sick, particularly during the plague of 1576. He also served his uncle, Pius IV, as secretary of state. Borromeo was canonized a saint in 1610.

The most important initiative of Pius IV's pontificate, however, was his reconvening, after a ten-year suspension, of the Council of Trent in 1562 (which he had pledged to do in the conclave that elected him) and his guiding the council to a successful conclusion the following year. One of the developments that contributed to its urgency was the advance of Calvinism in France. The only question facing the pope was whether to continue the old council, as the king of Spain, Philip II, preferred, or to call a new council, as the German emperor Ferdinand I wished, because Ferdinand still had hopes of forging some reconciliation with the Lutherans in his territories. Pius IV's bull of convocation (*Ad ecclesiam regimen*, November 29, 1560) evaded the issue, but when the council assembled at Trent on January 18, 1562, it basically resumed the agenda that had been set aside ten years earlier. Not without some difficulty, the pope maintained control over its proceedings, with the invaluable help of its president, Cardinal Morone. The council adjourned on December 4, 1563, at its twenty-fifth session, and Pius IV orally confirmed its decrees on January 26, 1564, and formally in his bull *Benedictus Deus* on June 30, 1564. Then began the difficult task of implementing the council's decrees.

The pope established a congregation of cardinals to supervise their enforcement, and he himself ordered bishops present in Rome to return to their dioceses and to take up residence there. In March 1564, he published the council's Index of Forbidden Books. Since the council had left the question of Communion in both kinds (consecrated bread and consecrated wine) to the pope's discretion, Pius IV allowed the practice of offering the chalice to the laity at the discretion of the bishops in Germany, Austria, Hungary, and other regions where Protestantism was strong. However, he deferred the question of married priests. On November 13, 1564, he ordered bishops, superiors, and professors to subscribe to the new "Tridentine Profession of Faith." He set in motion the compilation of a new catechism and the reform of the Roman Missal and the Divine Office.

In spite of all his efforts toward reform, Pius IV was unable to stem the Protestant tide in Germany, France, and England (he refrained from excommunicating Queen Elizabeth I in the hope of eventual reconciliation). Because the Papal States were in such poor financial condition (their treasury having been depleted from Paul IV's war against Spain), Pius IV had to raise new taxes, which, in turn, provoked widespread dissatisfaction with him and even a failed attempt on his life.

Unlike his predecessor, Pius IV revived the Renaissance tradition of papal generosity toward artists, architects, and scholars; revived the Roman university, staffing it with a strong faculty; established a printing press for the publication of Christian texts; and adorned the city, in collaboration with Michelangelo, with new buildings and churches such as the Porta Pia and Santa Maria degli Angeli within the Baths of Diocletian, and parts of the dome and other sections of the new St. Peter's. He also saw the completion of the Borgo Pio, a section of the city between the Castel Sant'Angelo and the Vatican, and the Villa Pia within the Vatican Gardens. After suffering over a long period of time with gout, Pius IV died on December 9, 1565. He was buried first in St. Peter's, but in January 1583 his remains were transferred to the church of Santa Maria degli Angeli, which he had built.

223 Pius V, St., *1504–72, pope from January 7, 1566, to May 1, 1572.*

Pius V enforced the decrees of the Council of Trent, published the *Roman Catechism,* reformed the Roman Missal and the Roman Breviary (Divine Office), and excommunicated Queen Elizabeth I of England. Although later canonized as a saint, he was a harsh enforcer of orthodoxy and probably an anti-Semite.

Born Antonio (Michele) Ghislieri of poor parents, he was a shepherd until he became a Dominican at age fourteen, taking as his religious name Michele. After ordination to the priesthood as a Dominican (1528), he served as an inquisitor for Como and Bergamo. So zealous was he that he came to the notice of Cardinal Gian (Giovanni) Pietro Carafa (later Paul IV), who recommended him to Julius III for appointment to the Roman Inquisition in 1551. When Carafa became pope, he named his protégé as bishop of Nepi and Sutri (1556), then a cardinal of the titular church of Santa Maria sopra Minerva (1557), headquarters of the Dominican order, and then grand inquisitor, or commissary general, of the Roman Inquisition (1558). Because of his closeness to the Carafa family and his severity as an inquisitor, he was not in favor with Pius IV, who appointed him bishop of Mondovi in 1560. Cardinal Alessandrino (as he was then called, after his native city, Alessandria) was elected pope on January 7, 1566, after a nineteen-day conclave, with the strong support of Cardinal (later St.) Charles Borromeo (d. 1584), who, for the good of the Church, overlooked the great differences between Alessandrino and his late uncle, Pius IV. Pius V was crowned on January 19. He did away with the traditional pomp and feasting, insisting that they were anachronistic and offensive to the poor.

The new pope's agenda was simple and straightforward: to implement the decrees of the Council of Trent, which had adjourned two years earlier. First, he imposed strict standards of lifestyle on himself, those in the Curia, and the city of Rome itself. He continued to follow a monastic regimen for himself (including the practice of simple, solitary meals, which remained a papal custom until the mid-twentieth century), and some of his contemporaries even accused him of trying to impose monasticism upon others as well, including the entire Roman citizenry. He continued to wear his white Dominican habit, which became the standard dress for subsequent popes. He opposed nepotism (although he made his grand-nephew and fellow Dominican Michele Bonelli a cardinal and secretary of state), insisted that clerics reside in their pastoral assignments, and maintained a careful watch over religious orders (he abolished the Humiliati altogether). Faithful to Trent's decrees, he published the *Roman Catechism* in 1566, a revised Roman Breviary in 1568, and a revised Roman Missal in 1570. The latter two brought uniformity for the first time to the celebration of the Mass and the recitation of the Divine Office. He restricted the use of indulgences (whose sale had been a major factor in provoking the Protestant Reformation) and dispensations (relaxations of church laws in individual cases). To promote the Tridentine reforms in Rome and in Italy generally, he personally visited the Roman basilicas and sent apostolic (papal) visitors to the Papal States and Naples. He also saw to the circulation of the decrees outside of Italy and beyond Europe.

Pius V's intense commitment to stamp out heresy (a throwback to his earlier years as an inquisitor, including grand inquisitor, or commissary general, of the Roman Inquisition) led him to an inordinate reliance upon the Inquisition and its often inhuman methods. He built a new palace for it (the old one having been destroyed by Roman mobs out of contempt for the deceased Paul IV), toughened its rules and practices, and personally attended its sessions. Many distinguished individuals were tried and sentenced under Pius V, but he still blamed himself for being too lenient! He was also unusually severe on the Jews. He allowed some to remain in Rome's ghettos and in Ancona for commercial reasons, but otherwise his policy was to expel Jews from the Papal States. In 1571, after he established the new Congregation of the Index, a curial office to oversee the Index of Forbidden Books, hundreds of printers fled to Germany and Switzerland. On the other hand, in 1567 he declared his fellow Dominican St. Thomas Aquinas (d. 1274) a Doctor of the Church and in 1570 sponsored the publication of a new edition of his works in seventeen volumes.

Pius V's political activities were largely counterproductive. He alienated the Catholic rulers, whose support and goodwill he needed, by rehabilitating the disgraced Carafa family and by his hard-line stand against state control of the Church, given in a bull that contained inflated claims of papal authority. His excommunication and putative deposition of Queen Elizabeth I of England—the last such papal excommunication of a reigning monarch—exposed English Catholics to persecution, imprisonment, torture, and execution. And it also antagonized Spain, France, and the empire. In France, Pius V gave financial and military assistance to the regent Catherine de Médicis to encourage her opposition to the Huguenots (French Calvinists), only to see her grant freedom of religion to the Huguenots in the Peace of Saint-Germain in 1570. The pope angered the emperor Maximilian II when he (the pope) presumed to nominate a new grand duke of Tuscany. And he was in constant conflict with his most natural ally, King Philip II of Spain, concerning royal control over the Church. His one significant achievement on the political-military front was the victory of his Holy League (with Spain and Venice) over the Turkish fleet at Lepanto in the Gulf on Corinth on October 7, 1571. The victory ended Turkish superiority in the Mediterranean. Because Pius V attributed his success to the Blessed Virgin (the Rosary Confraternity of Rome had met at the basilica of Santa Maria sopra Minerva to pray for victory), he declared October 7 the feast of Our Lady of Victory (changed by his successor, Gregory XIII, to the feast of the Most Holy Rosary).

Pius V died on May 1, 1572, at age sixty-eight and was buried first in St. Peter's; in 1588 his remains were transferred to a splendid tomb in the basilica of Santa Maria Maggiore (St. Mary Major). He was beatified on May 1, 1672, by Clement X and canonized on May 22, 1712, by Clement XI. Feast day: April 30.

224 Gregory XIII, *1502–85, pope from May 13, 1572, to April 10, 1585.*

Gregory XIII is best known for the Gregorian calendar (1582), still in use today, which reformed the Julian calendar by dropping ten days and introducing a leap year every fourth year. He also reconstructed and endowed the Jesuit-run Roman College, which was later (and still is) called the Gregorian University.

Born Ugo Buoncompagni, he was ordained a priest at about the age of forty. Given his strong legal and administrative experience, he undertook diplomatic missions for Paul IV in 1556 and 1557 and then was appointed bishop of Vieste in 1558. He took an active part in the Council of Trent from 1561 to 1563 and, in recognition of his services there, was created a cardinal-priest of San Sisto in 1565 and papal legate to Spain. His successful mission in Spain won the admiration of King Philip II, who exerted great influence on Cardinal Buoncompagni's election as pope on May 13, 1572, after a conclave of less than twenty-four hours. He took the name Gregory XIII out of respect for St. Gregory the Great (590–604), whom he had regarded as his protector since infancy. He was crowned on May 20, the feast of Pentecost. (The first choice of the conclave had been Cardinal Alessandro Farnese, nephew of Paul III, but he was vetoed by the king of Spain, Philip II. The veto was delivered to the conclave by Cardinal Granvella. The right of imperial veto was finally eliminated by Pius X in 1904.)

The new pope had a more accommodating personality than his predecessor (once again, contrary to conventional assumptions, a papal conclave had chosen someone clearly different from the previous pope). On the other hand, Gregory XIII, influenced by St. Charles Borromeo (d. 1584), was also determined to promote the decrees of the Council of Trent and Catholic reform generally. He placed a high priority on bishops' living in their dioceses, and he transformed nunciatures from purely diplomatic posts to instruments of church reform. To ensure a better-educated clergy, he established at great expense colleges in Rome and in other cities and entrusted them largely to the Jesuits. In Rome he reconstructed and generously endowed the Roman College (1572), which was later named the Gregorian University in his honor, secured the future of the German College, and established the English College (1579). He also founded a Greek, a Maronite, an Armenian, and a Hungarian college (the last was subsequently merged with the German College).

But like his predecessor, Pius V, there was a hard side to Gregory XIII as well. Thus, when news of the St. Bartholomew's Day massacre of Huguenots (Calvinists) in France reached Rome in late August 1572, he celebrated the event with a solemn *Te Deum* (a fourth-century hymn of praise sung on special occasions) and other thanksgiving services. He encouraged Philip II of Spain to consider launching an attack on Elizabeth I of England from the Netherlands or Ireland. When his hopes for an invasion from Ireland were dashed, he actively supported plots to assassinate the queen. He lost an opportunity to restore Sweden to communion with Rome when he rejected the Swedish king's request that priests be allowed to marry, that Communion be given under both kinds (consecrated bread and consecrated wine), and that the practice of invoking the saints be suppressed. The country remained—and remains—Lutheran.

Gregory XIII was a strong supporter of the Jesuits. He supported their missions in India, China, Japan, and Brazil as well as their work in Europe and completed work on the Gesù, the mother church of the Jesuits. He also approved the Congregation of the Oratory of Philip Neri (d. 1595) in 1575 and the reform of the Carmelites by Teresa of Ávila (d. 1582) in 1580 (the Discalced Carmelites, however, did not become a separate order until 1593). He saw to the production of a new edition of the *Corpus of Canon Law,* as mandated by the Council of Trent, and the reform of the Julian calendar in 1582. The new calendar involved the dropping of ten days (October 5–14, 1582) and the adding of a leap year. The calendar, subsequently named after him (thus, the Gregorian calendar), was adopted by Catholic states, but Protestant states waited for more than a century. He also declared a Jubilee year in 1575 that brought over three hundred thousand pilgrims to Rome.

His support of schools and missions, of various military enterprises against England and the Turks, and of various building projects in Rome cost the papacy great sums of money. In the last years of his pontificate, he faced serious disorders and banditry in Rome and the Papal States as nobles, dispossessed of their lands by a pope in need of revenue, struck back in desperation. Gregory XIII died on April 10, 1585, and was buried in St. Peter's.

225 Sixtus V, *1520–90, pope from April 24, 1585, to August 27, 1590.*

Sixtus V set the maximum number of cardinals at seventy, a total not exceeded until the pontificate of John XXIII (1958–63), reorganized the Roman Curia in a fashion that remained unchanged until the Second Vatican Council (1962–65), and instituted the practice of bishops' visiting the Holy See at least once every five years to submit reports on the state of their dioceses.

Born Felice Peretti, a farmworker's son, he joined the Franciscans at age twelve, was ordained a priest, earned a doctorate in theology, and soon earned a reputation as a great preacher. He served as inquisitor for

Venice, procurator general and then vicar general of the Franciscan order, and bishop of Sant'Agata dei Goti before his appointment by Pius V as cardinal in 1570. (He was the pope's confessor.) Cardinal Montalto (as he was known because he had been educated by the Franciscans of Montalto) was appointed bishop of Fermo the next year, but, because he was out of favor with the new pope, Gregory XIII, he spent most of his time in semiretirement at his villa on the Esquiline. (Gregory XIII suspended his pension, but the grand duke of Tuscany made up for the loss.) As a result he was an unknown quantity at the conclave following Gregory's death—except to a small but powerful circle of friends, who exploited the division in the College of Cardinals between the Medici and Farnese factions, on the one hand, and the French and Spanish, on the other, and saw to his unanimous election as pope on April 24, 1585. He took the name Sixtus V out of respect for his fellow Franciscan Sixtus IV (1471–84). He was crowned on May 1.

The new pope immediately addressed the problem of lawlessness in the Papal States. Employing the harshest measures of repression, including public executions and the exposure of bandits' heads on the bridge of Sant'Angelo, he finally brought the situation under control over a period of two years. He also replenished the papal treasury by shrewd economic and agricultural policies, cutting expenditures, raising new taxes, selling church offices (the sin of simony), and floating loans. He established himself as one of the richest and most financially independent princes in all of Europe.

His place in papal and church history, however, is linked with his reorganization of the Roman Curia. In 1586 he fixed the maximum number of cardinals at seventy (not exceeded until the pontificate of John XXIII [1958–63]). His own appointments to the College of Cardinals were of generally high quality, but he shocked his contemporaries when he appointed his fifteen-year-old nephew. He reorganized the Secretariat of State in 1588, with fifteen permanent congregations of cardinals, six to supervise secular affairs and eight for spiritual affairs. As a result, the consistory of cardinals (a body that sometimes regarded itself as coruler with the pope) declined in importance. In 1585 he revived the requirement that bishops visit the Holy See at least once every five years to report on the state of their dioceses. These visits, still in force, are known as *ad limina* visits (Lat., "to the thresholds [of the tombs of the Apostles]"). He also hastily published a revised version of the Vulgate Bible, in accordance with the mandate of the Council of Trent, but it was so filled with errors that it had to be withdrawn after his death. Unlike his predecessor, Gregory XIII, Sixtus V was generally cool to the Jesuits while partial to his fellow Franciscans. He made St. Bonaventure (d. 1274) a Doctor of the Church.

On the political and international fronts, Sixtus was less successful. He made no headway against the Turks (although he imagined himself creating a Christian state around the Holy Sepulchre in Jerusalem), saw the Spanish Armada (whose building he aided) defeated by the English in 1588, and failed in his efforts to stem the tide of Protestantism in France. He did promote missionary efforts in Japan, China, the Philippines, and South America.

Sixtus V devoted himself to the transformation of the city of Rome from a Renaissance to a Baroque city. He changed the layout of its main streets, linking the seven pilgrimage churches and placing four great obelisks at key sites (including St. Peter's Square), drained marshes, and built twenty-mile-long aqueducts for a new water supply. He rebuilt the Lateran Palace, enlarged the Quirinale (or Quirinal) Palace, and completed the dome of St. Peter's. He also constructed a new building for the Vatican Library and founded the Vatican Press. He died on August 27, 1590, at age sixty-nine, after several successive attacks of malaria. On hearing the news of his death, Roman mobs toppled his statue on the Capitol. He was buried in the basilica of Santa Maria Maggiore (St. Mary Major).

226 Urban VII, *1521–90, pope from September 15 to September 27, 1590.*

The pontificate of Urban VII was one of the shortest in history. He died before his coronation. Born Giovan Battista Castagna, he was the nephew of Cardinal Verallo. He served as papal legate to France, a curial official, archbishop of Rosanno (Rozzano), governor in the Papal States, an active participant in the Council of Trent (1562–63), nuncio to Spain, governor of Bologna, consultor (later inquisitor general) to the Holy Office, and a cardinal-priest of San Marcello al Corso (1583). When he was elected pope on September 15, 1590, many had great hopes that his would be a reformist but temperate pontificate. Although he had been in good health, the new pope contracted malaria the night after his election and died before his coronation could take place. Urban VII was buried in the basilica of Santa Maria sopra Minerva in Rome. He left a large amount of money for the care of impoverished girls.

227 Gregory XIV, *1535–91, pope from December 5, 1590, to October 16, 1591.*

The pontificate of Gregory XIV was one of the least popular and least successful in history, marred as it was by the appointment of his incompetent nephew as cardinal-secretary of state and by plague, food shortages, and lawlessness in Rome. Born Niccolò Sfondrati, he was a friend of

St. Charles Borromeo (d. 1584), was named bishop of Cremona at age twenty-five, served as an active participant on the side of reform at the third and last period of the Council of Trent (1562–63), and was appointed a cardinal in the title of Santa Cecilia in 1583. Although he had little curial experience, he was elected pope with the support of the pro-Spanish cardinals from a list of seven candidates after a faction-ridden conclave of more than two months. He took the name of the pope who made him a cardinal, Gregory, and was crowned on December 8.

Although only fifty-five years of age, he was physically weak and often in pain. The state of his health and his own insecurity about his lack of experience in the Curia led him to name his own twenty-nine-year-old nephew, Paolo Emilio Sfondrati, cardinal-secretary of state. Paolo, however, was more interested in his own and his family's well-being than in that of the Church. Resentment developed quickly among the other cardinals.

Politically, Gregory XIV abandoned the balanced approach of his predecessor, Sixtus V, to the rivalry between Spain and France and came down strongly on the side of Spain, which had supported his candidacy for the papacy. Ironically, his hard-line position against the Protestant King Henry IV brought moderate Catholics in France to Henry's side, and that hastened his eventual conversion to Catholicism.

Problems in the city of Rome—especially food shortages—were exacerbated by his nephew's incompetent administration. As he grew progressively weaker, Gregory XIV continued to fulfill his papal responsibilities from a sickbed. He called for the enforcement of residency requirements for bishops and defined the qualifications of candidates for the hierarchy, forbade Mass from being celebrated in private houses, and arranged for the revision of Sixtus V's defective edition of the Vulgate Bible. He also banned all gambling on papal elections, the length of a pontificate, or the creation of cardinals—practices that were evidently popular at the time. Gregory XIV died on October 16, 1591, and was buried in St. Peter's, in the Gregorian chapel next to the tomb of Gregory XIII.

228 Innocent IX, *1519–91, pope from October 29 to December 30, 1591.*

The third pope elected in a space of thirteen months, the elderly Innocent IX served only two months. Born Giovanni Antonio Facchinetti, he was bishop of Nicastro (which he later resigned for reasons of health), took an active part in the third and last phase of the Council of Trent (1562–63), was papal nuncio in Venice, where he helped forge the anti-Turkish alliance that defeated the Turks in the famous sea battle at Lepanto in 1571, served in the Roman Curia (including the Inquisition), was appointed titular patriarch of Jerusalem, and then was named a cardinal of Santi Quattro Coronati in 1583. Cardinal Facchinetti had been a serious candidate at previous conclaves. Although he was on Spain's list of acceptable candidates, even the anti-Spanish cardinals acceded to his election because of his age and fragile health. He was elected on October 29, 1591, and was crowned on November 3.

The new pope, as expected, pursued a pro-Spanish policy like his predecessor, Gregory XIV. Accordingly, he provided financial and military support to keep the pressure on the still Protestant Henry IV, king of France. He also took steps to deal with the persistent problem of lawlessness in Rome, regulated the course of the Tiber River, and completed work on the dome of St. Peter's. Within the Curia, he divided the Secretariat of State into three sections: one for France and Poland, one for Italy and Spain, and a third for Germany. Honoring a new tradition, he appointed his grandnephew Antonio Facchinetti to the College of Cardinals. Innocent IX fell ill on December 18 but insisted on making a pilgrimage to the seven pilgrimage churches of Rome. He died a few days later, on December 30, and was buried in a simple tomb in the crypt of St. Peter's Basilica. Perhaps because religious people often confuse a melancholic and withdrawn personality with sanctity, the deceased pope was venerated as a saint by many Romans. He was never beatified or canonized, however.

229 Clement VIII, *1536–1605, pope from February 3, 1592, to March 3, 1605 (the Vatican's official list begins his pontificate on the day of his election, January 30, but he was not yet a bishop and could not become Bishop of Rome until consecrated on February 3).*

The fourth pope elected within the space of only a year and four months, Clement VIII issued a corrected edition of the Vulgate Bible, expanded the Index of Forbidden Books, and increased the severity of the Inquisition.

Born Ippolito Aldobrandini, he served in a number of curial posts under Pius V (1566–72) and Sixtus V (1585–90), who made him a cardinal-priest in the title of San Pancrazio in 1585. A papal legate to Poland in 1588–89, he was a serious candidate for the papacy in the three previous conclaves of 1590–91. Although not a favorite of the pro-Spanish party, he had enough of its support to be elected on January 30, 1592. (The Spanish cardinals had tried to elect Cardinal Sartorio by acclamation, or "adoration," but they were blocked by Cardinals Altemps, Gesualdi, and Colonna, who demanded a regular canonical election.) The pope-elect was consecrated as Bishop of Rome on February 3 and crowned on February 9. He took the name Clement because his friend Philip Neri had once predicted that he would become pope someday and would take that name.

An ascetical person afflicted with gout, Clement VIII lived a traditionally pious and austere life, traveling on foot each month to the seven pilgrimage churches of Rome. He was a close friend of St. Philip Neri (d. 1595), founder of the Oratorians, and the celebrated historian Cesare Baronius (d. 1607) was his confessor. Among the cardinals he named were Baronius himself and the famous Jesuit theologian Robert Bellarmine (d. 1621), later canonized a saint. On the other hand, he had a taste for display and was inappropriately generous to his family. Although he had been a strong critic of nepotism when he himself was a cardinal, he named his nephews Cinzio and Pietro Aldobrandini to the College of Cardinals and turned the affairs of the Church over to them almost entirely. He also appointed a fourteen-year-old grandnephew to the college.

Clement VIII at least attempted to carry forward the reform movement launched by the Council of Trent (1545–63). He promoted the reform of religious houses, published a corrected version of the Vulgate Bible (which remained in force until the newer, more critical translations of the mid–twentieth century), and issued revised editions of a number of liturgical books, including the Pontifical, the Breviary, the Ceremonial, and the Roman Missal. However, he also expanded the Index of Forbidden Books, including a ban on all Jewish books. He increased the severity of the Inquisition which, during his pontificate, sent more than thirty people to the stake, including the former Dominican philosopher Giordano Bruno (1600). But his concern for orthodoxy was matched by an unnerving indecisiveness. Thus, he watched carefully the bitter theological dispute between the Jesuits and the Dominicans over the foreknowledge of God and the relationship between grace and free will (Does God know whether we will be saved or not? If so, what role does God play in the outcome? If a decisive role, what about our free will?), but he came to no conclusion about the debate, even after personally presiding over the commission he appointed to resolve the controversy.

In the political area, he came grudgingly in 1595 to recognize the now Catholic Henry IV as king of France and to absolve him of the excommunication imposed by Sixtus V ten years earlier. This meant, however, that Clement VIII had to accept the Edict of Nantes (1598) that granted religious freedom and civil equality to the Protestant Huguenots. At the same time, this act of recognition of Henry IV also freed the papacy from Spanish domination. Clement VIII mediated a peace between Spain and France in 1598 (the Treaty of Vervins). He failed, however, to organize an effective alliance of Christian powers against the Turks, who were then threatening Hungary and Austria. His hopes for James I's conversion and England's return to the Catholic fold also foundered, as did his dream of a Catholic restoration in Sweden.

Regarding matters more directly ecclesiastical, Clement VIII endorsed in 1595 proposals that were subsequently accepted by the Synod of Brest-Litovsk (1596), whereby millions of Orthodox Christians in Poland would join the Roman Catholic Church while retaining their liturgy. He appointed St. Francis de Sales (d. 1622) as coadjutor, then bishop of Geneva, to strengthen the Counter-Reformation in Switzerland. The Jubilee year he proclaimed for 1600 brought millions of pilgrims to Rome. Eighty thousand alone witnessed the opening of the Holy Door at St. Peter's on December 31, 1599. Clement VIII died on March 3, 1605, and was buried in St. Peter's. In 1646 his remains were transferred to a magnificent tomb in the Borghese Chapel (or "Paolina") in the basilica of Santa Maria Maggiore (St. Mary Major).

230 Leo XI, *1535–1605, pope from April 1 to April 27, 1605.*

A nephew of Leo X (1513–21), Leo XI was old and in poor health when elected and he served less than a month. Born Alessandro Ottaviano de' Medici, he was a favored disciple of St. Philip Neri (d. 1595), was named bishop of Pistoia in 1573, archbishop of Florence in 1574, cardinal in 1583, papal legate to France in 1596, cardinal-bishop of Albano in 1600, and then cardinal-bishop of Palestrina in 1602. He was elected pope on April 1, 1605, with strong support from France and equally strong opposition from Spain. (On the first ballot ten cardinals voted for the Jesuit theologian Robert Bellarmine, and twenty voted for the Oratorian Cesare Baronius. After Baronius's votes rose to thirty-seven in the second ballot, he urged his supporters not to vote for him.) Cardinal de' Medici took the name Leo XI out of respect for his uncle, Leo X, and was crowned on April 10. He became sick while taking possession of the Lateran Basilica (the pope's cathedral as Bishop of Rome) and died before the end of the month, on April 27. He was buried in St. Peter's.

231 Paul V, *1552–1621, pope from May 16, 1605, to January 28, 1621.*

In spite of his positive accomplishments, Paul V is best remembered as the pope who censured the famous astronomer Galileo for teaching that the earth revolves around the sun and for placing Copernicus's treatise on the Index of Forbidden Books.

Born Camillo Borghese, he served in the Roman Curia, was sent on a diplomatic mission to Spain, and was named a cardinal at age forty-four in the title of Sant'Eusebio in 1596, bishop of Iesi in the March of Ancona (1597–99), and vicar (i.e., the effective bishop) of Rome and inquisitor in 1603. His election to the papacy on May 16, 1605, at age fifty-three the youngest cardinal, was a great surprise to most people. The conclave of some fifty-nine cardinals present in Rome at first seemed ready to elect Cardinal Toschi di Modena, governor of Rome and an eminent jurist, by acclamation ("adoration" was the canonical term), but Cardinal Cesare Baronius intervened and strongly argued that Toschi was unworthy. Then the suddenly disoriented cardinals turned to Baronius himself, but he refused (as he had in the previous conclave). Cardinal Borghese was seen as an acceptable compromise between the rival factions, and he was elected. He was crowned on May 29 and took possession of the Lateran Basilica (the pope's cathedral in Rome) on November 6.

The new pope immediately had problems with the contemporary political powers, Catholic as well as Protestant, because of his inflated view of papal authority, particularly in the temporal order. Some Italian states yielded to him at first (Savoy, Genoa, Naples), but Venice resisted. It forbade the erection of new churches and the acquisition of land by the Church without permission from the senate. It also allowed two clerics (a bishop and an abbot) to go on trial in the secular courts. When Paul V's protests of December 1605 and March 1606 went unheeded, he excommunicated Venice's senate and placed the city under interdict (a canonical penalty denying the sacraments to those within the territory covered by the interdict). Venice, however, declared the interdict invalid, and most of the local clergy ignored it. The Jesuits, Theatines, and Capuchins observed it and were expelled for doing so. Other clergy were imprisoned. A spirited war of pamphlets ensued, with Cardinals Robert Bellarmine (d. 1621) and Cesare Baronius (d. 1607) defending the pope's position, and Fra Paolo Sarpi (d. 1623) defending the Republic of Venice's argument that the pope had no temporal authority. Only the intervention of King Henry IV of France prevented the defection of Venice to Protestantism. In April 1607 the interdict was lifted. Even though the imprisoned clergy were released, Paul V had suffered a serious moral defeat. The Jesuits continued to be excluded from the republic.

Paul V also confronted political problems in England and France. When the English Parliament required Catholics to swear an oath denying the pope's right to depose princes, Paul V denounced the oath and, with the support of the Jesuits (including Cardinal Robert Bellarmine), he forbade English Catholics from taking it. But this only divided the Catholics of that country because their archpriest George Blackwell had advised them to swear to it. He was replaced in 1608. In France, the pope's condemnation of Gallicanism (the view that the French Church is largely autonomous from Rome) provoked the Estates-General in 1614 to declare that the French king derives his authority from God alone, not the pope. The Estates-General also prohibited the promulgation of the decrees of the Council of Trent (1545–63) in France. The French clergy, however, voted to approve their publication in 1615.

On matters of church reform, Paul V renewed the obligation of episcopal residence (bishops' living in their dioceses), published the revised Roman Ritual, and tightened discipline in religious orders. He approved the use of the vernacular in the liturgy in China in 1615, and indefinitely postponed the debate between the Jesuits and the Dominicans over grace, free will, and God's foreknowledge that had erupted during the pontificate of Clement VIII (1592–1605). He approved the Congregation of the Oratory of St. Philip Neri in 1612, and the French Oratory of Pierre de Bérulle in 1613. On November 1, 1610, he canonized the great reformer cardinal Charles Borromeo (d. 1584) and Frances of Rome (d. 1440) and beatified other prominent reformers, namely, Ignatius of Loyola (d. 1556), Francis Xavier (d. 1552), Philip Neri (1595), and Teresa of Ávila (d. 1582).

In the city of Rome, Paul V completed the nave, façade (where he placed his name in giant letters), and portico (porch) of St. Peter's, erected many fountains (including one in St. Peter's Square), and improved the water supply to them by restoring two aqueducts, including the aqueduct of Trajan (renamed "Acqua Paoli"). He extended the Vatican Library and established a collection of secret Vatican archives. Alas, he was also vigilant in favor of the financial interests of his own family. By the end of his pontificate, the Borghese family was as wealthy and as powerful as the Orsini and Colonna families. The pope's nephew Cardinal Scipioni Cafarrelli Borghese, who served as the papal secretary of state, became so rich that he was able to build the famous Villa Borghese in Rome.

Unfortunately for his memory and place in history, Paul V is best remembered for having censured the famous astronomer Galileo Galilei (d. 1642) for advocating a scientific theory (valid, but not provable until the nineteenth century) espoused by the great Polish astronomer Nicolaus Copernicus (d. 1543), namely, that the earth revolves around the sun, not vice-versa. The Inquisition declared the theory incompatible with Sacred Scripture and ordered Galileo not to teach or seek to prove the theory. Copernicus's works were placed on the Index of Forbidden Books on March 5, 1616. (Galileo was brought before the Inquisition again in 1633, forced to renounce his position, and placed under house arrest for the remainder of his life. In 1979 John Paul II conceded that the Church had erred in its judgment against Galileo and in 1984 made all the relevant documents public.)

Paul V suffered a stroke while in procession during a service to celebrate a military victory over the Protestant Frederick V, short-lived king of Bohemia, in the battle of the White Mountain near Prague and died of a second stroke on January 28, 1621. He was buried first in St. Peter's and then in the magnificent Borghese Chapel (or "Paolina") in the basilica of Santa Maria Maggiore (St. Mary Major).

232 Gregory XV, *1554–1623, pope from February 9, 1621, to July 8, 1623.*

The first Jesuit-trained pope, Gregory XV decreed that papal elections should be conducted by secret ballot (a practice that remains in force today), founded the Sacred Congregation for the Propagation of the Faith, and canonized Teresa of Ávila, Philip Neri, and the two great Jesuits Ignatius of Loyola and Francis Xavier.

Born Alessandro Ludovisi, he held a variety of posts in the Roman Curia, served in diplomatic missions, became archbishop of Bologna in 1612 (where he initiated a number of reforms, especially in the area of the training and supervision of clergy), and was named a cardinal-priest in the title of Santa Maria in Trastevere in 1616 in recognition of his successful efforts in negotiating a peace between Savoy and Spain. In the conclave that followed Paul V's death, the cardinals first turned to Cardinal Robert Bellarmine, who refused election. Then they threw their support to Cardinal Frederico Borromeo, cousin of Charles (Carlo) Borromeo, but he, too, decisively refused. Finally, the cardinals turned to Cardinal Ludovisi, who was sixty-seven years old and in frail health. He accepted and was elected by acclamation on February 9, 1621, largely through the politicking of Paul V's nephew, Cardinal Borghese. He took the name Gregory XV in honor of Gregory XIII. He was crowned on February 14.

The new pope continued the now standard practice of appointing a trusted nephew as cardinal-secretary of state, the twenty-five-year-old Ludovico Ludovisi, who became extremely wealthy in office. He also moved to reform the system of papal elections out of concern for the external influences brought to bear upon them. In two separate decrees in 1621 and 1622, he ordered that, while election by acclamation should not be excluded (he himself had been elected in that manner), elections should normally occur after the conclave has been closed off from the public and that voting should be conducted by secret written ballot. No candidate can vote for himself; a two-thirds majority is required for victory; and each cardinal must take an oath that he is not voting for a candidate he thinks unqualified for the papacy.

In order to coordinate the Church's widespread missionary efforts, Gregory XV established the Congregation for the Propagation of the

Faith in 1622 and assigned thirteen cardinals to it. The new congregation became a virtual headquarters of the Counter-Reformation since the missionary efforts were directed not only to non-Christian lands but to those now under the control of Protestantism. Gregory XV also sent Cardinal Carlo Carafa to the imperial court to enlist the support of the emperor and the Catholic princes to the cause of Catholic restoration. Catholicism was reimposed in Bohemia and secured a majority among the five Palatine electors. The pope rewarded the anti-Calvinist policies of the French crown by raising Paris to a metropolitan see (1622).

On March 12, 1622, Gregory XV canonized as saints four well-known individuals beatified by his predecessor, Paul V, twelve years earlier: Teresa of Ávila (d. 1582), Philip Neri (d. 1595), and the two great Jesuits Ignatius of Loyola (d. 1556), founder of the Society of Jesus, and Francis Xavier (d. 1552), one of the Church's greatest missionaries of all time.

Gregory XV died in the Quirinale Palace on July 8, 1623, and was buried first in St. Peter's Basilica, but the remains of this Jesuit-trained pope were later moved (in 1634) to the newly completed church of Sant'Ignazio in Rome.

233 Urban VIII, *1568–1644, pope from August 6, 1623, to July 29, 1644.*

Although known for consecrating the new St. Peter's Basilica in 1626 and for selecting Castel Gandolfo as a papal summer residence (still in use today for that purpose), Urban VIII was a reckless nepotist who too often placed his family's interests ahead of the Church's.

Born Maffeo Barberini of wealthy parents, he served in the Roman Curia, then as nuncio to France (twice) and titular archbishop of Nazareth. In 1606 he was named a cardinal in the title of San Pietro in Montorio (exchanged in 1610 for San Onofrio), then bishop of Spoleto (1608), papal legate of Bologna (1611), and prefect of the Signatura of Justice, the highest court in the Church's judicial system (1617). He was elected pope on August 6, 1623, with fifty out of fifty-five votes after a literally and figuratively heated conclave, in which twelve of the cardinals became gravely ill with malaria. He was crowned on September 29.

The new pope appointed a brother and two nephews to the College of Cardinals, promoted other brothers to lucrative positions, and generally enriched all of his relatives so extravagantly that he suffered pangs of conscience in old age and consulted theologians about his use of papal revenues and whether it was lawful for his relatives to retain their possessions. (He was assured each time that everything was legally proper.) He consecrated the new St. Peter's Basilica on November 18, 1626, and commissioned the famous sculptor and architect Giovanni Lorenzo Bernini

(d. 1680) and other artists to beautify the basilica and the streets and pi-
azzas of Rome. He fortified the port of Civitavecchia and Castel Sant'Angelo and selected Castel Gandolfo, some fifteen miles southeast of Rome,
as a summer residence.

Urban VIII's pontificate overlapped with the Thirty Years' War
(1618–48), fought mainly in Germany. On one side were the German
Protestant princes and foreign powers (France, Sweden, Denmark, England), and on the other was the Holy Roman Empire, represented by the
Hapsburgs and the Hapsburg empire, which included Austria, Spain, Bohemia, most of Italy, and the southern part of the Netherlands. Although
Urban VIII strove to maintain neutrality in the conflict between France
and Spain, his sympathies were clearly with France because he feared
Hapsburg domination in Italy. Thus, he held back crucial financial and
political support from the emperor and tilted in favor of France and its
wily Cardinal Richelieu (d. 1642), even though Richelieu was siding with
the German and Swiss Protestant princes against the Catholic Hapsburgs
in order to maintain French independence from Rome. But the pope and
the Catholic Church paid a high price for such one-sided "neutrality" in
the Thirty Years' War. The Counter-Reformation in the empire was over.

Urban VIII took a personal role in the revising of the Breviary (Divine
Office), even rewriting some of the hymns himself. (His reforms were to
remain in place until the next reform, of Pius X in 1912.) He also revised
the Roman Missal and the Pontifical and significantly reduced the number of holy days of obligation (to thirty-four, not including Sundays!). He
also set down the procedures for canonizations and beatifications (the
latter were now reserved to the Holy See, as canonizations had been since
1234) and specified the grounds for excommunication. To promote the
Church's missionary work, he founded the Urban College of Propaganda
in Rome (1627) to train missionaries, enlarged the work of the Congregation for the Propaganda of the Faith, established a polyglot printing press,
and sent missionaries, including non-Jesuits for the first time, to the Far
East. In a bull dated April 22, 1639, he prohibited slavery of any kind
among the Indians of Brazil, Paraguay, and the entire West Indies. He approved new religious orders, including the Vincentians (founded by St.
Vincent de Paul) and the Visitation order (founded by St. Francis de Sales
and St. Jane Frances de Chantal). In fidelity to the Council of Trent
(1545–63), he decreed that all bishops, including cardinals, should reside
in their dioceses. It was also under Urban VIII that Galileo Galilei (d.
1642), although a personal friend, was condemned for a second time and
forced to renounce the Copernican system under threat of torture (1633).

In 1642 the pope censured the views of Cornelius Jansen (d. 1638) as
expressed in his work *Augustinus*. (The work, published two years after

Jansen's death, was controversial because its understanding of the relationship between grace and free will, with its apparent depreciation of
free will, seemed closer to Protestantism than to the Catholic tradition.)
The issue of Jansenism, however, would continue to disrupt and divide
the Church for decades and even generations to come, especially in
France and northern Europe.

As Urban VIII's pontificate drew to a close, he was drawn by his
greedy nephews into a disastrous war. On the pretext that the holder of
the papal fief of Castro had defaulted on his debts, the pope reclaimed
the fief for himself. The holder, Odoardo Farnese, the duke of Parma,
won support for his claim in France and in a league comprised of Venice,
Tuscany, and Modena. The pope suffered a humiliating defeat, not only
on the battlefield but in the treasury of the Papal States. The pope's use of
the bronze girders of the Pantheon for the making of guns and other ar-
maments prompted the epigram, "What the barbarians did not do the
Barberini did." When Urban VIII died on July 29, 1644, the Roman people, disgusted with his extravagances and shameless nepotism, were utterly jubilant. He was buried in St. Peter's and his monument was done
by the great Bernini himself.

234 Innocent X, 1574–1655, pope from September 15, 1644, to January 7, 1655.

Innocent X condemned Jansenism, a movement, based largely in France,
that many regarded as more Protestant than Catholic because of its
seeming depreciation of human free will.

Born Giovanni Battista Pamfili (Pamphili or Pamphilj), he served for
a long time as a judge of the Roman Rota (the second highest court in the
Holy See, which deals primarily with marriage cases), papal nuncio to
Naples and then to Spain, and titular patriarch of Antioch and was appointed a cardinal *in pectore* (Lat., "in the [pope's] breast," or secretly) in
1627 (announced in 1629). He was elected pope on September 15, 1644,
after a conclave lasting thirty-seven days because of the torrid Roman
heat and the outbreak of malaria among the cardinals. Once again, the
cardinals wanted to elect someone very different from his predecessor. In
this case, they wanted someone less pro-French than Urban VIII. Although Cardinal Pamfili's election was opposed by the French crown,
Cardinal Jules Mazarin's veto arrived too late. He took the name Innocent X in honor of his uncle, Cardinal Innocenzo del Bufalo. The new
pope was crowned on October 4.

Innocent X, already seventy years old, vented the anger and frustra-
tions of the cardinals against the Barberini family, which had been so
shamelessly enriched during Urban VIII's pontificate. He appointed a

commission to investigate their wealth and possessions, but Cardinal Mazarin, the powerful French minister, took the Barberini family under his personal protection and induced the pope to pardon them. Innocent X was not immune from the bug of nepotism, but he appointed none of his relatives to fill the now traditional role of the cardinal-nephew (whom popes from Paul III [1534–49] until the late seventeenth century employed as their most intimate adviser). A much more sinister influence in his papal court was his ambitious and greedy widowed sister-in-law, Donna Olimpia Maidalchini. Innocent X did nothing without consulting her. She was known around Rome as the "*papessa*" and was maliciously referred to as "*Olim pia*" (Lat., "formerly pious"). The pope, however, did not use her son and his nephew, Cardinal Camillo Pamfili, as his secretary of state, but gave that job instead to Cardinal Panciroli and then to Fabio Chigi (later Alexander VII), the first secretary of state who functioned as a normal diplomat, corresponding directly with nuncios and legates and signing letters and instructions.

The Thirty Years' War (1618–48) came to an end during Innocent X's pontificate, but he was unhappy with the terms of peace (the Peace of Westphalia) because they seemed to make too many concessions to the Protestants. The pope formally denounced the terms in a document dated October 24, 1648, but he delayed its publication until August 20, 1650, to avoid prejudicing the position of Catholics in Germany. The protest was ignored in any case. The war between France and Spain continued in spite of the peace, and the pope tended to favor Spain because it was a declining power that posed less of a threat to the Church in Italy.

Innocent X continued his predecessors' support of the missions. He increased the authority of the Congregation for the Propagation of the Faith and elevated the Dominican College in Manila to university status. However, he also approved a decree of the Propaganda that Chinese rituals were not to be used in the liturgy in China. On another matter, he established a commission in 1651 to examine Cornelius Jansen's *Augustinus* (published in 1640, two years after the author's death). The pope himself participated in some of the commission's sessions. On May 31, 1563, he published a bull, *Cum occasione,* that unconditionally condemned five propositions extracted from the work. Jansen's supporters, led by Antoine Arnauld (d. 1694), accepted the papal condemnation, but insisted that the condemned propositions were not to be found in the *Augustinus.*

During Innocent X's pontificate the interior decoration of the newly consecrated St. Peter's Basilica was completed, the Piazza Navona was restored and adorned with its famous fountains, and the Villa Doria Pamfili was erected at the Porta San Pancrazio. He also tried to make the prisons in the Papal States more humane, installing the cell system for separate living quarters. He proclaimed a Jubilee year in 1650 that was very successful. He died in the Quirinale Palace on January 7, 1655, but his body remained in the sacristy for a few days because his sister-in-law refused to pay the funeral expenses. He was buried in St. Peter's with simple ceremonies, but his remains were transferred in 1730 by a distant nephew, Cardinal Camillo Pamfili, to the Pamfili family crypt in the church of Sant'Agnese in Agone on the Piazza Navona in Rome.

235 Alexander VII, *1599–1667, pope from April 7, 1655, to May 22, 1667.*

Alexander VII allowed the Jesuit missionaries in China to use Chinese rites and commissioned the great sculptor and architect Bernini to enclose St. Peter's Square with two semicircular columns.

Born Fabio Chigi, he served a vice-legate in Ferrara, bishop of Nardò, inquisitor and apostolic delegate in Malta, and, for thirteen years, papal nuncio in Cologne, where he participated in the negotiations leading to the Peace of Westphalia, which ended the Thirty Years' War in 1648. (He vigorously protested provisions that he regarded as anti-Catholic.) Chigi was named secretary of state by Innocent X in 1651, and the next year a cardinal and bishop of Imola. When Innocent X died, the College of Cardinals was, for the first time, at its full complement of seventy members. But after the pope's funeral, there were only sixty-two cardinals in Rome ready to enter the conclave. There were at least four different factions, none of which could agree with the rest. Cardinal Chigi was elected pope on April 7, 1655, after a conclave that lasted some eighty days and against the strong initial opposition of France. He took the name Alexander VII in honor of the great twelfth-century pope Alexander III (1159–81) and was crowned by Cardinal Trivulsi on April 18. He took possession of his cathedral church, the Lateran Basilica, on May 9. One of his first moves as pope was to order Innocent X's "*papessa*," Donna Olimpia, to return to Orvieto, where she died in 1657.

Although the new pope began his pontificate by forbidding his own relatives from visiting Rome, by the next year he relented, with the encouragement of the Curia, and showered favors of all kinds upon his family: church offices, palaces, estates, and money. His relations with France were sour from the start. Because Rome gave refuge to Cardinal de Retz, the despised rival of the French minister Cardinal Jules Mazarin, France threw its support behind claims of the Farnese and Este families on papal territories. Mazarin also excluded the pope from participation in the Peace of the Pyrenees (1659) between France and Spain. After Mazarin's death, King Louis XIV accused the Holy See of violating French diplomatic immunity in Rome and of threatening his ambassador's life by Corsican troops in papal service. The king thereupon withdrew his ambassador to Rome, expelled the papal nuncio in Paris, occupied the papal enclaves of Avignon and Venaissin, and threatened an invasion of the Papal States. Since Alexander VII was without any allies, he was forced to apologize and accept the terms of the Treaty of Pisa (1664), which included the erection of a pyramid in Rome as an admission of his soldiers' guilt. The pope was also required to submit to the king's wishes on episcopal appointments. Moreover, the French king refused to cooperate with the pope's call for a crusade against the Turks because Louis XIV was more interested in weakening his German rivals, the Hapsburgs.

The pope's relations with other foreign powers were mixed. For example, relations with the Republic of Venice improved enough to have the Jesuits return (they had been expelled during Paul V's conflict with Venice in 1606). Spain, however, refused to receive the papal nuncio. When the pope did not accept the king's nominees to various dioceses, the king left them unfilled and appropriated their income.

The most important achievement of Alexander VII's pontificate, however, was in the realm of the missions, not politics. He decreed on March 23, 1656, that the Jesuit missionaries in China be allowed to use Chinese rites and, over three years later, dispensed the native Chinese clergy from having to pray the Divine Office in Latin. The same year he also confirmed Innocent X's condemnation in 1653 of the five propositions in Cornelius Jansen's *Augustinus,* insisting against Jansen's defenders (particularly Antoine Arnauld) that the five propositions were, in fact, to be found in the *Augustinus.* (Following St. Augustine's more rigid views on the relationship between grace and free will, the Jansenists held that the role of free will in salvation is, for all practical purposes, negated by the overriding power of God's grace.) In 1665, at the request of King Louis XIV, he issued a constitution requiring all French clergy to accept the pope's decisions and to reject Jansen's five propositions unreservedly. He did not condemn probabilism (a moral system favored by the Jesuits, namely, that a Catholic can safely follow a moral opinion supported by at least one reputable theologian, even if there are other, more numerous, and apparently stronger opinions on the other side), but did condemn (in 1665 and 1666) forty-five moral propositions that he considered laxist (an extreme form of probabilism, whereby one can always follow the easier moral course so long as there is at least some reason to do so).

Alexander VII had a special devotion to the writings of Francis de Sales (d. 1622), whom he beatified in 1661 and canonized in 1665. A friend of scholars and a patron of artists, he commissioned the incomparable Giovanni Lorenzo Bernini (d. 1680) to enclose St. Peter's Square within two grand semicircular colonnades. Alexander VII died on May 22, 1667, and was buried in St. Peter's in a tomb designed by Bernini himself.

236 Clement IX, *1600–1669, pope from June 20, 1667, to December 9, 1669.*

Clement IX's brief and undistinguished pontificate was preoccupied with politics, but he does have the distinction of having created the comic opera as a dramatic form. He wrote poetry and religious drama, some of which was publicly performed.

Born Giulio Rospigliosi, he spent his early years in the Roman Curia and then was appointed titular archbishop of Tarsus and papal nuncio to Spain. In 1653 he was named governor of Rome and then secretary of state and cardinal-priest of San Sisto under Alexander VII (1657). In spite of the French government's hostility to Alexander VII, Cardinal Rospigliosi maintained a mutually respectful relationship with the French court. Thus, upon Alexander VII's death, he had expected not only the support of Spain, but also that of France. Since the cardinals wanted someone capable of mediating between the two nations, they gladly turned to Rospiglioni, who was elected on June 20, 1667. He took the name Clement IX and was crowned on June 26. He took possession of his cathedral church, the Lateran Basilica, on July 3.

Unlike many of his predecessors, the new pope gave very little to his relatives. That was probably the only real achievement of his pontificate: to have liberated the papacy, if only for a short time, from the corrupting grip of nepotism. Otherwise, his pontificate was mired in political maneuvering that had little or no positive outcome. Thus, Clement IX was forced to allow the French crown a free hand in ecclesiastical appointments. The pope's involvement in peace negotiations between France and Spain showed that he was no match for the crafty Hugues de Lionne, Cardinal Mazarin's successor as France's foreign minister. The so-called Clementine Peace (1669) was also the work of de Lionne. He arranged to have the pope accept the (not entirely convincing) subscription of four Jansenist bishops to Alexander VII's condemnation in 1665 of the five propositions in Cornelius Jansen's *Augustinus*. The four bishops had written defiant pastoral letters and the king, fearing a schism, persuaded the bishops to sign their acceptance of Alexander's bull while keeping their reservations private. For allowing the bishops to do so without any retraction of their views, Clement was said to have been "more generous than the father of the prodigal son." In any case, the "peace" was interpreted as a sign of papal weakness in the face of French pressure. Finally, Clement IX's efforts to mount a campaign to liberate the island of Crete from Turkish occupation ended in defeat, with the Venetians being forced to surrender their last stronghold on the island, the capital, Candia, on September 6, 1669. The Holy See was left with overwhelming financial debts to Venice and the other participants (Spain and the empire).

It is said that the pope's death on December 9, 1669, following a stroke in the Quirinale Palace, was hastened by the news from Crete. He was buried first in St. Peter's, but his remains were transferred in 1680 to the basilica of Santa Maria Maggiore (St. Mary Major).

237 Clement X, *1590–1676, pope from April 29, 1670, to July 22, 1676.*

Elected at age seventy-nine, Clement X canonized an unusually large number of saints, including Rose of Lima, South America's first canonized saint.

Born Emilio Altieri, he served in the nunciature in Poland, then as bishop of Camerino and nuncio to Naples. He was recalled from Naples, however, by Innocent X in 1652 after eight years. The next pope, Alexander VII, rehabilitated Bishop Altieri and appointed him secretary of the Congregation of Bishops and Regulars (members of religious orders) and as a consultor of the Holy Office (formerly the Inquisition). A month before his death, Clement IX named Altieri a cardinal-priest without title. After a faction-ridden conclave of almost five months, with France and Spain exercising vetoes of certain candidates (the royal veto was abolished by Pius X in 1904), Cardinal Altieri, at age seventy-nine, was elected as a compromise candidate on April 29, 1670. He took the name of his patron, Clement IX, and was crowned on May 11.

The new pope assigned the role of cardinal-nephew (an unfortunate tradition that had developed whereby popes selected a relative to handle ecclesiastical affairs of state) to Cardinal Paluzzi degli Albertoni, whose nephew had married Clement X's niece. Unfortunately, Paluzzi took full advantage of his position, effectively nullifying the authority of the Secretariat of State and enriching himself and his family. He spent so much money, for example, on the Palazzo Altieri that the pope, in deference to acutely negative public opinion, never visited it.

Deeply concerned about the Turkish threat to Poland, Clement X and Cardinal Odescalchi (later Innocent XI) gave financial assistance to John Sobieski (d. 1696), who defeated the Turks at the Dniester (November 11, 1673) and was elected king the following May. Relations with King Louis XIV of France were no better in Clement X's pontificate than in his predecessor's. The king confiscated church property and diverted income from religious houses to the support of his military preparations against Holland. Clement's protests went unheeded. When Louis XIV later claimed an unrestricted right to make appointments to church offices and to receive the income of vacant dioceses and abbeys, the pope said nothing—leaving the problem for his successor to deal with.

The aged pope was also under heavy and sustained pressure from the Catholic powers to appoint their countrymen to the College of Cardinals. The French ambassador, for example, even threatened violence against the pope when asked to withdraw from a particularly unpleasant audience. When the French government decreed that members of exempt religious orders were subject to their local bishops, the pope ruled that religious must have the local bishop's permission for preaching or hearing confessions outside their own churches and religious houses. Clement X canonized an unusually large number of saints, including Cajetan (d. 1547), the founder of the Theatines, the Jesuit Francis Borgia (d. 1572), and Rose of Lima (d. 1617), South America's first canonized saint. He also beatified Pope Pius V (d. 1572) and the Spanish mystic John of the Cross (d. 1591). He died on July 22, 1676, at the age of eighty-six and was buried in St. Peter's, where his statue by Ercole Ferrata (d. 1685) is situated.

238 Innocent XI, Bl., *1611–89, pope from September 21, 1676, to August 12, 1689.*

Although regarded as the outstanding pope of the seventeenth century, Innocent XI manifested Jansenist and anti-Jesuit leanings. Born Benedetto Odescalchi, he held a series of appointments in papal service before being named a cardinal-deacon in the title of Santi Cosma e Damiano in 1645, legate of Ferrara in 1648, and bishop of Novara in 1650. Generous to the poor (he was called "the father of the poor"), he resigned his diocese in 1654 because of poor health and lived quietly in Rome while working in the Curia. He was surprised, therefore, when the cardinals elected him after another faction-ridden conclave of two months' duration. (His candidacy had been blocked at the previous conclave in 1670 because of opposition from King Louis XIV of France.) Cardinal Odescalchi accepted election on September 21, 1676, only after the cardinals subscribed to the program of reform he had proposed during the conclave itself (including completion of the work of the Council of Trent, defense of the freedom and rights of the Church, and defense of Christian Europe against the Islamic Turks). He took the name Innocent XI out of respect for the pope who created him a cardinal (Innocent X) and was crowned on October 4.

The new pope imposed severe reductions in the papal budget and called for evangelical preaching and catechesis, the strict observance of monastic vows, careful selection of priests and bishops, and the frequent reception of Holy Communion. His attempts to persuade the cardinals to outlaw nepotism ended in failure, and his prohibition of carnivals was ridiculed and ignored by the people. So ascetical was he in his personal life, that many suspected him of Jansenist leanings (that is, a rigid approach to the moral life). It was not surprising, therefore, that he condemned sixty-five laxist propositions in 1679 (any condemnation of laxism was regarded as an attack upon the Jesuits, the fiercest opponents of Jansenism). He was also impressed when a Jesuit theologian, Tirso González de Santalla, in Salamanca (Spain) turned against probabilism (the moral system, promoted by the Jesuits, that held that a Catholic could follow any "probable" opinion that had at least one reputable theologian in support of it). In 1687 he procured González's election as superior general of the Society of Jesus. On the other hand, Innocent XI backed off from his support of Miguel de Molinos (d. 1697), the Spanish Quietist whose work, *Spiritual Guide,* promoted an attitude of complete passivity (or "quiet"), that is, of leaving everything up to God. The Jesuit-dominated Holy Office (formerly the Inquisition) persuaded the pope to allow Molinos to be arrested in 1685. Innocent XI then denounced his views in the bull *Coelestis pastor* (1687).

On the political front, Innocent XI was in constant conflict with King Louis XIV of France. Since Innocent's predecessor, Clement X, had said nothing in response to the king's claim of the right to make appointments to church offices and to the income of vacant dioceses and abbeys, the French clergy took the pope's silence as consent and submitted themselves to the king's wishes. When two French bishops protested, however, Innocent XI rejected an extension of the arrangement. Louis XIV then ordered the assembly of clergy to meet and adopt the four so-called Gallican Articles on March 19, 1682. The Articles denied papal authority in temporal affairs or over kings, asserted the superiority of general, or ecumenical, councils over the pope, and reaffirmed the ancient liberties of the French (Gallican) Church. Innocent XI rejected the Articles on April 11 of the same year and refused to ratify the appointment of bishops who subscribed to the Articles. The king thought the pope might be more cooperative because of his (Louis's) brutal campaign against the Huguenots (Calvinists) and his revocation of the Edict of Nantes in 1685. (The Edict of Nantes was a grant of toleration to French Protestants in 1598 by King Henry IV.) But the pope, appalled by the inhumanity of the king's persecution of the Huguenots, did not become more cooperative. In 1687 the pope refused to receive the new French ambassador in Rome, and the following year he rejected the king's nominee as archbishop of Cologne and appointed the nominee of the emperor instead. By January 1688, there were thirty-five vacant dioceses in France. That same month Innocent XI

secretly informed Louis XIV that he and his ministers were excommunicated. The following September the king occupied the papal territories of
Avignon and Venaissin and imprisoned the papal nuncio. Open schism
was avoided only by the intervention of François Fénelon (d. 1715), later
archbishop of Cambrai, and the accession of William of Orange to the
English throne.

Unlike most popes before him, Innocent XI had greater success in the
campaign against the Turks. A papally arranged and financially sponsored
alliance between the emperor Leopold I and John III Sobieski of Poland
relieved Vienna from a Turkish siege (1683), and the liberation of Hungary
(1686) and the recovery of Belgrade (1688) followed, this time through the
efforts of the Holy League of the empire, which included Poland, Venice,
and Russia.

Although the Romans resented the pope's austerity measures during
his lifetime, many revered him after his death on August 12, 1689. He was
buried in St. Peter's under the altar of San Sebastiano. Efforts to beatify
him in the eighteenth century were suspended because of objections
from the French court. Innocent XI was eventually beatified, however, by
Pius XII in 1956. Feast day: August 12.

239 Alexander VIII, 1610–91, pope from October 6, 1689, to February 1, 1691.

Elected at age seventy-nine, the worldly Alexander VIII was greeted by
the Romans as a welcome contrast to the austere Innocent XI. Born
Pietro Ottoboni, he served in the Roman Curia, as a governor in the
Papal States, and as a judge in the Roman Rota (the second highest curial
court, dealing mostly with marriage cases) before being made a cardinal
in 1652. He was named bishop of Brescia in 1654, but returned to the
Curia ten years later, where he played a leading role as a trusted adviser of
Innocent XI, who appointed him grand inquisitor of Rome and secretary
of the Holy Office (formerly the Inquisition). At the conclave of 1689, fol-
lowing Innocent XI's death, special ambassadors of France and the empire were present. But the cardinals had already decided that the elderly
Cardinal Ottoboni's experience and character made him the logical
choice. He was elected pope on October 6 and chose the name Alexander
VIII out of deference to the nephew of Alexander VII (1655–67), Cardinal
Flavio Chigi, who had led the support for Ottoboni's election. Alexander
VIII was crowned on October 16.

The lavish personal style of the new pope was in stark contrast to that
of his ascetical predecessor, Innocent XI—yet one more indication of the
tendency of papal conclaves *not* to elect a carbon copy of a deceased
pope. Alexander VIII also revived the papal practice of nepotism that had
gone into eclipse during the previous two pontificates. He appointed his

grandnephew Pietro, at age twenty, as cardinal-nephew and appointed his nephew Giambattista as secretary of state, bestowing lucrative benefices (income-producing church offices) on both of them. He reduced taxes in the Papal States and lowered food prices, both of which made him very popular in those territories. His decision to draft troops to assist the Republic of Venice (his homeland) against the Turks, however, provoked angry resistance.

With his background in the Holy Office and as grand inquisitor of Rome, Alexander VIII made the defense of orthodoxy a high priority in his brief pontificate. In 1690 he condemned two laxist propositions that were currently advanced by the Jesuits: one that denied the necessity of an explicit act of love for God following attainment of the use of reason and another that held that sins committed without knowledge or thought of God were not real sins but only "philosophical sins." But later that same year he also condemned thirty-one Jansenist propositions (the morally rigid Jansenists were directly opposed to, and by, the Jesuits) that concerned such issues as Penance, Baptism, and the authority of the Church. He also imposed a life sentence on the followers of the Spanish Quietist Miguel de Molinos (d. 1697), who held that we attain salvation without any human effort at all, but rather by "quietly" and passively accepting the grace of God.

Alexander VIII made some effort toward reconciliation with King Louis XIV of France (for which he incurred the hostility of the emperor Leopold I). In return for Louis's withdrawal of his occupation forces in the papal territories of Avignon and Venaissin and other concessions, the pope named the bishop of Beauvais to the College of Cardinals, even though he had participated in the antipapal Gallican assembly of 1682. The pope also accepted the French ambassador to Rome, who had been rejected by Innocent XI. However, the pope and the king continued to disagree over the issue of the power of appointment of bishops. Like his predecessor, Alexander VIII refused to ratify the appointments of royally nominated bishops unless they repudiated the four antipapal Gallican Articles of 1682. The pope published on his deathbed a decree annulling the Gallican Articles and condemning the king's efforts to enforce these and other antipapal initiatives throughout his entire realm. Alexander VIII died on February 1, 1691, and was buried in St. Peter's under a sumptuous monument by Arrigo di San Martino.

240 Innocent XII, *1615–1700, pope from July 12, 1691, to September 27, 1700.*

Innocent XII was a reformist pope in the style of his hero, Innocent XI, striking especially at nepotism. Born Antonio Pignatelli, he served in the Roman Curia, as governor of Viterbo, and as nuncio to Tuscany, Poland,

and Vienna, before falling out of favor with Clement X, who sent him to
Lecce as bishop. He was recalled to Rome, however, in 1673 to become
secretary of the Congregation of Bishops and Regulars (members of religious orders), and was named a cardinal by Innocent XI in 1681, then
bishop of Faenza, legate of Bologna, and archbishop of Naples (1687).
The conclave following Alexander VIII's death lasted five months because
of the divisions between and within the pro-French and pro-imperial
factions. Under pressure of the unbearable summer heat and the impatience of the Roman people, Cardinal Pignatelli was elected as a compromise candidate (with fifty-one of sixty-one votes) on July 12, 1691, taking
the name Innocent XII out of respect for the pope who named him a cardinal and whose style he hoped to emulate as pope. He was crowned on
July 15.

The new pope introduced economies in the administration of Rome
and the Papal States, reformed the judicial system, insisting on impartial
justice for everyone, reduced (but did not eliminate) the sale of church
offices, established the Hospital of San Michele for poor youths, opened
the Lateran Palace as a refuge for disabled people unable to work, and declared that all of the poor and the needy were his "nephews." He established the Congregation for the Discipline and Reform of Regulars
(members of religious orders), and prohibited a practice common in
Germany of nominating bishops and abbots by electoral chapters. But
his most significant initiative was his decree *Romanum decet pontificem*
(June 22, 1692), which mandated that popes may never grant estates, offices, or revenues to relatives and that if such relatives are poor, they
should be treated like others in need. Moreover, only one relative may be
appointed to the College of Cardinals, if qualified, and his income should
be limited. Innocent XII encountered some resistance to the decree from
a number of cardinals, but they all eventually signed it.

Innocent XII also had some success on the political front. He broke a
fifty-year deadlock between France and the Holy See. On one side, the
pope ratified the appointment of those bishops nominated by the king
since 1682 who had not participated in the antipapal Gallican assembly
that year. Innocent XII also had to accept Louis XIV's extension to his entire realm of the right of regalia (that is, of royal administration of vacant
dioceses and abbeys). On the other side, the king promised to revoke the
declaration of the French clergy that required the French bishops to subscribe to the four antipapal Gallican Articles. The bishops who attended
the 1682 assembly also retracted their signatures from the Articles. (The
Articles themselves, however, remained intact.) By the end of 1693 the
French hierarchy was restored to the good graces of the Holy See, but
Gallicanism (the French Church's insistence on practical autonomy from

Rome) continued to affect relations between France and the papacy until the French Revolution at the end of the next century. Because of these accommodations reached between France and the Holy See, tensions were heightened between the emperor Leopold I and Innocent XII.

Toward the end of his pontificate, the pope was pressured by Louis XIV to make a negative judgment on the writings of Madame de Guyon (d. 1717), which influenced the thinking and writing of Archbishop François Fénelon (d. 1715) of Cambrai. On March 12, 1699, and at the urging of Bishop Jacques Bossuet (d. 1704), who was one of the judges in Guyon's case, Innocent XII published *Cum alias,* denouncing as dangerous Fénelon's work on the maxims of the saints. However, the pope refused to categorize the book as heretical.

Innocent XII died on September 27, 1700, and was buried in a simple tomb in St. Peter's Basilica. A monument, however, designed by Ferdinando Fuga with a sculpture by Filippo della Valle, was later erected in 1746.

241 Clement XI, *1649–1721, pope from November 30, 1700, to March 19, 1721 (the Vatican's official list begins his pontificate on the day of his election, November 23, but he was not yet a bishop and could not become Bishop of Rome until consecrated on November 30).*

Clement XI's long and largely ineffective pontificate was marred by his unfortunate and counterproductive decision to forbid missionaries in China from using Chinese rites, a prohibition that was not revoked until 1939, by Pius XII.

Born Giovanni Francesco Albani, he served in the Roman Curia and as governor in various parts of the Papal States, was secretary of papal briefs, and was named a cardinal-deacon in the title of Santa Maria in Portico in 1690 (he was not ordained a priest for another ten years, just before his elevation to the papacy). It was Cardinal Albani who drafted Innocent XII's important bull outlawing papal nepotism. The conclave that followed Innocent XII's death lasted forty-six days, divided once again between pro-French and pro-imperial factions. Albani was elected unanimously on November 23, 1700, at age fifty-one, as a compromise candidate with the support of independent cardinals who were committed to a nonpolitical pope. Because he felt himself unsuited for the office, he did not accept election immediately. He was consecrated as Bishop of Rome on November 30 and crowned on December 8. He took the name Clement XI because the day he accepted election was the feast of St. Clement, pope and martyr. He took possession of his cathedral church, the Lateran Basilica, on April 10.

At the instigation of King Louis XIV, the new pope would play a key role in the repression of Jansenism (a morally rigid movement that emphasized the workings of divine grace to the practical exclusion of human free will) in France. In 1705 he condemned the view, approved at the Sorbonne, that it was possible to reject the five Jansenist propositions censured by Innocent X but remain silent about whether or not those propositions were actually present in Cornelius Jansen's *Augustinus* (published in 1640, two years after the author's death). In 1708 the pope condemned a book of moral reflections by Pasquier Quesnel, a Jansenist leader, and on September 8, 1713, in a famous bull entitled *Unigenitus Dei Filius,* he condemned 101 allegedly Jansenist propositions extracted from Quesnel's book. After Louis XIV died in 1715, the Jansenist leaders called for a general council to deal with the question of their orthodoxy. The pope refused the appeal and in 1718 excommunicated those who made it. The Jansenist leaders, however, ignored the excommunication.

Clement XI was also committed to the missionary enterprise of the Church. He promoted missions in northern Germany (now under Protestant control), India, China, and the Philippines and the establishment of new missionary colleges in Rome. A particular problem festered in the Chinese mission, however. In their pastoral ministry, the Jesuit missionaries were using Chinese rites, such as the cult of Confucius and of ancestors (justifying them on the grounds that they were civic in nature), while the Dominicans opposed the practice. (Alexander VII had approved the use of Chinese rites in 1656.) On November 20, 1704, Clement XI accepted the judgment of the Holy Office (formerly the Inquisition) that missionaries in China were prohibited from using Chinese rites and repeated the judgment in 1715. Clement's action proved disastrous to the Church's missionary outreach in China. Chinese Catholics were persecuted and many missions were closed. Clement's action was not reversed until 1939, by Pius XII.

Clement XI appointed seventy cardinals during his pontificate, was a generous patron of the arts and scholarship, particularly archaeology, and was a munificent benefactor of the Vatican Library. He also made the feast of the Immaculate Conception (December 8) a universal holy day of obligation in 1708. Although elected as a nonpolitical pope, he was drawn inevitably into the political quagmire, particularly regarding the complicated matter of succession to the Spanish crown. He was caught in a crossfire between those backing the Bourbon, Philip V of Anjou, and those supporting the Hapsburg, Archduke Charles. The pope, who initially favored Philip and then tried to remain neutral, was forced to throw his support to Charles when the imperial troops invaded the Papal States, conquered Naples, and threatened Rome in January 1709. The pope's action precipitated a break in diplomatic relations with Spain, and he was thereafter systematically excluded from any involvement in important political decisions affecting papal interests in Sardinia, Sicily, Parma, and Piacenza. When the pope issued a bull protesting the establishment of a Sicilian monarchy, he was completely ignored. In 1717 he experienced a particularly keen humiliation when a Spanish fleet he had equipped to fight the Turks was diverted to conquer Sardinia from the empire.

Clement XI died on March 19, 1721, and was buried, according to his expressed wish, under the pavement of the Coro Chapel in St. Peter's. His heart, however, is preserved in the church of Santi Vincenzo e Anastasio in Rome (along with the entrails of dozens of other popes whose names are listed on the wall of the sanctuary), while other parts of his body are preserved in the church of San Francesco in his native Urbino.

242 Innocent XIII, *1655–1724, pope from May 8, 1721, to March 7, 1724.*

Innocent XIII's short and unproductive pontificate was marked by constant illness and personal aversion to the Jesuits. Born Michelangelo de' Conti (also dei Conti or simply Conti), he served in the Roman Curia, held three governorships in the Papal States, was nuncio to Switzerland (and titular archbishop of Tarsus) and then Portugal, and was named a cardinal-priest of Santi Quirico e Giulitta in 1706. After that he was named bishop of Osimo and then Viterbo, resigning the latter because of poor health. He was unanimously elected pope on May 8, 1721, after a lengthy conclave in which the emperor, through his delegate, Cardinal Althan, vetoed the favored candidate, Cardinal Fabrizio Paolucci, who had been Clement XI's secretary of state. (Imperial vetoes were prohibited by Pius X in 1904.) Cardinal Conti took the name Innocent XIII out of respect for Innocent III (1198–1216), from whose family he was descended. Innocent XIII was crowned by Cardinal Pamfili (Pamphili), senior cardinal-deacon, on May 18 and took possession of his cathedral church, the Lateran Basilica, on November 16.

Although educated by the Jesuits in Rome, the new pope developed a keen dislike of the Society of Jesus while serving as nuncio in Portugal. He even thought of suppressing the order because of their lack of compliance with Clement XI's ban (in 1704 and 1715) against the use of Chinese rites. He did forbid the Jesuits from accepting novices unless, within three years' time, he had satisfactory proof that they were complying with the papal ban. But he also reaffirmed Clement XI's condemnation of the Jansenists, fierce adversaries of the Jesuits. Indeed, when seven French bishops asked him to withdraw Clement's bull *Unigenitus,* Innocent XIII had the Holy Office (formerly the Inquisition) censure their petition and he asked the French king to take measures against the bishops.

On the political front, Innocent XIII mollified the emperor Charles VI by investing him with the kingdoms of Naples and Sicily (which Clement XI had refused to do) and placated the French regent by appointing his minister to the College of Cardinals. On the other hand, he failed to dissuade Charles VI from claiming supreme authority over the Church in Sicily and from investing the Spanish prince Don Carlos with the duchies of Parma and Piacenza, two traditionally papal fiefs.

Innocent XIII died on March 7, 1724, and was buried in a simple tomb in St. Peter's Basilica. No monument marks his resting place.

243 Benedict XIII, *1649–1730, pope from May 29, 1724, to February 21, 1730.*

Benedict XIII, a Dominican, was the last pope to have held two dioceses simultaneously, Rome and Benevento. His decision to retain Benevento had disastrous consequences for his pontificate because his associates from Benevento formed a corrupt ring around the pope.

Born Pietro Francesco Orsini, he renounced his inheritance as a youth and joined the Dominicans. Against his will, but through the machinations of his influential family, Vincenzo Maria (the name he took when he entered the Dominicans) was named a cardinal in 1672 at age twenty-three by Clement X, whose niece had married Pietro's brother. Although he continued to live the life of a friar, he was named archbishop of Manfredonia in 1675, bishop of Cesena in 1680, and archbishop of Benevento in 1686. He was unanimously elected pope on May 29, 1724, as a compromise candidate after the pro-French, pro-Spanish, and pro-Hapsburg factions failed over nine weeks to elect their own favored candidates. Cardinal Orsini at first refused election. He accepted only because he was, in effect, urged to do so by the master of the Dominican order, whom he still considered as his superior. At first he took the name Benedict XIV, in honor of another Dominican pope, Blessed Benedict XI (1303–4), but changed it to Benedict XIII because the previous bearer of the name Benedict had been an antipope (1394–1417) during the Great Western Schism. Benedict XIII was crowned on June 4 and took possession of his cathedral church, the basilica of St. John Lateran, on September 24.

In the most fateful—and unfortunate—decision of his pontificate, the new pope retained his archdiocese of Benevento after accepting election as Bishop of Rome. (Such a practice was considered an abuse around the time of the Protestant Reformation. It was known as pluralism, that is, holding more than one church office at a time.) Although he made visitations of a week's duration to Benevento in 1727 and 1729, Benedict XIII devoted himself to the pastoral care of Rome as well. In spite of his age (he was seventy-five when elected), he consecrated churches, visited the sick, administered the sacraments, and even gave religious instruction. He criticized the lifestyle and fastidious appearance of cardinals (their use of wigs, for example) and banned the profitable lottery in the Papal States. He personally presided over a provincial synod in the Lateran in the spring of 1725, at which he called for unconditional acceptance of Clement XI's bull against Jansenism, *Unigenitus* (1713), and had the synod's decisions printed and circulated immediately so that they might serve as an example to other bishops. However, the pope undermined his own reform efforts by opening his pontificate to unsavory influences from Benevento.

Benedict XIII retained Cardinal Paolucci as secretary of state (Paolucci had been the leading candidate for election to the papacy in 1721, but was vetoed by the emperor), but he also brought in Niccolò Coscia, his chancellor and secretary in Benevento, and made him a cardinal in 1725, against the protests of many cardinals. Coscia, in turn, appointed cronies from Benevento to influential positions and, on Cardinal Paolucci's death, had one of his own underlings made secretary of state. Coscia successfully isolated the pope from the cardinals as he enriched himself and his friends by selling church offices and by accepting bribes. As a result of Coscia's unscrupulous behavior, papal interests in Sicily and Sardinia were undermined, and the finances of the Papal States were in a state of collapse.

Some Jansenists (morally rigid Catholics, based mainly in France, who tended to exaggerate the effects of divine grace to the detriment of human free will) had hoped that with the election of a Dominican pope they would have a more sympathetic ear on the papal throne. But Benedict XIII disappointed them. Not only did he reaffirm Clement XI's anti-Jansenist bull, *Unigenitus,* but he also instructed the Dominicans to remain faithful to the teachings of St. Augustine (d. 430) and St. Thomas Aquinas (d. 1274). In 1727 he declared that the teaching of Aquinas and of the Thomist school had nothing to do with the Jansenist errors or with Quietism (the view that salvation will be given to those who await it "quietly" and passively, with no human effort at all).

Benedict XIII canonized many saints, including John of the Cross (d. 1591) and Aloysius Gonzaga (d. 1591). When he extended the feast of St. Gregory VII to the universal Church, he provoked an international crisis. Several governments were so offended by the reference in the feast's liturgical texts to Gregory's deposition of the emperor Henry IV that they banned their use.

In spite of his personal and pastoral sincerity, Benedict XIII was profoundly unpopular with the Roman people, particularly because of their hatred of Coscia and his cronies. When the pope died, at age eighty-one, on February 21, 1730, the Romans erupted in a rage against the Beneventans, who barely escaped with their lives. Benedict XIII was buried first in St. Peter's, but his remains were transferred in 1738 to the basilica of Santa Maria sopra Minerva, long associated with the Dominican order.

244 Clement XII, *1652–1740, pope from July 12, 1730, to February 6, 1740.*

The pontificate of Clement XII, elected at age seventy-eight and blind from the second year of his reign, was a failure, but he is remembered for having erected the famous Trevi Fountain in Rome.

Born Lorenzo Corsini, he renounced his inheritance after his father's death in 1685 and, with the aid of influential relatives, entered the service of the Roman Curia. In 1690 he was named titular bishop of Nicomedia, and nuncio to Vienna the following year. The emperor, however, refused to receive him because his nominees to the College of Cardinals had not been accepted by Alexander VIII. Lorenzo remained in Rome as treasurer of the apostolic chamber and in 1706 was named a cardinal-deacon in the title of Santa Susanna (later cardinal-priest of San Pietro in Vincoli and cardinal-bishop of Frascati) by Clement XI. At the conclaves of 1721 and 1724 he was considered a serious candidate for the papacy, and he was finally elected on July 12, 1730, at age seventy-eight, after a four-month-long conclave that was more contentious than usual (and there were many contentious conclaves during this period). Half the cardinals present were proposed at one point or another during the deliberations. Cardinal Corsini was eventually chosen unanimously and was crowned on July 16. He took the name Clement XII out of respect for Clement XI, who had made him a cardinal. He took possession of his cathedral church, the basilica of St. John Lateran, on November 19.

The new pope was often bedridden with gout and became blind in the second year of his pontificate, forcing him to rely excessively on his cardinal-nephew Neri Corsini. He brought Cardinal Niccolò Coscia (Benedict XIII's "evil genius") to trial. Coscia was sentenced to a large fine and ten years of imprisonment in the Castel Sant'Angelo. Clement XII revived the papal lotteries to raise much needed revenue for the Papal States, placed new taxes on imports, restricted the export of valuables, and issued paper money. To stimulate trade he created a free port at Ancona. But the papacy's financial problems were much bigger than any of these efforts could resolve, and the debts were still increasing by the time the pope died.

On the political front, the pope's fortunes turned from bad to worse. The Catholic powers continued to ignore the papacy, as they had under Clement XI. The emperor Charles VI declared his own sovereignty over

Parma and Piacenza (traditional papal fiefs). The Papal States were over-run by Spanish armies, which then recruited troops from Rome, inspir-ing a revolt among the people. In 1736 Spain and Naples broke off diplomatic relations with the Holy See. To restore those relations, the pope had to recognize Don Carlos of Spain as king of the Two Sicilies.

Because of his troubles on the international level, Clement XII at first created no cardinals outside of Italy in spite of pressures from various governments. He later relented. In the meantime, he limited by decrees in 1731 and 1732 the rights of cardinals in the financial administration of the Holy See during a papal vacancy. He also published in 1738 the first papal condemnation of Freemasonry, forbidding Catholics to belong to Ma-sonic lodges under pain of excommunication, because of their secret oaths, religious indifferentism, and naturalistic morality.

Unfortunately, he also renewed in 1735 Clement XI's prohibition of the use of Chinese rites by Jesuit missionaries in China and initiated a new investigation into the matter. To assist the Maronites, he sent a distin-guished Orientalist and Vatican librarian, Joseph Assemani, as a papal legate to Lebanon to preside over a synod in 1736 that reformed Maronite liturgical and canonical life. In 1737 he canonized Vincent de Paul (d. 1660), hailing him as a determined opponent of Jansenism.

With the help of his family's wealth, Clement XII beautified Rome, in-cluding the façade of the basilica of St. John Lateran, the Andrea Corsini chapel inside the basilica, the Piazza di Trevi, and the Trevi Fountain it-self, one of the city's most popular tourist attractions today. He enlarged the Vatican Library and added many valuable items to its collections. Clement XII died on February 6, 1740, just shy of his eighty-eighth birth-day. After a grand, military-style procession illuminated by lanterns and torches (one French writer reported that it was as if the pope were a gen-eral who had fallen in battle for his country), Clement XII was buried in the magnificent Corsini chapel (which he had commissioned) in the basilica of St. John Lateran.

245 Benedict XIV, *1675–1758, pope from August 17, 1740, to May 3, 1758.*

Elected after the longest conclave in modern times (six months), Bene-dict XIV was the author of the first papal encyclical, *Ubi primum* (1740), on the duties of bishops.

Born Prospero Lorenzo Lambertini of noble but poor parents, he was secretary of the Congregation of the Council (1708–27), Promoter of the Faith (in charge of canonizations), and archbishop of Ancona (1727) and was named a cardinal in 1728 (he had been named a cardinal *in pec-tore* ["in the (pope's) breast"], i.e., secretly, in 1726). In 1731 he became archbishop of Bologna, his birthplace, where he proved a successful and much admired pastor. He was elected pope on August 17, 1740, having emerged as a candidate only at the very end and to everyone's surprise. For the first forty days Cardinal Aldovrandi received thirty-one votes on every ballot, and Cardinal Lanfredini received twenty, both less than the two-thirds required for election. Then the cardinals turned to the general of the Capuchins, Father Barberini, but many objected because he was not a cardinal. More weeks passed and soon the terrible summer heat of Rome overcame them. At one point in the proceedings, the witty and good-humored Cardinal Lambertini remarked, "Do you wish to have a saint? Take Gatti. A politician? Take Aldovrandi. But if you wish a good man, take me!" Although it was clear from the tone of his voice and his general demeanor that he really was only joking, the cardinals eventually decided to elect him, unanimously, after Cardinal Aldovrandi asked his supporters not to vote for him any longer. (There had been 254 ballots, or scrutinies, on which Cardinal Lambertini had not received a single vote!) He took the name Benedict XIV in memory of the pope, Benedict XIII, who named him a cardinal. He was crowned by Cardinal Marini, senior cardinal-deacon, on August 22 in St. Peter's. He took possession of his cathedral church, the basilica of St. John Lateran, on August 30.

The new pope was conciliatory by nature and politically realistic. He signed concordats with Sardinia, Naples, Spain, and Austria (for Milan). All contained substantial concessions to the political rulers. In Spain, for example, the pope ceded almost all church appointments to the crown. By the same method, he also restored good relations with Portugal and Prussia. But he stumbled in his relations with Austria because of the complexities of the succession following the death of the emperor Charles VI in October 1740. Consequently, the pope had to suffer the confiscation of all benefices in Austria and the invasion of the Papal States by Austrian troops.

Two months after his election, Benedict XIV established a congregation to select worthy men as bishops and the following month another congregation to answer bishops' questions directed to the Holy See. He promoted improved clerical training, episcopal residentiality (evidently many bishops were still living away from their dioceses), and pastoral visitation. He addressed such topics as these in a circular letter written to all the bishops of the Catholic world. Entitled *Ubi primum* (Lat., "Where first"), it concerned the duties of bishops and is generally regarded as the first papal encyclical (December 3, 1740). In 1741 he exempted the marriages of non-Catholics and mixed marriages (between Catholics and non-Catholics) from the canonical form required by the

Council of Trent (that is, before a priest and two witnesses). In a letter to the Portuguese bishops of South America, also in 1741, he urged more humane treatment of the Indians. On July 11, 1742, he formally and finally suppressed the Chinese rites in use by the Jesuit missionaries in China, extending the ban even to the Malabar rites in India. Although he renewed Clement XII's condemnation of Freemasonry and condemned various writings of the Enlightenment, he published a new and improved edition of the Index of Forbidden Books in 1758, prescribing fairer and more scholarly standards of inclusion. A month before his death he instructed the patriarch of Lisbon to investigate the Jesuits in that country, because of the many (false) complaints he had been receiving about their neglect of their rule and their engaging in commercial trade.

Although Benedict XIV was a man of his time theologically and spiritually, many Protestants and agnostic scholars respected him for the breadth of his scholarly interests and for his support of the arts and sciences. He founded four scholarly academies, purchased manuscripts and books for the Vatican Library, and improved the University of Rome. Montesquieu (d. 1755) described him as "the scholars' pope," even though Benedict XIV had condemned his *The Spirit of Laws* (1748). His book on the making of saints, *De servorum Dei beatificatione et beatorum canonizatione* [Lat., "On the beatification of the servants of God and the canonization of the blessed"] (1738–48), was often reprinted and remained the classic treatment of the subject for many years. He also composed another enduring work on diocesan synods in 1748. The great Voltaire (d. 1778) even dedicated his tragedy *Mahomet* to the pope, which caused some consternation in conservative Catholic circles. Benedict XIV died on May 3, 1758, and was buried in St. Peter's, where he is memorialized by a striking monument by Pietro Bracci, erected through the financial contributions of the sixty-four cardinals he had created during his pontificate.

246 Clement XIII, *1693–1769, pope from July 6, 1758, to February 2, 1769.*

Clement XIII's pontificate was dominated by the issue of the Jesuits; he was under heavy pressure from Portugal and other Catholic countries to suppress the order, but he died before a special consistory met.

Born Carlo Rezzonico of an extremely rich commercial family in Venice, he served first in the Roman Curia, as a governor in the Papal States, and then as auditor of the Rota (a judicial body that handles mostly marriage cases) for Venice. He was named a cardinal-deacon in the title of San Niccolò in Carcere in 1737 by Clement XII (the title was later changed to cardinal-priest of Santa Maria in Ara Coeli, and then to

San Marco), and was appointed bishop of Padua in 1743, where he modeled himself on St. Charles Borromeo (d. 1584) and was regarded by some as a saint. The conclave that met after the death of Benedict XIV at first elected Cardinal Cavalchini on June 19, 1758, but the French cardinals presented a veto from the French crown. This action threw the conclave into confusion. For several days it lacked clear direction until a few of the cardinals recalled that Cardinal Rezzonico had received some votes on May 29. On July 4 he received twenty-two of the forty-four votes. After animated debate, on July 6, he received thirty-one votes, or just over the required two-thirds for election. Thus, after a conclave of some fifty-three days, Cardinal Rezzonico was elected pope by cardinal-electors who wanted a pope very different from Benedict XIV (that pattern again!) and not anti-Jesuit. He took the name Clement XIII in honor of his patron, Clement XII, and was crowned on July 16. The Venetians were so pleased by his election that they nullified all antipapal legislation dating back to 1754.

The new pope faced some old business from the previous pontificate, specifically an investigation of charges against the Jesuits in Portugal. The Bourbons in France, Spain, Naples, and Parma were now waging a full-scale offensive against the Society of Jesus. (At the time, the Jesuits had 23,000 members, 800 residences, 700 colleges, and 270 missions.) Portugal's powerful minister, the Marquis de Pombal, hated the Jesuits, mainly because he viewed them as a threat to the monarchy and because of their interference with Portugal's economic designs on South America, and on Paraguay particularly. Pombal thereupon confiscated Jesuit assets in Portugal and its colonies and then imprisoned some 250 Jesuits (60 were later freed) and deported some 1,100 others to the Papal States in 1759. When Clement XII protested, his nuncio was expelled and diplomatic relations were broken for a decade. France followed Portugal's lead, and again the pope resisted. His famous words to the Jesuit superior general Lorenzo Ricci were "*Sint ut sint aut non sint*" ("Let them be as they are or not be at all").

On December 1, 1764, the Society of Jesus was abolished in France by royal decree of Louis XV and almost all members were sent into exile. On January 7, 1765, Clement XII published a bull, *Apostolicum pascendi munus,* reaffirming his support for the Society, applauding its accomplishments, and insisting that an assault upon the Jesuits was tantamount to an assault upon the Church itself, but to no avail. The Jesuits were also expelled from Spain in 1767 and shipped to Civitavecchia, and then from Naples and Sicily the following year. Parma followed in 1768. The pope invoked Pius V's bull of 1568, *In coena Domini,* which condemned state control of the Church. The Bourbon courts protested. When Clement

XIII refused to back down, France occupied the papal enclaves of Avignon and Venaissin. In January 1769, Spain, France, and Naples were demanding that the pope suppress the order. Although he had no intention of doing so, he summoned a special consistory of cardinals for February 3, but he suffered a stroke and died the day before it was to meet.

The pope also had no success in persuading the German rulers or even the German bishops to condemn Febronianism, a movement comparable to Gallicanism (both of which sought to subordinate papal authority to local control). In other areas, the pope reacted against the Enlightenment by placing certain works on the Index of Forbidden Books (including Rousseau's *Émile* in 1763) and by releasing an encyclical in 1766 condemning all publications that were regarded as inconsistent with Catholic doctrine. He canonized Jeanne de Chantal (d. 1641), friend of St. Francis de Sales, and John Cantius (d. 1473), patron of Poland and Lithuania, and in 1765 authorized the Mass and Divine Office for the feast of the Sacred Heart for Poland and the Archconfraternity of the Sacred Heart in Rome, a devotion much favored by the Jesuits. Finally, although he supported the arts, he ordered the covering of certain nudities on statues and in paintings, including some of the frescoes in the Sistine Chapel. Clement XIII was buried in St. Peter's Basilica.

247 Clement XIV, *1705–74, pope from May 28, 1769, to September 22, 1774 (the Vatican's official list begins his pontificate on the day of election, May 19, but he was not yet a bishop and could not become Bishop of Rome until consecrated on May 28).*

A Franciscan who had been friendly with the Jesuits before his election, Clement XIV was the pope who finally acceded to the demands of the Catholic powers and suppressed the Society of Jesus in 1773.

Born Giovanni Vincenzo Antonio Ganganelli, he adopted his father's name, Lorenzo, as his religious name upon entering the Franciscans. He was a professor of theology, college rector, and a consultant to the Holy Office (formerly the Inquisition) before being named a cardinal in the title of San Lorenzo in Panisperna (later changed to Santi Apostoli) in 1759 by Clement XIII, who referred to him as a Jesuit in the clothes of a Franciscan. He was elected pope on May 19, 1769, after a contentious conclave in which the Catholic powers (particularly the Bourbon monarchs in France, Spain, Naples, and Parma) threatened to veto a pro-Jesuit candidate. The Bourbons rejoiced. There had been three groups among the cardinal-electors: those who favored the suppression of the Jesuits, those who opposed suppression, and those who were indifferent. The rules of secrecy laid down for conclaves by previous popes were breached. Certain cardinals were in open and frequent communication with the French and Spanish ambassadors. There was also a list of unacceptable candidates to be vetoed, and all the cardinals were categorized as "very good," "good," "bad," or "very bad." Cardinal Branciforte, a "great Sicilian lord," was chosen by acclamation ("adoration" is the technical term), but he was vetoed by the French cardinals on behalf of the crown. The conclave turned to the only cardinal who belonged to a religious order, Cardinal Ganganelli, who is said to have "trimmed his sails to the wind" on the matter of the Jesuits. He did not formally promise that he would suppress the order, but he did agree that such an act would be canonically possible and might even have certain advantages. Upon election, he took the name of the pope (Clement XIII) who had appointed him to the College of Cardinals. Since he was not yet a bishop, he was consecrated as Bishop of Rome on May 28 by Cardinal Lante, the subdean of the College of Cardinals. He was crowned on June 4 and took possession of his cathedral church, the basilica of St. John Lateran, on November 26. During the procession to the basilica the pope was thrown from his horse and fell so hard to the ground that he could not mount his horse again.

The new pope began to distance himself now from the Jesuits with whom he had once been friendly. (Indeed, he had dedicated one of his books to St. Ignatius of Loyola, the founder of the Society of Jesus, and its foreword included praise for the order.) He knew that his first order of business would be to satisfy the Catholic powers' thirst for Jesuit blood. Indeed, they formally reminded him of that unfinished business in July, two months after his election. After a ten-year break in diplomatic relations with Portugal, Clement XIV healed the breach by sending a compliant nuncio and by naming the brother of the ruthless Portuguese minister, the Marquis de Pombal, to the College of Cardinals (after the brother died, the pope named another of Pombal's friends) and by confirming eight of Pombal's nominees as bishops.

On Holy Thursday, 1770, Clement XIV omitted the reading of Pius V's famous bull, *In coena Domini* (1568), which condemned efforts by states to exercise control over the Church. (Clement XIII had used the bull to announce the excommunication of the duke of Parma in 1768, an act that provoked the ultimatum from the Bourbon states to dissolve the Jesuit order.) However, Clement XIV temporized for four years, hoping that the problem would somehow resolve itself. He advised bishops to withhold permissions for Jesuits to preach or hear confessions. Jesuits were removed from their positions at certain colleges in the Papal States. Jesuit exiles from Portugal were deprived of the pensions granted them by Clement XIII. But in the spring of 1773 the Bourbon states warned the pope that they would break diplomatic relations with Rome if he did not act against the Jesuits. Even the pro-Jesuit empress Maria Theresa moved into the neutral camp (but after the suppression of the order, she did allow them to remain in their houses as diocesan priests). On July 21, 1773, the pope issued the bull *Dominus ac Redemptor noster,* completely dissolving the Society of Jesus and extinguishing their remaining 11,000 members, 266 colleges, 103 seminaries, and 88 residences. The superior general, Lorenzo Ricci, and his assistants in Spain, Italy, Portugal, Germany, and Poland were imprisoned in the Castel Sant'Angelo for questioning the decision.

The reason Clement XIV gave for his action was that the Jesuits had incurred hostility and were at the center of controversy. The Jesuit order was crushed everywhere except in Prussia and Russia, whose sovereigns, Frederick II and Catherine II, forbade the promulgation of the papal bull. The Catholic school system in Europe and the missionary effort abroad suffered incalculable harm—all to satisfy the political and economic interests of grasping, nominally Catholic rulers. One might say that the pope's thirty pieces of silver consisted of the return of Avignon and Venaissin to papal control. (Naples also restored Benevento and Pontecorvo, but with humiliating conditions.) But the pope's action did not win him much more than that. In France a royal commission for the reform of religious orders continued its work, suppressing religious houses without papal approval. In Portugal, the secular authorities interfered with the work of the Church, and particularly the education of the young. The pope's efforts to improve economic conditions in the Papal States failed, largely because of the opposition of the cardinals and the Roman nobility, who could not forgive the pope for having suppressed the Jesuit order.

Elsewhere on the political front, Clement XIV failed to stop the partitioning of Poland among Prussia, Russia, and Austria in 1772, but he made politically astute moves regarding England by welcoming members of the royal family in Rome and by playing down papal support for the exiled Catholic Stuarts. During his last year he was severely depressed, in constant fear of assassination, and tormented by an acute skin disease. Clement XIV died in his summer residence, the Quirinale Palace, on September 22, 1774, and was buried at first in St. Peter's. In 1802 his remains were transferred to the Church of the Holy Apostles (Santi Apostoli), where they were entombed in a magnificent monument by Antonio Canova. Ironically, this church (known also as the Dodici Apostoli) is close to two major Jesuit institutions in Rome: the Pontifical Biblical Institute and the Pontifical Gregorian University. It was the custom of American seminarians studying in Rome to place flowers at the tomb of

Clement XIV after particularly difficult exams administered by their Jesuit professors at the Gregorian.

Clement XIV's eulogy made no mention of the suppression of the Jesuits. According to the historian J. N. D. Kelly, his pontificate "saw the prestige of the papacy sink to its lowest level for centuries." The great papal biographer Ludwig von Pastor called him "one of the weakest and most unhappy of the long line of popes."

248 Pius VI, *1717–99, pope from February 22, 1775, to August 29, 1799 (the Vatican's official list begins his pontificate on the day of his election, February 15, but he was not yet a bishop and could not become Bishop of Rome until consecrated on February 22).*

Pius VI was pope during the French Revolution, which he denounced and for which Napoleon invaded the Papal States and imprisoned him. His was the third longest pontificate in history (after Pius IX [1846–78] and Leo XIII [1878–1903]). Because of the circumstances in which he died, a prisoner of Napoleon Bonaparte, in exile, many thought he might be indeed "the last pope."

Born Giovanni Angelo Braschi of aristocratic parents of modest means, he served as secretary to Cardinal Antonio Ruffo in several different posts and then as private secretary to Benedict XIV (1740–58). He was not ordained a priest until 1758, at age forty-one. He was appointed treasurer of the apostolic chamber in 1766 (in charge of finances for the Papal States) and a cardinal-priest in the title of Sant' Onofrio in 1773 by Clement XIV. He was elected pope at the 134-day conclave following the death of Clement XIV, because he was perceived to be pro-Jesuit by the pro-Jesuit cardinals and anti-Jesuit by the anti-Jesuit cardinals. He was fifty-seven years of age and took the name Pius because he had a particular devotion to St. Pius V (1566–72). He was consecrated as Bishop of Rome and crowned on February 22. He took possession of his cathedral church, the basilica of St. John Lateran, on November 30.

The new pope was taken with the externals of his office and had a fondness for outdated protocols. He revived the practice of papal nepotism, bestowing substantial sums on his relatives and building the Palazzo Braschi for his nephew. He also spent great amounts on the sacristy of St. Peter's and the Museo Pio-Clementino, on road repairs, and on the (unsuccessful) draining of the Pontine marshes—all of which bankrupted the treasury.

Lacking special qualities of intellect or a gift for diplomacy, his early years were marked by various political setbacks. Naples refused to acknowledge him as a feudal lord, in spite of the pope's persistent demands, and claimed for its king the right to present episcopal nominees for dioceses. In the empire Joseph II imbibed the spirit of Febronianism and the Enlightenment, granting full toleration to all religions, limiting papal intervention to spiritual matters, forbidding his bishops to apply to Rome for dispensations, requiring candidates for the diocesan priesthood to take their course in state colleges, and subjecting the Church to the state. In 1781 the emperor promulgated an edict of toleration that suppressed certain religious orders and transferred certain monasteries from papal to episcopal jurisdiction. Pius VI traveled to Vienna in 1782 (the first pope to leave Rome since 1533, when Clement VII traveled to Marseilles to marry his grandniece to the son of King Francis I) to dissuade the emperor from his course. Although the emperor received the pope with courtesy, the pope had no success whatever in changing Joseph II's mind. When, four years later, the pope tried to establish a nunciature in Munich, the German archbishops opposed him, insisting that they could run their own Church without papal interference. The spirit of Febronianism (now called Josephinism) spread even to Italy when Tuscany, led by the emperor's brother, announced plans to make the local church independent of Rome. The Synod of Pistoia (September 1786) adopted the four Gallican Articles of 1682 (declaring the French Church independent of Rome in most matters) and exempted the local bishops from papal authority. The pope eventually asked the bishop who presided over the synod to resign and on August 28, 1794, formally condemned eighty-five of the articles of Pistoia. On the Jesuit matter, Pius VI tried to please the Bourbon monarchs by putting some pressure on Frederick II of Prussia and Catherine II of Russia (neither of whom were Roman Catholics), where the Jesuits still flourished in defiance of Clement XIV's declaration of suppression. But the pope failed here, too. Catherine established a novitiate for Jesuits in 1780. It is said that the pope tacitly approved the Jesuits' continued presence in Russia.

But the event that cast the darkest shadow over his pontificate was the French Revolution. At first the pope was cautious, although he regarded the revolution as an act of rebellion against a divinely sanctioned social order and a conspiracy against the Church. He said and did nothing when on July 12, 1790, the Civil Constitution of the Clergy reorganized the French Church and made clergy salaried officials of the state. But the following year he denounced the oath of loyalty the new regime imposed on the clergy and condemned the Civil Constitution as well as the Declaration of the Rights of Man (1789). He declared the ordinations of the new state bishops sacrilegious and suspended priests, bishops, and abbots who had taken the civil oath. Diplomatic relations between France and the Holy See were immediately broken off, and France annexed the papal enclaves of Avignon and Venaissin, where the citizens had already risen up against continued papal sovereignty there. The French Church became split between those sympathetic to the Revolution and those loyal to the monarchy. Pius VI did not help matters when he gave support to an alliance, known as the First Coalition, against the new France and by warmly receiving numerous royalists in Rome and the Papal States. When Napoleon Bonaparte occupied Milan in the spring of 1796, the French demanded that the pope withdraw his condemnation of the Civil Constitution and the revolution. The pope refused. Napoleon thereupon invaded the Papal States and defeated the pope's forces. By the Peace of Tolentino (1797), Pius VI was compelled to pay a huge indemnity, hand over valuable manuscripts and works of art, and cede substantial portions of the Papal States to France, including Ferrara, Bologna, and Romagna.

Matters, however, went from bad to worse. A French general was killed during a riot in Rome and the Directory (the revolutionary leaders in Paris) ordered the occupation of the Papal States. General Louis Berthier entered Rome on February 15, 1798, proclaimed the Roman Republic, deposed Pius VI as head of state, and forced him to withdraw to Tuscany. He lived for several months in Florence, cut off from almost all of his aides but using his nuncio to Florence as his secretary of state. When war broke out again, the Directory was concerned that troops would attempt to rescue the pope, so they had him moved from Florence on March 28, 1799, to Turin, then across the Alps to Briançon (April 30), and then to Valence (July 13).

Pius VI died a prisoner in Valence at age eighty-one on August 29, 1799, and was buried in the local cemetery with a simple inscription: "The body of Pius VI, supreme pontiff. Pray for him." His death provoked many expressions of sorrow around the world, and there were public funerals conducted in countries not under the control or influence of the Directory in Paris. His remains were transferred to St. Peter's in Rome in February 1802 and were moved later to the basilica crypt in 1983. Many thought that the papacy had at last come to an end with his death, that Pius VI was indeed "the last pope," but he had left careful instructions for the holding of the next conclave under emergency conditions.

249 Pius VII, *1742–1823, pope from March 14, 1800, to August 20, 1823.*

Like his predecessor, Pius VII endured imprisonment by Napoleon. He also restored the Jesuit order in 1814, after some forty years under suppression. His was the fifth longest pontificate in history, after Pius IX (1846–78), Leo XIII (1878–1903), Pius VI (1775–99), and Hadrian I (772–95).

Born Luigi Barnabà Chiaramonti of noble parents, he joined the Benedictines at age fourteen, taking the name Gregorio, was a professor of theology in Parma and at San Anselmo's in Rome, was named bishop of Tivoli in 1782 and then bishop of Imola in 1785, when he was also named a cardinal by Pius VI. Although the rules for papal conclaves dictated that the election of Pius VI's successor should technically take place where he died, namely, at Valence in France, the cardinals followed Pius VI's wishes that the senior cardinal should convene the conclave wherever he wished. With Rome now occupied by troops from the kingdom of Naples, the cardinals chose Venice, which was under Austrian protection. The conclave opened on December 1 with thirty-four cardinals in attendance. For weeks the balloting produced majorities of eighteen to twenty-two in favor of Cardinal Bellisomi, bishop of Cesena, and ten to thirteen voting for the Austrian candidate, Cardinal Mattei, archbishop of Ferrara. A fourteen-week deadlock was broken after the Mattei supporters agreed to name a Bellisomi voter acceptable to them. The choice fell on the Benedictine bishop of Imola, Cardinal Chiaramonti, and he was elected on March 14, 1800. He took the name Pius VII in honor of his predecessor, who had named him a cardinal, and was crowned on March 21 in Venice, in the same monastic church where the conclave had been held, San Giorgio Maggiore, because the Austrian emperor Francis II refused to give permission for the enthronement to take place in the cathedral of San Marco (as a sign of his displeasure at the outcome of the election, even though he had agreed to it). Since the church was so small, spectators were gathered in the piazza outside, while others observed from gondolas or peered through telescopes from further distances. Because the French had stolen the papal regalia, Pius VII was crowned with a papier-mâché tiara.

The new pope resisted pressure to move the seat of the papacy to Vienna. He left for Rome on July 3 and named an outstanding cardinal, Ercole Consalvi, to be his secretary of state. By the time the new pope reached Rome, after a difficult journey by sea and land arranged by the Austrian emperor, the Austrian troops had been defeated by Napoleon Bonaparte at the battle of Marengo in northwest Italy on June 14. Pius VII soon persuaded Austria and Naples to withdraw from occupied papal territories. The pope and Cardinal Consalvi then negotiated a concordat with Napoleon, now First Consul of the new French Republic, on July 16, 1801. The concordat restored Catholicism in France, although conditions later appended to the agreement by Napoleon (the so-called Organic Articles) strengthened the government's control over the Church and restricted papal interventions in France. In securing the power for the first time to remove a bishop from his diocese, however, the papacy moved yet another step toward the nearly absolutely monarchical status it has enjoyed over the Church in modern times. Indeed, the concordat with Napoleon may have laid the groundwork for the claims to papal autocracy that were made some seventy years later at the First Vatican Council.

Pius VII reached a similar agreement with the new Italian Republic in 1803, but failed in his attempt to do so with Germany. Against the advice of the Roman Curia, the pope went to Paris to take part in Napoleon's coronation as emperor on December 2, 1804. The gesture was not recip-rocated. Napoleon did not modify the limitations he had placed on the Church and the pope. And when the pope insisted on remaining neutral in the renewed European wars, Napoleon forced him to dismiss his secre-tary of state, Cardinal Consalvi. And when he refused to support the blockade of England, Napoleon occupied Rome on February 2, 1808, and annexed the remainder of the Papal States in May 1809. Pius VII there-upon excommunicated all the "robbers of Peter's patrimony" on June 10, but without mentioning Napoleon by name.

The pope was arrested on July 5 and placed in virtual solitary confine-ment in Savona, near Genoa, guarded by almost fourteen hundred sol-diers. He at first refused to approve the investiture of bishops nominated by Napoleon, but later succumbed to great pressure and agreed verbally to their investiture by the metropolitan archbishops. This was not enough for Napoleon, who had the pope transferred secretly from Savona to Fontainebleau (near Paris) in 1812, after a physically harrowing journey of some twelve days by horse-drawn carriage. The following January the pope, ill and exhausted, was forced to sign a draft convention (known as the Concordat of Fontainebleau), which included an implied renun-ciation of the Papal States. Napoleon published the document as if it were the final version. Two months later the pope retracted his signa-ture, and the following year, with Napoleon having suffered major defeats in Russia and then Leipzig, Pius VII was sent back to Savona and released on March 10, 1814. (Paris fell the same month and Napoleon abdicated on April 11.) The pope reentered Rome on March 24, and on May 7 he rein-stated Cardinal Consalvi as his secretary of state. At the Congress of Vi-enna, Consalvi negotiated the return of almost all of the Papal States, except Avignon and Venaissin, both of which were in French territory.

On August 7, 1814, the feast of St. Ignatius of Loyola (now celebrated on July 31), in spite of protests from the Catholic powers, Pius VII re-stored the Society of Jesus, after having regularized its status in Russia and Naples in 1801 and 1804, respectively. After Napoleon escaped from his exile on the isle of Elba, Pius VII had to seek refuge in Genoa in the spring of 1815. He returned to Rome on June 7. (Napoleon met his fa-mous Waterloo a few days later.)

The second part of Pius VII's pontificate was much less dramatic than the first. He was preoccupied with reorganizing the Papal States, while steering a middle course between the old ways and the newer ways introduced during the French occupation. The compromises satisfied neither the left nor the right, but at least the pope recognized that there were good as well as bad aspects to the French Revolution and the new wave of democracy sweeping the Western world. The pope was also concerned with the restoration of the Church in various countries.

After falling and breaking his thigh some six weeks earlier, Pius VII died on August 20, 1823, two years after his nemesis, Napoleon Bonaparte, and was buried in St. Peter's. His longtime, faithful secretary of state, Cardinal Consalvi, sold all of his own precious objects and had a grand monument by Antonio Canova erected in Pius VII's memory.

250 Leo XII, *1760–1829, pope from September 28, 1823, to February 10, 1829.*

Leo XII's pontificate was an extremely conservative one: he condemned religious toleration, reinforced the Index of Forbidden Books and the Holy Office (formerly the Inquisition), reestablished the feudal aristocracy in the Papal States, and confined Jews once again to ghettos.

Born Annibale Sermattei Della Genga of noble parents, he served after ordination to the priesthood in 1783 as private secretary to Pius VI. He was then ambassador to Lucerne (1784), titular archbishop of Tyre (1793), nuncio to Cologne and Bavaria (1794–1805), and special papal envoy in various other situations. While Pius VII was imprisoned by Napoleon in France, Cardinal Della Genga lived at the abbey of Monticelli, near Piacenza, as a virtual state prisoner. After Napoleon's first defeat and Pius VII's return to Rome in 1814, Della Genga was named nuncio to Paris, but he fell out of favor with the cardinal-secretary of state, Ercole Consalvi, for failing to negotiate the return of Avignon to papal control. He returned to Monticelli, but Pius VII named him a cardinal-priest in the title of Santa Maria in Trastevere and bishop of Sinigallia in 1816. Two years later he became bishop of Spoleto, in his home region. In 1820 he was named vicar of Rome and the head (prefect) of several curial congregations. He was elected pope on September 28, 1823, after a conclave of some twenty-five days due to the votes of reactionary cardinals (known as *zelanti*) who were unhappy with the secretary of state's liberal policies and wanted a return to more traditional papal rule.

The conclave following the death of Pius VII was held in the Quirinale Palace because of the torrid heat in the Vatican region of the city. The election itself was sharply contested, with Austria's vetoing the election of Cardinal Severoli (imperial vetoes were prohibited by Pius X in 1904). On

the afternoon of September 27, Cardinal Della Genga received twelve
votes. The next day his vote count increased to twenty-four and then to
thirty-four of forty-nine votes, the necessary two-thirds required for
election. At first, he tried to refuse election because of the poor state of
his health. Then he relented and took the name Leo XII, in honor of Pope
Leo the Great (440–61), to whom he had a special devotion. Once again,
the conventional assumption that popes are succeeded by duplicates of
themselves, especially if they have been in office many years (Pius VII had
been pope for more than twenty-three years), was thoroughly undermined. Leo XII was crowned on October 5. However, he fell gravely ill
soon thereafter and was given the last sacraments on Christmas Eve. (Another source says he fell ill about a week after his election and that he was
not crowned until after his recovery, very early in the new year.) It is said
that his friend Vincenzo Maria Strambi, the bishop of Macerata, offered
his own life if God would save the pope. Leo XII recovered and Strambi
died on New Year's Day.

The new pope shared the hard-line conservative views of the *zelanti*
who were instrumental in his election. Leo XII at once replaced the
cardinal-secretary of state, Ercole Consalvi, with the conservative Cardinal Della Somaglia and established a Congregation of State to advise him
on political and religious matters. In May 1825 he issued condemnations
of religious indifferentism, religious toleration, and Freemasonry. He also
reinforced the Index of Forbidden Books and the Holy Office (formerly
the Inquisition), restored the Gregorian University to the Jesuits, and established new chairs in theology, but with increased supervision over the
orthodoxy of the professors. He reinstated the feudal aristocracy, with
privileged positions, in the Papal States, as well as the pre-1800 ecclesiastical courts. He also put an end to the laicization of the administration of
the Papal States, restoring the dominance of clergy and nobility, and in
1826 Jews were once again confined to ghettos and their property confiscated. The modern state that Cardinal Consalvi had been trying to establish, without prejudice to the rights and interests of the Church, was now
dismantled in favor of a harsh police state, complete with press censorship, capital punishment, secret societies (the forerunner of the *Sodalitium Pianum* in the pontificate of Pius X in the early twentieth century)
that sniffed out the slightest hints of revolution. As a result of the new
pope's reactionary policies, the Papal States lost many productive citizens, including Jews, and suffered economic stagnation. The rising middle class was angry over the decline in their economic well-being and the
violations of their personal liberties, and the Papal States gained the reputation of being the most backward in all of Europe.

At first the European powers were concerned that Leo XII's election
signaled a reversal of Pius VII's more liberal attitude toward the world's

growing political pluralism. Some of the new pope's early moves confirmed those fears, but he soon came to realize that the Church needed to have good relations with other countries. He came to adopt a more conciliatory policy toward the European powers than with his own subjects in the Papal States. He even sought the advice of Cardinal Consalvi and appointed him prefect of the Congregation on the Propagation of the Faith (Propaganda)—which startled and unnerved the *zelanti* cardinals who had supported his election to the papacy. He returned to the practice of signing concordats with foreign powers, such as the Netherlands, but continued to favor conservative regimes in the hope of stemming the tide of liberalism.

His internal policy was designed to rejuvenate the spiritual vitality of the Church. He called a Holy Year in 1825 to reestablish contact between the papacy and the Catholic people and strove to raise the standards of clerical education and formation (which he addressed in his first encyclical, *Ubi primum*, on May 3, 1824). But his agenda was shaped by a rigidly clericalist theology and spirituality and an overriding fear of, and hostility toward, the modern world. He died on February 10, 1829, and was buried in St. Peter's. Pope Gregory XVI, whom Leo XII had made a cardinal, erected a grand monument to Leo in 1837, by the sculptor Giuseppe Fabris.

251 Pius VIII, *1761–1830, pope from March 31, 1829, to November 30, 1830.*

After Leo XII's generally reactionary pontificate, Pius VIII returned to the more liberal policies of Pius VII (1800–1823). He approved the decrees of the First Council of Baltimore in the United States (1830).

Born Franceso Saverio Castiglioni of noble parents, he was named bishop of Montalto in 1800, but was imprisoned from 1808 to 1814 for refusing to swear allegiance to the Napoleonic regime in Italy. Pius VII named him a cardinal and bishop of Cesena in 1816 and then called him to Rome in 1821 to become bishop of Frascati and grand penitentiary (in charge of absolutions, dispensations, indulgences, and so forth). Pius VII hoped that Cardinal Castiglione would succeed him to the papacy, but the conclave of 1823 chose Leo XII instead. Following Leo's death, the five-week conclave of 1829, dominated this time by moderate cardinals, elected Castiglione on March 31 with the backing of Austria and France and in spite of his poor health. He took the name Pius VIII in honor of his patron, Pius VII, and was crowned on April 5.

Although the new pope was committed to reviving the more liberal policies of Pius VII, his first and only encyclical, *Traditi humiliati nostrae* (May 24, 1829), blamed the breakdown of religion and the social order on indifferentism, the activities of Protestant Bible societies, attacks on

Catholic dogma and the sacredness of marriage, and the existence of secret societies. The next year he condemned Freemasonry's influence in education and in the declining moral standards of young people. On the other hand, he revoked most of Leo XII's harsh measures in the Papal States and made pastoral accommodations in the case of mixed marriages (between a Catholic and a Protestant) in Prussia. (He allowed priests to assist passively at ceremonies where the Protestant party had not promised to raise the children as Catholics. This did not satisfy Prussia and the problem rose again in the next pontificate.)

He appointed Cardinal Giuseppe Albani, the man most responsible for the pope's election in the conclave, as secretary of state. Albani was openly pro-Austrian, which meant that Pius VIII's policies toward the young churches in Latin America, formerly subject to the Spanish crown, were actually less progressive than Leo XII's. Albani's influence also placed the Church in opposition to emancipatory movements in Belgium, Ireland, and Poland in 1830. On the other hand, Pius VIII accepted, against the advice of his nuncio and the Curia, the July Revolution of 1830 in Paris, which deposed the highly unpopular King Charles X in favor of Louis-Philippe, who promised to respect the concordat of 1801 with Napoleon Bonaparte that restored Catholicism in France. He also reached an agreement with the Sultan of Turkey ensuring the religious and civil rights of Armenian Catholics and established an archbishopric of the Armenian rite in Constantinople in 1830. The same year he approved the decrees of the First Council of Baltimore, held in October 1829.

Pius VIII died on November 30, 1830, and was buried in St. Peter's. Cardinal Albani erected a monument to him, the work of Pietro Tenerani.

252 Gregory XVI, *1765–1846, pope from February 2, 1831, to June 1, 1846.*

A Camaldolese monk (and the last monk to be elected pope), Gregory XVI was one of the Church's most reactionary popes, employing Austrian troops on two occasions to crush uprisings in the Papal States and opposing Italian nationalism, freedom of conscience, freedom of the press, and the separation of Church and state. At the same time, he was a strong promoter of the missions. He may be best remembered, however, for having denounced and forbidden the use of railways in the Papal States, calling them, in a play on the French, *chemins d'enfer* ("roads of hell") rather than *chemins de fer* ("roads of iron"). He also banned streetlights, lest people gather under them to plot against the authorities. He was the last nonbishop to be elected pope.

Born Bartolomeo Alberto Cappellari, the son of an aristocratic lawyer, he entered a Camaldolese monastery (a reformed Benedictine community emphasizing fasting, silence, and solitude) at age eighteen, taking the name Mauro, was ordained in 1787, and became a professor of science and philosophy in 1780. He published a book upholding papal infallibility and the temporal authority and independence of the Holy See in 1799. (It has a lengthy title in Italian that begins: *Il trionfo della S. Sede e della Chiesa contro gli assalti dei novatori . . .* ["The Triumph of the Holy See and the Church Against the Attacks of the Innovators"].) In 1805 he became abbot of San Gregorio in Celio (on the Celian Hill in Rome) and two years later procurator general of his order. He taught outside of Rome during Pius VII's exile and imprisonment by Napoleon (1809–14) and was named vicar general of his order in 1823. Having declined appointment as bishop of Zante and of Tivoli, he was proclaimed a cardinal in the title of San Callisto in 1826 (he had been named cardinal the preceding year *in pectore* [Lat., "in the (pope's) breast," or secretly]) and appointed prefect of the Congregation for the Propagation of the Faith (Propaganda). He was considered a candidate for the papacy at the conclave of 1829, following the death of Leo XII, and received as many as twenty-two votes.

At the difficult and laborious fifty-day conclave following the death of Pius VIII, Cardinal Cappellari was elected on February 2, 1831, with the support of the *zelanti* (the ultraconservative, or reactionary, cardinals) and of the conservative Austrian statesman Klemens von Metternich (d. 1859), who argued that an absolutist pope would not yield to "the political madness of the age." (Cappellari was the third choice of the *zelanti*, after Cardinals DeGregorio and Giustiniani, the latter of whom was vetoed by Spain.) At first, Cardinal Cappellari resisted the possibility of election, but Cardinal Zurza, the general of his order, put him under obedience to accept if offered. He received thirty-two votes out of forty-five cast. He took the name Gregory XVI, in honor of Gregory the Great (590–604), because he was also a monk in the Benedictine tradition, of Gregory VII (1073–85), for his defense of the Church, and of Gregory XV (1621–23), founder of the Congregation for the Propagation of the Faith, which the new pope had headed. Since he was not yet a bishop, Gregory XVI was consecrated at once and then crowned on February 6.

The new pope was immediately confronted with a popular uprising in the Papal States and in the city of Rome. The people were calling for greater freedom and an Italian republic. Gregory XVI sought aid from the conservative Austrian government, which promptly crushed the revolts. But the other great European powers (Russia, England, France, and Prussia) intervened at that point and demanded substantial reforms in the Papal States. Gregory was prepared to concede on minor points, but stood firmly against elected assemblies and lay-dominated councils of state. New disorders erupted and Austrian troops were called in for a second time. France thereupon seized Ancona and for seven years the Papal States were under military occupation. In all of his international relations, the pope was aided by his two successive conservative secretaries of state, Tommaso Bernetti and Luigi Lambruschini.

Gregory XVI was as rigid in dealing with theological issues as he was in dealing with political ones. In his encyclical *Mirari vos* (August 15, 1832), a forerunner to Pius IX's famous *Syllabus of Errors* (1864), he denounced the concepts of freedom of conscience, freedom of the press, and separation of Church and state, particularly the liberal views associated with the French priest Félicité Robert de Lamennais (d. 1854) and his newspaper *L'Avenir*. (Lamennais favored religious liberty and the separation of Church and state and also regarded the common consent of all humanity as a norm of truth.) The pope seemed to erase the distinction between the hierarchical structures of the Church and the clericalized monarchical institutions of the Papal States. He accepted the basic assumptions of neo-Scholastic ecclesiology that the clericalized, monarchical structures of the Church were somehow divinely mandated and inferred that they were to be duplicated in the temporal order as well. Accordingly, he firmly supported monarchical regimes against the new democratic movements and declared that the divine origin of the papacy was the basis of the papacy's temporal sovereignty over the Papal States. Concerned about the effect of Lamennais's ideas on the political situation in Italy and the Papal States, Gregory XVI condemned him personally in *Singulari Nos* (1834) because he was dissatisfied with Lamennais's reaction to the previous encyclical. The pope also censured the teaching of the German theologian Georg Hermes (d. 1831) for emphasizing too much the role of reason in the understanding of faith, as well as the teachings of the French priest Louis Bautain (d. 1867) for emphasizing too much the role of faith at the expense of reason.

The pope found himself in conflict with Spain and Portugal for their anticlerical legislation, with Switzerland for the Articles of Baden (1834), which sought to eliminate papal authority over Swiss Catholics, and with Poland for revolting against the Russian czar. He acceded to the demands of the French government that the Jesuits be withdrawn from the country (1845) and eventually reached an accommodation with Prussia over the issue of mixed marriages (i.e., between a Catholic and a Protestant).

Gregory XVI, having headed the Congregation for the Propagation of the Faith (Propaganda) before his election as pope, was a strong promoter of the missions. During his pontificate some seventy dioceses and vicariates apostolic (local churches not yet ready to be made dioceses) were established, and almost two hundred missionary bishops were appointed. He encouraged the creation of a native clergy and a native hierarchy in mission lands. In his bull *Sollicitudo ecclesiarum* (1831) he insisted that, when there is a change of government, the Church will negotiate with the *de facto* government, whether it prefers that government or not. This meant that the Church would not wait until political wrangling was finished before appointing bishops to vacant dioceses in Latin America and India—much to the consternation of Spain and Portugal. It is also important to note that Gregory XVI, however reactionary a pope he may have been, clearly denounced slavery and the slave trade in a papal brief, *In supremo* (1839).

Gregory XVI founded the Etruscan and Egyptian museums in the Vatican and the Christian museum in the Lateran. By the end of this pontificate, however, the papal treasury had been depleted because of all the military expenditures to maintain order in the Papal States. Gregory XIV died on June 1, 1846, and was buried in St. Peter's, first in the crypt and then, in 1853, in the basilica proper, with a monument done by Luigi Amici and funded by the cardinals Gregory XVI had created during his pontificate.

Part VI

MODERN POPES FROM PIUS IX TO PIUS XII

HE TRANSITION TO A MODERN PAPACY IN THE mid-nineteenth century occurred primarily through the loss of the Papal States, an event that Pius IX (1846–78) interpreted at the time as gravely inimical to the Church, but that, in fact, allowed the Church, for the first time in centuries, to redirect its full energies to its spiritual mission and thereby to elevate the papacy's moral authority to levels theretofore rarely attained. Ironically, the first of the modern popes was the least modern of them all. Pius IX's pontificate was the longest in history: some thirty-one years, seven months, and twenty-one days. It was Pius IX who defined the dogma of the Immaculate Conception in 1854 and called the First Vatican Council (1869–70), which defined the primacy and infallibility of the pope. He also issued the famous "Syllabus of Errors" in 1864 that set the Church and the papacy at odds with most of the major developments of the modern world, including the principle of the consent of the governed. Although he was elected as a moderate progressive in 1846, as a welcome relief from his exceedingly conservative predecessor, Gregory XVI (1831–46), Roman mobs tried to throw Pius IX's body in the Tiber River after his death.

Because Pius IX had been the longest reigning pope in history and had created most of the cardinal-electors, according to the conventional wisdom he should have been succeeded by another conservative. He was succeeded instead by a moderate progressive, Leo XIII (1878–1903), the first pope of the twentieth century. Leo XIII was also the first pope seriously to attempt to bring the Church into the modern world. He opened the Vatican archives to scholars, with an expressed sense of confidence that the Church has nothing to fear from the truth. He supported biblical research and gave at least tentative approval to the new democratic movements. His most famous encyclical, *Rerum novarum* (Lat., "Of new things"), published in 1891, is still a historical benchmark in the field of moral theology and social ethics. Subsequent papal encyclicals on the social question (labor-management relations, social justice, the role of government, human rights, international relations, world peace) have always situated themselves in relation to that encyclical. Thus, the name of Pius XI's encyclical *Quadragesimo anno* ("After forty years") is derived from the fact that it was issued in 1931, forty years after Leo XIII's *Rerum novarum.* Paul VI's apostolic letter *Octogesima adveniens* ("The eightieth year") was issued in 1971, eighty years after *Rerum novarum.* And John Paul II's encyclical *Centesimus annus* ("The hundredth year") was released in 1991 to mark the centenary of Leo XIII's encyclical. During Leo XIII's pontificate, there was also a vast missionary expansion of the Church.

Although Leo XIII's was the second longest pontificate in history, the pendulum swung once again from a moderate to a conservative in the papal conclave following Leo XIII's death in 1903. Leo XIII had reigned so long that one cardinal exclaimed, "I thought we had elected a Holy Father, not an Eternal Father!" Nevertheless, the cardinals elected someone very much unlike Leo in theological, spiritual, and political outlook. Pius X (1903–14) once again took up the cause of emphasizing the rights of the Church over against the temporal authorities as well as the urgency of maintaining the purity of Catholic doctrine. The latter he enforced with an oath against Modernism and a vigorous, and sometimes cruel, prosecution of those suspected of heresy (which was itself broadly and often recklessly defined). On the more benign side, Pius X, who was canonized a saint by Pius XII in 1954, is remembered also as the pope who lowered the age for the reception of First Holy Communion to the "age of discretion (or reason)," or approximately seven years.

The papal pendulum swung yet again in 1914, just as the First World War was breaking out. The cardinals did not select another man just like Pius X, but turned instead to a moderate, Benedict XV (1914–22), who immediately called for an end to the bitter internecine conflicts between traditionalists and progressives in the Church. Benedict was, in turn, succeeded by an authoritarian pope, Pius XI (1922–39), who was bitterly opposed to Communism in Russia and Nazism in Germany, but supportive of Fascism in Spain. He also condemned contraception and concluded the Lateran Treaty with Mussolini, establishing Vatican City State as an independent political entity. He was the first pope to use the radio as a means of communication.

Although equally opposed to Communism, Pius XI's successor, Pius XII (1939–58), proved a generally more progressive pope than Pius XI. Pius XII had been secretary of state under Pius XI, and his diplomatic experience made him the inevitable candidate as Europe and the rest of the nations prepared for yet another world war. In spite of the terrible distraction of those war years, Pius XII promoted the renewal of biblical studies by endorsing the methods of modern critical scholarship, the renewal of the liturgy through greater participation of the laity, and the renewal of the theology of the Church through emphasis on the Church as the Mystical Body of Christ, with each member providing his or her own distinctive contribution to the missionary and ministerial work of the Body. Pius XII also defined the dogma of the Assumption of the Blessed Virgin Mary into heaven (1950), proclaimed a Marian Year (1954), and promoted devotion to the reported Marian apparition at Fátima in Portugal. Unfortunately, the pope's own pro-German bias (he had served there as nuncio in the 1920s and genuinely liked the German people and their culture) seems to have made him less sensitive to the terrible threat posed by Adolf Hitler and his Nazi movement and to the Holocaust perpetrated by the Nazis against the Jews. There was also a reactionary side to him, similar to that of Pius X, in his attitude toward modern theology. He condemned the so-called new theology in France (even though three future cardinals were leading figures in it) and allowed the Holy Office (formerly the Inquisition), under the leadership of Cardinal Alfredo Ottaviani, to persecute some of the Church's most distinguished theologians who would be among the future shapers of the documents of the Second Vatican Council: Yves Congar, O.P.; Karl Rahner, S.J.; Henri de Lubac, S.J.; Jean Daniélou, S.J.; M. D. Chenu, O.P.; John Courtney Murray, S.J.; and many others. (Congar, Daniélou, and de Lubac were later made cardinals.) At the same time, by increasing the number of native bishops in Asia and Africa and by internationalizing the College of Cardinals, Pius XII prepared the way for a truly global ecumenical council, Vatican II, which was the most important religious event of the twentieth century and one of the most important in the entire second Christian millennium. He was the first pope to use television as a means of pastoral communication.

It is the Second Vatican Council (1962–65) that separates the first set of modern popes, beginning with Pius IX, from the second, beginning with John XXIII (1958–63), perhaps the greatest pope of all time next to St. Peter himself (to the extent that the Blessed Apostle can be considered a pope in any strictly theological sense).

253 Pius IX, *1792–1878, pope from June 16, 1846, to February 7, 1878.*

The pontificate of Pius IX, also known as *Pio Nono* ("Pius the Ninth"), was the longest thus far in the history of the papacy (thirty-one years, and just over seven months). Elected as a moderate after Gregory XVI's reactionary pontificate, he soon established himself among the more reactionary popes of history. He called the First Vatican Council (1869–70), which defined papal primacy and papal infallibility; he defined the Immaculate Conception of Mary; and he published the "Syllabus of Errors," which condemned the major developments of the modern world.

Born Giovanni Maria Mastai-Ferretti, the son of a count and countess, after ordination to the priesthood (1819) he served on a diplomatic mission to Chile (1823–25), administered the Hospice of San Michele in Rome (1825–27), was named archbishop of Spoleto in 1827 and then bishop of Imola in 1832, and was proclaimed a cardinal in the title of Santi Pietro e Marcellino in 1840. He was considered a liberal during his years as a bishop in Spoleto and Imola because he supported administrative changes in the Papal States and sympathized with the nationalist movement in Italy.

Upon the death of Gregory XVI, there were forty-six cardinals present in Rome (of a total of sixty-two). The foreign cardinals decided not to come to Rome for the conclave because of the unsettled political situation in Italy. The conclave was sharply divided between the *intransigenti* cardinals, who were supporting Gregory XVI's reactionary secretary of state, Cardinal Luigi Lambruschini, and the *liberali* cardinals, who were supporting Cardinal Gizzi. Recognizing that the deadlock between these two candidates would not be broken, the conclave swung to the young (fifty-four-year-old) Cardinal Mastai-Ferreti, who had received fifteen votes on the first ballot, but who had little diplomatic and no curial experience. He was elected pope on June 16, 1846, after a two-day conclave. Mastai received thirty-six votes and Lambruschini received ten. The newly elected pope took the name Pius IX in honor of Pius VII (1800–1823), the pope who had encouraged his vocation to the priesthood in spite of a childhood problem with epilepsy and who had been one of his predecessors as bishop of Imola. Because the election occurred in the evening, it was too late to announce the decision to the Roman people. However, the signal of white smoke was already given, and many assumed that Cardinal Gizzi had been elected pope. His home town of Ceccano erupted in jubilation, with lighted street processions. His palace in Rome was plundered, in accordance with an ancient custom, and his servants joyously burned all of his cardinalatial purple vestments. On the morning of June 17, however, the senior cardinal-deacon announced the election of Cardinal Mastai, to tepid applause. After the newly elected pope appeared on the balcony of the Quirinale Palace to give his first blessing, the mood became more joyous. Pius IX was crowned on June 21 and chose Cardinal Gizzi as his secretary of state. Liberal Europe applauded his election.

One month after his election, the new pope granted amnesty to political prisoners and exiles and approved various reforms in the administration of the Papal States. These were designed only to correct abuses rather than to change structures. The next year he approved the establishment of city and state councils and gave various indications that he was in sympathy with Italian nationalism. He also reached an agreement with the Ottoman Empire that resulted in the reestablishment of the Latin patriarchate of Jerusalem the same year. Enthusiasm for the new pope was at its height in Italy, where any sign of resistance to the Hapsburgs and other reactionary regimes were hailed with cries of "Viva Pio Nono!" But after this initial period of euphoria, the citizenry of Rome and the Papal States turned against him when it became clear that he had no intention of agreeing to the establishment of a constitutional state.

Pius IX believed, like other popes before him, that the temporal sovereignty of the Holy See (the so-called Patrimony of St. Peter) was indispensable to its spiritual independence—a belief that has since been amply disproved. The reason the Papal States were regarded as such an obstacle to Italian unification was that they stretched across the whole of central Italy, cutting off the south from the north. In any case, the last straw was his refusal to support the war to expel Austria from Italy in 1848. With the Papal States in a state of economic crisis, Pius IX's prime minister, Count Rossi, was murdered on November 15, 1848. The pope was besieged by revolutionaries at the Quirinale Palace and was forced to flee in disguise to Gaeta, south of Rome, on November 24. On February 9, 1849, Giuseppe Mazzini and his followers proclaimed the Roman Republic.

The pope appealed to the Catholic powers of Europe for help. French troops restored papal rule to Rome on July 15, and Pius IX returned to the city on April 12, 1850. With Giacomo Antonelli now as his secretary of state, the pope established an antinationalist, paternalistic regime in the Papal States that alienated the educated citizenry and that his own counselor, Monsignor Giovanni Corboli-Bussi, described as "reactionary and maladroit." But one after another, the pope lost several of the Papal States (Romagna, Umbria, the Marches). Count Camillo Cavour, chief minister of Piedmont, took advantage of the situation and by September 1860, after the defeat of the papal army at Castelfidardo, all of the Papal States, with the exception of Rome and its immediate environs, had been taken over by the new kingdom of Italy. The pope remained in Rome under the protection of a French garrison, but after ten years the French had to leave with the outbreak of the Franco-Prussian War. (During this decade under French protection, he issued a decree on February 29, 1868, forbidding Catholics to take part in the political life of the "usurping" kingdom of Italy.)

On September 20, 1870, Italian forces under Victor Emmanuel occupied Rome. In an October plebiscite, Rome was incorporated into the Italian state. On May 13, 1871, the Law of Guarantees assured the pope of personal inviolability and left him with the Vatican and other buildings.

But Pius IX refused to accept the arrangement (which did not have the status of international law) and never again set foot outside the Vatican, considering himself a prisoner therein. He calmly and steadfastly viewed the events as a form of the ever raging battle between God and Satan, in which Satan's defeat was inevitable.

During his politically disruptive pontificate, the pope found time to carry on the ordinary business of the Church. Thus, he established over two hundred new dioceses and vicariates apostolic (ecclesiastical territories not yet ready for diocesan status) and reestablished the hierarchies in England (1850) and the Netherlands (1853). On December 8, 1854, he defined the dogma of the Immaculate Conception of the Blessed Virgin Mary (namely, that Mary was conceived without original sin), giving rise to a new wave of Marian devotions throughout the Western world. On December 8, 1864, he published the encyclical *Quanta cura* (Lat., "How much care") with the famous "Syllabus of Errors" attached. The eighty errors were concerned, first, with attempts to identify God with the world (pantheism) or to exclude God from it (naturalism); second, with the relationship between faith and reason, with a particular censure of all forms of rationalism; and, third, with liberalism and the rights of the Church. One of the errors read: "That in the present day, it is no longer necessary that the Catholic Church be held as the only religion of the State, to the exclusion of all other modes of worship: whence it has been wisely provided by the law, in some countries nominally Catholic, that persons coming to reside therein shall enjoy the free exercise of their own worship. . . . That the Roman Pontiff can, and ought to, reconcile himself to, and agree with, progress, liberalism, and modern civilization."

Then, in 1869 Pius IX convened the First Vatican Council (1869–70) which, in its dogmatic constitution *Pastor Aeternus* (Lat., "Eternal Pastor") and under intense personal pressure from the pope himself, defined the primacy of the pope over the universal Church as well as his infallibility. The pope, the council taught, has "full and supreme power of jurisdiction over the whole Church, not only in matters that pertain to faith and morals, but also in matters that pertain to the discipline and government of the Church throughout the whole world." Furthermore, this power is "ordinary [i.e., not delegated] and immediate [i.e., not exercised through some other party] . . . over each and every Church [and] over each and every shepherd and faithful." Regarding infallibility: "It is a divinely revealed dogma that the Roman Pontiff, when he speaks *ex cathedra* ["from the chair"], that is, when acting in the office of shepherd and teacher of all Christians, he defines, by virtue of his supreme apostolic authority, a doctrine concerning faith or morals to be held by the universal Church, possesses through the divine assistance promised to him in

the person of Blessed Peter, the infallibility with which the divine Redeemer willed his Church to be endowed in defining the doctrine concerning faith or morals; and that such definitions of the Roman Pontiff
are therefore irreformable of themselves, not because of the consent of
the Church." No definitions could have been further removed from the
teaching of the Council of Constance (1414–18), from the theology and
practice of the Eastern churches, and from the practice of the universal
Church, West and East alike, of the first Christian millennium. It should
be noted, however, that the council's other dogmatic constitution, *Dei Filius* ("the Son of God"), provided a more balanced theological program,
equally condemning rationalism, on the left, and fideism, on the right—
the one exaggerating the powers of reason to the detriment of faith; the
other exaggerating the powers of faith to the detriment of reason.

Unfortunately, Pius IX's extremely inflated notion of the papal office
created serious problems both within and outside the Church. A schism
developed in Holland and elsewhere (the Old Catholics, who rejected the
dogma of papal infallibility), and a wave of anticlericalism erupted
throughout Europe, exemplified particularly by the attacks of Protestant
Chancellor Otto von Bismarck on the Church in Germany (the so-called
Kulturkampf, or "culture war"). Austria repudiated its concordat with the
Vatican and religious confrontations broke out in Switzerland.

Ironically, by the time his record-long pontificate ended and in spite
of his own wishes, Pius IX had witnessed the creation of what is now
known as the modern papacy, freed of the deadweight of temporal sovereignty and exercising a more far-reaching spiritual authority perhaps
than ever before in its history. When Pius IX died on February 7, 1878,
however, he was an exceedingly unpopular pope with the people of Rome
and with the educated classes generally, even though he had been an extraordinarily popular pope with the Catholic masses, especially outside
of Italy, both because of his warmly pious personality and also out of
sympathy for all the troubles he had suffered with such serenity and
courage. On July 13, 1881, there was a disruption of the procession accom-
panying his body from its original burial place in St. Peter's to San
Lorenzo fuori le Mura (St. Lawrence's Outside the Walls). A mob tried
unsuccessfully to seize the body and throw it into the Tiber River.

254 Leo XIII, *1810–1903, pope from February 20, 1878, to July 20, 1903.*

Leo XIII was the first of the truly modern popes, seeking to bring the
Church into dialogue with the modern world, but also challenging the
modern world to live up to the standards of the gospel in terms of social
justice. His encyclical *Rerum novarum* (Lat., "Of new things," 1891) was

one of the most important papal pronouncements in history and has continued to shape the formation of Catholic social thought more than a century later. His was the second longest pontificate in history, after that of Pius IX, his predecessor.

Born Gioacchino Vincenzo Pecci, he served after ordination to the priesthood as governor of Benevento (1838–41) and then of Perugia (1841–43), where he had to engage in such activities as the control of banditry, the building of roads, and the establishment of a savings bank for farmers. Gregory XVI then sent him as papal nuncio to Belgium (1843–46), as titular archbishop of Damietta. In Belgium he witnessed the beginnings of the Industrial Revolution in Europe. However, the young archbishop was recalled from Belgium when his support for the local bishops against the king's prime minister on an educational matter led the king to ask for his removal. He was then named bishop of Perugia in 1846 and a cardinal in the title of San Crisogono in 1853. He remained in Perugia until 1878 (when he was elected pope) because Pius IX's ultra-conservative secretary of state, Cardinal Antonelli, did not trust him. As bishop of Perugia he modernized the course of studies in his seminary, promoted a revival of Thomism, and began, in a series of widely noticed pastoral letters, to argue for a reconciliation between the Church and modern culture. At the First Vatican Council (1869–70), he voted with the majority on papal infallibility but took no leadership position. After Cardinal Antonelli's death in 1877, Pius IX invited Archbishop Pecci back to Rome as the *Camerlengo* (It., "chamberlain") of the Holy Roman Church, the one who administers the Holy See when there is a vacancy in the Chair of Peter.

Pius IX died on February 7, 1878, and the cardinals worried that they could not hold a peaceful and free conclave in Rome, given the unfavorable political atmosphere. A move of the conclave to Malta was contemplated, but they received assurances from the government that they would not be disturbed in Rome. Sixty of the sixty-four cardinals attended. Among the absent was the cardinal-archbishop of New York, John McCloskey (d. 1885), the first American cardinal. At first, all eyes were on Cardinal Bilio as the favorite. But since he had been a major contributor to Pius IX's highly unpopular "Syllabus of Errors" (1864), he garnered only six votes on the first ballot, against nineteen for the favorite of the moderates, Cardinal Pecci, who was unpopular with the conservative friends of the late secretary of state, Cardinal Antonelli. Pecci's vote rose to twenty-six on the second ballot, and, on February 20, 1878, to forty-four on the third ballot, more than the required two-thirds for election. He took the name Leo XIII in honor of Leo XII (1823–29), although he had been a very conservative and unpopular pope. The new pope had to be crowned (on March 3) in the Sistine Chapel rather than in St. Peter's Basilica itself because the anticlerical government feared demonstrations in his favor if he blessed the Roman people from the outside balcony of St. Peter's. Nevertheless, immediately after the ceremony he gave his blessing *Urbi et Orbi* (Lat., "to the city and to the world") from the inside balcony of St. Peter's. Leo XIII was already sixty-eight years old and in weak health when elected. Many probably saw him as a transitional pope following Pius IX's record-long pontificate. But Leo himself would be in office for over twenty-five years, dying at age ninety-three—the second longest pontificate in history, after Pius IX's. The two popes together—Pius IX and Leo XIII—reigned for just over fifty-seven years! No two consecutive papal reigns have ever been so lengthy in the entire history of the Church.

Although the new pope was much more of a moderate than his predecessor, Leo XIII continued many of Pius IX's policies regarding, for example, socialism, Communism, and Freemasonry. He even increased the centralization of church government by actively intervening with national episcopates, strengthening the authority of his nuncios, and concentrating the headquarters of religious orders in Rome. Where Leo XIII was least like Pius IX was in his understanding of the relationship between Church and society and his general openness to scholarship and the intellectual life. With his 1879 encyclical *Aeterni Patris* (Lat., "Of the Eternal Father"), he encouraged the study of St. Thomas Aquinas (d. 1274), albeit through the lens of the current neo-Scholastic philosophy and theology and with the intention of employing Thomism against political and social liberalism. He promoted the study of astronomy (modernizing the Vatican Observatory) and the natural sciences at the Vatican, opened the Vatican archives to scholars of all backgrounds (1883), declaring that "the Church has nothing to fear from the truth," and urged Catholic historians to write objectively about the Church. He also laid down guidelines for the scientific study of Sacred Scripture in his 1893 encyclical *Providentissimus Deus* ("Most provident God"). He devoted several encyclicals to the social order: in 1881 his encyclical *Diuturnum illud* ("This long-lasting . . .") gave tentative recognition to democracy; in 1885 the encyclical *Immortale Dei* ("The immortal God") distinguished between the temporal and the spiritual realms, insisting that any form of government can be legitimate if it serves the common good; and in 1888 his *Libertas praestantissimum* ("Freedom") argued that the Church is the custodian of freedom, properly understood. But his most important and most enduring social encyclical was *Rerum novarum* ("Of new things"), published on May 15, 1891. Although it strongly defended the right to private property (against socialism), it also insisted (against laissez-faire capitalism) on the social responsibilities that accompany the private possession of property, namely, the obligation to pay workers a just wage and to honor workers' rights, especially the right to form trade unions.

At the same time Leo XIII was deeply concerned about recovering the Papal States and the temporal power of the Holy See. Some of his actions, however, were clearly counterproductive. Thus, by forbidding Catholics from participating in elections in the new Italian state, he undermined the capacity of the Church to influence political events. Otherwise, Leo XIII was a more astute diplomat and political realist than his predecessor had been. He secured a revision in 1886 and 1887 of the anticlerical laws passed in Germany during the *Kulturkampf* (Ger., "culture war") and reached accommodations with Belgium in 1884 and Russia in 1894. He also secured the withdrawal of anticlerical legislation in Chile, Mexico, and Spain. He had hoped for formal diplomatic relations with England, but that did not materialize during his pontificate. His efforts to rally French Catholics to the Third Republic also failed. Royalist Catholics in France were outraged, and the French government actually intensified its anti-Catholic legislation.

On the ecclesiastical (and especially missionary) front, Leo XIII's pontificate was more successful. He established 248 dioceses and 48 vicariates outside of Europe, for example, in North Africa, India, Japan, and the United States (where 28 new dioceses were erected). He published two encyclicals calling for an end to the enslavement of Africans, one to the Brazilian hierarchy in 1888 and another to all bishops in 1890. He appointed the first apostolic delegate to the United States in 1893 and, while praising some aspects of the Church in the United States, warned against idealizing the separation of Church and state in his 1895 apostolic letter *Longinqua oceani* (Lat., "An ocean apart"). On January 22, 1899, he also censured—in the apostolic letter *Testem benevolentiae* ("Witness of benevolence")—an opinion, misnamed as Americanism, for its too easy accommodation with modern ideas and practices, especially regarding the acceptance of religious pluralism. Historians today are generally convinced that the pope really had France in mind rather than the United States.

Ecumenically, Leo XIII's record was mixed, but more negative than positive. On the one hand, he was the first pope to speak of non-Catholic Christians as "separated brethren" and invited Protestants and Orthodox to return to union with Rome, but without mentioning heresy or schism. On the other hand, he followed the dominant ecclesiology of the Counter-Reformation period, which emphasized the hierarchical and structural elements of the Church, as well as the supreme authority of the pope. Thus, his 1896 encyclical *Satis cognitum* (Lat., "Known enough") stipulated that acceptance of the primacy of the pope was a necessary condition of Christian reunion. His 1895 letter *Ad Anglos* ("To the English people") was indicative of a special concern for the "conversion" of England. The same year he appointed a commission to investigate the validity of Anglican orders. Not surprisingly, the judgment was negative. The pope made the judgment official in his famous papal bull *Apostolicae curae* ("Of apostolic concern"), published on September 13, 1896. Anglican orders were declared "absolutely null and utterly void." The argument was that, in the consecration of Matthew Parker as archbishop of Canterbury in 1559, the form of ordination, based on the ordinal of King Edward VI (1550), omitted several necessary elements of the rite (later restored by Archbishop William Laud in the next century) and that the intention of the ordination as expressed in the Anglican ritual did not include the conferral of the power to offer sacrifice. Therefore, the line of apostolic succession was broken and subsequent ordinations to the Anglican episcopate and priesthood were invalid. In the light of current liturgical and theological understanding in the Catholic Church, however, neither argument (neither form nor intention) is regarded any longer as probative of the case against Anglican orders. (In 1879 Leo XIII had made the former Anglican John Henry Newman a cardinal.)

A man of traditional Catholic piety and devotion, Leo XIII issued ten encyclicals on the Rosary and consecrated the entire human race to the Sacred Heart of Jesus during the Jubilee year of 1900. Toward the end of his pontificate, his attitudes toward modern developments had hardened. Thus, he published new norms of censorship in 1897 and a new Index of Forbidden Books in 1900 and established the Pontifical Biblical Commission in 1902 to monitor the work of Catholic biblical scholars. Nevertheless, in spite of the limitations imposed by the continued conflict with the Italian government over the papacy's rights to its expropriated properties (the so-called Roman Question), Leo XIII brought increased international prestige to the papacy after long years of reactionary and separatist papal attitudes toward the newly emerging modern world.

The world took notice when Leo XIII died on July 20, 1903. He was buried temporarily in St. Peter's, but his body was later transferred, according to his wishes, to the basilica of St. John Lateran. Before his death, at age ninety-three and after more than twenty-five years as pope, one cardinal supposedly made the comment, "I thought we had elected a Holy Father, not an Eternal Father!"

255 Pius X, St., *1835–1914, pope from August 4, 1903, to August 20, 1914.*

Although Pius X was canonized a saint in 1954, his pontificate stands as one of the most controversial in the modern papacy. He assumed a negatively critical posture toward modern democratic governments and led a sometimes cruel and internecine campaign against Catholic theologians, biblical scholars, and historians (lumping them all under the umbrella of Modernism), from which the Church did not begin to recover until the Second Vatican Council (1962–65). On the other hand, Pius X was a deeply spiritual man in his personal life and is remembered as the "pope of frequent Communion," having lowered the age for First Communion to the "age of discretion" (approximately seven).

Born Giuseppe Melchiorre Sarto, the son of the village postman and a seamstress, he was ordained in 1858 and worked for the first eight years as a country curate and then nine years as a pastor. In 1875 he was named chancellor of his home diocese of Treviso and spiritual director of its major seminary. In 1884 he was appointed bishop of Mantua, a run-down diocese that he quickly revitalized. In 1893 he was named patriarch of Venice and a cardinal in the title of San Bernardo alle Terme. In Venice he devoted himself once again to pastoral tasks, generally steering clear of politics. However, his first pastoral letter to the Venetians presaged the approach he would later take as pope. In matters pertaining to the Vicar of Christ, he wrote, "there should be no questions, no subtleties, no opposing of personal rights to his rights, but only obedience."

Cardinal Sarto was elected pope on August 4, 1903, even though the clear favorite going into the conclave was Leo XIII's secretary of state for seven years, Cardinal Mariano Rampolla del Tindaro. On the first ballot on the morning of August 1, Rampolla received twenty-four votes; Cardinal Giuseppi Gotti, seventeen; and Cardinal Sarto, five. On the second ballot in the afternoon, Rampolla had twenty-nine votes; Gotti, sixteen; and Sarto, ten. The next day, when it appeared that no one could prevent Rampolla's election, the archbishop of Kraków, Cardinal Puzyna de Kozielsko, solemnly proclaimed the veto of Rampolla's candidacy by Franz Joseph, emperor of Austria and king of Hungary. The cardinals, especially the French and Rampolla himself, vigorously protested this intrusion into the business of the conclave and determined to continue with the voting. At which point Cardinal Vivos y Tuto proposed that the cardinals elect Rampolla by acclamation as a reply to the emperor's veto. But the third ballot had already begun, and the cardinals were obliged to count the votes. This time Sarto had twenty-one votes (more than double his support from the previous ballot). On the fourth ballot in the afternoon, Rampolla had thirty votes, and Sarto rose to twenty-four. The French cardinals felt that they had made their point against the imperial veto but now recognized that the election had taken a new course and that the situation had become uncertain. It began to look as if the cardinals wanted a different kind of pope from Leo XIII (the pendulum had swung once more!). The next morning (August 4) Rampolla's vote count dropped to ten; Gotti had two; and Sarto received fifty. He took the name Pius X out of respect for recent popes of that name who had courageously resisted persecution and fought against error. Like his predecessor, the new pope imparted his first papal blessing from the internal balcony of St. Peter's in order to make the point that the pope still considers himself a "prisoner" of the Italian government. Pius X was crowned on August 9. (The following January he decreed that vetoes of papal candidates by Catholic powers were henceforth prohibited.)

In adopting as his motto, "To restore all things in Christ" (Ephesians 1:10), the new pope made clear that he intended to be a pastoral rather than a political pope. Nevertheless, his "pastoral" outlook carried him inevitably into troubled political waters. He began by appointing a similarly conservative (some would say "reactionary") secretary of state, the Spanish Cardinal Rafael Merry del Val (d. 1930), in order to reverse Leo XIII's more accommodating approach to secular governments. This led the following year to a diplomatic break with France. In 1906 he denounced France's Law of Separation and, against the pleas of the French bishops, rejected any compromise settlement. The Church won its independence, but lost all its material support. The pope adopted the same stance toward Portugal in 1911, while his support for Catholic minorities in Ireland and Poland angered England and Russia. The pope's popularity in the United States plummeted when, in 1910, he refused to receive ex-president Theodore Roosevelt because Mr. Roosevelt was scheduled to speak at the Methodist church in Rome. He suspended the *Opera Dei Congressi,* which coordinated the work of Catholic associations in Italy in 1904, and in 1910 condemned the *Le Sillon,* a French social movement that tried to reconcile Catholicism with more liberal political views and that was ecumenical in composition. The pope also opposed trade unions that were not exclusively Catholic. At the same time, he was tolerant to a fault of the right-wing, monarchist *Action Française.* On the other hand, mainly out of fear of socialism in Italy, Pius X did relax the ban on the participation of Catholics in Italian elections.

Pius X's "pastoral" concept also included defending the flock against heresy. In the decree *Lamentabili sane exitu* (Lat., "A lamentable departure indeed"), issued by the Holy Office (formerly the Inquisition, now the Congregation for the Doctrine of the Faith) on July 3, 1907, sixty-five propositions concerning the nature of the Church, revelation, biblical exegesis, the sacraments, and the divinity of Christ were explicitly condemned. This decree was followed on September 8 by the encyclical *Pascendi Dominici gregis* ("Feeding the Lord's flock"), which characterized Modernism as the "synthesis of all heresies." On September 1, 1910, he continued his effort to root out Modernism from the Church by imposing, in

Sacrorum antistitum, an oath against Modernism on all clerics. He also gave encouragement in three papal letters to a network of informants, known as the *Sodalitium Pianum* (League of St. Pius V), to report on instances of deviations from doctrinal orthodoxy wherever and by whomever they occurred, leading in many instances to the dismissal of faculty from their teaching positions and in other cases to their suspension from the priesthood and/or their excommunication from the Church. The oath against Modernism required the cleric to agree that the existence of God can be known and proved by natural reason, that miracles and prophecies are certain signs of revelation, that the Church as an institution was founded by Jesus Christ, that there is a constant deposit of faith in which dogmas cannot change their meaning from one generation to another, and that faith involves a real assent of the intellect to truths presented from outside the believer. The oath was imposed on all Catholic clergy, and only about forty refused to swear to it. Professors of theology in Germany, however, were dispensed from the oath at the request of the German bishops. (An encyclical in 1910 dedicated to St. Charles Borromeo [d. 1584] had to be quickly withdrawn because of its vulgar polemics against German Protestantism.) The overall effect of the oath on Catholic scholarship was devastating—a blow from which it did not begin to recover until the pontificates of Pius XII (1939–58) and John XXIII (1958–63) and the Second Vatican Council (1962–65). The oath discouraged Catholic scholars from pursuing new lines of inquiry in their teaching and research and from publishing the results of their research, and at the same time it encouraged more fanatical elements in the Church to declare a kind of war on theologians and biblical scholars who did not toe the conservative line. Pius X's successor, Benedict XV (1914–22), had to declare an end to the internecine conflict in the Church, and the oath itself was finally rescinded by the Congregation for the Doctrine of the Faith in July 1967, during the pontificate of Paul VI (1963–78).

There were, of course, positive, less controversial initiatives taken during this pontificate. The Roman Curia was reorganized. The Code of Canon Law was revised (although not published until after the pope's death). Seminaries and their curricula were reformed. Catechetical instruction was improved. The Pontifical Biblical Institute was established in 1909. Laity were encouraged to cooperate with their bishops in the apostolates of the Church. Frequent Communion was encouraged (the seventeenth- and eighteenth-century Jansenists would have been appalled), and the age for First Communion was lowered to the "age of discretion" (approximately seven). Pius X also restored Gregorian chant as the model of church music and began a revision of the Breviary (Divine Office) and the Roman Missal.

After suffering a heart attack in 1913, Pius X lived in the shadow of death. He lapsed into a melancholia after learning of the events that would eventually precipitate the First World War, especially the assassination of the archduke Francis Ferdinand, heir apparent to the Austro-Hungarian throne, in Sarajevo on June 28, 1914. One month later Austria-Hungary declared war on Serbia, and other declarations of war followed. Pius X died on August 20, 1914, and was buried in a simple and unadorned tomb in the crypt of St. Peter's, in accordance with his wishes. However, a monument was erected in his memory in the basilica proper in 1923, the year the process of his canonization was begun. He was beatified on June 3, 1951 (the first pope to be beatified since Innocent XI [1676–89]), and canonized on May 29, 1954 (the first pope to be canonized since Pius V [1566–72]). His body was moved after his canonization to a place under the altar of the Chapel of the Presentation in St. Peter's. Because he had left instructions that his body not be embalmed, no subsequent popes have been embalmed after death, with sometimes unpleasant results (Pius XII's nose almost fell off; John Paul I's face turned green; and Paul VI's ears became black). Feast day: August 21.

256 Benedict XV, *1854–1922, pope from September 3, 1914, to January 22, 1922.*

Although his pontificate was overshadowed by the First World War, Benedict XV's greatest accomplishment may have been his calling to a halt the internecine war within the Church provoked by the vehement anti-Modernist campaign of his predecessor, Pius X. Benedict XV may well have been one of the finest popes in history, but surely one of the least appreciated, inside as well as outside the Church.

Born Giacomo della Chiesa, of patrician parents, he was not impressive in appearance because of an injury incurred at birth. One eye, one ear, and one shoulder were noticeably higher than the other. He was also short, extremely thin, stooped-shouldered, slightly bluish in complexion, and walked with a limp. Temperamentally, however, he was gentle and sympathetic and always approachable, even though he had occasional eruptions of temper for which he abjectly apologized. Ordained in 1878, he was assigned for study at the Academy of Noble Ecclesiastics (now called the Pontifical Ecclesiastical Academy, the training school for the Vatican's diplomatic corps) in Rome. From 1883 to 1887 he served as secretary to Archbishop Mariano Rampolla, who was then nuncio to Spain. When Rampolla became cardinal-secretary of state in 1887, della Chiesa remained with him, becoming undersecretary of state in 1901. He continued in that position even after Leo XIII died and Rampolla was succeeded by Cardinal Merry del Val in 1903. Although he cautioned against unwarranted condemnations of scholars in the anti-Modernist period, Pius X once referred to him as his "right arm in fighting Modernism." He had hoped to become nuncio to Spain, just as his mentor had been, but Merry del Val was suspicious of him because of his association with Rampolla and persuaded the pope to remove della Chiesa from the diplomatic service. Pius X thereupon appointed della Chiesa as archbishop of Bologna in 1907 and personally consecrated him in the Sistine Chapel. Not until May 1914, however, did the pope name him a cardinal (in the title of Santi Quattro Coronati), even though Bologna was traditionally a cardinalatial see. When the new cardinal came to Rome to take possession of his titular church on June 4, the pope was already gravely ill. Three months later, on September 3, 1914, della Chiesa himself would be elected pope.

On the first ballot of the conclave on the morning of September 1, Cardinals della Chiesa and Maffi each had twelve votes. Their votes each rose to sixteen on the second ballot. By the eighth ballot della Chiesa had thirty-two votes, Maffi had none. But Cardinal Serafini emerged meanwhile with twenty-four votes. On the tenth ballot on September 3, the votes for della Chiesa reached thirty-eight, sufficient for election. The newly elected pope took the name Benedict XV in memory of Prospero Lambertini, who like himself had been archbishop of Bologna when elected pope with the name Benedict XIV. Like his two immediate predecessors, he gave his first papal benediction from the internal balcony of St. Peter's to a crowd estimated at more than fifty thousand. His election was greeted with much surprise because he had been so recently named a cardinal. Undoubtedly, his diplomatic experience was an important consideration for those who voted for him, given the recent outbreak of the First World War. He was crowned not in St. Peter's Basilica proper, in accordance with the centuries-old tradition, but in the Sistine Chapel in order to give the event a more purely religious significance and to avoid the appearance of too much festivity during a time of war and human misery.

The new pope immediately took stock of the financial status of the Holy See, determined to dispense as much money as possible to those in need. He named Cardinal Domenico Ferrara as his secretary of state, but Ferrara died on October 10 and was replaced by Cardinal Pietro Gasparri. Cardinal Merry del Val was switched to the Holy Office as its secretary. As the war clouds continued to gather across Europe and beyond, the pope maintained a strictly neutral posture, refusing to condemn any side—with the result that both sides accused him of partiality. He sought in various ways to alleviate the sufferings caused by war, for example, by

attempting to reunite prisoners of war with their families and by persuading Switzerland to accept soldiers of all nations afflicted with tuber-
culosis. But when on August 1, 1917, he proposed a seven-point peace
plan, including the renunciation of war indemnities and the return of all
occupied territories, both the Allies and the Central Powers ignored it.
The Allies, in fact, suspected the pope of tilting toward Germany because
of Germany's promise to return Rome to the Holy See after defeating
Italy. Benedict XV also dreaded the expansion of Russian Orthodoxy if
Russia and the Allies triumphed. The Allies referred to him contemptuously as "*le pape boche*," or "the Kraut pope," while the Germans, in their
turn, dismissed him as "*der französische Papst*," or "the French pope."
When the armistice was actually reached in 1919, the pope was deliberately excluded from the negotiations in accordance with an agreement
reached between the Allies and Italy.

After the war Benedict XV pleaded for reconciliation among the nations and gave at least general support to the League of Nations. He sent
two future popes on diplomatic missions: Achille Ratti (later Pius XI) as
apostolic visitor to Poland and Lithuania and Eugenio Pacelli (later Pius
XII) as nuncio to Bavaria. Britain sent its first diplomatic representative
to the Holy See since the seventeenth century. The pope's canonization of
Joan of Arc (d. 1431) in 1920 helped in the restoration of diplomatic relations with France. With regard to the status of the Holy See within Italy,
he adopted a more moderate political course, allowing full participation
by Catholics in the political process (he gave his blessing to the Popular
Party founded by Don Luigi Sturzo) and lifting the ban on official visits
to the Quirinale Palace by Catholic heads of state. The palace had once
been the summer residence of the popes, but in 1870 was taken over as
the residence of the king of Italy. He also authorized a secret meeting between the Italian dictator Benito Mussolini and Cardinal Gasparri in the
home of Count Carlo Santucci, an old friend of the pope, in order to
begin the process of regularizing the place of the Holy See in Italy (the result would be the Lateran Treaty of 1929).

On June 28, 1917, he promulgated the new Code of Canon Law, whose
revision had been initiated by his predecessor, Pius X, and in September
established a commission to interpret it. Like many popes before him,
Benedict XV dreamed of a reconciliation between Eastern and Western
Churches. He thought, mistakenly, that the Russian Revolution opened
that possibility anew. He made the Congregation for the Oriental
Churches autonomous in May 1917 (it had been united previously with
the Congregation for the Propagation of the Faith), with himself as its
prefect, and established the Pontifical Oriental Institute in Rome the following October (he gave it over to the direction of the Jesuits in 1922). In

1920 he declared St. Ephraem (d. 373), the Syrian exegete and theologian, a Doctor of the Church. The Turks erected a statue of Benedict XV in Istanbul (formerly Constantinople) that hailed him as "the great pope of the world tragedy . . . the benefactor of all people, irrespective of nationality or religion." On the missionary front, he also pursued a more creative course, urging in his encyclical *Maximum illud* (Lat., "This greatest," 1919) that missionaries receive a better spiritual and theological preparation and that missionary bishops form a native clergy as quickly as possible and never place the interests of their native countries ahead of the pastoral needs of their people.

Perhaps the most important and abidingly relevant achievement of his pontificate occurred within two months of his election. On November 1, 1914, he issued his first encyclical letter, *Ad beatissimi Apostolorum* ("At [the threshold] of the most blessed Apostles"), in which he called a halt to the internecine warfare between so-called Integralist Catholics and progressive Catholics that had developed and intensified during the previous pontificate. The pope insisted, without using the name "Integralist," that the noun "Catholic" needed no qualification by "fresh epithets." In the end, he was a pope dedicated to healing and reconciliation, even if, on the political front, his ministrations were unappreciated.

Benedict XV died unexpectedly at age sixty-seven of influenza that developed into pneumonia on January 22, 1922. He was buried in the crypt of St. Peter's. A monument to him by Pietro Canonica was erected in the basilica proper in 1928.

257 Pius XI, *1857–1939, pope from February 6, 1922, to February 10, 1939.*

The first pope to use the radio as a means of communication and the first pope with a serious avocation of mountain climbing, Pius XI concluded the Lateran Pacts (also known as the Lateran Accords) with the Italian dictator Benito Mussolini, establishing the Vatican City State as a separate and independent political entity. So intense was his opposition to, and fear of, Communism that he signed agreements or concordats with two of the most notorious Fascist leaders of the twentieth century (Mussolini and Hitler) and gave his full support to another (Spain's Francisco Franco).

Born Ambrogio Damiano Achille Ratti, he was ordained in 1879, obtained three doctorates at the Pontifical Gregorian University, was a seminary professor in Padua (1882–88), and worked at the Ambrosian Library in Milan (1888–1911). He became pro-prefect of the Vatican Library in 1911 and prefect in 1914. In 1918 Benedict XV sent him to Poland as apostolic visitor, the next year promoting him to nuncio and titular archbishop of Lepanto. When the delicate political situation in the region made Archbishop Ratti a source of nationalist resentment because of his partiality toward Polish Catholics, Benedict XV appointed him in 1921 archbishop of Milan and a cardinal in the title of San Martino ai Monti (appropriate for a mountaineer). The next year, on February 6, 1922, he was elected pope as a compromise candidate on the fourteenth ballot.

The conclave opened on February 5, 1922, with the cardinals divided into two camps: those in support of the ultraconservative Spanish Cardinal Merry del Val, secretary of state under Pius X and head of the Holy Office under Benedict XV, and those in support of Cardinal Gasparri, Benedict's secretary of state. Merry del Val, however, could never get more than seventeen votes, and Gasparri's maximum was twenty-four. Support then shifted to Cardinal La Fontaine, the patriarch of Venice, who reached a maximum of twenty-three votes, and then, unexpectedly, support developed for Cardinal Ratti, who received twenty-four votes on the eleventh ballot. In the next three ballots, La Fontaine's support dropped from twenty-two, to eighteen, to nine, while Ratti's increased from twenty-seven, to thirty, and then to forty-two, sufficient for the two-thirds required for election. Ratti took the name Pius XI in honor of Pius IX, who had supported him in his early years of ecclesiastical formation, and of Pius X, who had called him to Rome for service in the Vatican Library. The new pope's first gesture was one of political reconciliation. He gave his pontifical blessing *Urbi et Orbi* (Lat., "To the city and to the world") from the external balcony of St. Peter's Basilica, the first time a pope had done so since 1870, when Italian forces occupied Rome and incorporated the city into the new Italian state. The crowd that had gathered in St. Peter's Square bellowed, "Viva Pio Undicesimo! Viva Italia!" He was crowned on February 12, 1922.

Pius XI took as his motto, "Christ's peace in Christ's kingdom," to make the point that the Church should be active in the world, not isolated from it. His first encyclical the following December, *Ubi arcano Dei consilio* ("Where [is] the hidden plan of God"), promoted Catholic Action, or the participation of the laity in the apostolate of the hierarchy. In 1925 he instituted the feast of Christ the King to counteract secularism, and for the same purpose he proclaimed Jubilee years in 1925, 1929, and 1933, as well as biennial eucharistic congresses. His numerous canonizations, particularly during the Jubilee year of 1925, were designed to promote the same end: John Fisher (d. 1535), Thomas More (d. 1535), John Bosco (d. 1888), and Thérèse of Lisieux (d. 1897), better known as "the Little Flower." He declared four theologians Doctors of the Church: Albertus Magnus (d. 1280), Peter Canisius (d. 1597), John of the Cross (d. 1591), and Robert Bellarmine (d. 1621).

Pius XI also had a strong commitment to the missions. He required every religious order to engage in missionary work. As a result, the number of missionaries doubled during his pontificate. He personally consecrated the first six native Chinese bishops in 1926, then a native Japanese bishop in 1927, and native priests for India, Southeast Asia, and China in 1933. The total number of native priests in mission lands rose from almost three thousand to over seven thousand during his pontificate. At the beginning of his pontificate there were no mission dioceses under the direction of a native bishop. Upon Pius XI's death, there were forty such dioceses. The Catholic population in mission countries rose from nine million to twenty-one million. He also established a faculty of missiology at his alma mater, the Pontifical Gregorian University.

Pius XI's ecumenical efforts bore less fruit. His calls for reunion between Rome and the Orthodox East fell on deaf, not to say hostile, ears. At the same time, he did everything he could to support Eastern-rite churches in union with Rome (sometimes referred to as Uniate churches, an opprobrious and unwelcome term). He promoted the work of the Oriental Institute in Rome, rebuilt the Ethiopian and Ruthenian Colleges in Rome, and in an encyclical, *Rerum Orientalium* (Lat., "Of matters of the Oriental [Churches]," 1928), called for a greater understanding of Eastern churches. The pope was negative, however, in his attitude toward Protestants and, in his encyclical *Mortalium animos* ("The souls of mortals," 1928), forbade any Catholic involvement in ecumenical conferences. His earlier tentative efforts toward outreach to Anglicans (he had approved, for example, the conversations between Catholics and Anglicans at Malines in 1921–26) foundered when, in 1930, his encyclical *Casti connubii* ("Of pure marriage") uncompromisingly condemned artificial birth control as immoral—in direct opposition to the position just taken by the Anglican bishops at their Lambeth Conference.

His most lasting encyclical, still studied today as an important part of the corpus of Catholic social teachings, was *Quadragesimo anno* ("After forty years," 1931), written on the occasion of the fortieth anniversary of Leo XIII's pioneering social encyclical *Rerum novarum* and in the midst of a terrible worldwide economic depression. Pius XI criticized both the excessive individualism of the capitalist right and the excessive collectivism of the socialist left. He insisted that the right to private property is a qualified right—qualified by the demands of social justice and of the common good. He also introduced one of Catholic social thought's most important principles, the principle of subsidiarity: nothing is to be done by a higher agency that can be done better or at least as well by a lower agency. In recent years Catholic theologians have begun to apply this principle to the Catholic Church itself in order to challenge the growing tendency toward recentralization of authority in the Vatican.

As a former librarian and scholar, Pius XI was committed to the advancement of science and of learning generally. He rehabilitated some scholars who had been punished during the anti-Modernist period under Pius X (1903–14), and he modernized and enlarged the Vatican Library, of which he had once been prefect. In 1925 he founded the Pontifical Institute of Christian Archaeology, erected the Pinocoteca for the Vatican's collections of pictures, and moved the Vatican Observatory to Castel Gandolfo, with added modern equipment. He installed a radio station (Vatican Radio) in Vatican City in 1931 and was the first pope to make use of radio as a means of pastoral communication. He admonished bishops to maintain their diocesan archives and introduced new reforms in seminary education. He founded the Pontifical Academy of Sciences in 1936 and opened its membership rolls to scientists from many countries.

Pius XI was not inactive politically. His first act, as noted above, was to signal a thaw in relations between the Holy See and the new Italian state. Aided by two secretaries of state, Cardinal Pietro Gasparri (until 1930) and Cardinal Eugenio Pacelli (the future Pius XII), he concluded concordats and other agreements with some twenty governments and improved relations with France, where he condemned the nationalistic and monarchistic Catholic movement *Action Française* (1926). His most important political initiative, however, was the Lateran Treaty (February 11, 1929), reached with the Italian prime minister Benito Mussolini after two and half years of difficult negotiations. Through the treaty the Vatican recognized for the first time since 1870 the kingdom of Italy, with Rome as its capital. Italy, in turn, financially compensated the Vatican for the loss of the Papal States and recognized Catholicism as the official religion of the country. Many anticlerical laws were repealed and religious instruction in secondary schools became obligatory. Vatican City State was established as a political entity, or sovereign state, independent of Italy. (After the fall of the Italian monarchy in 1946, the Lateran Treaty was incorporated into the new republican constitution of Italy. The concordat was renegotiated and formally ratified on June 3, 1985. By the new concordat, Catholic instruction is no longer mandatory in government schools, and the clergy are no longer paid salaries by the government.)

Pius XI's attention turned then from Italy to the new totalitarian states that had arisen in Russia and Germany. At the start of his pontificate, the pope had made a vain effort to stop the persecution of Christians in Russia. His effort, through the French Jesuit Bishop Michael d'Herbigny (d. 1957), to consecrate bishops secretly in the Soviet Union proved counterproductive. Bishop d'Herbigny was expelled from the country and the bishops he consecrated were sent to penal camps. In his encyclical *Divini Redemptoris* (Lat., "Of the Divine Redeemer," 1937) Pius XI condemned

Communism as atheistic. So intense was his revulsion for, and fear of, it that the pope even entered into a concordat with the ostensibly anti-Communist National Socialist (Nazi) Germany in 1933, trusting Hitler's assurances that the rights of the Church would be respected. As a result of that unfortunate agreement, Hitler's regime gained international prestige and domestic Catholic opposition to it was muted. Between 1933 and 1936, however, Pius XI was forced to address thirty-four notes to the Nazi government to protest its growing oppression of the Church. Most of the notes went unanswered. The break came in 1937 when he ordered his encyclical *Mit brennender Sorge* (Ger., "With searing anxiety"), denouncing the violations of the concordat and condemning Nazism as fundamentally racist and anti-Christian, to be read from every German pulpit. The letter, written largely by Michael von Faulhaber (d. 1952), the cardinal-archbishop of Munich, had to be smuggled into Germany. (Cardinal Faulhaber worked with the American occupation forces after the Second World War in the reconstruction of Munich and received the Grand Cross of the Order of Merit, the highest award that could be bestowed by the then West German Republic.) The Nazi leadership, caught completely off guard, was infuriated and intensified its persecution of the Church and especially of its priests. Many have wondered why Pius XI's successor, Pius XII, never made a similar gesture of protest against the Nazi outrages against humanity.

When Mussolini dissolved Catholic youth organizations in Italy in 1931, Pius XI began to change his attitude toward the Italian regime. He issued an encyclical critical of Italian Fascism, *Non abbiamo bisogno* (It., "We have no need"). The break became complete in 1938 when the regime adopted Hitler's racist doctrines, especially against the Jews. On the other hand, Pius XI never had a problem with Spanish Fascism, of the variety espoused by the Spanish dictator Generalissimo Francisco Franco, whom the pope supported during the civil war of 1936–39. The pope did not object when Mussolini intervened in that war on Franco's behalf. (After Franco's death in 1975 the Catholic Church by and large supported Spain's peaceful transition to democracy, which ultimately brought about the first complete separation of Church and state in the history of Spanish Catholicism.)

Although authoritarian in his exercise of the papal ministry and uninhibited in some of the more triumphalistic aspects of the office, he prepared the way, at least in part, for the renewal of the Catholic Church at the Second Vatican Council more than two decades later. Pius XI died on February 10, 1939, at age eighty-one and after seventeen years as pope. He was buried in the crypt of St. Peter's Basilica. The excavations in the crypt preparatory to the pope's burial accidentally broke through the floor, and subsequent investigations led to the discovery of a first-century cemetery and the putative grave of St. Peter. On February 9, 1941, Pius XI's remains were placed in a magnificent Carrara marble sarcophagus, underneath a statue of him by Giannino Castiglioni.

258 Pius XII, *1876–1958, pope from March 2, 1939, to October 9, 1958.*

Pius XII's pontificate spanned the entire Second World War and postwar period, when he devoted his energies to combating Communism through various means, including the promotion of Marian piety and devotion. Although largely traditional in his theological and pastoral views, Pius XII in fact laid much of the groundwork for the renewal that came to full flower in the Second Vatican Council (1962–65).

Born Eugenio Maria Giuseppe Giovanni Pacelli, the son of a lawyer, he studied, like several previous popes, at the Pontifical Gregorian University and the Capranica College. Ordained in 1899, he served from 1904 to 1916 as assistant to Cardinal Pietro Gasparri in the codifying of canon law, mandated by Pius X (1903–14). In 1917 he was appointed by Benedict XV (1914–22) as nuncio to Bavaria (whose capital was Munich) and titular archbishop of Sardes. In 1920 he was named nuncio to the new German republic, where he was dean of the diplomatic corps. He was created a cardinal in 1929 in the title of Santi Giovanni et Paolo. Less than two months later, on February 7, 1930, he succeeded his mentor, Cardinal Gasparri, as secretary of state. In this new capacity, Cardinal Pacelli was responsible for concluding concordats with Austria and National Socialist (Nazi) Germany in 1933. Hitler would flagrantly violate the latter. An accomplished linguist and world traveler, Cardinal Pacelli paid official visits to Argentina, France, and Hungary and an extensive private visit to the United States in 1936, which included a meeting with the newly re-elected president, Franklin D. Roosevelt.

With the Second World War about to erupt, Cardinal Pacelli was elected pope on March 2, 1939, on the third ballot of a one-day conclave, obtaining forty-eight of sixty-three votes (another source puts the total vote at fifty-three, not sixty-three). The resident Italian bishops were originally in favor of the cardinal-archbishop of Florence, Elia Dalla Costa. (Cardinal Pacelli had actually received sufficient votes for election on the second ballot, but he asked for a third ballot to confirm the will of the cardinal-electors. The brevity of the conclave stimulated the false rumor that he had actually been elected unanimously.) Pacelli was the best known of all the cardinals, especially among the non-Italians, and seemed to possess the diplomatic experience needed at that troubled time. He was also the first secretary of state elected to the papacy since

Clement IX in 1667. (After the death of his own first secretary of state in 1944, he would fill the position himself thereafter.) The new pope took the name Pius XII in grateful memory of Pius XI. The Romans were pleased with Pacelli's election because he was a native Roman himself ("*romano de Roma*"), the first one since Innocent XIII in 1721. Pius XII gave his first papal blessing from the central external balcony, or loggia, of St. Peter's Basilica and was the first pope to do so over the radio. He was crowned on March 12, 1939.

The new pope's central concern as he began his pontificate was world peace. He appealed to the nations to avoid war through diplomatic initiatives and urged the convening of an international conference to resolve differences peacefully. "Nothing is lost by peace," he said, "everything is lost by war." On August 24, 1940, he made a radio appeal to the world on behalf of peace (Italy itself had entered the war two months earlier). When his efforts failed and war broke out in earnest, Pius XII secured for Rome the status of an open city and he himself adopted an impartial stance. Although he was convinced that Communism was a greater evil than Nazism, the pope did not approve Hitler's attack on Russia. But he also opposed the Allies' demand at Casablanca (January 1943) for unconditional surrender. After Hitler occupied Rome on September 10, 1943, Vatican City became a sanctuary for many refugees, including Jews. However, Pius XII has been criticized severely for his failure to speak out and act more forcefully on behalf of the plight of the Jews.

Those who have written in defense of his wartime posture underscore his denunciation of the extermination of peoples based on race, albeit in general terms, his concern that stronger and more explicit denunciations would lead to even greater reprisals, and his personal support for efforts to render assistance and refuge to Jews. At the same time, however, in two separate statements (1944 and 1946) he implicitly exonerated Germany from any notion of collective guilt. The controversy will undoubtedly continue, but the judgment of history on this matter seems to have tilted against Pius XII. In a word, he could and should have done much more to protest the Holocaust—something akin to the strong denunciation of Nazism's racist policies and practices of his predecessor, Pius XI, in the encyclical *Mit brennender Sorge* (1937). Those who have taken a more critical view of the pope's position speculate that his experience as nuncio to Germany in the 1920s, his general partiality to Germans and German culture, and his contempt for Communism as more dangerous than Nazism had much to do with his reluctance to speak out against the atrocities against the Jews.

Although the Second World War and the pope's public attitude toward the Holocaust have dominated most of the secular interest in this pontificate, Pius XII was remarkably productive and successful in his pastoral and ecclesiastical activities. There were few religious and moral topics he did not touch upon in his allocutions, encyclicals, and other pronouncements. He clearly laid the groundwork for the extraordinary renewal of the Church wrought by the Second Vatican Council (1962–65). His encyclical on the Church as the Mystical Body of Christ, *Mystici corporis* (June 29, 1943), prepared the way for the council's teaching that the Church is the whole People of God (that is, including more than the hierarchy and clergy) and the Temple of the Holy Spirit (that is, a charismatic community as well as an institutional organization). His encyclical that same year on the renewal of biblical studies, *Divino afflante Spiritu* (Lat., "Inspired by the Divine Spirit," September 30, 1943), encouraged Catholic biblical scholars to make use of all the modern tools of critical, scientific scholarship in the interpretation of the Word of God. The consequent achievements of Catholic biblical scholarship enriched all of Catholic theology, and both together informed and shaped the central documents of the Second Vatican Council: on the nature and mission of the Church, on ecumenism, on the salvation of non-Christians, on revelation, and on religious liberty. In calling for greater participation by the laity in the worship of the Church, his encyclical *Mediator Dei* ("Mediator of God," November 20, 1947) prepared the way for the council's groundbreaking Constitution on the Sacred Liturgy and the many changes that document generated in the liturgical life of the Church following the council. Some of those changes, however, were already on course because of Pius XII's own reforms prior to the council: the reform of the Holy Week liturgy in the mid-1950s, the relaxation of the eucharistic fast (Catholics were no longer required to fast from midnight prior to the reception of Holy Communion, and water no longer broke the fast), and the introduction of evening Masses (which the wartime situation had first made necessary).

There was also, however, a conservative, even reactionary, side to Pius XII's theological and pastoral agenda. His Holy Office, under the leadership of Cardinal Alfredo Ottaviani, carried on a determined pursuit (some would say persecution) of some of the Church's most distinguished theologians: M. D. Chenu, O.P.; Yves Congar, O.P.; Henri de Lubac, S.J.; Jean Daniélou, S.J.; Karl Rahner, S.J.; John Courtney Murray, S.J.; and others. In his encyclical *Humani generis* ("Of the human race," August 12, 1950), Pius XII condemned the so-called new theology and warned that once the pope had spoken on a controverted matter, theologians were no longer free to discuss it. Ironically, three of the theologians who felt the lash of the Vatican at this time were rehabilitated and made cardinals by later popes: Daniélou (by Paul VI) and de Lubac and Congar (by John Paul II).

His personal devotion to the Blessed Virgin Mary and his conviction that she was the main spiritual bulwark against atheistic Communism led Pius XII to define the dogma of the bodily Assumption of Mary into heaven (*Munificentissimus Deus*, November 1, 1950), to promote devotion to Our Lady of Fátima (a town in Portugal where she was said to have appeared to three young children to urge the world to be converted, do penance, and pray the Rosary), to declare a Marian Year in 1954, and to leave open the question not only of her role as mediatrix of all grace but even as coredemptrix with Jesus Christ.

Pius XII canonized thirty-three persons during his pontificate, including Pius X (1903–14), and created an unusually large number of cardinals: thirty-two in 1946 and twenty-four in 1953. Here again, he anticipated the new, more international direction of the Church of Vatican II. The new cardinals were drawn from many countries of the world and the Italian contingent in the College of Cardinals was reduced to about one-third.

The pope took very few ecumenical initiatives during his pontificate. His attitude toward the World Council of Churches and Protestants generally was guarded, although he did permit Catholic scholars to engage in theological discussions with non-Catholic scholars. He tried to stimulate better relations between Eastern Catholic churches and the Orthodox, but with little discernible effect. There were little or no formal interfaith contacts with non-Christians, not even with Jews, but the pope did support the concept of tolerance toward others.

Because of the prevalence of radio, newsreels, and television (he had written an encyclical on these new media in 1957, *Miranda prorsus*, "Wholly to be wondered at"), Pius XII became the best known pope in history to that date. By the time of his death at Castel Gandolfo on October 9, 1958, he had gained considerable credibility and influence for the papacy and the Catholic Church among non-Catholics throughout the world. Pius XII was buried in the crypt of St. Peter's Basilica.

Part VII

MODERN POPES FROM JOHN XXIII TO JOHN PAUL II

NE HAS ONLY TO STUDY WITH SOME CARE AND detail the history of the two-thousand-year-old papacy of the Catholic Church to realize how singularly important was the pontificate of John XXIII (1958–63), who was elected at age seventy-six, a month short of his seventy-seventh birthday. Apart from the Blessed Apostle Peter himself, there has been no other pope quite like John XXIII. In a period of less than five years he almost single-handedly transformed the Catholic Church from a clericalistic, monarchical, unecumenical, and theologically rigid body to a community of radical equality in Christ—laity, religious, and clergy alike—open to dialogue and collaboration with other Christian and non-Christian communities, with nonbelievers, and with the world at large. He did so principally through the force of his own personal example—so different in style from his aloof and authoritarian predecessor, Pius XII—and the authentically pastoral manner in which he exercised the Petrine ministry: humbly, gently, compassionately, and always with warm humor. The institutional mechanism of this transformation of the Church was the Second Vatican Council (1962–65), which John XXIII conceived, convoked, and convened and which his successor, Paul VI (1963–78), guided to completion.

Paul VI was the first pope in history to travel by airplane as pope (Pius XII had done so while still a cardinal). Until John Paul II (1978–), Paul VI was the most widely traveled pope in history, visiting countries thousands of miles away from Rome. Although progressive in theology, social thought, and pastoral outlook, Paul VI's pontificate was unfortunately overshadowed by his divisive and widely rejected encyclical condemning all forms of artificial birth control. So distressed was he by the negative reaction to *Humanae vitae* (1968) that he vowed never to write another encyclical. And, indeed, Paul VI issued no other during the remaining ten years of his pontificate.

Paul VI was succeeded—not surprisingly—by a man very different from himself in personality. John Paul I, however, would have one of the shortest pontificates in all of history, serving just thirty-three days before he died suddenly of a heart attack. In spite of the brevity of his pontificate,

John Paul I made history on two counts, the one trivial, the other significant: he was the first pope in history to take a double name (out of respect for his two immediate predecessors, John XXIII and Paul VI), and
he was the first pope in at least a thousand years to dispense with the traditional crowning ceremony with the triple tiara following his election
(in order to emphasize the pastoral and ministerial nature of the papacy).
He was invested instead with the pallium of an archbishop, a woolen
vestment worn around the neck as a symbol of pastoral authority.

When, following John Paul I's sudden death, the cardinals were called
hurriedly back to Rome for another papal election, they were determined
to elect someone young enough and vigorous enough to handle the job.
At first they looked, as usual, to the list of Italian candidates. But when it
became clear that the Italians were unable to agree among themselves,
they turned outside the Italian minority in the College of Cardinals and
elected the first Slavic pope in history and the first non-Italian pope since
Hadrian VI (1522–23), the Polish cardinal Karol Wojtyła, archbishop of
Kraków. John Paul II quickly established himself as the most traveled
pope in history, surpassing the remarkable record of Paul VI. Through
the medium of his many foreign trips, his appearances on television and
video tapes, his many encyclicals and allocutions, and his books, he also
became the pope best known to his contemporaries in all of history. Although committed in principle to the renewal and reforms of the Second
Vatican Council, which he himself attended as a bishop, John Paul II devoted much of his pontificate to the containment of progressive ideas he
regarded as dangerous to the life and faith of the Church. For that reason,
some refer to his pontificate as restorationist, that is, committed to a
restoration of much of pre–Vatican II Catholicism, especially its centralization of power in the Vatican and its focus on the authority and personality of the pope himself. Others, however, are equally convinced that he
is one of the great popes of all time, leading the Church courageously and
without compromise of fundamental truths into a new century and a
new millennium.

More detailed attention is given here in Part VII than elsewhere in the
book to the process by which these modern popes were elected to the papacy. The wheeling and dealing, the coalition building, the strategizing,
and the blocking of one candidate or another deemed unacceptable to a
particular group of cardinals are all part of the drama of a papal conclave
and of events leading up to it. They also reinforce the point that the papacy is a very human and political institution, entered upon in very
human and political ways. All that happens in connection with a papal
election cannot simply, and naively, be attributed to the work of the Holy
Spirit.

259 John XXIII, *1881–1963, pope from October 28, 1958, to June 3, 1963.*

Perhaps the most beloved pope in all of history, John XXIII convened the Second Vatican Council (1962–65) and set the Catholic Church on a whole new pastoral course, emphasizing the role of the laity, the collegiality of bishops, the authentic faith and goodness of non-Catholic Christians and non-Christians, and the dignity of all human beings.

Born Angelo Giuseppe Roncalli, the third of thirteen children in a family of peasant farmers, he was ordained in 1904 and became secretary to his bishop in Bergamo, lecturing at the same time on church history at the diocesan seminary. He served as a conscripted hospital orderly during the First World War and then as a military chaplain. In 1921 Benedict XV appointed him national director of the Congregation for the Propagation of the Faith. Because of his interest in history, especially in St. Charles Borromeo (d. 1584), and his research at the Ambrosian Library in Milan, Father Roncalli came to the attention of its librarian, Achille Ratti, the future Pius XI (1922–39). It was Ratti, after being elected pope, who launched Angelo Roncalli on a diplomatic career in the Church, appointing him titular archbishop of Areopolis and apostolic visitor (1925) and then apostolic delegate (1931) to Bulgaria and apostolic delegate to Turkey and Greece (1934). In Turkey he established friendly relations not only with the government but also with the Orthodox churches. During the German occupation of Greece (1941–44), he did what he could to relieve the distress of the people and in particular to prevent the deportation of Jews. He was appointed nuncio to France on December 22, 1944, where he dealt tactfully with a number of difficult problems, including the resentment toward bishops who had collaborated with the pro-Nazi Vichy regime (he persuaded three bishops to resign) and the worker-priest movement (which he supported). He also served, while nuncio to France, as the Vatican's first permanent observer at the United Nations Educational, Scientific, and Cultural Organization (UNESCO) for nineteen months in 1951 and 1952. In 1953 he was named a cardinal in the title of Santa Prisca and the patriarch of Venice, where, in addition to his pastoral duties, he completed the fifth and last volume of his collection of documents of St. Charles Borromeo.

Upon the death of Pius XII there were fifty-one cardinals who gathered for the conclave that would elect a successor, of whom eighteen were Italian. (Cardinals Mindszenty of Hungary and Stepinac of Yugoslavia were not free to leave their Communist-controlled countries, and Cardinal Mooney of Detroit died suddenly just before the beginning of the conclave on October 25.) Although only a month short of his seventy-seventh birthday, the affable and jovial Cardinal Roncalli was considered by many the most likely candidate to be elected. He, too, recognized the possibility. (There were, after all, twenty-four cardinals in the conclave older than Roncalli himself.) In spite of his humble origins, Roncalli had wide diplomatic experience, was highly cultured, and was proficient in French, Bulgarian, Russian, Turkish, and modern Greek. The cardinals (once again!) were looking for someone different from the dead pope, whom they found aloof and autocratic. In his formal address on behalf of all the cardinals just prior to the start of the conclave, Cardinal Antonio Bacci said that the Church needed "a pope gifted with great spiritual strength and ardent charity," a man who can "embrace the Eastern and the Western Church," a man who "will belong to all peoples," especially those living under oppression or in poverty, a man capable of building "a bridge between all levels of society, between all nations—even those that reject and persecute the Christian religion." In other words, someone unlike Pius XII.

Although the secret of the conclave of 1958 has been well kept, there are clues to be read from various sources, including John XXIII's own posthumously published *Journal of a Soul*. He noted that the conclave wavered back and forth over the course of three days and that he "rejoiced when I saw the chances of my being elected diminishing and the likelihood of others, in my opinion truly most venerable and worthy persons, being chosen." By the end of the first day, Roncalli had twenty votes and Cardinal Gregory Peter Agagianian, an Armenian who had worked in the Roman Curia for many years and was disliked by his fellow Eastern-rite Catholics in Rome for being out of touch with Eastern Catholicism, had eighteen. Two votes were cast for a noncardinal, Archbishop Giovanni Battista Montini of Milan (the future Paul VI). It is said that Roncalli himself cast one of those votes for Montini. Cardinal Giacomo Lercaro of Bologna, considered the most progressive candidate, had only four (probably cast by the German cardinals), as did Cardinal Valerio Valeri. In any case, the non-Italian cardinals looked upon Agagianian as more Roman than Eastern so, even if they might have been disposed to a non-Italian pope, he was not their man. John XXIII later admitted, in a talk three months afterward at the Armenian College in Rome, that his name and Agagianian's "went up and down like two chickpeas in boiling water." By lunchtime on the second day, after two more ballots, the conclave was deadlocked. Lercaro had by now thrown his votes to Roncalli. Although Cardinal Eugene Tisserant (d. 1972), the dean of the College of Cardinals and prefect of the Congregation for the Oriental Churches, was strongly in favor of a non-Italian pope, he shifted his support from Agagianian to Cardinal Benedetto Masella. At that point, Roncalli may have slumped to fifteen votes or thereabouts. Two more ballots and still the smoke was black. No pope had been elected. At the beginning of the next day, October 28, Roncalli had thirty-four votes, still short of the necessary two-thirds. Cardinal Ottaviani, feared head of the Holy Office, was by now on Roncalli's side and brought a number of votes with him that had been cast for Masella. But it still took three more ballots to bring Roncalli to the necessary thirty-eight votes—on the eleventh ballot.

He took the name John XXIII (there had also been an antipope by the name of John XXIII, during the Great Western Schism of the fifteenth century) for a number of different reasons: it was his father's name; it was the name of the parish church where he was baptized; and it was the name of numerous cathedrals around the world, including the pope's own cathedral, St. John Lateran. The new pope pointed out that John was the most frequently used name by popes throughout history, and that nearly all had brief pontificates! He also explained that he loved the name John because it was borne by the two men closest to Jesus: John the Baptist and John the Evangelist. He called himself John, he said finally to the cardinals, in order to renew the exhortation of the Apostle John that we should love one another.

He gave his first papal blessing from the central external balcony, or loggia, of St. Peter's Basilica, where he was received with great joy by the assembled throng. For the first time in history, the blessing was televised. John XXIII was crowned on November 4, the feast of St. Charles Borromeo. At the coronation Mass, at which he himself preached (contrary to tradition), he insisted that he wanted to be, above all else, a good shepherd. Later, when he took possession of his cathedral church, the basilica of St. John Lateran, on November 23, he reminded the congregation that he was not a prince surrounded by the signs of outward power, but "a priest, a father, a shepherd." He proved true to his word. That Christmas, for example, he revived the custom, which had lapsed since the occupation of Rome in 1870, of visiting the prisoners at Regina Coeli (where he recalled the jailing of one of his own relatives) and the patients at one of the local hospitals. He also made frequent appearances in the parishes of his diocese, as well as other hospitals, convalescent homes for the elderly, and educational and charitable institutions. Every day he celebrated what was then known as a dialogue Mass (that is, with responses from the congregation). On Holy Thursday he washed the feet of selected members of the congregation, and on Good Friday he walked in the procession of the cross. More than any other pope since the earliest centuries, he recognized that he was, first and foremost, the Bishop of Rome. His example undoubtedly influenced John Paul II (1978–), who carried it to even broader levels of practice.

At his first consistory (or assembly) of cardinals John XXIII abolished the rule, established by Sixtus V (1585–90), limiting the maximum number of cardinals to seventy and named twenty-three new cardinals to the College of Cardinals. He also abandoned the old distinctions among cardinal-bishops, cardinal-priests, and cardinal-deacons. Henceforth, all cardinals would have to be or to become bishops. By 1962, after four more consistories, he had increased the total number to eighty-seven (plus three whose names had not been revealed because they were in Communist-controlled nations), with a more international composition than ever before in history. On January 25, 1959, he proposed three projects: a diocesan synod for Rome (it would be held the following January in the basilica of St. John Lateran, but without much discernible success), a revision of the Code of Canon Law (he created a pontifical commission for the revision of the code in 1963, but its work would not finally be completed until 1983 under John Paul II), and an ecumenical council (Vatican II, begun in October 1962 and completed under his successor, Paul VI). He attributed the last idea to a sudden inspiration of the Holy Spirit and referred to the council as a "new Pentecost."

John XXIII made it clear in his opening address to the council that it had not been called, as previous councils had been, to refute errors and to clarify points of doctrine. "The substance of the ancient doctrine of the deposit of faith is one thing," he said, "and the way in which it is presented is another. And it is the latter that must be taken into great consideration with patience if necessary, everything being measured in the forms and proportions of a magisterium which is predominantly pastoral in character." He acknowledged that the Church had punished those in error in the past with much severity, but he insisted that nowadays "the Spouse of Christ prefers to make use of the medicine of mercy rather than that of severity. She considers that she meets the needs of the present day by demonstrating the validity of her teaching rather than by condemnations." The most effective means of eradicating discord, and of promoting harmony, peace, and unity, he said, is through the spreading everywhere of "the fullness of Christian charity." The opening address, one of the most important pronouncements in his entire pontificate, placed John XXIII in direct opposition to leading figures in the Roman Curia who held to a more authoritarian, defensive, and punitive vision of the Church. "In the daily exercise of our office," he pointed out, "we sometimes have to listen, much to our regret, to voices of persons who, though burning with zeal, are not endowed with too much sense of discretion or measure. In these modern times they can see nothing but prevarication and ruin. They say that our era, in comparison with past eras, is getting worse, and they behave as though they have learned nothing from history, which is, nonetheless, the teacher of life. They behave as though at the time of former councils everything was a full triumph for the Christian idea and life and for proper religious liberty. We feel we must disagree with those prophets of gloom, who are always forecasting disaster, as though the end of the world were at hand. In the present order of things, Divine Providence is leading us to a new order of human relations which, by our own efforts and even beyond our very expectations, are directed toward the fulfillment of God's superior and inscrutable designs. And everything, even human differences, leads to the greater good of the Church." In one Italian word, which he himself gave us, the purpose of the council was *aggiornamento,* an updating of the Church. The metaphor he employed was that of a closed window suddenly thrust open "to let some fresh air in." We are not born to be "museum keepers," he once said, "but to cultivate a flourishing garden of life."

Official observers from eighteen non-Catholic Christian churches were present by invitation at the opening of the council. Although the pope himself did not attend the sessions, he intervened decisively on November 21, 1962, to rule that a theologically rigid document on revelation, rejected by more than half the council but short of the necessary two-thirds vote, should be redrafted by a new, mixed commission of bishops. He adjourned the first session of the council on December 8, but would never live to see the opening of the second session the following September. He was already suffering from a terminal cancer of the stomach, originally diagnosed on September 23, 1962. He said to a friend, "At least I have launched this big ship—others will have to bring it into port."

His encyclicals reflected the pastoral and ecumenical tone of his pontificate. *Ad Petri Cathedram* (Lat., "To the Chair of Peter," June 29, 1959), on the themes of truth, unity, and peace, greeted non-Catholics as "separated brethren." *Mater et magistra* ("Mother and teacher," May 15, 1961), released on the seventieth anniversary of Leo XIII's groundbreaking social encyclical *Rerum novarum* (1891) updated Catholic social teaching on property, the rights of workers, and the obligations of government. It struck a balance between the principles of subsidiarity (namely, that nothing should be done by a higher agency that can be done as well, if not better, by a lower agency) and socialization (namely, "the growing interdependence of citizens in society" requiring higher agencies, especially governmental, to meet needs that otherwise could not be met by lower or voluntary agencies). So progressive were the encyclical's ideas that one prominent American Catholic conservative writer retorted, "*Mater, si! Magistra, no!*" ("Mother, yes! Teacher, no!"). *Pacem in terris* ("Peace on earth," April 11, 1963), published less than two months before his death, insisted that the recognition of human rights and responsibilities is the foundation of world peace. Many saw this encyclical and other contemporaneous gestures (for example, his receiving in audience the son-in-law of Soviet premier Nikita Khrushchev) as signs that the pope harbored the hope of an eventual reconciliation between the West and the Communist East. Earlier, during the Cuban missile crisis, on October 25, 1962, he had broadcast a message over Vatican Radio to heads of states, urging both sides to exercise caution. The next day the Soviet newspaper *Pravda* carried a quotation from the address in a banner headline: "We beg all rulers not to be deaf to the cry of humanity." It has been said that John XXIII's appeal made it possible for Khrushchev to back down without losing face. The event also encouraged the pope to write his celebrated encyclical on peace, *Pacem in terris,* published the following spring. He was awarded the Peace Prize of the International Balzan Foundation in 1962, with the concurrence of the four Soviet members of the foundation's general council and with the approval, therefore, of Nikita Khrushchev himself. In 1963, after his death, he was awarded the U.S. Presidential Medal of Freedom.

No pope in history was so committed to Christian unity as John XXIII was. On June 5, 1960, he established the Secretariat for Promoting Christian Unity, with the venerable biblical scholar Cardinal Augustin Bea (d. 1968) as its first president. He formally received the Archbishop of Canterbury, Geoffrey Fisher, on December 20, 1960 (the first Anglican primate to be so received). He also sent two envoys to Istanbul (formerly Constantinople) to convey his greetings to Ecumenical Patriarch Athenagoras I on June 27, 1961, and exchanged greetings with Patriarch Alexis of Moscow. In November 1961, five official Catholic observers attended, with the pope's approval, the World Council of Churches meeting in New Delhi. With regard to the Jews, whom he had aided during the Second World War while a diplomat in Greece, he removed the offensive "perfidious" from the prayer for Jews in the Good Friday liturgy, and on one occasion greeted a group of Jewish visitors with the words, "I am Joseph, your brother."

John XXIII made his last public appearance from the window of his apartment on Ascension Thursday, May 23, 1963. At noon he intoned the prayer *Regina Coeli* (Queen of Heaven) in a voice that was still musical and strong. The applause from the crowd in St. Peter's Square was so strong that he was almost prevented from giving his blessing. The next several days were filled with pain, but the pope remained conscious and communicative, making statements that were relayed around the world, drawing the global human community into an unprecedented solidarity. He prayed for the council and for unity—not only of the Church but of all humankind. "It is not that the gospel has changed," he said, "it is that we have begun to understand it better." When John XXIII died on the evening of June 3, 1963, the whole world reacted with profound sorrow, so deeply had he touched the hearts of the entire human community. Even the Union Jack was lowered to half-mast in the bitterly divided city of Belfast. John XXIII was buried in the crypt of St. Peter's Basilica, where an Italian tour guide was once heard to say her party, "This is the tomb of Pope John XXIII, the most beloved pope in all of history." And so he was the most beloved pope in history. In the early Church he would have immediately been proclaimed a saint by popular demand. And so he was a saint.

260 Paul VI, *1897–1978, pope from June 21, 1963, to August 6, 1978.*

Paul VI continued the Second Vatican Council begun by John XXIII and became the first pope to travel around the globe by airplane. Although progressive in theology and social thought, his pontificate was marked by the ill-fated encyclical *Humanae vitae*, which condemned contraception.

Born Giovanni Battista Montini, son of a successful lawyer and politician, he was ordained in 1920 after taking his seminary courses at home because of poor health. After graduate studies in Rome, he served from 1922 in the Secretariat of State, with a brief period as an attaché in the Warsaw nunciature (1923) and contemporaneously as chaplain of the Catholic student movement (1924–33). In 1937 he was named assistant to the secretary of state, Cardinal Eugenio Pacelli (the future Pius XII), for internal church affairs. After Pius XII's first and only secretary of state, Cardinal Luigi Maglione, died in 1944, Monsignor Montini was placed in charge of internal church affairs. He was largely responsible for organizing the Holy Year of 1950 and the Marian Year of 1954. He was promoted to pro-secretary of state in 1952 (Pius XII acted as his own secretary of state after 1944), after declining appointment to the College of Cardinals.

In the midst of rumors that he had somehow fallen out of favor in Rome, Monsignor Montini was appointed archbishop of Milan in November 1954. (The rumors were given credence by the long delay between his appointment to Milan and the conferral of the cardinal's red hat.) He called himself "the workers' archbishop" and threw himself into the task of addressing Milan's many pastoral, social, and industrial problems. He was named a cardinal in the title of Santi Silvestro e Martino ai Monti by John XXIII on December 15, 1958. His name was at the top of the list of twenty-three new cardinals. Cardinal Montini made his second visit to the United States in 1960 (his first was in 1951), where he received an honorary degree, alongside President Dwight D. Eisenhower, from the University of Notre Dame. Although he spoke only twice at the first session of the Second Vatican Council (fall 1962), Cardinal Montini was one of its behind-the-scenes leaders.

John XXIII died on June 3, 1963. The conclave to elect his successor would be the largest in history. Eighty-one cardinals were eligible to vote, provided they could get to Rome. Fifty-seven were European (of whom twenty-nine were Italian). Twelve cardinals were from Latin America, seven from North America, three from Asia, two from Oceania, and a solitary one from Africa. The cardinals were divided into two groups: those who wanted to change the progressive course of the council and those who wanted to see John XXIII's project carried through to a successful conclusion. The candidate of the latter group was clearly Cardinal Montini, with some support also for Cardinal Giacomo Lercaro of Bologna. The public spokesman of the former group was the Spanish Cardinal Arcadio Larraona, a friend of the Fascist dictator Generalissimo Francisco Franco (d. 1975) and the Roman champion of Opus Dei, a secretive right-wing movement opposed to every progressive initiative at the council. This group's candidate was Cardinal Giuseppe Siri of Genoa, created a cardinal at age forty-five by Pius XII. Although he had supported John XXIII's election in 1958, he now regarded his pontificate as a disaster, saying that it would take four centuries for the Church to recover from it.

But the conservatives overplayed their hand at the outset. The traditional address on electing a new pope, given by a cardinal just before the conclave, was supposed to provide a job description of the new pope. Amleto Tondini, a Latinist whose official title was Secretary of Latin Briefs, savaged John XXIII in his discourse. He cast doubt on the enthusiastic applause John XXIII had received from around the world. Did it come, he asked, "from people who were true believers who accepted all the dogmatic and moral teachings of the Church?" He mocked the dead pope's optimism and offered a gloomy and apocalyptic view of the world, calling upon the cardinals to "affirm without uncertainty the sacred dogmas of the Catholic faith, to refute the errors contrary to dogma, to openly defend those who suffer persecution for the sake of justice." He implied that the new pope should suspend the council until the issues had matured. In attacking John XXIII, of course, Tondini and his conservative allies were really attacking Montini. But in Siri they did not have a credible alternative. So Siri shifted his support behind Cardinal Ildebrando Antoniutti, Prefect of the Congregation of Religious. The conservatives did not really expect Antoniutti to win, but they hoped to block Montini from the necessary two-thirds for election.

The first two votes on the morning of June 20 suggested that the strategy might succeed. Montini received roughly thirty votes, while Antoniutti was in the range of twenty. Lercaro also had about twenty. The remaining ten or so were scattered among various candidates. The curial dark horse, Cardinal Francesco Roberti, had enough to mark him as a possible compromise candidate if Antoniutti faltered. Cardinal Leo Josef Suenens of Malines-Brussels, Belgium, one of the leaders of the council, urged Lercaro's supporters to shift to Montini. But the third ballot was as inconclusive as the first two. Then something happened that was so striking and so memorable that the traditional secrecy of the conclave was later broken to tell of it. Cardinal Gustavo Testa, head of the Congregation for Oriental Churches and a man whom John XXIII had made a cardinal in 1959, was seated between Cardinal Carlo Confalonieri and Cardinal Albert Di Jorio. He suddenly lost his temper. He told his two neighbors in a voice loud enough for others to hear that they should stop their dishonorable maneuvering and think of the good of the Church. Cardinal Siri "hit the ceiling." Testa, he charged, had broken the rules. There was to be no discussion in the Sistine Chapel.

After Testa's "intervention," the fourth ballot went ahead. Montini picked up a few more votes, but was still substantially short of the fifty-four plus one necessary for election (Pius XII had changed the long-standing rule from two-thirds to two-thirds plus one). Some of the curial cardinals by now had come to admit their own failure to mount a credible alternative candidacy and concluded that they should support Montini. Even the old watchdog of orthodoxy, Cardinal Ottaviani, liked Montini personally and probably accepted the pragmatic argument. Cardinal Siri, however, rejected it and urged that Antoniutti be dumped in favor of Cardinal Roberti. The next morning, June 21, after a fifth indecisive ballot, Montini, at age sixty-five, finally got the two-thirds majority necessary for election: fifty-seven on the sixth ballot, or two more than required. It is significant that some twenty-two to twenty-five cardinals (mostly Italian and mostly in the Curia) refused to vote for Montini, even when his election was assured.

The newly elected pope chose the name Paul VI as a sign that he wanted to reach out to the modern Gentiles (that is, to the whole world), as Paul the Apostle had done. But his model as pope would not be John XXIII; it would be Pius XII, with whom he had worked so closely in the Secretariat of State. Indeed, when some of the council fathers, including the influential Cardinal Suenens, proposed that John XXIII be proclaimed a saint by the council, Paul VI resisted the idea, lest such an action reflect badly on Pius XII. In November 1965, with characteristic evenhandedness, Paul VI announced the initiation of procedures looking toward the beatification and canonization of *both* John XXIII and Pius XII. Paul VI was crowned on June 30, 1963, delivering an allocution in nine languages. He was the last pope to be so crowned. He later sold the tiara to Cardinal Francis Spellman (d. 1967) of New York and distributed the money to the poor in various countries. (The tiara is now on display in the Basilica of the National Shrine of the Immaculate Conception in Washington, D.C.) Thereafter, he wore only the customary bishop's miter as ceremonial headdress. The new pope took possession of his cathedral church, the basilica of St. John Lateran, on November 10.

Nine years after his election Paul VI wrote: "Perhaps the Lord called me to this service not because I have any aptitude for it, or so that I can govern and save the Church in its present difficulties, but so that I can suffer something for the Church so that it will be clear that it is the Lord, and not anyone else, who guides and saves it." Paul VI's approach to his election was in striking contrast to one of his successors, John Paul II, who looked upon his election as a sign of God's providential hand not only upon the Church but upon Poland and the whole of Europe and the world.

Paul VI immediately announced that he would continue the council (he opened the second session on September 29), carry forward the revision of the Code of Canon Law, and work for the promotion of peace and justice in the temporal order and for the unity of the Christian family of churches. He admitted laymen as council auditors (women would be invited the following year) and invited the various non-Catholic Christian churches to send more observers. On January 4, 1964, he made an unprecedented trip by airplane to the Holy Land, where he met with the ecumenical patriarch Athenagoras I in Jerusalem. On September 6 he announced that lay and religious women would be invited to the council as auditors. The third session, however, ended with many of the council's leaders demoralized. The council had passed the Dogmatic Constitution on the Church (*Lumen gentium*), which contained the doctrine of collegiality, that is, the principle that the bishops share in the governance of the universal Church in collaboration with the pope. The conservatives were vehemently opposed to this doctrine, arguing that it contradicted the Church's divinely established structure, in which the pope is the successor of Peter and by that fact the unchallenged head of the Church. In an effort to mollify the conservatives, Paul VI authorized the addition of an appendix to the text (technically, a *nota praevia;* Lat., "prefatory note") reassuring the conservatives that nothing in the document diminished or in any way compromised the supreme authority of the pope. The pope also proclaimed, on his own and against the better judgment of the majority of the bishops, that the Blessed Virgin Mary is the Mother of the Church.

During the recess Paul VI flew to Bombay for the International Eucharistic Congress (December 2–5, 1964). During the fourth session he flew to New York (October 4, 1965) to plead for peace at the United Nations. The speech, given in French, contained the powerful words, "*Jamais plus la guerre! Jamais plus la guerre!*" ("Never again war!"). Before the council Mass on December 7, 1965, there was read out a joint declaration by the pope and the patriarch Athenagoras deploring the mutual anathemas hurled at one another's churches at Constantinople in 1054 and the schism that resulted. On the next day Paul VI solemnly confirmed all the decrees of the council and proclaimed an extraordinary Jubilee (January 1–May 29, 1966) for reflection and renewal in the light of the council.

The difficult task of implementing those decrees now faced the pope. Although many were unhappy with the changes, Paul VI did not water them down. He established several postconciliar commissions and authorized the use of the vernacular in the Mass and the sacraments. A new Order of the Mass went into effect with his approval in 1969, much to the chagrin of conservative Catholics who mistakenly believed that the Missal of Pius V (1566–72) could never be supplanted, as if it were somehow divinely mandated for all time. He also approved a new Liturgy of the Hours (Divine Office, or Breviary), new translations and revisions of other liturgical texts and rituals, and restored the permanent diaconate in the Roman Rite. He reduced the eucharistic fast to one hour before the reception of Holy Communion. He reorganized the Roman Curia and confirmed as permanent secretariats the Secretariat for Promoting Christian Unity, the Secretariat for Non-Christian Religions, and the Secretariat for Nonbelievers. He held an official meeting in Rome with the Archbishop of Canterbury, Michael Ramsey, on March 24, 1966, and with Ecumenical Patriarch Athenagoras I in Istanbul on July 25, 1967, and again in Rome on October 26, 1967. In order to render permanent the structure of the council, he decreed on September 15, 1965, that worldwide synods of bishops should meet in Rome at regular intervals to address pastoral issues of great concern to the universal Church, such as the priesthood, catechesis, and the family, and to provide opportunities for collaboration between the bishops of the world and the Bishop of Rome. (The revised 1983 Code of Canon Law provides for the synod's structure, responsibilities, and powers in canons 342–48.)

Paul VI's encyclicals were few, and mixed. His first in 1964, *Ecclesiam Suam* (Lat., "His Church"), pointed out that the Church must always be ready to correct its own defects through reform and that it should be marked by the spirit and practice of dialogue: among all Catholics, with other Christian churches, with non-Christian religions, and with the human community at large. The following year, however, he released a conservative encyclical, *Mysterium fidei* ("Mystery of faith"), in which he reaffirmed the traditional, neo-Scholastic teaching on the Real Presence of Christ in the Eucharist over against some new interpretations, based on a different philosophical worldview, that had been proposed by certain Dutch theologians and others. In 1967 he published *Populorum progressio* ("On the progress of peoples"), which highlighted and deplored the gap between rich and poor nations and which reminded readers that the goods of the earth are intended by God for everyone. The "new name for peace," he said, "is development." But three months later he issued *Sacerdotalis caelibatus* ("Priestly celibacy"), reaffirming the tradition of obligatory celibacy for Roman Catholic priests. The following June he issued a Credo of the People of God that was traditional in orientation, and the next month the fateful encyclical on birth control, *Humanae vitae* ("Of human life"), which declared that every act of sexual intercourse within marriage must be open to the transmission of life. In other words, there can be no artificial means of contraception. The encyclical created a storm of protest all over the world, but especially in North America and Europe. Many were aware of the findings and recommendation of the Papal Birth Control Commission in 1966; namely, that the pope should change the teaching, acknowledging that our understanding of the natural law has matured. There was a widespread expectation, therefore, that the pope would accept that recommendation and modify the traditional teaching. When he did not do so, there was profound shock and disappointment. Some punitive actions were taken against public dissenters, but most dissented quietly and in the privacy of their own homes. Survey after survey has shown from the beginning that in excess of 80 percent of Catholic married couples have ignored the encyclical. So shaken was Paul VI by the reaction that he vowed never again to publish an encyclical, and he did not.

There were to be other papal documents, however, even if not called encyclicals. Two of the most important were *Octogesima adveniens* (known by its English title as "A Call to Action"), released in 1971 on the occasion of the eightieth anniversary of Leo XIII's social encyclical *Rerum novarum* (1891), and *Evangelii nuntiandi* ("On Evangelization in the Modern World"), published in 1975, on the occasion of the end of a Holy Year, the tenth anniversary of the close of Vatican II, and the anniversary of the Third General Assembly of the Synod of Bishops, which had focused on evangelization. Some regard the latter document as the best of his pontificate. It linked the process of evangelization (literally, the proclamation of the gospel) with the Church's abiding concern for questions of social justice, human rights, and peace. Evangelization, Paul VI wrote, proclaims the coming of the reign of God as a form of liberation "from sin and the Evil One," but also from every form of economic, social, and political oppression. While it is of the essence of the Church's mission to evangelize, it must begin "by being evangelized itself."

Although the birth control encyclical had cast a shadow over his pontificate, Paul VI pursued many other pastoral initiatives before and after the release of the encyclical. He traveled to Portugal and Turkey (1967), to Bogotá, Columbia (1968), to Geneva (to address the World Council of Churches) and to Uganda (1969), and to Asia, the Pacific islands, and Australia (1970). During this last pilgrimage he escaped an assassination attempt in Manila. In 1968 he instituted the annual observance of World Day of Peace on January 1. He elevated St. Teresa of Ávila (d. 1582) and St. Catherine of Siena (d. 1380) to the status of Doctors of the Church, the first women to be so recognized, and canonized eighty-four saints, including two Americans: Elizabeth Ann Bayley Seton (d. 1821) and John Nepomucene Neumann (d. 1860). He fixed the retirement age for priests and bishops at seventy-five (although he himself did not retire at that age) and decreed that cardinals over the age of eighty should not participate in the business of the Roman Curia or in papal elections and that the maximum number of cardinal-electors could not exceed 120. He convened and presided over four international synods of bishops and continued John XXIII's example of enlarging and internationalizing the College of Cardinals. By 1976 it had 138 members, of whom Italians constituted a small minority.

In the last year of his life, Paul VI was profoundly shaken by the kidnapping and murder of his close friend Aldo Moro, former prime minister of Italy and prominent Christian Democratic leader. His last public appearance was to preside at Moro's funeral in the basilica of St. John Lateran. He died of a heart attack at Castel Gandolfo on August 6, 1978, and was buried in the crypt of St. Peter's Basilica. He had planned his own funeral and, in typical Italian fashion, paid careful attention to gesture (*figura*) and symbol. His coffin was at ground level, surmounted not by a tiara, or even by a miter or a stole, but by the open book of the Gospels, fluttering in the light breeze across St. Peter's Square.

261 John Paul I, *1912–78, pope from August 26 to September 28, 1978.*

The first pope to take a double name, John Paul I left his mark in history by being the first pope in more than a millennium to refuse to be crowned with the triple tiara. Although he was pope for only thirty-three days, his was not the shortest pontificate in history. There were ten (and possibly eleven) other popes who served for thirty-two days or less, the shortest being Urban VII, September 15–27, 1590, a pontificate of twelve days.

Born Albino Luciani, of poor, working-class parents, he was ordained in 1935, did doctoral studies at the Gregorian University in Rome, and served as a curate in his home parish in a village near Belluno. In 1937 he was appointed vice-rector and a member of the teaching faculty of his diocesan seminary and served also as vicar general of his diocese. In 1958 he was appointed bishop of Vittorio Veneto and was ordained by John XXIII himself in St. Peter's Basilica. Eleven years later he was named by Paul VI as patriarch of Venice. He attended the Second Vatican Council (1962–65) without playing a leading part in it. In 1973, he was named a cardinal in the title of San Marco (to whom Venice's cathedral is dedicated). During his nine years in Venice, he hosted five ecumenical conferences, including a meeting of the Anglican-Roman Catholic International Commission (ARCIC), which produced an Agreed Statement on authority in 1976. He also published a series of whimsical letters, entitled *Illustrissimi*, to various real and fictional characters to bring out various catechetical points. He served as vice president of the Italian Conference of Bishops from 1972 to 1975. He was generally conservative in theology (he strongly defended Paul VI's controversial encyclical on birth control, *Humanae vitae*), but he was sensitive to the poor and to social issues. This latter trait would later commend him to the Third World cardinals at the next papal conclave.

Upon the death of Paul VI on August 6, 1978, and after the traditional nine-day period of mourning, 111 cardinals entered the conclave to elect a successor—the greatest number of electors in history. The conclave would begin—and end—on Saturday, August 26. On the first ballot, Cardinal Luciani and Cardinal Siri of Genoa, a leading ultraconservative and a perennial candidate, received about the same number of votes. Siri, at twenty-five votes, had a few more than Luciani. Other votes were received by Cardinals Pignedoli (less than twenty), Baggio, Koenig (of Vienna), Bertoli, Pironio, and a couple for Felici and Aloísio Lorscheider (of Fortaleza, Brazil, and president of the Latin American Conference of Bishops), whom Luciani himself admitted to voting for. The second ballot was taken immediately after the announcement of the results. This time Luciani gained thirty votes, to a total of fifty-five. Many of his new votes came from middle-of-the-roaders who had come into the conclave unsure of how to cast their votes. When they saw Luciani's surprising first-ballot strength, they moved naturally to him. Siri remained at twenty-five. (One report says his vote went to zero as his supporters, by prior plan, shifted their votes to Luciani.) Pignedoli slipped back to fifteen, and Lorscheider rose to twelve. On the third ballot some of Pignedoli's and Siri's supporters shifted to Luciani, but he was still five or six votes short of the necessary two-thirds majority plus one. On the fourth and final ballot,

Luciani received about ninety votes, there was one vote for Lorscheider (Luciani's!), and twenty blank ballots cast by intransigent Siri supporters. At the previous conclave, which elected Cardinal Montini as Paul VI, Cardinal Suenens of Belgium acted as the grand elector, or "king-maker." At this conclave, that role seems to have been filled by Cardinal Giovanni Benelli of Florence and Cardinal Lorscheider, with Suenens playing a supporting role. It was evident, in any case, that the cardinals wanted a pastoral pope, someone not connected with the Roman Curia and someone (again!) different in style from the previous pope.

The new pope chose a double name, John Paul (the first pope to do so in history). He did so, he said, to honor the pope (John XXIII) who ordained him a bishop and who preceded him as patriarch of Venice and the pope (Paul VI) who named him a cardinal. "Be sure of this," he pointed out the next day before his Sunday papal blessing, "I do not have the wisdom of heart of Pope John. I do not have the preparation and culture of Pope Paul." In his address to the cardinals earlier that morning, he emphasized twice that the Church exists not for its own sake but for the service of the world. On the other hand, he continued, the Church must sometimes stand over against the world in prophetic protest. He pledged to continue to implement the Second Vatican Council, to revise the Code of Canon Law for the Latin and Oriental Churches, and to promote evangelization, ecumenism, dialogue with all people, and peace. The new pope broke a tradition of more than a thousand years' standing when he refused to be crowned with the triple tiara. On September 3 he was invested with the pallium (the woolen vestment worn around the neck of an archbishop as a symbol of pastoral authority) in a ceremony described as "the inauguration of his ministry as supreme pastor." He took possession of his cathedral, the basilica of St. John Lateran, on September 23. (Although he had also abandoned the *sedia gestatoria,* the portable chair on which popes had been carried aloft above the crowds, he allowed himself to be carried into the basilica on the chair because many complained they could not see him otherwise.) That was to be his last public appearance outside the Vatican.

Late in the evening of September 28, John Paul I died of a heart attack while reading in bed. His light was still on when his body was discovered early the next morning. Rumors about the cause of his death proliferated. Some charged that the pope had been poisoned to prevent him from exposing financial irregularities in the Vatican Bank. The failure to conduct an autopsy (linked to the mistaken idea that deceased popes cannot be embalmed) and the lack of truthfulness regarding the circumstances in which the body was discovered only served to feed such rumors. The Vatican claimed that the dead pope was found by his Irish priest-secretary, John Magee, when, in fact, it was Sister Vincenza, his housekeeper. The most likely truth is that the pope died prematurely, just short of his sixty-sixth birthday, because he needed treatment for some serious health problems and did not seek or receive it. In any case, the Romans had taken such a liking to this humble, smiling pope that they reacted more emotionally to his death than they had to Paul VI's only two months earlier. In his address at the pope's funeral, Cardinal Carlo Confalonieri said that John Paul I had "flashed like a meteor across the sky." He was buried in the crypt of St. Peter's Basilica, just across the aisle from another short-reigned pope, Marcellus II, whose pontificate lasted only twenty-one days.

262 John Paul II, *Polish, b. 1920, pope from October 16, 1978.*

The first Slavic pope in history and the first non-Italian since Hadrian VI (1522–23), John Paul II is the most traveled pope in history. Although committed to the Second Vatican Council (1962–65), in which he participated as a bishop, his pontificate has been dedicated to the containment and even repression of progressive interpretations and implementations of the council. While some have characterized him as the first postmodern pope, others have described his pontificate as restorationist, that is, one that seeks to restore the more monarchical style of the papacy, with all effective authority centered in the Vatican.

Born Karol Wojtyła in Wadowice, Poland, in a family of modest means, he was a university student, then a manual laborer, during the Nazi occupation of his homeland. He studied secretly for the priesthood during the Second World War and was ordained in 1946. He obtained his doctorate in theology from the Angelicum (University of St. Thomas) in Rome in 1948, writing a dissertation on St. John of the Cross (d. 1591) under the direction of one of Rome's most conservative theologians, Reginald Garrigou-Lagrange, O.P. (d. 1964). He served as a parish priest in Poland from 1948 to 1951, then returned to the Jagiellonian University in Kraków to study philosophy, publishing a thesis in 1960 on the philosopher Max Scheler. During these years he taught social ethics at the local seminary and in 1956 was appointed professor of ethics at Lublin University. Two years later he was appointed auxiliary bishop of Kraków by Pius XII. On December 30, 1963, Paul VI appointed him archbishop of Kraków, and three and a half years after that (June 26, 1967) he named him a cardinal in the title of San Caesareo al Palatino. Cardinal Wojtyła took possession of his titular church in Rome on February 21, 1968. He had been a relatively active member of the Second Vatican Council (1962–65) and served in various capacities on postconciliar bodies, including the world synods of bishops. In spite of the Communist control of Poland, Cardinal Wojtyła was able to travel freely and frequently around the world: to the eucharistic congress in Philadelphia in 1976, to the Middle East, Africa, South and East Asia, and Australia. In 1976, at the invitation of Paul VI, he gave the Lenten retreat to the pope and the papal household. His addresses were later published in English in 1979 under the title *Sign of Contradiction*. (He had already published a book on human sexuality in 1960 entitled *Love and Responsibility*, which had attracted Paul VI's attention.)

When John Paul I died suddenly on September 28, 1978, after only thirty-three days as pope, the cardinals who quickly returned to Rome, in virtual shock, were now looking to elect someone with the physical vigor to withstand the requirements of the office. The public discussion before the opening of the conclave centered on the seventy-two-year-old ultra-conservative Cardinal Giuseppe Siri of Genoa, probably as the result of a well-orchestrated effort on his behalf in the conservative Italian press. A coalition of centrist cardinals, including Leo Josef Suenens (Belgium), Bernard Alfrink (Holland), Franz Koenig (Austria), Narciso Jubany Arnau (Spain), Vicente Enrique y Tarancón (Spain), François Marty (France), Paulo Evaristo Arns (Brazil), Aloísio Lorscheider (Brazil), and others, agreed to support Cardinal Giovanni Benelli of Florence, with a Luciani (John Paul I)–like backup if Benelli faltered. They were thinking of someone like Cardinal Ugo Poletti, the vicar of Rome. But other members of the coalition, particularly the Brazilians, felt that this may be the time for a non-Italian and that if Benelli failed, they should move in that direction. Among the non-Italian names discussed were Jan Willebrands, of Holland, head of the Secretariat for Promoting Christian Unity, and Karol Wojtyła, archbishop of Kraków. Koenig, in particular, was interested in Wojtyła, and Cardinal John Krol of Philadelphia was thought to be able to deliver American votes for him. The Germans were also solidly behind Wojtyła as the one non-Italian they could support. They liked his toughness in the face of the Communists, his intelligence and charm, and his political pragmatism. It was thought they could bring along many of the Third World cardinals who depended upon the Germans for the financial support of their churches. Cardinal Lorscheider was also strongly in favor of the Polish cardinal, but for reasons different from the Germans. He appreciated Wojtyła's speeches at the world synods of bishops, his attentiveness to different cultures and nations, his commitment to evangelization, and his sensitivity to issues of social justice. Lorscheider, along with Koenig, became one of the conclave's grand electors, urging his fellow Third World cardinals to support Cardinal Wojtyła. (He would come to realize, some years after the election, that he and Cardinal Wojtyła actually shared far fewer positions than he had thought at the time of the conclave.) Although Cardinal Siri of Genoa did not have a realistic chance of winning two-thirds of the votes plus one, he utterly destroyed any chances he did have with an inflammatory interview he conducted with the *Gazetta del Popolo*. In the interview, he mocked Vatican II's doctrine of episcopal collegiality and spoke strongly against the democratization of the Church. The interview was not supposed to be published until after the cardinals had been sealed away in the conclave, but the embargo was broken and the cardinal-electors saw it in time.

At the end of the first ballot, on October 15, Cardinal Siri was in the lead, but in the thirties, far short of the fifty votes his supporters had hoped for. Cardinal Benelli was not far behind, also in the thirties. Other Italians had substantial blocs of votes: Corrado Ursi of Naples, Ugo Poletti of Rome, and Giovanni Colombo of Milan. Wojtyła had five votes. On the second ballot Siri fell by about six votes while Benelli moved into the lead, with the votes for the other Italian candidates moving his way. (Another report says that Siri also increased his vote by a little on the second ballot.) But the Italian curial cardinals held a stormy meeting, easily overheard by other cardinals, between the morning and afternoon balloting and concluded they must do everything possible to prevent Benelli's election. They regarded him as too pliant toward the non-Italians (the *stranieri*, or foreigners) and arrogant and ruthless in manner. They also resented the way he engineered the election of Cardinal Luciani (John Paul I) a month earlier. There were enough Italian cardinals, in other words, who would never accept Benelli, thereby making it impossible for him to attain the necessary two-thirds plus one needed to win. And that is exactly what happened. (Benelli would die two years later.)

On the third ballot, Siri continued to lose votes, some of which drifted to the seventy-six-year-old Cardinal Colombo of Milan, and Benelli peaked somewhere below the necessary seventy-five needed for election. Cardinal Poletti, vicar of Rome and head of the Italian Bishops Conference, received a bloc of some thirty votes. On the fourth ballot there was a surge of votes toward Colombo as a compromise acceptable to all Italians. Cardinal Pericle Felici is also said to have received some votes on this ballot. Wojtyła had about ten votes. But Colombo announced that, if elected, he would not accept. That evening Cardinal Franz Koenig of Vienna openly campaigned on behalf of Cardinal Wojtyła with the Germans, the Central Europeans, the French, the Spaniards, and the Americans. (It is significant that, in a frank interview given in late 1996, Koenig, by then retired as archbishop of Vienna, spoke in a highly critical way of the policies and governing style of John Paul II's pontificate.) The next day, October 16, Cardinal Wojtyła's votes doubled on the fifth ballot from about ten to about twenty. Poletti continued to receive support and there was also a surge in favor of Cardinal Willebrands. Siri and Benelli were now losing votes. It had become clear that an Italian could not be elected. On the sixth ballot, before lunch, Wojtyła's vote rose to about forty. Before the first afternoon ballot Willebrands told his supporters that he appreciated their votes but thought that they should unite behind Wojtyła. On the seventh ballot Cardinal Wojtyła was just short of the necessary two-thirds plus one for election. On the eighth ballot he received more than ninety votes (one report says ninety-nine), sufficient for election, but no one moved that it be unanimous. A handful of Siri supporters stubbornly voted for their candidate to the end.

The newly elected pope, at age fifty-eight, chose the name John Paul II because of his "reverence, love, and devotion to John Paul and also to Paul VI, who has been my inspiration, my strength." Significantly, he made no reference to John XXIII, who was the first pope whom John Paul I intended to honor with his double name. (It is said that he also considered taking the name Stanislaus, in honor of the patron saint of Kraków.) John Paul II, following the new example set by his predecessor, was "inaugurated" into his Petrine ministry, rather than crowned, on October 22. He was vested with the pallium, the woolen vestment worn around the neck of an archbishop as a symbol of pastoral authority. He took possession of his cathedral church, the basilica of St. John Lateran, on November 12.

John Paul II viewed his election to the papacy as providential, a compensation for Polish sufferings during the nineteenth century and then under the Nazis and the Communists in the twentieth. He even saw the failed assassination attempt against him on May 13, 1981, as another sign of God's providential hand at work, keeping him safe to accomplish his special mission. In his view, his special mission was twofold: to bring the insights and values of the suffering Church of the East (especially Poland) to the comfortable churches of the West and to bring an end to what he and other conservative cardinals and bishops regarded as the postconciliar drift of the Church, a pointed criticism of Paul VI (1963–78). When he named Sts. Cyril and Methodius (d. 869, 885) copatrons of Europe in 1985, it was to make the point that the Church must "breathe with two lungs," combining the Latin tradition of law and order with the more mystical Greek tradition. When he received the Soviet president Mikhail Gorbachev in the Vatican in December 1989, after the fall of the Berlin Wall, it seemed to the pope an answer to his prayer.

In his address to the cardinals the day after his election, the new pope promised to promote "with prudent but encouraging action" the reforms of the Second Vatican Council. In January 1979, he traveled to Mexico to attend the Latin American Conference of Bishops meeting at Puebla,

where he cautioned the bishops and their clergy against direct involvement in politics (taken as an indirect criticism of Latin American liberation theology). The three cochairmen of the meeting were selected by the
pope, not the bishops—another indication of John Paul II's regard for
episcopal collegiality and the autonomy of national episcopal conferences. A speech later at the old Palafox seminary left the audience of bishops, clergy, and some laypeople subdued. The pope warned, "We must
keep watch over the purity of doctrine. . . . This notion of a political
Jesus, a revolutionary, the subversive from Nazareth, is not in harmony
with the Church's teaching." In the second part of the speech, however, he
spoke passionately on behalf of justice, using the word liberation twelve
times. The message was clear: social justice, yes, but always within the
confines of Catholic orthodoxy as interpreted by the pope and the Vatican. This approach would remain constant during the pontificate of John
Paul II: socially liberal, theologically and doctrinally conservative, perhaps even ultraconservative. The triumphant tour of Mexico became a
kind of paradigm for all subsequent papal trips and established John Paul
II as a global superstar. In six days the pope gave twenty-six speeches and
homilies, presided over several public Masses, and met with numerous
groups, including the local Polish community (a practice he would follow in his subsequent trips abroad). He intended, beginning with this
trip to Mexico, to draw attention back to the person of the pope and
thereby to reinforce the spiritual authority of the center of the Catholic
Church, in the Vatican.

John Paul II published his first encyclical in March 1979. Entitled *Redemptor hominis* (Lat., "Redeemer of humanity"), it emphasized the dignity and worth of every human person, deplored the "exploitation of the
earth" and the destruction of the environment, and condemned consumerism, that is, the accumulation and misuse of goods by privileged
social classes and rich countries "to an excessive degree." It also condemned the arms race, especially for diverting essential resources from
the poor, and the violation of human rights around the globe.

In June he returned triumphantly to his native Poland to take part in
the ninth centenary of its patron St. Stanislaus. Almost one of every three
Polish citizens was able to see him personally during his eight-day visit.
On June 10 more than a million Poles attended his Mass in the meadow of
Błonie on the edge of Kraków. It would be the first of seven trips back to
Poland: the second in 1983, the third in 1987, the fourth and fifth in 1991,
the sixth, and least satisfying, in 1994, when he angrily scolded his fellow
Poles, now liberated from Communism, for their newly independent atti-
tude toward the authority of the Church and its strict moral norms, and
the last in June 1997. By the middle of 1997 the pope had made some
eighty pastoral visits abroad to well over a hundred different countries.

At the same time, he published several substantial encyclical letters. In 1981, a few months after the attempt on his life in St. Peter's Square, he published *Laborem exercens* (Lat., "On doing work," or "On Human Work") to mark the ninetieth anniversary of Leo XIII's *Rerum novarum*. In this encyclical the pope viewed human work as a form of collaboration in the creative work of God and, therefore, of infinite dignity. He insisted on the priority of work over capital and condemned what he called a "rigid" capitalism that exaggerates the rights of private ownership over the common good and the common use of goods. In 1985 he published *Slavorum Apostoli* ("Apostles of the Slavs"), honoring Sts. Cyril and Methodius as copatrons of Europe alongside St. Benedict of Nursia (d. ca. 547), who had been proclaimed patron of Europe by Paul VI. His second major social encyclical, *Sollicitudo rei socialis* ("Solicitude for social concerns," or "On the Social Concern of the Church"), was published in 1987 to mark the twentieth anniversary of Paul VI's *Populorum progressio* (1967). The encyclical emphasized the obligations of rich and developed nations toward poor and undeveloped countries and the "preferential option for the poor" as a guideline of moral action. The goods of the earth, he insisted, are destined for all. In 1991 he published two major encyclicals, one on the missions, *Redemptoris missio* ("Mission of the Redeemer"), and the other, his third major social encyclical, *Centesimus annus* ("The hundredth year"), to mark the centenary of Leo XIII's *Rerum novarum*. At the center of the Church's social message, he wrote, is the dignity of every human person—a point he had made already in his first encyclical in 1979. He reaffirmed the Church's "preferential option for the poor" and referred positively to democratic systems for ensuring the participation of citizens in a nation's political life.

Two major controversial encyclicals on moral theology appeared in 1993 and 1995, respectively: *Veritatis splendor* (Lat., "The splendor of truth"), which was critical of theological dissent in the public media, of moral relativism, and of a method of moral theology known as proportionalism, and *Evangelium vitae* ("The gospel of life"), which strongly condemned contraception, euthanasia, and abortion in language similar to that employed in infallible teaching. Significantly, the pope also condemned capital punishment, insisting that there are, for all practical purposes, no sufficient reasons ever to justify it. Also in 1995 he published what may have been his most remarkable encyclical—remarkable for its openness on the most sensitive of ecumenical topics, the papacy itself. In *Ut unum sint* ("That [all] may be one") he acknowledged that, while the Petrine office belongs to the essential structure of the Church, the manner in which the papal office is exercised is always subject to criticism and improvement. He invited his readers, especially those in the other Christian churches, to enter into dialogue with him about the manner in which his office is exercised and to recommend ways in which its exercise might conform more faithfully to the gospel.

In addition to these encyclicals John Paul II issued an apostolic letter, *Tertio millennio adveniente* (Lat., "On the approaching third millennium"), in 1994 to invite the Church to prepare for the coming new millennium, an approaching event that has engaged his deepest interest throughout his entire pontificate. John Paul II has been profoundly convinced from the start of his pontificate that he was destined by God to lead the Catholic Church into that new millennium and that it is a millennium that will see the walls between the various religious faiths of the world come down so that there will be a united religious front against atheism, materialism, and individualism. In 1994 he also issued a formal statement against the ordination of women, *Ordinatio sacerdotalis* ("Priestly ordination"), insisting that the Church is not authorized to ordain women as priests. His emphatic way of stating and enforcing this teaching has contributed in some measure to the sense of alienation many Catholic women have felt toward the institutional Church and toward John Paul II's pontificate in particular.

In 1996, in *Universi Dominici gregis* ("Of the Lord's whole flock"), John Paul II changed the rules governing papal elections. Dispensing with eight hundred years of tradition requiring a two-thirds majority for election, the pope decreed that, if after thirty-three votes taken over several days, no candidate has received a two-thirds majority, an absolute majority is sufficient for election. Some commentators have viewed this as a radical departure from church tradition, which has always encouraged compromise and consensus in the election of a new pope. Now an ideologically committed group, whether of the left or the right, conceivably can hold out until after the thirty-plus ballots have been taken and seek to elect its own candidate by a bare mathematical majority. Although the elections will continue to take place in the Sistine Chapel, the cardinal-electors will be housed in the newly erected Domus Sanctae Marthae instead of the small and uncomfortable cubicles in the Apostolic Palace.

Besides his encyclicals and apostolic letters, John Paul II has been a productive and commercially successful author. He published *Crossing the Threshold of Hope* in 1994 and *Gift and Mystery* in 1996. Several other meditative writings have also been published during his pontificate, as well as collections of his poems and plays.

Among the other major developments in this pontificate were the promulgation in 1983 of the revised Code of Canon Law, a project initiated by Pope John XXIII (1958–63); the publication, under the direction of Cardinal Joseph Ratzinger, of the *Catechism of the Catholic Church* in 1992 (the English translation was delayed until 1994 because of complaints from ultraconservative Catholics about the gender-inclusive language employed in the first translation); in 1985 the renegotiation of the Lateran Pacts of 1929 whereby the separation of Church and state in Italy was formally recognized, Rome was no longer to be regarded as a sacred city, Catholic instruction was no longer to be required in public schools, and the clergy were no longer to be paid salaries by the state; and the establishment of formal diplomatic relations with the United States in 1984 (the apostolic delegate is now the nuncio) and with the State of Israel in 1994. John Paul II was also the first pope to visit Rome's chief synagogue, where he acknowledged the Church's sins against the Jews, even on the part of some of his predecessors who were knowing accomplices in anti-Jewish campaigns and who confined Jews to ghettos in Rome and the former Papal States.

As of 1997, the pope had convened and presided over six world synods of bishops (one an extraordinary synod in 1985 to celebrate the twentieth anniversary of the adjournment of the Second Vatican Council), canonized more than 270 saints (most of them priests and nuns), beatified many more than that (including the controversial founder of the ultra-conservative Opus Dei movement, Josemaría Escrivá de Belaguer), and named over 120 cardinals to the College of Cardinals, bringing the total number to 154 as of August 1996, of whom 112 were eligible to vote in papal elections. (Paul VI decreed that the maximum number eligible to vote in papal elections is 120.)

At the end of his first full year in office, John Paul II startled the theological community by revoking Swiss theologian Hans Küng's status as a Catholic theologian. A similar action had been taken already against French theologian Jacques Pohier, who was forbidden to write, preach, or give lectures without explicit permission. The renowned Dutch theologian Edward Schillebeeckx, a Dominican, was subjected to severe Vatican scrutiny (he was attacked by one of his examiners on Vatican Radio *before* the hearing in the Vatican even began), and the Brazilian theologian Leonardo Boff, a Franciscan, was forbidden to write or teach for a year. He eventually left the Franciscan order and the priesthood in protest of the Vatican's actions against him. Charles Curran, the American moral theologian, was forced out of the theological faculty at The Catholic University of America. In January 1997, a well-known Third World theologian, Tissa Balasuriya, a seventy-two-year-old Sri Lankan priest, a member of the Marist order, was excommunicated from the Church for having "deviated from the integrity of the truth of the Catholic faith." He had questioned, among other things, certain excesses in Marian devotion and had refused to reject the possibility that women could be ordained to the priesthood.

The pope also intervened to prevent the Society of Jesus (Jesuits) from electing a successor to their superior general, Father Pedro Arrupe (d. 1991), and suspended the constitution of the order. He appointed an eighty-year-old conservative to act as his personal delegate until a new superior general could eventually be elected with his approval. Disciplinary procedures were also instituted against various bishops, including Raymond Hunthausen, archbishop of Seattle, Walter Sullivan, bishop of Richmond, and Jacques Gaillot, bishop of Evreux in France. Indeed, one of the most enduring legacies of this pontificate, for good or for ill, will be the vast numbers of conservative bishops appointed to various dioceses all over the world, many times in opposition to the wishes and recommendations of the local hierarchies and the priests and people of the various dioceses.

Beginning in 1992 a series of illnesses and accidents left the pope in a weakened physical condition. He could no longer engage in his favorite recreational activities of skiing, hiking, and mountain climbing and rumors began to circulate that he was far more seriously ill than the Vatican would admit. But there is an ancient adage that the only time one has a completely accurate report of a pope's health is when his death is announced. In past centuries even that information was kept secret for as long as possible because of the tradition of looting the papal apartments upon hearing the news of the pope's death. Not all traditions associated with the papacy have survived, including that one. Indeed, few, if any, traditions associated with the papacy have anything at all to do with the Apostle Peter, or with the Lord himself for that matter. If nothing else is clear from this lengthy review of the more than 260 popes, at least that should be clear.

1 St. Peter the Apostle (d. ca. 64).

2 St. Clement I (ca. 91–ca. 101).

3 St. Leo I, "the Great" (440–461), the first pope to claim to be Peter's heir.

4 St. Gregory I, "the Great" (590–604), one of the papacy's most influential writers.

5 St. Leo III (795–816), who crowned Charlemagne as emperor in 800.

3

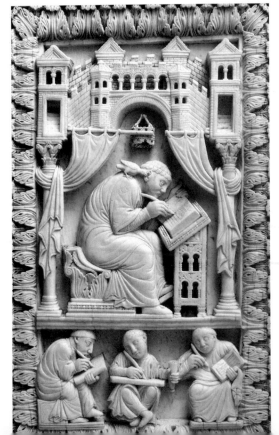

4

5

6

6 St. Gregory VII (1073–1085), whose reforms created the monarchical papacy of the second Christian millennium.

7 Bl. Urban II (1088–1099), who launched the First Crusade and established the Roman Curia.

8 Innocent III (1198–1216), one of the most powerful popes in history.

7

8

9 Boniface VIII (1295–1303), who claimed authority over the temporal as well as the spiritual realms.

10 Alexander VI (1492–1503), the most notorious pope in history.

11 Julius II (1503–1513), warrior-pope and patron of Michelangelo and Raphael.

9

10

11

12

13

12 Leo X (1513–1521), who excommunicated Martin Luther in 1521.

13 St. Pius V (1566–1572), who enforced the reforms of the Council of Trent and excommunicated Queen Elizabeth I in 1570.

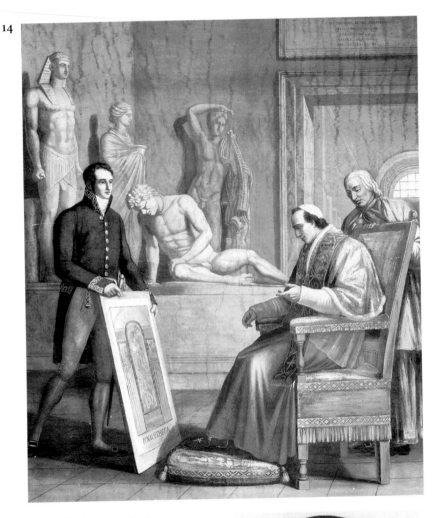

14 Pius VII (1800–1823), who restored the Jesuits in 1814 and suffered captivity under Napoleon.

15 Pius IX (1846–1878), the
longest-reigning pope in history,
who called the First Vatican
Council (1869–1870), defined the
dogma of the Immaculate Conception (1854), and issued the
"Syllabus of Errors" (1864).

15

16 Leo XIII (1878–1903), the first pope to bring the Catholic Church into the modern era and the author of the first major social encyclical, *Rerum novarum* (1891).

17 St. Pius X (1903–1914), the last pope to be canonized a saint and the "pope of frequent Communion," but also the initiator of a massive campaign against Catholic scholars.

18 Benedict XV (1914–1922), a peace-making pope who called a halt to the internecine warfare between traditionalists and progressives in the Church.

16

17

18

19

20

19 Pius XI (1922–1939), approved
the Lateran Pacts that established
Vatican City State in 1929.

20 Pius XII (1939–1958), pope
during the Second World War and
a firm opponent of Communism.

21 John XXIII (1958–1963), the
most beloved pope in history, who
called the Second Vatican Council
(1962–1965) and initiated the
modern renewal of the Church.

21

22   23

22 Paul VI (1963–1978), who
implemented the reforms of the
Second Vatican Council, but also
issued the controversial encyclical
on birth control (1968).

23 John Paul I (1978), the first
pope in a thousand years who
refused to be crowned.

24 John Paul II (1978–), the first
non-Italian pope since 1522 and
the most traveled pope in history.

24

25 John XXIII addressing the opening session of the Second Vatican Council on October 11, 1962. Cardinal Francis Spellman of New York (d. 1967) is seated to the pope's right.

26 Paul VI addressing the United Nations General Assembly during his historic visit to the U.S. on October 4, 1965.

25

26

27 John Paul I, shown here being carried on the traditional *sedia gestatoria,* was the first pope in centuries to refuse to be crowned as a temporal sovereign and instead was invested with the simple pallium and the miter.

28 John Paul II with Mikhail Gorbachev in Rome, December 1, 1989.

27

28

29

30

31

29 Council of Trent (1545–1563), the major response of the Catholic Church to the Protestant Reformation.

30 Vatican II (1962–1965), perhaps the most significant religious event since the Protestant Reformation and the most important of the twentieth century.

31 St. Peter's Basilica (Vatican City), Catholicism's principal church, built over the site on Vatican Hill where St. Peter is believed to have been buried. Although the original church was erected in the fourth century, the present church was dedicated in 1626.

32 The Sistine Chapel, named for Pope Sixtus IV (1471–1484), the principal chapel of the Vatican Palace where papal elections are held.

32

33

34

35

33 Basilica of St. John Lateran (Rome), the pope's cathedral church.

34 Basilica of St. Mary Major (Rome), founded by Pope Liberius in the mid-fourth century, with the present church erected the following century by Pope Sixtus III.

35 Hagia Sophia (Constantinople, now Istanbul), the principal church of Eastern Christianity until the Turkish conquest of the city in 1453, and the site of four ecumenical councils.

36 Avignon Palace (France), the papal residence from 1309 until 1377 and the headquarters of antipopes during the Great Western Schism (1378–1417).

36

37 The meeting of Sylvester I (314–335) and the first Christian emperor, Constantine the Great (d. 337).

38 Charlemagne (ca. 742–814), the first emperor of what was later called the "Holy Roman Empire."

39 Michelangelo Buonarroti (1475–1564) presenting the model of St. Peter's Basilica to Paul IV (1555–1559).

40 The trial of Galileo Galilei (1564–1642) before the Inquisition, 1633.

38

37

40

39

Epilogue

THE FUTURE OF THE PAPACY

N HIS ENCYCLICAL OF MAY 25, 1995, *UT UNUM sint* ("That All May Be One"), Pope John Paul II extended a remarkable invitation to pastoral leaders and theologians of non-Catholic Christian churches to enter into dialogue with him about papal primacy and the manner in which papal authority is exercised. He acknowledged, in accordance with the teaching of the Second Vatican Council, that everything the pope does as Bishop of Rome and as earthly head of the universal Church "must always be done in communion," because the papal ministry and office can never be separated from "the mission entrusted to the whole body of bishops, who are also 'vicars and ambassadors of Christ'" (Dogmatic Constitution on the Church, n. 27). The Bishop of Rome, John Paul II pointed out in the encyclical, is himself a member of the college of bishops and all of the other bishops are his "brothers in the ministry" (n. 95)

John Paul II indicated that, in a spirit of openness to a "new situation," the Church must "find a way of exercising the primacy" that would facilitate our common pilgrimage along the path toward Christian unity. Conceding that he cannot carry out this "immense task" by himself, he invited "church leaders and their theologians to engage with [him] in a patient and fraternal dialogue on this subject, a dialogue in which, leaving useless controversies behind, we could listen to one another, keeping before us only the will of Christ for his Church and allowing ourselves to be deeply moved by his plea 'that they may all be one . . . so that the world may believe that you have sent me' (John 17:21)" (n. 96).

What is the "new situation" to which the pope refers? What possible changes could there be in the exercise of the papal office that might serve to promote the unity of the Church without in any way compromising the essential mission, ministries, and structures of the Church? What sort of future might separated Christians work toward, in dialogue with the Bishop of Rome?

Speculation about the future, of course, is only that: speculation. By definition, the future is something that has not yet happened. It is a matter of promise, expectation (sometimes anxiety and even dread), and hope. In the meantime, we have only the past and the present from which to extrapolate possible future developments. Pope John XXIII (1958–63), himself a historian, said in his celebrated opening address to the Second Vatican Council on October 11, 1962, that history is the great "teacher of life." The lessons of history are consistently instructive and almost always liberating. History teaches us that things have not always been thus and that it is possible, therefore, to change them from what they have become. Nowhere is this principle more applicable than to the history of the papacy itself.

Catholics and non-Catholics alike have generally assumed that the popes with whom they are most familiar—the current and recent popes—have exercised authority in a certain manner (for all practical purposes, as if the authority were unlimited) because that is what Jesus Christ himself must have intended when he said to the Apostle, "You are Peter, and upon this rock I will build my church. . . . Whatever you bind on earth shall be bound in heaven; and whatever you loose on earth shall be loosed in heaven" (Matthew 16:18–19). The conventional assumption is that this authority, in exactly the same form in which it is exercised today, was conferred first upon Peter the Apostle and then transmitted in an unbroken line of succession to every individual whom the Catholic Church officially recognizes as a pope, from Linus (Peter's putatively immediate successor) to John Paul II. It is assumed, furthermore, that this line of succession has never been in doubt, that there has never been any serious question about the legitimacy of a particular claim to the papal chair, and that, if ever there has been a question, the Church readily resolved it.

History, "the teacher of life," teaches that there were no popes in the modern sense of the word (that is, as the sole Bishop of Rome) until the middle of the second century. Until then, the church of Rome was governed not by a single bishop but by a committee or council of elders and presbyter-bishops, perhaps with one individual acting as the body's convener or chair. Those prominent individuals in the Roman community may have been the ones whom the Catholic Church regards as the immediate successors of Peter himself: Linus, Anacletus, Clement, Evaristus, et al. But we cannot be certain. It is significant, for example, that when St. Ignatius of Antioch (d. ca. 107) addressed his famous letters to the various churches of the Mediterranean world, the letter to Rome was the only one in which the local bishop was not mentioned. Indeed, there is no evidence that Peter himself functioned in an episcopal role in Rome. Although traditionally regarded as the founder of the church there, along with the Apostle Paul, Peter was not even present when Christianity first came to Rome, probably in the early 40s, almost two decades before Peter arrived. Moreover, Paul makes no mention at all of Peter in his Letter to the Romans, written most likely in the winter of 57–58.

Furthermore, the popes of the first four centuries wielded relatively limited authority beyond Rome and its immediate environs. For example, Sylvester I (314–35) seems to have exercised no discernible influence over the first ecumenical council held at Nicaea in 325. He neither convened nor attended it. And yet this was the council that issued the Church's first definitive teaching on the divinity of Jesus Christ—as central a dogmatic issue as the Church would, or could, ever address in its entire history. The same can be said of Damasus I (366–84) with regard to the Council of Constantinople in 381, which reaffirmed the teaching of Nicaea and defined the divinity of the Holy Spirit, and of Celestine I (422–32) with regard to the Council of Ephesus in 431, which defined that Jesus Christ is one divine Person and that Mary is the Mother of God and not only the mother of the man Jesus. Not until the pontificate of Leo the Great (440–61) was the claim of universal papal jurisdiction (that is, over the whole Church, East as well as West) first articulated and an attempt made to exercise it in any really decisive manner.

The first pope who reached out to assert his authority beyond the borders of his own ecclesiastical community was Victor I (189–98), an African, who ordered other churches to conform to the Roman practice of celebrating Easter on the Sunday following the fourteenth day of Nisan (Passover). But when Victor threatened to excommunicate those who disagreed with his ruling, he was rebuked by no less a prominent figure of the early Church than St. Irenaeus of Lyons (d. ca. 200), who pointedly reminded the pope that all of his predecessors had been indulgent toward diversity of practice and had not dared to resort to the ultimate weapon of excommunication. And when popes first began to engage in theological disputes with the pastoral leaders of other churches, they were sometimes rebuffed as interlopers or, worse, as having erroneous views, as in the case of the clash between Stephen I (254–57) and Cyprian (d. 258), bishop of Carthage, over the question of the validity of baptism administered by heretics and schismatics.

Over the course of time, disputes and conflicts over pastoral practice developed into conflicts over doctrine. Thus, John II (533–35), under pressure from the Eastern emperor, contradicted the teaching of a previous pope, Hormisdas (514–23), on the two natures of Jesus Christ. Honorius I (625–38) became an unwitting adherent of Monothelitism, which held that there is only one (divine) will in Jesus Christ. After his death, Honorius was formally condemned by the Third Council of Constantinople (680)—an action subsequently ratified by Leo II (682–83). When the Monothelite controversy continued to divide Rome from Constantinople, Eugenius I (654–57) tried valiantly to reconcile the two sides. In doing so, however, he prematurely accepted a compromise that seemed to posit three wills in Christ. This provoked a firestorm of protest among the clergy and laity of Rome. The pope was prevented from continuing with Mass in the basilica of St. Mary Major (Santa Maria Maggiore) until he had promised to reject the compromise.

But doctrinal deviation was only one of the serious problems that surfaced in this early period of papal history. Between the beginning of the Carolingian Empire (800) and the end of the pontificate of Damasus II (1048), the papacy sunk to its lowest moral depths, stained by simony, i.e., the buying and selling of church offices, nepotism, lavish lifestyles, concubinage, brutality, even murder. It was also dominated for much of this time by German kings and by powerful—and corrupt—Roman aristocratic families. During this period at least five popes, and possibly a sixth, were assassinated. One pope, Sergius III (904–11), was himself a murderer, having ordered the killings of his predecessor, Leo V, and the antipope Christopher. Two popes were imprisoned and mutilated or starved before death (Stephen VIII [939–42] and John XIV [983–84], respectively), and the body of one pope (Formosus [891–96]) was even exhumed from its resting place, on orders of one of his successors, Stephen VI (896–97), and put on public trial in the so-called Cadaver Synod. Stephen himself was subsequently deposed, imprisoned, and strangled to death.

However, the "great turning point" in the history of the papacy, according to the distinguished Dominican theologian Cardinal Yves Congar (d. 1995), came with the pontificate of Gregory VII (1073–85). It was Gregory, more than any other pope, who substantially recast the papacy into the kind of monarchical and legalistic institution it is today. To be sure, Gregory VII faced overwhelming internal and external problems when he was elected in 1073: simony, nepotism, violations of clerical celibacy, and the interference of lay princes in the appointment and installation of bishops and abbots (also known as "lay investiture"). The pope had his canon lawyers comb the Roman archives for every trace or shred of support for the exercise of papal power that he deemed necessary to meet these challenges. Some of the uncovered material was authentic; other parts were spurious—forgeries. In seeking to rely on legal precedents for the exercise of what should be only spiritual authority, the pope transformed the Church principally into a juridical institution, with papal power as the basis of all of the Church's authority. As an unfortunate result, the Church came to adopt very much the same attitudes and to make very much the same claims as the temporal powers themselves. Gregory VII thereby set the second-millennial papacy on a legalistic, monarchical course, one completely foreign to that of the early Church and of the Eastern churches generally. So sharp a turn did the Roman Church make that two of Gregory's successors, Innocent III

(1198–1216) and Boniface VIII (1295–1303), claimed authority, indeed supremacy, not only over the whole Church, as Gregory VII had, but over the whole world as well—temporal and spiritual realms alike.

The conventional assumption that the papacy provides the Catholic with a direct conduit to and from Jesus Christ requires, of course, that the Catholic should be able to determine who the pope is. During the Great Western Schism (1378–1417) there were always two, and then three, contemporaneous claimants to the papal throne. After the death of Gregory XI in 1378, the election of a successor was interrupted by violence among the Roman people, who demanded an Italian pope following the papacy's seventy-year "captivity" in Avignon, France. The panic-stricken, mainly French cardinals elected Urban VI, an unstable man whose early behavior in office alienated the cardinals and prompted them to raise questions about the validity of his election. Virtually the same cardinals who had elected Urban now rejected him. They left Rome for Fondi (in the kingdom of Naples), where they formally declared Urban's election invalid and elected Cardinal Robert of Geneva (who was also French) as Clement VII. Although the three Italian cardinals did not vote in the election at the Fondi cathedral, they concurred in it by their presence.

England, the Holy Roman Empire, and most of Italy sided with Urban VI, but France, the kingdom of Sicily, Scotland, the kingdom of Naples, and Spain sided with Clement VII, who took up residence in Avignon, as popes had done for the previous seventy years. There was general confusion in the Church as heads of monasteries, religious orders, dioceses, and parishes appealed to one pope or the other as the basis for their authority. In 1409, some thirty-one years after the outbreak of the schism, adherents of both sides decided that a general council should be convened in order to bring the crisis to an end. Cardinals from both obediences (the Roman, headed now by Gregory XII, and the Avignon, headed now by Benedict XIII) called the Council of Pisa, which deposed both popes, denouncing them as schismatics, heretics, and perjurers, and elected a third, Alexander V. But neither Gregory XII nor Benedict XIII accepted the council's decision. So the Church now had three men claiming to be pope rather than two.

Gregory XII thereupon called his own council at Cividale, near Aquileia, but it was poorly attended and had to be adjourned after several sessions. Before it did adjourn, however, the council excommunicated the other two papal claimants, Benedict XIII (of the Avignon line) and now Alexander V (of the Pisan line). But Gregory XII, the pope of the Roman line, was so beleaguered and so little supported that he had to flee in disguise from Aquileia, whose local archbishop was hostile to him, to Gaeta, where he sought the protection of the king of Naples.

When the king of Naples, however, subsequently concluded a treaty with John XXIII, the second pope in the Pisan line, Gregory was banished from Naples. Eventually, with the help of the German king Sigismund, the Council of Constance (1414–18) was convened and deposed John XXIII. Gregory XII resigned (after being allowed to convoke the Council of Constance to make it official in his eyes); Benedict XIII (the pope in the Avignon line) fled to a well-fortified castle on the coast of Valencia, claiming to envoys of the council that this was now the true church, the ark of Noah; and Martin V was elected. It should be pointed out that, although the Catholic Church retrospectively recognizes Gregory XII and the other popes of the Roman line as the only legitimate popes during this confused and troubled period, their legitimacy was hardly obvious to all the Catholics of that time. For nearly forty years—a lifetime for most people of that day—Catholics could not be certain who the pope was, much less what he was teaching in the name of Christ. And yet the Church somehow survived and people made their way along the road to salvation under the power of God's grace, without benefit of guidance from the successor of Peter—whoever he might have been.

But the Great Western Schism was not the only period in church history in which the identity of the pope was in doubt. There have been thirty-nine antipopes in all, beginning with St. Hippolytus (yes, "St." Hippolytus), from 217 to 235, and ending with Felix V, from 1439 to 1449. The Vatican's own official list of popes, in the *Annuario Pontificio,* has occasionally shifted popes from one column to the other as it decides— many centuries later—that an individual it had always regarded as a legitimate successor of Peter was really not validly elected after all. Even with this correction process, four instances remain where the *Annuario* still cannot make up its mind.

Silverius (536–37) was still alive when Vigilius (537–55) was elected pope on March 29, 537. The *Annuario Pontificio* recognizes this date as the beginning of Vigilius's pontificate, even though it also marks the end of Silverius's pontificate as November 11, 537, the day he formally resigned, three weeks before his death. Were there two popes between March 29 and November 11?

Martin I's pontificate is listed as having ended with his death, in exile, on September 16, 655. But the beginning of the pontificate of his successor, Eugenius I, is listed as August 10, 654, the day he was elected by the Roman clergy and people after they concluded that Martin I would never return. They feared that if they waited any longer, the Byzantine emperor would impose a thoroughly unacceptable new pope on them. Was Martin I still pope or not? If so, how could Eugenius I be a legitimate pope? If Martin I was no longer the real pope, by what canonical action did his pontificate come to an end? There is no evidence that he resigned, nor that he was validly deposed by a council of the Church.

The third case is that of the notorious John XII (elected to the papacy at the age of eighteen!). The *Annuario Pontificio* lists the end of his pontificate as May 14, 964, which was the day of his death. But it gives the beginning of the pontificate of his successor, Leo VIII (the first layman elected pope), as December 4, 963—while John XII was still alive. Leo's pontificate is listed as having ended on March 1, 965, but his successor, Benedict V, is said to have begun his own pontificate on May 22, 964—while Leo VIII was still alive. The 1997 *Catholic Almanac* and *Our Sunday Visitor's Catholic Encyclopedia* (1991), both of which reproduce the official list of popes and their dates as given in the *Annuario Pontificio*, acknowledge the confusion. They point out that John XII was deposed by a Roman council on December 4, 963. However, if the deposition was invalid, then Leo VIII was an antipope. If the deposition was valid, Leo was a valid pope and Benedict V was an antipope. But the Vatican's official list regards neither Leo VIII nor Benedict V as an antipope—and yet it records the end of John XII's pontificate as May 14, 964, some five months *after* the election of Leo VIII. So, too, Benedict V begins his pontificate over eight months before Leo's pontificate ended. According to the Vatican's own official list, therefore, we had a brief period toward the end of the tenth century when there were two popes governing the Church simultaneously.

Finally, there is the case of Benedict IX, the only pope to have held the papal office at three different times (1032–44, 1045, and 1047–48). If Benedict's forcible removal in 1044 was invalid, Sylvester III (January 20–March 10, 1045) was an antipope (but he is still listed with the legitimate popes). And if Benedict IX's resignation in 1045 and his removal by a synod in 1046 were not valid, then Gregory VI (May 5, 1045–December 20, 1046) and Clement II (December 25, 1046–October 9, 1047) were also antipopes (but, again, they are still listed with the legitimate popes in the *Annuario Pontificio*).

In the history of papacy there were not only doubts about *who* was pope but also about *when* a pope became pope. During most of the first Christian millennium, papal terms of office were reckoned not from the moment an individual accepted his election, as was the case during most of the second Christian millennium, but from the moment of his consecration as a bishop. This was so because, until Marinus I (882–84), no one who was elected to the papacy was as yet a bishop. They were either priests (presbyters) or deacons (and one subdeacon). Since the pope is, first and foremost, the Bishop of Rome, he could not have been regarded as the pope until he was consecrated as a bishop. Furthermore, for much of this period it was the Byzantine emperor, headquartered in Constantinople, not the papal electors, who determined when—and if—that consecration would take place. The emperor, in fact, often took his time notifying the newly elected pope of his approval for the consecration to proceed. John IV (640–42), for example, had to wait five months between his election and consecration. In the interim, the archpriest Hilarus and another John, the chief secretary (*primicerius*), continued to administer the Roman church as "vicegerents of the Apostolic See." And when the Roman church sent an official letter to certain Irish bishops and abbots regarding the proper date for the celebration of Easter, the pope-elect, John IV, was the second signatory, not the first. On the other hand, a number of popes in the second Christian millennium (the last being Gregory XVI in 1831) were not yet bishops when elected. However, according to the canon law in force through most of the millennium (until the revision of the Code of Canon Law in 1983), these individuals were considered to be the pope, even before being consecrated as a bishop. The Church of the first Christian millennium would have found this practice theologically and pastorally inconceivable.

What, then, of the papacy's future? The recent period of recentralization of papal authority and of the restoration of various pre–Vatican II styles of governance in the Catholic Church will in all likelihood have ended with the pontificate of John Paul II. The history of papal elections, especially (but not exclusively) during the nineteenth and twentieth centuries, makes clear that popes are usually not succeeded by carbon copies of themselves, no matter how long they may have been in office and no matter how many cardinals they may have appointed. The succession of Pius IX by Leo XIII in 1878, and of Leo XIII by Pius X in 1903 are two dramatic cases in point. Pius IX was the longest reigning pope in history (nearly thirty-two years), and Leo XIII had the second longest pontificate (over twenty-five years). Both were succeeded by popes markedly different from themselves—personally, theologically, and pastorally. And so it has been the case throughout most of papal history.

In the years before the beginning of the second Christian millennium and before the pontificate of Gregory VII in particular, popes functioned largely in the role of mediator, resolving disputes and conflicts over belief and discipline "by common consent" (John Paul II, *Ut unum sint*, n. 95). They did not claim for themselves alone the title Vicar of Christ. They did not appoint bishops (except in neighboring dioceses or in missionary dioceses founded by the Roman church). They did not govern through a Roman Curia. They did not impose or enforce clerical celibacy. They did not write encyclicals or authorize catechisms for the universal Church. They did not retain for themselves alone the power of canonization of saints. As a rule, they did not convene or preside over ecumenical councils—and certainly not the major doctrinal councils of Nicaea (325), Constantinople (381), Ephesus (431), and Chalcedon (451). The papacy of the third Christian millennium will more probably resemble the papacy of the first millennium than of the second, but it will surely be different from both as the Church faces new and currently unforeseen pastoral circumstances, challenges, and opportunities in the decades and centuries to come.

So, too, will ecclesiastical authority be exercised at points closest to the pastoral levels where its decisions will have their greatest impact. There will be an increasing decentralization of church governance, without prejudice to the need to signify and to maintain the unity of the universal Church, albeit through a differently structured papacy and through ecumenical councils and world synods that will also include clergy, religious, and laity as active, voting participants, as was the case at the Council of Constance in the fifteenth century.

The historically contingent, and often artificial, barriers between and among churches will also fall, as intercommunion and the mutual recognition of ordained ministries becomes a commonplace of the ecumenical Church of the twenty-first century and the beginning of the third Christian millennium. Outreach to non-Christian religions will intensify, with particular breakthroughs, now unimagined, in Christian-Jewish relations.

And the Church will recognize more fully than it does today that it is only a means, not an end. The Reign of God alone is absolute and supreme. All else, including the papacy itself, is subordinate to it and is in its service. The Church of the third Christian millennium will be content to make as its own the familiar petition in the Lord's Prayer, "Thy kingdom come, thy will be done on earth as it is in heaven."

The will of God may have a place for the Petrine ministry, or papacy, in the Church of the third Christian millennium, but precisely what place is not clear from this historical distance. What does seem beyond question is that the papacy of the future will function much differently from the papacy as we know it today.

Appendix A

HOW POPES ARE ELECTED

SOME CATHOLICS ASSUME THAT, BECAUSE IN THEIR MINDS POPES are God's unique representatives on earth, they are somehow chosen by the direct inspiration of the Holy Spirit. Thus, when the cardinals gather in conclave after the death of a pope, it is simply to pray for divine guidance and to select the one to whom that guidance points. Why more than one ballot is almost always required is not explained—nor are there explanations for the political maneuverings, the direct interference of temporal rulers to prevent certain cardinals from being elected, or the occasional giving of bribes and promises of other benefits to potential supporters.

But there *is* an explanation for all this. Although Catholic doctrine holds that the pope (more precisely, the Bishop of Rome) is the successor of St. Peter and the Vicar of Christ on earth (Vicar of Peter is the more traditional and more accurate title), the process by which he is selected is a human and, indeed, a political process. The electors choose from a number of possible, and often competing, candidates. Some electors prefer one candidate over the others because he seems to them to have qualities better suited to the needs of the Church at that particular time in history. Others firmly oppose a candidate because he seems to have qualities that they deem harmful to the mission and well-being of the Church at that time. The electors, of course, do not always succeed in getting their favored candidates elected. So they must compromise. Another candidate is chosen because he is more acceptable (or less unacceptable) to those whose votes are needed for victory.

Although the electors meet in conclave, separate from the outside world, the pressures of the outside world are not absent inside. The electors are part of that world and came in directly from that world, with all its pressures and counterpressures swirling about them. Some of those pressures are ecclesiastical, others are purely political. Usually they are a mixture of the two. And this is as one might expect, given Catholic belief in the Church as both a human and a divine institution. To the extent that the Church is divine in character, God is involved somehow in the process of selecting a pastoral leader as important as the pope. But to the extent that the Church is also human in character, human beings are involved in the selection of the pope. And where you have human beings involved, you have the human factors of politics, self-interest, greed, and desire for power. How the two—the divine and the human—precisely interact in a papal election, one cannot determine. It is in the interaction of the divine and the human, however, that one confronts the mystery of the Church.

The First Christian Millennium

For the first thousand years of the Church's existence, that is, for half its entire history, popes were elected by the clergy and people of Rome, because, before all else, the pope is the bishop of the local church, or diocese, of Rome. From the earliest centuries of the Church, the clergy and laity always selected their own pastors in every part of the Christian world. Rome was no exception. Thus, when Cornelius was elected pope in 251, St. Cyprian, bishop of Carthage, described the process in a letter to Antonianus: "Cornelius was made bishop by the judgment of God and of His Christ, by the testimony of almost all the clergy, by the vote of the people who were then present, by the assembly of venerable bishops and good men" (cited by Patrick Granfield, *The Papacy in Transition*, p. 126). In many other letters in which he referred to the election of bishops in North Africa, Rome, Spain, and almost all of the provinces of the Roman Empire, Cyprian indicated that these elections involved the whole community and that they proceeded in three stages: the *testimonium* (Lat., "witness"), by which the community testified to a candidate's qualifications; the *suffragium* ("vote"), by which the community manifested its preference for one candidate or another; and the *judicium* ("judgment"), by which the community ratified the vote that had taken place.

In the fourth and fifth centuries, popular elections of bishops, including the Bishop of Rome, continued, but now the bishops of neighboring (or suburbicarian) dioceses assumed a greater role. In his letter to the bishops of Gaul (modern-day France), Pope Celestine I (422–32) wrote: "Let no bishop be given to a community against its will; the consent and desire of the clergy, people, and nobility is required." And Pope Leo the Great (440–61) made the same point: "No consideration allows making bishops of those who have not been chosen by the clerics, sought for by the people, and consecrated by the provincial bishops with the consent of the metropolitan." It was Leo who articulated the basic canonical principle that is honored today in the breach, not in the practice: "He [the bishop] who is in charge of all should be chosen by all."

In the sixth and seventh centuries, the clergy and the bishops of the neighboring dioceses took a more prominent part in electing the Bishop of Rome. Influential laypersons, such as civil and military officials, also began to exercise a greater role than ordinary citizens, although the approval of the general populace was always deemed necessary. From the time of the Byzantine conquest of northern and extreme southern Italy and Sicily in 535–53 until the waning of their power with the ascendancy of the Lombards in the early eighth century, the Eastern emperors also exercised a profound, but rarely positive, influence over papal elections. Justinian (d. 565) forced through the election of Vigilius in 537 (a pope who would later be excommunicated by a synod of African bishops for his vacillation on crucial points of doctrine regarding the divinity of Christ). At the next papal transition in 556, the emperor's interference was even more egregious. Pelagius I, who had been papal legate in Constantinople, where Justinian came to know and admire him, was installed in the papacy without even an election. When Pelagius arrived in Rome prepared to assume his new responsibilities, he received a hostile reception, especially from many religious and nobles who broke communion with him. His consecration as a bishop (he was still only a deacon) had to be postponed because no bishop would at first officiate. Eventually the bishops of Perugia and Ferentino agreed to do the consecration, and a presbyter (priest) represented the bishop of Ostia, who was normally one of the papal consecrators. By the time the next pope, John III, was elected in 561, it was taken for granted that he could not be consecrated without approval from the emperor. And he had to wait four months until that approval arrived from Constantinople.

It is important to understand why imperial approval for the consecration (i.e., episcopal ordination) of a newly elected pope was, in effect, essential for the validity of the pope's claim to office. The pope is, first and foremost, the Bishop of Rome. It is because he is Bishop of Rome, which is the universal Church's primatial see and the one traditionally associated with the Apostle Peter, that he is also the pope. But if a newly elected pope is not yet a bishop (which none were until Marinus I, who came to Rome from another diocese in 882), he cannot be the Bishop of Rome until he is consecrated as such. And if the emperor's approval is necessary for that, his approval becomes at least as essential as the election itself. (It should be noted that all of the popes from Agapitus I in 535 until Deusdedit in 615 were deacons, and not even priests, at the time of their election to the papacy.)

Benedict I, John III's immediate successor, had to wait eleven months from the time of his election in July 574 until the imperial approval for his consecration arrived from Constantinople. Benedict's successor, Pelagius II, went ahead with his own consecration in 579 without waiting for the emperor's approval, because the city of Rome was under siege by the

Lombards at the time and there was a sense of urgency in the air. But the practice of awaiting imperial confirmation resumed with the next pontificate. The practice itself is of extraordinary interest in light of traditional papal claims about the supremacy of the Apostolic See. For example, Pope Siricius (384–99) decreed that no bishop should be consecrated without the knowledge of the Apostolic See. And yet there was a situation less than two centuries later where the Apostolic See itself could not have its own bishop, the successor of Peter, consecrated without the approval of a lay ruler, the Byzantine emperor, many hundreds of miles away in Constantinople. The only concession the papacy won from the emperor in this period was his allowing the imperial exarch (viceroy) in Ravenna, the seat of Byzantine authority in Italy, to ratify papal elections instead of the newly elected pope's having to await approval from Constantinople itself. This new arrangement, achieved by Benedict II (684–85), at least speeded up the confirmation process by narrowing the time gap between the election and consecration of the Bishop of Rome.

During this same period the level of politicking and jockeying for power became increasingly intense and disedifying. Boniface III held a synod in 607 that introduced one of the first formal regulations of papal elections. Henceforth, the penalty of excommunication would be imposed on anyone discussing a successor to a pope (or any other bishop) during the pope's (or other bishop's) lifetime and until three days after his death. Historians point out that the delay of more than a year between the death of Boniface's predecessor, Sabinian, and Boniface's own election as pope in 607 may have been the result of extensive campaigning and horse-trading between those loyal to the memory of Pope Gregory the Great (590–604) and the anti-Gregorians, who felt that Gregory had shown too much favoritism to clergy in religious orders at the expense of the diocesan, or secular, clergy.

In the early eighth century, the balance of military and political power shifted from the Byzantines to the Lombards and then to the Franks. Gregory III (731–41) was the last pope to seek the Byzantine emperor's approval for his consecration. With the pontificate of Stephen II (III) from 752 to 757, the papacy became completely detached from the Byzantine Empire and placed itself under the protection of the Frankish kingdom, ruled at the time by Pepin III. Stephen's successor, Paul I (757–67), simply notified Pepin of his election without seeking any formal approval as the Byzantine emperors had required. By the time Leo III was elected in 795, Charlemagne (d. 814) was king of the Franks. Leo sent him notification of his election, along with the keys of St. Peter's tomb and the banner of Rome in recognition of his sovereignty. In the interim, a Roman synod (769), under Pope Stephen III (IV), decided that only deacons and cardinal-priests (that is, priests who were pastors of the titular, or cardinal, churches of Rome) were eligible for election as Bishop of Rome and that henceforth only clergy could vote in a papal election. The laity's role was to be one of subsequent acceptance of their newly elected bishop.

By the beginning of the ninth century the new Carolingian Empire had been established under Charlemagne. After Charlemagne's death in 814, his successor, Louis the Pious, restored the role of the laity in papal elections. Acting through his son Lothair I, Louis promulgated a Roman constitution in 824, with the approval of Pope Eugenius II (824–27), decreeing among other things a revival of the ancient tradition, recently suspended by Pope Stephen III (IV) in 769, whereby the people of Rome as well as the clergy would participate in papal elections. The constitution also stipulated, however, that before being consecrated, the newly elected pope must take an oath of loyalty to the Carolingian emperor before the imperial legate. Pope Eugenius II ratified these terms in a synod held at the Lateran in 826. The next pope, Valentine (827), was unanimously elected by the clergy, nobility, and people of Rome. However, there was a sharp division within the laity of Rome at the next election. Upon Valentine's death some forty days later, the Roman people proclaimed a deacon named John as the new pope, seized the Lateran Palace, and enthroned him. The lay aristocracy, however, had other ideas. Meeting in the basilica of San Martino, they elected the elderly, but nobly born, archpriest Sergius as pope, ejected John from the Lateran, and quickly crushed the opposition. Because of the tense situation, Sergius II's consecration was rushed through without waiting for imperial approval. The emperor Lothair I was irate. The papal territories were plundered in punitive fashion and, at a synod in St. Peter's in which some twenty Italian bishops participated, Sergius II had to submit to a difficult and lengthy investigation of his claim to the papal throne. Although his election was eventually ratified, he had to swear allegiance to Lothair and accept the emperor's condition that newly elected popes could not be consecrated without the emperor's approval and in the presence of his representative. Sergius's successor, Leo IV (847–55), honored that condition, waiting six weeks from the time of his election for imperial approval for his consecration.

The new requirement of imperial approval, however, also provided opportunities for serious mischief making in papal elections. When Leo IV died in 855, the first choice of the clergy and people of Rome was Hadrian, cardinal-priest of the church of San Marco. But when Hadrian refused election, the clergy and people elected Benedict, the highly respected cardinal-priest of the church of San Callisto. An influential group close to the imperial court preferred Anastasius, a former cardinal-priest who had been degraded (i.e., his cardinal's title was taken away) and excommunicated by Leo IV. Exploiting the rule that Benedict could not be consecrated without imperial consent and in the presence of his representative, the imperialist faction declared Benedict's election null and void, held an election of their own at Orte, brought Anastasius to Rome in the company of imperial representatives, and had him installed in the Lateran. Benedict was dragged from the papal throne, ejected from the palace, and imprisoned. But the reaction of the people was so intense (there were three days of rioting) that the imperial representatives withdrew their support of Anastasius and allowed Benedict's consecration to go forward. Anastasius was stripped of his papal insignia and ejected from the Lateran. In accordance with the terms of an agreement reached between Benedict and the emperor's representatives, Anastasius received no other punishment than reduction to the lay state and confinement to the monastery of Santa Maria in Trastevere. (Anastasius would experience a remarkable rehabilitation, however, serving as an important counselor to the next three popes and as Librarian of the Roman church; hence his name in the history books, Anastasius Bibliothecarius.)

Marinus I's election in 882 was of immense historical significance because he was the first Bishop of Rome to have already been a bishop. In direct violation of canon 15 of the First Council of Nicaea (325), prohibiting a bishop from transferring from one diocese to another, Marinus left his diocese of Caere (now Cerveteri) in Etruria to accept election as Bishop of Rome. He also did not seek approval from the emperor, Charles III. (The issue of a bishop's transferring from one diocese to another became one of the central issues in the infamous "Cadaver Synod," at which the corpse of Pope Formosus was placed on trial in January 897. Formosus had been bishop of Porto when elected Bishop of Rome.)

The character of papal elections changed for the worse in the tenth century with the aristocratic families of Rome overwhelming not only the voice of the ordinary laity but that of the clergy as well. The papacy became the plaything of these families, especially the Theophylacts, the Crescentii, and the Tusculans. The Theophylacts controlled the papacy from the pontificate of Sergius III (904–11) through that of John XI (931–35/6). Alberic II, prince of Rome, patrician, and senator of all the Romans, ruled the city, including the papacy, with absolute control from 932 to 954, and his illegitimate son Octavian (who took the named John XII) was elected pope the year after his father's death. (On his deathbed Alberic summoned the pope, Agapitus II, the nobility, and clergy and forced them to swear that after Agapitus II's death, they would elect his son as pope—in direct violation of Pope Symmachus's decree of 499, forbidding such pacts.) The Holy Roman emperor Otto I (d. 973) controlled the next three elections, but after his death the powerful Crescentii family of Rome emerged as the new dominant force, without negating, however, the continued influence of Otto's successors. Indeed, Otto III's twenty-four-old relative would become the first German pope in history, Gregory V (996–99). But the influence of the Crescentii continued even into the early eleventh century, until the pontificate of Sergius IV (1009–12). Then the Tusculan family came to the fore, engineering the election of three successive laymen to the papacy in 1012, 1024, and 1032. During this chaotic tenth century there were some twenty-five popes and antipopes. The French bishops, meeting at the Council of Saint-Basle de Verzy in 991, bitterly asked: "Is it to such monsters, swollen with their ignominy and devoid of all knowledge human or divine, that the innumerable priests of God throughout the world who are distinguished by their knowledge and virtues should have to be submitted?"

The Second Christian Millennium

The power of the German emperor-kings reasserted itself in full force in the eleventh century with the election of four consecutive German popes in 1046, 1048, 1049, and 1055. Soon thereafter, Nicholas II, a French pope who remained bishop of Florence during his pontificate (1058–61), not only prohibited simony in papal elections (that is, gaining the office through bribery and promises of ecclesiastical preferments), but he also decreed that henceforth only cardinal-bishops could vote in papal elections. (Alexander III modified that latter provision in 1179 by including cardinal-priests and cardinal-deacons as papal electors and also by requiring a two-thirds majority for election.) The clergy and laity were to give their subsequent assent. The emperor would also be notified of the election, but would no longer have the right of confirmation. Pope Gregory VII (1073–85) would deal another major blow against continued interference by lay rulers in papal elections by striking out directly against lay investiture and excommunicating the German emperor-king Henry IV for resisting him. Nevertheless, the German kings continued to interfere for a while in papal elections, with Henry IV and Henry V supporting various antipopes. But the new arrangement held fairly well, except in Martin V's election by the Council of Constance in 1417, ending the Great Western Schism (1378–1417). Martin was elected by twenty-two cardinals, but also by thirty other prelates—six from each of the five major nations represented at the council: Italy, France, Spain, Germany, and England.

Gregory X, in order to avoid the repetition of long vacancies, decreed through the Second Council of Lyons in 1274 that papal elections were to be held ten days after the death of a pope (the current requirement is fifteen to twenty days after the beginning of a vacancy) and that the cardinal-electors should conduct the election in a secure place where they will have no contact with anyone else. He also stipulated that the election be held in the city or town where the pope died (a practice followed as late as the end of the eighteenth century). The cardinals were also warned that if they did not elect a pope within three days, their rations were to be reduced for five days. If after those five days they still had not elected a new pope, they were to be given only bread, wine, and water until they had elected a pope. Furthermore, during the entire conclave the cardinals were to derive no income whatever from the papal treasury or from any other ecclesiastical source.

The Fifth Lateran Council (1512–17) decreed that if an ecumenical council is in session when a pope dies, the council should be suspended immediately. (Pope John Paul II reaffirmed that rule in 1996, but also included synods of bishops.) Julius II (1503–13) decreed that simoniacal elections are not only illicit but invalid and that the candidate elected is an apostate (i.e., one who has completely rejected the faith). Significantly, Julius's own election was simoniacal. Pius X abrogated that latter stipulation in 1904, and Paul VI, while deploring simony in whatever form, revoked the decree of nullity in 1975 so that the validity of a papal election may not be challenged for this reason. In 1945 Pius XII modified the ancient two-thirds rule of Alexander III, given in 1179, by increasing the required two-thirds majority to two-thirds plus one. In 1996 John Paul II rescinded Pius XII's amendment, so that the required majority is back to two-thirds, but now with a major difference. In John Paul II's new rules for papal elections, it will be possible for a candidate to be elected pope by a simple majority if, after several days of voting and prayer (thirty-three ballots in all), a candidate still has not received the necessary two-thirds majority. In 1970 Paul VI decreed that only cardinals under the age of eighty are eligible to vote in papal elections, with the maximum number of cardinal-electors set at 120. John Paul II confirmed these norms in 1996.

The New Rules of John Paul II

[The following are excerpts and syntheses of norms and procedures for papal elections promulgated by John Paul II on February 22, 1996, the feast of the Chair of St. Peter, Apostle, in an apostolic constitution entitled Universi Domini gregis *(Lat., "Of the Lord's whole flock").]*

Introduction.

John Paul II confirmed Paul VI's rule that the only papal electors are cardinals under the age of eighty (as of the day the papacy became vacant) and are limited in number to 120. The election is to take place in the Sistine Chapel, but the living quarters of the cardinals may be in any "suitable places within Vatican City State." (This represents a change from the cramped and makeshift living quarters in the Apostolic Palace, in the areas proximate to the Sistine Chapel. The electors will now be housed in a newly constructed guest house named Domus Sanctae Marthae.) Strict secrecy is still to be observed regarding everything pertaining to the electoral process.

Election by acclamation (or "by adoration"), however, is no longer possible. This occurs when one or more cardinals arise and proclaim a candidate and then others follow until there is a general consensus to elect that candidate without a formal vote. John Paul II also ended election by compromise, where the cardinals select a small number of their fellow electors to reach an agreement among themselves regarding a candidate, with the understanding that the rest of the electors would then abide by that agreement. The only form of election, therefore, is by secret ballot, in which all the electors participate.

Part I: The Vacancy of the Holy See.

1. *College of Cardinals' Powers During the Vacancy.* During a vacancy of the Holy See (which John Paul II explicitly acknowledged could be by the death or "valid resignation" of the pope), the College of Cardinals has no power or jurisdiction in matters pertaining to the pope "during his lifetime or in the exercise of his office" (n. 1). The power of the college is limited to the conducting of "ordinary business and of matters which cannot be postponed, and for the preparation of everything necessary for the election of the new pope" (n. 2). No changes can be made in the rules for the election of a new pope. And actions that contradict this prescription are "null and void" (n. 4). In cases of doubts or controversy regarding anything contained in this apostolic constitution, a majority of the college will determine what is to be done (n. 5).

2. *Congregations of Cardinals Preparatory to the Election.* A general congregation of all the cardinals, held in the Apostolic Palace (or other suitable place in the Vatican) and presided over by the dean of the College of Cardinals, is to be held daily, beginning on a day fixed by the Camerlengo of the Roman church (who also has the responsibility for

administering the goods and temporalities of the Holy See during the vacancy), and the senior cardinal-bishop, senior cardinal-priest, and senior
cardinal-deacon (n. 11). On the first day, all the rules and norms pertaining to a papal election are to be reviewed and discussed, and an oath is to
be taken by all the cardinals to observe the prescriptions of the apostolic
constitution and to maintain secrecy (n. 12).

In one of the subsequent meetings of the congregation, the cardinals
fix the details of the deceased pope's funeral (to be celebrated for nine
consecutive days) and burial (nn. 13a, b). The congregation of cardinals
also selects two "ecclesiastics known for their sound doctrine, wisdom
and moral authority" for the task of presenting to the cardinals "two
well-prepared meditations on the problems facing the Church at this
time and on need for careful discernment in choosing the new pope"
(n. 13d). The congregation reads any documents left by the deceased pope
for the College of Cardinals (n. 13f) and arranges for the destruction of
the fisherman's ring and of the lead seal with which apostolic letters are
dispatched (n. 13g). The congregation also determines the assignment of
rooms for the cardinal-electors (n. 13h) and determines the day and the
hour for the beginning of the voting process (n. 13i).

3. *Concerning Certain Offices During the Vacancy.* The authority of those
who head curial departments ends with the death or resignation of a
pope, except for the Camerlengo of the Roman church, the Major Penitentiary, who is responsible for resolving matters pertaining to the sacra-
ment of Reconciliation, or Penance, and other officials, including the
cardinal–vicar general for the diocese of Rome (n. 14).

It is the Camerlengo's task to verify the death of the pope and to place
a seal on the pope's study and bedroom. After the burial, the entire apartment is sealed (n. 17). The dean of the College of Cardinals, upon being
informed of the pope's death, informs the other cardinals and convokes
them for the congregations (meetings) of the cardinals. He also commu-
nicates the news of the pope's death to the diplomatic corps accredited to
the Holy See and to the heads of the respective nations (n. 19). Certain officials of the Secretariat of State and other offices concerned with relations
with other nations (including papal representatives to those nations), as
well as the secretaries of the various curial departments, remain in office
during the vacancy (nn. 20, 21).

4. *Faculties of the Curial Dicasteries.* This section is concerned with the
authority (faculties) that is retained by various curial officials and offices
during the vacancy.

5. *Funeral Rites of the Roman Pontiff.* Funeral rites are to be celebrated
for nine consecutive days (n. 27). Photographs of the deceased pope may

only be taken with the permission of the Camerlengo and only if the pope is attired in pontifical vestments (n. 30).

Part II: Election of the Roman Pontiff

1. *The Electors.* The only valid electors are cardinals of the Catholic Church who have not yet reached the age of eighty on the day the papacy became vacant. The maximum number of cardinal-electors is 120. No one else may participate in the election, nor may there be any intervention (veto) by any lay power (n. 33). An ecumenical council or world synod of bishops must be suspended immediately once there is a vacancy in the papal office (n. 34).

From the moment the Apostolic See is vacant, the cardinal-electors must wait fifteen days for those who are absent, and the College of Cardinals may even defer the election up to a maximum of twenty days following the death or resignation of a pope (n. 37). A cardinal who arrives after the electoral process has begun, but before a new pope has been elected, may be admitted to the conclave with full voting rights (n. 39). If a cardinal is forced to leave the conclave because of illness and later seeks to be readmitted, he must be allowed to reenter, even if he has left Vatican City for some other "grave reason" that is acknowledged as such by the majority of the cardinal-electors (n. 40).

2. *Election Place and Those Admitted by Their Office.* Although the apostolic constitution stipulates that the conclave shall take place "within the territory of Vatican City, in determined areas and buildings closed to unauthorized persons" (n. 41), it later indicates that the election itself is to be conducted in the Sistine Chapel of the Apostolic Palace (n. 50). No one is to be allowed to approach any of the cardinal-electors while they are being transported back and forth between the Domus Sanctae Marthae and the Sistine Chapel (n. 43). The cardinal-electors themselves are not to communicate with anyone outside the conclave by any means of communication, "except in cases of proven and urgent necessity" duly acknowledged by the "particular congregation," composed of the Camerlengo and three other cardinals, one from each of the orders (cardinal-bishop, cardinal-priest, and cardinal-deacon), chosen by lot (n. 44).

In addition to the cardinal-electors, the conclave also includes: the secretary of the College of Cardinals, who acts as secretary of the electoral assembly, the master of papal liturgical celebrations with two masters of ceremonies and two religious attached to the papal sacristy, an ecclesiastic chosen by the dean of the college to assist him in his duties, a number of religious order priests for hearing confessions in different languages, two medical doctors, and staff for preparing and serving meals and for housekeeping. All these persons must be approved in advance by the Camerlengo and his three cardinal-assistants (n. 46). All must also take an oath of secrecy in case they learn of anything connected with the electoral process (n. 47).

3. *Beginning of the Election.* On the fifteenth day after the death or resignation of the pope, and no later than the twentieth, the cardinal-electors meet, preferably in the morning, in St. Peter's Basilica (or elsewhere, if the circumstances warrant) for a solemn eucharistic celebration with the votive Mass *Pro eligendo papa* (Lat., "For electing the pope"; n. 49). After this Mass the cardinals assemble in the Pauline Chapel of the Apostolic Palace, chant the *Veni Creator* ("Come, Creator [Spirit]"), and then process into the Sistine Chapel where the election is to be held (n. 50). A prior electronic screening of the chapel is to be conducted to ensure the complete privacy of the election (n. 51). When the cardinal-electors arrive in the Sistine Chapel, they take the oath while touching the Holy Gospels to observe the terms of John Paul II's apostolic constitution pertaining to the election. When the last cardinal has taken the oath, the master of papal liturgical celebrations announces, "*Extra omnes*" ("Everybody out"), and all those not taking part in the election leave the chapel, except for the papal master of liturgical celebrations and the ecclesiastic chosen to preach the second meditation in which the cardinals are urged to "act with the right intention for the good of the universal Church" (n. 52). After the ecclesiastic and the papal master of liturgical celebrations leave the chapel, the dean of the college asks the cardinals if they are ready to proceed with the vote. If they are, they do so at once (n. 54).

4. *Observance of Secrecy on All Election Matters.* This chapter repeats the terms of secrecy and the prohibition of all forms of communication with the outside world during the course of the conclave (nn. 55–57). The cardinal-electors are forbidden to reveal anything about the voting or about discussions of the electoral process before or during the time of election (nn. 59, 60).

5. *Election Procedure.* Since the forms of election known as acclamation and compromise are abolished, the only form of electing a pope is by vote (Lat., *scrutinium*). A two-thirds majority of the total number of electors present is required for valid election. One additional vote is required if the number of cardinals present is not divisible by three (n. 62). If the election begins on the afternoon of the first day, only one ballot is to be held. If no one is elected, two ballots are held the following morning, and two more the following afternoon (n. 63). If no one has been elected after three days of voting, voting is suspended for a maximum of one day for prayer, informal discussion, and a brief spiritual exhortation

given by the senior cardinal-deacon. Voting is resumed, but if, after seven more ballots, no one has been chosen, there is another pause for prayer, discussion, and an exhortation, this time by the senior cardinal-priest. Another series of seven ballots takes place. If there has been no election, there is another pause for prayer, discussion, and an exhortation given this time by the senior cardinal-bishop. Voting is then resumed for another seven ballots (n. 74).

If, after all these votes, there is still no election, the Camerlengo invites the cardinal-electors to express their opinion about the manner of proceeding. The election then proceeds "in accordance with what the absolute majority of the electors decides." But there can be no waiving of the requirement that "a valid election takes place only by an absolute majority of the votes or else by voting only on the two names which in the ballot immediately preceding have received the greatest number of votes; also in this second case only an absolute majority is required" (n. 75). Any violation of these procedures renders the election "null and void" (n. 76).

6. *Matters to Be Observed or Avoided.* Any elector guilty of simony is automatically excommunicated, but a simoniacal election is not invalid (n. 78). No cardinal may make plans concerning a successor or promise votes or make decisions in this regard in private gatherings during a pope's lifetime and "without having consulted him" (n. 79). Any cardinal-elector who accepts the task of presenting a veto of any kind from a civil authority is automatically excommunicated (n. 80). No cardinals may make any preelection pacts or commitments of any kind directing their votes for or against any candidate. Such agreements are null and void and those who engage in such activities are automatically excommunicated. However, an exchange of views concerning the election is not forbidden (n. 81). No cardinal may make any promises or commitments about the course of his pontificate should he be elected, and such promises, even if made under oath, are null and void (n. 82). Cardinals should not be influenced by friendship or aversion or by any other outside pressures in casting their vote. They are to "give their vote to the person, even outside the College of Cardinals, who in their judgment is most suited to govern the universal Church in a fruitful and beneficial way" (n. 83).

7. *Acceptance and Proclamation of the New Pope.* Upon the election of a new pope, the junior cardinal-deacon summons into the hall of election the secretary of the College of Cardinals and the master of papal liturgical celebrations. The dean of the college, or the most senior cardinal, asks the one elected, "Do you accept your canonical election as supreme pontiff?" As soon as he has received the consent, he asks the new pope, "By what name do you wish to be called?" The master of papal liturgical celebrations, with the two masters of ceremonies (who are

summoned at that point) acting as witnesses, draws up a document certifying acceptance by the new pope and the name taken by him (n. 87). The conclave officially ends with the new pope's acceptance of his election.

If the one elected is already a bishop, he is immediately Bishop of Rome, "true pope and head of the college of bishops," with "full and supreme authority over the universal Church." If the person elected is not already a bishop (someone from outside the College of Cardinals, since all cardinals are bishops), he is immediately ordained a bishop by the dean of the College of Cardinals. It is important to note that the 1983 Code of Canon Law resolves the theological and canonical question whether someone who is not already a bishop becomes pope as soon as he accepts his election. He does not. Since he is pope because he is Bishop of Rome, he is not yet the pope until he is ordained a bishop: "The Roman Pontiff obtains full and supreme power in the Church by means of legitimate election accepted by him together with episcopal consecration . . ." (can. 332.1). The 1917 Code of Canon Law had stipulated, by contrast, that a man becomes pope "as soon as he accepts election" (can. 219).

The cardinals then approach the newly elected pope to pay him "homage and obedience," and an act of thanksgiving is then rendered by all present. The senior cardinal-deacon announces the name of the new pope to those in St. Peter's Square, and the new pope immediately thereafter imparts the apostolic blessing *Urbi et Orbi* (Lat., "To the city and to the world") from the balcony of St. Peter's Basilica (n. 89).

A solemn ceremony of "the inauguration of the pontificate" (formerly coronation) takes places several days later, and that is followed, "within an appropriate time," by the new pope's taking possession of the patriarchal archbasilica of the Lateran, which is the pope's cathedral church as Bishop of Rome (n. 92).

Appendix B

HOW POPES ARE REMOVED FROM OFFICE

THE CHURCH'S CODE OF CANON LAW ANTICIPATES NO REASONS FOR A VACANCY in the papal office other than death or a resignation that is made "freely and . . . duly manifested," but not "accepted by anyone" (can 332.2). In other words, no one is authorized to receive the resignation; the pope just resigns. Ecclesiastical law makes no provision at all for situations where a pope may become mentally incompetent, lapse into a coma, or suffer some other radical disability that prevents him from exercising his office and ministry. Nor is there any process to be followed if, in the judgment of many, the pope has fallen into heresy or schism. The law simply assumes that, as supreme pastor of the Church, he "is always united in communion with the other bishops and with the universal Church" (can. 333.2). Indeed, the same canon makes clear that "There is neither appeal nor recourse against a decision or decree of the Roman Pontiff" (can. 333.3). Moreover, "One who takes recourse against an act of the Roman Pontiff to an ecumenical council or to the college of bishops is to be punished with a censure" (can. 1372).

In law, if not in theology, the pope is, in effect, an absolute monarch. What recourse does the Church have if it should ever happen that a pope gravely violates the sacred duties of his office or is no longer physically or psychologically able to exercise them? In the past, the Church and civil authorities alike have taken certain kinds of action, although not always in the higher interests of the gospel or in a manner consistent with the gospel. What follows are the cases of twenty-six popes who have been removed, permanently or temporarily, from office by means other than death or who have been declared excommunicated and/or deposed from office, without, however, recognition of that action by the wider Church.

1. *Pontian* (230–35) was the first pope to abdicate, or resign, the papal office. He did so only because he had been deported by the new, anti-Christian emperor Maximinus Thrax to labor in the mines on the island of Sardinia, known as the "island of death," from which few ever returned alive. The exiled pope did not want there to be a vacuum of leadership in the Roman church. According to the fourth-century Liberian Catalogue, Pontian abdicated on September 28, 235, the first precisely recorded date in papal history.

2. During the Diocletian persecution launched in 303, *Marcellinus* (296–304) complied with imperial orders to hand over copies of Sacred Scripture and other sacred books and to offer incense to the gods. Some historians think that he was deposed or abdicated before his death. For a time, his name was actually omitted from the official list of popes. The *Annuario Pontificio,* an official Vatican publication, identifies the date of his termination from office with his date of death, October 25, 304. The pope's actions, however, would have automatically disqualified him from the priesthood and, therefore, from the papacy as well, as of about May 303. If he was deposed or voluntarily abdicated, we have no date for either event.

3. *Liberius* (352–66) at first opposed the condemnation of St. Athanasius of Alexandria (d. 373) by the Arians at councils in Aquileia and Arles and then again in Milan in October 355. In retaliation, the Arian emperor Constantius deposed Liberius from office and sent him into harsh exile in Thrace. Although the Roman clergy initially refused to elect a new bishop, they eventually yielded to imperial pressure and elected the archdeacon Felix, who was consecrated as Bishop of Rome in the imperial palace in Milan by three bishops who had Arian tendencies. When Felix was installed at the Lateran in Rome, there was a strong popular reaction against him and in support of Liberius. The emperor Constantius, responding eventually to political reality, allowed Liberius to return to Rome in 358 (Liberius had by now abandoned Athanasius), with the understanding that Liberius and Felix would serve as cobishops. The people protested, "One God, one Christ, one bishop," and expelled Felix from the city. But it seems that from 357 to 365 Rome had two men functioning as bishops of the Apostolic See: Liberius occupying the Lateran Palace and Felix II established in the suburbs, with clergy and laity unequally divided in their loyalties. Felix died on November 22, 365, and his name was included for a time on the official lists of popes as Felix II. Indeed, the next Pope Felix took the name Felix III.

4. *Silverius* (536–37) resigned from office under pressure. The Monophysite empress Theodora, upset with the previous pope's deposing of the Monophysite patriarch Anthimus of Constantinople, had urged him to step down in favor of the Roman deacon Vigilius, the papal legate to Constantinople, with whom she had made a pact to restore Anthimus to Constantinople. When Silverius refused to resign, he was summoned to the headquarters of the emperor's general, where he was stripped of his pallium, degraded to the status of a monk, and deposed on March 11, 537. He was deported to Patara, a seaport town in Lycia, and was later ordered back to Rome to face trial. By this time, however, Vigilius had already been elected the new pope. When Silverius reached

Rome, Vigilius arranged to have him taken to Palmaria, an island in the Gulf of Gaeta, where he resigned from the papacy under threat on November 11. Silverius died less than a month later on December 2, probably from physical abuse and starvation designed to avoid a potentially embarrassing trial.

5. *Vigilius* (537–55) paid for his sin of complicity in the unjust deposition, forced resignation, and cruel death of his predecessor, Silverius. Because of his vacillation on the teachings of the Council of Chalcedon (451), he was arrested, exiled, and kept under house arrest by the pro-Chalcedonian emperor, Justinian, and then suffered two excommunications. He and the patriarch of Constantinople excommunicated one another during the pope's exile in Constantinople, but they later reconciled. Vigilius was also excommunicated by a synod of African bishops at Carthage in 550, but there is no record of a subsequent reconciliation. He continued as pope until his death in 555.

6. *Martin I* (649–54) was the first pope in decades to be consecrated without waiting for imperial approval, an act that infuriated the emperor Constans II, who refused to recognize him as a legitimate pope. A strong and resolute opponent of Monothelitism (the heresy that held that in Christ there is only one divine will, not two: human and divine), Martin I paid a heavy personal price for his defiance of the emperor and for his defense of Catholic orthodoxy. In the summer of 653, the imperial exarch seized the pope in the Lateran Basilica, where he had taken sanctuary and lay bedridden from gout. The exarch handed the clergy an imperial decree declaring that Martin was not the legal pope and was therefore deposed. The pope was smuggled out of Rome and taken by force to Constantinople, where he arrived sometime in September 653. After three months of solitary confinement, the pope was put on trial, not as a pope but as a rebellious deacon and former papal legate. He was publicly stripped of his episcopal robes, his tunic was ripped asunder from top to bottom, and he was put in chains. He was found guilty, condemned to death, and publicly flogged. Only because of the plea of the dying patriarch of Constantinople, Paul II, was the pope's sentence commuted to exile. After three more months in prison, the pope was taken by ship to Chersonesus in the Crimea, where he died on September 16, 655, from the effects of his cruel treatment.

While Martin I was in exile and still alive, the clergy and laity of Rome elected a successor, Eugenius I. Was Eugenius I a legitimate pope? There is no evidence that Martin I abdicated, or resigned, while in exile. Eugenius and his supporters probably concluded that Martin would never return to Rome and that, if they waited any longer, the emperor would impose a Monothelite pope on the Church. Just before his death on September 16,

655, Martin sent a letter to a friend in which he mentioned that he prayed especially "for the one who is now ruling over the Church." Was this a tacit acquiescence or approval of Eugenius's election? We do not know. One wonders, in the meantime, why the *Annuario Pontificio* marks the end of Martin's pontificate as September 16, 655, and the beginning of Eugenius I's as August 10, 654. Does the Vatican wish to affirm that the Catholic Church at one time had two legitimately elected and consecrated popes serving concurrently? While that is exactly what the Vatican's official list of popes implies, it is not the only instance in papal history. The same question applies, for example, to the previous case of Vigilius and Silverius in 537.

7. Although elected unanimously as Bishop of Rome, *Leo III* (795–816) had many enemies among the aristocratic families of Rome. On April 25, 799, he was violently attacked while in procession to Mass and an unsuccessful attempt was made to cut out his eyes and tongue. He was then formally deposed and sent off to a monastery, from which he later escaped with the help of friends. He made his way to Charlemagne's court in Paderborn and was warmly received. The Frankish king refused to recognize the pope's deposition from office, but representatives of the anti-Leonine faction arrived soon thereafter from Rome, bearing charges of perjury and adultery against the pope. Although many Franks regarded the charges as credible, they were inhibited from making a judgment about them because of the commonly accepted principle that no power could judge the Apostolic See.

A year later Charlemagne came to Rome and, on December 1, 800, held a council in St. Peter's to examine the charges against the pope. The assembly refused to do so on the grounds that it could not sit in judgment of the pope. On December 23 Leo III declared himself ready to be purged of these "false charges" and thereupon took an oath of purgation, swearing to his innocence. His accusers were sent into exile. Two days later, the pope crowned Charlemagne as "emperor of the Romans."

8. After deposing and excommunicating Photius, the newly named patriarch of Constantinople in 863, *Nicholas I* (858–67) made matters even worse by dispatching missionary bishops to Bulgaria in response to an appeal from its king, Boris I. Since Bulgaria had been evangelized originally by Byzantine missionaries, Photius felt that it fell under his own spiritual jurisdiction. After denouncing the Latin interference to the other patriarchs of the East, Photius convened a synod in Constantinople (867), which excommunicated and deposed Nicholas. The pope had died (on November 13, 867) before word of the synod's action reached Rome, but the mutual excommunications clearly laid the foundation for the East-West Schism of 1054—a schism that perdures to this very day.

9. *Stephen VI (VII)* (896–97) was the pope who ordered the exhumation of Pope Formosus's body and then presided over a mock trial (the so-called Cadaver Synod) of the deceased pope in January 897, nine months after the aged pope's death. For his disgraceful action, Stephen himself was later deposed, stripped of his papal insignia, imprisoned, and strangled to death.

10. *Romanus* (897) probably became a monk after his brief period on the papal throne. If so, he was also probably deposed by the same pro-Formosan faction that elected him in the hope of replacing him with a more vigorous and effective defender of their hero's memory.

11. *Sergius III* (904–11) was originally elected pope to succeed Theodore II in 897 and was even installed in the Lateran Palace. However, he was quickly ejected in favor of the pro-Formosan John IX, who had the support of the emperor Lambert of Spoleto. Sergius was deposed and driven into exile, but found himself with a second chance when, seven years later, the antipope Christopher overthrew Leo V. Sergius marched on Rome with an armed force, threw Christopher into prison, was acclaimed pope, and was consecrated on January 29, 904. Soon afterward, he had both Leo and Christopher strangled to death in prison. Sergius dated his own reign from December 897, when he was first elected, and he regarded all subsequent popes as intruders. However, the Vatican's official directory, the *Annuario Pontificio,* dates the beginning of his pontificate as 904. His deposition, therefore, would not have been as pope. On the other hand, it is not absolutely clear that his first election was either canonically or theologically invalid, his reprehensible character notwithstanding.

12. *John X* (914–28) ran afoul of Rome's powerful noble families, especially when, after the emperor Berengar's murder in 924, he made a pact with the new king of Italy, Hugh of Provence. This alarmed Marozia and her husband, Guido, the marquis of Tuscany, both of whom organized a revolt against the pope and his brother Peter, whom the pope had come increasingly to rely upon. Peter was killed in the Lateran before John X's eyes, and a half year later the pope himself was deposed and imprisoned at Castel Sant'Angelo. He died after several months (probably in early 929), almost certainly by suffocation on orders of Marozia.

13. *John XII* (955–64) found himself in difficulty with the Roman clergy because of the openly immoral character of his life, and with the German emperor, Otto I, because he (the pope) intrigued against the emperor with his (the emperor's) hated enemy Berengar, king of Italy. In November 963, the emperor returned to Rome, and John XII fled with the papal treasury to Tivoli. Otto presided over a synod in St. Peter's at which, after hearing charges from the clergy of the pope's unworthy

behavior, he accused the pope of perfidy and treason. The synod wrote to the pope three times asking him to appear before the synod. He refused and threatened excommunication. In his absence, he was deposed on December 4, 963. At the request of the synod, Otto proposed the name of Leo, a layman, as a worthy successor, and Leo was elected on December 4, 963, and was consecrated as Bishop of Rome two days later after receiving all the requisite Holy Orders in sequence. There is a serious canonical question, of course, whether this synod (or any other) had the right to judge the pope and to depose him—which, in turn, raises a question about the validity of Leo VIII's election and consecration.

Leo's own behavior in office made the people pine for John XII. Leo fled, and at another synod on February 26, 964, the previous imperial synod was nullified, Leo VIII was deposed, and his ordinations were declared invalid.

14. *Leo VIII* (963–65) was elected pope after the deposition of John XII. His election has been a matter of canonical debate because of the questionable nature of John XII's deposition by a Roman synod presided over by the German emperor on December 4, 963. Significantly, the official list of popes in the Vatican's *Annuario Pontificio* accepts the overlapping without resolving the canonical question. (This is not the only instance where the Vatican's official list of popes allows for such overlapping, as we have already seen.) In any case, Leo's performance in office provoked widespread disturbances in the city and he was forced to seek asylum in the imperial court, thereby allowing John XII to regain the papal throne. A synod convened by John XII in St. Peter's on February 26 deposed Leo as a usurper and declared his ordination and consecration invalid, as well as the Holy Orders of those whom Leo had himself ordained.

15. The one-month-long pontificate of *Benedict V* (May 22–June 23, 964) was canonically dubious because another claimant to the papacy, Leo VIII, was still alive. When John XII died on May 14, 964, the Roman people and many of the clergy ignored the wishes of the emperor Otto I to reinstate Leo VIII (whom John XII had deposed as a usurper). Instead, on May 22 they acclaimed Benedict, a learned reformist cardinal-deacon, as pope, had him consecrated as Bishop of Rome, and enthroned him in the Lateran Palace.

The emperor laid siege to the city of Rome, threatening to starve the people into submission. The people soon yielded and handed over Benedict to the emperor on June 23. A synod was immediately held in the Lateran, presided over jointly by Leo VIII and the emperor Otto I. Benedict was condemned as a usurper (which he was only if Leo VIII's own dubious election and consecration in December 963 had been canonically valid), was stripped of his pontifical vestments and insignia, and had his pastoral staff, or crozier, broken over his head by Leo himself as Benedict lay prostrate. The emperor allowed Benedict to retain the rank of deacon but deported him to Hamburg, where the local bishop treated him with courtesy and dignity.

16. No sooner had *John XIV* (983–84) been installed, following the death of Benedict VII, when the German emperor Otto II was stricken with malaria and died in the pope's arms. The empress, Theophano, immediately left Rome for Germany to defend the claim of her three-year-old son Otto III. John XIV was now completely defenseless against his enemies. The antipope Boniface VII returned from exile in Constantinople in April 984. John was arrested, beaten, deposed from office, and imprisoned at Castel Sant'Angelo. He died four months later of starvation.

17. Little is known of the pontificate of *John XVIII* (1003–9), but he may have abdicated shortly before his death and become a monk at the basilica of St. Paul's Outside the Walls, where he is buried. If John XVIII did abdicate before his death in late June or early July 1009, it is probable that he was forced to do so.

18. *Benedict IX* (1032–44, 1045, 1047–48) had one of the most canonically confusing pontificates in all of history. In September 1044, he fled Rome because of growing hostility toward him for his immoral lifestyle and toward his family (the Tusculans) for their interference in the affairs of the city. The following January (1045) even though Benedict had never formally been deposed, a branch of the rival Crescentii family installed John, bishop of Sabina, as pope. He took the name Sylvester III. Benedict promptly excommunicated him, and on March 10 managed to expel him from Rome and reclaim the papal throne. Two months later, however, for reasons that are not clear (perhaps it was the money he would earn from the sale of his office), he abdicated in favor of his godfather, John Gratian, who took the name Gregory VI. Now there were three claimants to the papal throne. Sylvester III and Gregory VI (both of whom are on the Vatican's official list of popes) were deposed at a synod in Sutri in 1046, and then Benedict IX himself was deposed at a Roman synod four days later, on Christmas Eve. The emperor then named Suidger of Bamberg as pope, who took the name Clement II. (Clement II is also on the Vatican's official list of popes.) Clement died suddenly eight months later, and the Roman people, perhaps encouraged by bribes, demanded that Benedict IX be restored to office.

Benedict IX was reinstated on November 8, 1047, and remained in office until July 16, 1048, when he was forced from the papal throne by order of the emperor. Poppo of Brixen was installed as Damasus II. Benedict retreated to his Tusculan homeland, continuing to regard himself as the lawful pope against the intruder Damasus and, later, against Damasus's successor, Leo IX. A Lateran synod in April 1049 summoned Benedict to face the charge of simony and when he refused to appear, excommunicated him. Benedict IX lived at least another seven and a half years after this, his third period in the papacy.

19. *Sylvester III* (January 20–March 10, 1045) was elected pope as the candidate of the Crescentii family, after Benedict IX had been expelled from Rome. But as soon as Benedict IX heard of Sylvester's election, he excommunicated him. Two months later Benedict returned to Rome and had Sylvester removed from the papal throne. Sylvester thereupon resumed his duties as bishop of Sabina, a post he had never relinquished. Eighteen months later Henry III, king of Germany, had Sylvester III condemned at the synod of Sutri on December 20, 1046, confined to a monastery, and stripped of his Holy Orders. The sentence must have been suspended, however, because Sylvester continued to function in Sabina until 1062, when a successor was named.

20. *Gregory VI* (1045–46) was deposed on December 20, 1046, by a synod in Sutri convened by the German king Henry III, who had earlier come down to Rome with the hope of being crowned emperor by the pope. But there were three claiming to be pope: Benedict IX, Sylvester III, and Gregory VI. The king and the synod pronounced Gregory guilty of simony and deposed him from office. Gregory VI was taken back to Germany, accompanied by his chaplain and friend, the future Pope Gregory VII, and placed under the supervision of the bishop of Cologne. He died toward the end of that same year.

21. *Gregory VII* (1073–85) was deposed twice during his pontificate, both times by synods of German bishops (with support in the first instance from the Lombard bishops) and at the instigation of the German king, Henry IV. The first time it was by a synod of twenty-six German bishops at Worms (January 24, 1076), who referred to him contemptuously as the "monk Hildebrand." The pope and the king had quarreled over the king's nomination of candidates for the archbishopric of Milan and for various bishoprics and abbacies in other parts of Germany and Italy. At the Lenten synod of 1076, Gregory excommunicated Henry, suspended him from the exercise of his royal powers, and released the king's subjects from all allegiance to him. Bishops who supported Henry were either excommunicated or suspended. The second time Gregory VII was deposed followed a dispute between himself and the king over who should be recognized as king of Germany, Henry or Rudolf, whom the German princes had elected as a rival king. Gregory eventually recognized Rudolf. Henry thereupon called a council of imperial bishops at Brixen on June 25, 1080. The council deposed Gregory and elected Guibert, archbishop of Ravenna, as Clement III to replace Gregory.

Henry was still open to compromise because he wanted to be crowned as emperor. But Gregory VII was inflexible, so much so that he lost many of his supporters, including thirteen cardinals. After Henry seized Rome in March 1084 following a two-year siege, the Roman clergy and laity elected Guibert (Clement III) pope and he was enthroned in the Lateran Basilica on March 24, 1084. A week later, on March 31, while Gregory VII was still at Castel Sant'Angelo, the antipope Clement III crowned Henry emperor in St. Peter's. But both Henry and Clement left Rome when Robert Guiscard, duke of Apulia, marched on Rome with Norman troops and rescued Gregory. However, the violent behavior of Robert's troops infuriated the Roman people and they turned on the pope who had invited them in. Gregory VII left Rome, going first to Monte Cassino and then to Salerno, where he died on May 25, 1085.

22. Everyone seems to know about the case of *Celestine V* (1294). Indeed, many continue to think of him as the one and only pope to have resigned the office. He was not. There were at least three others (Pontian in 235, Silverius in 537, and Gregory XII in 1415), and possibly a fourth (John XVIII in 1009). One must also recall that Benedict IX abdicated in favor of his godfather in 1045, but he was reinstated in 1047. When he realized how ill-equipped he was for the papacy, Celestine called a consistory on December 13, 1294, and read out the formula of abdication that Cardinal Caetani (who would succeed him as Boniface VIII) had prepared for him. He then stripped off his papal insignia and, in a final appeal, urged the cardinals to proceed immediately to the election of his successor. The resignation provoked a war of theological and canonical treatises for and against its validity.

23. Almost immediately after his election, *Urban VI* (1378–89) began to manifest a darker side of his personality, including uncontrollable tirades. The French cardinals withdrew to Anagni to consider their options. After a failed attempt to reach an accommodation with the new pope (a council of coadjutors or regents was proposed), they published on August 2, 1378, a declaration that the April election was invalid because it was conducted not freely but under threat of mob violence. The French cardinals invited Urban VI to abdicate. Five days later (August 9) they sent out a notice to the Christian world that the pope had been deposed as incompetent and as an intruder. They moved then from Anagni to Fondi, where they elected the French king's cousin, Cardinal Robert of Geneva, as pope on September 20. His coronation as Clement VII on October 31 began the Great Western Schism (1378–1417), which would not be settled until another ecumenical council, the Council of Constance (1414–18), disposed of three simultaneous claimants to the papal throne and elected Martin V (1417–31). However, the council never settled the

controversy over Urban's and Clement's claims to the papacy. The *Annuario Pontificio,* however, regards Clement as an antipope.

24. *Gregory XII* (1406–15) was deposed by the Council of Pisa in 1409 after he broke his preelection pledge not to appoint any new cardinals. He created four, two of whom were his nephews. Both he and Benedict XIII (the rival pope in the Avignon line) had been invited to attend the council, but both refused, each summoning councils of their own. On June 5, 1409, both Gregory XII and Benedict XIII were formally deposed as schismatics, intractable heretics, and perjurers. The Holy See was declared vacant, and on June 26 the cardinals who were assembled at Pisa elected a new pope, Alexander V. Meanwhile, Gregory XII opened his own council at Cividale, near Aquileia, on June 6, 1409. Very few attended, but before he brought it to a close on September 6, Gregory excommunicated both Benedict XIII and Alexander V.

After the Council of Constance (1414–18) deposed John XXIII on May 29, 1415, it sought to open negotiations with Gregory XII with a view to his abdication. He agreed to consider it on condition that he would be allowed formally to convoke the council, since he did not recognize the authority of John XXIII to have done so originally. The request was agreed to and, on July 4, 1415, Gregory's cardinal, John Dominici, read aloud Gregory's bull convoking the council and resigning from the papal office. The two colleges of cardinals (Rome and Avignon) were united, Gregory's papal acts were ratified, and he was appointed cardinal-bishop of Porto and legate of the March of Ancona for life. He was also declared ineligible for election as pope, but would rank next in precedence to the new pope.

25. *Eugenius IV* (1431–47) was first suspended and then deposed on January 24, 1438, and June 25, 1439, respectively, by the conciliar delegates who opposed the pope's transfer of the ecumenical council from Basel to Ferrara and then to Florence and who defiantly remained behind in Basel. The pope replied on September 4, 1439, challenging the ecumenicity of the earlier phases of the Council of Constance and condemning the Council of Basel. On November 5, 1439, those remaining in Basel elected a layman, Amadeus VIII, the duke of Savoy, as an antipope (Felix V). In the spring of 1443, when Eugenius IV recognized the claims of Alfonso V of Aragón to the throne of the kingdom of Naples, Alfonso ordered his bishops to withdraw their support from the antipope Felix V and made possible the pope's return to Rome from Florence in September, after an absence of some nine years.

26. The last instance of a putative papal deposition is that of *Pius VI* (1775–99) After a French general was killed during a riot in Rome, the French government ordered the occupation of the Papal States. General

Louis Berthier entered Rome on February 15, 1798, proclaimed the Roman Republic, deposed Pius VI as head of state, and forced him to withdraw to Tuscany. He lived for several months in Florence, cut off from almost all of his aides but using his nuncio to Florence as his secretary of state. When war broke out again, the French government was concerned that troops would attempt to rescue the pope, so they had him moved from Florence on March 28, 1799, to Turin, then across the Alps to Briançon (April 30), and then to Valence (July 13). Pius VI died a prisoner in Valence, at age eighty-one.

Appendix C

RATING THE POPES

The historian Arthur Schlesinger Jr. pointed out in an article in *The New York Times Magazine* (December 15, 1996) that the "game of ranking presidents is a popular pastime among scholars." In 1948 his father, Arthur Schlesinger Sr., invited fifty-five leading historians to render their verdicts. The results were published in *Life* magazine. In 1962 *Time* magazine prevailed upon the senior Schlesinger to repeat the poll. Again it sparked much interest and controversy. The polls asked historians to place each president (except for two who died soon after taking office) in one of five categories: great, near great, average, below average, and failure. The standard was not lifetime achievement but performance in the White House. There were three subsequent polls conducted under different auspices in 1981 and 1982. In 1996 *The New York Times Magazine* persuaded Arthur Schlesinger Jr. to do yet another poll, which it published in December of that same year.

It is that relatively recent tradition of rating the presidents of the United States that prompts (one dare not say "inspires") this attempt to do the same regarding the more than 260 officially listed occupants of the Chair of Peter. However, it would be impractical to rate every one of the popes, not only because there are so many more popes than U.S. presidents, but also because there is an unusually high number of abbreviated pontificates (44 popes, or almost 17 percent, served less than a year). Moreover, given the much more limited material historians of the papacy have to rely upon in comparison with what historians of the presidency have available to them, it would be difficult, if not impossible, to make such fine distinctions between great and near-great popes or between average and below-average popes. Indeed, Arthur Schlesinger Jr. points out that, in all the various polls since 1948, the "choice of the best and worst presidents has remained relatively stable through the years. There is much fluctuation in between." For that reason, we offer below only a chronologically arranged sample of the best and worst popes because any finer distinctions are simply too difficult to make, given the pronounced historical variations from pontificate to pontificate.

Four categories of popes are employed here: outstanding, good (or above average), worst, and a special category for historically important popes, some of whom do not appear on any of the other lists. Arthur

Schlesinger Jr. indicates that great presidents "possess, or are possessed by, a vision of an ideal America" and are determined "to make sure the ship of state sails on the right course." The same is true of outstanding and good, or above-average, popes. They possess, or are possessed by, a vision of an ideal Church and are determined that the Church follow a course consistent with that ideal. The two positive criteria for outstanding and good popes are: (1) the contributions the pope made (a) to the pastoral and spiritual welfare of the contemporary Church, (b) to the integrity of the papal office in his time period, and (c) to the common good of the contemporary society; and (2) the lasting contribution a pope made (a) to the long-term pastoral and spiritual welfare of the Church, (b) to the long-term development of the papal office in pastorally and spiritually enriching ways, and (c) to the common good of humanity itself. The two negative criteria for worst popes are: (1) the immediate harm the pope may have done (a) to the pastoral and spiritual welfare of the contemporary Church, (b) to the papal office of his time period, and (c) to the common good of contemporary society; and (2) the lasting harm the pope may have done, through counterproductive or even scandalous behavior, (a) to the long-term pastoral and spiritual welfare of the Church, (b) to the long-term development of the papal office, and (c) to the common good of humanity. (Unfortunately, the list of worst popes is longer than that of outstanding and good, or above-average, popes combined.) The criteria for historically important popes are their prominence in the history of the Church and their recognition as such by historians of the papacy. St. Peter the Apostle is not included in the ratings because popes are, by definition, his successors. He remains in a category by himself, not subject to comparison with others.

I. Outstanding Popes

1. *John XXIII* (1958–63). Probably the most beloved, ecumenical, and openhearted pope in history, he touched the worldwide human community in a way no other pope has ever done. "Good Pope John," as the late cardinal-archbishop of Boston, Richard Cushing (d. 1970), once called him, also disclosed to the Church and to the world the real point and purpose of the Petrine ministry. Every pope, before and after him, is to be measured against the standard he set.

2. *Gregory the Great* (590–604). Like John XXIII, a genuinely pastoral pope, with a profound concern for the poor, he helped to shape the evolution of ministry for centuries. His *Pastoral Care*, translated into Greek and Anglo-Saxon in his own lifetime, remained an extraordinarily influential

work well into the Middle Ages. In it he set out a vision of pastoral care that is adapted to the needs of the people and is rooted in personal example and preaching, with a fine balance between the contemplative and active aspects of all ministry. He was the first to refer to the pope as the "servant of the servants of God."

II. Good, or Above-Average, Popes (Chronologically Arranged)

1. *Sixtus II* (257–58). One of the most revered martyrs of the early Church, he was beheaded by imperial forces during the celebration of the Eucharist. During his brief pontificate, he successfully devoted his energies to healing the breach between Rome and the churches of North Africa and Asia Minor created by the issue of the rebaptism of heretics and schismatics who wished to enter or be reconciled to the Church and, in particular, by the intransigent approach taken by his predecessor, Stephen I. Although Sixtus II, like Stephen I, upheld the Roman policy of accepting the validity of baptisms administered by heretics and schismatics, he restored friendly relations with Cyprian (d. 258), bishop of Carthage, and the estranged churches of Asia Minor, probably by tolerating the coexistence of the two practices. Sixtus II saw his ministry as one of healing and reconciliation rather than of hardening divisions within the Church through strict and unreasonably rigid enforcement of discipline.

2. *Leo the Great* (440–61). One of only two popes in history to be called "the Great," Leo I established the papal office as one of leadership in the formulation of doctrine and in dealings with the secular powers. He was the author of a number of clear and theologically substantive homilies and letters, and his famous *Tome* was accepted by the Council of Chalcedon in 451 as the basis for its definitive teaching on the divinity and humanity of Christ. He is also celebrated for his courageous personal confrontation with Attila the Hun in 452, when the warrior was laying waste to northern Italy and preparing to move south toward Rome. Leo persuaded Attila to withdraw beyond the Danube. Three years later he also succeeded in preventing the Vandal king Gaiseric (or Genseric) from torching the city and massacring its people. On the other hand, his jealousy of papal prerogatives led him to delay for two and a half years his endorsement of the Council of Chalcedon's (451) momentous dogmatic teachings on the divinity and humanity of Jesus Christ. Leo was disturbed by the council's granting the see of Constantinople an ecclesiastical dignity almost equivalent to that of Rome. He was also the first pope to claim to be Peter's heir, which, according to Roman law, meant that all the rights and duties associated with Peter lived on in Leo. Previous popes

had spoken of their succession to Peter's chair or appealed to his martyrdom and burial in Rome as the basis of their authority. Thereafter, the
popes clearly regarded themselves as standing in the place of Peter, exercising authority not only over all of the faithful but over all of the other
bishops as well. Some regard this as Leo's great achievement, the raising of
the authority of the papacy to new and higher levels. In actuality, however, Leo's claims are largely responsible for the inflation of papal authority, which the East has never accepted and which was taken to excess in
the West during the Middle Ages and even into the late twentieth century.
(This last point is made not to diminish Leo I's positive achievements as
Bishop of Rome, but to provide an explanation for his exclusion from the
short list of "outstanding" popes, even though he is only one of two
popes in history to be called "the Great.")

3. *Boniface V* (619–25). Known for his compassion and generosity,
he distributed his entire personal fortune to the poor. He is buried in St.
Peter's, where his epitaph describes him as "generous, wise, pure, sincere,
and just." One only wonders why he was not eventually recognized as a
saint, since the title had been conferred on many less deserving popes before him.

4. *Theodore II* (November/December 897). Although he was in office
only twenty days, he held a synod invalidating the so-called Cadaver Synod
of 897, which had placed the corpse of Pope Formosus on trial. Theodore
II rehabilitated Formosus, recognized the validity of his ordinations and
papal acts, and ordered to be burned all the letters solicited by Pope
Stephen VI (VII) from the clergy—letters in which they were forced to renounce the validity of their ordinations by Formosus. Theodore then ordered the body of Formosus to be exhumed from the private grave in
which it had been placed after being flung into the Tiber River, reclothed
in pontifical vestments, and reburied with honors in its original grave in
St. Peter's. The pope's courageous acts probably cost him his life.

5. *Nicholas V* (1447–55). A peacemaker on both the political and ecclesiastical fronts, he restored order in the city of Rome, rid the Papal States
of mercenary troops, and won back the allegiance of various cities; he
also persuaded the antipope Felix V to abdicate and admitted several of
the antipope's cardinalatial appointees to the College of Cardinals as a
gesture of reconciliation. He was also devoted to church reform, sending
prestigious cardinals to Germany and France to promote reform in those
countries. At home with scholars and artists, he amassed a great personal library of books and manuscripts, which, upon his death, became
the basis of the Vatican Library. In the early Church he would probably
have been proclaimed a saint, given his morally upright life in the midst
of much contemporary corruption and brutality.

6. *Innocent XI* (1676–89). He imposed severe reductions in the papal budget and called for evangelical preaching and catechesis, the strict observance of monastic vows, careful selection of priests and bishops, and the frequent reception of Holy Communion. His attempts to persuade the cardinals to outlaw nepotism ended in failure, however, and his prohibition of carnivals was ridiculed and ignored by the people. So ascetical was he in his personal life, that many suspected him of Jansenist leanings (that is, a too rigid approach to the moral life).

7. *Innocent XII* (1691–1700). His most significant initiative was his decree *Romanum decet pontificem* (June 22, 1692), which mandated that popes may never grant estates, offices, or revenues to relatives, and that if such relatives are poor, they should be treated like others in need. Moreover, only one relative may be appointed to the College of Cardinals, if qualified, and his income should be limited. Innocent XII encountered some resistance to the decree from a number of cardinals, but they all eventually signed it, thereby driving a stake into the heart of papal nepotism.

8. *Benedict XIV* (1740–58). Two months after his election, he established a congregation to select worthy men as bishops. He also promoted improved clerical training, episcopal residentiality (evidently many bishops were still living away from their dioceses), and pastoral visitation. He exempted the marriages of non-Catholics and mixed marriages (between Catholics and non-Catholics) from the canonical form required by the Council of Trent (that is, before a priest and two witnesses). In a letter to the Portuguese bishops of South America, also in 1741, he urged more humane treatment of the Indians. On the other hand, he also formally and finally suppressed the Chinese rites in use by the Jesuit missionaries in China, extending the ban even to the Malabar rites in India. Although Benedict XIV was a man of his time theologically and spiritually, many Protestants and agnostic scholars respected him for the breadth of his scholarly interests and for his support of the arts and sciences.

9. *Pius VII* (1800–1823). He bravely suffered five years' imprisonment at the hands of Napoleon Bonaparte and restored the Jesuits in 1814. Although generally opposed to the new wave of modernity sweeping Europe, he nevertheless recognized some of the positive aspects of the French Revolution and tried to incorporate them in the governance of the Papal States.

10. *Leo XIII* (1878–1903). He was the first pope to attempt to reconcile the Catholic Church with the modern world. His encyclical *Rerum novarum* in 1891 marked the beginning of over a century of formal papal pronouncements on social justice, human rights, and peace. On the other hand, he rendered a negative and unecumenical judgment on the validity

of Anglican orders and condemned Americanism without really under-standing the difference between American democracy and certain views being expressed in France at the time.

11. *Benedict XV* (1914–22). Perhaps the most underrated of the modern popes, he called a halt to the internecine warfare within the Catholic Church that had pitted so-called Integralist Catholics against more pro-gressive Catholics during the obsessively anti-Modernist pontificate of his predecessor, Pius X. Benedict XV patiently suffered misunderstanding of his neutrality during the First World War and tried valiantly to pro-mote the reconciliation of the Churches of East and West. He successfully promoted the development of native hierarchies in missionary countries.

12. *Paul VI* (1963–78). Although he was personally conflicted, his pon-tificate was generally marked by compassion and reasonableness. Com-mitted to the implementation of the reforms of the Second Vatican Council—and at great personal cost because of the determined opposi-tion of rigidly conservative church leaders and laity—he instituted the World Synod of Bishops, reached out to the ecumenical patriarch of Constantinople and the archbishop of Canterbury in gestures of recon-ciliation, advanced the social teaching of the Church by emphasizing the obligations of rich nations to poor nations, and sold the papal tiara and distributed the money to the poor. Although the encyclical on birth con-trol, *Humanae vitae* (1968), cast a shadow over his entire pontificate, his refusal to act harshly against dissenters was a mark of his respect for free-dom of conscience rather than a sign of weakness. In planning his own funeral, he saw to it that his casket would be at ground level and that it would be surmounted not by a tiara or even a miter and stole, but by an open Gospel book.

III. Worst Popes
(Indeed, the "Worst" of the "Worst Popes," Chronologically Arranged)

1. *Marcellinus* (296–304). During the Diocletian persecutions, he com-plied with imperial orders to hand over copies of Sacred Scripture and to offer incense to the gods. Such individuals were known as *traditores* (Lat., "traitors"; literally, "those who give over, or deliver").

2. *Liberius* (352–66). A weak man, he yielded to Arian pressure and agreed to the excommunication of Athanasius, the principal defender of the teachings of the Council of Nicaea (325) on the divinity of Christ.

3. *Vigilius* (537–55). A devious and weak person, easily manipulated by the Byzantine empress Theodora, he was elected under suspicious cir-cumstances in which he compelled his predecessor to abdicate. His vacil-

lation on the teaching of the Council of Chalcedon (451) caused such great consternation in the West that he was actually excommunicated by a synod of North African bishops.

4. *Sabinian* (604–6). He sold grain to the hungry—for a profit. So unpopular was he by the time of his death that his funeral procession had to be diverted outside the city walls in order to reach St. Peter's.

5. *Stephen VI (VII)* (896–97). He ordered the body of one of his predecessors, Formosus, exhumed from its grave, robed in full pontifical vestments, and tried for alleged crimes against the Church in the infamous "Cadaver Synod." He himself was later deposed and strangled to death.

6. *Sergius III* (904–11). He ordered the murder of his predecessor, Leo V, and the antipope Christopher and reaffirmed the acts of the notorious "Cadaver Synod," thereby throwing the Church once again into chaos because all of Pope Formosus's sacramental acts were declared invalid, including all of his ordinations of bishops and priests. Throughout his ignoble pontificate, he consistently did the bidding of the powerful Roman families, especially the corrupt Theophylacts.

7. *John XII* (955–64). Elected at age eighteen, he led one of the most immoral lives of any pope in history and died of a stroke, allegedly in the bed of a married woman.

8. *Innocent IV* (1243–54). The first pope to approve the use of torture in the Inquisition to extract confessions of heresy, he followed the principle "the end justifies the means." He raised nepotism to a high art, placing relatives in key positions in order to create a network of loyal supporters, and erased the distinction between church revenues and personal revenues.

9. *Boniface VIII* (1295–1303). Although he made a lasting contribution to the field of canon law and reorganized the Curia and Vatican archives, he had a uniquely inflated sense of his own personal and political importance as well as of the papal office he held, albeit under suspicious electoral circumstances. He commissioned or permitted so many statues of himself that he was accused of encouraging idolatry. He declared that papal authority extends over every creature in the world, and he even dressed occasionally in imperial regalia because he regarded himself as much an emperor as a pope. Few popes in history veered so far from the Petrine norm of humble service to others as Boniface VIII did. He also did incalculable harm to the image of the papacy and the Church for centuries to come. Historically naive and theologically uninformed Catholics continue to cite him today as if his exaggerated claims of papal authority, even over the political realm, are, in fact, consistent with the will of Christ.

10. *Clement VI* (1342–52). His pontificate was modeled less on the example of the Apostle Peter, whose successor he claimed to be, than on that of a worldly prince. His court was bathed in luxuries and punctuated by sumptuous banquets and grand festivities. He shamelessly conferred church offices and gifts on relatives, friends, and fellow countrymen. Charges were raised about his own personal moral life. Nevertheless, when the Black Death struck Avignon, he defended Jews against the charge that they were somehow responsible and he also reached out to assist the poor.

11. *Urban VI* (1378–89). Mentally unstable, volatile, and abusive, he was so intransigent and unreasonable a pope that the cardinals who elected him declared him deposed and elected another in his place, thereby initiating the Great Western Schism (1378–1417). He had five of his cardinal-critics tortured and executed.

12. *Boniface IX* (1389–1404). Although an outstanding administrator, he was infamous for his blatant nepotism and financial skullduggery. Because of the papacy's desperate need for money, he openly sold church offices to the highest bidders. He also increased church taxes exorbitantly, sold indulgences during the Holy Years of 1390 and 1400, and authorized income-producing Jubilees in cities far beyond the city of Rome—always for a price.

13. *Callistus III* (1455–58). The blatant nepotism of Callistus III, the first of two Spanish popes and the uncle of the infamous Alexander VI (the other Spanish pope), whom he made a cardinal, generated deep resentment among the cardinals and other church officials. He also shamed his pontificate by reviving harsh anti-Jewish legislation, left moribund by his predecessors, banning all social communication between Christians and Jews. Upon his death, the Romans vented their wrath upon the Catalans, who fled the city in terror.

14. *Paul II* (1464–71). He reneged on his promises to promote church reform, was self-indulgent in terms of luxury, sport, and entertainment, and had contempt for scholars.

15. *Sixtus IV* (1471–84). Although he is best known as the builder of the Sistine Chapel, his pontificate was seriously marred by several blots: the establishment of the Spanish Inquisition and the appointment of the notorious Tomás de Torquemada as grand inquisitor; his involvement in the Pazzi conspiracy, in which Giuliano de' Medici was killed and his brother Lorenzo was wounded; his annulling of the decrees of the reformist Council of Constance (1414–18); his depleting of the papal treasury through vain military expeditions and an unseemly generosity toward his family that forced him to engage in the sale of indulgences

and other dubious forms of revenue raising (including the doubling of curial offices); and his exceedingly undistinguished appointments to the College of Cardinals, including six of his nephews. Although a lifelong Franciscan, Sixtus IV reigned like a Renaissance prince.

16. *Innocent VIII* (1484–92). A fitting prelude to the pontificate of Alexander VI, Innocent VIII's pontificate caused the papacy to sink to the depths of worldliness. Less than three months after being crowned as pope, he ordered the Inquisition in Germany to punish "witches" with the greatest severity. To overcome the enormous debts left by his predecessor, he created new and unnecessary offices in the Roman Curia and sold them to the highest bidder—a blatant act of simony. At the time of his death, the Papal States were in anarchy. As he lay dying, he begged the cardinals to elect someone better than himself.

17. *Alexander VI* (1492–1503). The most notorious pope in history. Nepotism and unbridled sensuality were the hallmarks of his pontificate.

18. *Julius II* (1503–13). Although a patron of Michelangelo and other artists, he was the antithesis of the Apostle Peter and of the ideals of the Petrine ministry. Elected through bribery and false promises, Julius II spent most of his time and energies engaged in military battle. He also paved the way for the Reformation by arranging for the sale of indulgences to raise money for the building of the new St. Peter's Basilica.

19. *Leo X* (1513–21). Blind to the gathering storm clouds of the Reformation, he missed a golden opportunity to address the need for reform at the Fifth Lateran Council (1512–17). He also agreed to the sale of indulgences for the building of the new St. Peter's Basilica and then ignited the Reformation by excommunicating Martin Luther in 1521.

20. *Paul IV* (1555–59). Triumphalistic to the core, he was bitterly anti-Protestant and anti-Semitic, confining Jews to a special quarter in Rome and forcing them to wear distinctive headgear. He lent his strong personal support to the Inquisition and created the Index of Forbidden Books. When he died, the Roman people stormed the headquarters of the Inquisition and toppled his statue.

21. *Clement XIV* (1769–74). Under political and economic pressures he suppressed the Jesuits, with disastrous consequences for the missionary, educational, and pastoral work of the Church all over the world. His "thirty pieces of silver" consisted of the return of Avignon and Venaissin in France to papal control. The great papal biographer Ludwig von Pastor called him "one of the weakest and most unhappy of the long line of popes."

22. *Leo XII* (1823–29). He reinforced the Index of Forbidden Books and the power of the Holy Office, reestablished the feudal aristocracy in the

Papal States, and confined Jews once again to ghettos—all as the modern world was coming into being.

23. *Gregory XVI* (1831–46). He was so opposed to modernity that he banned railways in the papal territories, condemned Italian nationalism, and crushed an uprising in the Papal States with the use of Austrian troops. He denounced freedom of conscience, freedom of the press, and the separation of Church and state. On the other hand, he also denounced slavery and the slave trade.

24. *Pius X* (1903–14). Although a personally spiritual man (he was canonized a saint in 1954), his intemperate campaign against theologians and biblical scholars, which included the use of secret informants, created an atmosphere of fear and mean-spiritedness in the Church that set back the progress of Catholic scholarship for half a century.

IV. Historically Important Popes (Chronologically Arranged)

1. *Leo the Great* (440–61). A good, or above-average, pope (see above), he was the first to establish the papacy as a spiritually and politically powerful office.

2. *Gregory the Great* (590–604). One of the two truly outstanding popes (see above), he reshaped the papacy into a ministry of service ("servant of the servants of God") and influenced the development of pastoral care for centuries.

3. *Gregory VII* (1073–85). His pontificate was a turning point in the history of the papacy and of the Church itself. In order to combat real challenges to the integrity of the Church (simony, nepotism, clerical corruption, and the interference of lay rulers in the internal life of the Church), he transformed the papacy itself into a legalistic and monarchical office. He influenced—albeit, mostly for ill—the evolution of the papacy through the entire second Christian millennium.

4. *Innocent III* (1198–1216). One of the most powerful—and pretentious—popes in history, he claimed authority not only over the whole Church, but over the whole Christian world. He thought of himself as pope placed somewhere between God and humankind—less than God but greater than ordinary men and women. Although he was a masterful political pope, he also had a clear ecclesiastical agenda: the Fourth Crusade (1202–4), church reform (which he carried out with energy and determination), and the combating of heresy (even by violent means, as it turned out). It is revealing of his mentality and that of the times that he also decreed that Jews and Muslims should wear distinctive dress.

5. *Boniface VIII* (1295–1303). Few popes in history have made greater claims for the spiritual *and* temporal powers of the papacy than Boniface

VIII, who declared that every creature is subject to the pope. As such, he was the last of the medieval popes, and one of three most powerful, along with Gregory VII (1073–85) and Innocent III (1198–1216). Boniface VIII made a lasting contribution to the field of canon law, reorganized the Curia and Vatican archives, and catalogued the papal library. Most of his pontificate, however, was taken up with political battles with Philip the Fair of France, in which Boniface VIII inflated papal claims beyond those of any previous or subsequent pope. He asserted that papal authority extends over every creature in the world, and he began dressing occasionally in imperial regalia, declaring himself as much an emperor as a pope (see also above).

6. *Pius V* (1566–72). He enforced the decrees of the Council of Trent, published the *Roman Catechism,* reformed the Roman Missal and the Roman Breviary (Divine Office), and excommunicated Queen Elizabeth I of England. The last proved exceedingly counterproductive, causing great harm to Catholics in England. His intense commitment to stamp out heresy (a throwback to his earlier years as a grand inquisitor) led him to an inordinate reliance upon the Inquisition and its inhuman methods. He practiced what he preached in his own life, however. He continued to follow a monastic regimen for himself (including the practice of simple, solitary meals that remained a papal custom until the mid-twentieth century), and some of his contemporaries even accused him of trying to impose monasticism upon others as well, including the entire Roman citizenry. He opposed nepotism (although he made his grandnephew and fellow Dominican Michele Bonelli a cardinal and papal secretary of state), insisted that clerics reside in their pastoral assignments, and maintained a careful watch over religious orders. In sum, his Counter-Reformation pontificate was a strange mixture of authentically evangelical and crudely prosecutorial impulses.

7. *Pius IX* (1846–78). His was the longest pontificate in history. Elected as a moderate after Gregory XVI's reactionary pontificate, he soon established himself as well among the more reactionary popes of history. He called the First Vatican Council (1869–70), which defined papal primacy and papal infallibility, defined the Immaculate Conception of Mary, and published a "Syllabus of Errors" that condemned the major developments of the modern world. Ironically, by the time his record-long pontificate ended and in spite of his own wishes, Pius IX had witnessed the creation of what is now known as the modern papacy, freed of the deadweight of temporal sovereignty (the Papal States) and exercising more spiritual authority perhaps than ever before in its history. By the time of his death, however, Pius IX was an exceedingly unpopular pope with the people of Rome and with the educated classes generally, even though he

had been an extraordinarily popular pope with the Catholic masses, especially outside of Italy, both because of his warmly pious personality and also out of sympathy for all the troubles he suffered with such serenity and courage.

8. *Leo XIII* (1878–1903). His was the second longest pontificate in history. Although he was much more of a moderate than his predecessor, he continued many of the policies of Pius IX regarding, for example, socialism, Communism, and Freemasonry. He even increased the centralization of church government by actively intervening with national episcopates, strengthening the authority of his nuncios, and concentrating the headquarters of religious orders in Rome. Where Leo XIII was least like Pius IX was in his understanding of the relationship between Church and society and his general openness to scholarship and the intellectual life. Indeed, Leo XIII was the first pope to attempt a reconciliation between the Church and the modern world. Although he rendered an unecumenical judgment against the validity of Anglican orders and issued an ill-conceived condemnation of what he mistakenly called Americanism, Leo XIII made a great and lasting contribution to the papacy and to the Church by initiating the practice of papal encyclicals highlighting the application of the gospel to economic and political life. His *Rerum novarum* in 1891 remains a benchmark of Catholic social teaching.

9. *John XXIII* (1958–63). The most outstanding pope in history, he called the Second Vatican Council and set the Catholic Church on a whole new pastoral course, emphasizing the role of the laity, the collegiality of bishops, the authentic faith and goodness of non-Catholic Christians and non-Christians, and the dignity of all human beings. Through the council and especially by the example of his own life and ministry, he also set a whole new pastoral standard for modern popes in the exercise of their Petrine office. His encyclicals reflected the pastoral and ecumenical tone of his pontificate. *Ad Petri Cathedram* (June 29, 1959), on the themes of truth, unity, and peace, greeted non-Catholics as "separated brethren." *Mater et magistra* (May 15, 1961), released on the seventieth anniversary of Leo XIII's groundbreaking social encyclical, *Rerum novarum* (1891), updated Catholic social teaching on property, the rights of workers, and the obligations of government. *Pacem in terris* (April 11, 1963), published less than two months before his death, insisted that the recognition of human rights and responsibilities is the foundation of world peace. No pope in history was so committed to Christian unity as John XXIII was. On June 5, 1960, he established the Secretariat for Promoting Christian Unity, with the venerable biblical scholar Cardinal Augustin Bea as its first president. He formally received the archbishop of Canterbury, Geoffrey Fisher, on

December 20, 1960 (the first Anglican primate to be so received). He also sent two envoys to Istanbul (formerly Constantinople) to convey his greetings to Ecumenical Patriarch Athenagoras I on June 27, 1961, and exchanged greetings with Patriarch Alexis of Moscow. When John XXIII died on the evening of June 3, 1963, the whole world reacted with profound sorrow, so deeply had he touched the hearts of the entire human community.

10./11. *Paul VI* (1963–78) and *John Paul I* (1978). In breaking one of the most anti-evangelical papal traditions of more than a thousand years' duration, that is, in refusing to be crowned as pope, John Paul I liberated the papacy at long last from its imperial pretensions. The way was prepared, however, by his predecessor Paul VI, who had sold the papal tiara and distributed the money to the poor.

12. *John Paul II* (1978–). The most traveled pope in history and the first Slavic and Polish pope, John Paul II has had a broad and profound impact on the world community through his pastoral visits to every part of the globe, his encyclicals on moral, social, and traditionally religious themes, his personal writings, and the *Catechism of the Catholic Church,* issued on his authority. He had a significant role in the eventual collapse of the Soviet empire, especially through his unflinching support of the Solidarity movement in his native Poland. His pontificate has also been marked by prophetic denunciations of social injustice and oppression in various parts of the world, an acknowledgment of the sins of the Church as it approached a new millennium, a remarkable openness to non-Christian religions (symbolized in his convening of a controversial interfaith conference at Assisi in 1986 to pray for world peace and his many gestures of reconciliation toward the Jews), and his 1995 encyclical *Ut unum sint* (Lat., "That all may be one"), in which he invited non-Catholic Christians to critique and then help improve the exercise of the papal ministry. But this pontificate has also had a less inclusive and less irenic side—one more akin perhaps to the pontificates of Innocent III and Boniface VIII in the Middle Ages and of Pius IX in the nineteenth century than of John XXIII or of Paul VI in the twentieth. John Paul II's skepticism of democracy (with its emphasis on freedom of expression and the right to criticize those in authority) has been present as a consistent thread throughout his life and his pontificate. His favorite virtues—patience in the face of suffering, obedience to one's superiors, and loyalty to the institutional Church—have served as criteria for most of his appointments to the hierarchy, for the punitive actions taken against certain bishops deemed to be insufficiently faithful to Vatican teachings and policies, and against so-called dissident theologians and independent-minded religious orders, as well as for rewards bestowed on favored

groups like Opus Dei through the stunningly hasty beatification of its founder. John Paul II's strongest supporters speak of him as the first post-modern pope (without clearly defining the meaning of the term), and his strongest critics speak of his pontificate as restorationist, that is, as dedicated to the restoration of much of pre–Vatican II Catholicism, especially its emphasis on the person of the pope and the juridical authority of the papacy and the Roman Curia in relation to the local churches and their bishops.

CHRONOLOGICAL LIST OF POPES

Dates in parentheses are those of the Vatican's *Annuario Pontificio*.

1 *Peter, Apostle, St.*, Galilean, d. ca. 64.

2 *Linus, St.*, ca. 66–ca. 78 (67–76).

3 *Anacletus [Cletus], St.*, Greek (?), ca. 79–ca. 91 (76–88).

4 *Clement I, St.*, ca. 91–ca. 101 (88–97).

5 *Evaristus, St.*, Greek, ca. 100–ca. 109 (97–105).

6 *Alexander I, St.*, ca. 109–ca. 116 (105–115).

7 *Sixtus [Xystus] I, St.*, ca. 116–ca. 125 (115–125).

8 *Telesphoros, St.*, Greek, ca. 125–ca. 136 (125–136).

9 *Hyginus, St.*, Greek, ca. 138–ca. 142 (136–140).

10 *Pius I, St.*, ca. 142–ca. 155 (140–155).

11 *Anicetus, St.*, Syrian, ca. 155–ca. 166 (155–166).

12 *Soter, St.*, ca. 166–ca. 174 (166–175).

13 *Eleutherius [Eleutherus], St.*, Greek, ca. 174–ca. 189 (175–189).

14 *Victor I, St.*, African, 189–198.

15 *Zephrynus, St.*, 198/9–217 (199–217).

16 *Callistus [Calixtus] I, St.*, 217–222.

17 *Urban I, St.*, 222–230.

18 *Pontian [Pontianus], St.*, July 21, 230–September 28, 235.

19 *Anterus, St.*, Greek, November 21, 235–January 3, 236.

20 *Fabian, St.*, January 10, 236–January 20, 250.

21 *Cornelius, St.*, March 251–June 253.

22 *Lucius I, St.*, June 25, 253–March 5, 254.

23 *Stephen I, St.*, May 12, 254–August 2, 257.

24 *Sixtus [Xystus] II, St.*, Greek, August 30, 257–August 6, 258.

25 *Dionysius, St.*, July 22, 260–December 26, 268.

26 *Felix I, St.*, January 5, 269–December 30, 274.

27 *Eutychian, St.*, January 4, 275–December 7, 283.

28 *Caius [Gaius], St.*, December 17, 283–April 22, 296.

29 *Marcellinus, St.*, June 30, 296–October 25, 304.

30 *Marcellus I, St.*, November/December 306–January 16, 308 (May 27 or June 26, 308–January 16, 309).

31 *Eusebius, St.*, Greek, April 18–October 21, 310 (April 18, 309–August 17, 309 or 310).

32 *Melchiades [Miltiades], St.*, African (?), July 2, 311–January 11, 314.

33 *Sylvester [Silvester] I, St.*, January 31, 314–December 31, 335.

34 *Mark [Marcus], St.*, January 18–October 7, 336.

35 *Julius I, St.*, February 6, 337–April 12, 352.

36 *Liberius*, May 17, 352–September 24, 366.

37 *Damasus I, St.*, October 1, 366–December 11, 384.

38 *Siricius, St.*, December 384–November 26, 399 (December 15 or 22 or 29, 384).

39 *Anastasius I, St.*, November 27, 399–December 19, 401.

40 *Innocent I, St.*, December 22, 401–March 12, 417.

41 *Zosimus, St.*, Greek, March 18, 417–December 26, 418.

42 *Boniface I, St.*, December 28, 418–September 4, 422 (December 28 or 29, 418).

43 *Celestine I, St.*, September 10, 422–July 27, 432.

44 *Sixtus [Xystus] III, St.* July 31, 432–August 19, 440.

45 *Leo I, "the Great," St.*, September 29, 440–November 10, 461.

46 *Hilarus [Hilary], St.*, November 19, 461–February 29, 468.

47 *Simplicius, St.*, March 3, 468–March 10, 483.

48 *Felix III (II), St.*, March 13, 483–March 1, 492.

49 *Gelasius I, St.*, African, March 1, 492–November 21, 496.

50 *Anastasius II*, November 24, 496–November 19, 498.

51 *Symmachus, St.*, November 22, 498–July 19, 514.

52 *Hormisdas, St.*, July 20, 514–August 6, 523.

53 *John I, St.*, August 13, 523–May 18, 526.

54 *Felix IV (III), St.*, July 12, 526–September 22, 530.

55 *Boniface II*, September 22, 530–October 17, 532.

56 *John II*, January 2, 533–May 8, 535.

57 *Agapitus I, St.*, May 13, 535–April 22, 536.

58 *Silverius, St.*, June 1 or 8, 536–November 11, 537.

59 *Vigilius*, March 29, 537–June 7, 555.

60 *Pelagius I*, April 16, 556–March 4, 561.

61 *John III*, July 17, 561–July 13, 574.

62 *Benedict I*, June 2, 575–July 30, 579.

63 *Pelagius II*, August 579–February 7, 590 (the Vatican's official list gives the beginning of his pontificate as November 26, the date of his imperial confirmation).

64 *Gregory I, "the Great," St.*, September 3, 590–March 12, 604.

65 *Sabinian*, September 13, 604–February 22, 606.

66 *Boniface III*, February 19–November 12, 607

67 *Boniface IV, St.*, August 25, 608–May 8, 615.

68 *Deusdedit [Adeodatus I], St.*, October 19, 615–November 8, 618.

69 *Boniface V*, December 23, 619–October 25, 625.

70 *Honorius I*, October 27, 625–October 12, 638.

71 *Severinus*, May 28–August 2, 640.

72 *John IV*, Dalmatian, December 24, 640–October 12, 642.

73 *Theodore I*, Greek, November 24, 642–May 14, 649.

74 *Martin I, St.*, July 5, 649–August 10, 654 (the day a successor, Eugenius I, was elected; the Vatican's official list gives as the end of his pontificate September 16, 655, the day of his death in exile).

75 *Eugenius [Eugene] I, St.*, August 10, 654–June 2, 657.

76 *Vitalian, St.*, July 30, 657–January 27, 672.

77 *Adeodatus II*, April 11, 672–June 17, 676.

78 *Donus*, November 2, 676–April 11, 678.

79 *Agatho, St.*, June 27, 678–January 10, 681.

80 *Leo II, St.*, August 17, 682–July 3, 683.

81 *Benedict II, St.*, June 26, 684–May 8, 685.

82 *John V*, Syrian, July 23, 685–August 2, 686.

83 *Conon*, Thracian, October 21, 686–September 21, 687.

84 *Sergius I, St.*, Syrian, December 15, 687–September 8, 701.

85 *John VI*, Greek, October 30, 701–January 11, 705.

86 *John VII*, Greek, March 1, 705–October 18, 707.

87 *Sisinnius*, Syrian, January 15–February 4, 708.

88 *Constantine*, Syrian, March 25, 708–April 9, 715.

89 *Gregory II, St.*, May 19, 715–February 11, 731.

90 *Gregory III, St.*, Syrian, March 18, 731–November 28, 741 (March 18, 731–November 741).

91 *Zacharias [Zachary], St.*, Greek, December 10, 741–March 22, 752.

92 *Stephen II (III)*, March 26, 752–April 26, 757.

93 *Paul I, St.*, May 29, 757–June 28, 767.

94 *Stephen III (IV)*, August 7, 768–January 24, 772.

95 *Hadrian [Adrian] I*, February 9, 772–December 25, 795.

96 *Leo III, St.*, December 27, 795–June 12, 816 (the Vatican's official list marks the beginning of his pontificate on December 26, the day of his election, but he was not consecrated as Bishop of Rome until December 27).

97 *Stephen IV (V)*, June 22, 816–January 24, 817.

98 *Paschal I, St.*, January 25, 817–February 11, 824.

99 *Eugenius [Eugene] II*, May 11 (?), 824–August 27 (?), 827 (May 824–August 827).

100 *Valentine*, August–September 827.

101 *Gregory IV*, March 29, 828–January 25, 844 (827–January 844).

102 *Sergius II*, January 844–January 27, 847.

103 *Leo IV, St.*, April 10, 847–July 17, 855 (the Vatican's official list marks the beginning of his pontificate in January, the month of his election, but he was not consecrated as Bishop of Rome until April 10).

104 *Benedict III*, September 29, 855–April 17, 858.

105 *Nicholas I, St.*, April 24, 858–November 13, 867.

106 *Hadrian [Adrian] II*, December 14, 867–December 14, 872.

107 *John VIII*, December 14, 872–December 16, 882.

108 *Marinus I*, December 16, 882–May 15, 884.

109 *Hadrian [Adrian] III, St.*, May 17, 884–September 885.

110 *Stephen V (VI)*, September 885–September 14, 891.

111 *Formosus*, October 6, 891–April 4, 896.

112 *Boniface VI*, April 896.

113 *Stephen VI (VII)*, May 896–August 897.

114 *Romanus*, August–November 897.

115 *Theodore II*, November/December 897 (December 897).

116 *John IX*, January 898–January 900.

117 *Benedict IV*, February 900–July 903.

118 *Leo V*, July/August–September 903.

119 *Sergius III*, January 29, 904–April 14, 911.

120 *Anastasius III*, ca. June 911–ca. August 913 (April 911–June 913).

121 *Lando [Landus]*, ca. August 913–ca. March 914 (July 913–February 914).

122 *John X*, March/April 914–May 928 (March 914–May 928).

123 *Leo VI*, May–December 928.

124 *Stephen VII (VIII)*, December 928–February 931.

125 *John XI*, March 931–December 935, or January 936 (March 931–December 935).

126 *Leo VII*, January 3, 936–July 13, 939.

127 *Stephen VIII (IX)*, July 14, 939–October 942.

128 *Marinus II*, October 30, 942–May 946.

129 *Agapitus II*, May 10, 946–December 955.

130 *John XII*, December 16, 955–May 14, 964.

131 *Leo VIII*, December 6, 963–March 1, 965.

132 *Benedict V*, May 22–June 23, 964.

133 *John XIII*, October 1, 965–September 6, 972.

134 *Benedict VI*, January 19, 973–July 974 (January 19, 973–June 974).

135 *Benedict VII*, October 974–July 10, 983.

136 *John XIV*, December 983–August 20, 984.

137 *John XV*, August 985–March 996.

138 *Gregory V*, Saxon, May 3, 996–February 18, 999.

139 *Sylvester [Silvester] II*, French, April 2, 999–May 12, 1003.

140 *John XVII*, May 16–November 6, 1003 (June–December 1003).

141 *John XVIII*, December 25, 1003–June/July 1009 (January 1004–July 1009).

142 *Sergius IV*, July 31, 1009–May 12, 1012.

143 *Benedict VIII*, May 18, 1012–April 9, 1024.

144 *John XIX*, April 19, 1024–October 20, 1032 (May 1024–1032).

145 *Benedict IX*, October 21, 1032–September 1044; March 10–May 1, 1045; November 8, 1047–July 16, 1048 (1032–1044; April 10–May 1, 1045; November 8, 1047–July 17, 1048).

146 *Sylvester [Silvester] III*, January 20–March 10, 1045 (January 20–February 10, 1045).

147 *Gregory VI*, May 5, 1045–December 20, 1046.

148 *Clement II*, Saxon, December 25, 1046–October 9, 1047.

149 *Damasus II*, Bavarian, July 17–August 9, 1048.

150 *Leo IX, St.*, Alsatian, February 12, 1049–April 19, 1054.

151 *Victor II*, Swabian, April 13, 1055–July 28, 1057 (April 16, 1055–July 28, 1057).

152 *Stephen IX (X)*, French, August 2, 1057–March 29, 1058 (the Vatican's official list marks the beginning of his pontificate on August 3, the day of his enthronement, rather than August 2, the day of his election and consecration).

153 *Nicholas II*, French, December 6, 1058–July 27, 1061 (the Vatican's official list begins this pontificate on January 24, 1059, the day of enthronement, rather than the day of his acceptance of election).

154 *Alexander II*, September 30, 1061–April 21, 1073 (the Vatican's official list gives October 1 as the starting point of this pontificate; it is the day of enthronement rather than election).

155 *Gregory VII, St.*, June 30, 1073–May 25, 1085 (although April 22, 1073, is given as the beginning of his pontificate, the day on which he was elected by popular acclaim,

Gregory VII was still only a deacon at the time; he was not consecrated as Bishop of Rome until June 30).

156 *Victor III, Bl.*, May 9, 1087–September 16, 1087 (the Vatican's official list begins his pontificate on May 24, 1086, the date of his first election—an election he did not formally accept—and almost a year before his consecration as Bishop of Rome on May 9, 1087).

157 *Urban II, Bl.*, French, March 12, 1088–July 29, 1099.

158 *Paschal II*, August 14, 1099–January 21, 1118.

159 *Gelasius II*, March 10, 1118–January 28, 1119 (January 24, 1118–January 28, 1119, in the Vatican's official list; January 24 is the date of election; consecration as Bishop of Rome did not occur until March 10).

160 *Callistus [Calixtus] II*, French, February 2, 1119–December 13, 1124.

161 *Honorius II*, December 21, 1124–February 13, 1130.

162 *Innocent II*, February 23, 1130–September 24, 1143 (the Vatican's official list gives the date of the beginning of his pontificate as February 14, the day of his election, but he was not consecrated as Bishop of Rome until February 23).

163 *Celestine II*, October 3, 1143–March 8, 1144 (the Vatican's official list marks the beginning of his pontificate on September 26, the day of his election, but he was not consecrated as Bishop of Rome until October 3).

164 *Lucius II*, March 12, 1144–February 15, 1145.

165 *Eugenius [Eugene] III, Bl.*, February 18, 1145–July 8, 1153 (the Vatican's official list gives the date of his election, February 15, as the beginning his pontificate, but he was not consecrated as Bishop of Rome until February 18).

166 *Anastasius IV*, July 12, 1153–December 3, 1154.

167 *Hadrian [Adrian] IV*, English, December 4, 1154–September 1, 1159.

168 *Alexander III*, September 20, 1159–August 30, 1181 (the Vatican's official list takes the date of his election, September 7, as the beginning of his pontificate, but he was not consecrated as Bishop of Rome until September 20).

169 *Lucius III*, September 1, 1181–November 25, 1185 (the Vatican's official list gives the date of his death as August 25, 1185).

170 *Urban III*, November 25, 1185–October 20, 1187.

171 *Gregory VIII*, October 25–December 17, 1187 (the Vatican's official list begins his pontificate on the day of his election, October 21, but he was not consecrated as Bishop of Rome until October 25).

172 *Clement III*, December 19, 1187–March 1191.

173 *Celestine III*, April 14, 1191–January 8, 1198.

174 *Innocent III*, February 22, 1198–July 16, 1216 (according to the Vatican's official list, canonically he was pope once he accepted election on January 8; theologically he was not pope until consecrated as Bishop of Rome on February 22).

175 *Honorius III*, July 24, 1216–March 18, 1227.

176 *Gregory IX*, March 19, 1227–August 22, 1241.

177 *Celestine IV*, October 25–November 10, 1241.

178 *Innocent IV*, June 28, 1243–December 7, 1254 (the Vatican's official list marks the beginning of his pontificate on the day of his election, June 25, but he was not consecrated as Bishop of Rome until June 28).

179 *Alexander IV*, December 12, 1254–May 25, 1261.

180 *Urban IV*, French, August 29, 1261–October 2, 1264.

181 *Clement IV*, French, February 5, 1265–November 29, 1268.

182 *Gregory X, Bl.*, March 27, 1272–January 10, 1276 (the Vatican's official list marks the beginning of his pontificate on September 1, 1271, the day of his election, but he was not consecrated as Bishop of Rome until March 27, 1272).

183 *Innocent V, Bl.*, French, January 21–June 22, 1276.

184 *Hadrian [Adrian] V*, July 11–August 18, 1276.

185 *John XXI*, Portuguese, September 8, 1276–May 20, 1277.

186 *Nicholas III*, December 26, 1277–August 22, 1280 (the Vatican's official list gives the beginning of his pontificate as the day of his election, November 25, but he was not consecrated as Bishop of Rome until December 26).

187 *Martin IV*, French, March 23, 1281–March 28, 1285 (the Vatican's official list begins his pontificate on the day of his election, February 22, but he was not consecrated as Bishop of Rome until March 23).

188 *Honorius IV*, May 20, 1285–April 3, 1287 (the Vatican's official list begins his pontificate on the day of his election, April 2, but he was not consecrated as Bishop of Rome until May 20).

189 *Nicholas IV*, February 22, 1288–April 4, 1292.

190 *Celestine V, St.*, August 29–December 13, 1294 (the Vatican's official list begins his pontificate on July 5, the day of his election, but he was not consecrated as Bishop of Rome until August 29).

191 *Boniface VIII*, January 23, 1295–October 11, 1303 (the Vatican's official list begins his pontificate on December 24, 1294, the day of his election, but he was not consecrated as Bishop of Rome until January 23, 1295).

192 *Benedict XI, Bl.*, October 22, 1303–July 7, 1304.

193 *Clement V*, French, June 5, 1305–April 20, 1314.

194 *John XXII*, French, August 7, 1316–December 4, 1334.

195 *Benedict XII*, French, January 8, 1335–April 25, 1342 (the Vatican's official list begins his pontificate with his election on December 20, 1334, but he was not consecrated as Bishop of Rome until January 8, 1335).

196 *Clement VI*, French, May 7, 1342–December 6, 1352.

197 *Innocent VI*, French, December 18, 1352–September 12, 1362.

198 *Urban V, Bl.*, French, November 6, 1362–December 19, 1370 (the Vatican's official list marks the beginning of his pontificate on the day of his election, September 28, but he was not consecrated as Bishop of Rome until November 6).

199 *Gregory XI*, French, January 4, 1371–March 27, 1378 (the Vatican's official list begins his pontificate on the day of his election, December 30, 1370, but he was not consecrated as Bishop of Rome until January 4, 1371).

200 *Urban VI*, April 8, 1378–October 15, 1389.

201 *Boniface IX*, November 9, 1389–October 1, 1404 (the Vatican's official list marks the beginning of his pontificate on the day of his election, November 2, but he was not consecrated as Bishop of Rome until November 9).

202 *Innocent VII*, October 17, 1404–November 6, 1406.

203 *Gregory XII*, December 19, 1406–July 4, 1415 (the Vatican's official list begins his pontificate on the day of his election, November 30, but he was not consecrated as Bishop of Rome until December 19).

204 *Martin V*, November 21, 1417–February 20, 1431 (the Vatican's official list marks the beginning of his pontificate on November 11, the day of his election, but he was not consecrated as Bishop of Rome until November 21).

205 *Eugenius [Eugene] IV*, March 11, 1431–February 23, 1447 (the Vatican's official list begins his pontificate on March 3, but he was not consecrated as Bishop of Rome until March 11).

206 *Nicholas V*, March 6, 1447–March 24, 1455.

207 *Callistus [Calixtus] III*, Spanish, April 8, 1455–August 6, 1458.

208 *Pius II*, August 19, 1458–August 15, 1464.

209 *Paul II*, August 30, 1464–July 26, 1471.

210 *Sixtus IV*, August 25, 1471–August 12, 1484 (the Vatican's official list begins his pontificate on the day of his election, August 9, but he was not consecrated as Bishop of Rome until August 25).

211 *Innocent VIII*, August 29, 1484–July 25, 1492.

212 *Alexander VI*, Spanish, August 26, 1492–August 18, 1503 (the Vatican's official list begins his pontificate on the day of his election, August 11, but he was not consecrated as Bishop of Rome until August 26).

213 *Pius III*, October 1–18, 1503 (the Vatican's official list marks the beginning of his pontificate on the day of his election, September 22, but apparently, although he had been appointed archbishop of Siena, he had not yet been ordained a priest or a bishop; his consecration as Bishop of Rome did not occur until October 1).

214 *Julius II*, November 1, 1503–February 21, 1513 (the Vatican's official list begins his pontificate on October 31, but he was actually elected the next day, November 1).

215 *Leo X*, March 17, 1513–December 1, 1521 (the Vatican's official list begins his pontificate on March 9, the day of his election, but he was not consecrated as Bishop of Rome until March 17).

216 *Hadrian [Adrian] VI*, Dutch, January 9, 1522–September 14, 1523.

217 *Clement VII*, November 19, 1523–September 25, 1534.

218 *Paul III*, October 13, 1534–November 10, 1549.

219 *Julius III*, February 8, 1550–March 23, 1555.

220 *Marcellus II*, April 10–May 1, 1555 (the Vatican's official list begins his pontificate on the day of his election, April 9, but he was not consecrated as Bishop of Rome until the following day).

221 *Paul IV*, May 23, 1555–August 18, 1559.

222 *Pius IV*, December 25, 1559–December 9, 1565.

223 *Pius V, St.*, January 7, 1566–May 1, 1572.

224 *Gregory XIII*, May 13, 1572–April 10, 1585.

225 *Sixtus V*, April 24, 1585–August 27, 1590.

226 *Urban VII*, September 15–27, 1590.

227 *Gregory XIV*, December 5, 1590–October 16, 1591.

228 *Innocent IX*, October 29–December 30, 1591.

229 *Clement VIII*, February 3, 1592–March 3, 1605 (the Vatican's official list begins his pontificate on the day of his election, January 30, but he was not consecrated as Bishop of Rome until February 3) .

230 *Leo XI*, April 1–27, 1605.

231 *Paul V*, May 16, 1605–January 28, 1621.

232 *Gregory XV*, February 9, 1621–July 8, 1623.

233 *Urban VIII*, August 6, 1623–July 29, 1644.

234 *Innocent X*, September 15, 1644–January 7, 1655.

235 *Alexander VII*, April 7, 1655–May 22, 1667.

236 *Clement IX*, June 20, 1667–December 9, 1669.

237 *Clement X*, April 29, 1670–July 22, 1676.

238 *Innocent XI, Bl.*, September 21, 1676–August 12, 1689.

239 *Alexander VIII*, October 6, 1689–February 1, 1691.

240 *Innocent XII*, July 12, 1691–September 27, 1700.

241 *Clement XI*, November 30, 1700–March 19, 1721 (the Vatican's official list begins his pontificate on the day of his election, November 23, but he was not consecrated as Bishop of Rome until November 30).

242 *Innocent XIII*, May 8, 1721–March 7, 1724.

243 *Benedict XIII*, May 29, 1724–February 21, 1730.

244 *Clement XII*, July 12, 1730–February 6, 1740.

245 *Benedict XIV*, August 17, 1740–May 3, 1758.

246 *Clement XIII*, July 6, 1758–February 2, 1769.

247 *Clement XIV*, May 28, 1769–September 22, 1774 (the Vatican's official list begins his pontificate on the day of election, May 19, but he was not consecrated as Bishop of Rome until May 28).

248 *Pius VI*, February 22, 1775–August 29, 1799 (the Vatican's official list begins his pontificate on the day of his election, February 15, but he was not consecrated as Bishop of Rome until February 22).

249 *Pius VII*, March 14, 1800–August 20, 1823.

250 *Leo XII*, September 28, 1823–February 10, 1829.

251 *Pius VIII*, March 31, 1829–November 30, 1830.

252 *Gregory XVI*, February 2, 1831–June 1, 1846.

253 *Pius IX*, June 16, 1846–February 7, 1878.

254 *Leo XIII*, February 20, 1878–July 20, 1903.

255 *Pius X, St.*, August 4, 1903–August 20, 1914.

256 *Benedict XV*, September 3, 1914–January 22, 1922.

257 *Pius XI*, February 6, 1922–February 10, 1939.

258 *Pius XII*, March 2, 1939–October 9, 1958.

259 *John XXIII*, October 28, 1958–June 3, 1963.

260 *Paul VI*, June 21, 1963–August 6, 1978.

261 *John Paul I*, August 26–September 28, 1978.

262 *John Paul II*, Polish, October 16, 1978– .

LONGEST AND SHORTEST PONTIFICATES

The beginning of each pontificate in the lists below is determined by the date of the individual's consecration if he was not already a bishop when elected. The Vatican's official list in the *Annuario Pontificio* begins each pontificate, in accordance with the canon law in force during most of the second Christian millennium, with the date of election, not consecration, even if the individual was not already a bishop. That may be appropriate canonically, but not theologically. The pope is the Bishop of Rome. He cannot become Bishop of Rome until he is consecrated as a bishop, if he was not already a bishop. Today canon law and theology coincide once again. An individual is not considered to be pope until he is consecrated as Bishop of Rome, if he was not already a bishop when elected (can. 332.1).

Longest Pontificates (as of October 16, 1997)

1 Pius IX (June 16, 1846–February 7, 1878), or 31 years, 7 months, 3 weeks.
2 Leo XIII (February 20, 1878–July 20, 1903), or 25 years, 5 months.
3 Pius VI (February 22, 1775–August 29, 1799), or 24 years, 6 months, 1 week.[1]
4 Hadrian I (February 9, 772–December 25, 795), or 23 years, 10 months, 2 weeks+.
5 Pius VII (March 14, 1800–August 20, 1823), or 23 years, 4 months, 2 weeks+.
6 Alexander III (September 20, 1159–August 30, 1181), or 21 years, 11 months, 13 days.[2]
7 Leo the Great (September 29, 440–November 10, 461), or 21 years, 1 month, 12 days.
8 Urban VIII (August 6, 1623–July 29, 1644), or 20 years, 11 months, 3 weeks+.
9 Sylvester I (January 31, 314–December 31, 335), or 20 years, 11 months.
10 Leo III (December 26, 795–June 12, 816), or 20 years, 5 months, 2 weeks+.
11 Clement XI (November 30, 1700–March 19, 1721), or 20 years, 3 months, 11 days.[3]
12 Pius XII (March 2, 1939–October 9, 1958), or 19 years, 7 months, 1 week.
13 John Paul II (October 16, 1978–), or 19 years.

Shortest Pontificates

1 Urban VII (September 15–27, 1590), or 12 days.
2 Boniface VI (April, 896), or 15 days (?).
3 Celestine IV (October 25–November 10, 1241), or 16 days.

---

[1] The *Annuario Pontificio* begins his pontificate on February 15, the day of his election, rather than February 22, the day of his consecration as Bishop of Rome.
[2] The *Annuario* begins his pontificate on September 7, the day of his election.
[3] The *Annuario* begins his pontificate on November 23, the day of his election.

4 Pius III (October 1–18, 1503), or 17 days.[1]

5 Sisinnius (January 15–February 4, 708), or 20 days.

6 Theodore II (November/December, 897), or 20 days (?).

7 Marcellus II (April 10–May 1, 1555), or 21 days.[2]

8 Damasus II (July 17–August 9, 1048), or 23 days.

9 Leo XI (April 1–27, 1605), or 26 days.

10 Benedict V (May 22–June 23, 964), or 32 days.

11 John Paul I (August 26–September 28, 1978), or 33 days.[3]

---

[1] The *Annuario* begins his pontificate on September 22, the day of his election.

[2] The *Annuario* begins his pontificate on April 9, the day of his election.

[3] The *Annuario* differs from other historical sources in calculating the end of Sylvester III's pontificate as February 10, 1045, rather than March 10. If the former, his pontificate was only twenty-one days, making his and Marcellus II's the seventh shortest pontificates, and John Paul I's the twelfth shortest. On the other hand, Benedict V's pontificate was canonically dubious. John Paul I's could also be regarded someday as the tenth shortest in history.

PAPAL "FIRSTS" AND "LASTS"

1 The first pope who was a martyr and the first to be recognized by the Church as a saint: *Peter the Apostle* (d. ca. 64).

2 The first of eleven Greek popes: *Evaristus* (ca. 100–109). The last of the Greek popes: *Zacharias* (741–52).

3 The first pope to function as the sole Bishop of Rome: *Pius I* (ca. 142–ca. 155). (The form of governance in the Roman church before Pius I was collegial rather than monoepiscopal.)

4 The first of six Syrian popes: *Anicetus* (ca. 155–ca. 166). The last of the Syrian popes: *Gregory III* (731–41).

5 The first of two, and possibly three, African popes: *Victor I* (189–198); the third (or second) was *Gelasius I* (492–96). (Melchiades, 311–14, was possibly African.) Victor I was also the first pope to assert his authority beyond his own diocese, demanding that certain churches follow the Roman practice of celebrating Easter on the Sunday following Passover rather than on the fourteenth day of the month of Nisan.

6 The first pope to abdicate (after being arrested and deported): *Pontian* (230–35). The last pope to abdicate, or resign, was not *Celestine V* (1294), but *Gregory XII* in 1415. Other popes who have abdicated, or resigned, include Silverius in 537, John XVIII in 1009, and Benedict IX in 1045 (reinstated in 1047).

7 The first pope to use the Lateran Palace as a papal residence (given him by the emperor Constantine): *Melchiades* (311–14).

8 The first pope not to be listed among the saints (under imperial pressure, he had approved the excommunication of St. Athanasius during the Arian controversy): *Liberius* (352–66).

9 The first pope to issue decretals in the style of imperial edicts: *Siricius* (384–99).

10 The first (and only) pope to succeed his father as pope: *Innocent I* (401–17). His father was *Anastasius I* (399–401). Both are recognized as saints. (*Hormisdas* [514–23] also had a son who became pope, but not as his immediate successor: *Silverius* [536–37]. Both are honored as saints.)

11 The first of two popes to be called "the Great" and also the first pope forcefully to claim jurisdiction over the universal Church, East and West alike: *Leo I* (440–61). The other pope called "the Great" was *Gregory I* (590–604)

12 The first pope to be called Vicar of Christ: *Gelasius I* (492–96).

13 The first pope to bestow the pallium (a symbol of pastoral authority) on a bishop outside of Italy: *Symmachus* (498–514).

14 The first pope to leave Italy for the East (Constantinople): *John I* (523–26).

15 The first pope of Germanic stock (though born in Rome): *Boniface II* (530–32). Five German-born popes would later serve, beginning with *Gregory V* (996–99) and ending with *Victor II* (1055–57).

16 The first pope to take a different name upon being elected to the papacy (his birth name was that of a pagan God, Mercury): *John II* (533–35). The last pope to take his own name as pope was *Marcellus II* (1555).

17 The first pope to be excommunicated (by an African synod of bishops for vacillating over the teaching of the Council of Chalcedon [451]): *Vigilius* (537–55).

18 The first pope to be consecrated with the approval of the Byzantine emperor (required for validity after the Byzantine conquest of Italy): *Pelagius I* (556–61). (Pelagius I was also the first and only pope to be installed in the papacy by imperial action, without a prior election). The last pope to seek imperial approval for his consecration was *Gregory III* (731–41).

19 The first pope (of several) to have been a monk: *Gregory the Great* (590–604).

20 The first (and only) pope to be excommunicated by an ecumenical council (the Third Council of Constantinople in 680, for his unwitting adherence to the heresy of Monothelitism): *Honorius I* (625–38).

21 The last pope to be recognized as a martyr: *Martin I* (649–54).

22 The first (and only) pope to ratify an ecumenical council's (Constantinople III in 680) condemnation of a predecessor (Honorius I [625–38]): *Leo II* (682–83).

23 The first man elected pope whose name does not appear on the official list of popes because he died before he could be consecrated as Bishop of Rome: *Stephen II* (752).

24 The first pope to rule the Papal States: *Stephen II (III)* (752–57).

25 The first pope to succeed his brother as pope (Stephen II [III]): *Paul I* (757–67). The other was *John XIX* (1024–32), the younger brother of *Benedict VIII* (1012–24)

26 The first pope to be assassinated: *John VIII* (872–82). Other popes whose lives ended through murder: possibly *Hadrian III* (884–85), *Stephen VI [VII]* (896–97), *Leo V* (903), *John X* (914–28), possibly *Sergius IV* (1009–12), *Benedict VI* (973–74), and possibly *Urban VI* (1378–89). Two other popes died after brutal treatment in prison: *Stephen VIII [IX]* (939–42) and *John XIV* (983–84).

27 The first (and only) pope to offer obeisance to a Western emperor: *Leo III* (795–816).

28 The first pope to anoint an emperor: *Stephen IV (V)* (816–17).

29 The first bishop of another diocese to be elected Bishop of Rome and therefore pope—in violation of canon 15 of the First Council of Nicaea (325): *Marinus I* (882–84).

30 The first (and only) pope whose body was exhumed from his grave and placed on trial (the "Cadaver Synod") by one of his successors (Stephen VI [VII]) for various alleged offenses, including having accepted election as Bishop of Rome while already serving as bishop of another diocese: *Formosus* (891–96).

31 The first (and only) person to be elected pope after having previously been defrocked from the subdiaconate and the priesthood for immorality: *Boniface VI* (896). (He died fifteen days after his election, which was canonically dubious in the first place.)

32 The first pope to be deposed from office by other than imperial action: *Stephen VI (VIII)* (896–97), the pope who presided over the so-called Cadaver Synod, which found the late Pope Formosus guilty of various offenses. The first pope to be

deposed by a Roman synod (and later reinstated) was *John XII* (963 and 964, respectively).

33 The first (and only) pope to have ordered the murder of his predecessor (Leo V): *Sergius III* (904–11).

34 The first (and only) illegitimate son of a pope who was also elected pope: *John XI* (931–35/6). His father was *Sergius III* (904–11).

35 The first (and only) pope to have been elected while still a teenager: *John XII* (955–64), elected at age eighteen. He was also the second pope to change his name (Octavian) upon election as pope.

36 The first layman elected pope (although the legitimacy of his election has been a matter of canonical debate): *Leo VIII* (963–65). Three successive laymen (whose elections are not in doubt) were elected pope in the next century: *Benedict VIII* (1012–24), *John XIX* (1024–32), and *Benedict IX* (1032–44; 1045; 1047–48).

37 The first of two popes to be elected with the baptismal name Peter and who, out of respect for the Blessed Apostle, changed his papal name: *John XIV* (983–84). The other was *Sergius IV* (1009–12).

38 The first pope formally to canonize a saint (Ulric of Augsburg in 993): *John XV* (985–96).

39 The first of five German popes: *Gregory V* (996–99). The last German pope was *Victor II* (1055–57).

40 The first of sixteen French popes: *Sylvester II* (999–1003). The last of the French popes was *Gregory XI* (1371–78).

41 Only 5 of the 123 second-millennial popes have been canonized saints. The first was *Leo IX* (1049–54), and the last, *Pius X* (1903–14). The other three were: *Gregory VII* (1073–85), *Celestine V* (1294), and *Pius V* (1566–72).

42 The first (and only) pope whose term of office consisted of three separate time segments: *Benedict IX* (1032–44; 1045; 1047–48).

43 The first clearly legitimate pope to retain his former diocese while serving as Bishop of Rome: *Clement II* (1046–47), who retained his diocese of Bamberg. The three German popes who succeeded him did the same: *Damasus II* (1048) retained the see of Brixen; *Leo IX* (1049–54) retained the see of Toul; and *Victor II* (1055–57) retained the see of Eichstätt. So, too, did *Nicholas II* (1058–61) remain bishop of Florence. *Stephen IX [X]* (1057–58) remained abbot of Monte Cassino after his election as pope. *Urban III* (1185–87) retained his archdiocese of Milan to prevent the revenues from passing into the imperial treasury, and *Benedict XIII* (1724–30) retained his diocese of Benevento, the last pope to hold two dioceses simultaneously—a condemned practice known as pluralism. (Sylvester III retained his diocese of Sabina in 1045, but he may have been an antipope.)

44 The first pope to restrict the election of a pope to the College of Cardinals: *Nicholas II*, in 1059. *Alexander III* decreed in 1179 at the Third Lateran Council that a two-thirds majority was necessary for election. (*Pius XII* in 1945 changed that to two-thirds plus one. *John Paul II* in 1996 changed it back to two-thirds, while also decreeing that only an absolute majority is necessary after thirty-three inconclusive ballots.) *Gregory X* (1272–76) decreed that a papal election must be held within ten days after the death of the pope, in the city where he died, and with the

cardinal-electors having no contact with the outside world. *Gregory XV* (1621–23) decreed that such elections should be conducted by secret ballot.

45 The first pope to claim temporal as well as spiritual authority over the whole Christian world, and also the first pope to require metropolitan archbishops to come to Rome to receive the pallium: *Gregory VII* (1073–85). *Innocent III* (1198–1216) was the first pope to claim such authority over the whole world.

46 The first pope to be beatified without subsequently being canonized a saint: *Victor III* (1086–87). The last one to date is *Innocent XI* (1676–89).

47 The pope who established the Roman Curia (1089) and the first pope to call for a Crusade to liberate Jerusalem from the Muslims: *Urban II* (1088–99).

48 The first Cistercian pope: *Eugenius III* (1145–53).

49 The first (and only) English pope: *Hadrian [Adrian] IV* (1154–59).

50 The first of many popes who were lawyers: *Alexander III* (1159–81).

51 The first pope to establish procedures for the Inquisition for the suppression and punishment of heretics: *Lucius III* (1181–85). *Gregory IX* (1227–41) established the papal Inquisition under the direction of the Dominicans, and *Paul III* (1534–49) established the Congregation of the Roman Inquisition (Holy Office).

52 The first pope to be elected by a conclave consisting of less than ten cardinals: *Celestine IV* (1241). (When Urban IV was elected in 1261, there were only eight cardinals left in the college.)

53 The first Dominican pope and the first pope to adopt the white cassock (the Dominican habit) as normal papal dress: *Innocent V* (1276). The custom of the white papal cassock became normal after the pontificate of another Dominican, St. Pius V (1566–72). (When Urban V was elected in 1362, he retained his Benedictine black habit as pope.)

54 The first (and only) Portuguese pope and the only medical doctor who served in the papacy: *John XXI* (1276–77).

55 The first pope to make the Vatican Palace his residence: *Nicholas III* (1277–80).

56 The first Franciscan pope: *Nicholas IV* (1288–92).

57 The first (and only) hermit elected pope: *Celestine V* (1294).

58 The first pope to proclaim a Holy Year (1300): *Boniface VIII* (1295–1303).

59 The first of the Avignon popes: *Clement V* (1305–14). The last was *Gregory XI* (1371–78).

60 The last noncardinal elected pope: *Urban VI* (1378–89).

61 The first of the Renaissance popes: *Nicholas V* (1447–55).

62 The first of two Spanish popes: *Callistus III* (1455–58). The second was the infamous *Alexander VI* (1492–1503).

63 The pope who built the Sistine Chapel and established the Vatican archives: *Sixtus IV* (1471–84).

64 The pope who first commissioned plans for the rebuilding of St. Peter's Basilica: *Julius II* (1503–13).

65 The first pope of the Reformation, who excommunicated Martin Luther in 1521: *Leo X* (1513–21).

66 The first (and only) Dutchman elected pope and the last non-Italian pope until John Paul II in 1978: *Hadrian [Adrian] VI* (1522–23).

67 The last pope to have retained his baptismal name as pope: *Marcellus II* (1555).

68 The pope who created the Index of Forbidden Books in 1557: *Paul IV* (1555–59).

69 The pope who reformed the Julian calendar into the Gregorian calendar: *Gregory XIII* (1572–85).

70 The pope who consecrated the new St. Peter's Basilica and who first used Castel Gandolfo as a summer residence: *Urban VIII* (1623–44).

71 The first (and only) pope to suppress a major religious order, the Society of Jesus, in 1773: *Clement XIV* (1769–74). (The Jesuits were restored in 1814 by *Pius VII.*)

72 The first (and only) Camaldolese monk elected pope and the last person elected who was not yet a bishop: *Gregory XVI* (1831–46).

73 The first pope to attempt to reconcile the Church with the modern world: *Leo XIII* (1878–1903).

74 The first pope to use radio for pastoral communication: *Pius XI* (1922–39).

75 The first pope to use television as means of pastoral communication: *Pius XII* (1939–58).

76 The first pope to travel by airplane and to visit countries thousands of miles away from Rome: *Paul VI* (1963–78).

77 The first pope to take a double name, and the first pope in more than a thousand years to forgo the traditional coronation rite: *John Paul I* (1978).

78 The first Slavic (Polish) pope and the first non-Italian pope since Hadrian VI (1522–23): *John Paul II* (1978–).

KEY PAPAL ENCYCLICALS

A papal encyclical is, in principle, a circular letter sent by the Bishop of Rome to the whole Church concerning doctrinal, moral, pastoral, or disciplinary matters. However, most encyclicals through the pontificate of Pius X (1903–14) were written to particular churches about national or regional problems and were not of concern to the universal Church. Several of those that were more universal than local proclaimed a Holy Year or Jubilee year for the universal Church or outlined a new pope's plans for his pontificate. Until the 1960s encyclicals were addressed only to bishops and other church officials; only much later were they to all of the Catholic faithful, and finally, with Pope John XXIII's *Pacem in terris* (1963), to all non-Catholic Christians and to all people of good-will. The Latin names of the encyclicals are taken from the first two or three words in the original Latin text, which are usually meaningless when literally translated. The authority of an encyclical depends upon its content, the audience intended, and the magisterial force with which its central teachings are presented. It is generally agreed that the first papal encyclical was issued by Benedict XIV in 1740. The following list, chronologically arranged, contains only a sample of the more important encyclicals. The lists of the encyclicals of John XXIII, Paul VI, and John Paul II, however, are complete. For a complete list of all papal encyclicals, see the annual *Catholic Almanac* (Huntington, IN: Our Sunday Visitor Publishing Division).

Benedict XIV (1740–58):

Ubi primum (Lat., "Where first"), on the duties of bishops (December 3, 1740).

Gregory XVI (1831–46):

Mirari vos (Lat., "You wonder"), which condemned (without mentioning by name) the social and political principles espoused in *L'Avenir* (Fr., "The Future"), the Catholic newspaper edited by liberal French Catholics, including Father Félicité Robert de Lamennais (d. 1854), who advocated social liberty, separation of Church and state, and freedom of religion and of the press (August 15, 1832).

Singulari Nos (Lat., "We singular"), which condemned Lamennais personally because the pope was dissatisfied with Lamennais's reaction to the previous encyclical (June 25, 1834).

Pius IX (1846–78):

Ubi primum (Lat., "Where first"), which anticipated the pope's proclamation of the dogma of the Immaculate Conception of the Blessed Virgin Mary in 1854 (June 17, 1847).

Cum nuper (Lat., "Lately with"), which defended the Holy See's right to the Papal States, which were about to be expropriated by the new Italian state (June 18, 1859).

Quanta cura (Lat., "How much care"), which condemned certain modern errors and included, as an appendix, the famous "Syllabus of Errors," containing eighty previously condemned propositions (December 8, 1864)

Ubi Nos (Lat., "Where we"), which restated the Holy See's claim to the Papal States, recently expropriated—including, finally, even Rome itself—by the new Italian state (May 15, 1871)

Leo XIII (1878–1903):

Aeterni Patris (Lat., "Of the Eternal Father"), on the restoration of Christian philosophy and particularly that of St. Thomas Aquinas (August 4, 1879).

Diuturnum illud (Lat., "This long-lasting . . ."), on the origins of civil authority, giving tentative recognition to democracy (June 29, 1881).

Immortale Dei (Lat., "The immortal God"), which distinguished between the temporal and the spiritual realms, insisting that any form of government can be legitimate if it serves the common good (November 1, 1885).

Libertas praestantissimum (Lat., "Freedom"), on the Church as the custodian of freedom, properly understood (June 20, 1888).

Magni Nobis (Lat., "Great to us"), to the bishops of the United States on the opening of the new Catholic University of America (March 7, 1889).

Sapientiae Christianae (Lat., "Of Christian wisdom"), on Christians as citizens (January 10, 1890).

Catholicae Ecclesiae (Lat., "Catholic churches"), against slavery in the missions (November 20, 1890).

Rerum novarum (Lat., "Of new things"), the classic social encyclical. Although it strongly defended the right to private property (against socialism), it also insisted (against laissez-faire capitalism) on the social responsibilities that accompany the private possession of property, namely, the obligation to pay workers a just wage and to honor workers' rights, especially the right to form trade unions (May 15, 1891).

Providentissimus Deus (Lat., "Most provident God"), which laid down guidelines for the scientific study of Sacred Scripture. It was a cautious document, affirming that Scripture was written "at the dictation" of the Holy Spirit and that every interpretation of the Bible must be in conformity with the teachings of the Church (November 18, 1893).

Longinqua oceani (Lat., "An ocean apart"), which warned the U.S. Church against idealizing the separation of Church and state. This document, like many others on the list of encyclicals found in the *Catholic Almanac,* may not belong on the list of encyclicals, since it was more in the nature of an apostolic letter (January 6, 1895).

Satis cognitum (Lat., "Known enough"), which stipulated that acceptance of the primacy of the pope was a necessary condition of Christian reunion (June 29, 1896).

Divinum munus (Lat., "This divine function"), on the Holy Spirit (May 9, 1897).

Annum Sacrum (Lat., "Holy Year"), on consecration to the Sacred Heart (May 25, 1899).

Tametsi futura prospicientibus (Lat., "Although those looking toward future things"), on Jesus Christ the Redeemer (November 1, 1900).

Graves de communi re (Lat., "Serious matters concerning a common reality"), on Christian democracy (January 18, 1901).

In amplissimo (Lat., "In the fullest"), to the bishops of the United States on the Church in the United States (April 15, 1902).

Mirae caritatis (Lat., "Wonders of love"), on the Eucharist (May 28, 1902).

Pius X (1903–14):

E supremi (Lat., "From the highest"), his first encyclical, on the restoration of all things in Christ, the motto for his pontificate (October 4, 1903).

Vehementer Nos (Lat., "We vehemently"), to the bishops, clergy, and people of France, condemning the French law of separation of Church and state (February 11, 1906).

Pascendi Dominici gregis (Lat., "Feeding the Lord's flock"), which condemned Modernism as "the synthesis of all heresies," commended the teaching and study of Scholasticism, and defended the censorship of writings (September 8, 1907).

Benedict XV (1914–22):

Ad beatissimi Apostolorum (Lat., "At [the threshold] of the most blessed Apostles"), his first encyclical, in which he called a halt to the internecine warfare between so-called Integralist Catholics and progressive Catholics that had developed and intensified during the previous pontificate. The pope insisted, without using the name "Integralist," that the noun "Catholic" needs no qualification by "fresh epithets" (November 1, 1914).

Maximum illud (Lat., "This greatest"), which insisted that missionaries receive a better spiritual and theological preparation, and that missionary bishops form a native clergy as quickly as possible and never place the interests of their own native countries ahead of the pastoral needs of their people (November 30, 1919).

Pacem, Dei munus pulcherrimum (Lat., "Peace, the most beautiful work of God"), which pleaded for international reconciliation following the First World War (May 23, 1920).

Pius XI (1922–39):

Ubi arcano Dei consilio (Lat., "Where [is] the hidden plan of God"), his first encyclical, which promoted Catholic Action, or the participation of the laity in the apostolate of the hierarchy (December 23, 1922).

Quas primas (Lat., "Those first things"), written on the occasion of the establishment of the feast of Christ the King, to counteract atheism and secularism (December 11, 1925).

Rerum Ecclesiae (Lat., "Of matters of the Church"), which developed the themes in Benedict XV's encyclical *Maximum illud* (1919) on the missions (February 28, 1926).

Mortalium animos (Lat., "The souls of mortals"), which offered a negative assessment of the nascent ecumenical movement, forbade any Catholic involvement in ecumenical conferences, and insisted that Catholicism not be considered on par with other religions (January 6, 1928).

Rerum Orientalium (Lat., "Of matters of the Oriental [Churches]"), which called for a greater understanding of Eastern churches and promoted Oriental studies (September 8, 1928).

Casti connubii (Lat., "Of pure marriage"), which affirmed the Church's doctrine that marriage is chaste, monogamous, and faithful and which, in response to the less restrictive approach of the Anglican Lambeth Conference of 1930, strongly condemned contraception. However, the encyclical also introduced, as the secondary end or purpose of marriage (after procreation), the mutual help of the spouses (December 31, 1930).

Quadragesimo anno (Lat., "After forty years"), which commemorated the fortieth anniversary of Leo XIII's *Rerum novarum* (1891). The pope criticized both the excessive individualism of capitalism and the deadening collectivism of socialism, insisted on the social responsibilities that go hand in hand with the right of private property, and introduced the principle of subsidiarity, whereby nothing is to be done by a higher agency (for example, the government) that can be done as well, if not better, by a lower agency (May 15, 1931).

Non abbiamo bisogno (It., "We have no need"), which condemned Italian Fascism and promoted Catholic Action in Italy, a lay movement of cooperation with the hierarchy (June 29, 1931).

Ad Catholici sacerdotii (Lat., "Concerning the Catholic priesthood"), a restatement of traditional teachings of the Church on the priesthood (December 20, 1935).

Vigilanti cura (Lat., "Vigilant care"), written to the bishops of the United States, the first papal encyclical wholly devoted to motion pictures (June 29, 1936).

Mit brennender Sorge (Ger., "With searing anxiety"), which denounced the violations of the concordat between the Holy See and the German Third Reich and which condemned Nazism as fundamentally racist and anti-Christian. The encyclical was smuggled into Germany and read from every Catholic pulpit in the country (March 14, 1937).

Divini Redemptoris (Lat., "Of the Divine Redeemer"), which condemned Communism as atheistic (March 19, 1937).

Pius XII (1939–58):

Summi pontificatus (Lat., "Of the supreme pontificate"), his first encyclical, issued on the threshold of the Second World War, which presented a Christian vision of a harmonious society (October 20, 1939).

Mystici Corporis Christi (Lat., "Of the Mystical Body of Christ"), which not only reaffirmed the institutional hierarchical structure of the Church but also insisted on its interior and charismatic dimension. Real membership belongs to those who have been baptized, profess the true faith, and are in union with the pope. Therefore, the Church is identical with the Catholic Church, a position later modified by the Second Vatican

Council's Dogmatic Constitution on the Church and Decree on Ecumenism in 1964 (June 29, 1943).

Divino afflante Spiritu (Lat., "Inspired by the divine Spirit"), which commemorated the fiftieth anniversary of Leo XIII's *Providentissimus Deus* and promoted the historical-critical study of Sacred Scripture among Catholic biblical scholars, directing them to determine the literal sense of the Bible, that is, "what the writer intended to express." The various directives in this encyclical were incorporated into the Second Vatican Council's Dogmatic Constitution on Divine Revelation in 1965 (September 30, 1943).

Deiparae Virginis Mariae (Lat., "Of Mary the Virgin Mother of God"), which raised the possibility of defining the dogma of the Assumption of Mary into heaven, a dogma that was later defined in 1950 (May 1, 1946).

Mediator Dei (Lat., "Mediator of God"), which encouraged full participation of the laity in the Eucharist and established a pastoral and theological basis for reforming the liturgy. It was the first papal encyclical devoted entirely to the topic of worship (November 20, 1947).

Humani generis (Lat., "Of the human race"), which attempted to halt new theological and pastoral trends (particularly among French theologians writing on the relationship between nature and grace, original sin, ecumenism, and liturgical renewal), to expose errors in contemporary philosophy and science (existentialism, historicism, evolutionism), and again to propose Thomism as the true Christian philosophy. The encyclical is also important for the claims it made for the teaching authority of papal encyclicals, insisting that when the pope takes a stand on a disputed point, it is no longer a subject for discussion among theologians. This latter statement was proposed for inclusion in the Second Vatican Council's Dogmatic Constitution on the Church, but the council fathers rejected it (August 12, 1950).

Evangelii praecones (Lat., "Proclaimers of the gospel"), on the promotion of the missionary work of the Church, with special emphasis on the need to implant the gospel in every culture (June 2, 1951).

Sempiternus Rex Christus (Lat., "Christ the eternal King"), which commemorated the fifteen-hundredth anniversary of the Council of Chalcedon, which taught that in Jesus Christ there are two natures, human and divine, hypostatically united in one divine Person (September 8, 1951).

Fulgens corona (Lat., "Shining crown"), which proclaimed a Marian Year to commemorate the one-hundredth anniversary of the definition of the dogma of the Immaculate Conception (September 8, 1953).

Sacra virginitas (Lat., "Holy virginity"), on the Christian vocation to consecrated virginity (March 25, 1954).

Ad Caeli Reginam (Lat., "To the Queen of Heaven"), which proclaimed the queenship of Mary (October 11, 1954).

Musicae sacrae" (Lat., "Of sacred music"), which contains directives on the uses of music in the liturgy (December 25, 1955).

Haurietis aquas (Lat., "You draw waters"), on the theological foundation for devotion to the Sacred Heart of Jesus (May 15, 1956).

Fidei donum (Lat., "Gift of faith"), on the current state of Catholic missions, especially in Africa, and the need to adapt to native cultures (April 21, 1957).

Miranda prorsus (Lat., "Wholly to be wondered at"), which was concerned with radio, television, and motion pictures and with the pastoral problems posed by the modern communications media (September 8, 1957).

John XXIII (1958–63):

Ad Petri Cathedram (Lat., "To the Chair of Peter"), the pope's first encyclical, which treated the themes of truth, unity, and peace and greeted non-Catholics as "separated brethren" (June 29, 1959).

Sacerdotii Nostri primordia (Lat., "The foundation of Our priesthood"), on the priestly example of St. John Vianney (August 1, 1959).

Grata recordatio (Lat., "Grateful memory"), on the Rosary as an effective prayer for the Church, the missions, and world justice and peace (September 26, 1959).

Princeps Pastor (Lat., "Chief Pastor"), on the missions, the need for native clergy, and the importance of lay participation (November 28, 1959).

Mater et magistra (Lat., "Mother and teacher"), released on the seventieth anniversary of Leo XIII's *Rerum novarum* (1891), an update on Catholic social teaching on property, the rights of workers, and the obligations of government. It also struck a balance between the principles of subsidiarity, namely, that nothing should be done by a higher agency that can be done as well, if not better, by a lower agency, and socialization, namely, "the growing interdependence of citizens in society" requiring higher agencies, especially governmental, to meet needs that otherwise could not be met by lower or voluntary agencies (May 15, 1961).

Aeterna Dei sapientia (Lat., "The wisdom of the Eternal God"), on the see of Peter as the center of Christian unity, written on the fifteenth centenary of the death of Pope Leo the Great (November 11, 1961).

Paenitentiam agere (Lat., "To do penance"), on the need for the practice of interior and exterior penance (July 1, 1962).

Pacem in terris (Lat., "Peace on earth"), an encyclical published less than two months before the pope's death, which insisted that the recognition of human rights and responsibilities is the foundation of world peace (April 11, 1963).

Paul VI (1963–78):

Ecclesiam Suam (Lat., "His Church"), the pope's first encyclical, which called upon the Church to be ready to correct its own defects and to enter into dialogue with fellow Catholics, with other Christians, with non-Christians, and with all of humanity (August 6, 1964).

Mense maio (Lat., "The month of May"), on prayers during May for the preservation of peace (April 29, 1965).

Mysterium fidei (Lat., "Mystery of faith"), which was written to counter erroneous opinions and practices regarding the Eucharist and to reaffirm the traditional doctrine of transubstantiation, namely, that through the priest's words of consecration at Mass the bread and the wine become fully and without remainder the very Body and Blood of Jesus Christ (September 3, 1965).

Christi Matri (Lat., "Of the Mother of Christ"), on prayers for peace during October (September 15, 1966).

Populorum progressio (Lat., "On the progress of peoples"), which highlighted and deplored the gap between rich and poor nations and which reminded readers that the goods of the earth are intended by God for everyone. The "new name for peace," the pope said, "is development" (March 26, 1967).

Sacerdotalis caelibatus (Lat., "Priestly celibacy"), reaffirming the tradition of obligatory celibacy for Roman Catholic priests (June 24, 1967).

Humanae vitae (Lat., "Of human life"), which declared that every act of sexual intercourse within marriage must be open to the transmission of life. In other words, there can be no artificial means of contraception. The encyclical created a storm of protest all over the world, but especially in North America and Europe. So shaken was Paul VI by the reaction that he vowed never again to publish an encyclical, and he did not (July 25, 1968).

John Paul II (1978–):

Redemptor hominis (Lat., "Redeemer of humanity"), the pope's first encyclical, which emphasized the dignity and worth of every human person, deplored the "exploitation of the earth" and the destruction of the environment, and condemned consumerism, that is, the accumulation and misuse of goods by privileged social classes and rich countries "to an excessive degree." It also condemned the arms race, especially for diverting essential resources from the poor, and the violation of human rights around the globe (March 4, 1979).

Dives in misericordia (Lat., "Rich in mercy"), on the mercy of God (November 30, 1980).

Laborem exercens (Lat., "On doing work"), which viewed human work as a form of collaboration in the creative work of God and, therefore, of infinite dignity. It insisted on the priority of work over capital and condemned what the pope called a "rigid" capitalism that exaggerates the rights of private ownership over the common good and the common use of goods (September 14, 1981). The encyclical was originally intended for publication on May 15, to commemorate the ninetieth anniversary of Leo XIII's *Rerum novarum,* but the attempt on the pope's life in St. Peter's Square the previous spring delayed its publication.

Slavorum Apostoli (Lat., "Apostles of the Slavs"), which honored Sts. Cyril and Methodius as copatrons of Europe alongside St. Benedict of Nursia, who had been proclaimed patron of Europe by Paul VI (June 2, 1985).

Dominum et vivificantem (Lat., "And the lifegiving Lord"), on the Holy Spirit in the life of the Church and the world (May 18, 1986).

Redemptoris Mater (Lat., "Mother of the Redeemer"), on the role of Mary in the mystery of Christ and her active presence in the life of the Church (March 25, 1987).

Sollicitudo rei socialis (Lat., "Solicitude for social concerns," also known as "On the Social Concern of the Church"), which commemorated the twentieth anniversary of Paul VI's *Populorum progressio.* It emphasized the obligations of rich and developed nations toward poor and undeveloped countries and the "preferential option for the poor" as a guideline of moral action. The goods of the earth, the pope insisted, are destined for all (December 30, 1987).

Redemptoris missio (Lat., "Mission of the Redeemer"), on the abiding missionary responsibility of the Church (January 22, 1991).

Centesimus annus (Lat., "The hundredth year"), written to mark the centenary of Leo XIII's *Rerum novarum*. At the center of the Church's social message, the pope declared, is the dignity of every human person—a point he had made already in his first encyclical, *Redemptor hominis,* in 1979. He reaffirmed the Church's "preferential option for the poor" and referred positively to democratic systems for ensuring the participation of citizens in a nation's political life (May 1, 1991).

Veritatis splendor (Lat., "The splendor of truth"), which was critical of theological dissent in the public media, of moral relativism, and of a method of moral theology known as proportionalism (August 6, 1993).

Evangelium vitae (Lat., "The gospel of life"), which strongly condemned contraception, euthanasia, and abortion in language similar to that employed in infallible teaching. Significantly, the pope also condemned capital punishment, insisting that there are, for all practical purposes, no sufficient reasons ever to justify it (March 25, 1995).

Ut unum sint (Lat., "That [all] may be one"), which acknowledged that, while the Petrine office belongs to the essential structure of the Church, the manner in which the papal office is exercised is always subject to criticism and improvement. The pope invited his readers, especially those in the other Christian churches, to enter into dialogue with him about the manner in which his office is exercised and to recommend ways in which its exercise might conform more faithfully to the gospel (May 25, 1995).

LIST OF ANTIPOPES

If an antipope shares the same name and number as a legitimate pope, his number is given in parentheses.

St. Hippolytus (217–35)
Novatian (251–58)
Felix II (355–65)
Ursinus (366–67)
Eulalius (418–19)
Lawrence (498–99, 501–6)
Dioscorus (530)
Paschal (687)
Theodore (687)
Constantine (767–68)
Philip (768)
John (844)
Anastasius Bibliothecarius (855)
Christopher (903–4)
Boniface VII (974, 984–85)
John XVI (997–98)
Gregory (VI) (1012)
Benedict X (1058–59)
Honorius (II) (1061–64)
Clement (III) (1080, 1084–1100)
Theodoric (1100–1101)
Albert (1101)
Sylvester IV (1105–11)
Gregory (VIII) (1118–21)
Celestine (II) (1124)
Anacletus II (1130–38)
Victor IV* (1138)
Victor IV (1159–64)
Paschal III (1164–68)
Callistus (III) (1168–78)

Innocent (III) (1179–80)
Nicholas (V) (1328–30)
Clement (VII) (1378–94)
Benedict (XIII) (1394–1417)
Alexander V (1409–10)
John (XXIII) (1410–15)
Clement (VIII) (1423–29)
Benedict (XIV) (1425–?)
Felix V (1439–49)

---

* Note that there are two Victor IVs among the antipopes. The second Victor IV took no note of the first one because he was "in office" less than two months.

GLOSSARY

For a more complete list of relevant ecclesiastical terms and definitions, consult *The HarperCollins Encyclopedia of Catholicism* (HarperCollins, 1995), Richard P. McBrien, general editor.

abdication, the renunciation of an ecclesiastical office. The term was commonly used at a time when the prevailing model of ecclesiastical office, including the papacy, was monarchical. The current term in canon law is resignation.

Acacianism, the fifth-century split between Rome (the center of the Western Church) and Constantinople (the center of the Eastern Church) over a theological document, the Decree of Union, known as the *Henoticon* (482), drawn up by Acacius, patriarch of Constantinople, and Peter Mongus, patriarch of Alexandria, in order to achieve union between Orthodox Catholics and Monophysites. Rome felt that the document did not do justice to the teaching of the Council of Chalcedon (451), because it did not mention the two natures of Christ. The Acacian Schism began in 484 when Pope Felix III (II) excommunicated Acacius for recognizing Peter Mongus as patriarch of Alexandria. The schism continued until 519, when it was finally resolved by the emperor Justinian.

Action Française, a nationalistic, monarchistic, and anti-Semitic French political movement begun in the late nineteenth century that emphasized the importance of Catholicism in national culture. It was supported by Pius X (1903–14), but condemned by Pius XI in 1926. Nevertheless, it continued to influence French politics via the pro-German Vichy government during the Second World War.

ad limina visits (Lat., *ad*, "to"; *limina*, "thresholds"), the visit each diocesan bishop is regularly required to make to Rome ("to the thresholds [of the tombs of the Apostles, Peter and Paul]") in order to meet with the pope and curial officials to report on the status of his diocese. Such visits became common beginning with the pontificate of Benedict VII (974–83).

Adoptionism, a general term for theological views that look upon Jesus Christ as the purely human, "adopted" son of God. More specifically, it applies to an eighth-century view, widely circulated in Spain and condemned by Hadrian I as well as the Council of Frankfurt in 794, that there is a dual sonship in Christ, one natural and the other adopted.

aggiornamento (It., "bringing up to date"), a term that became synonymous with Pope John XXIII's program of church renewal and reform leading up to and including the Second Vatican Council (1962–65).

Albigensianism, a dualist heresy that viewed all reality as an eternal battle between the world of the spirit created by the infinitely good God and the world of the flesh created by the infinitely evil Satan. Albigensianism flourished in southern France and northern Italy from the mid-twelfth to the fourteenth century. Its followers championed an austere asceticism, rejecting all sexual activity and the eating of meat, eggs, and milk and practicing rigorous fasts. They regarded themselves as holier than the Church and rejected its authority. The Cistercians and Dominicans preached against it, but without success. It was eventually overcome by the Albigensian Crusade (1209–19) and the Inquisition.

allocution, papal, an address given by the pope to a department of the Roman Curia or to some other group of persons.

Americanism, an ill-defined and widely misunderstood movement associated with the efforts to adapt Catholicism to American culture. It was condemned by Leo XIII in *Testem benevolentiae* (Lat., "Witness of benevolence"; 1899). Cardinal James Gibbons of Baltimore (d. 1921), to whom the papal letter was addressed, denied that such a heresy ever existed in the United States.

annates, taxes on a benefice's first year of income. By the fourteenth century annates paid to the papal treasury were common and became a source of great tension between the papacy and various local churches and nations.

Annuario Pontificio (It., "papal yearbook"), official annual publication by the Vatican of a complete list of members of the hierarchy, offices and officials of the Roman Curia, and names of dioceses and religious institutes with pertinent statistics. It also contains a list of the popes with the dates of their pontificates.

antipope, an individual whose claim to the papacy has been rejected by the Church as invalid. Because the rules for papal elections have changed over the course of history and in some cases have been bypassed, it is not always easy to distinguish between valid and invalid claimants to the papal office. There have been thirty-nine antipopes. The first antipope was St. Hippolytus (217–35); the last was Felix V (1439–49).

Apollinarianism, the fourth-century heresy, named after Apollinarius of Laodicea, that denied the existence of a rational soul in Jesus Christ. The heresy was condemned by the Council of Constantinople in 381.

Apostolicae curae (Lat., "Of Apostolic concern"), the encyclical of Leo XIII in 1896 in which Anglican orders were declared invalid because the ordinal of Edward VI (1550) omitted several necessary elements of the rite and because the ritual did not include the intention of conferring the power to offer sacrifice.

apostolic constitution, a papal document that is solemn in form and legal in content and ordinarily deals with matters of faith, doctrine, or discipline that are of import for the universal Church or for a particular portion thereof. It may be signed by the pope himself or by a curial official.

apostolic delegate, a cleric or layperson who acts as an emissary of the pope to the church in a particular area or country with whom the Holy See does not have formal diplomatic relations.

Apostolic See. *See* Holy See.

Arianism, a fourth-century heresy that denied the divinity of Jesus Christ, regarding him as only the greatest of creatures. It was condemned by the Council of Nicaea in 325, but it continued to divide the empire throughout most of the remainder of the century as it went in and out of favor with successive emperors. The heresy was finally vanquished at the Council of Constantinople in 381, thanks in large part to the careful theological work of the Cappadocian Fathers: Basil the Great, Gregory of Nazianzus, and Gregory of Nyssa.

audience, papal, a visit or reception given by the pope to a person or a group of persons visiting the Holy See. General and public papal audiences are ordinarily held on Wednesdays in the Audience Hall on the south side of St. Peter's Basilica. Semiprivate or private audiences are held in the papal residence by arrangement of the Prefecture of the Pontifical Household. During the summer, audiences are held at the pope's summer residence at Castel Gandolfo, fifteen miles outside of Rome.

Avignon, a city and archdiocese in southeastern France that was the seat of the papacy from 1309 to 1377 (a period also described as the "Babylonian captivity" of the papacy) and also of rival popes during the Great Western Schism (1378–1417). This was not the only time that the papacy established its headquarters outside of Rome. Rome was often dangerous and popes had to settle temporarily in various cities throughout Italy, as well as in Avignon. Some popes, in fact, were forced to spend their entire pontificates outside of Rome because of unfavorable conditions in the city.

basilica (Gk., "king's hall"), a church of greater than average importance. There are four major basilicas in Rome: St. Peter's, St. John Lateran, St. Paul's Outside the Walls, and St. Mary Major. There are hundreds of minor basilicas around the world. The term originally designated an official building in the Roman Empire.

beatification, the second-to-last step in the official process of proclaiming an individual a saint. The person beatified is called "Blessed."

benefice, an income-producing ecclesiastical office. The Second Vatican Council and the 1983 Code of Canon Law urged the suppression of benefices.

bishops, college of, the body of bishops headed by the pope who are said to succeed the college of the apostles in teaching authority and in the pastoral governance of the Church.

brief, papal (or apostolic), a papal letter, less formal than a bull, signed for the pope by a secretary and impressed with the seal of the papal ring, also known as the Fisherman's Ring.

bull, papal (Lat., *bulla,* "lead seal"), since the thirteenth century, the common term for an important papal document stamped with a lead seal embossed with the facial imprints of the Apostles Peter and Paul on one side and the name of the pope in block letters on the other. Bulls may be used, for example, to confer titles on bishops and cardinals, to promulgate canonizations of saints, or to proclaim Holy Years.

Byzantine, pertaining to Byzantium, the original name of the city of Constantinople (now Istanbul). The adjective applies to the Byzantine Empire once centered in Constantinople (but also extending to parts of Italy) and to the Byzantine rite (also known as the Greek rite), which originated in the Orthodox patriarchate of Constantinople.

Caesaro-papism, a political system in which the temporal ruler has sovereignty over the Church as well as the state. It reached its zenith under the emperor Justinian (527–65) and remained a governing principle of Byzantine rulers for a millennium. It contributed to tensions between Rome and Constantinople that eventually led to the East-West Schism of 1054.

Camerlengo (It., "chamberlain"), a title held by a cardinal who holds an office with specific financial duties. There are the Camerlengo of the Holy Roman Church and the Camerlengo of the College of Cardinals. The former administers the property and finances of the Holy See during a vacancy, and the latter oversees the financial assets of the College of Cardinals and records the business of its official meetings, or consistories, called by the pope and conducted in his presence.

canonization, the process by which an individual is raised to sainthood in the Catholic Church. Since the word "canon" is derived from a Greek word meaning "rule" or "list," canonization is literally the process of adding someone to the official "list" of saints. The first papal canonization was in 993 by John XV. In 1234 Pope Gregory IX decreed that only the pope can canonize a saint. Before that, saints were proclaimed locally and their cults developed naturally among the people themselves.

cardinal (Lat., *cardo,* "hinge"), the title given to a member of the College of Cardinals, all of whom are appointed directly by the pope and who serve as his close advisers and as papal electors. The title was originally given to members of the Roman clergy who administered certain key ("hinge") churches in Rome. Cardinals who had no pastoral responsibilities in the city of Rome were made titular pastors of these churches. Thus, one is named a cardinal "in the title of" a particular church. There are four categories of cardinals: cardinal-deacons, who originally had care of the poor in the seven districts of Rome but who are now titular bishops assigned to full-time service in the Roman Curia; cardinal-priests, who served as pastors of the key parishes of Rome but who now are bishops of dioceses outside of Rome; cardinal-bishops, who were heads of the neighboring (or suburbicarian) dioceses around Rome but who are now engaged in full-time service in the Roman Curia; and cardinal-patriarchs, who are heads of sees of apostolic origin with ancient liturgies. In 1962 Pope John XXIII decreed that all cardinals would also have to be bishops.

cardinal-nephew, an informal title for a nephew or other close relative of a pope who served as his closest collaborator and adviser, sometimes as his official or unofficial secretary of state. The arrangement existed from the time of Paul III (1534–49) until the late seventeenth century, when Innocent XII (1691–1700) decreed that the pope should never grant estates, offices, or revenues to relatives, that only one relative should be eligible for appointment to the College of Cardinals, assuming he is qualified, and that his income should have a modest ceiling.

Cardinals, College of, the body of cardinals responsible for (since 1059) electing a new pope (although voting rights are restricted to those cardinals under the age of eighty) and assisting the pope in the governance of the universal Church. The elected dean of the college by tradition holds title to the diocese of Ostia, the seventh of the neighboring dioceses of Rome, in addition to his own suburbicarian see. The dean ordains to the episcopate the person elected pope if he is not already a bishop. The first cardinal-deacon announces the name of the new pope.

Carolingian reform, reforms of the Church and of society carried out by the emperor Charlemagne (d. 814) and his successors involving the renewal of monastic life, the replacement of the Gallican liturgy with the Roman liturgy, the establishment of new diocesan and provincial structures, and provision for the education of clergy.

Castel Gandolfo, papal summer residence about fifteen miles southeast of Rome, on the shore of Lake Albano. It is also the site of the Vatican Observatory. The entire estate is under the extraterritorial rights of Vatican City State.

celibacy, clerical, the canonically enforced, lifetime renunciation of marriage by ordained priests in the Roman, or Latin, rite. The discipline of obligatory celibacy had a spotty history until the pontificate of Gregory VII (1073–85), who imposed a more uni form observance in the West. In the Eastern churches, priests are allowed to marry before ordination, but not after. Bishops may not be married.

Chalcedon, Council of, the ecumenical council of 451 that definitively taught that in Jesus Christ there is only one divine Person but two natures, one divine and one human.

Chinese rites controversy, a bitter conflict between the Jesuits and the Dominicans in the seventeenth and eighteenth centuries over the legitimacy of various accommodations of Catholic liturgy and devotional practices to Chinese culture. At the center of the controversy were the methods of Matteo Ricci (1552–1610), a Jesuit missionary, who was the principal advocate of ritual adaptation. The use of Chinese rites was prohibited by Benedict XIV in 1742, but the prohibition was lifted by Pius in 1939, long after China was "lost" to Catholicism.

Cluny, French Benedictine monastery founded near Mâcon in Burgundy in 909 and the center of monastic reform during the tenth and eleventh centuries. By the mid-twelfth century there were over one thousand Cluniac monasteries. It was eventually eclipsed by new orders and was finally suppressed by the French Revolution in 1790.

Code of Canon Law, a codification of canons, or laws, of the Roman Catholic Church, originally promulgated by Benedict XV in 1917 and promulgated in revised form by John Paul II in 1983. A Code of Canons of the Eastern Churches was promulgated by John Paul II in 1990.

College of Cardinals. *See* Cardinals, College of.

collegiality, a doctrine that asserts that the worldwide episcopate, together with the pope, the Bishop of Rome, has supreme teaching and pastoral authority over the universal Church. The bishops do not simply help the pope govern the Church; they govern it in collaboration with him, although he is the head, or president, of the college of bishops, with his own distinctive authority within the college and over the universal Church.

conciliarism, a view emanating from canonists of the twelfth and thirteenth centuries according to which a general, or ecumenical, council is regarded as the highest ecclesiastical authority, superior even to the pope. Conciliarism was officially taught by the Council of Constance in 1415 and reached its high point at the Council of Basel (1431–49).

conclave (Lat., *cum clavis,* "with the key"), the meeting of cardinals to elect a new pope. It also refers to the separate, locked portion of the Vatican where the election occurs. The conclave originated in 1271 in Viterbo when local authorities, wearied by a delay of two years and nine months in electing a new pope, locked up the cardinals in confined quarters until they succeeded in choosing a new pope.

concordat, a formal agreement between the Holy See and a political entity. The most famous example in recent times is the Lateran Accords of 1929, guaranteeing the Holy See's sovereign and independent rights over Vatican City State.

congregation, a department of the Roman Curia. There are nine such congregations in the Curia, including, for example, the Congregation for the Doctrine of the Faith, the Congregation for Bishops, and the Congregation for the Evangelization of Peoples.

consistory (Lat., *consistere,* "to stand together"), a formal meeting of cardinals convoked and presided over by the pope. The term originated in Roman times to designate meetings with the emperor in the antechamber of the imperial palace.

Constance, Council of (1414–18), sixteenth ecumenical council of the Church, which ended the Great Western Schism (1378–1417) by deposing or securing the resignation of three simultaneous claimants to the papal office and then electing Martin V. The council was significant also for including lower clergy, religious, theologians, and laity among its active participants. It decreed that councils should be held at regular intervals and declared that a general council receives its authority directly from Christ, without papal approval.

Constantine, Edict of (313), sometimes called the Edict of Milan, a document from Constantine the Great granting toleration to all religions, including Christianity. By this act, all confiscated properties were returned to the Church, and the Church was recognized as a legal entity, capable of owning and disposing of property.

Constantinople, the traditional seat of Eastern Christianity. The emperor Constantine transferred the capital of the Roman Empire from Rome to Constantinople in 330, building the new city on the site of the Greek city of Byzantium. It remained the capital of the Eastern, or Byzantine, empire until 1453, when it fell to the Turks. The Council of Chalcedon in 451 granted Constantinople patriarchal status equivalent to Rome because both were imperial cities. Four ecumenical councils have been held in Constantinople, in 381, 553, 680–81, and 869–70.

constitution, papal (or apostolic), a document in which a pope enacts or promulgates a law for the universal Church. (There are also constitutions, both dogmatic and pastoral, issued by an ecumenical council.)

coronation, papal, the crowning of a new pope with the tiara, that is, a formal head covering (which developed eventually into a triple crown), some days after his election. The bishops of Rome probably began wearing a tiara in the third century. The coronation ceremony was eventually modeled after that of secular rulers. Between the sixth and eighth centuries, that is, after the wars against the Goths (535–53), a newly elected pope could not be crowned without the emperor's approval. And until he was crowned, he was not regarded as pope. That arrangement ended after the pontificate of Gregory III (731–41), the last pope to seek approval for his consecration and coronation from the Byzantine emperor. However, in 824 the Carolingian emperor, Louis the Pious, imposed a Roman constitution in which, in addition to restoring the laity's role in papal elections, required that a newly elected pope swear an oath of allegiance to the emperor, in the presence of his representative, before being consecrated and crowned. This arrangement was more or less enforced until the tenth century, when the aristocratic families of Rome began to exercise a decisive, although also temporary, control over papal elections. Nicholas II (1058–61) decreed that imperial confirmation was no longer necessary. Since Paul VI (1963–78), who sold his tiara, and John Paul II (1978–), who rejected the coronation rite, popes are no longer crowned, but simply "inaugurated" into their Petrine ministry by being vested with the pallium (the woolen vestment worn around the neck of an archbishop as a sign of pastoral authority).

council, official assembly of church leaders. Ecumenical, or general, councils are assemblies drawn from the entire Church and exercise supreme teaching and pastoral authority in union with the Bishop of Rome. There are, and have been, many other kinds of councils in the Church: local, provincial, regional, and national (plenary).

Counter-Reformation/Catholic Reformation, the renewal and reform of the Catholic Church undertaken after the outbreak of the Protestant Reformation in the early sixteenth century. Among its elements were the Council of Trent (1545–63), the founding of new religious orders such as the Jesuits (1540), and the establishment of seminaries for the education and training of future priests. Among its less pleasing elements were the Inquisition and the Index of Forbidden Books.

Crusades, a series of wars fought initially to recover or to defend Christian territory and holy sites in the Holy Land (Palestine), Spain, and Sicily. The First Crusade was called by Urban II in 1095, and the Fifth Crusade ended in 1221. Many of the medieval popes were almost obsessed with the need to launch crusades and push back the Turks and other Muslims from one place or another, including Italy itself. Unfortunately, the Crusades were transformed into economic and political enterprises and did much to widen the rift between the Eastern and Western Churches.

curia, the administrative network that assists the pope or any bishop in the governance of his diocese or, in the case of the pope, of the universal Church. *See also* Roman Curia.

decretal, a papal letter issued in response to a question or to resolve a matter of controversy. Papal decretals were first issued in the fourth century and were an important source of canon law in the Middle Ages.

dicastery (Gr., *dikastēs,* "judge," "law court"), generic term for a department or agency of church government, especially in the Roman Curia.

Dictatus papae (Lat., "pronouncement of the pope"), a collected series of statements, dated March 1075 and associated with Gregory VII, describing a papacy with vast powers in both the religious and secular spheres. They assert, for example, that the pope may depose emperors and that he himself can be judged by no one else (except, presumably, God).

diocese, a Christian community within a given geographical territory under the pastoral care of a bishop. It is also known as a see. A larger diocese is known as an archdiocese and its bishop as an archbishop.

Docetism (Gk., *dokein,* "to seem"), a second-century heresy that held that Jesus Christ only seemed to have a human body. It had much in common with Gnosticism, a contemporary heresy that also denied the full humanity of Christ.

Doctor of the Church, a canonized saint officially recognized by the pope (or an ecumenical council) as an eminent teacher of the faith, for example, Sts. Augustine of Hippo, Athanasius, Basil the Great, Thomas Aquinas, Bonaventure, John of the Cross, Teresa of Ávila, and Catherine of Siena.

doctrine, an official teaching of the Church, though not necessarily definitive, or infallible.

dogma (Gk., "what seems right"), a definitive, or infallible, teaching of the Church. The promulgation of a dogma is the prerogative of the pope acting as earthly head of the Church or of an ecumenical council in union with the pope.

Donation of Constantine, the emperor Constantine's alleged bequest to Pope Sylvester I (314–35) of temporal domain over Italy and other Western regions. It enjoyed widespread credibility for centuries and was used as the basis of various claims by the Church to temporal sovereignty, but it came to be regarded as inauthentic in the mid-1400s.

Donation of Pepin. *See* Papal States.

Donatism, a North African schismatic movement of the fourth and fifth centuries tending to moral rigorism. The schism arose from a dispute over the election of Caecilian as bishop of Carthage in 311. The Donatists (or followers of Donatus) argued that

Caecilian's consecrator had been a *traditor*, i.e., one who had "handed over" the Scriptures during the time of the Diocletian persecution (303–12). The schism lingered until the Muslim conquest of North Africa in the seventh century.

Eastern churches, those Christian churches of the Eastern rite whose origins were in the eastern half of the Roman Empire or beyond the empire's eastern frontiers. From the fifth century various controversies led to the separation of various Eastern churches from the Western, or Latin-rite, Church, centered in Rome.

East-West Schism, the disruption of the bonds of ecclesiastical communion between Rome and Constantinople beginning already with the Christological controversies of the fifth century but coming to a climax in 1054 with the mutual excommunications by the patriarch of Constantinople, Michael Cerularius, and the Bishop of Rome, Leo IX. The schism was sealed by the Crusades (1095–1221) and the Orthodox rejection of the Decree of Union of the Council of Florence in 1439.

ecumenical council, the assembly of all the world's bishops, under the presidency of the Bishop of Rome, and the highest earthly authority in the Church.

election, papal. *See* papal election.

Eminence, the title of honor given to a cardinal, for the first time by Pope Urban VIII in 1630.

encyclical, a formal pastoral letter (lit., a circular letter) written by, or under the authority of, the pope concerning moral, doctrinal, or disciplinary issues and addressed to the universal Church (and now to the whole human community). They were first employed by Benedict XIV in 1740 and have become a standard means of ordinary papal teaching in modern times.

encyclicals, social, papal letters circulated to the whole world concerning matters of social justice, human rights, and peace. The first major social encyclical was Leo XIII's *Rerum novarum* in 1891. The centenary of its issuance was marked by John Paul II's *Centesimus annus* in 1991.

Enlightenment, the philosophical, political, and scientific movement of eighteenth-century Europe in which the ideas of great seventeenth-century thinkers were carried forward by such figures as Rousseau, Hume, and Kant. Enlightenment thinkers rejected tradition and authority, especially religious authority, and relied instead on human reason. The Church and its popes reacted strongly against the movement, but came to adopt a more sympathetic attitude toward its many valid aspects at the Second Vatican Council (1962–65).

Ephesus, Council of (431), the third ecumenical council of the Church, which defined (against the Nestorians) that in Christ there is only one divine Person, and that Mary is, therefore, the Mother of God, not only the mother of Jesus.

episcopate, both the office of bishop and the collective body of bishops.

ex cathedra (Lat., "from the chair"), the highest level of papal teaching; an infallible teaching, i.e., one immune from error. There are three conditions for an *ex cathedra* statement: (1) it must concern a matter of faith and morals; (2) the pope must be speaking as earthly head of the Church; and (3) he must have the clear intention of binding the whole Church.

excommunication, the penalty in canon law that excludes a member of the Church from full participation in its sacramental and ministerial life. It can be imposed automatically, as in the case of a bishop who ordains a bishop without papal approval, or it can be imposed after a canonical proceeding, as in the case of a theologian whose writings are deemed heretical.

Exsurge Domine (Lat., "Rise up, Lord"), the papal bull of Leo X, June 15, 1520, that condemned Martin Luther as a heretic. He was excommunicated the following year.

False Decretals, a series of papal letters and canonical documents that were forged around 850 in France and falsely attributed to St. Isidore of Seville (d. 636). They were used by Gregory VII (1073–85) and his canonists to support their arguments that the pope and the other bishops were independent of lay control.

Febronianism, an eighteenth-century movement in Germany that subordinated the Church to national interests. Originated by an auxiliary bishop of Trier who wrote under the pen name of Justinus Febronius, it argued, among other things, that papal pronouncements are binding only if they receive episcopal consent. Pius VI condemned this view in 1778. The bishop recanted, but the movement continued into the nineteenth century.

Filioque (Lat., "and of the Son"), a Latin term added to the Nicene-Constantinopolitan Creed in the West in the ninth century that created serious conflict, and continues to do so to this day, between Eastern and Western Churches. The East insists on the original version, "the Holy Spirit who proceeds from the Father," in order to preserve the Father's unique role within the Trinity as the source of divine life.

Fisherman's Ring, a signet ring engraved with the image of St. Peter fishing from a boat and encircled with the name of the current pope. The ring is not worn by the pope, but is used to seal papal briefs and other official documents. It is destroyed upon the death of each pope.

Florence, Council of (1438–45), an ecumenical council, begun in Ferrara and ended in Rome, that attempted to heal the breach between Eastern and Western Churches, but ultimately failed. The Decree of Union, accepting the *Filioque* (see above), was signed by some of the Greeks, but most changed their minds after the council and then Constantinople fell to the Turks in 1453, cutting short whatever progress toward union was achieved.

Gallicanism (Lat., *Gallia,* "Gaul," or modern-day France), a movement that claimed for the French Church an independence from papal intervention. It regarded a general council as superior to the pope and insisted that papal pronouncements are subject to subsequent episcopal approval. The movement was essentially dissolved with the French Revolution, although it was revived in some form after the restoration of the monarchy in the nineteenth century. The First Vatican Council (1869–70) directed a part of its teaching on papal infallibility against Gallicanism when it declared that infallible teachings are authoritative in themselves and not from the consent of the Church.

Gnosticism (Gk., *gnosis,* "knowledge"), the earliest of Christian heresies, which denied that the Word of God had taken on human flesh (the incarnation). Besides stressing the role of inner enlightenment or saving knowledge of God, available only to the few, it also denied the goodness of creation and the material order.

grand elector, a cardinal who plays a major role in the election of a new pope, functioning as a kind of campaign manager in a conclave, pointing out his candidate's virtues and qualities of leadership and successfully urging significant blocs of cardinal-electors from various countries and/or the Roman Curia to throw their support to his candidate.

Gregorian reform, the movement of church renewal beginning in the tenth century but linked most directly to its strongest exponent, Gregory VII (1073–85). It included the combating of simony, nepotism, clerical marriage, and lay investiture of church officials.

Henoticon, formula of union between Orthodox Catholics and Monophysites drawn up in 482 between Acacius, patriarch of Constantinople, and Peter Mongus, patriarch of Alexandria, at the instigation of the emperor Zeno. Pope Felix III (II) later excommunicated Acacius, thus provoking the Acacian Schism.

heresy, the knowing and obstinate denial of a defined dogma of the Church.

hierarchy (Gk., "rule by priests"), the ordered body of clergy (bishops, priests [presbyters], deacons) or, more usually, of bishops alone.

Holiness, His, a title since the fourteenth century restricted in the Catholic Church to the pope. For the first several centuries, it was used of all bishops.

Holy Father, a title of the pope, first used in English in the 1830s. The Latin is more expansive, *Beatissimus Pater* ("The Most Holy Father").

Holy Office, originally the Congregation of the Inquisition, established by Paul III in 1542. It became the Congregation for the Doctrine of the Faith in 1967 under Paul VI.

Holy Roman Empire, the European state founded by the German king Otto I in 962 as a successor to Charlemagne's empire. Its core consisted of the German principalities, Austria, Bohemia, and parts of Italy and the Netherlands. Emperors were elected by the more powerful princes and then were crowned by the pope in Rome, a practice discontinued in 1562. The empire was dissolved in 1806.

Holy See (Lat., *sancta sedes,* "holy chair"), a term originally related to the ceremony for installing the Bishop of Rome in his chair of authority, but now referring only to the Apostolic See, or the diocese of Rome, including especially its bishop, i.e., the pope, and the Roman Curia. The term also refers to the Catholic Church as a moral and juridical entity, including the spiritual and diplomatic authority exercised by the pope. It is not to be confused with Vatican City State, which is the political entity and territory in which the Holy See is located and which guarantees the Holy See's independence. The diplomatic relations that more than one hundred nations have with the Vatican are with the Holy See, not with Vatican City State.

Holy Year, a year of prayer, pilgrimages to Rome, and special spiritual benefits proclaimed by the pope at various intervals (originally every hundred years) and for special reasons of need or celebration. The first Holy Year was proclaimed by Boniface VIII in 1300.

iconoclasm, destruction of religious images ordered by the Byzantine emperors from emperor Leo III (717–41) to 843 when their use was restored by the empress Theodora. The controversy between iconoclasts and iconophiles—a replay of the Christological controversies of the fifth through seventh centuries—was bitter and intense, the former insisting that any representation of Christ constituted an assault on his divinity, while the latter insisted that, in keeping with the principle of the Incarnation, the divine is always capable of being embodied, or imaged, in the human or the material.

Index of Forbidden Books, list of books that Catholics were forbidden to read or to possess under pain of excommunication. Established in 1557 by Paul IV and later supervised by the Congregation on the Index founded by Pius V in 1571, and then by the Holy Office in 1917, the Index was abolished by Paul VI in 1966.

indulgences, the remission of temporal punishment for sins already forgiven, achieved through prayer or other good works. They became a source of great controversy just before and during the Protestant Reformation because the popes of that time in effect placed indulgences on sale in order to raise money for the building of the new St. Peter's Basilica. Martin Luther and others protested this, and the rest is history. In a reformulation of the theology and practice of indulgences in 1967, Paul VI tried to put them in their proper perspective—which means that they were reduced in importance for the spiritual lives of Catholics.

infallibility, a charism, or gift, of the Holy Spirit by which the Church is protected from error when it defines a matter of faith or morals to be held by the whole Church. The pope is infallible when he speaks as earthly head of the Church, on a matter of faith and morals, and with the clear intention of binding the whole Church. So, too, is an ecumenical council—under the same conditions.

Inquisition, a now defunct institution established in the Middle Ages for the eradication and punishment of heresy. Sometimes the punishment included torture and death. The Roman Inquisition established and maintained by the popes is to be distinguished from the even more infamous Spanish Inquisition, established by Ferdinand and Isabella in 1479. The latter was directed especially against converted Muslims and converted Jews who had secretly returned to the practice of their respective faiths. It was abolished by royal decree in 1834. The most famous victim of the Roman Inquisition was the Italian astronomer and mathematician Galileo (d. 1642), who was rehabilitated posthumously by John Paul II in 1992. The Roman Congregation of the Inquisition, along with the Holy Office, was renamed and folded into the Congregation for the Doctrine of the Faith by Paul VI in 1965.

Integralism, a nineteenth- and early-twentieth-century ultraconservative movement in France that opposed ecumenism, modern biblical studies, and historically based theology. The movement was supported and encouraged by Pius X (1903–14), but denounced by his successor, Benedict XV, in his first encyclical, *Ad beatissimi Apostolorum* (1914).

interdict, an ecclesiastical penalty that prohibits a person from ministerial participation in public worship and from reception of the sacraments and sacramentals of the Church. In the past, interdicts were applied to whole communities, cities, and entire regions.

investiture controversy. *See* lay investiture.

Jansenism, a seventeenth-century Catholic reform movement originating in the Low Countries and France but expanding into the territories of the Hapsburgs and Italy during the eighteenth century. It was pessimistic about human nature and free will and emphasized the need for rigid asceticism, which set it against the Jesuits, who took a more pastorally realistic approach to the moral life. It also opposed the centralizing tendencies of the Counter-Reformation, which set it against the hierarchy of the Church, and the absolutist tendencies of the French government, which set it against the temporal authorities as well. It was condemned by various popes, including Alexander VII (1656 and

1665) and Clement XI (1713). Jansenism disappeared in France after the death of a sympathetic archbishop of Paris in 1729, but it produced a schism in Holland in 1723 and survives today as a branch of the Old Catholic Church.

Joan, "Pope," subject of a medieval fable that was widely accepted in the thirteenth century and until the seventeenth, when a French Protestant, David Blondel (d. 1655), disproved the belief in a treatise published in Amsterdam in 1647 and 1657. It was thought that Pope Victor III (d. 1087) was succeeded by a woman who, having disguised her gender, had worked in the Curia and been named a cardinal. She is said to have been elected pope, but that her disguise was disclosed when she gave birth to a child while mounting her horse. In another version of the story, Pope Leo IV (d. 855) was succeeded by John Anglicus, who was in fact a woman but whose brilliant lectures in Rome and whose edifying life resulted in her unanimous election as pope. She is said to have served as pope for more than two years. Like the other putative female pope, this one also was exposed when, riding in procession from St. Peter's to the Lateran, she gave birth to a child in a narrow street between the Colosseum and the church of San Clemente. She died and was buried on the spot. The tradition developed that popes thereafter avoided that narrow street in processions. The problem with the story in both instances is that there is no place to fit a Pope Joan into papal history. The two popes she was alleged to have succeeded had other successors who functioned as popes and whose activities are clearly recorded in history.

Josephenism, an eighteenth-century effort of the Austrian emperors to subordinate the Church to national interests. The name is derived from the Holy Roman emperor Joseph II (d. 1790), who instituted a policy of state control over the Church. The policy was withdrawn in 1850.

Jubilee, Year of, a term used in Catholicism since 1300 in connection with, and as generally synonymous with, a Holy Year.

keys, power of the, a reference to Jesus' commissioning of Peter and the authority conferred upon him in Matthew 16:13–20.

Lateran Basilica and Palace, the cathedral church of the pope as Bishop of Rome and the highest-ranking Catholic church in the world. It is one of the four major basilicas in Rome. It was first built in the early fourth century on Monte Celio (Celian Hill), on a site formerly occupied by the palace of the Laterani, a noble Roman family. The property was donated to the Church by the emperor Constantine in ca. 312. The basilica and papal dwelling served as the official papal residence from the fourth century until the removal of the papacy to Avignon, France, in 1309. After being destroyed by earthquakes and fires, it was rebuilt and rededicated to St. John the Baptist in 905. Two more fires in the fourteenth century kept it in a state of disrepair until the late 1500s, when Clement VIII commissioned a baroque renovation. The façade dates to 1735.

Lateran councils, five ecumenical councils that were held in the Lateran Palace between 1123 and 1517. Lateran III (1179) decreed that a two-thirds majority is necessary for the election of a pope. Lateran IV (1215), the most important of the councils, mandated annual confession and Communion for all Catholics. Lateran V (1512–17) missed a crucial opportunity to promote church reform and avert the disruptions of the Protestant Reformation.

Lateran Treaty, agreement signed on February 11, 1929, between the Holy See and the Italian government settling the Roman Question. The Holy See was financially compensated for the loss of the Papal States, Vatican City State was established as an independent political entity within Italy, and Catholicism was declared the official religion of Italy. The concordat based on the treaty was renegotiated in 1985. Rome was no longer to be a sacred city; Catholicism was no longer to be the official religion of the state; religious instruction was no longer to be mandatory in the public schools; and priests were no longer to be salaried employees of the state.

laxism, a moral attitude, with origins in the seventeenth century, that attempts to find ways of circumventing Christian obligations and that always resolves the doubt in favor of exemption even when good reasons for the exemption are not present. Associated unfairly with the Jesuits by the Jansenists, laxism was condemned by Alexander VII in 1665 and 1666, and again in 1679 by Innocent XI.

lay investiture, a medieval practice whereby bishops and abbots were appointed to, and then installed ("invested") in, their offices by temporal rulers. During the ceremony the bishop or abbot would pay homage to the lay ruler and the lay ruler would give the ecclesiastic the crosier and ring as symbols of office. In 1075 Gregory VII issued a decree forbidding lay investiture. The decree was strongly opposed by the German emperor Henry IV, whom the pope thereupon excommunicated. A compromise was finally worked out at the Diet of Worms in 1122 between Pope Callistus II and Henry V. The practice of lay interference in ecclesiastical appointments continued, however, into the twentieth century when the Austro-Hungarian emperor submitted a veto of a papal candidate in the conclave of 1903. The veto was ignored, and thereafter such imperial vetoes were forbidden.

Leonine City, the walled-in section of Rome on the right bank of the Tiber River encompassing St. Peter's and much of Vatican Hill, erected by Pope Leo IV in 846 to protect papal Rome from future Saracen attacks.

Macedonianism, a fourth-century heresy, named after Bishop Macedonius of Constantinople, that denied the divinity of the Holy Spirit. It was condemned by the Council of Constantinople in 381.

magisterium, the teaching office and authority of the Church. It is exercised by the hierarchy, by theologians, and by ordinary members of the Church (parents, catechists, etc.). The term is most commonly applied, however, to the hierarchy.

martyrology, a list of feast days of saints with all applicable names for any give date. The martyrology gives some biographical data, such as place of birth, death, and burial.

Master of the Sacred Palace, the title given to the one who serves as the pope's personal theologian, traditionally a member of the Dominican order. The Master also serves as theologian to the Secretariat of State and other offices of the Roman Curia.

mendicants, also known as friars, religious with the privilege of begging (Lat., *mendicare*) in the dioceses where they have been established. Mendicant orders, first founded at the beginning of the thirteenth century, are vowed to communal and personal poverty. The first mendicant orders were the Franciscans and Dominicans. The Carmelites, Augustinians, Servites, and others were also given the mendicant title and privileges. Unlike traditional monks in the Benedictine tradition, the friars were allowed to work in the world, outside their monastic foundations, where they engaged in preaching, hearing confessions, and other ministerial work.

metropolitan, noun or adjective applied to the chief local church of a region or to its bishop (usually an archbishop).

Middle Ages, the historical period spanning the millennium between the collapse of the Roman Empire in 476 and the birth of the modern world at the end of the fifteenth century.

miter (Lat., *mitra,* "headband"), the head covering worn by bishops and some abbots during liturgical rites.

Modalism, a general theological approach to the Trinity, during the third, fourth, and fifth centuries, that viewed the three Persons as three different modes, aspects, or energies of the one God's operations, but not as three distinct Persons. In the East, it was known as Sabellianism; in the West, as Patripassianism.

Modernism, the name given to the doctrinal and disciplinary crisis in the Catholic Church in the early years of the twentieth century, particularly during the pontificate of Pius X (1903–14). The crisis arose because various theologians, biblical scholars, historians, and social philosophers were led, through their research, to revise their understanding of some traditional church teachings. They proposed a more critical reading of the Bible, a more experientially based theology, and a more positive attitude toward democracy. Modernism, an umbrella term for all these various approaches, was condemned by Pius X and an oath against Modernism was imposed on all bishops, clergy, and theologians in 1910. A secret spy network, called the *Sodalitium Pianum,* encouraged individuals to report suspected heretics to Rome. Pius X's successor, Benedict XV (1914–22), disbanded the spy network and called upon ultraconservative, or Integralist, Catholics to stop their warfare against more progressive Catholics. But the anti-Modernist movement had a chilling effect on Catholic scholarship until the Second Vatican Council (1962–65).

Monarchianism, a second- and third-century heresy that so stressed the unity of God in divine rule (Gk., *monarchia*) that it denied the distinctly divine personhood of the Son and the Holy Spirit. Various forms of the heresy were known as Sabellianism, Patripassianism, and Modalism.

monasticism (Gk., *monos,* "one, alone"), an institutionalized form of ascetical religious life in which individuals take vows of poverty, chastity, obedience, and (as in the Benedictines) stability, separating themselves from society either singly (eremitic form) or in community (cenobitic form).

Monophysitism (Gk., *monos,* "one"; *physis,* "nature"), the fifth-century heresy that held that Jesus Christ had only one divine nature, and not a human nature as well. The heresy was condemned by the Council of Chalcedon in 451, but the view continued to be held by many in the East and was the source of serious political as well as ecclesiastical problems.

Monothelitism (Gk., *monos,* "one"; *theleis,* "will"), a seventh-century heresy that held that Jesus Christ possessed only one divine will. Pope Honorius I (625–38) found himself espousing this view in an effort to reconcile the Monophysites with the Church, for which he was posthumously excommunicated by the Third Council of Constantinople (680–81).

Montanism, a second-century apocalyptic and charismatic movement, identified with Montanus of Phrygia, that stressed the imminent end of the world and imposed an austere morality in preparation for the event. Its most famous convert was Tertullian (d. ca. 225), the Latin Christian writer and apologist from Roman Africa.

motu proprio (Lat., "on his own initiative"), papal document originating from the pope's own office concerning various administrative and pastoral matters. Many of the changes brought about by the Second Vatican Council (1962–65) were given practical application by this type of papal document.

neo-Scholasticism, a term used for the revival, from 1860 to 1960, of the philosophical tradition of the medieval and baroque universities. It also describes a very conservative type of theology that was generally abstract, nonexperiential, and unhistorical in method.

nephew, cardinal-. *See* cardinal-nephew.

Nestorianism, the fifth-century heresy, named after Nestorius, bishop of Constantinople, that held that in Christ there are two persons, one divine and one human. Mary, therefore, is the mother of the human Jesus only, not the Mother of God. The Council of Ephesus condemned this heresy in 431.

Nicaea, First Council of, the first ecumenical council of the Church, held in 325 at the invitation of the emperor Constantine to deal with the problem of Arianism, which taught that Christ was only the greatest of creatures. The council defined the divinity of Christ, declaring him to be "of the same substance" (Gk., *homoousios*) as God the Father. (The Second Council of Nicaea in 787 validated the practice of venerating images. It was the last ecumenical council recognized by the East.)

Nicene Creed, also known as the Nicene-Constantinopolitan Creed, a statement of Christian belief formulated by the Council of Nicaea in 325 and affirmed, with some modification, by the Council of Constantinople in 381. It is the same creed recited each week at Mass.

Noble Guards, aristocratic bodyguards of the pope, founded in 1801 and dissolved by Paul VI in 1970. Not to be confused with the Swiss Guard, founded in 1505, and still serving the pope.

nuncio (Lat., *nuntius*, "messenger"), a papal legate who represents the Holy See to a state or nation and also represents the pope to particular churches in that state or nation. A nuncio is to be distinguished from an apostolic delegate, who represents the pope to the particular churches of a state or nation with whom the Holy See does not have formal diplomatic relations.

Orthodox Christianity, the original apostolic churches and the later churches they founded in the Eastern half of the Roman Empire and in other Eastern territories beyond the imperial frontiers. The term "orthodox" originally was applied only to those who accepted the teachings of the Council of Chalcedon (451) on the divinity and humanity of Christ. Today the term applies more commonly to Christian churches of the East that are not in communion with Rome, particularly the Russian Orthodox and Greek Orthodox.

Osservatore Romano, official daily newspaper of the Vatican, founded in 1861.

pallium, the woolen vestment worn around the neck and shoulders of an archbishop as a sign of pastoral authority. It consists of a narrow circular band of white lamb's wool marked with six dark purple crosses, with two hanging strips front and back. Its conferral is now reserved to the pope. The early history of the pallium is obscure. Derived from imperial insignia, it was at first worn by archbishops and had no connection with Rome or with the investment of papal authority. Only later did the pope assume it for himself. Not until the ninth century were all metropolitan archbishops required to petition him for it.

papal blessing, a benediction or blessing bestowed by the pope. The term also applies to the parchment certificate bearing the words of the blessing for particular persons on special occasions in their lives.

papal coronation. *See* coronation, papal.

papal election, the election of a pope by members of the College of Cardinals under the age of eighty in a conclave, or secret meeting. The conclave begins between fifteen and twenty days after the death of a pope. The dean of the college convokes and presides over the conclave. Before 1059, a pope was elected by the Roman clergy and people, then by the Roman clergy alone with the subsequent approval of the people. For several centuries, the emperor's approval of the election was essential because, without his approval, the pope could not be consecrated as Bishop of Rome and crowned. Since 1179 a two-thirds majority of the cardinal-electors has been necessary for election. Pope Pius XII changed that to two-thirds plus one in 1945. In 1996 John Paul II changed the procedures once again. A two-thirds majority (without the plus one) is sufficient, but an absolute majority is also sufficient after thirty-three ballots have been conducted over the course of several days, interrupted by an occasional day of prayer with no voting.

papal legate, a representative of the pope to a particular church or civil government or to an international council or conference.

Papal States, also known as the Patrimony of St. Peter, parts of central Italy and the territory of Avignon and Venaissin in southern France that were once under the temporal sovereignty of the Holy See and of the pope as its temporal as well as spiritual head. The Papal States began with a donation of lands, taken from the Lombards, by Pepin III, king of the Franks, to Pope Stephen II in 754 and 756: Ravenna and the cities of the Byzantine exarchate, the Pentapolis (Rimini, Pesaro, Fano, Senigallia, and Ancona, with adjacent territories), and Emilia. Papal control over these lands was sporadic, however, until Julius II (1503–13) established firm papal authority over them through a series of military campaigns. The French portion of the Papal States, purchased by Pope Clement VI from Joanna, queen of Naples, in 1348, were absorbed by the new French Republic in 1791. In 1860 the remaining territories in Italy, except for Rome, became part of the kingdom of Italy, and in 1870, after the withdrawal of French protection, Rome itself also became part of the Italian kingdom. In 1929 the Lateran Pacts provided financial compensation for the loss of certain papal territories and properties and Vatican City State was recognized as a separate and independent political entity.

patriarch, title for the highest-ranking bishop of an autonomous church or federation of local churches (known as dioceses or eparchies). In 451 the Byzantine emperor Justinian determined the five chief patriarchal sees as Rome, Constantinople, Alexandria, Antioch, and Jerusalem. In the East the title became restricted to those sees. There is also a patriarchal structure in the six Eastern Catholic rites: Armenian, Chaldean, Coptic, Maronite, Melkite, and West Syrian.

Patrimony of St. Peter. *See* Papal States.

Pelagianism, a fifth-century heresy, linked with the name of Pelagius (d. ca. 425), a British monk ministering in Rome, that held that salvation is possible through human effort alone, without the aid of grace. The heresy was vigorously opposed by Augustine of Hippo (d. 430), the North African bishops, and Pope Zosimus (d. 418).

Peter's Pence, annual financial contributions by Catholics from around the world for the support of the Holy See and the apostolic works of the pope. It began in England in 787 as a penny tax on all except the poor, to be given to the pope. The practice was revived in 1860 by Pius IX after the loss of all of the Papal States, except Rome.

Petrine ministry, the ministry that the Bishop of Rome exercises in his capacity as Vicar of Peter. It is concerned with the unity of the universal Church and with the strengthening of the faith of his brother bishops.

Petrine succession, the complex process by which the bishops of Rome follow in the line of St. Peter as his vicars and as earthly heads of the universal Church. As St. Cyprian of Carthage (d. 258) pointed out, however, in a sense all bishops are successors of St. Peter in their own dioceses—they are signs of unity and bearers of the tradition.

pluralism, holding more than one ecclesiastical office at the same time, an abuse common in the Middle Ages. The first pope to retain his former diocese while serving as Bishop of Rome was Clement II (1046–47), who retained his diocese of Bamberg. The three German popes who succeeded him did the same: Damasus II (1048) retained the see of Brixen; Leo IX (1049–54) retained the see of Toul; and Victor II (1055–57) retained the see of Eichstätt. So, too, did Nicholas II (1058–61) remain bishop of Florence. Stephen IX [X] (1057–58) remained as abbot of Monte Cassino after his election as pope. Urban III (1185–87) retained his archdiocese of Milan to prevent the revenues from passing into the imperial treasury, and Benedict XIII (1724–30) retained Benevento, the last pope to retain his diocese.

Pontifex Maximus (Lat., "Supreme Pontiff," or "bridge builder"), a title of honor accorded to the Bishop of Rome since the late fourth century, but originally a pagan title given to the emperor as head of the college of (pagan) priests in Rome.

pope (It., *papa,* "father"), the Bishop of Rome and the earthly head of the Church. In earlier centuries the title was used of any bishop in the West, while the East applied it to priests as well. In 1073 Gregory VII prohibited its use for all but the Bishop of Rome.

pope, titles of the, Bishop of Rome, Vicar of Jesus Christ, Successor of the Chief of the Apostles (Vicar of Peter), Supreme Pontiff of the Universal Church, Patriarch of the West, Primate of Italy, Archbishop and Metropolitan of the Roman Province, Sovereign of Vatican City State, and Servant of the Servants of God.

Pope Joan. *See* Joan, "Pope."

Pragmatic Sanction of Bourges (1438), a decree negotiated between the Council of Basel and the French king Charles VII whereby papal rights to French benefices were curtailed, as well as papal power to intervene in canonical disputes and to levy taxes. It remained a source of tension between the papacy and the French government and French Church for many years thereafter.

prelate, a priest who has the power of governance in the external (public) forum of the Church, that is, over some canonical portion or agency of the Church.

primacy, papal, the honorary and jurisdictional authority possessed by the Bishop of Rome and exercised over the universal Church. The primacy, however, is always exercised within the college of bishops, over which the pope presides.

Priscillianism, a heresy of the fourth to sixth centuries that regarded the human body as evil, insisted that Christ did not have a human body, and held that the three Persons of the Trinity are three modes or facets of one divine Being. The movement, which derived its name from Priscillian, an ascetic who taught and became a bishop in Spain in the late fourth century, was condemned by the Council of Braga in 563.

probabilism, a moral system for the formation of conscience in cases of doubt that holds that one can safely follow a theological opinion if it is proposed by someone having sufficient theological authority and standing. It became a source of controversy in the seventeenth century when its proponents were accused of laxism, which, unlike probabilism, held that one could always resolve moral doubts in favor of freedom even when good reasons were not present.

pro-nuncio, a now defunct term for the papal ambassador in countries where the representative of the Holy See is not head of the diplomatic corps (as is the case in the United States, for example). The pro-nuncio represented the Holy See not only to the government but to the Church and its hierarchy in that country.

Propaganda Fide (Lat.), or Congregation for the Propagation of the Faith, a department of the Roman Curia originally established by Pius V (1566–65) and Gregory XIII (1572–85) to promote the missions to non-Christians in the Orient and later also to Protestants in Europe. It is now called the Congregation for the Evangelization of Peoples.

Quartodecimans (Lat., "fourteenth"), those, especially in Asia Minor, who celebrated Easter on the fourteenth day of the Jewish month of Nisan (what they called Christian Passover), instead of on the following Sunday, in accordance with the practice in Rome and elsewhere in the Church. The dispute preoccupied the popes of the first four centuries. Victor I (189–98) even threatened to excommunicate them, but he was rebuked by St. Irenaeus of Lyons (d. ca. 200) for making such a threat. The First Council of Nicaea (325) settled on the Sunday celebration of Easter, but the Quartodeciman practice continued until the fifth century.

Quirinale (or Quirinal) Palace, the original summer residence of the popes (before Castel Gandolfo), whose construction was begun by Gregory XIII (1572–85). A few summer papal conclaves were held there because of its cooler location, situated atop the Quirinal Hill. In 1870, during the pontificate of Pius IX (1846–78), it was expropriated by the new Italian state and used as the official residence of the king of Italy. Benedict XV (1914–22) lifted Pius IX's ban on papal visits to the Quirinale Palace.

Ravenna, northern Italian city that first served as the site of an imperial residence in 404 and then as the capital of the Byzantine exarchate from 540 until 751, when it fell to the Lombards. Its geographical location and former political status gave its medieval archbishops a special importance.

Religious orders and congregations, groups living under a religious rule and publicly professing the vows of poverty, chastity, and obedience or their equivalents.

rescript, papal, a written reply by the pope to a specific question or request addressed to him. Its provisions bind only those to whom the rescript is sent.

Roman Curia, the network of secretariats, congregations, tribunals, councils, offices, commissions, committees, and individuals who assist the pope in his responsibilities as earthly head of the universal Church. Although popes of the early centuries had assistants in their capacity as Bishop of Rome, the Roman Curia as such was first organized by Sixtus V in 1588.

Roman Empire, the territory around the Mediterranean and in Europe that was ruled by Rome from the first century before Christ to the end of the fourth century after Christ (395), when the empire was divided into East and West. The Western empire ended in 476 when the last emperor of the West, Romulus Augustulus, was deposed by the Goths under Odoacer. The early Church adopted some of the organizational framework of the Roman Empire for its own organizational plan of provinces, metropolitan sees, dioceses, and the like. Constantine moved the capital of the empire to Constantinople in 330, where it became the seat of the Byzantine Empire (from the name of the town, Byzantium, on which the new city of Constantinople was erected). The latter survived until the fall of Constantinople to the Turks in 1453. In the West the Roman Empire gave way to the new Germanic kingdoms in 476. The Holy Roman Empire began under the German king Otto I in 962, as a successor to Charlemagne's empire, begun in 800. The Holy Roman Empire came to an end in 1806.

Roman Question. *See* Lateran Treaty.

Sabellianism, a third- and fourth-century heresy, named after the Roman cleric Sabellius, that held that God is triune only in relation to the world. Because of its exaggerated emphasis on the oneness of God, it has often been associated with Monarchianism; and because of its insistence that the three divine Persons are merely modes of the one divine Person exercising three different operations, it has also be associated with Modalism.

Saint John Lateran Basilica. *See* Lateran Basilica.

Saint Mary Major (also Santa Maria Maggiore), one of Rome's four major basilicas, founded in the fourth century by Pope Liberius on the Esquiline Hill. The present church was rebuilt by Sixtus III in the fifth century.

Saint Paul's Outside the Walls, one of the four major basilicas in Rome, first built over the relics of St. Paul by Constantine in the fourth century and later enlarged. The basilica burned to the ground in 1823 and was rebuilt and rededicated in 1854.

Saint Peter's Basilica, one of the four major basilicas in Rome and the Catholic Church's principal church. Built over the site of St. Peter's grave on Vatican Hill, it was originally constructed during the reign of the emperor Constantine (d. 337). The present church was begun in 1506 and dedicated in 1626. The plans for the new church, including its great dome, were designed by its chief architect, Michelangelo (d. 1564). The colonnade enclosing St. Peter's Square, or piazza, was designed by Bernini (d. 1680), who became architect of St. Peter's in 1629, where he designed its interior details as well as the piazza. The crypts and altars contain the burial places of more than 130 popes.

schism (Gk., *schisma,* "tear"), a formal breach of church unity. Unlike heresy, a schism is not directed against orthodoxy of doctrine but against communion. The most famous schisms in the history of the Church have been the East-West Schism (begun in 1054) and the Great Western Schism (1378–1417).

sedia gestatoria (Lat., "portable chair"), the chair on which the pope can be carried through a crowd so that he can easily be seen by all. It was last used by John Paul I (1978) for his entrance into St. John Lateran Basilica when taking possession of his cathedral church after his election.

see (Lat., *sedes*, "seat"), a local church, or diocese. The Latin word refers to the bishop's chair as symbolic of his episcopal authority.

Servus servorum Dei (Lat., "servant of the servants of God"), papal title first used by Gregory the Great (590–604) and in general use since Gregory VII (1073–85).

simony, the buying and selling of church offices, named after Simon Magus, who tried to buy the power of laying on hands from Peter (Acts 8:9–24). It was a major problem for the Church in general and the papacy in particular during the Middle Ages.

Sistine Chapel, named for Pope Sixtus IV (1471–84), the principal chapel of the Vatican Palace, famous for its frescoed walls by various artists but best known for its ceiling and altar wall (depicting the Last Judgment) by Michelangelo. The Sistine Chapel is used for papal elections.

Subordinationism, a second- and third-century heresy that held that the Son and the Holy Spirit are less than the Father, and therefore less divine, because they proceed from the Father. The councils of Nicaea (325) and Constantinople (381) condemned the Subordinationist teachings associated with the Alexandrian priest Arius.

subsidiarity, principle of, an element of Catholic social doctrine, first proposed by Pius XI in his encyclical *Quadragesimo anno* (1931), that holds that nothing should be done by a higher agency in society, government, or the Church that can be done as well, or better, by a lower agency.

suburbicarian sees, the neighboring dioceses of Rome: Ostia, Palestrina, Porto-Santa Rufina, Albano, Velletri-Segni, Frascati, and Sabina–Poggio Mirteto. These are now titular sees, held by the various cardinal-bishops. The dean of the College of Cardinals is the titular bishop of Ostia as well as one of the other suburbicarian sees. Today he is the one who consecrates a newly elected pope if the pope is not already a bishop. In the first eight and a half centuries, when no one who was already a bishop was elected pope, the newly elected pope would be consecrated a bishop by the bishops of Ostia, Albano, and Porto.

suppression, a canonical term that pertains to the removal of a saint's feast from the Church's liturgical calendar; the abolition of a clerical order (e.g., the subdiaconate); the redrawing of diocesan boundaries in such a way that an existing diocese no longer exists under its former name but becomes incorporated into another, differently configured diocese; and the formal closing down of a religious order or an ecclesiastical institution such as a monastery.

Swiss Guard, soldiers in the employ of the Vatican as a small security force for the papal palace and the person of the pope. Originally recruited from Switzerland as mercenaries in the service of the papacy in the early sixteenth century, they wear uniforms that were designed by Michelangelo. New recruits must be Swiss, Catholic, unmarried, and under the age of twenty-five.

Syllabus of Errors, a document attached to Pope Pius IX's 1864 encyclical *Quanta cura* (Lat., "How much care"), containing eighty previously condemned theses, including the condemnation of freedom of the press and of democracy generally.

synods, gatherings of church leaders to address matters of concern to the life and mission of the Church. After Vatican II, Paul VI established the World Synod of Bishops which meets at regular intervals to advise the pope on matters of concern to the universal Church.

tiara, papal, a generic papal head covering that has taken different forms in the course of centuries. From the fifteenth century, the papal triple-tiered crown, resembling a beehive, was used in papal coronation ceremonies. Paul VI (1963–78) was the last pope to be crowned with the tiara in 1963. He subsequently sold it and gave the money to the poor. Since John Paul I in 1978 popes are "inaugurated" into their ministry with the vesting of the pallium, the woolen vestment worn around the neck of an archbishop as a sign of pastoral authority.

title (Lat., *titulus,* "inscription"), a classical inscription denoting a claim to a particular building or territory. The term applies to the suburbicarian dioceses of Rome and to the churches and deaconries (aid stations) of Rome to which cardinals are assigned as honorary bishops, pastors, or administrators. Thus, a cardinal is appointed "in the title of San Marco," for example, that is, as honorary pastor of the church of St. Mark, in memory of the time when the cardinals were the actual pastors of various key churches in the city of Rome.

Tome of Leo, the letter sent in June 449 by Pope Leo the Great to Flavian, patriarch of Constantinople, articulating the Church's doctrine of the two natures (human and divine) and the one divine Person in Jesus Christ. The letter was adopted as the basis for the teaching of the Council of Chalcedon in 451.

Trent, Council of, the Counter-Reformation council held in three different segments from 1545 to 1563. It defined the seven sacraments, the Real Presence of Christ in the Eucharist, and the role of tradition alongside that of Scripture, and decreed the establishment of seminaries for the training of future priests and a catechism for the universal Church. The council shaped Catholic life and worship until the Second Vatican Council (1962–65).

two-swords theory, the medieval belief that the pope has power in both the temporal and the spiritual realms. The theory found its extreme expression in Boniface VIII's bull *Unam Sanctam* (1302).

Ultramontanism (Lat., "beyond the mountains"), a nineteenth-century movement in European countries beyond the Alps (France, Germany, Spain, and England) that exalted the papacy as the great bulwark against political liberalism and philosophical and ethical relativism. Initially, many liberal Catholics were Ultramontane because they saw the papacy as the guardian of the Church's independence against hostile secular regimes. Ultramontanism reached its high point in the pontificates of Gregory XVI (1831–46) and Pius IX (1846–78) and was a driving force behind the papal doctrines of Vatican I (1869–70).

Vatican, the shorthand term for the central headquarters of the Roman Catholic Church, including the pope and the Roman Curia. It takes its name from Vatican Hill, which in classical Rome was located outside the city walls and was the site of Nero's circus and a cemetery. Tradition holds that St. Peter was martyred in Nero's circus and buried in the nearby cemetery. St. Peter's Basilica was built over that site.

Vatican City State, the political entity that governs the territory where the Holy See is located. It is the smallest sovereign state in the world (108.7 acres in all) and is completely surrounded by the city of Rome. It contains St. Peter's Basilica, the Vatican Palace, the Vatican Museum, the Vatican Library, Vatican Radio, the Vatican Television Center, the Vatican Gardens, a post office, a bank, a newspaper, a railroad station, and various other offices and galleries. Its extraterritorial rights also extend to the three other major basilicas in Rome (St. John Lateran, St. Paul's Outside the Walls, and St. Mary Major), various offices of the Roman Curia in the city of Rome proper, and to the papal villas and the Vatican Observatory at Castel Gandolfo, fifteen miles southeast of Rome. Vatican City State was established by the Lateran Pacts of 1929 as a final settlement of the dispute between the papacy and the Italian government over the loss of the Papal States in the nineteenth century.

Vatican Council I (1869–70), the ecumenical council that defined the dogmas of papal primacy and papal infallibility.

Vatican Council II (1962–65), the ecumenical council that ended the Tridentine era (beginning with the Council of Trent in the sixteenth century) and inaugurated a new era of renewal and reform marked by an emphasis on the Church as the whole People of God, on the collegiality of the bishops (governing the Church in collaboration with, rather than under, the pope), on the social mission of the Church on behalf of the poor and the oppressed, on the participation of the laity in the worship and ministries of the Church, and on the Church's need to dialogue and collaborate with other Christian churches, other religions, and humankind at large.

Vatican Library, founded by Pope Nicholas V (1447–55), library that contains some 70,000 manuscripts, about 800,000 printed books, and many other documents, including all the Vatican archives, which were opened to scholars by Leo XIII in 1881.

Vatican Radio and Television Center, radio station, founded by Pius IX in 1931, and television station, founded by John Paul II in 1983, of the Vatican. Vatican Radio was designed and supervised by the famous Guglielmo Marconi, inventor of the radio, until his death in 1937. The station broadcasts in some thirty-four languages to every part of the world.

Vicar of Christ, the traditional title for a bishop, although now reserved to the Bishop of Rome since Eugenius III (1145–53). Innocent III (1198–1216) appealed especially to this title as the basis of his universal authority, even over temporal rulers. The more proper distinctive title for the pope is Vicar of Peter.

Vicar of Peter, the most traditional title designating the function of the Bishop of Rome. It was commonly accepted by popes since the end of the fourth century, but was displaced by the title Vicar of Christ (which originally applied to all bishops, not just the pope) during the pontificate of Eugenius III (1145–53), who reserved the latter title to the Bishop of Rome. The title Vicar of Peter underscores the point that the pope does not replace Peter, because the pope is not an eyewitness to the Resurrection. He and the other bishops can only keep alive what they have received. As Peter's vicar, the pope continues Peter's mission to serve the unity of the whole Church and to strengthen the faith of his brother bishops.

zucchetto, the white skullcap worn by the pope. The color for bishops is purple; for cardinals, scarlet; and for others, such as abbots, black.

SELECT BIBLIOGRAPHY

The literature on the popes and the papacy is voluminous. Since this book is not intended for scholars but for a general, nonspecialist audience, the listing of titles below is included to provide a representative sample of scholarly, encyclopedic, and popular works. The bibliography contains no references to scholarly or popular articles, which far outnumber the monographs and collections. All of the listed books, however, provide ample bibliographies of their own. Moreover, an annual bibliography on the papacy appears in the *Archivum Historiae Pontificiae* (Rome). If the author of this book could recommend another comprehensive, one-volume, historical, theological, canonical, and pastoral treatment of the popes and the papacy geared to the nonspecialist reader, he would do so. But that is precisely the gap this book is intended to fill.

Scholarly Works

Casper, Erich. *Geschichte des Papstums von den Anfängen bis zur Höhe der Weltherrschaft* (A History of the Papacy from the Beginning to [the mid-Eighth Century]), 2 vols. Tübingen: Mohr, 1930–33.

Davis, Raymond, trans. and ed. *The Book of Pontiffs (Liber Pontificalis)*. Liverpool: Liverpool University Press, 1989.

Mann, Horace K. *The Lives of the Popes in the Early Middle Ages*, 18 vols. London: Kegan Paul, Trench, Trübner, 1902–32.

Pastor, Ludwig von. *The History of the Papacy from the Close of the Middle Ages*, 40 vols. St. Louis: Herder, 1899–1933.

Seppelt, Franz Xaver. *Geschichte der Päpste von den Anfängen bis zur Mitte des zwanzigsten Jahrhunderts* (The History of the Popes from the Beginnings to the Middle of the Twentieth Century), 5 vols. Munich: Kösel, 1954–59.

———, and G. Schwaiger. *Geschichte der Päpste von den Anfängen bis zur Gegenwart* (The History of the Popes from the Beginnings to the Present). Munich: Kösel, 1964.

Encyclopedias, Encyclopedic Dictionaries, and Dictionaries

Cross, Frank L., and Elizabeth A. Livingstone, eds. *The Oxford Dictionary of the Christian Church*, 3d ed. London: Oxford University Press, 1997.

Gelmi, Josef. *Die Päpste in Lebensbildern* (The Popes in Their Life Profiles). Vienna: Verlag Styria, 1989.

Gligora, Francesco, and Biagia Catanzaro. *Storia dei Papi a degli Antipapi da San Pietro a Giovanni Paolo II* (The History of the Popes and Antipopes from St. Peter to John Paul II), 2 vols. Rome: Panda Edizioni, 1989.

Kelly, John N. D. *The Oxford Dictionary of Popes*. New York: Oxford University Press, 1986.

Levillain, Philippe, ed. *Dictionnaire historique de la papauté* (Historical Dictionary of the Papacy). Paris: Fayard, 1994.

McBrien, Richard P., ed. *The HarperCollins Encyclopedia of Catholicism*. San Francisco: HarperCollins, 1995.

McDonald, William J., ed. *The New Catholic Encyclopedia*, 14 vols. (plus an index vol. and four supplementary vols.). Washington, DC: The Catholic University of America, 1967.

Mondin, Battista. *Dizionario Enciclopedico dei Papi* (Encyclopedic Dictionary of the Popes). Rome: Città Nuova Editrice, 1995.

General Works on the Papacy

The Petrine Ministry in the New Testament.

Brown, Raymond, et al. *Peter in the New Testament*. Minneapolis, MN: Augsburg, 1973.

Caragounis, Chrys C. *Peter and the Rock*. New York: W. De Gruter, 1990.

Cwiekowski, Frederick J. *The Beginnings of the Church*. New York: Paulist Press, 1988.

The Papacy Through History

Brezzi, Paolo. *The Papacy: Its Origins and Historical Evolution*. Westminster, MD: Newman Press, 1958.

Eno, Robert B. *The Rise of the Papacy*. Wilmington, DE: Michael Glazier, 1990.

Hughes, John Jay. *Pontiffs: Popes Who Shaped History*. Huntington, IN: Our Sunday Visitor, 1994.

Schatz, Klaus. *Papal Primacy: From its Origins to the Present*. Translated by John A. Otto and Linda M. Maloney. Collegeville, MN: Liturgical Press, 1996.

Schimmelpfennig, Bernhard. *The Papacy*. Translated by James Sievert. New York: Columbia University Press, 1992.

Tierney, Brian. *Origins of Papal Infallibility 1150–1350*. Leiden: Brill, 1972.

Theological Studies of the Papacy

Bertrams, Wilhelm. *The Papacy, the Episcopacy and Collegiality*. Westminster, MD: Newman Press, 1964.

Granfield, Patrick. *The Papacy in Transition*. Garden City, NY: Doubleday, 1980.

———. *The Limits of the Papacy: Autonomy and Authority in the Church*. New York: Crossroad, 1987.

Tillard, Jean-M. R. *The Bishop of Rome*. Wilmington, DE: Michael Glazier, 1983.

Ecumenical Approaches

Anglican-Roman Catholic International Commission. *The Final Report*. Washington, DC: United States Catholic Conference, 1982.

Dionne, J. Robert. *The Papacy and the Church: A Study of Praxis and Reception in Ecumenical Perspective*. New York: Philosophical Library, 1987.

Empie, Paul C., et al., eds. *Papal Primacy and the Universal Church: Lutherans and Catholics in Dialogue V*. Minneapolis, MN: Augsburg, 1974.

———. *Teaching Authority and Infallibility in the Church: Lutherans and Catholics in Dialogue VI*. Minneapolis, MN: Augsburg, 1978.

McCord, Peter J., ed. *A Pope for All Christians: An Inquiry into the Role of Peter in the Modern Church*. New York: Paulist Press, 1976.

Modern Popes

Greeley, Andrew M. *The Making of the Popes 1978: The Politics of Intrigue in the Vatican*. Kansas City, MO: Andrews and McMeel, 1979.

Hebblethwaite, Peter. *Paul VI: The First Modern Pope*. New York: Paulist Press, 1993.

———. *Pope John Paul II and the Church*. Kansas City, MO: Sheed & Ward, 1995.

———. *Pope John XXIII: Shepherd of the Modern World*. Garden City, NY: Doubleday, 1985.

———. *The Year of Three Popes*. Cleveland, OH: William Collins, 1979.

Zizola, Giancarlo. *The Utopia of Pope John XXIII*. Translated by Helen Barolini. Maryknoll, NY: Orbis, 1978.

The Vatican Today

Reese, Thomas J. *Inside the Vatican: The Politics and Organization of the Catholic Church*. Cambridge, MA: Harvard University Press, 1996.

PHOTOGRAPH CREDITS

1: Masaccio, *The Tribute Money* (detail of St. Peter and Jesus). Brancacci Chapel, S. Maria del Carmine, Florence. Photo: Erich Lessing/Art Resource, NY.

2: Raphael, *St. Clement I Between Moderatio and Comitas.* Stanze di Raffaello, Vatican Palace, Vatican City. Photo: Alinari/Art Resource, NY.

3: Raphael, *Meeting of Leo the Great and Attila the Hun.* Stanze di Raffaello, Vatican Palace, Vatican City. Photo: Scala/Art Resource, NY.

4: *St. Gregory and Three Scribes.* German, tenth-century ivory panel. Kunsthistorisches Museum, Kunstkammer, Vienna. Photo: Erich Lessing/Art Resource, NY.

5: *Coronation of Charlemagne at Rome.* In *Grandes Chroniques de France,* French, fourteenth century. Musée Goya, Castres, France. Photo: Giraudon/Art Resource, NY.

6: *Gregory VII.* Photo: New York Public Library Picture Collection.

7: *Council of Clermont: Arrival of Pope Urban II in France.* Miniature from the *Roman de Godefroi de Bouillon,* 1337. Ms. fr. 22495, fol. 15. Bibliothéque Nationale, Paris. Photo: Giraudon/Art Resource, NY.

8: *Pope Innocent III with the Papal Bull of the Donation to the Monastery* (detail of fresco). Cacro Speco, Subiaco, Italy. Photo: Scala/Art Resource, NY.

9: Giotto di Bondone, *Pope Boniface VIII.* Fresco. St. John Lateran, Rome. Photo: Alinari/Art Resource, NY.

10: Bernardino Pinturicchio, *Pope Alexander VI Borgia Kneeling in Prayer.* Sala dei Misteri della Fede, Appartamento Borgia, Vatican Palace, Vatican City. Photo: Scala/Art Resource, NY.

11: Raphael, *Portrait of Pope Julius II,* 1511. Uffizi, Florence. Photo: Erich Lessing, Art Resource, NY.

12: Raphael, *Portrait of Pope Leo X with Two Cardinals.* Uffizi, Florence. Photo: Nicolo Orsi Battaglini/Art Resource, NY.

13: Leonardo Sormanno, monument to Pope Pius V (detail). St. Mary Major, Rome. Photo: Alinari/Art Resource, NY.

14: Domenico De Angelis, *Pius VII Forming the Collection of the Museum and Art Gallery.* Biblioteca Apostolica Vaticana, Vatican City. Photo: Scala/Art Resource, NY.

15: Catholic News Service.

16: Corbis-Bettmann.

17: UPI/Corbis-Bettmann.

18: Catholic New Service.

19: Corbis-Bettmann.

20: Art Resource, NY.

21: Catholic News Service.

22: Catholic News Service.

23: Catholic News Service.

24: Reuters/Corbis-Bettmann.

25: UPI/Corbis-Bettman.

26: Catholic News Service.

27: UPI/Corbis-Bettmann.

28: Fabian/Sygma.

29: Reuters/Corbis-Bettmann.

30: Titian, *The Council of Trent.* Venetian School, sixteenth century. Louvre, Paris. Photo: Bettmann Archive.

31: Catholic News Service.

32: Catholic News Service.

33: UPI/Corbis-Bettmann.

34: Michelangelo Buonarroti, interior view, Sistine Chapel, Vatican Palace, Vatican City. Photo: Scala/Art Resource, NY.

35: UPI/Corbis-Bettmann.

36: Ferdinando Fuga, south facade, St. Mary Major, Rome. Photo: Alinari/Art Resource, NY.

37: Interior view toward the altar, St. Paul's Outside the Walls, Rome. Photo: Scala/Art Resource, NY.

38: Exterior view, Hagia Sophia, Istanbul. Photo: Vanni/Art Resource, NY.

39: Exterior view, Palace of the Popes, Avignon, France. Photo: Erich Lessing/Art Resource, NY.

40: *Encounter of Pope Silvester and Emperor Constantine.* Twelfth-century fresco. Quattro Santi Coronati, Rome. Photo: Art Resource, NY.

41: Albrecht Dürer, *Portrait of Charlemagne.* Germanisches Nationalmuseum, Nuremberg, Germany. Photo: Giraudon/Art Resource, NY.

42: Domenico Passignano, *Michelangelo Presenting the Model of St. Peter's to Paul IV.* Casa Buonarroti, Florence. Photo: Scala/Art Resource, NY.

43: Anonymous, *Trial of Galileo before the Inquisition in 1633.* Seventeenth century. Private collection, NY. Photo: Erich Lessing/Art Resource, NY.

INDEXES

Index of Popes *(See also* Personal Names Index)

Personal Names Index

Index of Subjects

and church reform, 176, 191, 259; and
the French Revolution, 329–30; and
Gallicanism, 311–12; and the Great
Western Schism, 248; heresy in, 246;
independence of, 185, 261, 299–300;
and the Protestant Reformation, 288;
restoration of Catholicism in, 336;
and suppression of the Society of Jesus,
324, 325. *See also* Gallicanism; Gaul,
Church in
Franciscan order, 211, 212, 220, 224, 225,
226, 227, 233, 236–37, 239; Conventuals,
224, 234–35, 236; and poverty, 21–22, 185,
210, 224, 225, 230, 236–37; Spiritual, 224,
230, 235, 236, 237, 242
Frankfurt, Synod of, 125
Franks, 119, 122, 123, 130, 133, 136; bishops
of, 125, 135; and control of papacy, 134;
kingdom of, 74
Freemasonry, 321, 323, 334, 336, 349, 440
French Revolution, 276, 277, 329–30, 333,
433

Gallican Articles, 311, 313, 314, 329
Gallicanism, 22, 102, 314–15, 325, 475
Gaul, Church in, 26, 41, 49, 50, 64, 67, 70,
75, 76, 78, 84, 94, 97. *See also* France,
Church in
German College, 284, 291
Germany, Church in, 145, 156, 158, 259,
285; and Communion under both
kinds, 288; and conflicts with the
papacy, 179, 203, 225, 261, 262, 329; and
the Great Western Schism, 248; heresy
in, 246; and lay investiture, 187, 193, 195,
258; and the *Kulturkampf*, 347, 350; mission to, 118, 120; and Moravia, 144; and
Nazism, 361–62; and the oath against
Modernism, 354; and the see of Trier,
116, 206
Gnosticism, 18, 38, 39, 475
Gratian, *Decretals* of, 58
Great Western Schism, 182, 247, 371, 397,
398; beginning of, 183, 248, 254, 425, 436;
end of, 185, 228, 253, 409; and the Protes-

tant Reformation, 275
Greek Church. *See* Eastern churches
Gregorian calendar, 40, 277, 291, 292
Gregorian University, 277, 291, 327, 360;
restoration of, 334

Hagia Sophia, 86, 93
Henoticon, 79, 82, 476
Holocaust, 343, 364
Holy Office, 282, 311, 334, 343, 437. *See also*
Doctrine of the Faith, Congregation for
the
Holy Roman Empire, 157, 18, 303, 476
Humanae vitae, 367, 375, 380, 434, 464
Humani generis, 365, 462
Humiliati, 289
Hundred Years' War, 239–40, 241, 245
Hungary, Church in, 167, 188, 248, 288

Iconoclasm, 18, 119, 123, 125, 133, 134, 142,
476
Immaculate Conception, dogma of, 439,
458, 462; feast of, 316, 341, 346
Index of Forbidden Books, 276, 285, 286,
287, 288, 290, 297, 300, 323, 325, 334, 351,
437, 477
India, Church in, 237, 316, 339, 359
Indulgences, 182, 183, 231, 240–41, 249,
250–51, 260, 265, 270, 272, 273, 289, 436,
437, 477
Infallibility of the Church, 20, 22, 23. *See
also* Pope, infallibility of
Inquisition, 183, 276, 285–86, 439, 477;
establishment of, 212, 282; Franciscan
victims of, 236; and Galileo, 300; reform
of, 287; and torture, 215, 239, 289–90,
297, 435. *See also* Spanish Inquisition
Integralism, 358, 477
Ireland, Church in, 70, 104, 201, 336, 353
Israel, State of, 391

Jansenism, 22, 303–4, 305, 307, 308, 311,
313, 316, 317–18, 319, 477–78
Jerusalem, Council of, 29, 140
Jesuits. *See* Society of Jesus